ENCYCLOPEDIA OF
EMANCIPATION
AND ABOLITION
IN THE TRANSATLANTIC WORLD

VOLUME TWO

EDITED BY JUNIUS RODRIGUEZ

SHARPE REFERENCE
an imprint of M.E. Sharpe, Inc.

SHARPE REFERENCE

Sharpe Reference is an imprint of M.E. Sharpe, Inc.

M.E. Sharpe, Inc.
80 Business Park Drive
Armonk, NY 10504

Library of Congress Cataloging-in-Publication Data

Encyclopedia of emancipation and abolition in the transatlantic world / Junius Rodriguez, editor.
  p. cm.
Includes bibliographical references and index.
ISBN 978-0-7656-1257-1 (alk. paper)
  1. Slavery—History—Encyclopedias. 2. Liberty—History—Encyclopedias. I. Rodriguez, Junius P.

HT985.E53 2008
306.3′6203—dc22   2006035834

Cover images: Clockwise from top left corner, provided by Getty Images and the following: English School/The Bridgeman Art Library; MPI/Stringer/Hulton Archive; FPG/Taxi; Stringer/Hulton Archive; MPI/Stringer/Hulton Archive; Henry Guttmann/Stringer/Hulton Archive; MPI/Stringer/Hulton Archive.

Printed and bound in the United States

The paper used in this publication meets the minimum requirements of American National Standard for Information Sciences Permanence of Paper for Printed Library Materials, ANSI Z 39.48.1984.

BM (c) 10 9 8 7 6 5 4 3 2 1

Publisher: Myron E. Sharpe
Vice President and Editorial Director: Patricia Kolb
Vice President and Production Director: Carmen Chetti
Executive Editor and Manager of Reference: Todd Hallman
Senior Development Editor: Jeff Hacker
Development Editor: Gina Misiroglu
Project Editor: Laura Brengelman
Program Coordinator: Cathleen Prisco
Text Design: Carmen Chetti and Jesse Sanchez
Cover Design: Jesse Sanchez

Contents

Topic Finder

Abolitionists, American

Allen, Richard (African American bishop)
Allen, William G.
Anderson, Osborne Perry
Beecher, Henry Ward
Benezet, Anthony
Birkbeck, Morris
Birney, James Gillespie
Blanchard, Jonathan
Bowditch, Henry Ingersoll
Brown, John
Buffum, Arnold
Burleigh, Charles Calistus
Butler, Benjamin Franklin
Channing, William Ellery
Child, David Lee
Cornish, Samuel E.
Cuffe, Paul
Dawes, William
Day, William Howard
Delany, Martin Robison
Dillwyn, William
Downing, George Thomas
Du Bois, W.E.B.
Forten, James, Sr.
Foster, Stephen Symonds
Garnet, Henry Highland
Garrison, William Lloyd
Gatch, Philip
Gay, Sydney Howard
Gibbons, James Sloan
Gibbs, Mifflin Wistar
Grinnell, Josiah B.
Grosvenor, Cyrus Pitt
Hamilton, William
Hayden, Lewis
Hopkins, Samuel
Johnson, Oliver
Langston, John Mercer
Lay, Benjamin
Lovejoy, Elijah P.
Lovejoy, Owen
Lundy, Benjamin

May, Samuel Joseph
McKim, James Miller
Miller, Jonathan Peckham
Mott, James, and Lucretia Coffin Mott
Nell, William Cooper
Norton, John Treadwell
Olmsted, Frederick Law
Owen, Robert Dale
Paine, Thomas
Paul, Nathaniel
Pennington, James W.C.
Phillips, Wendell
Pillsbury, Parker
Purvis, Robert
Ray, Charles B.
Realf, Richard
Reason, Charles L.
Reason, Patrick H.
Rock, John Sweat
Rush, Benjamin
Smith, Gerrit
Spooner, Lysander
Steward, Austin
Stroyer, Jacob
Sunderland, La Roy
Tappan, Arthur
Tappan, Benjamin
Tappan, Lewis
Torrey, Charles Turner
Vaux, Roberts
Ward, Samuel Ringgold
Washington, Bushrod
Weld, Theodore Dwight
Whitting, William
Woolman, John
Wright, Elizur
Wright, Henry Clarke
Wright, Theodore Sedgwick

Abolitionists, Brazilian

Gama, Luís
Lacerda, Carlos de
Menezes, José Ferreira de

Historical Events, Periods, and Occasions

Laws, Decrees, and Governing Documents

Newspapers, Periodicals, Editors, and Publishers

Gibbs, Mifflin Wistar
Greeley, Horace
Johnson, Oliver
Lacerda, Carlos de
Lovejoy, Elijah P.
Lundy, Benjamin
Macaulay, Zachary
Menezes, José Ferreira de
Mirror of Liberty
Mystery, The
National Anti-Slavery Standard
Nell, William Cooper
North Star, The
Owen, Robert Dale
Palladium of Liberty, The
Patrocínio, José do
Pennsylvania Freeman
Philanthropist, The
Pillsbury, Parker
Price, Thomas
Ray, Charles B.
Russwurm, John B.
Shadd Cary, Mary Ann
Stone, Lucy
Swisshelm, Jane Grey Cannon
Tappan, Arthur
Tappan, Lewis
Webb, Richard Davis
Weekly Anglo-African Magazine, The
Wells-Barnett, Ida B.
Whittier, John Greenleaf
Wright, Elizur
Wright, Frances ("Fanny")

Novels, Novelists, Playwrights, and Poets
Beattie, James
Behn, Aphra
Brown, William Wells
Castro Alves, Antônio de
Day, Thomas
De Gouges, Marie Olympe
Gama, Luís
Gilbert, Ann Taylor
Harper, Frances Ellen Watkins
Howe, Julia Ward
Hugo, Victor
Kemble, Frances Anne
Manzano, Juan Francisco
Novels, Antislavery
Novels, Proslavery
Oroonoko (1688)

Realf, Richard
Sancho, Ignatius
Stowe, Harriet Beecher
Uncle Tom's Cabin (1852)
Valdés, Gabriel de la Concepción
Wheatley, Phillis
Whitfield, James Monroe
Whittier, John Greenleaf
Wilson, Harriet E.
Yearsley, Ann

Pamphlets, Tracts, Nonfiction Works, and Writers
Abdy, Edward Strutt
Adams, William Edwin
Allen, William G.
Anderson, Osborne Perry
Assing, Ottilie
Benezet, Anthony
Birkbeck, Morris
Candler, John
Chandler, Elizabeth Margaret
Chapman, Maria Weston
Child, David Lee
Child, Lydia Maria Francis
Clarkson, Thomas
Day, Thomas
Delany, Martin Robison
Dillwyn, William
Du Bois, W.E.B.
Estlin, John Bishop
Follen, Eliza Lee Cabot
Forten, James, Sr.
Gage, Frances Dana
Grimké, Angelina Emily
Grimké, Charlotte Forten
Grimké, Sarah Moore
Helper, Hinton Rowan
Heyrick, Elizabeth
Keckley, Elizabeth
Lay, Benjamin
Liberty Bell, The
Madden, Richard Robert
Malvin, John
Martineau, Harriet
May, Samuel Joseph
Mercer, Margaret
More, Hannah
Murray, Orson S.
Nabuco, Joaquim
Olmsted, Frederick Law

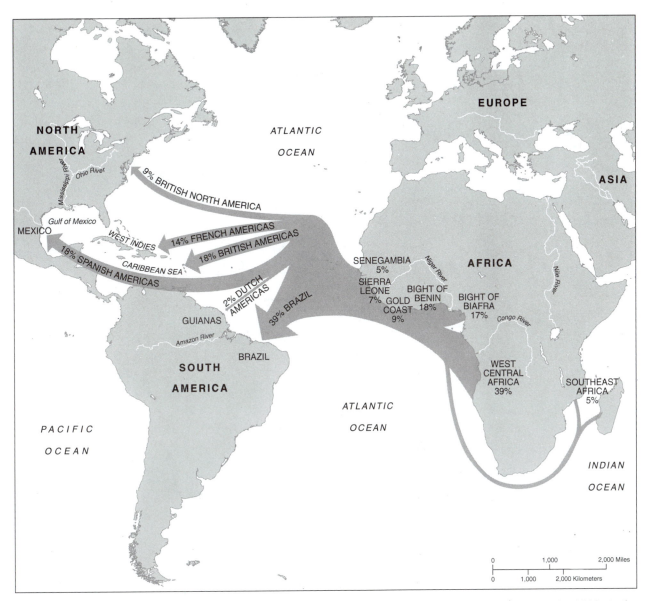

The transatlantic slave trade was a vast commercial enterprise that prospered for some 350 years, from the 1510s to the 1860s. Most of the slaves were captured in West and Central Africa, and transported by ship—the notorious Middle Passage—to South America and the Caribbean to work on plantations. Less than 10 percent were shipped directly from the African continent to the British colonies of North America or, after 1776, to the new United States. *(Cartographics)*

ENCYCLOPEDIA OF
EMANCIPATION
AND ABOLITION
IN THE TRANSATLANTIC WORLD

VOLUME TWO

Habsburg Emancipation Decree (1781)

Serfdom was abolished within the Habsburg Empire by an emancipation decree issued on November 1, 1781, by Emperor Joseph II. The proclamation reflected the influence of Enlightenment ideas on policies in Europe.

Until the mid-eighteenth century, when Empress Maria Theresa and her son, Joseph II, took the throne, conditions for peasants living in Habsburg-ruled lands varied from the relatively modernized village life of suburban Vienna to the late medieval feudalism of rural Hungary. Legally, peasants were subject to their noble lord's authority if they wished to move, marry, or engage in a trade, and they were liable for *robot,* or personal labor on the lord's lands or in his service. Many rural lords also held patrimonial courts, judging civil and criminal cases. Thus, the peasants were serfs who had little personal freedom and no legal recourse.

Maria Theresa, who ruled the Habsburg Empire from 1740 to 1780, reformed the laws restricting the peasantry, taking the paternalistic view that improving their legal status and education would also improve their loyalty to the Crown, taxable industry, piety, and reliability as conscripts in her long and costly wars. At the same time, her rival for the throne, King Charles VII of Bavaria, offered the peasants their freedom if they would join his invasion of Austria.

Once secure on the throne, Empress Maria Theresa issued commands requiring accurate censuses and surveys of noble and peasant land, preventing nobles from reclaiming the land and collecting higher taxes on peasant holdings. In 1770, the July Decree offered peasants impartial imperial justice through local royal officials rather than the patrimonial courts, and the Patent of 1772 gave peasants the right to appeal to the empress for justice. Addressing the robot and the freedom to move, Maria Theresa limited the robot to three days a week and a maximum of twelve hours a day. In 1773, the October Decree fixed the maximum sums that lords could demand for letters of release.

Following her death in 1780, Maria Theresa was succeeded by her far more radical son, Joseph II, who approached the peasants as an enlightened monarch, anxious to build a power base outside the nobility and to improve the lives of his people through rationality and modernization. In 1781, he abolished serfdom in all Crown lands, giving all people the right to move (so long as they remained registered for conscription), marry, and pursue any vocation. The new emperor cracked down on the nobles who attempted to deny that they practiced serfdom, and he followed up on his decree by offering provincial "subject's advocates" to help newly freed peasants pursue their rights—such as paying the robot owed on leased land in cash or using mills other than the lord's—in the courts. Joseph II encouraged the peasants to migrate to the cities and to own small farms that would be inherited by their eldest son. In an attempt to shape social norms, he forbade peasants to bow to their former lords or kiss their hands in subordination, and he opened the parks and social services to former serfs. Foreign observers were torn, simultaneously approving of the enlightened policy and, like the revolutionary comte de Mirabeau, horrified by the freedom of thousands of brutish, uneducated commoners.

When Joseph II died in 1790, his conservative brother, Leopold II, repealed many of his reforms and made substantive changes to the system of tax collection, but he did not dare reverse the emancipation decree. The robot remained legal if not paid in cash, however, until it was abolished by the radical government established during the revolution of 1848, which offered a one-time compensation to nobles in return for their loss. By 1848, most peasants had already enjoyed several generations of freedom, and thus they remained loyal to the Habsburg family rather than the radicals who completed their emancipation.

Margaret Sankey

Further Reading

Blum, Jerome. *Noble Landowners and Agriculture in Austria, 1815–1848.* Baltimore: Johns Hopkins University Press, 1948.

Link, Edith Murr. *The Emancipation of the Austrian Peasant,*
1740–1798. New York: Columbia University Press, 1949.

Wright, William. *Serf, Seigneur, and Sovereign: Agrarian Reform*
in Eighteenth-Century Bohemia. Minneapolis: University of
Minnesota Press, 1966.

Haitian Revolution (1791–1804)

The slave rebellion and anticolonial revolt that came
to be known as the Haitian Revolution are remembered with pride among the Haitian people, who re-
vere its heroes as the founders of their nation. Unlike
the maroon uprisings that occurred elsewhere in the
Caribbean, the revolution that took place on the western third of the island of Hispaniola accomplished
feats of epic proportions: It marked the success of the
first large-scale slave rebellion, the total abolition
of slavery in the colony of Saint-Domingue, and the
founding of the world's first black republic and the
second independent nation in the Americas.

Such revolutionaries as Toussaint L'Ouverture,
Henri Christophe, Jean-Jacques Dessalines, Alexandre Sabès Pétion, and other intrepid individuals led
the anticolonial struggle. The dream of freedom that
led to independence in 1804 endures in the national
myth of Haiti some 200 years hence.

History of Tension

The decline of Hispaniola's aboriginal population
during the first thirty years of colonization prompted
the Spanish to begin transporting enslaved Africans,
mainly from Africa's west coast, to do the work of
mining and planting as early as 1593. Later, in the
French colony of Saint-Domingue, plantations owned
by the aristocratic class of *grands blancs* (elite merchants and landowners) produced indigo, tobacco,
coffee, and, most notably, sugar, making it the most
lucrative and prosperous of France's overseas possessions. The island's landed groups also included thousands of mulatto *affranchis* (freedmen of mixed white
and African blood) who owned plantations and slaves
and enjoyed French citizenship. By 1789, more than
500,000 slaves were laboring in the colony's fields
and mills, far outnumbering the 40,000 whites and
28,000 affranchis.

Numerous uprisings took place during the
eighteenth century, setting the stage for the upheaval
of the revolution decades later. From 1753 to 1757,
the slave and *bokor* (conjurer) Mackandal led a revolt
in the Northern Plain during which slaves attempted
to poison their white masters. For his instigation and

leadership of the rebellion, Mackandal was captured,
brought to Cap-Français, and burned at the stake—
though many slaves believed that he survived in the
form of an animal or insect so that he could continue
to lead the uprising.

In October 1790, mulattoes Vincent Ogé, the
affranchi commissioner to the National Assembly, and
Jean-Baptiste Chavannes led an anti-French insurgency in the North. The two were backed by *La Société*
des Amis des Noirs (Society of Friends of the Blacks),
which had been founded in Paris in 1788 and was
committed to the gradual abolition of slavery. When
the revolt was suppressed, Ogé and Chavannes fled to
Santo Domingo but were captured and brought back
to Saint-Domingue, where they were tortured on the
wheel in February 1791. Mulatto revolts continued in
the South under the leadership of André Rigaud.

The outbreak of the French Revolution in 1789
gave ideological direction to the resistance of free

Born into slavery, Toussaint L'Ouverture joined the rebellion against the French colonial power in Saint-Domingue
(now Haiti) in 1791. Later captured by the French, he died
in prison just months before the island was declared
independent on January 1, 1804. *(Time Life Pictures/Getty*
Images)

mulattoes, who desired equality with the whites, and to the slaves, who simply desired the most elemental freedoms. The whites made use of Enlightenment ideals to justify their control of the colony over and against the impositions of the French republicans. The revolutionary motto "liberty, equality, and fraternity," which had divergent meanings for Saint-Domingue's blacks and mulattoes, inspired the mulatto rebellion of 1791, a precursor to the slave revolution led by Toussaint.

Rebellion Begins

On August 14, 1791, black plantation representatives of the Central Plain met in solidarity and secrecy at the Bois Caïman (Cayman Woods) on the Morne Rouge River. United in their fight by an African-based ritual, they heard the conjurer Boukman (Bouckman) Dutty exhort in his speech, "Throw away the thoughts of the white god who thirsts for our tears, listen to freedom that speaks from our hearts." Bearing in mind the ideals of the Declaration of the Rights of Man and of Citizen, which the French National Assembly had adopted in 1789, the slaves set out from the meeting to spread the word.

The slaves began their revolt on August 22, 1791, unleashing violence and destruction against the whites who had enslaved them. Within a week, some 50,000 slaves in the Northern Plain had risen up in arms, killing whites and burning plantations. In the first ten days of revolt, some 1,000 whites and 10,000 blacks lost their lives. Thousands of white planters abandoned the island, many of them leaving with their slaves for Santiago de Cuba.

The battles fought among the rich whites, poor whites, blacks, and mulattoes, as well as the intervention of the colonizing nations, would figure in the conflict, making the island a scene of internal and international power struggle. In view of the violence unleashed against the colony, the French National Assembly voted to grant eligibility rights to all affranchis for a seat in their body.

Significantly, the struggle for control of Saint-Domingue occasioned a renewal of hostilities between the British and the French in the region. The grands blancs were aided by the English in Jamaica, who aimed to restore Saint-Domingue to its antebellum condition and return the blacks to slavery. Although they generally voiced support for Enlightenment ideals, the grand blancs sought to distance themselves from the radical revolution, market interests, and, of

course, abolition, as all of these went against their interests. The *petits blancs* (mostly overseers, craftsman, and artisans) and the affranchis saw in the revolt an opportunity to join or supplant the aristocracy. The mulattoes sought to defend their rights and maintain equality with the whites, which had been decreed in 1792. Spain supported the rebels against the French; North Americans watched in the wings, wanting to resume trade with the lucrative colony but fearing a spread of "Haitianization" to other slaves in the region.

Many blacks joined the Spanish against the French. In 1792, Spain launched an invasion of the western portion of the island, with Toussaint, who had been among the anti-French forces in September 1791, as one of its generals. To aid in their defense, the French colonists invited the British to invade.

The Jacobins sent Léger-Félicité Sonthonax, son of a wealthy merchant, to the colony to lead a revolutionary commission, accompanied by 6,000 soldiers. Representing the French National Assembly, Sonthonax's commission parleyed with the leaders of the insurrection over the terms of peace and emancipation. A member of the Société des Amis des Noirs, Sonthonax favored the mulattoes and suspected the whites who were loyal to the monarchy.

In June 1793, the blacks sacked and destroyed Cap-Français and sent the whites fleeing the island. The Spanish invaded Cap-Français in late August, followed by the English army, which was led by William Pitt the Younger. The latter faced an army commanded by Toussaint, which succeeded in expelling the English from the northern region. Indeed, were it not for the Saint-Domingue slaves, the French colony would most likely have succumbed to British control. The French National Assembly debated the liberty of the slaves, who had defended their part of the island against the British and defended their right to liberty from the French plantation owners. Sonthonax unilaterally declared the slaves emancipated on August 29, 1793.

On February 4, 1794, the National Assembly voted to abolish slavery in all French colonies. Toussaint thus had reason to reverse his allegiance, now allying himself with the French, and he led a successful fight to restore Saint-Domingue to French control. The victory was formalized by the Treaty of Basel (1795), by which Spain ceded the whole of the island to France. The action was moot, however; by this time, the former slaves had wrested control of the colony from France.

Fighting for the French—but still holding out for full emancipation, if not independence—Toussaint was key not only in removing the British but also in putting down the rebellion of mulattoes led by Rigaud, who had declared the independence of the South. Battered by Toussaint's forces, the British troops were scourged by mosquitoes carrying yellow fever. All told, some 100,000 British soldiers were struck down, half of them dead, in the West Indian campaign: Saint-Domingue had stood in the way of their domination of the region. Toussaint had thwarted Pitt's plan, securing a pledge of noninterference and withdrawal from the island from British commander in chief Thomas Maitland.

Toussaint led his troops into the Cap, where the French showed him their appreciation for saving the colony: General Étienne-Maynard Laveaux named him governor general, and Sonthonax appointed him commander in chief of the French forces in Saint-Domingue. Under Toussaint's command, the British were forced to evacuate the Môle Saint-Nicolas in August, and Gabriel Hédouville, commissioner of the colony, was dismissed and sent away to France.

Toussaint L'Ouverture and Haitian Autonomy

Governor General Toussaint next took a bold move: He ordered the Haitian army to invade Santo Domingo in January 1801, temporarily joining the two colonies under one government and making the island *une et indivisible* (one and indivisible). Under Toussaint's authorization, the Haitian Assembly ratified the country's first constitution in 1801 and granted citizenship with no restrictions of race or national origin. In their constitution, the Haitians declared their autonomy from France, and Toussaint proclaimed himself governor general for life. The following year, in response to these moves, Napoleon Bonaparte sent his brother-in-law, Charles-Victor-Emmanuel Leclerc, to subdue the Haitians and neutralize Toussaint.

In their campaign to retake the colony, the French scored a decisive victory at La Crête-à-Pierrot in March 1802. Up to this point, Christophe, Dessalines, and Pétion had fought on the side of the republicans. Yet on October 13, Dessalines and Pétion held a council at Haut-du-Cap to determine their strategy for the war against France, making the decision to desert Leclerc and fight for independence. Black leaders organized the resistance to Leclerc's forces. Led by Dessalines, they vanquished Napoleon's

troops, killing some 50,000 soldiers and forcing their withdrawal in 1803, although the French remained in Santo Domingo until 1809.

In November 1802, Leclerc died of yellow fever, and his command was taken over by General Donatien-Marie-Joseph de Rochambeau. Infamous for his ferocity in seeking out and punishing rebels, Rochambeau brought 10,000 troops and mastiffs bred to "eat blacks," intending to replace the rebels with new *bossals,* or imports of fresh slaves.

Amid this readjustment of relations between France and the insurgents, Toussaint was betrayed and captured in June 1802. Transported to France, he died of pneumonia in his prison cell in Joux, near the Swiss border, on April 7, 1803. After his death, Dessalines, Christophe, and Pétion continued to lead the fight for independence.

Revolution Ends

External forces intervened in the battle for Hispaniola. England launched another series of attacks against the colony in May 1803, and the British blasted its port garrisons in June. Dessalines' campaign of counterattack aimed at nothing less than the extermination of the whites. A total of 50,000 Frenchmen died in the Saint-Domingue campaign before France capitulated on November 19, 1803. This was followed by an evacuation of the island by both French soldiers and white citizens. The colony's population had shrunk by 50 percent, from nearly 500,000 inhabitants to about 250,000. The end of French rule in Saint-Domingue had come, though the French maintained a military presence in Santo Domingo.

On January 1, 1804, Dessalines proclaimed the independence of Haiti at Gonaïves, renaming the country with the island's indigenous name, meaning "mountainous." On the same occasion, he announced the nationalization of all the island's territory. During the first three months of 1804, Dessalines oversaw the massacre of the country's white residents. On October 8, 1804, Dessalines was crowned emperor of his nation, just as Napoleon had done in France that May. Jean-Jacques I, as he was recognized, ordered the death of all whites remaining in the country and defined Haitian citizenship on the basis of race. He ruled as absolute leader until his assassination in 1806.

The Haitian Revolution successfully resisted metropolitan attempts to re-instate slavery and colonial rule in the former French possession. In 1789, freed mulattoes had advocated their equality with the whites and, in league with the whites, sought an easing of metropolitan-imposed restrictions on trade and political involvement. In spite of troubles that continue to face the modern, impoverished, violence-plagued Haiti, the enslaved masses of Saint-Domingue went on to realize a more radical dream that persists today: the dream of freedom and self-determination.

Eugenio Matibag

See also: Toussaint L'Ouverture, François-Dominique.

Further Reading

Bellegarde-Smith, Patrick. *Haiti: The Breached Citadel.* Boulder, CO: Westview, 1990.

Heinl, Robert Debs, Jr., and Nancy Gordon Heinl. *Written in Blood: The Story of the Haitian People, 1492–1995.* 2nd ed. Lanham, MD: University Press of America, 1996.

Knight, Franklin W. *The Caribbean: The Genesis of a Fragmented Nationalism.* New York: Oxford University Press, 1990.

Williams, Eric. *From Columbus to Castro: The History of the Caribbean 1492–1969.* New York: Vintage Books, 1984.

Hamilton, William (1773–1836)

William Hamilton was one of the most influential leaders of the free black community in New York City during the early nineteenth century. He was actively involved in the self-help movement that began through community associations, and, for a time, was a supporter of the colonization of free blacks in Liberia.

Born in 1773, Hamilton was long rumored to be the illegitimate son of Alexander Hamilton, later the nation's first secretary of the treasury, and a free black woman. Trained as a carpenter, he spent most of his life engaged as a social activist. As early as 1796, Hamilton took a public stand against racism. Frustrated by a series of indignities to which blacks were subjected at the John Street Methodist Church in New York City, Hamilton joined with James Varick and Peter Williams, Sr., to split from the white Methodists and establish the African Methodist Church, also in New York City, in 1796.

In 1808, Hamilton helped reorganize the African Society for Mutual Relief, the most effective mutual aid association in the city. On June 6 of that year, he was chosen to be a charter member of the society and was elected its first president. He clearly understood the importance of black mutual aid associations, ar-

guing in 1809 for the "necessity of societies to lessen the miseries of mankind."

To commemorate the first anniversary of the abolition of the African slave trade in 1809, the African Society selected Hamilton as its orator. Although his address briefly mentioned self-help as a means of moral uplift, Hamilton was more concerned with the issues of identity and institution building within the free black community.

Urging his people to view themselves as Africans, Hamilton boldly argued for unity among all African peoples, regardless of their geographic location. He believed they should embrace the term "African" because "it makes no kind of difference whether the man is born in Africa, Asia, Europe, or America, so long as he is proginized {sic} from African parents." Reflecting an early pan-African philosophy, he sought to unify all African people throughout the diaspora based on their shared identity and heritage.

Hamilton also demonstrated a tendency toward black nationalism; he issued bold calls for black unity within the United States. Using the African Society as a model, he argued that building institutions, such as churches, schools, and businesses, would strengthen the black community and provide hope for the future. He commended the African Society for its cohesion, dedication to moral uplift, and fight against poverty. Without community, Hamilton remarked, life would be miserable and advancement nearly impossible. By stressing African pride, he hoped that blacks would use their common identity and heritage as a foundation for collective political action.

In 1815, Hamilton gave another public address in which he criticized those who had participated in and benefited from slavery. He suggested that blacks (and Africans elsewhere in the diaspora) could play a role in their own destiny, arguing that Africa should be the seat of global political power in the future.

Hamilton was a convener of the 1834 gathering of the National Negro Convention movement, during which black leaders met to develop strategies for contesting slavery and racism in the United States. By the 1830s, Hamilton had dramatically reversed his position on emigration. In 1832, he addressed the convention and attempted to convince delegates that supporting Canadian emigration was a serious strategic error. Anticolonization had become a watchword of the black community and influenced every aspect of its political activism. Later that year, when the headmaster of the African Free School, Charles Andrews, espoused procolonization views, Hamilton led a boy-cott of the school until Andrews was fired from his position.

Among the most dramatic episodes of Hamilton's life was the 1834 anti-abolition riot in New York City, during which he took up arms to defend his home and family. He died two years later.

Leslie M. Alexander

See also: Anti-Abolition Riots.

Further Reading

Hamilton, William. *Address to the Fourth Annual Convention of the People of Color of the United States.* New York: S.W. Benedict & Co., 1834.

Hargrave, Francis (ca. 1741–1821)

Francis Hargrave was one of five advocates who appeared on behalf of James Somersett in *Knowles v. Somersett,* the 1772 case that determined the legal status of slaves in England.

Hargrave was born in London and educated in the law at Lincoln's Inn. When the abolitionist Granville Sharp began the legal campaign that would culminate in the *Somersett* case, Hargrave wrote to Sharp with an offer of help. On May 14, 1772, the young lawyer delivered a speech—the first that he had ever given in court—that made a vital contribution to Somersett's cause.

Hargrave polished his notes from the oration, which appeared in print shortly thereafter as *An Argument in the Case of James Somersett* (1772). Much of the speech centered on the argument that an old form of slavery, *villenage* (the type of bondage that characterized the feudal system), had already been outlawed under English law, and that new forms of slavery, such as the enslavement of Africans, could not be legal in England unless legislation were expressly enacted by Parliament.

Hargrave recognized that such legislation was in place for the British colonies in North America, but he pointed out that no such laws had been enacted with respect to England: "By an unhappy concurrence of circumstances, the slavery of negroes is thought to have become necessary in *America;* and therefore in *America* our Legislature has permitted the slavery of negroes. But the slavery of negroes is unnecessary in *England,* and therefore the Legislature has not extended the permission of it to *England;* and

not having done so, how can this court be warranted to make such an extension?"

Hargrave's arguments were grounded in a thorough knowledge of English legal history, but his style was polished and diplomatic as well. He concluded his speech by observing, "This court, by effectively obstructing the admission of the *new* slavery of *negroes* into England, will in *these times* reflect as much honor on themselves, as the great judges, their predecessors, *formerly* acquired, by contributing so uniformly and successfully to the suppression of the *old* slavery of *villenage.*"

Although the case was Hargrave's first, his efforts secured his reputation, and his arguments were widely reported and admired in the newspapers. "Mr Hargrave's speech," the *Morning Chronicle and London Advertiser* reported on May 15, 1772, "was one of the most learned and elaborate we have ever heard." Hargrave was appointed King's Counsel and thereafter specialized in legal history and commentary. He did not play a prominent part in the later abolitionist campaign in Britain, but his *Argument* went through three editions, and manuscript notes in Hargrave's own copy of the first edition (now archived in the British Library) show that he continued to take a keen interest in the legal status of slaves in later years.

In 1797, Hargrave was appointed recorder of Liverpool, though he had already embarked on a career as a legal historian, publishing many works and amassing a substantial collection of legal books and manuscripts. He fell ill in 1813, probably with a form of dementia, and his collection was bought by the government and deposited in the British Library. He died on August 16, 1821, and was buried in the chapel of Lincoln's Inn.

Brycchan Carey

See also: Sharp, Granville; *Somersett* Case (1772).

Further Reading

Anstey, Roger. *The Atlantic Slave Trade and British Abolition 1760–1810.* London: Macmillan, 1975.

Fryer, Peter. *Staying Power: A History of Black People in Britain.* London: Pluto, 1984.

Nadelhaft, Jerome. "The Somersett Case and Slavery: Myth, Reality, and Repercussions." *Journal of Negro History* 51 (1966): 193–208.

Oldham, James. "New Light on Mansfield and Slavery." *Journal of British Studies* 27 (1988): 45–68.

Walvin, James. *Black Ivory: A History of British Slavery.* London: HarperCollins, 1992.

Harper, Frances Ellen Watkins (1825–1911)

Frances Ellen Watkins Harper was a well-known African American writer, lecturer, and political activist who promoted abolition, civil rights, and women's rights during the nineteenth century. She was the cofounder and leader of several national progressive organizations for the advancement of African American and women's rights. After a period of neglect during the mid-twentieth century, her poetry and fiction were rediscovered in the 1980s and 1990s.

Harper was born into a free black family on September 24, 1825, in Baltimore, Maryland. Her parents remain unknown, but it is clear that she endured the oppressive laws and widespread discrimination that typified her time. After her mother's death when Harper was only three years old, the young girl was entrusted to the care of her aunt and uncle. Her uncle, the Reverend William Watkins, was an abolitionist and a teacher at the Academy for Negro Youth, a free school for colored children that Harper attended until the age of thirteen. Her uncle's views on abolition and civil rights had a profound influence on the young woman.

After leaving school, Harper worked as a maid for a Quaker family who allowed her to use their library and supported her literary ambitions. Eventually, her poems began to appear in newspapers, and, in 1845, they were collected in a volume titled *Autumn Leaves* (also published as *Forest Leaves*). The Watkins family left Baltimore after the passage of the Fugitive Slave Law of 1850, which threatened free blacks in the slave state of Maryland. Harper separated from her aunt and uncle and moved around the free states of Ohio and Pennsylvania, where she worked as a teacher.

In the 1850s, Harper became actively involved in the abolitionist movement. In Ohio, she worked at the Union Theological Seminary, where the abolitionist John Brown was the principal. In Pennsylvania, she joined the Pennsylvania Abolition Society and helped fugitive slaves along the Underground Railroad on their way to Canada. In 1854, Harper was much in demand on the abolitionist lecture circuit due to her rhetorical skills, and she traveled extensively before the outbreak of the U.S. Civil War.

Despite her heavy speaking schedule, she continued to pursue her writing career as well, publishing the volume *Poems on Miscellaneous Subjects* in 1854. The collection was praised by literary critics and became her most important commercial success. The

A free black from Baltimore, Frances Harper promoted the abolitionist cause with her poetry, fiction, and other writings. At public gatherings, she stirred audiences with readings of the popular "Bury Me in a Free Land" and other original verse. *(Library of Congress)*

poems attacked racial and gender discrimination, and the majority of her earnings were donated to the cause of helping freed slaves.

During and after the Civil War, Harper continued to write extensively, both literary and journalistic pieces, and lectured in favor of the rights of African Americans and women. Unlike other campaigners for women's suffrage, such as Susan B. Anthony and Elizabeth Cady Stanton, Harper supported the Fourteenth Amendment, which granted the right to vote to African American men but not to women. She argued that such a compromise was needed to secure an immediate political voice for the African American community so that further political and economic advancements would be possible. Harper died on February 22, 1911, nine years before the Nineteenth Amendment gave women the right to vote.

Much of the prose and poetry that Harper wrote after the Civil War dealt with Reconstruction. The poems in *Sketches of Southern Life* (1872) tell the story of Reconstruction from the point of view of an elderly freed slave, Aunt Chloe. In 1892, her novel *Iola Leroy* was published at the height of the Jim Crow laws and lynching. The book dramatized the developing racial awareness of the title character, a mulatto. Brought up as white girl, Iola is sold into slavery with her mother, prompting her to become an advocate of African American rights and racial mixing.

Perhaps because of the predominance of mixed-race characters in her fiction, critics dismissed Harper's novels and short stories for much of the twentieth century. Some critics characterized her style as excessively sentimental and Victorian. Toward the end of the century, however, the literary community rediscovered her works. Despite their sentimental surface, critics argued, her stories encode powerful antiracist and protofeminist messages.

Luca Prono

See also: Reconstruction; Women's Rights and the Abolitionist Movement.

Further Reading

Boyd, Melba Joyce. *Discarded Legacy: Politics and Poetics in the Life of Frances E.W. Harper.* Detroit, MI: Wayne State University Press, 1994.
Graham, Maryemma. *The Complete Works of Frances E.W. Harper.* Oxford, UK: Oxford University Press, 1988.
Harper, Frances E.W. *Iola Leroy.* Boston: Beacon, 1999.

Harpers Ferry Raid (1859)

The raid on Harpers Ferry, Virginia (now part of West Virginia), that began on the evening of October 16, 1859, did not accomplish the immediate goal that its instigators had envisioned. It did not incite a massive slave uprising in the South and thereby end the institution of slavery in the United States. Indeed, the raid was a spectacular failure—although that fact does not detract from its significance in the history of American slavery and the abolitionist movement.

For slave owners, the raid symbolized the lengths to which some abolitionists were willing to go in support of their cause, a prospect that caused great apprehension. For ardent abolitionists, it epitomized the selfless dedication that they urged among adherents and set an inspirational example. For all Americans, it moved the nation to the edge of civil war.

For its planner and leader, John Brown, the Harpers Ferry raid was the culmination of an adulthood spent in the cause of abolition. Brown was born in West Torrington, Connecticut, in 1800. Both his mother and father imbued him with a powerful religious faith rooted in Calvinism and a deeply felt opposition to slavery.

As a young man, Brown became a vocal opponent of slavery. He went so far as to claim blacks as friends, attempted to adopt a black child, and became acquainted with leading abolitionists such as William Lloyd Garrison. Although he admired men like Garrison, Brown believed that slavery should be attacked more directly and with more violent means than many abolitionists advocated. Despite frequent moves and business failures, two constants remained in Brown's life: his strict and fervent Calvinism and his desire to eradicate slavery. Predictably, these two forces combined to set the stage for the raid at Harpers Ferry.

For Brown, the road to Harpers Ferry began more than twenty years earlier. Following the murder of Illinois abolitionist newspaper editor Elijah P. Lovejoy in 1837, Brown publicly dedicated his life to destroying slavery in the United States. He became more active in abolitionist circles, and, by 1855, he was in Kansas fighting for the territory to enter the Union as a free state. He played a leading role in violence committed against proslavery agitators from Missouri, gaining a reputation as a man who was willing to kill for the cause of freedom. Brown increasingly came to view himself as an instrument of God, commissioned by the Almighty to end slavery by the sword, regardless of the cost. On the lam for his activities in Kansas, he returned to the East and began to plan a deathblow against slavery.

Brown's ambitions were large, but his scheme was relatively simple. As early as 1857, he began recruiting an abolitionist army, though the number never rose above thirty men. With this devoted band, he hoped to attack slave interests in the South and incite, arm, and lead a massive slave rebellion that would eradicate the institution in the United States. To back his plan, Brown secured support from a number of prominent New Eng and abolitionists, including Gerrit Smith and Frederick Douglass. Most were impressed by his passion, though some believed him to be a bit unstable.

After developing a number of different plans, Brown finally settled on a raid at Harpers Ferry, Virginia, as the first battle in his war against slavery. A federal arsenal in the town made it an attractive target, as it would provide weapons for the thousands of slaves whom Brown hoped to rally (despite the fact that the region had only a modest slave population). Convinced of his divine calling, Brown pressed ahead.

Harpers Ferry, Virginia, on the banks of the Potomac and Shenandoah rivers, was an attractive target for the radical abolitionist John Brown. The federal arsenal there was expected to provide arms for the slave uprising he attempted to incite in 1859. *(©Private Collection/Peter Newark American Pictures/The Bridgeman Art Library)*

A fugitive from federal authorities, Brown carried out the preliminary planning for the raid in secret. At least one of his men arrived in Harpers Ferry in summer 1858 to familiarize himself with the town and its surroundings. With such information in hand, Brown leased a nearby farm the following summer, took an assumed name, and made final preparations for the raid. He ordered 950 pikes and a large quantity of rifles with which to arm his men and the slaves whom he expected to join the revolt. Recruits continued to arrive at the farm throughout the summer and into the fall. In mid-October, Brown announced that the time to strike had come.

On the evening of October 16, Brown ordered twenty-one followers, including five blacks, to ready their weapons and move toward Harpers Ferry. Marching in a driving rain, they reached the town and captured the railroad engine house, armory, arsenal, and rifle works. They also captured about sixty residents whom they held as hostages.

Just after dawn, a railroad engineer whose train had been delayed by the raiders telegraphed his company with the news. They, in turn, telegraphed Virginia governor Henry Wise and President James Buchanan. Closer to Harpers Ferry, area residents mustered local militia companies, and these troops skirmished with Brown's followers.

By the evening of October 17, a number of Brown's men had been killed or wounded, and the militia surrounded the rest; their wounded leader was under siege in the engine house. Despite his grand designs, Brown's raid caused little more than temporary chaos and a number of dead and wounded on both sides. Not a single slave rallied to his cause. In fact, most of the slaves in the area were likely unaware of the raid until it was over.

The next morning, Colonel Robert E. Lee led a detachment of U.S. federal troops to Harpers Ferry. Lee took charge of the engine house siege and demanded Brown's surrender. When he refused, the troops charged the building and put a quick end to the situation. Five of Brown's men who were not in the engine house made their escape, but ten of his compatriots were killed and most of the remaining survivors were wounded. Brown himself was captured, tried in state court for treason, convicted, and sentenced to death. On December 2, he was hanged in Charlestown; six of his followers were later executed as well.

The raid at Harpers Ferry had profound consequences. It heightened slave owners' fears about a slave insurrection and boosted the morale of Northern abolitionists. Political tensions between the North and South worsened as the nation entered the presidential election year. Conflicting images of Brown portrayed him either as a martyr to the abolitionist cause or as a crazed and bloodthirsty criminal. The raid was the most notorious attempt to end slavery through violence, and it moved the nation closer to the brink of disunion.

Richard D. Starnes

See also: Brown, John.

Further Reading

Finkelman, Paul, ed. *His Soul Goes Marching On: Responses to John Brown and the Harpers Ferry Raid.* Charlottesville: University of Virginia Press, 1995.

Oates, Stephen B. *To Purge This Land With Blood: A Biography of John Brown.* New York: Harper & Row, 1970.

Quarles, Benjamin. *Allies for Freedom: Blacks and John Brown.* New York: Oxford University Press, 1974.

Haughton, James (1795–1863)

Born in 1795, Dublin corn merchant James Haughton supported a wide variety of social reform movements in the early nineteenth century, including abolitionism, temperance, and Irish nationalism. More so than any of his antislavery colleagues in Dublin, he was responsible for influencing the Unitarian Church to maintain a staunch opposition to slavery.

Haughton first encountered his antislavery colleagues, Richard Allen and Richard Davis Webb, through his work with the Dublin Temperance Society in the late 1820s and early 1830s. In 1837, the three men joined the newly formed Hibernian Anti-Slavery Society, through which they fought against the West Indian apprenticeship system that had been instituted at the time of emancipation. By the 1840s, when the attention of the society turned to opposing American slavery, Haughton had emerged as one its most influential leaders.

Throughout the 1840s and 1850s, Haughton wrote letters and editorials on behalf of the antislavery movement that appeared in prominent Dublin publications. He took a special interest in promoting the Free Produce movement, which discouraged the purchase of slave-grown cotton, tobacco, and sugar.

As a Unitarian, Haughton was concerned with promoting an active stance against slavery within his church. He maintained a correspondence with the American abolitionist and Unitarian minister Samuel May, and, in the 1840s, authored several addresses to American Unitarians on the subject of slavery. In 1847, when the American Unitarians rebuffed his entreaties, Haughton convinced the Irish Unitarian Christian Society to pass a resolution of censure against American Unitarians who failed to support abolitionism. That same year, Haughton criticized the selection of a South Carolina slaveholder, Joshua B. Whitridge, as a member of the board of vice presidents of the American Unitarian Association. The American Unitarians, as a result of a barrage of criticism from Unitarians across the Atlantic, eventually expelled Whitridge, but the incident resulted in lasting tension between the British and American branches of the church.

In the 1840s, Haughton was an active member of Daniel O'Connell's Loyal National Repeal Association, which was formed to repeal the union between Britain and Ireland and to establish an Irish parliament under the Crown. As a member, Haughton frequently introduced resolutions calling for an end to American slavery. He helped produce the *Address From the People of Ireland to Their Countrymen and Countrywomen in America,* a petition that encouraged Irish Americans to support abolitionism, and he used the established network of the Irish repeal association to circulate the petition around Ireland in 1841. The petition, which was eventually signed by approximately 60,000 Irish men and women, including O'Connell, failed to attract Irish Americans to the abolitionist cause.

Haughton continued to press for a continued commitment to antislavery among the repealers until the Young Irelanders, a more radical group of Irish nationalists, split away from the repeal movement in 1847. Haughton followed the Young Irelanders in this split, but he was less successful with them in encouraging an abolitionist agenda.

The Hibernian Anti-Slavery Society was dissolved after the Great Famine hit Ireland in the late 1840s, but Haughton maintained his commitment to the abolitionist cause. In 1850, when interest in American slavery was revived by the passage of the Fugitive Slave Law, he served as vice president of the Gentleman's Anti-Slavery Society in Dublin.

Haughton supported American abolitionists through the U.S. Civil War. When the war broke out, he was critical of the Northern effort to maintain its union with the South; however, he continued to work on behalf of American slaves. After the Emancipation Proclamation of 1863, he became active in the Freedmen's Aid movement in Ireland, which was dedicated to helping former slaves transition into American society as free men and women. Haughton died in 1863.

Angela F. Murphy

See also: Apprenticeship and Emancipation; Hibernian Anti-Slavery Society; O'Connell, Daniel; Webb, Richard Davis.

Further Reading

Ignatiev, Noel. *How the Irish Became White.* New York: Routledge, 1995.

Strange, Douglas Charles. *British Unitarians Against American Slavery.* Cranbury, NJ: Associated University Presses, 1984.

Hausa Uprising (1835)

The Hausa Uprising, variously known as the Malê Revolt and the Bahía Rebellion, was the largest and one of the most brutal slave insurrections in Brazilian history. The incident took place in and around the port city of San Salvador in the state of Bahía when an estimated 400–600 slaves nearly seized control of the city on January 25, 1835. This revolt was the last major slave insurrection to occur in Brazil before emancipation was finally legislated in 1888.

The 1835 uprising was the culmination of a series of nearly two dozen incidents that had occurred in the sugar-producing region of northeastern Brazil during the early decades of the nineteenth century. Two key factors, however, set the 1835 incident apart from previous slave uprisings: This incident was primarily an urban uprising with only marginal support from the hinterlands, and the successful organization of the revolt was largely attributable to networking among slaves who shared common Muslim heritage.

White Brazilians constituted only about 20 percent of the population in Bahía, whereas slaves and free blacks each made up about 40 percent of the region's inhabitants. As a result, African cultural influences were readily present and were deeply entrenched in the community. Due to Brazil's steady reliance on slave importation through the transatlantic trade, the country received a steady stream of newly enslaved Africans who were not acculturated to their new status and environment but were familiar with African ways. Thus, Bahía's African cultural identity was constantly being regenerated by the arrival of new slaves in the region.

Brazilian authorities and local planters and farmers initially tolerated some of the African cultural practices that were maintained within the slave community. Common characteristics such as language, religion, dance, and folk medicine were not perceived as subversive but rather as cultural traits that kept the slave population happy and complacent. By the 1830s, however, the Brazilian authorities had changed their attitude, as they began to restrict some of the traditional liberties that slaves had been allowed to enjoy in previous years.

Many of the Africans who were transported to Brazil as slaves had originated in a region of northern Nigeria belonging to the Hausa tribal group. In that area, many Africans who converted to Islam were known generally as Malê, regardless of their individual tribal identities. Many of these Hausa/Malê slaves were responsible for the uprising that took place in Bahía in early 1835.

Had the plot progressed as planned, it could have been lethal. Slaves hoped to start the revolt on a Sunday while white residents were attending church services. The plan called for the instigation of widespread arson in the city, signaling allies to the cause and occupying the attention of local authorities. The arson was designed to be a ruse that would distract white residents so that a scheduled counterattack could be mounted by a force of slaves. Two free black women alerted the Brazilian authorities of the plot shortly before it was to begin; despite advanced notice, leaders decided to continue with their plans.

Intense fighting went on in and around Bahía for an entire day, with casualties mounting on both sides of the conflict. The slaves, who believed they were protected by magical talismans that contained messages written in Arabic, used clubs, knives, and bows. Although the white forces were outnumbered, they had superior firepower and suppressed the uprising. Afterwards, the region saw the brutal application of extralegal justice, as hundreds of suspected rebels were executed without the benefit of a trial.

In the aftermath of the 1835 uprising, Brazilian authorities enacted more stringent ordinances associated with the management of slaves, and more stringent patrols were ordered throughout the affected region. In addition, the slaves' religious and cultural expressions, as well as other liberties, were severely curtailed. Under the new system of control, no comparable slave plot took place during the remaining half-century of enslavement in Brazil before emancipation.

Junius P. Rodriguez

See also: Brazil, Abolition in; Brazil, Emancipation in.

Further Reading

Diouf, Sylviane A. *Servants of Allah: African Muslims Enslaved in the Americas.* New York: New York University Press, 1998.

Goody, Jack. "Writing, Religion, and Revolt in Bahía." *Visible Language* 20 (Summer 1986): 318–43.

Kent, Raymond K. "African Revolt in Bahía." *Journal of Social History* 3 (Summer 1970): 334–56.

Reis, João José. *Slave Rebellion in Brazil: The Muslim Uprising of 1835 in Bahía.* Trans. Arthur Brakel. Baltimore: Johns Hopkins University Press, 1993.

Haviland, Laura Smith (1808–1898)

As an educator, missionary, nurse, and supporter of the Underground Railroad, Laura Smith Haviland played an important role in the abolitionist movement in Michigan.

Born in Ontario, Canada, on December 20, 1808, Smith was raised in Niagara County, New York. The daughter of Quaker farmers, she was educated in Society of Friends schools and grew up with the conscience of a Quaker. She married Charles Haviland, Jr., a fellow Quaker, in 1825, and, in September 1829, the couple relocated with their two small children to Lenawee Township, Michigan, an outpost on the Raisin River about thirty miles southwest of Ann Arbor.

Soon after they arrived, the Havilands befriended Elizabeth Margaret Chandler, a Quaker poet and editor of the ladies' page of an antislavery newspaper, the *Genius of Universal Emancipation*. The Havilands joined Chandler's Logan Female Anti-Slavery Society, a move that brought them into conflict with conservative Quakers in the community who felt their antislavery beliefs were too radical. Haviland ultimately split from the Quakers and joined the Wesleyan Methodist Church. In 1844, she became a minister of the faith.

Always interested in the plight of poor and orphaned children, in 1837, the Havilands opened their farm to a few of the country's indigent youth. Two years later, they turned the farm into the Raisin Institute, a co-educational, biracial preparatory school modeled after Oberlin College in Ohio. The school was the first to teach blacks in Michigan, providing basic education and skills aimed at moving blacks out of poverty, preparing them to teach, and demonstrating that whites and blacks could work together. It was also a refuge for runaway slaves.

In 1845, Haviland lost her husband, youngest child, father, mother, and sister in an epidemic that raged through the township. A widow at thirty-six, she had seven children to raise and a large debt to pay off. She turned over the institute to trustees and threw herself into antislavery work, traveling across the Midwest and Canada as a self-appointed missionary. She gave speeches, taught in schools for freed slaves, and ventured far into the South to provide nursing and aid where she could.

Haviland also became a conductor on the Underground Railroad—a secret network of safe hiding places that assisted fugitive slaves in escaping to freedom—personally escorting runaway slaves from Ohio to Canada. In 1846–1847, she foiled the efforts of Southern slave catchers to return a family of escaped slaves to their master; for doing so, the men offered a reward of $3,000 for her capture.

During the U.S. Civil War, Haviland put her nursing skills to work in the army hospitals and prison camps of the Midwest. Long before there was an infrastructure of services to assist them, she provided care and education to the countless slaves who fled to the North in the face of advancing armies. Haviland traveled to Mississippi to minister to wounded soldiers and former slaves, and she successfully intervened on behalf of 3,000 Union soldiers imprisoned on islands in the Gulf of Mexico.

The conclusion of the war did not end Haviland's mission. In the late 1860s and early 1870s, she worked to provide relief for former slaves and education for orphaned children. As an officer for the Freedmen's Aid Commission, she assisted in the relocation and adjustment to their new lives of former slaves in

Kansas. In 1871, she helped push a bill through the Michigan legislature that created the State Public School for Dependent and Neglected Children.

Later, Haviland turned her energies toward women's suffrage and temperance, and she worked for these movements for the remainder of her life. In her autobiography, *A Woman's Life Work* (1881), she asked, "Is it not the duty of every Christian to bring his or her religion into every line of life work, and act as conscientiously in politics as in church work?"

Haviland died on April 20, 1898. Having reconciled with the Quakers, she was buried in a Friends cemetery near Grand Rapids, Michigan.

Heather K. Michon

See also: Chandler, Elizabeth Margaret; Underground Railroad.

Further Reading

Hersh, Blanch Glassman. *The Slavery of Sex: Feminist-Abolitionists in America.* Urbana: University of Illinois, 1978.

Yellin, Jean Fagan. *Women and Sisters: The Anti-Slavery Feminists in American Culture.* New Haven, CT: Yale University Press, 1989.

Hayden, Lewis (ca. 1811–1889)

Lewis Hayden, an Underground Railroad agent, Boston merchant, and politician, was dubbed the abolitionist movement's "staunchest ally" by the noted antislavery activist William Lloyd Garrison. An example of the political activism and social power of blacks in nineteenth-century Boston, Hayden pressed for freedom and equality for all black Americans.

Hayden was born a slave in Lexington, Kentucky, to Millie and Lewis Hayden. Young Lewis learned the pain of slavery and separation from family at an early age when his father, who was owned by a different master, was forced to move away. Lewis and his mother were owned by the Reverend Adam Rankin, who sold Millie to a local man whose cruel treatment eventually drove her insane. When Hayden was about fifteen years old, Rankin decided to move to Pennsylvania, a free state. Rankin could not take his slaves—among them Hayden and his brothers and sisters—so he sold them all.

After being sold to another owner and seeing his wife and son sold to slave traders, in 1838, Hayden married Harriet Bell, also a slave, and raised her two-year-old son as his own. In 1842, Hayden was sold to two men who hired him out to temporary masters and earned rental fees for his labor. This arrangement brought him under the employ of a hotel manager, who trained Hayden as a waiter.

Through his work at the hotel, Hayden met Delia Webster and her close friend Calvin Fairbanks of Ohio, both abolitionists and Underground Railroad agents. With their help, Lewis and his family escaped to Ohio, a free state. Their trip by carriage was difficult and long, and they were almost discovered several times along the road. Upon reaching Ripley, Ohio, a well-known Underground Railroad stop across the Ohio River from Kentucky, the Haydens were hotly pursued.

After passing from one safe house to the next, the Haydens finally reached safety in Amherstburg in Ontario, Canada. Webster and Fairbanks, however, were both arrested and convicted for helping the Haydens to escape. Webster was released from prison within a few months, but Fairbanks was sentenced to fifteen years. Hayden would eventually help pay for Fairbanks's release.

Hayden quickly became active in the fugitive slave community in Canada. Before long, he and Harriet felt secure enough to move to Detroit, Michigan, where they participated in antislavery activities. After traveling to Boston to raise funds to build a black church in Detroit, Hayden's story of enslavement and escape began to attract much attention. The American Anti-Slavery Society eventually hired him as a speaker, but Hayden's disagreement with society president Garrison over his position of nonviolence forced the society to end Hayden's employment.

Hayden and his wife relocated to the predominantly black Beacon Hill district of Boston, where the couple became active in local antislavery politics. After the passage of the Fugitive Slave Law of 1850, which provided loose terms for the return of escaped slaves to their masters, Hayden helped form the Boston Vigilance Committee, which successfully raised money, provided legal counsel, and resisted federal marshals on behalf of runaway slaves. The committee comprised some of the most powerful antislavery activists in New England, including Wendell Phillips, Francis Jackson, and the Reverend Theodore Parker.

The Boston Vigilance Committee was instrumental in the rescue of Shadrach Minkins, the first fugitive slave to be captured in the city under the new Fugitive Slave Law. As a result of aiding Minkins, Hayden was indicted for his actions. Throughout the 1850s, the Haydens sheltered more than 100 runaways in their home on Beacon Hill, including the famous couple William and Ellen Craft.

Hayden supported the radical abolitionist John Brown and was one of the few insiders privy to Brown's plans for an attack on the federal arsenal at Harpers Ferry, Virginia, in 1859. A close friend of Massachusetts governor John Andrew, Hayden helped convince Andrew to form a regiment of black soldiers, the Fifty-fourth Regiment of the Massachusetts Volunteer Infantry, to fight in the U.S. Civil War. In the late 1850s, Hayden became the first African American hired by the Massachusetts state government when he was appointed messenger to the office of the secretary of state, a position he held for more than thirty years.

After the war, Hayden became active in the Freemason movement, and, in 1873, he was elected to the Massachusetts state senate. A fierce defender of civil and equal rights for both minorities and women, Hayden struggled to gain recognition for the contributions of African Americans to the nation's history. In 1887, he successfully led a petition to build a monument to Crispus Attucks, the first casualty of the American Revolution.

Despite his successes, Hayden's failing health, kept his family on the brink of poverty. He died on April 7, 1889.

Kate Clifford Larson

See also: Brown, John; Canada; Fairbanks, Calvin; Massachusetts Fifty-Fourth Regiment; Underground Railroad.

Further Reading

Blassingame, John W., ed. *Slave Testimony: Two Centuries of Letters, Speeches, Interviews, and Autobiographies.* Baton Rouge: Louisiana State University Press, 1977.

Quarles, Benjamin. *Black Abolitionists.* New York: Oxford University Press, 1969.

Ripley, C. Peter, et al., eds. *The Black Abolitionist Papers.* 5 vols. Chapel Hill: University of North Carolina Press, 1985–1992.

Robert, Stanley J., and Anita W. Robert. "Lewis Hayden: From Fugitive Slave to Statesman." *New England Quarterly* 46 (December 1973): 591–613.

Strangis, Joel. *Lewis Hayden and the War Against Slavery.* North Haven, CT: Linnett, 1999.

Helper, Hinton Rowan (1829–1909)

An abolitionist, writer, businessman, diplomat, and racist ideologue, Hinton Rowan Helper is best known as the author of *The Impending Crisis* (1857), which, along with Harriet Beecher Stowe's novel *Uncle Tom's Cabin* (1852), was one of the two most important literary works to come out of the antislavery movement. Perhaps the most influential Southerner to join the abolitionist cause, Helper nevertheless left a legacy tainted by virulent lifelong racism. His negrophobia was clearly manifest in all of his postwar writings, which reveal an almost rabid desire to expel the black race from the United States after emancipation.

Born in Davie County, North Carolina, on December 27, 1829, Helper came of age in his native state. At the age of twenty, he moved to New York City briefly before traversing the continent to California in 1851, where he remained for the next three years. There, he observed differences in the economics, politics, society, and especially race relations of the Far West, as contrasted with those of his native region. In 1855, he published his first book, *The Land of Gold,* which chronicled his sojourn to the Pacific Coast.

By far his most influential work came two years later, when he wrote *The Impending Crisis of the South: How to Meet It* (1857), which was reprinted as a campaign document by the Republican Party as the election of 1860 approached. In it, Helper made a case for abolishing slavery for economic reasons. As the title implies, he believed that a conflict pitting abolitionists and Free Soilers against Southern slave owners was inevitable. Moreover, he believed that the sooner it happened, the better it would be for the South, because the conflict would surely hasten the demise of slavery, which kept the South in economic shackles.

In his book, Helper proposed a solution to the problem: Get rid of slavery immediately, before the inevitable conflict arises. He argued that although slaveholders complained about the need for financial compensation in the event of a government-coerced emancipation, the exact opposite was needed. Slaveholders, he maintained, should compensate Southern white society for decades of retarded economic growth at their hands. Realistically, of course, he knew that would never happen, but he believed that if slavery were abolished, the value of land in the South would rise more than fivefold to compensate everyone—slaveholder and yeoman alike.

Most Southerners simply dismissed Helper's book as the ravings of an abolitionist fanatic, yet it also frightened them, to the extent that Southern state governments banned the book and threatened to punish anyone caught reading it. They lumped it in with the so-called "incendiary" abolitionist literature coming out of the Northern states, such as William Lloyd Garrison's newspaper *The Liberator* and David Walker's *Appeal,* which precipitated the worst slave uprising in American history—Nat Turner's Rebellion in Virginia—in 1831.

Unlike Garrison and most other abolitionists, Helper was not interested in the welfare of blacks but in the welfare of the South and the working-class whites who lived there. He believed that the average white Southerner had become culturally and economically backward because of the debasing influence of slavery. He wanted the South to catch up with the progress the North had made, both economically and culturally. In his mind, the only way to do that was to get rid of the institution that was responsible for holding the South down, as well as to purge its political system of the pernicious influence of slave power. He believed that liberated slaves should be shipped en masse to Liberia, Central or South America, or the Western United States at the slaveholders' expense.

Helper looked down on women writers and their literature in general, but he especially disdained Stowe's fictional masterpiece on slavery, *Uncle Tom's Cabin,* considering it an example of the sentimental and misguided zealousness that pervaded the abolitionist movement in the 1850s. He believed it did no harm for women writers to contribute to the abolitionist movement with such literature, but he thought that it would ultimately require factual accounts of the institution and its impact on the South—written by men—to effect any great change.

Helper considered himself a Southerner, both by birth and by choice, yet he also regarded himself as an unconditional abolitionist, an immediate emancipationist, a patriotic Free Soiler, and an empathetic racial colonizationist. He was careful to avoid being identified with the likes of John Brown and other fanatical abolitionists who advocated the violent overthrow of slavery. But neither did he belong to the contingent of abolitionists headed by Garrison who favored moral suasion as the best approach to ending slavery. He associated with certain other abolitionists, although he did not always agree with their methods.

President Abraham Lincoln initially refused to reward Helper or anyone who endorsed his controversial book with any political office. Late in 1861, as a result of Helper's persistence in seeking patronage, however, Lincoln relented and appointed him U.S. consul to Argentina, a post Helper held until 1867. He resigned at that time because radicals had taken control of the Republican Party and began pushing their civil rights agenda. He subsequently left the party permanently and became one of its foremost critics. In 1868, he led the movement to create a third party devoted to fighting for the working class.

From his resignation as consul in Buenos Aires in 1867 to his death in 1909, Helper became a special agent hired by private Americans and companies to collect debts owed them by South American governments. He became well acquainted with Latin America and spent a good deal of time there promoting the idea of the Three Americas Railway, a railroad connecting North and South America.

Helper's post–Civil War writings include *Nojoque, a Question for a Continent* (1867) and *The Negroes in Negroland, the Negroes in America, and the Negroes Generally* (1868). Both of these works set forth his vision for a segregated America that must eventually expel blacks altogether. He died on March 9, 1909.

Thomas Adams Upchurch

See also: Immediatism; Racism.

Further Reading

Bailey, Hugh. *Hinton Rowan Helper: Abolitionist and Racist.* Tuscaloosa: University of Alabama Press, 1965.

Cardoso, J.J. "Hinton Rowan Helper as a Racist in the Abolitionist Camp." *Journal of Negro History* 55 (October 1970): 323–30.

Robertson, James I., Jr. "The Book That Enraged the South." *Civil War Times Illustrated* 7 (September 1969): 20–22.

Henson, Josiah (1789–1883)

Regarded by many as the model for the character of Uncle Tom in Harriet Beecher Stowe's antislavery novel *Uncle Tom's Cabin* (1852), Josiah Henson was a slave who escaped to Canada with his family in 1830. He became a leading advocate for the rights of fugitives settling in Canada.

Henson was born on June 15, 1789, on a farm in Charles County, Maryland. Sometime during the mid-1820s, Henson was loaned to his master's brother, Amos Riley, in Kentucky. For three years, Henson worked in Kentucky and became a licensed preacher of the Methodist Episcopal Church. In 1829, he purchased his freedom from his master, but Riley intended to have him sold in New Orleans. In defiance of his master's plan, Henson and his wife and children escaped to Waterloo, Canada, in October 1830.

In Canada, Henson continued preaching, and his small band of religious followers began to grow

Romantics of the nineteenth century identified literature as an instrument of social activism. Like some transcendentalists in the United States, Hugo proved the effectiveness of novels and poems in promoting humanitarian causes. In 1818, the young Hugo began writing *Bug-Jargal* (1826), a novel about the 1791 slave insurrection in Saint-Domingue (present-day Haiti). He compared the lives of the slaves with those of their masters through the actions and thoughts of Bug-Jargal, a heroic slave who fights and dies for freedom. Hugo's concern for the plight of the enslaved placed him squarely in French Romantic tradition's concentration on global social issues.

Hugo's insistence on the human dignity of slaves informed his later works on capital punishment and poverty. Like slavery, the practice of capital punishment contradicted the humanitarian element of French Romanticism. Through the characters and themes of *Le dernier jour d'un condamné* (The Last Day of a Condemned, 1829) and *Claude Gueux* (1834), Hugo expressed his opinion that criminals are the product of social conditions. He criticized societies for abetting poverty and then punishing the poor for trying to survive. In *Les Contemplations* (1856), he reminded readers to treat the poor with respect and compassion by describing *le meniant,* or the beggar, as a silent person, representative of Jesus Christ.

In his masterpiece *Les Misérables,* Hugo integrated his concern for human suffering and dignity in the character of Jean Valjean. The protagonist is imprisoned for stealing a loaf of bread, after which he experiences a spiritual awakening and becomes a benevolent contributor to society. Hugo saw in Valjean the possibility of improving the lives of the downtrodden through individual and social reform.

In 1859, John Brown's militant actions at Harpers Ferry, Virginia, compelled Hugo to denounce slavery and capital punishment in the United States. Brown had led a violent raid against an army arsenal in an effort to instigate a slave insurrection; ultimately, he was arrested and sentenced to death by hanging. Hugo responded to Brown's predicament with a plea to the humanitarian sensibilities of both Europeans and Americans. "If we can save this man," Hugo argued, "this hero, this martyr, what joy! and above all, to save this man would be to save this republic." His letters were published as far away as Haiti, and he made a personal plea to the president of the United States, James Buchanan.

After Brown was executed that December and the American Civil War began in 1861, Hugo enjoyed a prominent political career in France as a leader of the Liberal Party. Upon his death on May 22, 1885, more than 2 million people viewed his body under the Arc de Triomphe, remembering him as one of France's most celebrated Romantic thinkers and activists.

Michael Pasquier

See also: Brown, John.

Further Reading

Frey, John Andrew. *A Victor Hugo Encyclopedia.* Westport, CT: Greenwood, 1999.
Gavronsky, Serge. *The French Liberal Opposition and the American Civil War.* New York: Humanities, 1968.

Immediatism

One of the key tenets of the radical abolitionist philosophy was the belief that emancipation, when effected, must be immediate rather than gradual. This philosophy, which came to be called "immediatism," advocated that the abolition of slavery should not be associated with any form of compensated emancipation for slaveholders or with the removal of emancipated blacks through any colonization scheme. Battle lines were drawn within the antislavery movement between the proponents of immediatism and more conservative abolitionists who favored a gradual approach.

The immediatists charged that if slavery was indeed evil, it was unacceptable for the gradualists to oppose slavery but work to prolong its effects. The question of gradualism versus immediatism quickly became one that divided abolitionists. The English Quaker Elizabeth Heyrick wrote a pamphlet titled *Immediate, Not Gradual Emancipation* (1824) as Parliament began to discuss the fate of slavery in the colonies. Americans became familiar with the argument as Heyrick's tract was reprinted and published in serial installments, starting in November 1825, by abolitionist Benjamin Lundy in the antislavery paper the *Genius of Universal Emancipation*. Heyrick's message had a transatlantic appeal, and many followers in Britain and the United States adopted the immediatist philosophy as their own.

Heyrick charged that gradualism was a "masterpiece of satanic policy," because "the great interests of truth and justice are betrayed rather than supported by the softening, qualifying concessions [to slaveholders] . . . Truth and justice make their best way in the world, when they appear in bold and simple majesty." Such strident rhetoric moved the abolitionist argument beyond the realm of mere philosophical debate and made it a question of good versus evil.

It is no coincidence that the immediatist philosophy began to crystallize in the 1820s, just as a religious revival known as the Second Great Awakening was sweeping large parts of the United States. For those who found themselves "born again" in the evangelical fury of the time, the characterization of slavery as sin was a statement of fact that appealed to both faith and reason. Within such a moral universe, anyone who sought to prolong the existence of slavery was aiding and abetting the worst type of evil.

Radical abolitionists such as William Lloyd Garrison believed the gradualists were effectively no better than slaveholders, as both groups sought to perpetuate an institution that was rooted in sin. Not surprisingly, Garrison devoted much editorial space in *The Liberator* to condemnations of slavery, but he also included vituperative attacks against the antislavery gradualists, whom he viewed as tacit supporters of the institution. Garrison's argument, language, and incessant pleading for the immediate abolition of slavery were all couched in the crusading spiritual zeal of one who sensed that he was part of a divine mission. One of the most beneficial aspects of immediatism to the general antislavery debate was that it promoted a sense of urgency that was necessary to further the abolition of slavery—a point that Garrison and other immediatists advanced in their relentless propagandizing.

Opponents of immediatism charged that the radical abolitionists were either unaware of the adverse effects that unconditional and immediate emancipation might have on the nation or dismissed them too blithely. Some even charged that full, unfettered freedom could have negative consequences for emancipated slaves who were ill-prepared for the transition to their new role as wage laborers. Others believed that the social, economic, and political effects of immediate emancipation would be untenable without adequate time to prepare society for such a consequential change.

The ongoing debate between the gradualists and the immediatists created a schism within the antislavery movement that made unified action impossible. Their philosophical duality and factional infighting diluted their message and thwarted their efforts. When emancipation finally did come to the United States, it was based on the immediate, uncompensated model that Garrison and other radical abolitionists had long promoted.

Junius P. Rodriguez

See also: Garrison, William Lloyd; Gradualism; Heyrick, Elizabeth; Lundy, Benjamin.

Further Reading

Davis, David Brion. "The Emergence of Immediatism in British and American Antislavery Thought." *Mississippi Valley Historical Review* 49 (September 1962): 209–30.

Fladeland, Betty. *Men and Brothers: Anglo-American Antislavery Cooperation.* Urbana: University of Illinois Press, 1972.

Loveland, Anne C. "Evangelicalism and Immediate Emancipation in American Antislavery Thought." *Journal of Southern History* 32 (May 1966): 172–88.

MacLeod, Duncan J. "From Gradualism to Immediatism: Another Look." *Slavery and Abolition* 3 (September 1982): 140–52.

Pease, Jane H., and William H. Pease. "Anti-Slavery Ambivalence: Immediatism, Expediency, Race." *American Quarterly* 17 (Winter 1965): 682–95.

Imperial Act (1793)

The Imperial Act of 1793, also known as the Act Against Slavery, was passed by the legislature of Upper Canada (present-day Ontario) to prohibit slavery. Upper Canada thus became the first British territory to pass an antislavery act; by 1800, other Canadian provinces had limited slavery through court rulings. The act remained in force until 1833, when the British Parliament passed the Abolition of Slavery Act (commonly known as the British Emancipation Act), abolishing slavery in all parts of the British Empire.

Spearheaded by John Graves Simcoe, the first lieutenant governor of Upper Canada, and introduced by Attorney General John White as a bill in Upper Canada's House of Assembly, the Imperial Act of 1793 repealed the Imperial Statute of 1790, which allowed white settlers to immigrate to Canada with their enslaved Africans. The 1793 law stipulated that those already in Canada who were slaves would remain slaves, and those who currently owned slaves had to provide them with food and clothing. It stated that if a slave was given his or her freedom, the slave must be able to function independently upon emancipation. It further indicated that any child born of a slave mother would be free at the age of twenty-five. The Imperial Act also placed a nine-year limit on the terms of indentured servants.

Although the Imperial Act did not free a single slave, it did curtail the growth of Canada's slave community and helped pave the way for the end of chattel slavery worldwide. It also fostered a perception of Canada as a safe haven for the enslaved, and as a result, many African defenders of the War of 1812 flocked to Canada. The territory also provided a terminus for the Underground Railroad, a loosely organized network of abolitionists who assisted enslaved African Americans in their journey northward to free Canada.

In 1833, the few slaves who remained in Canada were freed by Abolition of Slavery Act. The first global human rights legislation, this act abolished slavery throughout the British Empire. Just as the Imperial Act of 1793 raised awareness of the potential for slaves to be transported from a British colony edging toward abolition, the Abolition of Slavery Act was the model from which other global slave powers took their lead in ending the "peculiar institution."

Rosemary Sadlier

See also: Canada.

Further Reading

Alexander, Ken, and Avis Glaze. *Towards Freedom: The African-Canadian Experience.* Toronto, Ontario, Canada: Umbrella, 1996.

Craig, Gerald M. *Upper Canada: The Formative Years, 1784–1841.* Toronto, Ontario, Canada: McClelland and Stewart, 1963.

Macdougall, Donald V. "Habeus Corpus, Extradition and the Fugitive Slave in Canada." *Slavery and Abolition* 7 (September 1986): 118–28.

McCalla, Douglas. *Planting the Province: The Economic History of Upper Canada, 1784–1870.* Toronto, Ontario, Canada: University of Toronto Press, 1993.

Murray, Alexander L. "The Extradition of Fugitive Slaves from Canada: A Re-Evaluation." *The Canadian Historical Review* 43 (December 1962): 298–314.

Winks, Robin W. *The Blacks in Canada: A History.* New Haven, CT: Yale University Press, 1971.

Isabel, Princess Regent of Brazil (1846–1921)

As regent of Brazil, Princess Isabel, the only woman to rule a nation in the Western Hemisphere during the nineteenth century, signed the *Lei Áurea* (Golden Law) in 1888, abolishing slavery in Brazil.

Born into an aristocratic family on July 29, 1846, Isabel became the official heiress of the Brazilian Empire when her brother died as an infant in 1850. Isabel's father, Dom Pedro II, became emperor of Brazil in 1831 upon the abdication of his father,

Pedro I. During his rule, Dom Pedro II relied on the support of the regional elite and the sugar planters, who viewed the empire as a guarantee of the survival of the slavery system.

By 1870, however, Dom Pedro II was facing pressure from abolitionists to support the complete emancipation of slaves and the simultaneous demand of slave owners to delay granting their slaves freedom for as long as possible. As the abolitionist movement began to gain momentum in Brazil, Dom Pedro II advocated a slow transition from slavery to conditional freedom.

Isabel ruled Brazil as regent on three occasions when her father was out of the country between 1871 and 1888; during two of his absences, she signed anti-slavery laws. This was a crucial period in Brazilian history, as the abolitionist movement was gaining strength. Isabel was an ardent abolitionist, and her advocacy earned her the support of the masses, who gave her the popular title *A Redentora* (the Redemptress).

During her first regency, Isabel sympathized with the work of abolitionists such as Joaquim Nabuco, and she signed the *Lei do Ventre Libre* (literally "Law of the Free Womb," or "Free Birth Law," as it came to be known) on September 28, 1871, a measure that freed the newborn children of slave women. Although Isabel signed the law, the groundwork had been laid by the emperor before his departure.

The landed elite did not revolt against the measure, because it included clauses that required current slave children to continue serving their masters until they reached the age of twenty-one. Abolitionist groups in Brazil denounced the law as a government ploy to delay true emancipation.

The process of abolition intensified in 1884 when the provinces of Ceará and Amazonas decreed the emancipation of all slaves. With mounting pressure from abolitionists, on September 25, 1885, Pedro II approved the Sexagenarian Law, another incremental measure that granted freedom to *sexagenários* (slaves over sixty years old). Again, sugar planters and other slave owners did not oppose the measure, because most slaves did not live long after reaching sixty years of age.

Isabel's third regency began in 1887, when her father traveled to Europe to receive medical attention. This time, she faced more challenging events and took a more assertive role in ruling the colony. The abolitionist movement had gained widespread support, and its leaders were calling for full emancipation. The Brazilian Parliament met to address the issue of slavery, voted overwhelmingly for abolition, and then drafted a law that Isabel approved. On May 13, 1888, she signed the Golden Law, which declared the full and final abolition slavery in Brazil. "From the date of this law," the document stated, "slavery is declared abolished in Brazil. All contrary provisions are revoked. Signed by Princess Isabel, ruling as Regent for Dom Pedro II." With the passage of the Golden Law, Brazil became the last country in the Americas to abolish slavery.

The Golden Law made Isabel immensely popular with the Brazilian masses. The monarchy was no longer useful to the regional elite and the sugar planters, however, as they believed their interests were no longer protected. Their response was quick and strong. On November 4, 1889, the imperial family was overthrown in a bloodless military coup, and a new republic was established. Two days later, Dom Pedro II, Isabel, and the rest of the royal family set sail for Europe, where they lived in exile.

It is the paradox of Isabel's life that her boldest exercise of power—signing the Golden Law—led directly to her exile from Brazil and her discharge from public life. Yet she never regretted her decision, stating, "If abolition is the cause for this, I don't regret it; I consider it worth losing the throne for." She died in France on November 14, 1921.

Javier A. Galván

See also: Brazil, Abolition in; *Lei Áurea* (Golden Law, 1888).

Further Reading

Barman, Roderick J. *Princess Isabel of Brazil: Gender and Power in the Nineteenth Century.* Wilmington, DE: Scholarly Resources, 2002.

Skidmore, Thomas E. *Brazil: Five Centuries of Change.* New York: Oxford University Press, 1999.

Jacobs, Harriet (1813–1897)

By publishing her autobiography of slave life, *Incidents in the Life of a Slave Girl* (1861), Harriet Jacobs exposed the sordid exploitation that was associated with the treatment of enslaved women in nineteenth-century America. Her narrative, one of the few written in book-length form, provides readers with an early female view of slavery, described by the abolitionist Lydia Maria Child as "a peculiar phase of Slavery [that] has generally been kept veiled; but the public ought to be made acquainted with its monstrous features." Jacobs's narrative is a testimony to the author's determination to free herself from bondage.

Harriet Jacobs was born into slavery in 1813 in Edenton, North Carolina, to Delilah Horniblow and Elijah Knox. Her mother died in 1819, and Jacobs later remembered that it was only then that she understood she was a slave. Her first mistress, Margaret Horniblow, taught her to read and spell, activities that would become illegal for slaves in North Carolina in 1830. Jacobs and her grandmother, Molly, hoped her mistress would free the young girl, but upon Horniblow's death in 1825, she left Jacobs to her niece, Mary Matilda Norcom.

James Norcom, Mary Matilda's father, made sexual advances toward Jacobs. To better resist his advances and to gain a protector, Jacobs entered into a sexual relationship with Samuel Tredwell Sawyer, a white lawyer in Edenton. They had two children: Joseph in 1829 and Louisa Matilda in 1833.

Jacobs's relationship with Sawyer did not thwart Norcom. To intimidate Jacobs, he sent her to work at a nearby plantation that he had purchased for his son and threatened to send her children, who were legally his property, there as well. Jacobs believed that if she ran away, Norcom would lose interest in her children and perhaps sell them to Sawyer. In 1833, she escaped, eventually hiding herself in a crawl space below the roof of her grandmother's house. With only a blanket and what food and water could be secretly provided to her, she spent the next seven years in that dark, stifling space, which was so small she could barely move.

In June 1842, a friend of Jacobs's uncle located a sea captain who was willing to assist her in her escape North. Jacobs sailed north to Philadelphia and soon settled in New York, where she went to work as a baby nurse for the author Nathaniel Parker Willis and his wife Mary. There, she also reunited with her daughter Louisa, whom Sawyer had sent to live with his cousins in Brooklyn. Jacobs was being hunted by Norcom; several times, she left New York when he threatened her with re-enslavement.

In 1849, she traveled to Rochester, New York, where her brother, John S. Jacobs, worked in the Anti-Slavery Office and Reading Room, located above the offices of Frederick Douglass's abolitionist newspaper, *The North Star.* She became involved in western New York's large abolitionist community, befriending Amy Kirby Post, founder of the Western New York Anti-Slavery Society, whose home served as a station on the Underground Railroad. In 1852, Cornelia Willis, Nathaniel Parker Willis's second wife, arranged to purchase Jacobs for $300 in order to free her.

Jacobs began writing her story in 1853. In February, she rejected an offer from Harriet Beecher Stowe to include her story in the book *A Key to Uncle Tom's Cabin* (1854), which Stowe had written to refute claims that her novel was false or exaggerated. In June and July of that year, Jacobs published three articles about her experiences in the *New York Tribune* under the pseudonyms "A Fugitive" and "A Fugitive Slave."

Jacobs finished a draft of *Incidents in the Life of a Slave Girl* in 1858. Child penned the preface to the book and edited the manuscript, which was published in 1861. It appeared in England as *The Deeper Wrong* the following year and received wide attention in abolitionist circles in both Great Britain and America. Though Jacobs had used the pseudonym Linda Brent, her authorship of the book was widely known.

When the text was re-examined in the twentieth-century scholarship of Jean Fagan Yellin, many critics doubted that a former slave could have written such a lucid account. However, letters between Jacobs and Child held in the University of Rochester's special collections make it clear that *Incidents* was written by

Jacobs herself, with a "desire to arouse the women of the North to a realizing sense of the condition of two millions [sic] of women at the South, still in bondage, suffering what I suffered, and most of them far worse."

After the book's publication, Jacobs worked actively on behalf of her race. Beginning in 1862, she and her daughter worked in camps for refugees and freed slaves in Alexandria, Virginia. She opened the Jacobs School there in 1864 to teach the emancipated slaves in the region. She and Louisa continued their relief work in Savannah, Georgia, in 1865.

In later years, Jacobs ran boardinghouses in Cambridge, Massachusetts, and Washington, D.C., and worked at the New England Women's Club. She died in Washington on March 7, 1897, and was buried at Mount Auburn Cemetery in Cambridge.

Katherine L. Culkin

See also: Education of Former Slaves; Stowe, Harriet Beecher.

Further Reading

Garfield, Deborah M., and Rafia Zafar, eds. *Harriet Jacobs and* Incidents in the Life of a Slave Girl: *New Critical Essays.* New York: Cambridge University Press, 1996.

Jacobs, Harriet. *Incidents in the Life of a Slave Girl, as Written by Herself.* Ed. Henry Louis Gates, Jr., New York: Oxford University Press, 1988; ed. Jean Fagan Yellin, Cambridge, MA: Harvard University Press, 2000.

Sánchez-Eppler, Karen. *Touching Liberty: Abolition, Feminism, and the Politics of the Body.* Berkeley: University of California Press, 1993.

Smith, Valerie. *Self-Discovery and Authority in Afro-American Narrative.* Cambridge, MA: Harvard University Press, 1987.

Jamaica, Abolition in

The Spanish island colony of Jamaica was acquired by Great Britain in 1655 and thereafter relied on slave labor for the production of sugar and coffee. England, in turn, came to rely on the colony for much of its economic growth, at the expense of millions of lives. Although Jamaica had become the jewel of the British Empire by the mid-eighteenth century, many in England resented the system of slavery that was behind the colony's success. Thus, as antislavery sentiment increased, Jamaica became a central target of the abolitionist cause.

Despite rising abolitionist sentiment in England during the mid-eighteenth century, Jamaican planters were more concerned with production and output than they were with threats to the slave trade.

Though the Quakers freed their slaves in the American colonies in 1774 and disavowed those connected with the slave trade, it was business as usual on the Jamaican estates. It was not until 1783, when the Quakers presented the British Parliament with the first petition to abolish the slave trade that the Jamaican planters seriously began to consider the question of abolition. Over the next few years, such petitions increased in number, and support for abolitionism intensified; the Jamaican planters gradually comprehended that their labor supply was in danger.

At first, the Jamaican planters responded by buying more slaves, and the number of Africans imported into the colony increased with each passing year. At the same time, many recognized that changing their strategy was the only means of counteracting the abolitionist threat to the slave supply.

Although the slave population grew steadily, the increase came primarily from the transatlantic slave trade. Jamaica's slaves experienced extremely high mortality rates, and the number of deaths far outweighed the number of births each year. Hard labor, harsh treatment, and low birthrates made a natural increase impossible. In fact, planters of the period discouraged slave women from having children, because they had meager chances for survival. Rather than risk investing in children who probably would not reach working age, the Jamaican planters preferred to purchase Africans who were more "field ready" from the slave markets.

Although importing more slaves was a quick solution, those slaves died quickly and still had to be replaced. In the seasoning process, during which Africans adjusted to life and work on the plantation over a period of one to three years, nearly one-third of all Africans died. Many of those who survived the seasoning process began working in the fields too soon and died not long after entering the workforce. With such high mortality rates among the Jamaican slave population, many planters grew dependent on the slave trade, convinced that their plantations would not be profitable without constant imports from Africa.

At the same time, abolitionists continued to petition Parliament for the abolition of the slave trade. The planters knew that if one of the petitions were passed and the trade ended, the Jamaican labor force would gradually disappear unless the slave population began to sustain itself. Therefore, in 1788, members of the Jamaican Assembly began to look more closely at the slave population in an effort to ascertain

ABOLITION OF SLAVERY IN JAMAICA.

PROCESSION of the BAPTIST CHURCH and CONGREGATION in SPANISH TOWN under the Pastoral care of THE REV.ᵈ J.M PHILLIPPO, with about 2000 Children of their Schools and their Teachers, to the Government House on the 1ˢᵗ August 1838, when they were received by His Excellency the Governor SIR LIONEL SMITH who after addressing them, read to them the PROCLAMATION of FREEDOM, amidst the hearty rejoicing of not less than 8000 persons, the majority of whom had previously attended Divine Worship, and who subsequently retired to their respective homes peaceful and happy. — The Governor, The Rev.ᵈ J.M Phillippo and the Bishop are seen standing in front of the Portico thus representing the happy Union of Civil & Religious feeling on this joyful occasion.

Full emancipation came to Jamaica on August 1, 1838. A crowd of 8,000 gathered in the main square of the capital, Spanish Town, for a reading of the Proclamation of Freedom by Governor Lionel Smith. *(©Private Collection/©Michael Graham-Stewart/The Bridgeman Art Library)*

the reasons behind its decrease. After a series of investigations and inquiries, they concluded that in addition to high mortality and low birthrates, Jamaica's slaves could not sustain themselves because of the disproportion of the sexes on Jamaican estates.

Within months, slave births were not only being encouraged, but the island's legislature took measures to reward and increase live births, secure healthy children, and limit the importation of Africans above the age of twenty-five. Jamaican planters also began purchasing as many "breeding wenches" and young boys and girls from Africa as possible. The Jamaican Assembly began to pass laws ameliorating the condition of the slave population, with specific laws requiring additional provisions, clothing, and medical attention for children.

By the time the English trade was effectively abolished in 1808, the lives of Jamaican slaves reflected these changes for the better in medical, social, and quantitative terms. By 1793, smallpox inocula-

tions were standard practice on the estates. Planters built hospitals and clinics on their estates, and doctors performed regular rounds among the slave population. Slave children received lighter work, better clothing, and more food. Pregnant women performed lighter work and gained a longer lying-in period. Not only did the number of births increase, these children also had a greater chance of survival.

Although these legislative efforts and the granting of rewards to slave women for live births increased the number of slave children, the Jamaican planters still were not satisfied. Following the abolition of the slave trade, English activists set their sights on ending slavery in all of the English colonies. The Jamaican planters, meanwhile, unable to import Africans, impatiently waited for the island's slave population to grow.

Influenced by visiting missionaries, the Jamaican "plantocracy" became convinced that the slow increase in the slave population was rooted in promiscuity and paganism. Some were convinced that promiscuity prohibited slave women from becoming pregnant. Others felt that unless the slave community understood the importance of marriage and the Christian ideals of family, the number of children would never increase. Therefore, starting in 1815, planters and missionaries began to impress Christianity upon the slave population, and the number of marriages and baptisms increased throughout the island.

Again, however, the planters realized that the abolitionists would soon bring an end to the institution of slavery in the English colonies, as it had the slave trade. Facing a life without slaves, the Jamaican plantocracy planned for the future. Although the planters knew that their way of life was coming to an end, they were more fearful of losing control of their labor force. It was the oppressive system of slavery that ensured the slave population knew its place. Where would their place be when slavery was made illegal, they wondered. What would become of a colony overrun with immoral savages and illiterates?

In the 1820s, planters and missionaries began to impose English values and beliefs on the slave population in the hope of socializing and de-Africanizing them into a more manageable class of people. Planters placed slave children in schools, either in the towns or on the estates, where they were taught English and etiquette alongside free black and colored children. At the same time, missionaries and parish rectors visited the estates weekly to provide the slave population with religious instruction and services.

Slave children were extremely important to the abolitionist movement. Abolitionists focused their attention on ending slavery in all British dominions by centering their arguments on the fate of slave children. Their solution to the gradual end of slavery was to free all slave children born after a certain date, as these children had done nothing to forfeit their freedom. Ironically, the same abolitionists applauded efforts to Christianize and de-Africanize slave children so that a happy, manageable, free peasantry could be created.

As slavery was coming to an end in July 1834, the Jamaican planters braced themselves for the backlash. As they awoke on the morning of August 1, the white population imagined that the day would rival the worst moments of the Haitian Revolution, expecting the newly freed slave population to take the island by storm. In the weeks that followed, however, their biggest fight was for monetary compensation from Parliament.

Meanwhile, the newly freed slave population adjusted to life without chains. Although they were no longer slaves, they were forced into a life of apprenticeship until their full emancipation in 1838. As they would come to see, slavery had ended in name only.

Colleen A. Vasconcellos

See also: Abolition of Slavery Act (1833); Abolition of the Slave Trade Act (1807); Apprenticeship and Emancipation; British West Indies, Abolition in the; Jamaica, Emancipation in.

Further Reading

Anstey, Roger. *The Atlantic Slave Trade and British Abolition, 1760–1810.* London: Macmillan, 1975.
Mathieson, William Law. *British Slavery and Its Abolition, 1823–1838.* London: Longman, Green, 1932.
Walvin, James. *Slavery and British Society, 1776–1846.* Baton Rouge: Louisiana State University Press, 1982.

Jamaica, Emancipation in

In December 1831, small groups of slaves moved throughout the Jamaican parishes of Saint James, Trelawney, Hanover, Saint Elizabeth, and Westmoreland, burning estates and sugar fields. Following the rebel leader Samuel Sharpe, the slaves traveled through the Jamaican countryside for a month. When the rebellion was finally quelled, 750 square miles and 226 estates had sustained property damage of $3.5 million. Although the rebels failed in bringing an immediate end to slavery in Jamaica, the rebellion disturbed the Jamaican "plantocracy" and the British legislature. It also caught the attention of British abolitionists, who felt the time was right to strike while the iron was hot.

By 1832, the Jamaican planters had realized that the abolition of slavery was unavoidable. Increased industrialization in Great Britain had created empathy for the slaves as the British working class began to gain control of the abolitionist movement and, with it, parliamentary support. Just as the British abolitionists had ended the transatlantic slave trade, there was no doubt among the Jamaican planters that they would end the institution of slavery as well. Rather than wait for the inevitable, the West Indian interest in Parliament and the Jamaican Assembly felt that another Haitian Revolution would occur unless they took control of the process. When the abolitionists sent 5,000 petitions to Parliament with 1.5 million signatures calling for an end to slavery in the British colonies the following year, Parliament acquiesced and set the wheels in motion.

In September 1833, Parliament passed the Abolition of Slavery Act (commonly known as the British Emancipation Act), presented by Edward Stanley, head of the Colonial Office. Drafted by James Stephen, son of the prominent abolitionist James Stephen, the plan provided for the immediate abolition of slavery, followed by a six-year apprenticeship period for former slaves. Beginning on August 1, 1834, the laborers worked for wages while being supported, clothed, and fed by their estates. All children under the age of six would be freed unless their parents consented to their apprenticeship and were considered the complete responsibility of their parents.

Special magistrates from Britain, chosen by the Jamaican governor, would preside over the system to ensure its fairness and smooth transition. With an average of two magistrates per parish, these men also would preside over any complaints voiced by the planters and their laborers. In addition to the magistrates, a special plantation police force made up of free blacks was appointed to enforce discipline within the revamped public workhouse system. As flogging females was prohibited by law, a treadmill was installed in each workhouse to be used as a form of punishment. Finally, Britain granted £20 million in compensation to planters who filed by a certain date.

Meanwhile, Jamaica set out to devise a plan for a smooth transition. The Jamaican plantocracy had already been making preparations for a future without slaves. In 1815, planters and missionaries began to impose British values and beliefs on slave children in the hope of socializing and de-Africanizing them into a more manageable class of people. Planters placed slave children in schools, either in the towns or on the estates, where they were taught English etiquette alongside free black and colored children. At the same time, missionaries and parish rectors visited the estates weekly to provide the slave population with religious instruction and services. From 1815 to 1826, numerous baptisms filled the pages of the parish registers as entire estates brought Christianity to their slave quarters. By 1826, every infant was being baptized soon after birth.

After the apprenticeship system began in August 1834, the Jamaican plantocracy only intensified these efforts. With a £20,000 education grant from Britain, the Jamaican Assembly built schools and churches by the score. If children under the age of six were not allowed to work, the planters argued, they would be socialized with the proper morals, work ethic, and beliefs for the future. Some magistrates and planters tried to persuade parents to apprentice their children, whereas missionaries persuaded them to place their children in the plantation schools. Mothers were caught in a tug-of-war, tempted by promises of lighter hours, extra wages, medical care, and food for their children. Although most mothers did not allow their children to be apprenticed, a small number agreed, and a few children under the age of six found themselves taken out of school and placed in the fields.

The apprenticed community made efforts to resist the intentions and influence of the white community, but they were largely unsuccessful. For example, apprenticed women were constantly under attack for not allowing the education of their children in the estate schools and for impeding the religious instruction of their children. Although many women preferred to work extra hours in the field rather than consent to the apprenticeship of their children, the period also witnessed a sharp increase in the education of plantation children. These women tried to keep their children away from a life of servitude and British influence, but their new situation motivated them to place their children in school, where they would receive meals and care that the parents could not provide. As a result, the children became increasingly more British, erasing what little culture they had retained from their parents and kinship groups.

Furthermore, the apprenticed community came to resent the magistracy system. Because the magistrates had been sent to ensure that the apprentices worked, their presence fostered resentment among the newly freed laborers. Although a few magistrates had the apprentices' best interests in mind, many took advantage of their power. As a result, the apprentices openly defied the system, and magistrates frequently reported cases of insolence and insubordination to the Colonial Office. In addition, the apprentices increasingly refused to work more than the forty hours required of them each week, and a few estates experienced open acts of violence.

By 1836, it had become obvious that the system was not working. With sugar production declining, the Jamaican planters pushed their apprentices hard in the fields and punished them harder on their estates. They docked free time and pay for the slightest production loss. The magistrates were no better, as they abused their power, sent thousands to the treadmills and workhouses, and ignored the complaints of the apprentices. It became clear to the apprentices that, despite abolition, they were still slaves. As a result, more and more of them violently resisted, refused to work, and ran away.

Throughout the apprenticeship period, Britain watched as Jamaica tried desperately to cling to the old system of labor. Between reports of insubordination and resistance from the apprentices, Parliament became increasingly enlightened as to the ineptitude of the magistracy and apprenticeship systems. Meanwhile, the Jamaican Assembly grew tired of Britain's control over its internal affairs.

In June 1838, the Jamaican Assembly passed a bill granting immediate abolition to all apprentices. On August 1, 1838, Jamaica's apprentices finally gained their full freedom and left the plantations in droves.

Colleen A. Vasconcellos

See also: Abolition of Slavery Act (1833); Apprenticeship and Emancipation; Jamaica, Abolition in.

Further Reading

Burn, William L. *Emancipation and Apprenticeship in the British West Indies.* London: Jonathan Cape, 1937.

Green, William A. *British Slave Emancipation: The Sugar Colonies and the Great Experiment, 1830–1865.* Oxford, UK: Clarendon, 1976.

Holt, Thomas C. *The Problem of Freedom: Race, Labor, and Politics in Jamaica and Britain, 1832–1938.* Baltimore: Johns Hopkins University Press, 1992.

Mathieson, William Law. *British Slavery and Its Abolition, 1823–1838.* London: Longman, Green, 1932.

Jamaica Rebellion (1831–1832)

Shortly after Christmas 1831, a slave rebellion in western Jamaica destroyed $3.5 million in property and brought economic ruin to many sugar planters on the island. Variously known as the Jamaica Rebellion, the Great Jamaican Slave Revolt, the Christmas Uprising, the Baptist War, the Native Baptist War, and Samuel Sharpe's Rebellion, the event was one of the largest slave insurrections to occur in the British West Indies. The rebellion helped hasten the British Parliament to decide the monumental question of whether or not slavery should be maintained in the British colonial possessions.

Periodic episodes of unrest had plagued Jamaica during the previous century. The First Maroon War (1729–1739), Tacky's Rebellion (1760–1761), and the Second Maroon War (1795–1796) had demonstrated a general restlessness among the island's enslaved inhabitants. During the 1820s, several hundred fugitives ran away to maroon villages of the Blue Mountains in the interior during the so-called Argyle War, and some viewed this as a sign of growing dissatisfaction among the slaves.

The rebellion appears to have been a homegrown plot organized and led by West Indian–born slaves. Many of the movement's leaders were Christianized slaves. Samuel Sharpe, the rebellion's principal leader, was described as an itinerant preacher who gained adherents to his plot by arguing, "no man can serve two masters." Sharpe would later testify that his intent had been to launch a massive strike among laborers in the sugar fields of Jamaica in order to prompt a general emancipation, but when this plan proved unworkable, he saw armed revolt as the only viable alternative.

The rebellion began in the parish of Saint James and quickly engulfed seven other sugar-producing parishes of western Jamaica. Slaves were told that the governor, the earl of Belmore, was suppressing a proclamation of general emancipation (a ruse that had been used similarly in Barbados in 1816). This news enraged the island's slaves, swelling the ranks of the rebels.

The scale of destruction wrought by the rebellion was massive, as tens of thousands of slaves participated in the well-organized uprising. When the Jamaican militia was unable to contain the massive revolt, the colonial governor ordered two companies of the 84th Regiment to Montego Bay to suppress the uprising at all costs. Even with such well-trained troops in the field, the fighting continued for almost two weeks before order was restored to western Jamaica.

After calm was restored, the disruptive influence of retributive justice continued to shake the colony. Slaves who were suspected of having been involved in organizing the rebellion were executed without the benefit of trial, and a wave of arson attacks followed, as whites destroyed several Baptist and Methodist churches in the area.

William Knibb, an English missionary, had been sent to Jamaica by the Baptist Missionary Society in the late 1820s. His duties included teaching free blacks and some slave children at a school in Kingston and later ministering to a slave congregation at Falmouth on the northern side of Jamaica. Although he had not arrived in the Caribbean an abolitionist, Knibb's experiences in serving his congregants and his observation of the slave regimen on the sugar plantations of the British West Indies convinced him that slavery was evil. In the aftermath of the rebellion, white planters in Jamaica alleged that

Knibb and his associates had planted the seeds of insurrection among the island's slaves.

The missionaries denied any involvement with the rebellion. Having had the opportunity to interview Sharpe in prison, Knibb wrote *Facts and Documents Connected with the Late Insurrection in Jamaica* (1832) to clear the Baptists of rumors that alleged their preaching had fomented the Jamaica Rebellion. Despite his efforts, the suspicions persisted, and Knibb left Jamaica in April 1832.

Returning to Britain, Knibb became a leading antislavery advocate, pressing Parliament to abolish slavery throughout the British West Indies. Arguing that the recent uprising was merely a small-scale version of the next revolt that would occur if nothing was done, Knibb presented a persuasive case for emancipation.

Although it is impossible to prove a clear cause-and-effect relationship between the Jamaica Rebellion and Parliament's passage of the Abolition of Slavery Act of 1833, it is safe to say that events in Jamaica hastened Parliament's action on general emancipation in the British West Indies.

Junius P. Rodriguez

See also: British West Indies, Abolition in the; Sharpe, Samuel; Tacky's Rebellion (1760–1761).

Further Reading

Craton, Michael. *Testing the Chains: Resistance to Slavery in the British West Indies.* Ithaca, NY: Cornell University Press, 1982.

Genovese, Eugene D. *From Rebellion to Revolution: Afro-American Slave Revolts in the Making of the Modern World.* Baton Rouge: Louisiana State University Press, 1979; New York: Vintage Books, 1981.

Hall, Catherine. *Civilising Subjects: Colony and Metropole in the English Imagination, 1830–1867.* Chicago: University of Chicago Press, 2002.

Higman, B.W. *Slave Population and Economy in Jamaica, 1807–1834.* Kingston, Jamaica: The Press, University of the West Indies, 1995.

Reckerd, Mary. "The Jamaican Slave Rebellion of 1831." *Past and Present* 40 (July 1969): 108–25.

Reid, C.S. *Samuel Sharpe: From Slave to National Hero.* Kingston: Bustamante Institute for Public and International Affairs, 1988.

Short, K.R.M. "Jamaican Christian Missions and the Great Slave Rebellion of 1831–2." *Journal of Ecclesiastical History* 27 (1976): 57–72.

Turner, Mary. *Slaves and Missionaries: The Disintegration of Jamaican Slave Society, 1787–1834.* Urbana: University of Illinois Press, 1982.

Wright, Philip. *Knibb "The Notorious": Slaves' Missionary, 1803–1845.* London: Sidgwick and Jackson, 1973.

Jocelyn, Simeon Smith (1799–1879)

A devout Congregationalist and an engraver by trade, Simeon Smith Jocelyn was a leader in the antebellum movement to expand African Americans' access to education.

Born in New Haven, Connecticut, Jocelyn first followed the path blazed by his father, also named Simeon, and worked alongside his brother Nathaniel as a commercial engraver. Though he never achieved the success of Nathaniel, who became New Haven's premier portrait painter, Simeon Jocelyn continued his work as an engraver for several years.

In his early twenties, Jocelyn enrolled in nearby Yale College to prepare for the ministry. At this time, he began to conduct religious services for blacks inside his home. In 1824, he joined with a handful of his congregants to form the African Ecclesiastical Society, which in less than a year grew to twenty-one members, and secured a modest wood building on Temple Street for their meetings. In 1829, the Western Association of New Haven County recognized Temple Street as the first African church in New Haven and ordained Jocelyn as its minister. He would continue in that position until 1834, when former slave James W. C. Pennington would assume the position.

About 1830, Jocelyn joined a budding movement to dismantle the American Colonization Society, which had a strong following among New Haven's clerical and intellectual elite. Calling colonization "the great obstacle to emancipation," he organized the New Haven Anti-Slavery Society as an alternative to the American Colonization Society in 1833. The same year, the New England Anti-Slavery Society appointed Jocelyn as its agent for New Haven. He declined the post, however, preferring to concentrate on his local organization.

Though Jocelyn formed close ties with such notable abolitionists as William Lloyd Garrison, Amos Phelps, and Arthur and Lewis Tappan, he focused his energies on African American education in New Haven. In 1831, he led an interracial campaign to open the first black college in the United States. Planned as a men's institution in New Haven, it was to combine training in manual labor and classical academics. Unfortunately, however, the college planners disclosed their intentions the same week that news of Nat Turner's slave rebellion in Virginia reached New Haven. Upon learning of the proposal, Mayor Dennis

Kimberly swiftly organized an opposition; three days later, white townsmen rejected the plan by a vote of 700 to 4. Backers of the project conceded defeat, but Jocelyn succeeded in opening a black primary school in the city three years later.

In 1833, Jocelyn became embroiled in another controversy over black education in the state of Connecticut, when he tendered his support to Prudence Crandall, a young white woman who was operating a boarding school for black girls in the town of Canterbury despite violent local opposition. Jocelyn counseled Crandall, penned editorials in her support, and enrolled a black teenager, who resided with his family, in the reviled institution. White opposition to black education prevailed again, however, as Crandall's school folded under local pressure one year later.

Jocelyn's public association with these contentious endeavors put him at the center of the anti-abolitionist backlash that was fomenting in Connecticut during the mid-1830s. In 1836, he experienced the full force of these frustrations when a mob, enraged by an antislavery lecture, stormed his home and began shattering the windows and ripping up the fence. Despite the attack, Jocelyn remained steadfast in his commitment to abolitionism and black education.

In 1839, he joined with the Tappan brothers, Joshua Leavitt, and Roger Sherman Baldwin to form the Amistad Committee, a group dedicated to the release and return of the African captives detained in New Haven from the *Amistad* slave ship. In 1846, he helped launch the American Missionary Association, an organization devoted to disseminating Christianity and literacy to people of African descent throughout the world. He would serve as the association's secretary for more than a decade, helping it to become the largest sponsor of freedmen's education in the aftermath of the U.S. Civil War. Jocelyn died in Tarrytown, New York, on August 17, 1879.

Hilary J. Moss

See also: American Colonization Society; Crandall, Prudence; Garrison, William Lloyd.

Further Reading

Gibson, Robert A. "A Deferred Dream: The Proposal for a Negro College in New Haven, 1831." *New Haven Colony Historical Society Journal* 37:2 (1991): 22–29.

McQueeny, Mary Beth. "Simeon Jocelyn, New Haven Reformer." *New Haven Colony Historical Society Journal* 19 (September 1970): 63–68.

Warner, Robert Austin. *New Haven Negroes: A Social History.* New Haven, CT: Yale University Press, 1940.

Johnson, Andrew (1808–1875)

Succeeding to the presidency upon the death of Abraham Lincoln, Andrew Johnson, the seventeenth president of the United States (1865–1869), began the process of restoring the Union in the aftermath of the U.S. Civil War. Although the Thirteenth Amendment to the U.S. Constitution, which abolished slavery, took effect during his administration, President Johnson vetoed a number of bills introduced by the U.S. Congress to assist freedmen in making the transition from slavery to freedom.

Early Political Career

Andrew Johnson was born in poverty in Raleigh, North Carolina, on December 29, 1808. He never attended school and only learned to read and write as an adult. After moving with his family to eastern Tennessee in 1826, he opened his own tailoring shop in Greenville.

Johnson's shop soon became the center of political discussion among the working class of the community, and he began to participate in public service as a Jacksonian Democrat. Johnson served as a state senator from 1835 to 1837 and from 1839 to 1841, and he was elected to Congress in 1843, serving five terms. He returned to Tennessee in 1853 and was elected governor; during his term, he worked to establish the first tax-funded public schools in the state. In 1857, he was elected to the U.S. Senate as a Democrat.

Rise to Presidency

When the Civil War broke out in 1861, Johnson was serving in the U.S. Senate. He defended the institution of slavery, having supported the Fugitive Slave Law of 1850, which mandated that the courts and ordinary citizens must assist in the recapture of runaway slaves. Unlike his colleagues from the South, however, Johnson publicly denounced secession. After Tennessee withdrew from the Union in June 1861, Johnson broke with his home state and was the only Southerner to retain his seat in the U.S. Senate.

Johnson showed strong support for the recently elected Republican administration of Abraham Lincoln. For his loyalty, Lincoln rewarded Johnson by appointing him military governor of Tennessee in 1862. Coming from a slave state and being a slave owner himself, Johnson believed that slavery was protected by the Constitution and beyond the jurisdiction of Congress; yet later in his career, he would argue for abolition on purely economic grounds. As military governor, he encouraged the legislature of Tennessee to pass amendments to the state constitution that, among other things, granted blacks who had served in the war the right to vote.

In 1863, Johnson supported Lincoln's radical approach to the war effort under the Emancipation Proclamation, which freed the slaves in the rebelling states as a war measure. Again, Lincoln was so impressed with Johnson's devotion to the Union cause that he chose him as his running mate in the 1864 election.

Just forty-one days after taking office as vice president, Johnson became president when Lincoln was assassinated. Many scholars feel that the words Johnson spoke upon his inauguration, "I feel incompetent to perform . . . duties so unexpectedly thrown upon me," characterized his term in office.

Reconstruction

As the war was drawing to a close, Lincoln had begun to make plans to reconstruct the South. He believed that the North should forgive and forget past offenses and welcome the rebels back with open arms. Johnson agreed with this view and began Reconstruction by appointing temporary federal governors in each former Confederate state, giving them orders to oversee the drafting of new constitutions that would abolish slavery, renounce secession, and pledge loyalty to the Union. Within a matter of months, the states had begun to rebuild their governments, and Johnson felt that the time had come to allow Southerners to manage their own affairs.

Johnson's soft approach to Reconstruction, however, allowed many abuses of power in the South. For example, the new Southern governments were strikingly similar to the old ones. Their new constitutions made no mention of African American rights. Many Southern politicians pointed to the U.S. Supreme Court ruling in *Dred Scott v. Sandford* (1857), which stated that African Americans were not citizens and therefore not entitled to the rights guaranteed in the Constitution. Although the Thirteenth Amendment abolished slavery in 1865, the Southern states passed "Black Codes" that were intended to keep freed African Americans from voting and in a state of perpetual servitude. In many Southern states, the Ku Klux Klan—founded in Pulaski, Tennessee, by former Confederate soldiers who believed the white race to be superior to all others—terrorized former slaves who owned property or tried to vote.

To address the Southern abuses and to ally themselves with black voters, whom they saw as crucial to their power base in the South, members of the U.S. Congress, led by the Radical Republican faction, passed two bills in early 1866. The Freedmen's Bureau Bill provided shelter and provision for former slaves and protected their rights in court. The Civil Rights Bill, which stated that all Americans (with the exception of American Indians) were entitled to citizen rights, gave former slaves the rights to own property, enforce contracts, and submit evidence in courts, rights that were not specifically guaranteed in the Thirteenth Amendment. Johnson, not wishing to see former slaves gain full equality, responded to both bills with a presidential veto. To his surprise, Congress was able to garner enough votes to override his vetoes, and the measures became law. With this political setback, Johnson's control of Reconstruction began to slip out of his hands and into the hands of Congress, which continued to override Johnson's vetoes and press forward with its plan for Radical Reconstruction.

The Reconstruction Acts of 1867–1868 divided the former Confederacy into five military districts in the seceded states. Each of the districts was run by an army commander who oversaw elections in order to block the prewar planter class from the polls. In 1868, in an effort to further solidify the issue of citizenship, Congress passed the Fourteenth Amendment, which nullified the 1857 *Dred Scott* ruling and provided for equal protection under the law for all citizens. Voters, including freedmen and white men who took an extended loyalty oath, were required to be registered. State constitutional conventions, made up of elected delegates, were required to draft new governing documents providing for black male suffrage, and states were required to ratify the Fourteenth Amendment before re-admission to the Union.

In 1867, Congress attempted to limit the president's power even further by passing the Tenure of Office Act. The legislation denied Johnson the right to fire any of his cabinet members without approval from the Senate. Johnson immediately challenged the law by firing Secretary of War Edwin M. Stanton. This action resulted in the first presidential impeachment in U.S. history, and Johnson was tried in the Senate. Although he was ultimately acquitted and remained in office, this incident further undermined Johnson's political clout.

Although racism continued to abound in the South, African Americans were able to gain some political power under Radical Reconstruction. The

Reconstruction Acts extended suffrage to formerly enslaved male African Americans. Hundreds of black delegates participated in state constitutional conventions; in 1870, Hiram Revels of Mississippi became the first African American to be elected to the U.S. Senate. By 1870, all of the states had returned to the Union.

Legacy

Although turbulent, Johnson's administration began the reunification of America after four years of civil war. During his presidency, the Thirteenth and Fourteenth Amendments were added to the Constitution. Although Johnson sought to carry out Lincoln's policy of Reconstruction, he lacked his predecessor's political savvy and oratorical skills. Johnson's presidency became noted for his ongoing conflict with the Radical Republicans who dominated Congress.

In 1870, one year after Johnson had left office, Congress passed the Fifteenth Amendment, which gave African American men the right to vote. Johnson died in Carter County, Tennessee, on July 31, 1875, six months after being reelected to the U.S. Senate.

Rolando Avila

See also: Amendments, Reconstruction; Reconstruction.

Further Reading

Bowen, David Warren. *Andrew Johnson and the Negro.* Knoxville: University of Tennessee Press, 1989.

Castel, Albert. *The Presidency of Andrew Johnson.* Lawrence: Regents Press of Kansas, 1979.

McKitrick, Eric L. *Andrew Johnson and Reconstruction.* New York: Oxford University Press, 1988.

Trefousse, Hans L. *Andrew Johnson: A Biography.* New York: W.W. Norton, 1989.

Johnson, Oliver (1809–1889)

Oliver Johnson was one of the most influential journalists associated with the antislavery movement in the United States during the pre–Civil War years. He was a close personal friend and editorial collaborator of William Lloyd Garrison, and he traveled and lectured widely in support of the abolitionist movement. He was also involved in other social reform campaigns, including the women's rights and peace movements.

Johnson was born on December 27, 1809, in Peacham, Vermont, the son of Ziba Johnson and Sally Lincoln. He was raised on his parents' farm, a Quaker household in which he was taught that all people are called to serve their neighbors. Johnson brought this moral imperative to all aspects of his work, helping to make him, in the words of the Congregationalist reformer Henry Ward Beecher, "a wheel horse in every humanitarian movement for almost half a century."

Johnson first met William Lloyd Garrison at age nineteen, when he was working as a printer's apprentice in the newspaper office of the *Vermont Watchman* in Montpelier. Thus acquainted with the budding abolitionist editor, Johnson began to learn more about the antislavery movement by reading issues of the *Journal of the Times,* the newspaper that Garrison was editing from an office in Burlington. The young apprentice soon became a heartfelt disciple of the abolitionist cause, and he formed a lasting personal and professional association with Garrison.

When Garrison moved to Boston to begin publishing *The Liberator* in 1831, he shared the same building and the same press with Johnson, who was then editing a religious newspaper, the *Christian Soldier,* which had an anti-Universalist theme. Johnson remained involved in the work of abolition and was one of the twelve original founders of the New England Anti-Slavery Society in 1832. Within four years, he had been selected as the organization's traveling agent and was lecturing frequently on behalf of the antislavery movement.

Johnson served as interim editor of *The Liberator* during the summers of 1837 and 1838, when illness prevented Garrison from carrying out his duties. In addition, when Garrison visited Europe in 1833 and 1840, he left the entire task of editing and managing *The Liberator* in Johnson's hands.

Johnson left Boston in 1844, but he remained active in the abolitionist movement by working for publications with an antislavery focus. He worked with abolitionist editor Horace Greeley on the *New York Tribune* from 1844 to 1848 before moving on to edit such other abolitionist papers as the *Anti-Slavery Bugle* of Salem, Ohio, and the *Pennsylvania Freeman.*

In 1853, Johnson accepted the prestigious position of associate editor of the *National Anti-Slavery Standard,* which was published in New York as the official organ of the American Anti-Slavery Society. He would hold this position until 1865, when the end of the U.S. Civil War and the reality of emancipation negated the need for the abolitionist publication.

In the years following the Civil War, Johnson wrote for a number of newspapers, including the *Independent, New York Weekly Tribune, Christian Union,* and *New York Evening Post.* He also wrote the biography

William Lloyd Garrison and His Times, or Sketches of the Anti-Slavery Movement in America (1880).

Johnson was a dedicated humanitarian and philanthropist who remained active in many nineteenth-century reform movements. Besides his antislavery efforts, he supported the women's rights campaign and remained a committed pacifist until his death on December 10, 1889.

Junius P. Rodriguez

See also: Garrison, William Lloyd.

Further Reading

Raffo, Steven M. *A Biography of Oliver Johnson, Abolitionist and Reformer, 1809–1889.* Lewiston, NY: Edwin Mellen, 2002.

Jones v. Van Zandt (1847)

In the 1847 case *Jones v. Van Zandt,* the U.S. Supreme Court affirmed the constitutionality of the federal Fugitive Slave Act (1793), which allowed slave hunters to recapture escaped slaves in any territory or state with only an oral confirmation before a state or federal judge that the person was a runaway. Under that legislation, John Van Zandt of Kentucky had been required to pay Wharton Jones for his role in assisting in the escape of one of Jones's slaves.

The lower court ruling was appealed to the Supreme Court, which concurred that the law was constitutional and that Van Zandt was responsible to Jones for the lost property. The decision came as a blow to the abolitionist cause, but it stiffened the resolve of many antislavery activists, who vowed to continue resisting efforts to enforce laws that required citizens to aid in the recovery and return of fugitive slaves.

The incident in question took place in April 1842, when Van Zandt was driving his wagon and came upon a group of black men at the side of the road. Van Zandt offered the men a ride, which they accepted, and he took them from Boone County, Kentucky, into Ohio. The wagon was intercepted by two slave catchers who claimed the men were fugitive slaves and attempted to recapture them. All of the men were caught except one.

Van Zandt denied knowing that the black men were escaped slaves, testified that he had discovered them in Ohio—a free state—and said they had expressed no sense of urgency upon boarding the wagon. In short, nothing in their behavior would have led Van Zandt to believe that he was doing anything more than giving a ride to a group of free black men. Thus,

he maintained, he could not be charged with assisting in their escape. He was charged and found guilty, however, and appealed the case to the Supreme Court.

Van Zandt's lawyer, Salmon P. Chase, argued that the institution of slavery was illegal and violated the basic principles of American government articulated in the Declaration of Independence and the Bill of Rights. According to the U.S. Constitution, Chase argued, the government had no right to aid in the return of escaped slaves. The Court disagreed with Chase's claims, maintaining that slavery was a state issue and that its protection had allowed the South to participate in the writing and ratification of the Constitution. Speaking for the majority, Associate Justice Levi Woodbury cited Article IV of the Constitution, which permitted the recapture of fugitive slaves as one of the "sacred compromises" of the founders. Van Zandt was ordered to pay Jones for the cost of the slave and his recapture, plus a $500 fine.

This decision angered abolitionists, who had already suffered a series of legal defeats. In a letter to Senator Charles Sumner (R-MA), Chase said that the Supreme Court "cannot be trusted at all when the great corporate interest [i.e., slavery] is in question . . . and all attempts to compromise the matter by getting the court committed on such matters as the locality of slavery, in decisions of leading questions in favor of the slaveholders, will be found as unavailing as the efforts of the Philistines with their green with[e]s upon Samson."

The gauntlet had been thrown down. It was clear that legal battles were not going to lead to the abolition of slavery.

Philine Georgette Vega

See also: Chase, Salmon P.; Fugitive Slave Act of 1793.

Further Reading

Sanders, Carl. *History of the Supreme Court of the United States: The Taney Period, 1836–1864.* New York: Macmillan, 1974.

Wiecek, William M. "Slavery and Abolition Before the United States Supreme Court, 1820–1860," *Journal of American History* 65 (June 1978): 34–59.

Julian, George Washington (1817–1899)

Among the most radical of the Radical Republicans who served in Congress during Reconstruction, George Washington Julian believed that the federal government had a responsibility to aid freedmen in making the transition from slavery to freedom. He was also one of the most outspoken critics of the administration of President Andrew Johnson.

Julian was born on May 5, 1817, near Centreville, in Wayne County on the eastern Indiana border. He was the son of Isaac and Rebecca (Hoover) Julian. His father died when he was six years old, and he was raised by his mother, a Quaker with antislavery convictions. He was exposed to the theological teachings of the great Unitarian minister William Ellery Channing, who stimulated his interest in a number of important antebellum social reform movements, the most significant of which was abolitionism.

Although he worked briefly as a teacher, Julian felt called to the legal profession. Upon finishing his legal studies in Illinois, he returned to Indiana, practicing law briefly in New Castle and Greenfield. Julian then returned to his childhood home of Centreville, where he established a legal practice.

Entering the political arena as a Whig, Julian was elected to Indiana's state assembly in 1845. Three years later, however, Julian became disillusioned with the Whig Party's explicit failure to condemn slavery, as well as its nomination of a Southern slaveholder, Zachary Taylor, for president. As a result, Julian joined the newly formed Free Soil Party in 1848. That same year, Julian was elected as a Free Soil representative to Congress from Indiana. Defeated for re-election in 1850, he became the vice presidential nominee of the Free Soil Party in 1852.

Many members of the Free Soil Party stressed the gradual abolition of slavery by preventing the "peculiar institution" from following settlers into the territories of the United States. Arguing that the founding fathers had never intended slavery to be a permanent institution, many Free Soilers cited the Northwest Ordinance of 1787 and the Missouri Compromise of 1820 as examples of how the United States intended to limit and eventually eliminate slavery in the United States.

Although Julian endorsed the principle of free territories, his position on slavery was much more radical than that of his colleagues. He refused to sanction the legitimacy of slavery and repeatedly attacked the institution on the grounds of its immorality. Julian supported equal social and political rights for blacks, even daring to interact socially with African Americans.

Julian eventually migrated to the Republican Party in the mid-1850s. Like many of his fellow Republicans, Julian was convinced that Southern slave-holders exercised disproportionate influence in the federal government. Julian used the image of the "slave power conspiracy" in many of the antislavery messages he delivered throughout the Midwest during the 1850s, arguing that Southerners constituted an illegitimate aristocracy with undue influence on the government. "The powers of government are in their keeping," he remarked, "and they determine all things according to the counsels of their own will. They say to the politicians of the North 'Go, and he goeth'; to the Northern priest, 'Do this, and he doeth it.'"

For Julian and other Republicans, the secession crisis was a logical outcome of the alleged slave power conspiracy. With the election of President Abraham Lincoln in 1860, he felt that Southern slaveholders had endorsed secession because they felt their power slipping away. It was important that Republicans concede nothing.

During the run-up to the U.S. Civil War, Julian was one of the most outspoken Radical Republicans in Congress. Elected to the U.S. House of Representatives in 1860, he would serve Indiana's Fifth Congressional District for five consecutive terms. He pressed for emancipation early in the war and applauded General John C. Frémont when he issued an emancipation decree on August 31, 1861, in the Department of the West. When President Lincoln countermanded Frémont's order and later removed the Republican favorite from command, Julian bitterly denounced the administration. Frémont, according to Julian, recognized that slaveholders had perpetrated the rebellion for the sake of preserving their own interests.

As a member of the Joint Committee on the Conduct of the War, Julian aggressively criticized Democratic generals who returned fugitive slaves to their masters and did not actively endorse the emancipationist goals of the Republican Party. A supporter of every major piece of legislation against slavery, Julian, as did other Radical Republicans, pressed President Lincoln to make an emancipation decree, thereby formally committing the Union to the abolition of slavery. Though Julian was not enthusiastic about Lincoln's re-election, he eventually supported the president in his campaign for a second term. Julian saw the Thirteenth Amendment, which abolished slavery as a legal institution, passed by Congress and sent on to the states for ratification.

In agreement with other Radical Republicans, Julian did not believe that the end of the Civil War and the ratification of the Thirteenth Amendment solved the problem of slavery in America. During

Reconstruction, he was a fervent but unsuccessful supporter of providing emancipated African Americans with free land. He continued to lobby for civil rights, supporting black suffrage and the Fifteenth Amendment. He was a bitter antagonist of President Andrew Johnson and was prominently involved in the attempt to remove him from office.

After leaving Congress in 1870, Julian aligned himself with the Liberal Republican revolt against Ulysses S. Grant. Eventually, he drifted into the Democratic Party, where he became a proponent of free trade and tariff reform. He died on July 7, 1899, in the Indianapolis suburb of Irvington.

Bruce Tap

See also: Free Soil Party; Reconstruction.

Further Reading

Julian, George W. "The Strength and Weakness of the Slave Power—The Duty of Anti-Slavery Men." In *Speeches on Political Questions,* by George Washington Julian. 1872. Westport, CT: Negro Universities Press, 1970.

Riddleberger, Patrick W. *George Washington Julian, Radical Republican: A Study in Nineteenth-Century Politics and Reform.* Indianapolis: Indiana Historical Bureau, 1966.

Tap, Bruce. *Over Lincoln's Shoulder: The Committee on the Conduct of the War.* Lawrence: University Press of Kansas, 1998.

Juneteenth

The holiday known as Juneteenth, so called because it is celebrated annually on June 19, is the oldest commemoration of the end of slavery in the United States. Recognized as Emancipation Day among African Americans, it marks the anniversary of the official freeing of slaves in Texas on June 19, 1865, in Galveston. Just as the Fourth of July celebrates liberty for all American people, for descendants of former slaves, Juneteenth symbolizes the attainment of freedom. Honoring the legacy of struggle and perseverance on the part of African Americans throughout their enslavement, Juneteenth also serves as a day of reflection on African American progress.

On June 19, 1865, Major General Gordon Granger and a regiment of Union soldiers arrived in Galveston. Gathering a crowd of slaves and slave owners, Granger read General Order No. 3, which officially declared the emancipation of Texan slaves. Despite widespread rumors of liberation, this declaration of freedom came nearly two and a half years after President Abraham Lincoln issued the Emancipation Proclamation on January 1, 1863, giving freedom to all slaves who resided in states in rebellion against the Union. Due to several factors—including poor communication technology and the minimal number of Union troops to enforce the proclamation (they were made available only after General Robert E. Lee's surrender in April 1865)—slaves in Texas were the very last to be freed.

Upon hearing the news, African Americans had many different reactions to their newfound freedom. Some experienced shock; others began to sing, dance, and pray, rejoicing that their prayers had been answered. Amid the widespread jubilation, many African Americans were rendered virtually penniless and homeless, sometimes possessing only the clothes on their backs. Despite these conditions, many ex-slaves fled their masters. They moved to Louisiana, Arkansas, and Oklahoma in search of economic opportunities and family members from whom they had been separated and sold from during captivity.

Juneteenth was first celebrated in the Texas state capital in 1867 under the direction of the Freedmen's Bureau; by 1872, it had become an official municipal event. The same year, the Reverend Jack Yates and other black leaders marked the earliest documented land purchase for Juneteenth, successfully raising $1,000 for the purchase of ten acres of land known today as Emancipation Park. In earlier years, with interest resting mainly within the southwestern African American community, many Juneteenth celebrators had found their activities barred from public property. Many celebrations were relocated to church grounds and rural areas, allowing a variety of activities, such as fishing, horseback riding, rodeos, dances, and barbecues, to become associated with the event. As Juneteenth was commemorated throughout generations, many former slaves and their descendants made annual pilgrimages to Galveston on the date of their declared freedom.

Juneteenth festivities continue to expand nationally, with the participation of many African Americans. Despite declining interest in the holiday, a result of ongoing economic and cultural changes sweeping the nation, during the Civil Rights movement of the 1960s, many African Americans began to link their struggles with those waged by their enslaved ancestors. During the Atlanta civil rights campaign, for example, student demonstrators donned Juneteenth freedom buttons.

The Juneteenth holiday underwent a resurgence following the Poor People's March to Washington, D.C., in 1968, after which many African American attendees returned home and, seeking to commemorate their heritage, began Juneteenth celebrations in their own hometowns. On January 1, 1980, Juneteenth became an official state holiday in Texas through the efforts of African American state legislator Al Edwards.

Since then, interest in Juneteenth celebrations has grown locally and nationally because of the widespread growth of such national organizations as the National Association of Juneteenth Lineage and the National Juneteenth Observance Foundation. Many institutions across the country, including the Smithsonian Institution and the Henry Ford Museum, have also been instrumental in sponsoring Juneteenth activities.

Sowandé Mustakeem

See also: Freedom Celebrations, International; Freedom Celebrations, U.S.

Further Reading

Pemberton, Doris Hollis. *Juneteenth at Comanche Crossing.* Austin, TX: Eakin, 1983.

Wiggins, William H., Jr., and Douglas DeNatale, eds. *Jubilation! African American Celebrations in the Southeast.* Columbia: McKissick Museum, University of South Carolina, 1993.

Keckley, Elizabeth (1818–1907)

Although it was common for freedwomen of the U.S. Civil War and Reconstruction eras to find domestic work in the homes of white families, there was nothing ordinary about the life of former slave Elizabeth Keckley, a seamstress, entrepreneur, author, and confidante of former first lady Mary Todd Lincoln.

Born in the town of Dinwiddie Court House, Virginia, in 1818, Elizabeth Hobbs Keckley learned the craft of sewing from her mother, Agnes Hobbs, a slave who worked as the family seamstress for Colonel Armistead Burwell. Elizabeth eventually managed to escape bondage by purchasing her own freedom, but not before she had experienced the brutalities of slavery, including rape and violence. Her only child, George, resulted from a forced sexual encounter with a friend of her owner.

After spending several years working for her owner's son in Hillsborough, North Carolina, Elizabeth returned to Virginia. She later moved to Saint Louis, Missouri, with one of Burwell's daughters, where she entered into a short-lived marriage to James Keckley in 1852.

Elizabeth Keckley gained a notable reputation as a seamstress in Saint Louis. Her patrons included some of the wealthiest white women in the area. Keckley's relationships with her patrons often blurred the boundaries of race and class during the antebellum period. For example, when Keckley's owner set the terms for her manumission, she was able to secure the necessary funds to purchase her own freedom and that of her son with the aid of donations raised by one of her white customers in 1855.

As a freedwoman, Keckley relocated to Washington, D.C., in 1860, where she established a profitable business as a seamstress. Her skills garnered her high regard within Washington's elite circles. Commissioned to create a gown for Mary Todd Lincoln to attend the inaugural ball for President Abraham Lincoln, Keckley earned an appointment as the first lady's regular seamstress.

The relationship between Keckley and Mrs. Lincoln soon proceeded from business to personal friendship. Keckley's ties to the White House and her success as a businesswoman earned her a secure and respected position in black middle-class society. In 1862, with the aid of the first lady and such patrons as Frederick Douglass, Keckley established the Contraband Relief Association to assist former slaves seeking refuge in Washington, D.C., during the Civil War.

Keckley supplied Mrs. Lincoln with beautiful gowns, and in turn, the first lady provided Keckley access to social networks of empowerment. The friendship between the two women became the focal point of Keckley's autobiography, *Behind the Scenes: Thirty Years a Slave and Four Years in the White House,* published in 1868.

After her husband's assassination, Mrs. Lincoln enlisted Keckley's help in selling her wardrobe to generate income. When that venture proved unsuccessful, Keckley published her life story in order to support both Mrs. Lincoln and herself. Though her contemporaries, including Mrs. Lincoln, criticized and dismissed the authenticity of her memoirs, Keckley's writing challenged the social conventions that denied black women the authority to speak publicly about their intimate knowledge of prominent whites.

Following the publication of her book, many of Keckley's predominately white clients declined to use her services. At the urging of black clergyman and educator Daniel A. Payne, she took a position at Wilberforce University as head of the Department of Sewing and Domestic Science Arts in 1892. During her tenure, she organized a dress reform exhibit for the Chicago World's Fair of 1893.

After suffering a stroke in the late 1890s, Keckley returned to Washington, D.C. She spent her final years in the national Home for Destitute Colored Women and Children until her death on May 26, 1907.

Kennetta Hammond Perry

See also: Lincoln, Abraham.

Further Reading

Fleischner, Jennifer. *Mrs. Lincoln and Mrs. Keckley: The Remarkable Story of the Friendship Between a First Lady and a Former Slave.* New York: Broadway, 2003.

Hoffert, Sylvia D. "Jane Grey Swisshelm, Elizabeth Keckley, and the Significance of Race Consciousness in American Women's History." *Journal of Women's History* 13 (Autumn 2001): 8–33.

Keckley, Elizabeth. *Behind the Scenes: Thirty Years a Slave and Four Years in the White House.* 1868. New York: Arno, 1968.

Sorisio, Carolyn. "Unmasking the Genteel Performer: Elizabeth Keckley's *Behind the Scenes* and the Politics of Public Wrath." *African American Review* 34 (Spring 2000): 19–38.

Kellogg, Hiram H. (1803–1881)

Hiram Huntington Kellogg, a Presbyterian minister and educator, was the first president of Knox College in Illinois, an abolitionist-founded institution of higher education. Kellogg was one of the most prominent figures in Illinois antislavery circles.

Kellogg was born on February 26, 1803, in Clinton, New York. After attending Hamilton College and Auburn Theological Seminary, he began working as a Presbyterian minister in his hometown. He fervently supported Charles Grandison Finney's efforts during the religious revival known as the Second Great Awakening and assisted him by preaching in the towns located in a region of western New York that came to be known as the "Burned-Over District," so called for the frequency and intensity of the revivals held there.

Kellogg became involved in various benevolent organizations and took a particular interest in the cause of female education. In 1833, he opened the Young Ladies' Domestic Seminary in Clinton. The school was run on the manual labor system, which meant that students performed physical labor in exchange for their tuition. The manual labor concept was considered egalitarian, because it provided an opportunity to students who otherwise could not afford to attend school. Kellogg's seminary was reputedly the first manual labor institution for women in the United States and was notable for admitting women of African descent.

The seminary at Clinton was located near the Oneida Institute in Whitesboro, New York, a manual labor college for men founded by George Washington Gale in 1827. Gale had been a mentor to Finney and believed that the spread of manual labor education would usher in the millennium. Therefore, he relinquished leadership of the Oneida Institute in 1834 and, with Kellogg's assistance, made plans for the establishment of a college on the Western prairie.

In 1836, Gale led a colony to Knox County, Illinois, where he founded the town of Galesburg. A charter was obtained for Knox Manual Labor College in 1837, and Kellogg was elected its first president in 1841, when he sold his seminary and moved to Galesburg.

From its inception, Knox College was a center of radical antislavery activity. As Kellogg pointed out in his inaugural address, manual labor education was an affront to the idea that only slaves were suited to perform physical labor. The college, its preparatory academy, and its female seminary provided a liberal education to those willing to work, regardless of their race or class.

Kellogg had joined the American Anti-Slavery Society while living in New York, but he became much more active in the abolitionist movement after moving to Illinois. He corresponded with fellow abolitionist James G. Birney and aided the fledgling Liberty Party in Illinois. In 1842, he served on key committees during the annual meeting of the Illinois Anti-Slavery Society and was appointed vice president of the organization. That same year, Gale and others associated with the college were indicted for harboring fugitive slaves on the Underground Railroad. Though Kellogg was not indicted, he helped the fugitives involved in the incident obtain legal counsel.

In spring 1843, the Illinois Anti-Slavery Society appointed Kellogg as its delegate to the Second World Anti-Slavery Convention in London. He gave a keynote address at the convention on June 19, 1843, in which he discussed racial prejudice and the history of slavery in American legislation and judicial decisions. He contended that racial discrimination was not uniformly practiced, that the founding fathers had been antislavery at heart, and that the abolitionist movement was making progress. When the convention was over, Kellogg traveled throughout Britain, making speeches and raising money for the college.

In May 1845, Kellogg resigned as president of Knox College and was succeeded by the Reverend Jonathan Blanchard, a noted abolitionist and fellow delegate to the London convention. Though he was often in poor health, Kellogg continued to work as a minister and educator in New York, Iowa, Wisconsin, and Illinois until his death on January 1, 1881.

Matt Norman

See also: Birney, James Gillespie; Blanchard, Jonathan; Finney, Charles Grandison; Liberty Party.

Further Reading

Finney, Charles Grandison. *Memoirs of Charles G. Finney, Written by Himself.* 1876. New York: AMS, 1973.

Kemble, Frances Anne (1809–1893)

The British-born writer and actress Frances Anne ("Fanny") Kemble drew on her short residence in antebellum Georgia to write a vivid denunciation of the institution of slavery.

Born into a famous acting family in London on November 27, 1809, Kemble became well known for her acting talent, as well as her published journals about life in America. In addition to her *Journal of a Residence on a Georgian Plantation* (1863), she published other diaries, memoirs, a novel, and dramatic works. Her personal fame helped her abolitionist writings obtain international acclaim.

In August 1832, Kemble sailed to America with her father—the noted actor and theater manager Charles Kemble—to begin a theatrical tour in New York City. Throughout the multistate tour, she met with some of the most influential Americans of the day, including Presidents Andrew Jackson and John Quincy Adams, former first lady Dolley Madison, and novelist Catharine Maria Sedgwick. Early in the tour, Kemble met Pierce Butler of Philadelphia.

Butler, the heir to a large Georgia plantation and nearly 1,000 slaves, courted Kemble, and the two married in June 1834. After living for a time in Philadelphia and traveling to Great Britain, the family went to Butler Island, near Darien, Georgia, in December 1838. In February 1839, they settled on the family plantation on Saint Simons Island. Although the contentious Butler marriage would officially end in 1849, Kemble's brief experiences on the extensive rice and cotton plantation would shape her future.

Life on the Georgia plantation opened Kemble's eyes to the daily realities of slavery. Her background had not prepared her for life in the Sea Islands. At the suggestion of her abolitionist friend, Elizabeth Sedgwick, she recorded her experiences in an extensive and detailed journal. In particular, she detailed the daily traumas caused by slavery, especially those that affected women. Kemble expressed her horror at the division of slave families, the high rate of infant mortality and miscarriages in the slave community, the sexual exploitation of slave women, and the general mistreatment of female slaves. For her part, Kemble tried to alleviate the misery of her slaves by establishing a slave hospital and nursery at Butler Place.

Kemble routinely opposed the norms of the American South, and Butler faced ridicule and public humiliation for his wife's refusal to embrace the region's "peculiar institution." Kemble, in open defiance of her husband, paid her domestic slaves for the labor they performed for her and taught another slave to read. In her journal, she remarked that slavery and Southern society not only took their toll on the African American population but also on Southern white women. To demonstrate this position, she pointed to the tyrannical nature of her husband and other brutal slave masters, who treated everyone in their households as property subject to their whims. Husbands expected their wives and slaves to obey them without question.

Kemble would not remain on the Georgia plantation or in the American South for long. Within a matter of months, the family returned to their home in Philadelphia. After years of circulating her journal in private, the eruption of the U.S. Civil War prompted Kemble to arrange for its publication, first in Britain and later in America.

Kemble's vivid eyewitness account of the treatment and living conditions of slaves greatly assisted the abolitionist war against slavery and helped sway Europeans to the Union cause at a crucial point in the Civil War. She died in London on January 15, 1893.

Lisa Tendrich Frank

See also: Women's Rights and the Abolitionist Movement.

Further Reading

Clinton, Catherine. *Fanny Kemble's Civil Wars.* New York: Oxford University Press, 2000.
———, ed. *Fanny Kemble's Journals.* Cambridge, MA: Harvard University Press, 2000.
Kemble, Frances Anne. *Journal of a Residence on a Georgian Plantation in 1838–1839.* 1863. Ed. John A. Scott. Athens: University of Georgia Press, 1984.

Ku Klux Klan

Originally founded by returning Confederate army officers as a social fraternity, the Ku Klux Klan (KKK) quickly emerged as a violent white supremacist organization. Although the society has evolved and shifted in its purpose since its original founding, its identifying characteristic has always been to protect its ideal of ethnic and racial purity and to preserve religious and political distinctions based on principles of American nativism and white supremacy.

Throughout its history, the Klan has spurred three national movements characterized by clandestine acts of terror. Periods of growth have corresponded with times of abrupt social change in American history, whereas periods of decline have generally stemmed from corrupt or ineffectual leadership. The first Ku Klux Klan was founded in 1866 as a secret society in Pulaski, Tennessee, and it was active in the Reconstruction-era South. The second Klan existed from 1915 into the 1920s. The third Klan movement formed after World War II, and its splinter groups have persisted into the twenty-first century.

Early Klan

The name Ku Klux Klan is derived from the Greek word *kuklos,* meaning "circle" or "band." What distinguished the Klan from other white supremacist organizations, such as the Knights of the White Camellia, was its liturgical character. Klansmen were involved in an organization that was highly secretive and cultish.

Originally, the Klan was divided into subgroups called realms, dominions, provinces, and dens. Titles of authority, such as grand dragon, titan, giant, cyclops, and ghoul, were given to members. Klansmen dressed as the ghosts of dead confederates in long white robes, white masks, and conical hats, and they engaged in initiation ceremonies, burning crosses, giving secret salutes, and holding secretive meetings, typically at night. Their rituals were closely modeled on those of the Kuklos Adelphon, a college fraternity with widespread membership throughout the South during the antebellum period.

The early Ku Klux Klan was organized by former Confederate general and cavalry commander Nathan Bedford Forrest. Forrest was an antebellum slave trader from Mississippi who mixed the secretive nature of the Klan with regimented discipline. The Klan's first grand wizard, he recruited heavily throughout the Southern states but found the greatest number of recruits in the Piedmont region.

Despite its secretive nature, the Klan was able to increase in membership during the years following the U.S. Civil War. The society's beliefs were representative of the growing fear among white Southerners who perceived racial intermingling as detrimental to the moral fabric of society.

Early members of the Ku Klux Klan display the traditional costume of white hoods and robes. The secret white supremacist society was founded in Tennessee in 1866 and terrorized blacks throughout the South during Reconstruction and beyond. (*©Dallas Historical Society, Texas, USA/The Bridgeman Art Library*)

In addition to their fears of miscegenation, white Southerners abhorred the political power granted to blacks following the Civil War. Shortly after emancipation and during Reconstruction, black ex-slaves began to take an increasingly prominent role in elections and public offices under the supervision of the Radical Republicans in the U.S. Congress.

Many Southern whites perceived blacks' newfound political participation as directly threatening the social order, and they responded with acts of clandestine terror. A number of violent, secret white protective societies emerged after 1867, including the Knights of the White Camellia, the Black Horse Cavalry, the

White Brotherhood, and the Pale Faces. The Ku Klux Klan and such other Klan-like organizations were responsible for the deaths of hundreds of blacks by lynching. During Reconstruction, the Klan also lynched scalawags, carpetbaggers, and others whom they saw as challenging Southern mores or helping African Americans to gain political, educational, or economic power.

In the decades after the Civil War, lynching became a common social phenomenon in the South, and this practice continued into the 1900s. Klansmen also used other forms of vigilantism and terrorism—committing murder, arson, and rape—to advance their cause. As the power of the local chapters and dens grew, even the formidable Forrest was unable to maintain order among the increasingly unruly Klansmen. In 1869, faced with a complete loss of control, he ordered the disbandment of the Klan and resigned as grand wizard.

Congress responded to the increasing violence and disorder by passing the Civil Rights Act of 1871 (also known as the Ku Klux Klan Enforcement Act), which made night riding a crime and gave the president of the United States the power to suspend habeas corpus and order the use of federal troops to put down conspirators by force. Although government officials prosecuted and convicted hundreds of Klan members in 1871 and 1872, the act initially did little to contain the Klan's hateful tactics. During the rest of the 1870s, however, the Klan declined in influence, as arrests, combined with the return of white political dominance in the South, diminished its activity.

Later Movements

The second Ku Klux Klan was founded in 1915 by William J. Simmons, a former minister who claimed to have had a night vision of Klansmen passing across his wall. Simmons organized the first meeting of the new Ku Klux Klan in Stone Mountain, Georgia. This second incarnation of the Klan had strong anti-Catholic and anti-Semitic elements. Some of its members were closely affiliated with the American (Know-Nothing) Party movement that was popular in the mid-nineteenth century.

The release of the controversial film *Birth of a Nation* (1915) was influential in cementing the Klan's place in American popular culture. Based on Thomas Dixon's 1905 novel *The Clansman,* the motion picture glorified the Klan as an agency that aimed to protect American civilization—and the South in particular—

from deranged African Americans who sought to undermine the social structure and compromise white womanhood.

At the same time, the Klan underwent a national resurgence, coinciding with an increase in lynchings that continued well into 1919. By the following year, the movement had become a nationwide threat that terrorized groups in every region of the United States. Klan membership peaked in the 1920s, with estimates reaching between 4 million and 5 million members nationwide.

During this period, the Klan exerted considerable political influence, helping to elect sympathetic candidates to state and national offices. The group dominated such Southern states as Alabama, Georgia, Louisiana, and Texas, but it also had a presence in California, Colorado, Illinois, Indiana, Kansas, Missouri, New Jersey, New York, Ohio, Oklahoma, Oregon, and Pennsylvania. Strongly opposed to the arrival of immigrants from Southern and Eastern Europe, the Klan helped to secure strict the immigration quotas set forth in the Emergency Quota Act of 1921 and the Immigration Act of 1924.

The third Ku Klux Klan formed after World War II, when Samuel Green of Georgia led a concerted effort to revive the white supremacist group. His attempt proved largely unsuccessful, however, as the group had splintered and states had begun to outlaw Klan activity.

Following the 1954 U.S. Supreme Court decision in *Brown v. Board of Education,* many whites, disturbed by racial advances that were perceived as a threat to Southern values, became involved in scattered Klan groups such as Mississippi's White Knights of the Ku Klux Klan, led by Robert Shelton. These newly revived Klan groups were responsible for violent attacks against blacks and civil rights workers in cities throughout the South during the 1960s, including Jacksonville and Saint Augustine, Florida; Birmingham and Montgomery, Alabama; and Meridian, Mississippi. By the end of the decade, membership again dwindled.

Although the early 1990s saw a modest resurgence of Klan support—as former Klan leader David Duke was elected to the Louisiana state legislature—the combined membership of Klan organizations was estimated to be only in the low thousands as the United States entered the twenty-first century.

Seneca D. Vaught

See also: Lynching; Reconstruction.

Further Reading

Chalmers, David Mark. *Hooded Americanism: The History of the Ku Klux Klan.* 3rd ed. Durham, NC: Duke University Press, 1987.

Fisher, William Harvey. *The Invisible Empire: A Bibliography of the Ku Klux Klan.* Metuchen, NJ: Scarecrow, 1980.

MacLean, Nancy. *Behind the Mask of Chivalry: The Making of the Second Ku Klux Klan.* New York: Oxford University Press, 1995.

Trelease, Allen W. *White Terror: The Ku Klux Klan Conspiracy and Southern Reconstruction.* Baton Rouge: Louisiana State University Press, 1971, 1995.

Lacerda, Carlos de (fl. 1880s)

Carlos de Lacerda, also known as Luís Carlos de Lacerda, was a leading radical abolitionist in Brazil during the 1880s. As a journalist and political activist, he led the antislavery movement in the prosperous sugarcane-producing region of Campos in the state of Rio de Janeiro.

Lacerda published an abolitionist newspaper, organized mass rallies, and used all legal means to free slaves; however, he was also one of the foremost proponents of extralegal direct-action tactics. He vigorously encouraged slaves to flee the plantations, arm themselves in self-defense, and sabotage their masters' property. Together with like-minded activists such as Antonio Bento in São Paulo, Lacerda's combative activities played a key role in destabilizing the slave economy and mobilizing broad sectors of slaves, free blacks, and white urban workers in favor of abolition.

Minor abolitionist measures had been introduced by the Brazilian government in the 1870s, but the continued power of the "slavocracy" prompted the resurgence of an urban-based abolitionist movement in the 1880s. Most abolitionist groups focused on newspaper publicity, public rallies, petitions to higher authorities, and formal legislative activity. By the mid-1880s, however, many abolitionists had become frustrated with the slow progress of these legal campaigns and turned to more radical methods.

Lacerda was the son of a prominent Campos physician. Like most Brazilian abolitionists, he was influenced by the secular critique of slavery, which denounced the institution as an impediment to moral, political, and economic progress. Initially, he favored a moderate abolitionist strategy, but, in the face of slaveholders' intransigence, he adopted a decidedly more radical stance that centered on the activities of the slaves themselves. As he expressed it, "The resolution of the problem of servitude is not subordinated to the government, legislative power or the will of the owners of captives. It is dependent exclusively on the complete disorganization of slave labor which can only be achieved by a unique power—the resolution of the slaves."

In 1884, Lacerda founded a local newspaper, *Vinte e Cinco de Março,* which called for the immediate abolition of slavery through a diverse combination of legal and illegal means. Lacerda advocated the use of all judicial methods to free the slaves, personally facilitating legal action against slave owners for abuse. In public meetings, he fiercely denounced the brutalities of slavery by graphically exhibiting the leg irons and other tools of punishment used by plantation masters. He and his followers organized mass rallies that attracted the participation of many slaves, free blacks, and white urban workers.

Yet it was Lacerda's extralegal tactics that gained him the ardent support of slaves and abolitionists and drew violent opposition from plantation owners. Lacerda openly advocated and aided slave escapes, the creation of *quilombos* (free communities of ex-slaves), armed insurrections, and sabotage of the sugar cane farms. From 1884 until the abolition of slavery in 1888, such radical tactics were adopted in other slaveholding states, such as São Paulo and Minas Gerais, and helped to undermine the slave economy and encourage widespread political unrest. Fearing continued upheaval, most proslavery politicians and plantation owners soon saw abolition as the only realistic solution.

Lacerda succeeded in building a formidable campaign against slavery in the Campos region. Working with more well known moderate abolitionists such as Joaquim Nabuco and Ruy Barbosa, both of whom worked on the formal political level, Lacerda played a significant part in the eventual abolition of slavery in Brazil.

Sean Purdy

See also: Brazil, Abolition in; Nabuco, Joaquim.

Further Reading

Azavedo, Celia M. *Abolitionism in the United States and Brazil: A Comparative Perspective.* New York: Garland, 1995.

Conrad, Robert E. *The Destruction of Brazilian Slavery, 1850–1888.* Berkeley: University of California Press, 1972; 2nd ed., Malabar, FL: Krieger, 1993.

Toplin, Robert Brent. *The Abolition of Slavery in Brazil.* New York: Atheneum, 1972.

Lafayette, Marquis de (1757–1834)

A French soldier and statesman, the marquis de Lafayette was heralded throughout the transatlantic world as a champion of Enlightenment thought and its application to human rights. Lafayette became an advocate for liberal reform and the abolition of slavery following his service in the American Revolution.

The marquis was born Marie-Joseph-Paul-Yves-Roch-Gilbert du Motier on September 5, 1757, to a noble family in the Auvergne region of central France. Although he was orphaned at the age of thirteen, Lafayette's formative years were not unlike those of other young aristocrats of his day. He was educated at the College of Louis le Grand in Paris and secured an officer's commission in the Royal Army while still a teenager. At the age of sixteen, he married the noblewoman Marie Adrienne Françoise de Noailles.

Following the outbreak of war in British North America in 1775, Lafayette joined other young French military officers who were eager to seek action against British forces in the colonies. The Continental Congress commissioned Lafayette at the rank of major general in July 1777, and he served with distinction in the Continental army until the end of hostilities in October 1781. His notable achievements included the maneuvering of forces at the Battle of Barren Hill in May 1778, a move that allowed him to escape entrapment at the hands of the British, and the successful command of an American brigade at the siege of Yorktown in September and October 1781.

Prior to his service in the American war for independence, Lafayette had little reason to question the class structure or racial ideologies of the period. His participation in the American Revolution, however, effected a reorientation of his political beliefs, leading him to accept the notion that the natural rights of man supersede the traditional class system. In 1783, he began openly to oppose chattel slavery, as it conflicted with the principles of liberty and equality championed in the war. His opposition to slavery also was influenced by his personal knowledge of the service of blacks—both slave and free—in the Revolutionary War.

In February 1783, Lafayette wrote to his friend and former commander, General George Washington, proposing that the two work jointly on a plan for the gradual emancipation of black slaves in America. Although the project with Washington never came to fruition, Lafayette did pursue a plan for gradual emancipation in partnership with his wife. In 1786, the couple purchased two slave plantations near Cayenne in French Guiana, with the intention of assisting slaves in becoming free tenant farmers after a period of preparation. The couple instituted several reforms on the plantations, such as banning the flogging and sale of slaves, paying slaves for their work, and establishing educational programs. Lafayette took over the supervision of the plantations in the late 1780s, but the Cayenne project ended prematurely a few years later when the couple lost their lands during the Reign of Terror, the radical phase of the French Revolution. Although the project's success remained unclear, the marquis and his wife believed that their efforts had eased racial tensions in French Guiana, as the colony did not see the same level of interracial violence as Saint-Domingue (Haiti) did during the 1790s.

Early in 1788, Lafayette joined with like-minded liberal reformers in France seeking to abolish the slave trade in the French colonies. Although the founders of the *La Société des Amis des Noirs* (Society of Friends of the Blacks) had initially wished to avoid any entanglements with the French nobility, Lafayette soon convinced them to allow him to join the organization. Along with his wife, Lafayette brought other French liberal leaders and intellectuals into the organization. In addition to his public support for the society, Lafayette corresponded with abolitionists in the United States and Great Britain. He maintained contact with Benjamin Franklin and the Philosophical Society in Philadelphia, and he became an honorary member of the New York Manumission Society.

After establishing a relationship with the Society for the Abolition of the Slave Trade in Great Britain, Lafayette met Thomas Clarkson, one of the group's leading spokesmen. Clarkson traveled to Paris in August 1789, hoping to have the slave trade outlawed as part of the reform movement that was developing during the first phase of the French Revolution. Ultimately, Clarkson's six-month sojourn in Paris was unsuccessful. The *Société* did not have the political clout to effect the abolition of the slave trade, a result of the lack of consensus on slavery in France. On one hand, the conservative factions in the National Assembly had strong economic ties to the proslavery planters' group, the Massiac Club; on the other hand, the radical factions were far more concerned about the success of social and political reforms within France.

The political activities of *La Société des Amis des Noirs* waned after the Jacobins gained control of the Legislative Assembly in August 1792. All of the leading members of the *Société* subsequently committed suicide, fled France, or were executed. Lafayette himself was condemned and evaded arrest by escaping to an Austrian camp. Imprisoned by the Austrians, he spent five years in captivity and three years in exile before returning to France in 1800.

In the decades following the French Revolution, Lafayette continued to correspond with abolitionists in Great Britain and the United States, offering them both public and private support. After the two countries ended the slave trade in 1807 and 1808, respectively, Lafayette assisted British abolitionists such as Clarkson in pressuring French officials to end the trade in the French colonies. Minor progress was achieved with passage of the Law of April 1818, which suppressed the slave trade in principle, if not in practice. Lafayette also actively supported the Nashoba gradual emancipation project, spearheaded by his close friend Frances Wright in the United States.

In France, Lafayette's public activism on slavery in the Chamber of Deputies was muted after his loss of political influence in 1820. Nonetheless, he continued to correspond with abolitionist friends and colleagues, keeping them informed of developments on the issue in France and debating the future of freed slaves after emancipation.

Although Lafayette did not live to see the abolition of slavery in the French colonies in 1848, he did see a strengthening of the legal measures suppressing the slave trade, beginning in the early 1830s. He died in Paris on May 20, 1834.

Melinda Marie Jetté

See also: Clarkson, Thomas; Enlightenment; *Société des Amis des Noirs, La;* Society for the Abolition of the Slave Trade.

Further Reading

Gottschalk, Louis. *Lafayette and the Close of the American Revolution.* Chicago: University of Chicago Press, 1942.

Gottschalk, Louis, and Margaret Maddox. *Lafayette in the French Revolution.* 2 vols. Chicago: University of Chicago Press, 1969, 1973.

Kennedy, Melvin D., ed. *Lafayette and Slavery: From His Letters to Thomas Clarkson and Granville Sharp.* Eaton, PA: American Friends of Lafayette, 1950.

Kramer, Lloyd. *Lafayette in Two Worlds: Public Cultures and Personal Identities in an Age of Revolution.* Chapel Hill: University of North Carolina Press, 1996.

Lamartine, Alphonse de (1790–1869)

Best known as a man of letters, Alphonse de Lamartine became a leader in the French government following the revolution of 1848. It was this reformist government that abolished slavery throughout the French Empire.

Born on October 21, 1790, at Mâcon Saône-et-Loire, Lamartine was the only son of a minor noble family with connections to the duke of Orleans. Lamartine was brought up Roman Catholic and a monarchist, but he was exposed to the liberal leanings of the Orleans household through his mother, who had lived with the Orleans family since childhood.

The family survived the French Revolution with its wealth intact, and Lamartine avoided conscription during the Napoleonic Wars by serving as mayor of Milly, the family's estate, from 1812 to 1815. After the wars, Lamartine, whose family had dropped the aristocratic "de" but remained landed and wealthy, drifted into diplomatic posts in Naples and Florence, writing and enjoying the life of an aristocrat. Although he supervised the Naples embassy, Lamartine avoided politics and declined government posts in the Polignac ministry.

In 1820, Lamartine published his first successful work, *Les méditations poétiques,* considered by scholars to be the first work of Romantic poetry in French. The collection of twenty-four poems became a popular and financial success, giving him the means to marry Englishwoman Mary-Ann Birch in 1823. In 1830, he was elected to the French Academy on the strength of his plays and poetry, including *La morte de Socrates* (1823) and *Les harmonies poétiques et religieuses* (1830).

His 1831 *Sur la politique rationelle* advocated equal rights provided by a society guided by reason and built on moral principles. Active in antislavery societies beginning in 1834, Lamartine's views on emancipation stemmed from his deep belief in the fundamental equality of men.

Lamartine was elected to the Chamber of Deputies in 1839, but he spent little time in the legislature, preferring to write and cultivate a broad circle of political allies. That year, he penned a poetic appeal for the lives of Armand Barbés and Louis-Auguste Blanqui, who had been caught in an aborted rebellion against the monarchy. Lamartine's multivolume *Histoire des Girondins* (1847) offered a history of the French Revolution, praising its leaders without approving of their crimes and allowing readers to interpret the work on several different levels. In addition, Lamartine and his circle founded a newspaper, *Bien Public,* which supported equality and social reform.

In 1847, Lamartine took part in the Banquet Campaign (dinner meetings held across France), expounding a policy of free education, freedom of conscience, and prison reform. He appeared in the Chamber of Deputies after the abdication of King Louis-Philippe in February 1848 to propose a provisional government rather than a regency or republic. As the acting head of that provisional government, Lamartine presided over immediate reforms, including the formation of a committee to draft an emancipation decree for all French colonies. The final decree was promulgated on April 27, 1848, ordering the emancipation of all slaves within two months of the receipt of the decree in all French lands.

Lamartine had been correct to push through such reforms before an election could be held: The Constituent Assembly convened in May 1848 was conservative and began to remove the more radical members of the government, such as the reform-minded Alexandre-Auguste Ledru-Rollin, without whom Lamartine refused to continue serving. Lamartine's popularity faded with this reactionary swing in politics, and after losing the October 1848 presidential election, he served in the Chamber of Deputies until the coup d'état of Louis-Napoleon Bonaparte (Napoleon III) in 1851.

In his later years, Lamartine wrote a wide variety of works, including a *Histoire de la Revolution de 1848,* thinly disguised autobiographical romantic novels, biographies of famous men meant to educate the working class, and histories of Turkey and Russia. All but forgotten as a politician, he died in Paris on February 28, 1869.

Margaret Sankey

See also: French West Indies, Abolition and Emancipation in the.

Further Reading

Drescher, Seymour. "British Way, French Way: Opinion Building and Revolution in the Second French Slave Emancipation." *American Historical Review* 96 (June 1991): 709–34.

Fortescue, William. *Alphonse de Lamartine: A Political Biography.* New York: St. Martin's, 1983.

Lombard, Charles M. *Lamartine.* New York: Twayne, 1973.

Langston, John Mercer (1829–1897)

Second only to Frederick Douglass in importance among African American spokesmen of the nineteenth century, John Mercer Langston spent his early life working for the emancipation of his people and his later years working for their equality. He organized antislavery societies at both the state and local levels, assisted fugitive slaves along the Ohio section of the Underground Railroad, recruited blacks for the 54th and 55th Regiments of the Massachusetts Volunteer Infantry, and formed the 127th Colored Ohio Volunteer Infantry during the U.S. Civil War. In 1864, as leader of the National Equal Rights League, Langston implemented suffrage campaigns in Ohio, Kansas, and Missouri. Later, he ran for political office, becoming the first African American congressman from Virginia.

Langston was born in Virginia on December 14, 1829, the son of a wealthy white planter and a free black mother. When he was only four years old, both of his parents died, and Langston and his siblings inherited their father's substantial estate. Adopted by a family friend in Ohio, Langston grew up among the free blacks of Chillicothe and Cincinnati. In 1849, he graduated from Oberlin College (the first abolitionist and co-educational college in America) and earned a master's degree in theology there three years later.

Unable to circumvent the racial discrimination that kept African Americans from entering the legal profession, he studied law independently until 1854, when he became the first black man admitted to the Ohio bar. Langston remained a resident of Ohio for the next fifteen years, becoming a successful lawyer, as well as a respected and prominent citizen.

Langston entered the ranks of the Ohio abolitionists while still a teenager, making his first major antislavery speech in Cleveland in 1848 at the behest of Frederick Douglass. He organized abolitionist societies and participated in the Underground Railroad in Ohio. Unsure of the proper course his people should take in responding to their collective oppression, Langston waffled in his racial ideology, first favoring emigration and colonization, then militancy and violent rebellion, and finally working within the system. He was among those blacks who conferred with the radical abolitionist John Brown before Brown launched his infamous raid on Harpers Ferry in 1859.

When the Civil War erupted in 1861, Langston immediately began recruiting black soldiers in Ohio

A lawyer, educator, orator, congressman, and tireless worker for abolition and black suffrage, John Mercer Langston is also recognized as the first African American to hold elective office. He was elected town clerk in Brownhelm, Ohio, in 1855. *(Library of Congress)*

and Massachusetts, organizing the now-famous black 54th Regiment of the Massachusetts Volunteer Infantry. In 1864, Langston was elected president of the National Equal Rights League, which campaigned for black suffrage, ultimately achieving that aim within three years.

He then immersed himself in his next job, inspecting educational facilities for blacks under the auspices of the Freedmen's Bureau. In 1868, he helped establish the first law school designed especially for blacks—part of the newly created Howard University in Washington, D.C.—and served as its dean for the next three years. He later served as vice president and interim president of the university and sought the preeminent position permanently, though he was denied the job on the basis of his race. After an eight-year stint as U.S. consul to Haiti, Langston returned to Virginia in 1885 to serve as president of the Virginia Normal and Collegiate Institute.

Langston was among the first black elected officials in the history of the United States, having been elected to the position of town clerk in Brownhelm, Ohio, before the Civil War. After moving back to Oberlin, he held local offices there from 1865 to 1868 while also serving in his national capacities.

In 1888, Langston ran as a Republican for Congress in Virginia's Fourth District. William Mahone, who controlled the Republican Party in Virginia throughout the 1880s, opposed Langston's candidacy—an ironic move, considering that Langston had been among the original organizers of the Republican Party in the mid-1850s. Mahone forced Langston to run as an independent.

The Democrats ran Edward Venable and committed fraud at the ballot box to defeat Langston, who appealed the outcome to the U.S. House of Representatives, where Republicans held the majority. In the case of *Langston v. Venable* (and sixteen similar cases), Speaker of the House Thomas B. "Czar" Reed of Maine employed his revolutionary "Reed Rules," which allowed unusually brief debate on the merits of the case before the vote was taken. The Republican House unseated Venable and, eighteen months after the election of 1888, awarded the seat to Langston; he served for five and a half months until his term expired. He thus became the first African American elected to Congress from Virginia. On the day that Langston was seated, the Democrats completely vacated the House in a show of protest. In 1890, he was not re-elected.

Langston retired to Washington, D.C., where he wrote his autobiography, *From the Virginia Plantation to the National Capitol*, which was published in 1894. He died on November 15, 1897. Among the many honors bestowed on this great black leader, the town of Langston, Oklahoma, was named for him, as was the school located there, Langston University.

Thomas Adams Upchurch

See also: Freedmen's Bureau; Massachusetts Fifty-Fourth Regiment; Underground Railroad.

Further Reading

Bromberg, Alan B. "John Mercer Langston: Black Congressman from the Old Dominion." *Virginia Cavalcade* 30 (Summer 1980): 60–67.

Cheek, William F. "A Negro Runs for Congress: John Mercer Langston and the Virginia Campaign of 1888." *Journal of Negro History* 52 (January 1967): 14–34.

Cheek, William F., and Aimee Lee Cheek. *John Mercer Langston and the Fight for Black Freedom, 1829–1865.* Urbana: University of Illinois Press, 1989.

Langston, John M. *From the Virginia Plantation to the National Capitol.* 1894. New York: Johnson Reprint, 1968.

Lay, Benjamin (1677–1759)

The Anglo-American Quaker reformer Benjamin Lay was an early abolitionist in eighteenth-century Pennsylvania.

Born in 1677 to poor Quaker parents in Colchester, England, Lay was a farmer and sailor before becoming a glove maker. In 1718, he married Sarah Smith of Deptford, England, an itinerant minister in the Society of Friends. An almost constant critic of his fellow Quakers, whom he judged to be lacking in piety, Lay had long been considered a chronic troublemaker in Quaker meetings.

Lay and his new wife sailed to Barbados in the West Indies in 1718. Quakers had been on the wealthy sugar-producing island since 1655. Although their numbers had fallen to a few hundred from a peak of more than 1,000 in the early 1680s, the island Quakers were maintaining a vital religious community when the Lays arrived. Shocked by the brutal treatment of slaves on the island, however, the Lays remained less than two years. They sailed back to England, where Benjamin Lay again faced admonishment for his disorderly behavior at Quaker meetings, as well as in Anglican, Presbyterian, and Baptist congregations.

In 1732, Lay moved again, this time to Pennsylvania, where he and his wife established a home in Abington, a small community just north of Philadelphia. While running a small clothing shop, Lay spent most of his time working to eradicate the evil institution that he had encountered on Barbados.

The seventeenth-century Quaker founders George Fox and William Edmondson had argued that owning humans was incompatible with the ideals of universal redemption. By the eighteenth-century, however, leaders of the Society of Friends on both sides of the Atlantic, many of whom owned slaves, sought to stifle abolitionist agitation, seeing it as a threat to the hard-won tolerance accorded them by the English government.

Contemporary Quakers who criticized Society of Friends leaders for their complicity in slavery were ostracized or disowned. Never one to be intimidated, Lay took up the challenge. He distributed antislavery literature, disrupted Quaker meetings with his antislavery harangues, refused to dine with slave owners or wear clothing produced by slaves, and fasted in protest for more than forty days, a tactic that almost cost him his life.

Lay published a collection of his abolitionist thoughts in 1737. In *All Slave-Keepers, That Keep the Innocent in Bondage*, he drew on his short stay on Barbados, what he had read and heard about the transatlantic slave trade, and his observations of slave ownership in and around Philadelphia to condemn slavery as the worst of all sins. He called on Quaker masters to instruct their slaves in the principles of the faith, teach them reading and writing and a trade, and then set them free. Most important, Lay called on the Quaker leadership to disown all who refused to manumit their slaves. The leaders of the Quaker Yearly Meeting in Philadelphia placed ads in newspapers condemning Lay for his failure to submit his manuscript to the Society's Overseers of the Press before publication—an act that actually contributed to the circulation of Lay's arguments.

The diminutive agitator—he stood only four feet seven inches tall—finally saw some success. In early 1758, the Pennsylvania Yearly Meeting encouraged members of the Society of Friends to free their slaves and ruled that all Quakers who participated in the slave trade would be disowned. Although it would be another generation before the Quakers actually prohibited members from owning slaves, Lay kept the issue front and center in Quaker politics until his death on February 3, 1759.

Larry Gragg

See also: Fox, George; Quakers (Society of Friends).

Further Reading

Drake, Thomas E. *Quakers and Slavery in America.* New Haven, CT: Yale University Press, 1950.

Gragg, Larry. "The Making of an Abolitionist: Benjamin Lay on Barbados, 1718–1720." *Journal of the Barbados Museum and Historical Society* 47 (2001): 166–84.

Nash, Gary B. *Forging Freedom: The Formation of Philadelphia's Black Community, 1720–1840.* Cambridge, MA: Harvard University Press, 1988.

Soderlund, Jean R. *Quakers and Slavery: A Divided Spirit.* Princeton, NJ: Princeton University Press, 1985.

Lei Áurea (Golden Law, 1888)

On May 13, 1888, after four centuries of operation, slavery was abolished in Brazil. Princess Regent Isabel signed the *Lei Áurea* (Golden Law) on behalf of her father, Emperor Dom Pedro II, freeing the remaining slaves in the country. The law freed approximately 700,000 slaves, a small number compared with the almost 4 million African slaves trafficked from Africa to the Americas from the mid-sixteenth century to the nineteenth century.

The law was the culmination of a long process of discussion and negotiation in Brazil's parliament and among different sectors of Brazilian society. The process of abolition began in the 1830s with the unsuccessful prohibition of the importation of African slaves. Later, in 1850, a new prohibition was issued, putting an end to four centuries of transatlantic slave trade. In 1871, Brazil passed the *Lei do Ventre Libre* (Law of the Free Womb, or Free Birth Law, as it became known), which freed the newborn children of slave women. As a result of this law, families were separated and the government became responsible for the care of the free children of slaves. In 1885, the Sexagenarian Law was passed, freeing any slave over sixty years of age. In this way, slave owners no longer had any responsibility for elder slaves, leaving them abandoned without any kind of compensation or means to survive. Abolitionists viewed these measures as temporary solutions to the complete emancipation of all slaves.

In most provinces, slave labor had been almost eliminated by rising slave prices after the end of the transatlantic slave trade; therefore, the abolition of slavery was not seen as a threat. In the coffee-producing regions of Brazil—São Paulo, Rio de Janeiro, and Minas Gerais—that relied heavily on slave labor, the elite landowners of these regions joined the anti-abolitionist campaign.

In the 1880s, sparked by the publication of Joaquim Nabuco's book *Abolitionism*, the abolitionist movement gained ground and saw several laws passed in the Brazilian Parliament. The slaves also resisted, abandoning the coffee plantations, damaging tools, and working at a slow pace to disturb production. By 1887, slave flights had become endemic in Brazil, further slowing the production and harvesting of coffee. In the face of this problem, the plantation owners of São Paulo broke with the anti-abolitionist coalition and, for the first time, considered freeing their slaves. These instabilities accelerated the approval of the Golden Law of 1888, which abolished slavery without financial compensation for the plantation owners.

Following passage of the Golden Law, the masses celebrated in the streets and threw balls in honor of the princess and emperor. Decades later, Isabel was portrayed as the historical figure who was most responsible for the emancipation, and she was referred to as the redemptress (*A Redentora*) of Brazilian blacks in newspapers and schoolbooks. As modern historians have studied the events leading up to the passage of the Golden Law, however, they have come to view Brazilian abolition in the broader context of international pressure and the spread of the abolitionist movement in the Americas.

The abolition of slavery in Brazil was a milestone event, but it provided little social and economic integration for this new group of freedmen and women. The distribution of land and universal education, two of the abolitionist movement's strongest demands, still had not been met.

Mariana P. Candido

See also: Brazil, Abolition in; Isabel, Princess Regent of Brazil; Nabuco, Joaquim.

Further Reading

Bethell, Leslie. *The Abolition of the Brazilian Slave Trade: Britain, Brazil and the Slave Trade Question, 1807–1869.* Cambridge, UK: Cambridge University Press, 1970.

Reis, Jaime. *Abolition and the Economics of Slaveholding in North East Brazil.* Glasgow, UK: Institute of Latin American Studies, 1974.

Scott, Rebecca. *The Abolition of Slavery and the Aftermath of Emancipation in Brazil.* Durham, NC: Duke University Press, 1988.

Toplin, Robert Brent. *The Abolition of Slavery in Brazil.* New York: Atheneum, 1972.

Lei do Ventre Libre (Free Birth Law, 1871)

The *Lei do Ventre Libre* (literally, Law of the Free Womb, or Free Birth Law, as it came to be known) of 1871 was part of a plan by the emperor Pedro II (known as Dom Pedro) and the Liberal Party to abolish slavery gradually in Brazil. The abolition of African slavery had become an important issue in the aftermath of the Paraguayan War (1865–1870), as Brazilian political leaders and intellectuals saw the persistence of slavery as the country's key vulnerability. Also known as the Rio Branco Law, after Brazilian prime minister Viscount Rio Branco, José Maria da Silva Paranhos, the measure represented a compromise between complete emancipation and the continuation of the slave system.

The Free Birth Law freed all children born to slave mothers. Slave owners were responsible for looking after the children until the age of eight, at which time the owners would receive compensation from the government. Furthermore, owners could choose to keep the children until they reached the age of twenty-one by declining government compensation. The law also required owners to allow their slaves to purchase their freedom at the prevailing market price. In addition, it created a government emancipation fund to be used for the manumission of slaves and created a national slave register.

In 1871, Dom Pedro appointed Rio Branco to the post of prime minister. Although Rio Branco was a member of the Conservative Party, which generally opposed abolition, he remained flexible on the issue of slavery. After appointing Rio Branco, Dom Pedro left Brazil for Europe so that he might be less directly associated with any decision that led to the emancipation of slaves. The issue was hotly debated in the Brazilian Parliament, and representatives engaged in intense shouting matches that often came close to physical violence. The debate also involved the Brazilian public, as the press covered the issue closely, and the government produced propaganda leaflets. Public meetings on the law attracted thousands of people.

The slaveholders who opposed the law did not argue against the abolition of slavery; rather, they felt the government had no right to take their private property away from them. Slave owners argued that the constitution and laws of Brazil protected their property rights to keep the children born to slaves, just as it protected any other private property.

Some slave owners complained that the compensation offered was insufficient. Others feared that the law would foment rebellion, as the Afro-Brazilians would no longer be passive and subordinate. The opposition also pointed to the potential for economic upheaval, as the law would change the existing economic order and decrease land values. Finally, some opposed the measure simply to challenge the power of the emperor, whom they saw as imposing his own ideas on slave owners.

Some abolitionists believed the law was too conservative and cautious. They argued that slave owners would simply ignore the well-being of the children. They also claimed that the government should compensate the former slaves, not the owners.

Supporters of the law argued that it was the best solution for both sides. They claimed that the law would actually stabilize the economy and maintain the supply of labor, while providing for the eventual abolition of slavery. To convince the planters of the merits of the law, supporters argued that the children would grow accustomed to life and work on the plantation and would continue to stay and work there even when freed. Furthermore, proponents believed that free labor would be much more efficient than slave labor.

Supporters also pointed out that gradual abolition would help avoid a civil war, such as the one that took place in the United States, and that world opinion toward Brazil would become more favorable. Finally, abolitionists made moral and religious arguments that questioned the legitimacy of owning human beings.

Rio Branco appealed to both sides. By late September 1871, the debates had come to an end, and the measure was put to a vote. The law narrowly passed the Chamber of Deputies. Princess Regent Isabel, daughter of Dom Pedro, signed the bill into law, acting on his behalf. Conservatives generally accepted the law, despite their opposition to the abolition of slavery. They felt that if the law were defeated, abolitionists would propose a more radical emancipation measure that would completely abolish slavery.

Many Brazilians celebrated the passing of the law in 1871. In reality, however, the Free Birth Law was quite conservative and contained a number of loopholes. To some degree, this new law even served as an obstacle to complete abolition, as slave owners often ignored it and the government did not consistently enforce it. As antislavery groups voiced their agitation over the law's limitations, they adopted a more radical approach to abolition during the 1880s, which eventually led to full abolition in Brazil with the passage of the *Lei Áurea* (Golden Law) in 1888.

Ronald E. Young

See also: Brazil, Abolition in.

Further Reading

Burns, E. Bradford. *A History of Brazil*. 3rd ed. New York: Columbia University Press, 1993.

Conrad, Robert E. *The Destruction of Brazilian Slavery, 1850–1888*. Berkeley: University of California Press, 1972; 2nd ed., Malabar, FL: Krieger, 1993.

Toplin, Robert Brent. *The Abolition of Slavery in Brazil*. New York: Atheneum, 1972.

Liberia

Following the successful establishment of the colony of Sierra Leone as a refuge for newly freed slaves from Great Britain, the wealthy African American businessman Paul Cuffe attempted to found a settlement for free blacks from the United States. The result was the launching of the colony of Liberia, which was part of an effort to return African Americans to Africa and to spread Western culture, including Christianity, among the peoples of the region.

Founding of a Colony

Although Cuffe failed to fulfill his dream, his ideas encouraged a group of leading American politicians and abolitionists to form the American Colonization Society (ACS) in 1816. The aim of the ACS was to create a settlement in Africa that would serve as a haven for repatriated former slaves and other free blacks.

In 1820, the ACS dispatched a small group of settlers to an area of Sierra Leone. The territory proved inhospitable and disease infested, and the ACS had to relocate its colony farther north of the original settlement. The ACS was able to purchase a strip of land three miles wide and thirty-six miles long from local chiefs in exchange for about $300 in trade goods.

This area became the foundation for the colony of Liberia, and the settlers moved to their new home in April 1822. From the beginning, slavery and the slave trade were outlawed in the settlement; however, the colonists were unable to end slavery in the interior regions of Liberia, and the slave trade continued both in those inland regions and in some areas along the coast.

The ACS's first governor, Jehudi Ashmun, was an authoritarian figure who sparked a brief revolt in the colony. The ACS dispatched a mediator who resolved the dispute by developing a constitution and legal framework that granted significant local autonomy. Despite these measures, a succession of ACS-appointed, white governors retained ultimate political authority.

In 1824, the capital of the colony, Christopolis, was renamed Monrovia in honor of American president James Monroe, and the colony officially became known as Liberia. The free blacks who settled in Liberia were referred to as Americo-Liberians. This group would dominate the political and economic structures of the country for most of its history.

Beginning in 1827, a number of American states began to form their own colonization societies in an effort to relocate their free black populations. Pennsylvania, Maryland, Virginia, and Mississippi all formed state societies and corresponding settlements in Liberia. In some Southern states, slave emancipations or manumissions were allowed only on the condition that the newly freed slaves relocate to Liberia.

In 1838, most of the state settlements and the areas controlled by the ACS merged to form the Commonwealth of Liberia, and a new constitution was adopted. (The Mississippi colony did not join the com-

The Danish steamer *Horsa*, with some 200 freed slaves on board, gets ready to leave Savannah, Georgia, for Liberia in 1895. Rising racial tensions in the 1890s brought a revival of the back-to-Africa movements among Southern blacks. (*©Library of Congress/The Bridgeman Art Library*)

monwealth until 1842, and the Maryland colony remained autonomous from Liberia until 1857.) In 1841, Joseph Jenkins Roberts, a former Virginian, became the first black governor of the colony.

Anti–slave trade patrols of the U.S. Navy repatriated newly freed slaves to Liberia after they captured slave ships. In all, the navy dispatched about 5,000 former slaves to the colony, and this group became commonly known as the "Congoes."

Independence

The mid-nineteenth century witnessed frequent disputes between the Liberian government and the British merchants from Sierra Leone who did business in the colony. The British increasingly refused to pay customs duties on imports, because, they argued, the colony was controlled by the ACS and this private organization lacked the authority to levy taxes. This issue prompted the business and planter elites in the colony to support independence.

In an October 1846 referendum, Liberians voted

overwhelmingly in favor of independence. On July 26, 1847, they adopted their own Declaration of Independence and declared themselves a free and sovereign people. The country also adopted a new constitution, modeled on that of the United States. Roberts was elected the country's first president; in 1884, the first native-born president, Hilary Johnson, was elected.

Great Britain, with its neighboring colony in Sierra Leone, was the first country to recognize the new nation; the United States did not recognize Liberian independence until 1862. In the 1860s, immigration to Liberia slowed dramatically, especially after slavery was abolished in the United States. In 1865, one last wave of immigrants arrived in Liberia from Barbados. In addition, during this period, its government launched an extensive campaign to assert its control over the interior regions of the country through both diplomacy and force.

The effort to achieve effective control of the interior was a response to the colonization efforts of the French and British, who threatened to claim most of Liberia's hinterland. French forces forcibly seized former areas of Liberia in 1892. The potential for foreign intervention led to a rapprochement with the United States, and the Liberians asked the U.S. government to serve as a mediator in several territorial disputes.

Turmoil and Oppression

A highly rigid class system developed in the country, dividing the 15,000 or so Americo-Liberians and their allies the Congoes from the 2 million natives, who were referred to as simply "Africans." In 1869, the True Whig Party was formed and became the political power base of the Americo-Liberians. The party remained in power until 1980 and worked to exclude Africans from access to political power. For example, the full right to vote was not extended to all Africans until 1946. There were also economic disparities based on a system of semislavery and forced labor that remained in place into the twentieth century.

In 1908, the government created the Liberian Frontier Force military unit to protect the country's borders. In reality, however, the force was used as a means of oppression. It supported local commissioners who abused their powers and created plantations based on forced labor. There was a brief effort to reform local governments by hiring commissioners from the United States and other Western nations, but, in 1921, the foreign commissioners were forced out. The League of Nations conducted an investigation in 1929, concluding that public officials in Liberia had improperly benefited from forced labor. It was not until 1962 that the government repealed the forced labor laws and removed the power of local officials to forcibly recruit workers.

In 1980, a military coup led by Samuel Doe, a member of the long-suffering African class, overthrew the Americo-Liberian government. An extended period of civil war and ethnic unrest followed, during which Doe was overthrown and executed by forces led by Charles Taylor, an Americo-Liberian. Taylor was elected president in 1997 but was forced from office in 2003 as a result of international pressure and the presence of United Nations–sponsored peacekeeping forces. In January 2006, Ellen Johnson-Sirleaf took office as president, making her the first elected female head of state in Africa.

Tom Lansford

See also: American Anti-Slavery Society; Cuffe, Paul.

Further Reading

Eltis, David. *Economic Growth and the Ending of the Transatlantic Slave Trade.* New York: Oxford University Press, 1987.

Gershoni, Yekutiel. *Black Colonialism: The Americo-Liberian Scramble for the Hinterland.* Boulder, CO: Westview, 1985.

Schick, Tom. *Behold the Promised Land: A History of Afro-American Settler Society in Nineteenth-Century Liberia.* Baltimore: Johns Hopkins University Press, 1977.

Smith, James Wesley. *Sojourners in Search of Freedom: The Settlement of Liberia by Black Americans.* Lanham, MD: University Press of America, 1987.

Staudenraus, P.J. *The African Colonization Movement, 1816–1865.* New York: Columbia University Press, 1961; New York: Octagon, 1980.

Liberty Bell, The

Created by abolitionist Maria Weston Chapman, *The Liberty Bell* was an antislavery gift book that was published more or less annually from 1839 to 1858. The first page of every volume featured an engraving of the Liberty Bell followed by a poem dedicated to liberty. Authorship of the volumes was attributed to "Friends of Freedom" and the place of publication as Boston. The publishers varied, however, including such organizations as the American Anti-Slavery Society, the Massachusetts Anti-Slavery Society, and the National Anti-Slavery Bazaar.

Modeled on the fashionable gift books of the mid-nineteenth century and containing true stories, poems, letters, and speeches, *The Liberty Bell* was produced and sold at fairs and bazaars throughout New England to raise money for the antislavery cause and to help fund antislavery societies. Chapman, the assistant to abolitionist William Lloyd Garrison and the wife of wealthy Boston merchant Henry Grafton Chapman, served on the business and executive committees of the Massachusetts Anti-Slavery Society, the New England Anti-Slavery Society, and the American Anti-Slavery Society. Her sisters, Anne Warren Weston and Caroline Weston, worked with her to produce the annual. Like others in the so-called Boston Circle, the sisters were committed to the immediate and uncompensated end of slavery and full rights for blacks. In 1832, they formed the Boston Female Anti-Slavery Society to express their views and to agitate for the antislavery cause.

To keep production costs low, the engravings and other illustrations were minimal, but the paper and printing were always of high quality. As many as 200 individuals contributed their writings to the publication, most of them well-known male abolitionists, including Garrison, Wendell Phillips, and Frederick Douglass. Other notable contributors included Elizabeth Barrett Browning, Ralph Waldo Emerson, James Russell Lowell, Lucretia Mott, Henry Wadsworth Longfellow, Alexis de Tocqueville, Lady Byron, Thomas Clarkson, and James Haughton.

Charles A. D'Aniello and Gina Misiroglu

See also: Chapman, Maria Weston; Garrison, William Lloyd; Women's Rights and the Abolitionist Movement.

Further Reading

Pease, Jane H., and William H. Pease. *Bound With Them in Chains: A Biographical History of the Antislavery Movement.* Westport, CT: Greenwood, 1972.

Thompson, Ralph. *American Literary Annuals and Gift Books, 1825–1865.* 1936. Hamden, CT: Archon, 1967.

———. "The *Liberty Bell* and Other Anti-Slavery Gift-Books." *New England Quarterly* 7 (March 1943): 154–68.

Liberty Party

Formed in 1840, the Liberty Party was the first political party in the United States founded specifically to oppose slavery. Its members strongly believed that working within the political system was the only way to succeed in abolishing slavery. The party had some success at the state and local levels, but it had little influence at the national level. By 1848, most members of the Liberty Party had joined the Free Soil movement.

Birth

The growth of the antislavery movement during the 1830s threatened to disrupt the political balance of power maintained by the dominant two-party system of Democrats and Whigs. A number of abolitionists had broken with their more radical colleagues, such as William Lloyd Garrison, who felt strongly that there could be no peaceful political end to slavery in the United States. Garrison's moderate counterparts wanted to explore the political options, free from the constraints that hampered the antislavery actions of the two major parties.

In July 1839, at the national convention of the American Anti-Slavery Society, members discussed the possibility of forming a third political party dedicated to the destruction of slavery. Though the idea of a third party appealed to a number of the convention's participants, they did not act on the matter. When members of the society reconvened in Cleveland several months later, they voted down two resolutions to form an abolitionist party.

The struggle between the radical abolitionists, who felt that political action under the U.S. Constitution was useless in the struggle to end slavery, and those who wished to remain a viable part of the constitutional process split the American Anti-Slavery Society and led to the founding of the Liberty Party. The party was inspired by the editorials of Joshua Leavitt, editor of the New York abolitionist paper *The Emancipator* (the official organ of the American and Foreign Anti-Slavery Society), who wrote that abolitionists needed to learn to *use* the political system, just as Southern slave owners had done.

A faction of the American Anti-Slavery Society—led by abolitionists and philanthropists Gerrit Smith, Judge William Jay, Myron Holley, and Arthur Tappan, along with the Ohio antislavery agitator and attorney Salmon P. Chase—met in Warsaw, New York, in November 1839 to form a new political party dedicated solely to the abolition of slavery. Antislavery editor James G. Birney, a former Kentucky slaveholder, and Francis Lemoyne of Pennsylvania were nominated as the party's presidential and vice presidential candidates, respectively. Because only a few members of the American Anti-Slavery Society had offered their support to a third-party candidacy, Birney and Lemoyne declined the nomination. Undeterred by their refusal, Smith and other members of the antislavery faction called for a convention to be held in Albany, New York, on April 1, 1840.

Representatives of six states sent delegates to the convention, formalizing the creation of the Liberty Party. The new party's platform had only one plank—the end of slavery in America—but its goals targeted specific aspects of the institution: to pressure legislators into taking firmer positions on antislavery issues, to end slavery in the District of Columbia, to cease the interstate slave trade, and to bar slavery from all territories. The party opposed the three-fifths compromise in the Constitution, as well as the Fugitive Slave Law, and it promised to be active at the local and state levels in the quest to end slavery.

1840 and 1844 Presidential Campaigns

In the 1840 presidential campaign, William Henry Harrison, a hero of the War of 1812, stood as the candidate of the Whig Party against President Martin Van Buren, the Democrats' standard-bearer. The Liberty Party had officially nominated Birney, now living in Michigan, and Thomas Earle of Ohio, as the party's presidential and vice presidential candidates, respectively.

Although Birney accepted the Liberty Party's nomination, he traveled to Britain in May 1840, attending antislavery conferences. He did not return to the United States until November. With the party's unorganized campaign, the spirited race mounted by the Whigs and Democrats, and intense campaigning to a white male–dominated electorate, the results of the 1840 presidential election surprised few people: Birney polled slightly more than 7,000 votes. Harrison easily defeated Van Buren, carrying the Whigs to their first presidential victory.

Part of the difficulty the Liberty Party experienced with the electorate came from divisions within its own ranks. Party purists wanted to retain the abolition of slavery as their only goal. Other members began to call for a broader platform that would address other national issues besides slavery. By 1844, members of the Liberty Party had readied themselves for a more intense campaign for the presidency. Again, the party chose Birney as its candidate, although Chase urged the party to nominate John Quincy Adams of Massachusetts or William Seward of New York as its presidential nominee.

Birney disenchanted some of his followers when he also accepted the Democrats' nomination for the Michigan legislature. The Whigs eagerly attacked Birney's candidacy; the Whig press circulated a letter purportedly written by Birney stating that he would not agitate against slavery.

The Whigs chose Henry Clay of Kentucky as their candidate, and the Democrats nominated James K. Polk of Tennessee. The campaign's major issue soon became the proposed annexation of Texas. Polk supported the annexation, whereas Clay opposed it. The mood of the nation, especially the South, favored bringing Texas into the Union, which members of the Liberty Party believed would become another slave state if it were admitted. The Liberty Party received more than 62,000 votes, including enough from New York to lose that state—and ultimately, the election—for Clay and the Whigs. The presidency went to Polk.

With another defeat but a much better showing at the polls, the Liberty Party gained more confidence. It fared well at the local level in some of the Northern states, as the Mexican-American War, which began in 1846, made many Northern voters feel that the influence of slavery had expanded too far. When Pennsylvania congressman David Wilmot proposed a proviso forbidding any territory taken from Mexico to allow slavery, a number of Liberty Party supporters thought that a coalition between their party and the Democrats would be advantageous to the antislavery cause. Others called for an alliance with the New York Anti-Rent Party, which had gained significant political influence in the state of New York through its land-reform agenda, which called for replacing the system of tenanted estates with owner-operated farms, and the National Reform Association, a New York City–based land-reform organization.

Decline

Dissension over a proposed coalition with antislavery Democrats and a growing rift over the one-issue platform caused increasing tensions within the ranks of the Liberty Party. Although it did well in the off-year election of 1846, it became obvious that the party was beginning to disintegrate. Factions within the party that wanted to adopt a broad platform of universal reform began to call themselves the Liberty League.

By 1848, the Liberty Party had fallen into further disarray. John P. Hale and Leicester King accepted the party's nomination for president and vice president; however, both men withdrew from the race when former president Van Buren formed the Free Soil Party, which opposed slavery in the territories acquired from Mexico. Hale joined the Democrats and won a seat as a senator from New Hampshire.

Smith tried in vain to keep the Liberty Party to one issue. Gamaliel Bailey, editor of the *National Era*, also defended the one-issue focus of the party. Ultimately, however, the Liberty Party fell prey to the divisive issues that plagued antebellum America, and the Free Soil Party absorbed the majority of its members.

Although short-lived, the Liberty Party was a unique American political experiment that forced both the Democrats and the Whigs to examine their stands on slavery. It endeavored to stay within the constitutional system of the United States when more radical abolitionists such as Garrison looked for any means to end human bondage.

Ron D. Bryant

See also: American Anti-Slavery Society; Birney, James Gillespie; Free Soil Party.

Further Reading

Harrold, Stanley C., Jr. "The Southern Strategy of the Liberty Party." *Ohio History* 87 (Winter 1978): 21–36.

Johnson, Reinhold O. "The Liberty Party in Massachusetts, 1840–1848: Antislavery Third Party Politics in the Bay State." *Civil War History* 28 (1982): 237–65.

———. "The Liberty Party in New Hampshire, 1840–1848: Antislavery Politics in the Granite State." *Historical New Hampshire* 33 (Summer 1978): 123–59.

———. "The Liberty Party in Vermont, 1840–1848: The Forgotten Abolitionists." *Vermont History* 47 (Fall 1979): 258–75.

Volpe, Vernon L. *Forlorn Hope of Freedom: The Liberty Party in the Old Northwest, 1838–1848.* Kent, OH: Kent State University Press, 1990.

Lincoln, Abraham (1809–1865)

The sixteenth president of the United States, Abraham Lincoln held office throughout the American Civil War (1861–1865), a conflict that effected the abolition of slavery in the United States and ushered in an era of emancipation. Lincoln's views on emancipation and abolition became encapsulated in myth, following his assassination in April 1865, as posthumous monikers such as the "Great Emancipator" shrouded Lincoln's private thoughts in the popular memory and influenced interpretation of his actions.

Regardless of whether Lincoln was a *true* abolitionist or whether he was the *ultimate* abolitionist remain points of scholarly debate. Some view his conversion to the antislavery cause as merely a wartime necessity rather than an ideological shift in his views on slavery.

Early Life and Rise in Politics

Lincoln was born on February 12, 1809, in Hardin County, Kentucky, a slaveholding region. Soon, the Lincoln family moved to southeastern Indiana, where young Abraham's views were shaped by the egalitarian character of the frontier experience.

As a young man, he traveled by flatboat to New Orleans, where he observed the operations of the largest slave market in the United States. Lincoln's later profession—"As I would not be a slave, so I would not be a slave owner"—was a manifestation of his frontier ethos and his personal observation of slave societies in operation. When the Lincoln family moved again to Illinois, Abraham settled in New Salem, near Springfield, where he established a homestead.

Lincoln operated a general store and served briefly as a militiaman during the Black Hawk War of 1832. He read the law in order to become trained as a country lawyer and won election to the Illinois state legislature in 1834, serving there until 1842. One of Lincoln's key achievements as a legislator was successfully relocating the Illinois state capital from Vandalia to Springfield.

Lincoln was elected to serve one term in the U.S. House of Representatives (1847–1849), during which time the United States was involved in the Mexican-American War. It was Lincoln's insistence that President James K. Polk respond to his so-called spot resolution questioning the United States' justification for war with Mexico that drew attention to the freshman congressman from Illinois. This challenge, and the circumstances of acquiring vast new territories in the Southwest as a result of the war, prompted Lincoln to focus on the central question of national life: whether the expansion of slavery into the territories should be permitted.

Despite his legislative experience at the state and federal levels, Lincoln was best known in central Illinois as a circuit-riding lawyer who frequented courthouses in small towns across the state. Lincoln's clients included both slaveholders and slaves, and he apparently showed no bias or antipathy toward either side in the question over slavery's legality as an institution in the United States. Neither did he express any real association with the small but vocal abolitionist contingent that existed within the state.

Political Leanings

Politically, Lincoln viewed himself as a Whig who supported the probusiness agenda of Henry Clay's

President Abraham Lincoln presents the original Emancipation Proclamation to his cabinet on September 22, 1862. The official freeing of slaves in the Confederate states, effective January 1, 1863, marked a major turning point in the Civil War. *(Hulton Archive/Getty Images)*

"American System," which endorsed the tariff, the national bank, and federal support for internal improvements. On the divisive issue of slavery, Lincoln recognized its legality in the states where it existed and enjoyed constitutional protection, but he was decidedly against the expansion of slavery into newly acquired Western territories. This position placed Lincoln squarely within the ranks of the growing "Free Soil" movement, which sought to stop the spread of slavery into the territories.

The passage of the Kansas-Nebraska Act of 1854 and the dissolution of the Whig Party were catalysts for the formation of the Republican Party, which Lincoln joined. The Republicans were a coalition of dissident elements—some Whigs, some Free Soilers, and some "Conscience" Democrats—who stood opposed to the uncontrolled expansion of slavery into the Western territories. Although Southerners portrayed the Republicans as a pro-abolitionist party, that description was not accurate, though politically minded antislavery supporters did find common cause within the Republican ranks. Lincoln campaigned on behalf of Republican candidate John C. Frémont in an unsuccessful bid for the presidency in 1856, but he found himself the party's nominee for a U.S. Senate seat from Illinois in the 1858 election.

Lincoln's campaign against Democratic senator Stephen A. Douglas not only helped make Lincoln a national political figure but also provided him with an opportunity to hone his views on slavery and its possible expansion. During a series of seven debates that Lincoln and Douglas held across the state of Illinois in late summer and fall 1858, Lincoln articulated a position that challenged the expansion of slavery while recognizing its right to exist as a legally protected institution in the states of the South. Although Lincoln was unable to defeat Douglas, the positions that he defended during the debates were widely reported in newspapers across the country, and his views came to embody the Republican Party's position on the expansion of slavery.

Civil War President

Lincoln received the Republican Party's presidential nomination in 1860. He faced a divided field that included his nemesis Douglas as the nominee of the Northern Democrats, sitting vice president John C. Breckenridge representing the Southern Democrats, and Tennessee congressman John Bell for the Constitutional-Union Party. In actuality, the election of 1860 was two separate contests folded into one: Lincoln and Douglas competed for votes in the Northern states while Breckenridge and Bell competed for Southern votes. Because the Southern states viewed Lincoln and the Republicans as a pro-abolition association, Lincoln's name was left off of the ballot in ten states. Nonetheless, Lincoln won a plurality of the popular votes and a wide electoral majority, making him the president-elect in November 1860.

Lincoln's election sparked a process of secession by seven slaveholding states in the Deep South, led by South Carolina in December 1860. By the time Lincoln took the oath of office and delivered his first inaugural address on March 4, 1861, the seceded states had formed the Confederate States of America (known as the Confederacy), with Jefferson Davis as their president and a capital in Montgomery, Alabama.

Lincoln's inaugural address sounded a firm stance against disunion but hinted that reconciliation was still possible. After acknowledging that he would not interfere with slavery, Lincoln cautioned, "In *your* hands, my dissatisfied fellow countrymen, and not in *mine*, is the momentous issue of civil war." The war came five weeks later when Confederate forces fired upon United States troops who were stationed at Fort Sumter in the harbor at Charleston, South Carolina.

Issuing a call for 75,000 volunteers to put down the rebellion and restore the Union, Lincoln pursued the war vigorously as commander in chief, but the Union forces stumbled during the war's early campaigns, and Lincoln had difficulty finding competent generals to lead the U.S. forces. Lincoln faced tremendous criticism, even among Northerners and fellow Republicans, for his expansion of presidential powers, an action that he justified as necessary because of the exigencies of war. These new powers, whereby he imposed a military draft and an income tax while suspending the constitutional protection of habeas corpus rights, would eventually lead Lincoln to free the slaves through executive proclamation.

Shortly after the Union victory at the Battle of Antietam, on September 22, 1862, President Lincoln issued a preliminary draft of his Emancipation Proclamation. The document stated the president's intent if the war had not concluded by January 1, 1863, 100 days after the preliminary draft was issued. Lincoln stated that he would end slavery in those areas that remained in rebellion against the United States government on January 1, 1863, but the proclamation carefully avoided freeing slaves in the border states and in regions of the southern Confederacy that were already in the control of Union forces. Lincoln supported congressional efforts to create a Thirteenth Amendment to the U.S. Constitution that would effectively abolish slavery.

The moral apogee of Lincoln's presidency came on November 19, 1863, when he spoke at the dedication ceremonies for a military cemetery held at the site where the Battle of Gettysburg had been fought just months earlier. In his Gettysburg Address, as the remarks became known, Lincoln connected the Civil War with the revolutionary cause of freedom that the generation of 1776 had labored to attain. By prophesying a "new birth of freedom," Lincoln elevated the cause of the Civil War beyond partisan squabbling and made the war a crusade for righteousness.

Abraham Lincoln was elected to a second term in office in November 1864, and he lived to see the successful conclusion of the Civil War just weeks after he delivered his second inaugural address in March 1865. Just days after Confederate forces surrendered to Union General Ulysses S. Grant at Appomattox, Virginia, Lincoln fell victim to an assassin's bullet on the night of April 14. He died the following morning.

Junius P. Rodriguez

See also: Civil War, American (1861–1865); Emancipation Proclamation (1863).

Further Reading

Beck, Warren A. "Lincoln and Negro Colonization." *Abraham Lincoln Quarterly* 6 (September 1959): 162–83.

Breiseth, Christopher N. "Lincoln and Frederick Douglass: Another Debate." *Illinois State Historical Society Journal* 68 (February 1975): 9–26.

Donald, David H. *Lincoln*. New York: Simon & Schuster, 1995.

Findley, Paul. *A. Lincoln: The Crucible of Congress*. New York: Crown, 1979.

Oates, Stephen B. *With Malice Toward None: The Life of Abraham Lincoln*. New York: Harper & Row, 1977.

Paludan, Phillip Shaw. *The Presidency of Abraham Lincoln*. Lawrence: University Press of Kansas, 1994.

Planck, George R. "Abraham Lincoln and Black Colonization: Theory and Practice." *Lincoln Herald* 72 (Summer 1970): 61–77.

Locke, John

See Enlightenment

Lovejoy, Elijah P. (1802–1837)

The abolitionist and journalist Elijah Parish Lovejoy was murdered in Alton, Illinois, on November 7, 1837, as he defended his press against attack by an armed proslavery mob. As a result of his tragic death, Lovejoy became a martyr for the cause of freedom of the American press, and his murder drew attention and adherents to the fledgling antislavery movement.

Born in Albion, Maine, on November 9, 1802, Lovejoy studied at Waterville (now Colby) College, graduating with honors in 1826. After a brief teaching stint in Maine, he moved to Missouri, where he hoped to continue teaching, but he soon became interested in the ministry. He returned to the East to pursue his studies and attended the Theological Seminary at Princeton University. By 1833, he was licensed to preach by the Presbyterian Church, and he returned to Saint Louis, Missouri, to pursue a career in the ministry.

Shortly after returning to Missouri, Lovejoy began to publish a religiously oriented newspaper called the *Observer* in Saint Louis. The first edition appeared on November 21, 1833, to mixed reviews. As a Presbyterian minister turned editor, Lovejoy's newspaper focused largely on theological themes, and the early issues of his weekly paper displayed a decidedly anti-Catholic bias. The focus of the *Observer* shifted with the editor's interests, and by 1835, it had become clear that Lovejoy and his publication had adopted a strong antislavery stance.

The Midwest was certainly not a bastion of abolitionist sympathy in the 1830s, and operating an antislavery press in Missouri—a slave state—was a risky venture. Even though the mercantile and urban interests of Saint Louis did not rely on slavery, critics within the city found Lovejoy's publications to be at odds with the community's standards. When Lovejoy took a two-week break from his duties to attend to business outside the city, the assistant editor of the *Observer* noted in the October 8, 1835, issue that the publication would not publish antislavery materials while Lovejoy was away.

Lovejoy was not unaware of the antipathy the *Observer* faced in Saint Louis, but he believed that the larger principle of freedom of the press stood in the balance if he allowed himself to be silenced by the anti-abolition mobs. In an editorial published on November 5, 1835, he wrote, "The truth is, my fellow-citizens, if we give ground a single inch, there is no stopping place. I deem it, therefore, my duty to stand upon the Constitution."

Lovejoy responded to his critics in Saint Louis within the pages of the *Observer*, but the growing litany of anti-abolition sentiment convinced the editor that neither his publication nor his family was safe in Missouri. On July 21, 1836, Lovejoy announced his intention to move the *Observer* to Alton, Illinois, where he would continue the publication of the antislavery newspaper from the safe confines of a free state. Though Illinois was a free state, its southern portion was home to a substantial number of proslavery sympathizers.

Despite its critics, the *Observer* boasted a significant number of subscribers in both Missouri and Illinois. By September 1837, Lovejoy claimed that more than 2,100 subscribers were receiving his weekly newspaper. Lovejoy believed that the community of Alton, which was home to many pioneer settlers who had New England roots, would be a more supportive environment in which to openly espouse antislavery sympathies.

The move from Saint Louis to Alton did not completely alleviate the problems that Lovejoy had faced from his anti-abolition critics. Essentially, he had moved his press across the Mississippi River but only about thirty miles upstream from Saint Louis. The enemies whom Lovejoy had accumulated during his time in Saint Louis were still close enough to harass the press once it relocated to Alton, Illinois.

Lovejoy's press was destroyed on three occasions by anti-abolition mobs that wanted to silence any criticism of slavery, but with the help of the Ohio Anti-Slavery Society, Lovejoy was able to replace each destroyed press with a new one. He vowed that he would not be silenced.

Meanwhile, Lovejoy's views as an abolitionist grew more bold: On July 6, 1837, he wrote an editorial in the *Alton Observer* calling for a statewide meeting to form an Illinois State Anti-Slavery Society; on October 26, such an organization was formed at a meeting held in Alton. This action proved to be too much for Lovejoy's critics.

The final attack occurred on November 7, 1837, as Lovejoy and his supporters defended the arrival of his fourth press. An armed mob stormed the warehouse

Proslavery militants attack and burn the press building of the *Alton* (Illinois) *Observer,* an abolitionist newspaper, on November 7, 1837. Publisher Elijah Lovejoy, killed in the incident, became a martyr to the antislavery cause. *(Hulton Archive/Getty Images)*

where Lovejoy and about twenty supporters had gathered to defend the new press from enemies who had vowed to destroy it. Despite Lovejoy's belief in pacifism, he had decided to defend his press, if necessary, by force of arms against those enemies who were attempting to silence him. Lovejoy died during the ensuing battle.

Symbolically, Lovejoy's abolitionist voice was more strident in death than it ever had been through his editorial pen. Abolitionists around the country held memorial services to honor their fallen comrade. In the process, a new generation of recruits was drawn into the antislavery cause.

Junius P. Rodriguez

See also: Anti-Abolition Riots; Lovejoy, Owen.

Further Reading

Beecher, Edward. *Narrative of Riots at Alton.* New York: E.P. Dutton, 1965.

Blight, David W. "The Martyrdom of Elijah P. Lovejoy." *American History* 12 (November 1977): 20–27.

Curtis, Michael Kent. "The 1837 Killing of Elijah Lovejoy by an Anti-Abolition Mob: Free Speech, Republican Government, and the Privileges of American Citizens." *UCLA Law Review* 44 (April 1997): 1109–84.

Mabee, Carlton. *Black Freedom: The Nonviolent Abolitionists From 1830 Through the Civil War.* New York: Macmillan, 1970.

Merideth, Robert. "A Conservative Abolitionist at Alton: Edward Beecher's *Narrative.*" Pts. 1 and 2. *Journal of Presbyterian History* 42 (March 1964): 39–53; 42 (June 1964): 92–103.

Richards, Leonard L. *Gentlemen of Property and Standing: Anti-Abolition Mobs in Jacksonian America.* New York: Oxford University Press, 1970.

Lovejoy, Owen (1811–1864)

The American memory readily associates the name Lovejoy with abolitionism and freedom of the press because of Elijah Parish Lovejoy, the Alton, Illinois, activist killed by an anti-abolition mob in 1837. Owen Lovejoy, embracing the mantle of his martyred brother, was a self-described "ultra-abolitionist." For him, the slave system denigrated and dehumanized the master as well as the slave. He believed that the responsibilities of the abolitionist included aiding runaway slaves, preaching and lecturing against slavery, and seeking political, legal, and social change. His home was an advertised stop on the Underground Railroad, and his runaway-aiding activities landed him in court on several occasions.

Lovejoy was born on January 6, 1811, in Albion, Maine, the sixth of eight children of Elizabeth Gordon Pattee and Daniel B. Lovejoy. He attended Bowdoin College but, after his father's death in 1833, failed to graduate.

In 1836, Lovejoy moved to Alton, Illinois, to pursue theological studies. Following a period of study, he sought ordination in the Episcopal Church; however, he was asked to pledge not to preach on the subject of slavery. He refused, and his ordination was deferred.

After considering ordination under the Presbytery of Alton, Lovejoy heard from the Reverend Edward Beecher of a temporary pastoral position at the Hampshire Colony Congregational Church in Princeton, Illinois. Initially appointed as minister for one year in summer 1838, Lovejoy went on to hold the position for seventeen years. Ignoring the Illinois state law prohibiting abolitionist meetings, he spoke boldly from his pulpit and in meeting halls on the antislavery cause, often experiencing open hostility from agitated crowds.

While working with the Illinois Anti-Slavery Society, Lovejoy realized the need to use the political system to advance the cause of abolitionism in state and national legislatures. In Illinois, Lovejoy helped establish the short-lived Liberty Party during the early 1840s. Because of its singular focus on abolitionism, the Liberty Party failed to make any significant political advances and had begun to dissolve by 1848, as members were absorbed into the Free Soil Party.

Following the creation of the Republican Party in 1854, Lovejoy was elected to the Illinois House of Representatives. As a resident of the state's Third Congressional District, he presided over the most populated district in the country, which included much of northern Illinois.

Seeing the decline of the Whig and Liberty parties, Lovejoy encouraged abolitionists, particularly those in Illinois, to broaden their perspectives and join the Republican ranks, although he believed the Republican platform of gradual emancipation and the moderate position of nonextension of slavery into the territories did not advance the abolitionist cause strongly enough. In the early years of the Republican Party, Lovejoy sought to draw Abraham Lincoln into its ranks, with little success. He eventually succeeded, but the party remained divided between the former Whigs and abolitionists.

As his state term ended, Lovejoy pursued a seat in the U.S. Congress. Drawing on his strong oratory skills, which he had acquired as a preacher and an antislavery lecturer, Lovejoy campaigned successfully and was elected in 1856 as a Republican to the 35th Congress, where he served from the following January until his death. Although the districts in Illinois would change over the next decade, Lovejoy was re-elected three times, representing Illinois's Third, Fourth, and Fifth districts. Once he assumed his seat, Lovejoy wasted no time in distinguishing himself, debating on the House floor within his first weeks in Washington. With some of his antislavery speeches reprinted nationally, Lovejoy rose in prominence.

By 1858, the Republican Party had begun to solidify, and Lovejoy continued to be a firebrand in Congress. In April 1860, a bitter battle erupted as Lovejoy debated the slavery question. Southern legislators resented his debating an issue that was not linked to any specific matter before the House. Angry exchanges ensued, during which Lovejoy became entangled in a shoving match with some of his Southern colleagues.

Meanwhile, Lovejoy's relationship with Lincoln grew stronger, so much so that Lovejoy worked unceasingly for Lincoln's presidential nomination and election in 1860, neglecting his own campaign. Despite his militant abolitionism, during the 1862 campaign, Lovejoy expressed his exigent political moderation by stressing that the U.S. Civil War was meant to quell the Southern rebellion, not strictly to end slavery. During this tumultuous period, Lovejoy became one of Lincoln's confidants.

Lovejoy's election to the 38th Congress in 1862 would be his last. Although the Southern states had seceded, political wrangling still occupied the House, and Lovejoy continued to fight for freedom for the enslaved. In 1863, he introduced House Resolutions 21 and 22, bills proposing universal emancipation and freedmen's protection. He also submitted a resolution calling for equal pay among soldiers without distinction of color.

Throughout his last session of Congress, Lovejoy's health failed, at one point causing him to return to Illinois. He returned to Congress but died while recuperating in Brooklyn, New York, on March 25, 1864.

David B. Malone

See also: Amendments, Reconstruction; Lincoln, Abraham; Lovejoy, Elijah P.

Further Reading

Magdol, Edward. *Owen Lovejoy: Abolitionist in Congress.* New Brunswick, NJ: Rutgers University Press, 1967.

Lundy, Benjamin (1789–1839)

Benjamin Lundy was a publisher of several antislavery newspapers and a leading Quaker abolitionist during the 1820s and 1830s. He worked to limit the expansion of slavery and explored the feasibility of establishing a colony of freed slaves outside the United States. His ideas inspired William Lloyd Garrison, another prominent abolitionist and newspaper editor.

Lundy was born on January 4, 1789, in Sussex County, New Jersey. Raised as a devout Quaker, he was exposed early on to the antislavery sentiment of the Society of Friends' teachings, which emphasized strong opposition to the practice of slavery. At age nineteen, he relocated to Wheeling, Virginia, and spent eighteen months working as an apprentice saddle maker. His passion for the abolitionist cause was fueled by his experiences in Virginia, where he observed slavery firsthand, as slave traders traversed the route from Virginia and Maryland to the lower Mississippi River Valley region.

After completing his apprenticeship, Lundy moved to Mount Pleasant, Ohio, a community of devout Quakers and an important link on the Underground Railroad, which smuggled slaves from the Southern states to freedom in the North. Four years later, he moved a short distance to Saint Clairsville, Ohio. There, he organized the Union Humane Society, an antislavery association, in 1815.

In 1819, Lundy established the *Philanthropist*, a short-lived antislavery periodical. That same year, he relocated to Saint Louis, Missouri, where he worked to prevent the expansion of slavery in that state. As a result of his experience in Missouri, Lundy recognized that it was possible to influence public opinion in the direction of an antislavery majority. In 1821, he returned to Mount Pleasant.

At this time, Lundy founded the periodical the *Genius of Universal Emancipation* as a forum for his abolitionist writings. The first issue, published in June 1821, generated much controversy. Lundy wrote passionately about his opposition to slavery, showing little concern for the feelings of slaveholders and expressing no interest in seeking a middle ground on the slavery question. One of the earliest abolitionist periodicals, the *Genius* was dedicated to describing the evils of slavery and emphasizing the need for political pressure to bring an end to the institution. The *Genius* reflected Lundy's basic belief that a widely circulated and effectively edited newspaper could influence public opinion in the direction of antislavery.

In 1829, Garrison, who was inspired by Lundy's antislavery rhetoric, was named co-editor of the *Genius*. Because of disagreements and a lawsuit against the co-editors of the periodical by slaveholders, Garrison moved to Boston the next year to publish a new periodical, *The Liberator* (1831–1865), which would later emerge as the most prominent abolitionist periodical. Lundy remained with the *Genius* until it ceased publication in late 1835.

Lundy subscribed to the view that settling free blacks in rural regions could effectively solve the slavery problem. As a proponent of gradual emancipation, he saw the need to establish settlements of freed slaves until full national emancipation could be achieved. He visited Haiti on two occasions and the Wilberforce Colony of fugitive slaves in Canada, and he made three trips to Texas between 1830 and 1835 in the hopes of obtaining land for a settlement of freed slaves.

While in Texas, Lundy visited with free blacks, farmers, and Mexican officials. He traveled to Nacogdoches, San Antonio, the Brazos region, and Rio Grande region. He concluded that several areas of Texas, especially the Corpus Christi and Laredo areas, were ideally suited to his colonization experiment. The Mexican government responded favorably to his proposal. The start of the Texas Revolution, however, prevented Lundy from implementing his plans. Soon after the revolution, the Republic of Texas legalized slavery. Lundy viewed the outcome of the Texas Revolution as a slaveholders' plot to remove Texas from Mexico and to add slave territory to the United States. In 1836, he began another newspaper in Philadelphia, the *National Enquirer and Constitutional Advocate of Universal Liberty*, which was dedicated to exposing this plot.

In August 1836, he published *The War in Texas*, a pamphlet highlighting his arguments against the annexation of Texas by the United States. Lundy won over many with his arguments, including former president and then-congressman John Quincy Adams, who articulated his views in the U.S. House of Representatives.

Adams, Lundy, and other advocates were successful in delaying the annexation of Texas for nine years.

Lundy continued to publish the *National Enquirer* until March 1838, when it was sold and its name changed to the *Pennsylvania Freeman*. After relocating to Illinois, where his family resided, Lundy became active in the state's local antislavery societies and re-established the *Genius*, publishing twelve issues before his death on August 22, 1839. His descendants collected a portion of his writings, including details of his Texas journeys, and published them as *The Life, Travels and Opinions of Benjamin Lundy* (1847).

J.B. Watson, Jr.

See also: Quakers (Society of Friends).

Further Reading

Lilly, Stephen R. *Fighters Against American Slavery*. San Diego, CA: Lucent, 1999.

Stewart, James Brewer. *Holy Warriors: The Abolitionists and American Slavery*. Rev. ed. New York: Hill and Wang, 1996.

Wixom, Robert. *Benjamin Lundy (1789–1839): The Pioneer Quaker Abolitionist*. Columbia: University of Missouri Press, 1971.

Lynching

Lynching is a violent crime in which one or more persons are apprehended by a mob and then tortured or executed, often by hanging. The act is often justified by its perpetrators as vigilante justice.

The term *lynch law* was first used to describe the actions of Colonel Charles Lynch and his Virginia associates during the American Revolution, as they persecuted Tories and Loyalists. Although it has been widely practiced in the United States, this form of mob violence is specifically associated with racial unrest in the South during the late nineteenth and early twentieth centuries. Lynching was practiced extensively after the U.S. Civil War, most commonly between 1880 and 1930.

Lynching became symbolic of white economic, political, and social frustration directed toward African Americans. Although the lynch law was imposed for a variety of offenses—ranging from serious crimes such as grand theft or murder to petty personal crimes—its most common purpose was to administer mob rule over African Americans. Historians estimate that between 1880 and 1920, an average of two African Americans were lynched per week in the United States. From 1882 to 1968, just under 5,000 Americans died of lynching, 3,400 of them black men and women.

The Scourge of the South

At the close of Reconstruction in the late 1870s, Southern whites focused on ending Northern interference in the region's affairs, and Northerners displayed a growing indifference to the civil rights of Southern blacks. Taking its cue from this regional disharmony, the federal government abandoned its oversight of constitutional protections. Southern and border states responded by enacting Jim Crow laws in the 1890s—segregating blacks and whites in public schools, restaurants, theaters, hotels, and restrooms, as well as on public transportation—and white vigilante mobs, set on taking the law into their own hands, flourished. With blacks barred from voting, public office, and jury service, Southern law enforcers disregarded minority interests and failed to protect the lives of minority men and women. In addition to lynchings of individuals, dozens of race riots that victimized blacks erupted throughout the Southern United States, from Wilmington, North Carolina, in 1898 to Tulsa, Oklahoma, in 1921.

Although white men and black women were sometimes the victims of lynching, it became primarily a mode of oppression directed at black males. At the hands of angry mobs or white supremacist organizations such as the Ku Klux Klan and the Knights of the White Camellia, black men were lynched in Alabama, Georgia, Louisiana, and Texas. Although lynching was characteristic of the South during the post-Reconstruction years, it spread to virtually every state, with the exception of a few northeastern states.

Typically, lynchings were prompted by an accusation that an African American had raped a white woman, killed a white person, or posed some economic threat to property or commerce. Underlying many of these accusations was a fear that blacks would attain equal social and economic status with whites. In her article "Lynch Law in America" (1900), the crusading black journalist Ida B. Wells-Barnett described the practice as "the cool, calculating deliberation of intelligent people who openly avow that there is an 'unwritten law' that justifies them in putting human beings to death without complaint under oath, without trial by jury, without opportunity to make defense, and without right of appeal."

Lynching was often regarded as a family function, in which both parents and children were present to witness or participate in the atrocity. Victims of lynching were often beaten, stripped naked, castrated, dismembered, coated with tar, burned alive, shot repeatedly,

The lynching of African Americans reached epidemic proportions in the period 1880–1930. As evidenced by this hanging of an alleged rapist in Minneapolis in 1882, mob justice was not confined to the South. *(©Private Collection/Peter Newark American Pictures/The Bridgeman Art Library)*

and hung to die. Newspapers announced public lynchings, and railroad agents sold tickets. Some participants even took home victims' body parts as souvenirs.

Efforts to End Lynching

As enlightened citizens and activists became disgusted by the practice, antilynching campaigns were organized. Antilynching organizations, such as the Association of Southern Women for the Prevention of Lynching, the National Association of Colored Women, the Council for Interracial Cooperation, and the National Association for the Advancement of Colored People (NAACP), undermined the traditional justifications for lynching and mobilized middle- and upper-class white Southerners who opposed the practice.

Black women played a key role in exposing the fallacies that lynch mobs often used to justify the practice—namely, that black men were predators of white women. Key writings of the time denounced the practice, including Frances E.W. Harper's "Duty to Dependent Races" (1892), Wells-Barnett's *A Red Record* (1895), and Mary Church Terrell's "Lynching From a Negro's Point of View" (1904).

Wells-Barnett spoke out against the inhumanity of the lynch laws in her book *Southern Horror: Lynch Law in All Its Phases* (1892), appealing to civilized people everywhere to end the practice. Like the antilynching organizations to which she belonged, Wells-Barnett sought to combat lynching through education. Recognizing that there was strong state and community support for the practice, she appealed to the U.S. Congress to pass a federal antilynching law.

In 1900, G.H. White, an African American representative from North Carolina, introduced a bill to Congress to make lynching a federal crime; however, the bill died in committee that year—the same year in which 105 African Americans were lynched. In 1918, Congressman Leonidas Dyer (R-MO) introduced an antilynching bill known as the Dyer Bill; although the House of Representatives voted in favor of the measure in January 1922, final passage was blocked by a filibuster in the Senate. In the meantime, between June and December 1919—a period that included the so-called Red Summer, which was marked by race riots and racial violence nationwide—a total of seventy-six African Americans were lynched.

Years later, the NAACP lobbied for an antilynching bill that failed to pass the Senate, as the Costigan-Wagner Bill and the Wagner-Gavagan Bill were filibustered and abandoned in 1935 and 1940, respectively. Despite these legislative failures, as a result of the efforts of the NAACP and other antilynching organizations, the number of lynchings declined sharply after 1935, though isolated instances were reported throughout the South and parts of the West. Even though the antilynching campaign never achieved its legislative goal, it did draw attention to an ethical issue that stirred the nation's conscience and laid the groundwork for future civil rights activism.

Seneca D. Vaught

See also: Ku Klux Klan; Reconstruction; Wells-Barnett, Ida B.

Further Reading

Allen, James. *Without Sanctuary: Lynching Photography in America.* Santa Fe, NM: Twin Palms, 2000.

Giddings, Paula. *When and Where I Enter: The Impact of Black Women on Race and Sex in America.* New York: William Morrow, 1996.

Shay, Frank. *Judge Lynch: His First Hundred Years.* New York: Biblo and Tannen, 1969.

Waldrep, Christopher. *The Many Faces of Judge Lynch: Extralegal Violence and Punishment in America.* New York: Palgrave, 2002.

Zangrando, Robert L. *The NAACP Crusade Against Lynching, 1909–1950.* Philadelphia: Temple University Press, 1980.

networks, communication with drums and horns, and strategies for rapid attack and withdrawal.

The maroon communities not only defended themselves but also attacked plantations and European settlements, freeing slaves and stealing provisions. Constant military incursions undermined the plantation system in Suriname. The planters and colonial government were simply unable to afford the military resources needed to subdue their ex-slave adversaries. After a series of intense conflicts in the 1750s and 1760s, the maroons' military successes obliged the Dutch authorities to sign peace treaties with the Ndjuka in 1760, the Saramaka in 1762, and the Matawai in 1767.

The Aluka tribe, led by the great warrior Boni Kikindo from 1765 to 1793, continued to fight and, in the mid-1770s, moved en masse across the border to French Guiana, where military conflicts stretched out for a century. Only in 1860 did the French and Dutch colonial governments agree to peace terms with the Aluka. The peace treaties generally provided for peace and political freedom, in exchange for which the maroons agreed to return escaped slaves.

The Maroon Wars in Suriname represent some of the most extraordinary feats of black resistance to slavery in the transatlantic world. According to historians Kenneth Bilby and Diana Baird N'Diaye, "Maroons were among the first Americans in the wake of 1492 to resist colonial domination, striving for independence, forging new cultures and identities, and developing solidarity out of diversity—processes which only later took place, on a much larger scale, in emerging nation states."

Sean Purdy

See also: Maroons; Suriname, Abolition in; Suriname, Emancipation in.

Further Reading

Bilby, Kenneth L., and Diana Baird N'Diaye. "Creativity and Resistance: Maroon Culture in the Americas." 1992 Smithsonian Festival of American Folklife, Smithsonian Institute, Washington, DC. http://www.folklife.si.edu/resources/maroon/presentation.htm.

Brana-Shute, Gary, ed. *Resistance and Rebellion in Suriname: Old and New*. Studies in Third World Societies 43. Williamsburg, VA: College of William and Mary, 1990.

Goslinga, Cornelis C. *The Dutch in the Caribbean and in Surinam, 1791/5–1942*. Assen, Netherlands: Van Gorcum, 1990.

Hoogbergen, Wim. *The Boni Maroon Wars in Suriname*. Leiden, Netherlands: Brill, 1990.

Price, Richard. "Maroons: Rebel Slaves in the Americas." 1992 Smithsonian Festival of American Folklife, Smithsonian Institute, Washington, DC. http://www.folklife.si.edu/resources/maroon/educational_guide/23.htm.

Maroons

An escaped slave (or a descendant of one) living in the wilderness in an independent, autonomous community was known as a maroon. The term was originally used in the context of the West Indies and Central America, but eventually it came to be used in slave societies throughout the Americas.

The term "maroon" came into the English language from the Spanish word *cimarrón* ("wild"). The Spaniards adopted the expression in the sixteenth century from the Taino, a native people of the Greater Antilles, who used it to refer to undomesticated plants and animals. The sixteenth-century conquistadors retained this original connotation, as indicated by their references to cimarrón (wild) vegetation and (untamed) cattle, dogs, and cats proliferating in the backwoods of Hispaniola, Cuba, and Puerto Rico.

The conquistadors justified their colonial enterprise as a spiritual, civilizing crusade, and they eventually extended the designation of *cimarrón* indiscriminately to captive Amerindians and Africans who fled to the hinterland to evade European control. Seen from their imperial eyes, the fugitives had reverted to a wild, rebellious, savage state. Willfully debasing them as roving, troublemaking, idolatrous brutes gave the Europeans an expedient pretext for taking coercive and punitive actions against them.

The Europeans built their fortunes by exploiting the Amerindians and Africans, especially in the mining and agricultural sectors of the American colonial economy. Because slaves were considered valuable property, particularly those with highly specialized training, their loss for whatever reason—fatigue, disease, accident, malnourishment, suicide, or desertion—often paralyzed or shut down production altogether. Hence, colonial legislatures across the Americas had a large stake in preventing *marronage*, or the creation of maroon communities.

Black codes severely penalized slaves who traveled without permits, held clandestine meetings, deserted, refused to work, or engaged in other forms of resistance. These codes fined, jailed, or otherwise punished anyone harboring, feeding, employing, or trading with fugitive slaves. Judging by the runaways' continuing quest to recover their freedom, none of these stringent measures put an end to individual or collective flight.

The oppressive circumstances that triggered flight varied widely and included overwork, mistreatment, separation from relatives or friends, insufficient food allowances, and loss of privileges. Initially, Native American cimarrónes possessed an advantage over their African counterparts. They were acquainted with the fauna and flora, topography, and climatic conditions of the New World, all of which significantly enhanced their chances of escaping and remaining free. By contrast, newly imported Africans were thrust into an unfamiliar terrain. Despite the constraints of bondage, however, they caught on quickly to their new surroundings.

Domestics, porters, artisans, petty traders, lumbermen, cattle herders, and those linked to maritime occupations—ship cooks, caulkers, shipbuilders, sail makers, sailors, and anglers—frequently came into contact with each other and with the world of the free. For example, the enslaved Africans who manned trading ships servicing the transatlantic world gained valuable access to information about local, regional, and international affairs that they used to improve their lot or to flee slavery altogether.

Bondsmen and women brought news and rumors acquired from their everyday contacts that they used to calculate the odds of regaining their freedom, and they acted accordingly. They plotted their escapes carefully, determining the best dates, times, and places to break out, as well as which means of transportation, guides, weapons, tools, provisions, clothing, and valuables to take. Next, they mapped their escape routes as best as they could and selected specific destinations that would suit their new lives as liberated men and women.

Successful escapes depended on many factors, such as the runaway's gender, health, age, skills, and access to resources. Some fell short of their objectives, unable to break ties with loved ones left behind or to withstand the daily deprivations of life on the run. In some cases, slave owners lured them back by offering to ameliorate their living and working conditions.

Those who were able to elude the private or state-paid bounty hunters blended into the free population, joined up with peers in remote areas, or sought shelter in colonies occupied by rival European powers. As the fugitives consolidated their control over a given territory, runaway bands frequently coalesced into maroon communities.

Maroon communities in Spanish America, the West Indies, and the United States frequently comprised Amerindians, Africans, and persons of mixed racial background living on the periphery of Euro-Creole colonial authority. During the sixteenth century, the Taino *cacique* (ruler) Enriquillo and his band of cimarrónes successfully held the Spaniards at bay on the island of Hispaniola (present-day Dominican Republic and Haiti). Black runaways built large, well-organized, self-sufficient, and enduring maroon communities in the Blue Mountains of Jamaica.

By contrast, most of the islands of the Caribbean archipelago were too small and thickly settled or lacked the natural resources needed for the establishment and long-term viability of permanent maroon communities. In such cases, maritime marronage, or escape by sea, became an alternative, especially for runaways with navigational skills. Amerindians were the first recorded maritime maroons. Driven by hardship and a desire to escape Spanish control, the Tainos of Hispaniola sought shelter in Cuba and Puerto Rico during the conquest period. When the Spaniards next

Runaway slaves known as "maroons" established independent settlements in remote areas of Jamaica—pictured here in the early 1900s—and throughout the Americas. Some communities survived for centuries. (*©Royal Geographical Society, London, UK/The Bridgeman Art Library*)

tried to subdue the Taino in Puerto Rico, many of the natives fled to the interior of the island or sailed to the eastern Caribbean.

Seaborne flight in the Caribbean became particularly widespread among the islands that had undergone the "sugar revolution," that is, the conversion to slave-based plantation agriculture that started around the middle of the seventeenth century. As the plantation system expanded, it denuded forests, leveled pastures, and devoured provision grounds, destroying natural sanctuaries on many of the small islands. Amerindians, European indentured servants, and enslaved Africans fleeing the harsh social and working conditions in the Caribbean formed alliances with other subaltern groups or capitalized on interimperial rivalries. For example, black escapees from French-occupied Martinique navigated south to the British colonies of Dominica and Saint Lucia, hoping to team up with Black Caribs. In turn, those from the British and Danish Virgin Islands fled to Puerto Rico, where some tried to disguise themselves as Indians or free coloreds.

Many were caught, perished en route, or suffered re-enslavement in their new destinations. Others received asylum after completing several years of indentured service in the host colony. In some cases, the Spaniards reluctantly congregated maroons in towns to assist with defense needs, harness their labor, and convert them to Catholicism. The towns of San Lorenzo de los Minas and San Mateo de Cangrejos, founded by the Spaniards in Hispaniola and Puerto Rico, respectively, typified this imperial strategy. Ultimately, however, the choice between short-term and permanent flight, as well as the type of sanctuary—swamps, forests, mountains, ships, cities, and nearby colonies—rested on individual perseverance and the options available to runaways.

Rebel slave societies spanned the length and breath of the Americas. Known as *palenques, quilombos, cumbes,* and *mocambos,* well-entrenched maroon strongholds took root in hard-to-reach areas of the Southern and southeastern United States, the Caribbean, and Central and South America. Their guerrilla-fighting tactics and ability to overcome formidable environmental hurdles foiled slave catchers and the larger, better-equipped military parties deployed against them. Maroons not only blocked the advance of plantations, cattle ranches, and mining operations into the hilly interior, but they also descended periodically on adjacent European settlements to socialize, trade, pillage, and harass white colonists or to lure away enslaved Africans in order to increase their ranks.

After long stretches of prolonged but futile attempts to defeat them, European colonials in the Americas were forced to cut their losses and sue for peace with the rebels. Such was the case with the British in Jamaica in 1739 and the Dutch in Suriname in 1761.

Jorge L. Chinea

See also: Maroon Wars, Jamaica (1729–1739, 1795–1796); Maroon Wars, Suriname (1600s–1800s).

Further Reading

Campbell, Mavis C. *The Maroons of Jamaica, 1655–1796: A History of Resistance, Collaboration, and Betrayal.* Granby, MA: Bergin & Garvey, 1988.

Heuman, Gad J., ed. *Out of the House of Bondage: Runaways, Resistance, and Maroonage in Africa and the New World.* London: Frank Cass, 1982.

Okihiro, Gary Y., ed. *In Resistance: Studies in African, Caribbean, and Afro-American History.* Amherst: University of Massachusetts Press, 1986.

Price, Richard. *Maroon Societies: Rebel Slave Communities in the Americas.* Baltimore: Johns Hopkins University Press, 1996.

Martineau, Harriet (1802–1876)

As the author of *Society in America* (1837), the English traveler Harriet Martineau offered an insightful critique of the United States and its social institutions, including slavery. Like Alexis de Tocqueville in *Democracy in America* (1835), Martineau found the institution of slavery incompatible with the American ideals of freedom and liberty.

Martineau was born of Huguenot ancestry in Norwich, England, on June 2, 1802. Her father was a manufacturer, and her mother came from a family of sugar refiners. The progressive and Unitarian Martineaus educated Martineau and her brothers equally. By age fifteen, she had read the work of English economist Thomas Malthus and was already "becoming a political economist without knowing it." By the time she was sixteen, her increasing deafness had become "very noticeable, very inconvenient, and excessively painful," but she discovered how to manage it in ways that were unobtrusive to others.

After her father died in 1825, Martineau began to support herself by writing. She became a prolific and vastly popular journalist who conveyed to readers her own political and sociological understandings. Her first successful works were *Illustrations of Political Economy* (1832–1834), twenty-four stories that illustrated the thought of Malthus, James Mill, David Ricardo, and Adam Smith. She began to write these sketches after the death of her fiancé in 1827 and published them in monthly installments. They outsold the work of Charles Dickens and supported her move to London in 1832.

Her first attacks on slavery appeared in the *Monthly Repository,* a Unitarian critical journal, and in *Illustrations.* She argued both the immorality and inefficiency of slavery in her fourth story, "Demerara," in which she revealed slavery as a system that wasted both capital and labor while engendering intense human suffering.

From 1834 to 1836, Martineau traveled in the United States, rousing admiration and controversy everywhere. Her *Society in America,* like Tocqueville's better-known work, described and explained widespread features of American behavior, institutions, and daily life. Despite her generally leftist politics, Martineau argued that moral values gird social institutions. In the United States, she claimed that the institution of slavery made a mockery of the ideals of freedom. In her chapter on the "Morals of Slavery," she reiterated proslavery arguments only to destroy them, questioning whether "social virtues are possible in a society of which injustice is the primary characteristic."

Martineau chose irony over outrage in her critique of slavery. On slaveholders, for example, she wrote, "I could not but marvel at their mild forbearance under the hourly provocations to which they are liable in their homes . . . their rooms dirty, their property wasted, their plans frustrated, their infants slighted, themselves deluded by artifices . . ." Forbearance was their single virtue, for "the inherent injustice of the system extinguishes all others, and nourishes a whole harvest of false morals toward the rest of society."

In plain, harsh language—explosive for her time—Martineau exposed the sexual degradation of women (slave and free), the damage to children, the coercion of conscience and behavior, and a society pervaded by hypocrisy, suspicion, and restriction of liberty. New England did not escape her slashing critique, as she described the condition of free people of color.

By 1855, after a period of illness and remission, Martineau had become housebound, but invalidism did not stop her fight to end American slavery. In 1857, for example, she wrote to her friend George Combe that despite "many bodily troubles . . . I earn lots of money for the American abolitionists by fancy-work." Her "last piece of embroidery fetched 100 dollars for 'the cause' in America."

Martineau was the English correspondent for the *American Anti-Slavery Standard* before the U.S.

Civil War, producing a continuous flow of antislavery articles founded not only on moral principle, but also on her own social and economic research. These writings reveal an acute observer and critic of the politics of slavery and antislavery in the United States.

Like her contemporary Joseph Sturge, Martineau recognized the link between abolitionism and chartism (the reform movement that sought to create a charter of liberties), with which she had both agreements and disagreements. Like Sturge, she urged immediate rather than gradual emancipation and abandoned her earlier laissez-faire market principles in favor of governmental action to end chattel slavery, wage slavery, and class oppression.

Martineau's other important writings include *Retrospect of Western Travel* (1838), another account of her U.S. travels; *Deerbrook* (1839), a novel; and *Eastern Life Present and Past* (1848), a book on the history and practice of Judaism, Christianity, and Islam. Her intelligent, socially conscious journalism interpreted for a broad readership the politics and society of her time.

In 1831, she disclaimed Christianity and Unitarianism in favor of freethinking. In 1851, she began to study Auguste Comte's positivism, publishing an abridged translation of his *Cours de philosophie positive* in 1853. An optimist, Martineau embraced positive science as the foundation of a new morality. She continued to write and publish until her death in 1876.

Riva Berleant

See also: Sturge, Joseph.

Further Reading

David, Deirdre. *Intellectual Women and Victorian Patriarchy.* Ithaca, NY: Cornell University Press, 1987.

Fladeland, Betty. "'Our Cause Being One and the Same': Abolitionists and Chartism." In *Slavery and British Society, 1776–1846,* ed. James Walvin. Baton Rouge: Louisiana State University Press, 1982.

Hoecker-Drysdale, Susan. *Harriet Martineau: First Woman Sociologist.* New York: Berg, 1992.

Martineau, Harriet. *Harriet Martineau's Autobiography.* Ed. Maria Weston Chapman. Boston: James R. Osgood, 1877.

Sanders, Valerie. *Harriet Martineau: Selected Letters.* Oxford, UK: Clarendon, 1990.

Massachusetts Fifty-Fourth Regiment

The Fifty-fourth Regiment of the Massachusetts Volunteer Infantry was the first African American military unit raised to fight for the Union cause during the U.S. Civil War. The regiment is perhaps best known for its role in the attack on Battery Wagner in Charleston Harbor, South Carolina, in July 1863, and for the role it played in changing the nation's outlook on the abilities of African American soldiers.

Less than a month after President Abraham Lincoln issued the Emancipation Proclamation on January 1, 1863, the United States allowed the federal army to recruit African American soldiers into its ranks. On January 26, Secretary of War Edwin M. Stanton authorized Massachusetts governor John A. Andrew to raise a regiment that included black enlisted men and white officers.

Andrew chose officers with impressive military records, offering commissions only to those who had proved themselves in battle and who came from wealthy antislavery families. The backgrounds of the officers would help enlist popular support and monetary backing for the new unit. The governor appointed Robert Gould Shaw, a captain in the Second Massachusetts Regiment and the son of prominent abolitionists, to command the Fifty-fourth Regiment.

Andrew also organized a committee to help recruit men, raise money, and advise on issues concerning the regiment. He named wealthy businessman and abolitionist George L. Stearns to head the recruiting committee; other prominent abolitionists, including Shaw's father, soon joined him. The committee created a network of prominent African Americans who traveled, spoke, and signed up recruits who were sent on to Boston. Frederick Douglass played an active role in this recruiting network.

Governor Andrew and Captain Shaw, promoted to colonel, intended the Massachusetts regiment to become a model for future black units. They wanted it to exemplify the abilities of African American soldiers so as to help overcome racist sensibilities across the nation. To ensure a healthy regiment, army doctors carefully examined the recruits and rejected about one-third of the volunteers on the basis of their medical condition.

On February 21, the recruits began training at Camp Meigs in Readville, Massachusetts. Only 113 of the 1,007 original enlistees came from Massachusetts; the remainder came from other Northern states, four border states, five confederate states, Canada, and the West Indies. The governor made sure that the camp was well supplied.

Although the War Department prohibited commissions for black officers, Andrew promised the black recruits that he would guarantee them equal treatment. He pledged that they would be given the same equipment, be eligible for the same benefits and bounties, and receive the same pay as all other Union soldiers. He also assured his recruits that he would award commissions to those who performed well in

A monument to the heroic Massachusetts Fifty-Fourth Regiment, the first all-black unit in the Union Army, and its white commander, Colonel Robert Gould Shaw, was dedicated on the Boston Common in 1897. (©Massachusetts Historical Society, Boston, Massachusetts, USA/The Bridgeman Art Library)

battle. The regiment's white officers appointed fifty-four sergeants and eighty corporals from among the black enlistees.

Despite promises of equal treatment, the federal government failed to give African American soldiers the same pay as their white counterparts. Instead of the $13 a month awarded to white enlisted men, the black soldiers of the Fifty-fourth Regiment were offered only $7 a month ($10 per month pay, minus an additional $3 per month deduction for their clothing)—the same pay given to contraband laborers.

This discrepancy came as a harsh blow to both the soldiers and officers, and most of the former refused to accept anything less than full pay. No increases were offered even after the regiment proved itself in battle, and the members of the Fifty-fourth Regiment, still refusing to be treated as second-class soldiers, went eighteen months without any pay at all. Those who survived the war were paid in full only after congressional authorization in March 1865.

The Fifty-fourth Regiment was mobilized in the same manner as other Union troops. On May 18, the governor presided over an elaborate ceremony for the presentation of flags to the regiment. When it prepared to leave Boston for the South on May 28, 1863, the city held a parade that drew approximately 20,000 onlookers. The regiment set sail later that day for Hilton Head, South Carolina. The soldiers joined Colonel James Montgomery's Second South Carolina Contraband Regiment in Beaufort, and the two units headed to Saint Simons Island, Georgia. With Montgomery's men, the Fifty-fourth Regiment participated in the destruction of Darien, Georgia.

The regiment's biggest test came during the assault on Battery Wagner, off the coast of Charleston, South Carolina. The Fifty-fourth led a column of 6,000 Union soldiers in a frontal assault on the Confederate facility on the evening of July 18, 1863. The beachfront attack resulted in more than 1,500 Union casualties, 272 of whom came from the Fifty-fourth. Despite the staggering loss of life, the regiment had proved itself in battle. As a result, it gained both fame and new recruits, the latter mostly from Massachusetts.

The regiment faced enemy fire again at the Battle of Olustee in northern Florida in February 1864. Although Confederate troops defeated the Union at both Battery Wagner and Olustee, observers and soldiers in other units commended the Fifty-fourth Regiment's performance. Soldiers continued to enlist

in the regiment, and by the end of the war, more than 1,300 white and black men had served in it.

Lisa Tendrich Frank

See also: Civil War, American (1861–1865); U.S. Colored Troops.

Further Reading

Blatt, Martin H., Thomas J. Brown, and Donald Yacovne, eds. *Hope and Glory: Essays on the Legacy of the Fifty-Fourth Massachusetts Regiment.* Amherst: University of Massachusetts Press, 2001.

Duncan, Russell. *Where Death and Glory Meet: Colonel Robert Gould Shaw and the Fifty-Fourth Massachusetts Infantry.* Athens: University of Georgia Press, 1999.

May, Samuel Joseph (1797–1871)

Unitarian minister Samuel Joseph May spent his life ministering to others and serving the reform movements of the early and mid-nineteenth century in America, including education reform, temperance, the peace movement, civil liberties, penal reform, Native American rights, and women's rights. Despite his wide-reaching influence in these areas, his most intense commitment was to the abolitionist movement.

Born in Boston on September 12, 1797, to Colonel Joseph and Dorothy May, he graduated from Harvard College in 1817 and from Harvard Divinity School in 1820. As a pastor, he led congregations in Brooklyn, Connecticut, from 1822 to 1836; South Scituate, Massachusetts, from 1836 to 1842; and Syracuse, New York, from 1847 to 1867.

He was brought into the abolitionist movement in 1830 by William Lloyd Garrison and, like him, May opposed gradualism, instead advocating the immediate emancipation of all slaves. He worked with Garrison to form the New England Anti-Slavery Society in 1832 and helped revise Garrison's Declaration of Sentiments for the society. In addition, he served as general agent and secretary for the Massachusetts Anti-Slavery Society; in this position, he lectured frequently on the need to abolish slavery, often to angry mobs. May's antislavery stance isolated him from his more moderate Boston Unitarian colleagues and frequently from the public at large.

May was an important figure in the Liberal Persuasion movement. This constellation of ideas grew out of Unitarianism and focused on fighting racial prejudice and advocating the emancipation of African Americans and women, freedom of religion, civil liberties, and social, economic, and political rights for workers. Opposed to the Mexican-American War (1846–1848), May encouraged men of the laboring class to refuse military service.

May also was committed to educational reform. He organized the first statewide convention for school reform in Connecticut in 1827, and, from 1842 to 1844, served as principal of the Normal School in Lexington, Massachusetts, admitting the first black student to the school.

In 1832, when Prudence Crandall opened a school for girls in Canterbury, Connecticut, and admitted a black farmer's daughter, the town erupted in disapproval. The school was forced to close and then reopened; in the midst of the scandal, the Connecticut legislature passed a law forbidding the founding of schools for nonresident blacks. Because many of Crandall's students were from Boston, New York, and Philadelphia, she was arrested, and May secured the financial support of Arthur Tappan for her defense. Although the case was dismissed on a technicality in an appeal in 1834, Crandall closed the school and left Canterbury. May later wrote of the event, "I felt ashamed of Canterbury, ashamed of Connecticut, ashamed of my country, ashamed of my color."

Over time, antislavery issues commanded an increasing amount of May's attention. On October 1, 1851, in Syracuse, May played a key role in orchestrating the rescue of runaway slave William "Jerry" McHenry. In accordance with the Fugitive Slave Law of 1850, McHenry had been captured by the authorities and was awaiting return to his owner. May openly advocated political action against the Fugitive Slave Law, which allowed slave owners the right to organize a posse anywhere in the United States to aid in recapturing fugitive slaves.

May's Syracuse home was a stop on the Underground Railroad, and he safely sheltered hundreds of runaway slaves and led them North into free Canada. He toured free black settlements in Canada to confirm that the living conditions were satisfactory to those he sent North.

When the Emancipation Proclamation was issued in 1863, May argued that blacks should be accorded full equality and that rebel lands should be confiscated and redistributed to free blacks. He advocated the enlistment of free blacks into the Union army—but not ex-slaves, whom he believed had already sacrificed enough. He credited President Abraham Lincoln with bringing public opinion around to a point where the Emancipation Proclamation could be issued. During the U.S. Civil War, May was a solid Lincoln supporter,

organized one of the nation's first freedmen's relief associations, supported Radical Reconstruction, and repudiated President Andrew Johnson.

In 1869, he published *Some Recollections of Our Anti-Slavery Conflict,* and in 1870, he donated his substantial collection of antislavery pamphlets, books, newspapers, and manuscripts to Cornell University, where today they comprise the Samuel J. May Anti-Slavery Collection. May died in Syracuse on July 1, 1871.

Charles A. D'Aniello

See also: Free Soil Party; Fugitive Slave Act of 1850; Garrison, William Lloyd.

Further Reading

Baros-Johnson, Irene. *The Just Demands of the Other: An Introduction to Samuel Joseph May.* Syracuse, NY: Syracuse University, Kellogg Project/Center for the Study of Citizenship, 1989.

Galpin, W. Freeman. "Samuel Joseph May: God's Chore Boy." *New York History* 21 (April 1946): 144–46.

Yacovone, Donald. "Samuel Joseph May, Antebellum Reform, and the Problem of Patricide." *Perspectives in American History* 2 (1985): 99–124.

———. *Samuel Joseph May and the Dilemma of the Liberal Persuasion, 1797–1871.* Philadelphia: Temple University Press, 1991.

McKim, James Miller (1810–1874)

The abolitionist, writer, and Underground Railroad agent James Miller McKim was born on November 14, 1810, in Carlisle, Pennsylvania, to James McKim and Catherine Miller. An exceptional student, he graduated from Dickinson College in 1828 at the age of eighteen, continued his studies at Princeton Theological Seminary and Andover Theological Seminary, and finally received his ordination from the Wilmington Presbytery in 1835.

By the time of his ordination, McKim had already become actively and passionately involved in the antislavery movement. An early proponent of William Lloyd Garrison's call for immediate emancipation, he took a stance that was in direct conflict with that of the Presbyterian Church. His congregation in Carlisle supported him, however, and most became converts to the abolitionist cause.

McKim was the youngest delegate at the founding meeting of the American Anti-Slavery Society in Philadelphia in 1833, and he was drawn into a small but powerful circle of leading abolitionists. He became particularly close to James and Lucretia Mott, both Quakers. His lecturing for the American Anti-Slavery Society created a conflict with the church, which led to his resignation from the Presbytery by the end of the decade.

In 1840, McKim married Sarah A. Speakman, a Quaker, and the couple moved to Philadelphia. He established himself as publishing agent for the Pennsylvania Anti-Slavery Society, editing the influential *Pennsylvania Freeman* after John Greenleaf Whittier retired from its helm. When the *Freeman* merged with the *National Anti-Slavery Standard* in 1854, McKim became a regular contributor.

Serving as the Anti-Slavery Society's corresponding secretary, an office he held until 1862, he worked closely with William Still, Philadelphia's most famous black abolitionist and Underground Railroad agent. The McKims were actively involved in helping fugitive slaves escape bondage, and after the passage of the Fugitive Slave Law of 1850, they helped found the Vigilant Committee of Philadelphia to aid fleeing bondsmen and women. McKim's and Still's records of the many enslaved people they had assisted later formed the foundation for Still's monumental book, *The Underground Railroad* (1872). In 1859, McKim and his wife accompanied Mary Brown to Harpers Ferry to see her husband, John Brown, and to claim his body after he was executed by Virginia authorities.

The McKims had two children, Charles Follen and Lucy. The latter married Wendell Phillips Garrison, the son of McKim's close ally, William Lloyd Garrison; the former became a prominent architect and designer in the neoclassical style. During early winter 1862, McKim helped found the Philadelphia Port Royal Relief Committee to aid the freed and fleeing slaves who were flooding Union encampments in the Port Royal District in South Carolina. He coordinated the call for volunteers, money, and supplies to be sent to the Union encampments in the South, providing educational, economic, and physical support to tens of thousands of newly freed people.

McKim reported on the situation in the Sea Islands and Hilton Head in *The Freedmen of South Carolina* (1862), which was used to plan relief operations in the district. McKim was appointed corresponding secretary of the Pennsylvania Freedmen's Relief Association in 1863, a position he leveraged to raise awareness and support in the North for the establishment of schools for newly liberated slaves in the South. He was an early proponent of the enlistment of African American soldiers, helping to establish Camp William

Penn outside Philadelphia for the recruitment and training of black men.

In 1865, McKim became the corresponding secretary of the American Freedmen's Union Commission in New York. He was one of the early investors and founders of the *Nation*, and his son-in-law, Wendell Garrison, became its literary editor and later editor in chief. McKim died at his home at Llewellyn Park, New Jersey, on June 13, 1874.

Kate Clifford Larson

See also: Brown, John; Garrison, William Lloyd; *Pennsylvania Freeman*; Port Royal Experiment.

Further Reading

Brown, Ira V. "Miller McKim and Pennsylvania Abolitionism." *Pennsylvania History* 30 (January 1963): 56–73.

Gara, Larry. *The Liberty Line: The Legend of the Underground Railroad.* Lexington: University Press of Kentucky, 1996.

Rose, Willie Lee. *Rehearsal for Reconstruction: The Port Royal Experiment.* Indianapolis, IN: Bobbs-Merrill, 1964; Athens: University of Georgia Press, 1999.

Still, William. *The Underground Railroad.* 1872. Chicago: Johnson, 1970; Medford, NJ: Plexus, 2005.

Menezes, José Ferreira de (1845–1881)

José Ferreira de Menezes was the editor of one of the leading abolitionist newspapers in Brazil during the 1880s, *Gazeta da Tarde (Afternoon Gazette)*. One of the few mulattoes to gain a distinguished position in the abolitionist campaign, he was also a popular orator and poet. During Menezes' brief tenure as editor, *Gazeta da Tarde* became the most influential newspaper of the antislavery movement in Brazil's capital city, Rio de Janeiro.

Born in 1845 to a lower-middle-class family, Menezes studied law at the prominent São Paulo Faculty of Law. It was his skill as a journalist and a poet, however, rather than his business acumen, that contributed to Brazil's burgeoning abolitionist movement of the 1870s and 1880s.

Antislavery sentiment intensified in the late 1870s, as slave owners remained intransigent to meaningful reform, as the free labor force expanded, and as liberal ideas of progress and civilization spread among the professional urban elite. In this period, abolitionist clubs and newspapers proliferated in Brazil's major cities, giving impetus to a movement that would play a key part in the final abolition of slavery in 1888.

Menezes shared the concerns of most abolitionists, a group largely drawn from the ranks of the urban professional elite. In addition to abhorring the brutality and inhumanity of slavery and the treatment of blacks, he believed that slavery blocked the moral, political, and economic advancement of the country. Along with the majority within the movement at the time, he supported the use of moderate tactics in the struggle for abolition, such as newspaper propaganda, rallies, concerts, and poetry readings. In 1880, he was a founding member of one of the first abolitionist groups in Rio de Janeiro, the Central Emancipation Association, and spoke widely at meetings and events organized by other abolitionist groups.

The abolitionists took advantage of technical innovations in the production of newspapers that allowed them to produce more copies at a cheaper price. The traditional newspapers of Brazil's large cities were almost exclusively proslavery and dependent on the economic and politic patronage of the "slavocracy." The leaders of the abolitionist movements of the 1870s and 1880s believed it was crucial to reach a wider audience and thus established popular newspapers devoted to critiques of slavery and coverage of the abolitionist campaign across the country. Newspapers were particularly key in Rio de Janeiro, as it was the chief center of political activity in the Brazilian Empire and geographically close to the slave-based coffee and sugar plantations in southeast Brazil.

Menezes founded *Gazeta da Tarde* in July 1880 and edited it with up-and-coming young writers such as Augusto Ribeiro, Hugo Leal, João de Almeida, and Adelino Fontoura. In addition to reports on legislative activity and abolitionist events, the paper regularly published antislavery columns by the leading activists of the day, including Ruy Barbosa, Joaquim Nabuco, and André Rebouças. Though its daily circulation reached only 2,000 under Menezes' leadership, the newspaper was an intellectual point of reference among abolitionists.

Menezes died suddenly in 1881, and the passionate young black abolitionist José do Patrocínio bought the newspaper. Under Patrocínio, the paper became harsher in its antislavery critique and made direct appeals to both slaves and the large free population of color. Within a few years, daily circulation had increased to 12,000. Building on the reputation that Menezes had established, Patrocínio would become one of the country's leading abolitionists and a pioneer politician and writer in the Afro-Brazilian community.

Sean Purdy

See also: Brazil, Abolition in; Nabuco, Joaquim; Patrocínio, José do; Rebouças, André.

Further Reading

Drescher, Seymour. *From Slavery to Freedom: Comparative Studies in the Rise and Fall of Atlantic Slavery.* London: Macmillan, 1999.

Toplin, Robert Brent. *The Abolition of Slavery in Brazil.* New York: Atheneum, 1972.

Mercer, Margaret (1791–1846)

As an antislavery advocate, educator, and author, Margaret Mercer was considered Virginia's strongest female supporter of the American Colonization Society and its efforts to resettle free blacks in Liberia.

Margaret Mercer was born on July 1, 1791, in Annapolis, Maryland, to a distinguished Maryland family. Her Virginian father, John Francis Mercer, was a close friend of James Madison, James Monroe, and Thomas Jefferson; he later served as a representative in the U.S. Congress, helping to draft the Maryland state constitution. By the time Margaret was a young child, her father had become a notable Maryland governor, and he reared his daughter under his strict and arduous tutelage. Benefiting from a comprehensive family library, she developed a voracious appetite for reading early on.

As an ardent member of the Protestant Episcopal Church, Mercer had an eagerness for religious and social undertakings in the local community. As a Sunday school teacher, Mercer's passion for education and pedagogy grew, and soon she left home to take a position as a drawing and painting instructor at a relative's school. During this independent period, Mercer pledged to care for and guide all children, just as Jesus had demonstrated in the Gospels. She devoted her life to instilling biblical principles in her pupils.

In 1836, Mercer purchased the Belmont Plantation in Ashburn, Virginia, in order to found a girls' Christian school that would provide a distinctive, comprehensive education for those who could not afford it. The curriculum exposed young women to untraditional subjects for females, including agriculture, public health, religion, astronomy, mathematics, science, and medicine. During this period, Mercer wrote *Popular Lectures on Ethics or Moral Obligation for the Use of Schools* (1837).

Although her school was prospering, Mercer turned her attention to "the condition of the Negro." She broke Virginia law to ensure that all black persons under her employment, including sharecroppers on surrounding lands, received literacy training and were welcomed at religious services. She was convinced that slavery was an evil institution, but the grueling and complicated task of eliminating the corrupt system was frustrating for Mercer.

She deemed slavery a destructive influence on both the master and the slave, but, having been reared in an environment that was inherently supportive of slavery in Southern daily culture, Mercer supposed that the obstacles of deep prejudice and degradation toward black persons would forever be maintained as long as the two races lived on the same soil. Turning her attention to colonization as a solution, she supported the American Colonization Society, which initiated an African resettlement movement in Liberia, and served as cofounder of the Virginia Colonization Society.

Mercer personally funded the education of promising young blacks, such as medical student William Taylor, whom she hoped could take his new skills and missionary fervor to Liberia. As a testament to her efforts in these resettlement projects, a ship built to transport black American settlers to West Africa and an African school in Monrovia, the capital of Liberia, were named in her honor.

Mercer died, most likely from tuberculosis, in 1846. She was buried beneath the chapel of her Belmont school.

Howell Williams

See also: American Colonization Society; Liberia.

Further Reading

Staudenraus, P.J. *The African Colonization Movement, 1816–1865.* New York: Columbia University Press, 1961; New York: Octagon, 1980.

Mexican Emancipation Decree (1829)

The Mexican government used the tenth anniversary of its independence from Spain as an occasion to proclaim the abolition of slavery. President Vicente Guerrero took this action on September 15, 1829, issuing the Mexican Emancipation Decree. By choosing September 15, a date traditionally associated in Mexican history with the *Grito de Delores* of 1810, when Father Miguel Hidalgo rang the church bells to signal the beginning of Mexico's independence movement, Guerrero hoped to shroud his action in the mantle of nationalism.

Guerrero's decree followed a pattern that had emerged in most of the Latin American nations created after a series of revolts led by landed Creoles overthrew Spanish colonial rule and established independent republics. Finding the institution of slavery inconsistent with the ideal of liberty on which they had based their rebellions, many Latin American leaders instituted programs of graduated emancipation to bring an end to slavery.

Mexico was a poor country in 1829, with a tremendous national debt outstanding to several European powers. Therefore, the Mexican government could not afford to institute a system of compensated emancipation, as was its goal, but instead had to make a promise of compensation at a later date. The third section of the decree stated, "When the financial situation of the republic admits, the proprietors of slaves shall be indemnified, and the indemnification regulated by a law." This promise of compensation was never fulfilled by the Mexican government.

The population of slaves in Mexico proper was relatively small in 1829, but a significant number of slaves recently had been introduced in the province of Texas as Mexican authorities sought to promote emigration to that region by foreign settlers. Many of the Texas emigrants came from Southern slaveholding states of the United States, and they brought their slaves with them when they moved to Texas. Other poor emigrants had no slaves but hoped that the productive cotton lands of east Texas would help them to make the transition to the class of planter. Wealth in Texas had the potential to transform social stratification by allowing poor dirt farmers to join the planter class through the purchase of slaves. For these reasons, the Mexican Emancipation Decree aroused anger among the Texas settlers.

On December 2, 1829, following protests by such settlers from the United States who had emigrated to Texas, Guerrero exempted Texas from the antislavery proclamation. Several years later, when Mexican president Antonio López de Santa Anna announced his intention to establish a unified constitution for Mexico on December 15, 1835, he threatened to eliminate the special exemption that had allowed slavery to persist in Texas. American settlers in Texas, particularly those who were slaveholders, vowed they would fight a war of secession from Mexico rather than surrender their right to hold slaves. This action prompted the Texas Revolution (1835–1836), which led to the establishment of the independent Republic of Texas.

Indirectly, the Mexican emancipation had much to do with the "Free Soil" debate that emerged in the United Sates after the Mexican territorial cession of 1848. As politicians debated whether slavery should be allowed to extend into the territories acquired as a result of the Mexican-American War (1846–1848), many found the idea abhorrent that the United States would consider re-introducing slavery into a territory where it had previously been abolished. Efforts such as the failed Wilmot Proviso (1846) were designed to recognize the status quo of former Mexican lands in the Southwest as free territories, a condition that had first been effected by Guerrero's proclamation in 1829.

Junius P. Rodriguez

See also: Mexico; Wilmot Proviso (1846).

Further Reading

Ellsworth, Clayton Sumner. "The American Churches and the Mexican War." *American Historical Review* 45 (January 1940): 301–26.

Sprague, William. *Vicente Guerrero, Mexican Liberator: A Study in Patriotism.* Chicago: R.R. Donnelley, 1939.

Mexico

The country of Mexico became a haven for blacks who escaped from slavery in the American South. The first known case involved nine enslaved Africans who went to Mexico, taking with them horses and ammunition, from Natchitoches, Louisiana, in 1803. Blacks who were slaves—and some who were formerly free—left Texas for Mexico in numbers into the thousands after the Fugitive Slave Law of 1850 made escape to the North more problematic. Though definitive numbers are unknown, historians estimate that as many as 5,000 blacks crossed the southwestern border of the United States between 1836 and 1855.

After gaining independence from Spain in 1821, the Mexican government acknowledged its hatred of slavery and prohibited its practice within its borders. By 1822, at least 20,000 whites from America had settled in the Mexican territory of Texas, many with their slave property. Mexico's efforts to restrict slavery resulted in the Mexican Constitutional Convention decree of July 13, 1824, which outlawed the domestic slave trade and declared all black fugitives arriving in Mexico freedmen.

White slaveholders began to push for an extradition treaty that would require Mexico to return fugitive slaves. From 1825 until the end of the U.S. Civil War, Mexican authorities opposed attempts by slaveholding settlers to conclude fugitive extradition treaties. During this period of strained relations between the Mexican and American governments, Mexico forbade the institution of slavery within its territory, officially abolishing it in 1829.

In 1834, the former Mexican congressman Colonel Juan N. Almonte, while conducting an inspection of Texas, assured the American abolitionist Benjamin Lundy of Mexico's antislavery stance, indicating that no slave who reached Mexican territory would be reclaimed. Abolitionists spread the word and aided blacks in traveling south via the Underground Railroad, whose southernmost point was the so-called Freedom Station in the city of Mazamitla in Jalisco, Mexico.

Mexico's hospitable welcome—which included incentives for foreigners settling within its borders, such as lenient immigration policies and tax-free land—made settlement there desirable. In addition, some Mexican officials, wary of American military intervention, began to encourage the formation of runaway slave colonies along the country's Northern border, reasoning that fugitives who settled there would fight to protect their newfound freedom during times of conflict.

After Texas declared itself an independent, slaveholding republic in 1836, its slave population increased. As a result, the number of fugitives who crossed the Texas border into northern Mexico increased as well. Once Texas was annexed to the United States in December 1845, slavery grew in unprecedented numbers. The 1850 Census listed some 58,000 slaves, increasing to 182,000 (30 percent of the state's total population) by the 1860 Census. Texas slaves had no property rights or legal rights of marriage, and they had no legally prescribed method of gaining their freedom.

As men and women desired to flee from bondage, the Texas-to-Mexico route to freedom became an informal Underground Railroad, as *Tejanos* (Mexicans living in Texas) helped facilitate the escape of slaves into Mexico. In 1850, in a new treaty with the United States, Mexico again refused to provide for the return of fugitive slaves, making the country a safe haven—so much so that, by 1855, as many as 5,000 formerly enslaved Africans had escaped from Texas to Mexico.

Slaveholders, frustrated by the loss of valuable property, posted large rewards for information leading to the return of fugitive slaves. In October 1855, Texas slaveholder James Callahan led an expedition to reclaim fugitive slaves who had fled to northern Mexico. That year, slaveholders requested and received a U.S. Army command along the Texas–Mexico border in a vain effort to halt the flow of runaways. The Mexicans stood their ground, continued aiding escaping slaves, and refused to return them. In 1857, the Mexican constitution granted freedom to enslaved Africans who escaped to Mexico and gave them the right to protection under the nation's laws.

After crossing the Rio Grande border, runaways found shelter in settlements of fugitive slaves, free blacks, and Indians among whom they might live. Some found refuge in the colony of a Seminole refugee named Coacoochee, who, in 1850, persuaded Mexican authorities to support his colony in Coahuila as a buffer against Indian or Anglo incursions. Black fugitives also were able to found legally free settlements at Nacimiento in Coahuila, at Eureka in Vera Cruz, and elsewhere in Mexico.

Marilyn D. Lovett and Gina Misiroglu

See also: Mexican Emancipation Decree (1829).

Further Reading

Schwartz, Rosalie. *Across the Rio to Freedom: U.S. Negroes in Mexico.* El Paso: Texas Western, 1975.

Mill, John Stuart (1806–1873)

John Stuart Mill was one of the foremost British philosophers, economists, and social reformers of the nineteenth century. His writings on the economic doctrine of utilitarianism dominated much of European intellectual thought.

Mill was born in Pentonville, Yorkshire, England, on May 20, 1806. His earliest education was at the hands of his father, James Mill, who was a close friend of Jeremy Bentham. As the founder of utilitarianism, Bentham espoused a philosophical tradition based on the doctrine of "the greatest happiness for the greatest number." From an early age, Mill read widely in disparate authors, both ancient and modern.

His own writings disseminated utilitarian philosophy, which he shaped in specific ways—for example, by differentiating higher from lower pleasures. His major works include *System of Logic* (1843), *Principles of Political Economy* (1848), *On Liberty* (1859), *Considerations on Representative Government* (1861), *Utilitarianism* (1863), *The Subjection of Women* (1869), and

his *Autobiography* (1873), but he also contributed numerous essays to periodicals such as the *Westminster Review* and the *Edinburgh Review*. Given his reforming tendencies and lifelong commitment to social justice, it is not surprising that a number of Mill's writings address the subjects of slavery, abolitionism, and emancipation.

Slavery was a social phenomenon and human experience that Mill would have witnessed during his long career with the East India Company. His essay "The Negro Question," first published in *Fraser's Magazine* in January 1850, was prompted by Thomas Carlyle's "Occasional Discourse on the Negro Question." Mill's moral disdain for chattel slavery is perhaps at its clearest here. He challenged Carlyle's assessment of the inferiority of blacks and wrote of slavery in the West Indies, "I have yet to learn that anything more detestable than this has been done by human beings towards human beings in any part of the earth." Mill provided a spotted history of the British abolitionist movement and gave particular attention to "the great ethical doctrine" of Carlyle's discourse, "that one kind of human beings are born servants to another kind." To Carlyle's assertion that their age contained too much benevolence, Mill replied, "It is precisely because we have succeeded in abolishing so much pain, because pain and its infliction are no longer familiar as our daily bread, that we are so much more shocked by what remains of it than our ancestors were, or than in your contributor's opinion we ought to be."

Mill also hinted that he had been giving some thought to the institution of slavery in America: "That this country [England] should turn back, in the matter of negro slavery, I have not the smallest apprehension. There is, however, another place where that tyranny still flourishes, but now for the first time finds itself seriously in danger." Mill wrote of the "crisis of American slavery, when the decisive conflict between right and iniquity seems about to commence," a topic that he took up at greater length elsewhere.

Mill's most philosophically compelling discussion of slavery can be found in his 1859 work *On Liberty.* In chapter 5, "Applications," Mill argued, "In this and most other civilised countries . . . an engagement by which a person should sell himself, or allow himself to be sold, as a slave, would be null and void; neither enforced by law nor by opinion." Mill reasoned that "by selling himself for a slave, he abdicates his liberty; he foregoes any future use of it beyond that single act. He therefore defeats, in his own case, the very purpose which is the justification of allowing him to dispose of himself . . . The principle of freedom cannot require that he should be free not to be free." Scholars have debated the philosophical merits of Mill's position on slave contracts.

In "The Contest in America," which was first published in *Fraser's Magazine* in February 1862, Mill aimed to explain the American Civil War to an English audience. He interpreted the conflict as "a war of principle" and argued that it was the North, not the South, whose principles English readers ought to support.

Mill made a similar case in his 1862 review of J.E. Cairnes's *The Slave Power; Its Character, Career, and Probable Designs: Being an Attempt to Explain the Real Issues Involved in the American Contest*, published in the *Westminster Review*. In it, he favorably reviewed Cairnes's book, in large measure by summarizing its arguments. He warned that if the South should "succeed in making good their independence . . . nothing is to be expected but the spread of the institution [of slavery] by conquest." Therefore, Mill reasoned, "That peace should be made by giving up the cause of quarrel, the exclusion of slavery from the territories, would be one of the greatest calamities which could happen to civilization and to mankind".

From 1865 to 1868, Mill was a Member of Parliament for Westminster. In Parliament, he promoted a number of liberal causes, including suffrage for women—the focus of his *Subjection of Women*, a book in which Mill compared the plight of women to slaves. He also showed that he continued to interpret slavery and other "rights" questions through the lens of historical development: "The course of history, and the tendencies of progressive human society, afford not only no presumption in favour of this system of inequality of rights, but a strong one against it." Mill died in France on May 7, 1873.

Mark G. Spencer

Further Reading

Bain, Alexander. *James Mill: A Biography.* London: Longman, Green, 1882; New York: Augustus M. Kelley, 1967.

Mill, John Stuart. *Collected Works of John Stuart Mill.* Ed. John M. Robson. 33 vols. Toronto, Ontario, Canada: University of Toronto Press, 1963–1991.

———. *On Liberty; With "The Subjection of Women" and Chapters on Socialism.* Ed. Stefan Collini. Cambridge, UK: Cambridge University Press, 1989.

Packe, Michael Saint John. *The Life of John Stuart Mill.* New York: Macmillan, 1954.

Miller, Jonathan Peckham (1796–1847)

Few American abolitionists were so wholeheartedly inspired by the Romantic movement of the early nineteenth century as Jonathan Peckham Miller. As a freedom fighter who fought with British poet Lord Byron in the Greek Civil War, Miller proved his unquestionable faith in liberty over oppression, and when he returned to the United States, he committed himself with the same passion to the fight against slavery and the slave trade.

Miller was born on February 24, 1796, in Randolph, Vermont, and later gained military training by serving briefly as a private in the U.S. Army. He attended the University of Vermont for a time but did not find the excitement that he sought in his academic experience. Circumstances outside the United States would provide that opportunity for him.

He traveled to Greece as a mercenary in 1824, aiding the Greeks in their struggle for freedom from the Turks. Two years later, Miller returned to Vermont to raise money and obtain supplies that might assist the Greek people in their cause. He lectured in support of the Greek cause throughout New York and New England, and he was able to return to Greece with much-needed provisions. After the Greeks won their independence, Miller came back to the United States with the sword of his fallen compatriot, Lord Byron.

Known as "the American Dare Devil," Miller's experience in Greece was intense, and he distinguished himself as a fighter. He was present during the siege on Missolonghi and witnessed the massacre of many Greeks there. He later produced a pamphlet, *Turkish Barbarity* (1828), which recounted the poignant tale of Sophia Mazro and her daughters, who had been made prisoner by the Turks during the siege. Miller learned to speak the Greek language, and he wore the uniform of the Greek fighters (the *foustanella*) in battle. In 1828, he published an account of his experiences in Greece, *The Condition of Greece in 1827 and 1828*, which had wide popular appeal.

Miller became involved in the antislavery cause shortly after he returned to Vermont in 1827. His conversion to the abolitionist movement was largely the result of Miller's conversations with antislavery advocate Orson S. Murray. As editor of the *Vermont Telegraph*, a religious newspaper that supported the antislavery cause, and secretary of the Vermont Anti-Slavery Society, Murray was the most influential abolitionist leader in Vermont.

Settling in Montpelier, Miller studied law and was soon admitted to the Vermont bar. By 1833, he had been elected to the state legislature representing the community of Berlin. Miller began his political career as a Jacksonian Democrat, but his antislavery views turned him into a reform-minded Whig. As a state legislator, he introduced a resolution that called on Vermont's congressional delegation to demand the abolition of both slavery and the slave trade within the District of Columbia. He lectured frequently on abolition throughout Vermont and often hid fugitive slaves in his home.

In 1836, Miller was instrumental in protecting the abolitionist lecturer Reverend Samuel J. May when he was nearly assaulted by a proslavery mob at the Vermont State House in Montpelier. Miller further helped guarantee May's safety while he remained in Vermont.

After Murray moved to Ohio, Miller became the leader of the Vermont abolitionists and was considered one of the leading antislavery supporters in New England. Miller was present at the 1840 World Anti-Slavery Convention in London, which was attended by delegates from the United States and Great Britain. Upon returning to the United States, he remained actively involved in the abolitionist movement as a speaker and organizer. He died in Montpelier on February 17, 1847.

Junius P. Rodriguez

See also: May, Samuel Joseph.

Mirror of Liberty

The quarterly periodical *Mirror of Liberty,* published in New York City from 1838 to 1841, was the first African American magazine in the United States. Aimed at black readers, it was published and edited by David Ruggles.

Ruggles was born to a free black family in Connecticut in 1810, and he moved to New York City at the age of seventeen. While working as a grocer, he became involved in the growing antislavery movement. Ruggles became known as the general agent for the antislavery newspaper *Emancipator and Public Morals,* the official voice of the American Anti-Slavery Society. In 1835, he helped establish the New York Anti-Slavery Society and served as its founding secretary. Ruggles traveled throughout New York and New England lecturing to antislavery groups and earned a reputation as one of the most radical black abolitionists in America.

In 1834, Ruggles opened New York City's first African American–owned bookstore, on Broadway. The store specialized in abolitionist literature and included a special reading room for free blacks, who, at the time, were not permitted to use the city libraries. Ruggles also published antislavery literature in pamphlet and tract form; his best-known works include *Extinguisher, Extinguished* (1834) and *Abrogation of the Seventh Commandment by the American Churches* (1835).

In 1838, William Whipper and other black leaders began publishing the *National Reformer,* a journal of the Moral Reform Society that advocated nonviolence in the abolition of slavery. That same year, Ruggles began publishing the *Mirror of Liberty,* whose motto was "Liberty is the word for me—above all, liberty." Modeled after the *Freedom's Journal,* the periodical pledged to avoid "the greedy appetite of scandal and abuse" but to "fearlessly attack vice and immorality, in high places and in low places." Like other early black papers and periodicals of the era, *Mirror of Liberty* espoused a strong antislavery ideology, but it also opposed colonization efforts that were designed to send free blacks to Liberia. The publication took a strong editorial position against segregation on public transportation and at religious services.

For a subscription price of $1 per year, readers could follow developments in the antislavery movement in the United States and elsewhere. For example, articles in the *Mirror of Liberty* chronicled the story of the African captives who had been taken from the slave ship *Amistad* in 1839. In addition, the publication was able to devote attention to the World Anti-Slavery Convention held in London in 1840 and the growing schism that had begun to develop within the American antislavery movement.

In a fashion that was typical of nineteenth-century quarterly magazines, the *Mirror of Liberty* offered more than a recapitulation of news stories. The magazine also published a selection of literary miscellany, poetry, and guest commentary written by social reformers.

The decline of the *Mirror of Liberty* nearly coincided with Ruggles's declining health. At that time, he appointed William Cooper Nell as secretary of a committee to obtain subscribers for the publication. Starting in 1841, Ruggles began to suffer from a medical condition that caused temporary blindness, an ailment that would last until his death in 1849. With his eyesight failing, he abandoned the publication of the *Mirror of Liberty*.

Junius P. Rodriguez

See also: *Amistad* Case (1841); Douglass, Frederick; Nell, William Cooper.

Further Reading

Porter, Dorothy. "David Ruggles: An Apostle of Human Rights." *Journal of Negro History* 28 (January 1943): 23–50.
Pride, Armistead, and Clint Wilson. *A History of the Black Press.* Washington, DC: Howard University Press, 1997.
Wolseley, Roland. *The Black Press, U.S.A.* Ames: Iowa State University Press, 1990.

Missionary Agents

See American Missionary Association; Church Missionary Society

Missouri Compromise (1820)

During the contentious period from 1819 to 1821, when the Missouri Territory sought statehood, the U.S. Congress wrestled with the divisive issue of whether slavery should be permitted in the states carved out of the Louisiana Purchase territory. The series of legislative measures enacted to remedy this situation and to preclude further debate on the expansion of slavery became known as the Missouri Compromise (1820). The agreements reached as part of this compromise would be effectively overturned by passage of the Kansas-Nebraska Act of 1854, and portions of the measure would be nullified by the U.S. Supreme Court's decision in *Dred Scott v. Sandford* (1857).

On January 26, 1819, Congress considered a measure to create the Arkansas Territory out of Arkansas County in the Missouri Territory. The action was approved, but not before Congress defeated an amendment, proposed by New York representative

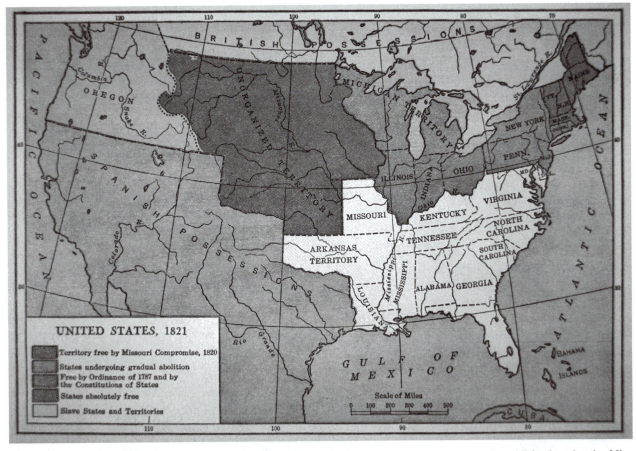

A map of the United States in 1821 defines the areas in which slavery would be allowed and prohibited under the Missouri Compromise. It would be barred in all new states north of the Arkansas Territory, except Missouri. (*©Private Collection/Peter Newark American Pictures/The Bridgeman Art Library*)

John W. Taylor, that would have prohibited slavery in the Arkansas Territory.

Nearly two weeks later, when the Missouri Territory sought admission to the Union as a slave state on February 13, 1819, the action was challenged by New York congressman James Tallmadge, Jr. He proposed that two antislavery amendments be attached to the bill proposing Missouri's statehood. The first would have prevented the further importation of slaves into Missouri; the second would have emancipated, at the age of 25, all those born to slaves in Missouri after its admission as a state. Although the House of Representatives approved both amendments, the Senate defeated both measures. It was clear, however, that the admission of Missouri into the Union would be mired in controversy.

The question of Missouri's statehood languished for an entire year as Congress debated the merits of slave or free status should the region be admitted as a state. On February 17, 1820, the Senate passed a measure that became known as the Missouri Compromise. According to this legislation, it was understood that Missouri would enter the Union as a slave state and that Maine would enter the Union as a free state, thus maintaining the delicate balance of votes in the Senate chamber. Senator Jesse B. Thomas of Illinois introduced an amendment to the bill calling for the prohibition of slavery in the areas of the Louisiana Territory that lay above the 36°30' north latitude line. The measure passed as amended in the Senate.

Less than two weeks later, the House of Representatives defeated the Senate version of the legislation. Members of the House attempted to pass a modified version that included the controversial Taylor Amendment, which would have barred slavery in all of the Western territories. (The latter measure had been introduced—and defeated—for the first time in January 1819.)

By March 3, 1820, after effective cajoling by Speaker of the House Henry Clay, the House agreed to the version the Senate had passed, allowing Missouri to enter the Union as a slave state, provided that Maine entered as a free state. The measure also prohibited slavery in any territories located north of the 36°30' parallel. (In developing the Missouri Compromise, the Thomas Amendment had been incorporated and the Taylor Amendment rejected.)

Despite Clay's apparent success in getting Congress to accept the compromise, Missouri's path to statehood still faced an uncertain future. The Missouri Territory drafted a constitution for the proposed state, but the document included a discriminatory prohibition keeping mulattoes and free blacks from entering. This controversial provision presented problems when Congress reviewed the proposed constitution in November 1820.

Finally, on March 2, 1821, Clay negotiated a last-minute caveat to the Missouri Compromise agreement, as Congress balked at the discriminatory provisions in the proposed constitution. Congress voted to approve statehood for Missouri, provided that state officials did not attempt to limit the rights of citizens, especially free blacks, as guaranteed by the U.S. Constitution. On June 26, 1821, the Missouri legislature approved this stipulation, and on August 10, 1821, Missouri entered the Union as a slave state.

At this point, the United States comprised twenty-four states, evenly divided: twelve free states and twelve slave states. Despite the apparent solution of 1820, the issue of permitting slavery's expansion within new states was one that would continue to plague the nation until the U.S. Civil War.

Junius P. Rodriguez

See also: Tallmadge, James, Jr.; Taylor, John W.; 36° 30' North Latitude.

Further Reading

Brown, Richard H. "The Missouri Crisis, Slavery, and the Politics of Jacksonianism." *South Atlantic Quarterly* 65 (Winter 1966): 55–72.

Moore, Glover. *The Missouri Controversy, 1819–1821.* Lexington: University Press of Kentucky, 1953.

Montesquieu, Baron de La Brède et de (1689–1755)

A leading philosopher, jurist, and political theorist of the French Enlightenment, Charles-Louis de Secondat Baron de La Brède et de Montesquieu greatly influenced the thinkers of the American and French revolutions. A longtime resident and leading citizen of the French port city of Bordeaux, Montesquieu must have witnessed the slave trade at close quarters, and commentators have speculated about how that environment influenced his ideas on the topic. Montesquieu not only made reference to slavery in much of his writing, but his extended discussion of it in *The Spirit of the Laws* (1748) formed the foundation of most significant philosophical discussions that followed in the eighteenth and nineteenth centuries.

However, because of Montesquieu's tendency to use satire—and also because he appears ambivalent toward slavery at times—his contemporaries and near contemporaries did not always agree on how best to interpret his writings.

Montesquieu was born on January 18, 1689, to a noble family of Bordeaux. His grandfather was president of the Bordeaux Parliament, and his father was a member of the royal bodyguard. From 1700 to 1711, the young Montesquieu was educated at the Oratorian College at Juilly, where he received a literary and classical education. Although he became a councilor of the Bordeaux Parliament, his life's work centered on his writing.

Montesquieu's principal works include the satirical *Lettres Persanes* (Persian Letters, 1721), *Causes de la grandeur des Romains et de leur décadence* (Reflections on the Causes of the Rise and Fall of the Roman Empire, 1734), and *L'Esprit des lois* (The Spirit of the Laws), whose 600-plus chapters are grouped in thirty-one books. *The Spirit of the Laws* is a compilation of general principles and particular observations in which Montesquieu attempted to explain human laws and social institutions. His writings introduced liberal concepts into the thinking of the day, including the separation of executive, legislative, and judiciary powers; the condemnation of slavery and torture; tolerance in religious belief; and freedom of worship.

In his *Persian Letters,* Montesquieu criticized the Spanish treatment of slaves in South America, but he also documented the utility of slavery to the Romans. He continued his justification of slavery on cultural and geographic grounds in *The Spirit of the Laws,* in which he argued that the laws of many countries should be more liberal and more humane and that religious persecution and slavery should be abolished. He rejected Aristotle's justification of slavery and generally opposed the practice, writing in book 15, "The state of slavery is in its own nature bad. It is neither useful to the master nor to the slave." Though he maintained that slavery was not appropriate in countries such as France, Montesquieu did identify locations and circumstances in which he believed it could be justified—for example, in southern regions where the climate is warmer and people may tend to be people lazy ("indolent"). He goes on to note that slavery is "more tolerable" in "despotic countries," where inhabitants are "already in a state of political servitude." Because "every one ought to be satisfied in those countries with necessaries and life. . . . the condition of a slave is hardly more burdensome than

that of a subject." For slavery's apologists, such as Thomas Cobb, Edward Long, and Gordon Turnbull, Montesquieu's discussion provided a convenient jumping-off point for a defense of slavery on the grounds of relativity.

Other passages of *The Spirit of the Laws* were put to use by proslavery advocates, although modern commentators generally agree that they were written in a spirit of satire. For example, Montesquieu introduces a section titled "Of the Slavery of the Negroes" as follows: "Were I to vindicate our right to make slaves of the negroes, these should be my arguments: . . . These creatures are all over black, and with such a flat nose that they can scarcely be pitied; . . . It is hardly to be believed that God, who is a wise Being, should place a soul, especially a good soul, in such a black ugly body." That Montesquieu was speaking satirically is given away by his suggestion that "the color of the skin may be determined by that of the hair, which, among the Egyptians, the best philosophers in the world, was of such importance that they put to death all the red-haired men who fell into their hands."

Montesquieu died in Paris on February 10, 1755. His writings made the topic of slavery a central focus of Enlightenment debate in Europe and in America, where his texts were widely disseminated and admired. He gave the debate direction, pointing it toward a discussion of utilitarian considerations. Although some misread Montesquieu's satire, mistaking him for a fellow defender of the institution of slavery, most often, his pages were incorporated into the arguments against slavery. Those who borrowed from him in this way included James Beattie, William Blackstone, T.R.R. Cobb, William Dickson, Adam Ferguson, Granville Sharp, George Wallace, and William Wilberforce, among others.

Mark G. Spencer

See also: Enlightenment.

Further Reading

Davis, David Brion. *The Problem of Slavery in Western Culture.* Ithaca, NY: Cornell University Press, 1966.

Fletcher, F.T.H. "Montesquieu's Influence on Anti-Slavery Opinion in England." *Journal of Negro History* 18 (October 1933): 414–26.

Montesquieu, Charles de Secondat, Baron de. *The Spirit of the Laws.* 1900. Trans. Thomas Nugent. New York: Hafner Library of Classics, 1949.

Pangle, Thomas. *Montesquieu's Philosophy of Liberalism: A Commentary on "The Spirit of the Laws."* Chicago: University of Chicago Press, 1973.

Morant Bay Rebellion (1865)

The Morant Bay Rebellion began on October 11, 1865, when the Baptist deacon Paul Bogle led approximately 400 black Jamaicans armed with sticks and machetes into the town of Morant Bay, the capital of the island of Saint Thomas. There, a vestry meeting at the courthouse was being held under the chairmanship of the parish's principle magistrate, Baron von Ketelhodt. Bogle and his men descended on the courthouse to protest events that had occurred a few days earlier.

On October 7, a black man named Lewis Miller had been put on trial and imprisoned for trespassing on an abandoned plantation. When one member of a group of black protesters from the village of Stony Gut was arrested, the protesters, who included Bogle, became unruly, scuffled with police, and broke Miller free from prison. When he returned home, Bogle learned that warrants had been issued for the arrest of him and twenty-eight of his men for rioting, resisting arrest, and assaulting the police.

During the postemancipation period, Jamaica was in a state of increasing economic decline, and Ketelhodt had removed or transferred mulattoes who were sympathetic to the peasantry's land and wage problems from the parish vestry. Bogle and his followers believed justice was impossible to obtain in local courts, because the magistrates were themselves planters; as a result, employers often judged the cases of their own employees who complained of low and irregular payment on sugar estates.

When Bogle and his followers descended on the courthouse, Ketelhodt read the Riot Act amid the hurling of glass bottles and stones. A number of volunteer militiamen were beaten and lost their guns. Most of the militia and vestrymen locked themselves inside the courthouse for safety, but others escaped. Urged by the women among them, Bogle's band of protesters burned down the courthouse to force out their adversaries. Several of the volunteers and vestrymen were wounded as they fled the burning courthouse. Ketelhodt was among those killed. Bogle led his supporters to the district prison and liberated all fifty-one inmates.

The protesters were highly organized and marched through Morant Bay in military formation, referring to their leader as General Bogle. The level of respect given to Bogle stemmed from his position in the Native Baptist Church, which attracted hundreds of worshippers and was perhaps the largest association of blacks led by Afro-Jamaicans on the entire island.

Upon returning to Stony Gut, Bogle led his congregation in prayers of thanks to God for the day's events, despite the death of seven of his supporters.

The next morning, the troops that Ketelhodt had requested from the governor—he had anticipated trouble following the events of October 7—arrived to discover eighteen officials and militiamen dead and thirty-one others wounded. The government responded to the rebellion with reprisals, aided by the maroon communities of the eastern parishes, who hoped to revive the privileged status that they had lost in the aftermath of the abolition of slavery. Over the next several weeks, 600 blacks were flogged and more than 400 were put to death. In addition, roughly 1,000 homes were destroyed.

Bogle, who had unsuccessfully sought backing from the maroons before October 11, was caught, tried, and hanged, along with several members of his family and his associates. Edward John Eyre was dismissed as governor of Jamaica after his violent way of putting down the rebellion caused a sensation in Britain. To make way for a strong government that would prevent further rebellion, the Jamaican Assembly renounced its charter, and Jamaica became a colony of the British Crown.

David M. Carletta

See also: Bogle, Paul; British West Indies, Abolition in the.

Further Reading

Heuman, Gad J. *The Killing Time: The Morant Bay Rebellion in Jamaica.* Knoxville: University of Tennessee Press, 1994.

Holt, Thomas C. *The Problem of Freedom: Race, Labor, and Politics in Jamaica and Britain, 1832–1938.* Baltimore: Johns Hopkins University Press, 1992.

Lumsden, Joy. "'A Brave and Loyal People': The Role of the Maroons in the Morant Bay Rebellion in 1865." In *Working Slavery, Pricing Freedom: Perspectives from the Caribbean, Africa, and the African Diaspora,* ed. Verene A. Shepherd. New York: Palgrave, 2002.

More, Hannah (1745–1833)

The religious writer and philanthropist Hannah More was a pioneer of the British abolitionist movement. Her publication of *Cheap Repository Tracts* led to the formation of the Religious Tract Society in Great Britain in 1799. Her morally edifying tracts sold millions of copies and were reprinted in England and the United States well into the nineteenth century.

Born on February 2, 1745, in a suburb of Bristol, England, the fourth of five daughters of an impecunious teacher, More was educated and then became a teacher at a school for girls established by her eldest sister, Mary. More left teaching and began to write full time after receiving an annuity of £200 from a man who had broken off an engagement with her after six years.

In 1774, she traveled to London and became a friend of theater producer David Garrick, who produced her tragedy *Percy,* a great success on the London stage. Nevertheless, Garrick's death in 1779 and her growing sense that the world of the theater was immoral—a belief derived from her conversion to evangelicalism—prompted her to move away from writing drama in favor of moralistic essays and poetry.

She became involved in the antislavery cause during the 1780s after meeting Charles and Margaret Middleton, leaders of the antislavery movement in Bristol, and John Newton, a former master of a slave ship who had become an evangelical preacher in London. More's personal correspondence from this period reveals her early efforts, along with her friends, to raise awareness of the horrors of slavery and the need for an abolitionist crusade.

At social gatherings, she would show fellow guests abolitionist Thomas Clarkson's layout of the African slave ship *Brookes.* Though she was still uncomfortable with the theater, she urged that Thomas Southerne's stage adaptation of Aphra Behn's tragedy *Oroonoko, or the History of the Royal Slave* be performed at Drury Lane as a means of exposing the issue. More also traveled to London to look for support of abolition among Members of Parliament; this mission led to her friendship with the evangelical William Wilberforce.

At the urging of fellow abolitionists who thought that it would be useful to have a literary work appear at the same time that Wilberforce introduced the first bill in Parliament to ban the slave trade, More wrote *Slavery, a Poem* (1788). She felt rushed and dissatisfied with the completed work, but as she informed her sister, "If it does not come out at the particular moment when the discussion comes on in parliament, it will not be worth a straw." In the poem, More emphasized the humanity of the Africans and the moral corruption brought on all who were connected to the slave trade.

In the decade after the poem appeared, More's commitment to the campaign was superseded by her growing fear that revolutionary ideas would spread to England, prompting her to write *Village Politics* (1792), a refutation of Thomas Paine's *Rights of Man.* From 1795 to 1798, she wrote about fifty of the 114

Cheap Repository Tracts that she published as part of a plan to bring politically safe reading material to the lower classes.

More's pamphlets, of which more than 2 million were distributed, provided a mixed message on slavery. One of the tracts, *The Sorrows of Yamba; or, the Negro Woman's Lamentation* (1795), is a traditional abolitionist poem about an enslaved woman who looks back longingly at her life in Africa as compared to the horrors of her life in captivity. At least two other tracts are more ambivalent on the slavery question: In *Babay, a True Story of a Good Negro Woman* and *A True Account of a Pious Negro,* both published in 1795, no abolitionist message is provided; instead, the tracts focus on how religion is the only true source of comfort, a position that was sometimes taken by proslavery advocates.

These tracts would be the last that More would write on the issue of slavery. Her later years were taken up with philanthropic work such as founding Sunday schools among the laboring classes, writing moralistic essays, and writing her only novel. She died on September 7, 1833 in Clifton, England.

Kenneth Pearl

See also: American Tract Society; Newton, John; Wilberforce, William.

Further Reading

Ford, Charles Howard. *Hannah More.* New York: Peter Lang, 1996.
Scott, Anne. *Hannah More: The First Victorian.* Oxford, UK: Oxford University Press, 2003.

Mott, James (1788–1868), and Lucretia Coffin Mott (1793–1880)

Influential reformers in both the abolitionist and women's rights movements, James Mott and Lucretia Coffin Mott used the social calling of their Quaker heritage to effect change in antebellum America. For fifty-seven years, the couple pooled their considerable talents to fight for the causes in which they believed.

James Mott and Lucretia Coffin met in 1805 at Nine Partners, a Quaker boarding school near Poughkeepsie, New York. Lucretia, born on the island of Nantucket, Massachusetts, on January 3, 1793, was the daughter of a whaling shipmaster. James, born on Long Island, New York, on June 20, 1788, was the son of farmers. They married in Philadelphia on April 10, 1811, and continued to live and work in Pennsylvania.

Lucretia Mott

Lucretia Coffin Mott, a pioneer of the women's rights movement, began her career as a social reformer in the 1820s, campaigning against slavery with her husband and fellow Quaker, James Mott. *(Hulton Archive/Getty Images)*

James Mott joined the Pennsylvania Abolition Society in 1812; there and in his local Quaker meetings, he was a perennial favorite when a committee needed a chair or a petition needed circulation. Lucretia was more spiritually driven than her husband, especially after the death of their infant son in 1817. By 1821, she had been designated a minister in the Society of Friends.

The Motts were caught up in the painful Quaker schism of 1827, known as the Great Separation. A group of Quakers led by Elias Hicks argued that the Friends had grown away from their roots and had become too evangelical in their views. This was a persuasive argument to Lucretia, who was not particularly interested in theology and preached a message of "practical righteousness." When the break finally came, the Motts resigned from the Orthodox meeting and joined the Hicksites, an act of conscience that cost them many old friends.

As Hicksites, the Motts became more involved in abolitionism. Hicks promoted a doctrine of "free pro-

duce," urging his followers not to purchase items that came from slave labor, such as sugar, molasses, and cotton. James Mott, then a cotton trader, embraced the Free Produce movement. In 1830, he abandoned cotton for wool and made it a success.

Throughout the 1830s, the Motts were at the forefront of the abolitionist movement. In 1833, they joined with fellow abolitionist William Lloyd Garrison to found the American Anti-Slavery Society, which became the most radical of the abolitionist groups by calling for the immediate emancipation of black slaves. The society organized meetings, generated civil petitions, printed and distributed antislavery literature, and organized and promoted antislavery lecture tours. By 1840, the society had 250,000 members, published more than twenty journals, and had 2,000 local chapters.

At the time of the society's founding, women were not admitted to its membership; in response, Lucretia launched an auxiliary group called the Philadelphia Female Anti-Slavery Society later that year. Lucretia scandalized Philadelphians—and even some fellow abolitionists—by inviting ladies of color to these meetings, inviting black families to her supper parties, and preaching in black churches on her travels. The Motts were also active in the Underground Railroad, sometimes hiding escaped slaves in their home for weeks at a time.

The Motts were chosen as delegates to the first World Anti-Slavery Convention, held in London in June 1840. Upon their arrival, Lucretia found herself banned from participating in the proceedings, both because some British and American delegates were determined to keep women out and because her allegiance with the Hicksites had branded her a heretic in the eyes of the British Quakers. Female delegates were finally allowed to attend the sessions, sitting silently behind a curtain at the back of the convention hall. There, Lucretia met a young lady named Elizabeth Cady Stanton. Discussing the unfairness of the situation, the two resolved to hold a women's rights convention when they returned to America.

In summer 1848, the Motts made a trip to upstate New York. Traveling through Waterloo, Lucretia again met Stanton. Their conversation turned to the women's rights convention that they had discussed eight years before, and they impetuously decided to organize a meeting "to discuss the social, civil, and religious condition and rights of woman." Giving themselves just five days, they called a meeting for July 19 and 20, 1848, in nearby Seneca Falls.

Both ladies panicked when they suddenly realized the large scale of the undertaking. Lucretia turned to James, an expert meeting organizer; he led them through an abbreviated planning process, helped them set an agenda, and at their request, chaired the two-day meeting.

The convention ended with the passage of the "Declaration of Sentiments," which included a historic call for women's suffrage. The former slave Frederick Douglass, editor of the *Rochester North Star*, worked with Mott to convince the attendees to agree to the resolution on women's suffrage. Douglass commented on the groundbreaking nature of the event in his *North Star*, noting, "A discussion of the rights of animals would be regarded with far more complacency by many of what are called the wise and the good of our land, than would be a discussion of the rights of woman."

Years of relentless activity and stress compromised Lucretia's health, and, by the 1850s, she was suffering from frequent stomach problems and headaches. In 1857, James retired from business and purchased a large home just north of Philadelphia. Christened "Roadside," it became a place of refuge for the aging couple for the duration of the U.S. Civil War.

When the war ended in 1865, Lucretia worked with the Friends Association of Philadelphia for the Aid and Elevation of the Freedmen, helping to fund elementary schools across the South. She continued her work for higher education and women's rights, helping to found the co-educational Swarthmore College in 1864 and serving as a speaker and organizer for virtually every suffrage and women's rights convention held between 1850 and 1880.

James Mott died on January 26, 1868, following a brief illness. Not long after his death, Lucretia wrote, "In a true marriage relation the independence of the husband and the wife is equal, their dependence is mutual and their obligation reciprocal." Lucretia continued to lecture until her death on November 11, 1880. She was buried next to James in Germantown, Pennsylvania.

Heather K. Michon

See also: Quakers (Society of Friends); Stanton, Elizabeth Cady; Women's Rights and the Abolitionist Movement.

Further Reading

Bacon, Margaret Hope. *Valiant Friend: The Life of Lucretia Coffin Mott.* New York: Walker, 1980.

Lutz, Alma. *Crusade for Freedom: The Women of the Antislavery Movement.* Boston: Beacon, 1968.

Murray, Orson S. (1806–1885)

The Reverend Orson S. Murray was a controversial Baptist minister and printer who was actively involved in the antislavery movement in Vermont and Ohio for more than three decades. The *Vermont Telegraph*, a religious newspaper that he edited, became one of the most staunchly pro-abolition papers in the country. Touring Vermont in 1843, the noted black abolitionist Frederick Douglass paid special tribute to Murray's work when he said, "the way had been prepared for us by such stalwart antislavery workers as Orson S. Murray."

Born in 1806, Murray was a Calvinistic Free-Will Baptist minister who preached in Orwell and later Brandon, Vermont. He was attracted to many social reform movements of his day, including abolitionism, temperance, anti-Masonry, women's rights, economic communitarianism, and pacifism. He was considered an eccentric in many respects, as he was a committed vegetarian who wore his hair unstylishly at full length, never permitting it to be cut. Murray was also attracted to the faddish notion of spiritualism that was popular in some areas during the early nineteenth century.

Murray was converted to the abolitionist cause in 1832 when he read William Lloyd Garrison's *Liberator* and *Thoughts on African Colonization*. The following year, he was a delegate to the convention that established the American Anti-Slavery Society, and he became secretary of the Vermont Anti-Slavery Society, which was formed shortly thereafter. He soon earned a reputation as an ardent antislavery man, organizing more than twenty local antislavery chapters throughout the northeastern states at his frequent public lectures. He traveled as a paid agent of the New England Anti-Slavery Society who tried to persuade others to join the antislavery crusade.

Never one to mince words or hide from a fight, Murray was known as a blunt spokesman for the cause who used inflammatory language and vitriolic rhetoric in his passionate antislavery orations. Typically, he offended practically everyone in his audience except those like-minded radicals who supported his extreme positions. On several occasions, Murray was physically attacked by mobs after delivering controversial lectures.

The *Vermont Telegraph* was established in 1828 as a religious newspaper that covered items of interest to Baptist readers. Murray purchased the newspaper in 1834 and changed its focus dramatically, making it the first newspaper in Vermont to advocate openly for the abolitionist cause. Murray believed that his efforts were representative of Vermont's historic antislavery stance. (The state abolished slavery within its borders in its constitution of July 8, 1777.) In spite of this legacy, many considered the editorial position of the *Vermont Telegraph* to be quite extreme.

In 1840, Murray acquired a second antislavery paper, the *Voice of Freedom,* from fellow Vermont abolitionist Joseph Poland. Murray's second paper was edited by Jedediah Holcombe until it ceased publication in 1843.

Having been licensed to preach by the Baptist Church in 1837, Murray's license was suspended in 1842 because his views had become too extreme. By the 1850s, Murray had repudiated Christianity and become an atheist, preferring to call himself a freethinker.

Murray moved from Vermont to Foster's Crossings (today New Richmond) in Clermont County, Ohio, to continue his work in support of the abolitionist movement. For a short time, he published another newspaper called the *Regenerator,* but that venture failed. In his new home along the Ohio River, he was able to work within the secret network known as the Underground Railroad, helping fugitive slaves to escape from captivity and make their way toward freedom.

Murray continued to deliver stirring addresses on antislavery topics. One of his orations, *The Struggle of the Hour; A Discourse Delivered at the Paine Celebration in Cincinnati, January 29, 1861,* was published in pamphlet form and distributed by several antislavery groups.

Junius P. Rodriguez

See also: Underground Railroad.

Further Reading

Hamm, Thomas D. *God's Government Begun: The Society for Universal Inquiry and Reform, 1842–1846.* Bloomington: Indiana University Press, 1995.

Ludlum, David M. *Social Ferment in Vermont.* New York: Columbia University Press, 1939.

Mystery, The

Pittsburgh's first African American newspaper, *The Mystery,* was published by antislavery editor and physician Martin Robison Delany from 1843 to 1847. It was one of a handful of African American antislavery weeklies that emerged in the United States during the 1840s. Reflecting its editor's dual commitment to the abolition of slavery and the uplift of free African Americans, *The Mystery* played a role in unifying Pittsburgh's black community.

The origins of *The Mystery* can be traced to the August 1841 state Convention of the Colored Freemen of Pennsylvania, held in Pittsburgh. "In the opinion of this Convention," the delegates resolved, "a newspaper conducted by the colored people, and adapted to their wants, is much needed in this state; and that we request their general cooperation, especially in the east, in establishing such a paper." Two years later, Delany, one of the convention's principle organizers and already a leader in the city's African American community at the age of thirty-one, followed through on the resolution, putting out the first edition of *The Mystery* in September 1843.

The Mystery was published regularly through the end of 1847. The four-page paper consisted of material written by its reporters (often Delany), as well as stories taken from papers that it counted as exchange partners (as was the custom of the time), such as *The Hampshire Herald.* The front page typically reproduced speeches and covered major news events, from urban fires to the exploits of escaped slaves. Pages two and three consisted largely of letters, editorials, and advertisements—mostly for African American boarding houses, merchants, and professional services, such as "Leeching, Cupping, and Bleeding," offered by Delany himself. Announcements were found on page four.

As was the case with most African American newspapers in the nineteenth century, *The Mystery* struggled to keep afloat economically. A subscription to the paper cost $1.50 per year. The paper held fundraisers during the celebration of events such as British Emancipation Day (August 1) to supplement the money it made from subscriptions.

The circulation of *The Mystery* is unknown, but Delany claimed that he put out 1,000 copies of the first edition in Pittsburgh alone. Nevertheless, the paper's influence extended beyond Pittsburgh. Many of its articles, for example, were reprinted in more widely circulated journals such as William Lloyd Garrison's *The Liberator.* Moreover, *The Mystery* had more than fifty agents who promoted it in eight states (Illinois, Indiana, Massachusetts, Michigan, New York, Ohio, Pennsylvania, and Virginia) and one territory (Iowa).

The paper was equally devoted to fostering black elevation in the North and combating the institution of slavery in the South. An early issue of *The Mystery* declared, "the paper shall be free, independent, and untrammeled" and would work for black uplift through different channels, including the "Literary Sciences, the Mechanical Arts, Agriculture and the elevation of labor." At first, Delany took a biblical verse as the paper's motto: "And Moses was learned in all the wisdom of the Egyptians." Later, he changed it to the well-known call of English poet Lord Byron: "Hereditary bondsmen! Know ye not who would be free, themselves must strike the blow."

The Mystery frequently reported on slave escapes, whether successful or not, and warned fugitives about the activities of slave catchers in the Pittsburgh area. One such article precipitated a lawsuit against Delany. Thomas ("Fiddler") Johnson, an African American whom he had accused of assisting slave catchers, sued Delany for libel. An all-white jury found Delany guilty, fining him $150 and court costs. A group of Pittsburgh newspapers rallied around him, however, helping the city's African American community to raise money and successfully petitioning Governor Francis R. Shunk to remit the fine.

In 1847, Delany agreed to become co-editor of a new, more widely circulated antislavery newspaper, *The North Star,* which Frederick Douglass had begun publishing the previous December. Delany explained his choice to join Douglass in his farewell to *The Mystery,* reprinted in the January 21, 1848, issue of *The North Star:* "For upwards of four year the paper has been afloat upon the breeze," he wrote, "the position that we assumed, was to claim for our oppressed fellow countrymen both bond and free, every right and privilege belonging to man." The time had come, Delany continued, for him to move on to what he hoped would be "a more useful and productive part of the moral vineyard" in "a union with the far famed and world renowned Frederick Douglass."

Although Delany hoped that *The Mystery* would persist after he resigned, it did not survive the year. By summer 1848, the African Methodist Episcopal Church had purchased the paper and merged it with *The Christian Herald* (later *The Christian Recorder*) as the national organ of the church.

Ethan J. Kytle

See also: Delany, Martin Robison; Douglass, Frederick.

Further Reading

Foner, Philip S., and George E. Walker, eds. *Proceedings of the Black State Conventions, 1840–1865.* Vol. 1, *New York, Pennsylvania, Indiana, Michigan, Ohio.* Philadelphia: Temple University Press, 1969.

Levine, Robert S., ed. *Martin R. Delany: A Documentary Reader.* Chapel Hill: University of North Carolina Press, 2003.

Ullman, Victor. *Martin R. Delany: The Beginnings of Black Nationalism.* Boston: Beacon, 1971.

Nabuco, Joaquim (1849–1910)

One of the most famous antislavery advocates in Brazilian history, Joaquim Nabuco worked tirelessly to speed abolition in that nation. As a diplomat, journalist, and cofounder of the Brazilian Anti-Slavery Society, he rallied support for the abolitionist cause throughout Brazil and was a major force in bringing an end to slavery in 1888.

Like many other abolitionist leaders in Brazil, Nabuco was the son of a prosperous family. His father, José Thomaz Nabuco de Araújo, was a deputy in Parliament and had an important role in the approval of the 1871 *Lei do Ventre Libre* (Law of the Free Womb, or Free Birth Law, as it became known), which freed the children of enslaved parents.

Born on August 19, 1849, in Pernambuco, Brazil, Nabuco spent his childhood on a sugarcane plantation in the northeastern part of the country and witnessed the slave experience at close hand from a tender age. While his parents were in Rio de Janeiro, the capital of the empire, Nabuco stayed on the family plantation in Recife. In 1857, he joined the family in Rio.

Nabuco had access to the best education available in Brazil at the time, and his training prepared him to continue the family tradition of life in politics. In 1866, he was admitted to law school in São Paulo, where he came into contact with leading antislavery figures, such as Ruy Barbosa and Antônio de Castro Alves. After graduation, Nabuco joined the liberal newspapers in promoting abolition and, while living in Rio de Janeiro and then São Paulo, he attested to the dependency on slave labor in the nation's urban centers.

Many of Nabuco's writings described scenes that he had witnessed on the family plantation as a child—for example, a slave who begged the eight-year-old boy to buy him from his physically abusive master. Nabuco never mentioned having slaves of his own, but as a member of the Brazilian elite, it is unlikely that he did not rely on slaves as servants or laborers. Slaves in Brazil were not costly, and almost everybody could afford to own one.

Between 1873 and 1878, Nabuco joined the Brazilian diplomatic mission to Washington, D.C., and London. After returning to Brazil, he was elected deputy, and his political goal was to abolish slavery gradually. With André Rebouças, he founded the Brazilian Anti-Slavery Society in 1880. The organization issued a monthly bulletin, the *Abolitionist,* to which Nabuco contributed articles advocating freedom for slaves. Beyond sharing the ideal of abolishing slavery in Brazil, he and Rebouças also defended legal emancipation without radical political change. In their opinion, the monarchal regime should be preserved.

Nabuco became the unofficial spokesman of the abolitionist movement, and, in 1880, he presented to Parliament a bill defining a ten-year window for the total abolition of slavery and financial compensation for slave owners. Republican abolitionists, who defended immediate freedom and no indemnification, opposed the measure. Without political support, the bill was rejected, and Nabuco lost in his re-election bid in 1881.

In self-exile in London, Nabuco wrote a polemic titled *O abolicionismo* (Abolitionism, 1883), in which he analyzed the slave trade, slavery, and abolitionism. Away from the Brazilian political scene, he could express his ideas about immediate abolition without any financial compensation to slave owners. But his position on the necessity of using legal means to achieve emancipation had not changed. The book had immediate repercussions and became an abolitionist pamphlet.

In 1884, Nabuco returned to Brazil and to politics. In 1887, he was re-elected to the deputy chamber and resumed his calls for the end of slavery. The following year, he traveled to Rome and demanded that the pope officially condemn the institution of slavery. By the time he returned to Brazil, however, slavery had already been brought to an end.

Because of his legalist position, Nabuco was considered a conservative abolitionist. His view was never based on the immorality of slavery or the recognition of abuses suffered by slaves. Like many Brazilian abolitionists, Nabuco's position was not a defense of slaves' rights; rather, his political goal was to pre-serve Brazil's international image. As the last country to banish slavery in the Americas, Brazil had acquired the reputation of not being "modern," a vital image for the urban elite. Nabuco believed that whites were superior to and more advanced than blacks, and he blamed the weaknesses in Brazilian society on its African element. To Nabuco, Brazil was a land of lazi-ness and superstition, which he associated with Africa. Like other abolitionists in Brazil, Nabuco advocated the benefits of emancipation in economic terms. In his view, free labor was essential to accelerate industrial-ization, improve agriculture, and bring the Brazilian economy into the modern world. Nabuco defended education, democratization of land, and European immigration after emancipation.

After the proclamation of the Brazilian Repub-lic in 1889, Nabuco refused to run for office or join the constitutional commission. He continued to ex-press his political opinions in several newspapers, in-cluding the *Jornal do Brasil* and the *Jornal do Commercio*. In 1900, he finally agreed to join the government, representing Brazilian interests in London and acting as an ambassador in Washington, D.C. He died in Washington, on January 17, 1910.

Mariana P. Candido

See also: Brazil, Abolition in; Brazilian Anti-Slavery Society; Rebouças, André.

Further Reading

Bethell, Leslie. *The Abolition of the Brazilian Slave Trade: Britain, Brazil and the Slave Trade Question, 1807–1869.* Cambridge, UK: Cambridge University Press, 1970.

Nabuco, Carolina. *The Life of Joaquim Nabuco.* Palo Alto, CA: Stanford University Press, 1950.

Nabuco, Joaquim. *Abolitionism: The Brazilian Antislavery Struggle.* Trans. and ed. Robert Conrad. Urbana: Univer-sity of Illinois Press, 1977.

Tapié, Victor Lucien. *Joaquim Nabuco, 1849–1910.* Trans. Jacob Bean. Paris: UNESCO, 1949.

Nashoba Experiment

See Wright, Frances ("Fanny")

National Anti-Slavery Standard

The official organ of the American Anti-Slavery Soci-ety, the *National Anti-Slavery Standard* was one of the leading abolitionist periodicals published in the United States during the nineteenth century. A forum for the ideas of William Lloyd Garrison, one of the most rad-ical antislavery advocates in antebellum America, the paper espoused the twin doctrines of disunion and nonresistance (a philosophy akin to Christian anar-chism). While this message appealed to some of the most militant abolitionists of the day, the paper alienated many Christian clergymen and other people of faith, who found its vociferous attacks on orga-nized religion much too strident.

The abolitionist movement in the United States suffered a tremendous schism in 1840. Multiple is-sues, including the role of women within the aboli-tionist movement and the place of direct political action in aiding the antislavery cause, resulted in fac-tions forming within the ranks of the abolitionists. The more radical abolitionists—those who supported women's rights and disavowed political action—remained loyal to Garrison's leadership and contin-ued to be a part of the American Anti-Slavery Society. The more traditional abolitionists organized them-selves into the American and Foreign Anti-Slavery Society, a rival organization to Garrison's group that embraced different views and used different tactics.

The American Anti-Slavery Society began pub-lishing the *National Anti-Slavery Standard* as its official journal in June 1840 to support the idea of immediate emancipation. The journal remained in operation as a weekly publication under various titles until mid-1870, when the society disbanded. The paper was pub-lished in New York City for most of its history, except for one interlude from July 1854 to November 1865, when it was published in Philadelphia.

Throughout most of the journal's history, it was clear that Garrison had extraordinary control over the publication's content and tone. He often handpicked the *Standard*'s editors, but these editors did not al-ways appreciate the level of oversight that Garrison maintained. David Lee Child and his wife Lydia Maria Child, two well-known New England abolitionists and close personal friends of Garrison, co-edited the paper for a time in the early 1840s, but they eventually resigned because of editorial disputes with Garrison.

The paper published letters, speeches, and ex-cerpts from antislavery tracts, as well as some elements of news, especially those associated with contemporary reforms such as the women's rights and temperance movements. Extended communications with leading abolitionist figures in the United States and Britain were often published (in serial form) to update readers on the progress being made within the movement. Be-cause of the publication's association with nonresistance and its opposition to the use of political action as a tool for the abolitionist cause, news coverage of political affairs was woefully incomplete and partisan in perspective.

Like many other abolitionist publications, the *National Anti-Slavery Standard* also published an array of miscellany, including puns, aphorisms, and miracle cures, as well as occasional literary selections. The British Romantic poet William Blake was first published in the United States in the pages of the *Standard* when his poem "The Little Black Boy" appeared in March 1842.

For three decades, the *National Anti-Slavery Standard* chronicled the history of the antislavery movement in the United States. From 1865 until its demise in 1870, when the editors acknowledged that direct political action had finally effected emancipation, the editorial tone of the paper changed. During this time, more balanced coverage of political affairs related to the struggles of the freedmen appeared in the weekly columns of the journal.

Junius P. Rodriguez

See also: Child, David Lee; Child, Lydia Maria Francis.

Further Reading

Baer, Helene G. "Mrs. Child and Miss Fuller." *New England Quarterly* 26 (June 1953): 249–55.

Karcher, Carolyn. "Censorship, American Style: The Case of Lydia Maria Child." *Studies in the American Renaissance* 9 (1986): 287–303.

Kraditor, Aileen S. *Means and Ends in American Abolitionism: Garrison and His Critics on Strategy and Tactics, 1834–1850.* New York: Pantheon, 1969.

Mills, Bruce. *Cultural Reformations: Lydia Maria Child and the Literature of Reform.* Athens: University of Georgia Press, 1994.

National Anti-Slavery Tract Society

The National Anti-Slavery Tract Society was founded by Benjamin Lundy in Baltimore, Maryland, in 1828. Building on the trend of establishing tract societies to disseminate literature with a moral message, Lundy hoped that publishing and distributing antislavery literature in pamphlet form would attract adherents to the abolitionist cause.

The initial concept of a tract society was first pioneered in Great Britain by the Religious Tract Society of London, which was founded in 1799. Two similar organizations, the New York Religious Tract Society

(founded in 1812) and the American Tract Society in Boston (formerly the New England Tract Society, founded in 1814), merged in 1825 to form the American Tract Society, with headquarters in New York City. Through its production of nonsectarian Christian pamphlets, the society became one of the largest publishing houses in early nineteenth-century America. Lundy's National Anti-Slavery Tract Society sought to achieve similar goals but with a more focused approach on attacking the evils of the domestic slave trade and the institution of slavery.

Tract societies were some of the many organizations that emerged in the United States during the antebellum reforms of the Jacksonian era, and they worked to remedy societal ills by targeting specific messages to particular transgressors. Included in the bevy of social ills that such tracts targeted was slavery. Although slaveholding was perceived as a sin, it was also believed to engender other ills, such as avarice, violence, rape, and drunkenness. Slaveholders throughout the South were regarded as having the potential of moral redemption, provided they could be reached.

Like other tract societies, the National Anti-Slavery Tract Society produced small antislavery pamphlets that could be easily printed and distributed. They were age-appropriate, as well as based on some level of literacy among adults, so that those who acquired them might read and understand the moral message. In addition, most of the tracts had illustrations and sketches, so that even those who might not understand the language could draw an understanding from the pictures.

The most problematic concern about the use and effectiveness of tracts was that they had to be delivered and read. Proselytizing against prostitution or the evils of alcohol, as many tracts did, was different from urging the slaveholders of the American South to distance themselves from the moral evils of slavery. Following the Great Postal Campaign of the 1830s, postmasters in Southern communities refused to deliver antislavery newspapers or other forms of abolitionist literature, including tracts. In many Southern cities, such materials were often confiscated and burned. The likelihood that members of the National Anti-Slavery Tract Society would be able to travel to the South to deliver such literature was practically none, as that would put them in danger of physical assault. Accordingly, the effectiveness of antislavery tracts was marginal in the American South.

The society's efforts were more successful in the North, where its tracts attracted abolitionist support for the antislavery movement. The language of the tracts presented the abolitionist message in a stark good-versus-evil context and made some realize that their failure to oppose slavery made them guilty of complicity in its continued existence. In this regard, silence about the sin of slavery was regarded as sin itself.

Tracts were often distributed at church revivals and camp meetings in communities along the Western frontier. Although the effectiveness of such large-scale distribution cannot be measured, it did guarantee that some forms of antislavery literature were reaching individuals who might not otherwise subscribe to or read the abolitionist newspapers of the day. This form of distribution also served to attract reform-minded women to the antislavery cause.

As the debate over slavery intensified, the changing political climate in the United States forced the American Tract Society to make a controversial decision. In 1848, the tract *Jacob and His Sons,* written by the Reverend Thomas H. Gallaudet, was dropped from circulation by the American Sunday School Union. Evidently, a Bible story that mentioned the sale of Joseph into slavery was a topic that was too controversial for inclusion in a religious tract.

For a time, the National Anti-Slavery Tract Society had the support of the leading abolitionists in the United States, including the philanthropic aid of abolitionists Arthur and Lewis Tappan, who criticized the American Tract Society for its avoidance of slavery in its tracts. The simple method of delivering a Christian message of hope to those who were the most at risk had popular appeal, but in the end, the effectiveness of tracts as an agent of moral suasion was questionable.

Junius P. Rodriguez

See also: American Tract Society; Great Postal Campaign; Lundy, Benjamin.

Further Reading

Boyer, Paul. *Urban Masses and Moral Order in America, 1820–1920.* Cambridge, MA: Harvard University Press, 1978.

Nell, William Cooper (1816–1874)

An African American educator, editor, abolitionist, and historian, William Cooper Nell devoted his life to advancing racial integration.

Born on December 20, 1816, in Boston, Massachusetts, Nell grew up on the back side of Beacon Hill in one of the most segregated neighborhoods of the city. There, he attended the Smith School, the sole grammar school available to Boston's African American community. As an adult, he would bitterly recall the inferior education he had received at this "refuge of colorphobia" and fought tenaciously for its destruction. Though it took Nell and his associates more than two decades to dismantle Boston's separate school system, that activism would serve as both inspiration and example for subsequent desegregation campaigns across the nation.

Nothing in Nell's early upbringing suggested that he would become a dogged opponent of segregation. In fact, his father, William G. Nell, was a vocal proponent of separate black institutions. In 1826, the elder Nell helped to launch the Massachusetts General Colored Association, an organization that promoted both abolitionism and African American activism.

In 1831, William Cooper Nell accepted a position as a printer's apprentice at a little-known abolitionist publication, *The Liberator.* There, he worked alongside its founder, William Lloyd Garrison. It was not long before Nell became swept up in Boston's burgeoning movement for immediate abolition.

At the same time, however, Nell's immediate attention remained focused on education. In addition to leading the charge for school desegregation, he supported such improvement-oriented organizations as the Young Men's Literary Society, the Boston Minor's Exhibition Society, and the Adelphi Union Library Association. He devoted whatever scarce time remained to his own improvement, studying law, literature, philosophy, and history, often from books borrowed from his friend and occasional patron, the young Wendell Phillips. In the 1840s, Nell embarked on one of the first serious studies of African American history, publishing *Services of Colored Americans in the Wars of 1776 and 1812* (1851) and *The Colored Patriots of the American Revolution* (1855) the following decade.

Still, despite his efforts at improvement and his close ties to Boston's abolitionist elite, Nell struggled to sustain himself on the modest wages available to African Americans at the time. Working alternately as a copyist, editor, accountant, and clerk, he grew deeply dissatisfied with his personal circumstances. In 1847, he accepted an offer from Frederick Douglass to leave Boston for upstate New York to edit his antislavery publication, *The North Star.*

Nell remained in Rochester from 1847 to 1849, becoming close friends with fellow abolitionist Amy

Kirby Post. Their relationship would remain one of the most valued in Nell's life. Although he had left for Rochester with nothing but admiration for Douglass, the growing rift between Douglass and Garrison would soon cause Nell to reconsider his estimation. Douglass's decision to lobby for "exclusive" organizations, most notably a Colored Men's Manual Labor College, drove the two men even farther apart.

When Nell returned to Boston in 1849, he re-inserted himself into the ongoing battle for school desegregation. Although the movement would face a series of stunning setbacks, he never relented in his determination to overthrow the system that had pained him throughout his childhood. In 1855, on the heels of an integration victory, Boston's African American community celebrated Nell for his role in their success. At a public ceremony in his honor, the city's free blacks presented him with a bouquet of flowers and a gold watch bearing the inscription, "A Tribute to William C. Nell, from the colored citizens of Boston, for his untiring efforts in behalf of Equal School Rights."

Nell remained in Boston for the rest of his life. From 1861 until his death on May 25, 1874, he served as a clerk in the Boston Post Office. He was one of the nation's first African Americans to hold such a federal position.

Hilary J. Moss

See also: Douglass, Frederick; Garrison, William Lloyd; *North Star, The;* Phillips, Wendell; Post, Amy Kirby.

Further Reading

Brown, Patrick T.J. "'To Defend Mr. Garrison': William Cooper Nell and the Personal Politics of Antislavery." *New England Quarterly* 70 (September 1997): 415–42.

Nell, William C. *The Colored Patriots of the American Revolution.* 1855. New York: Arno, 1968.

Smith, Robert P. "William Cooper Nell: Crusading Black Abolitionist." *Journal of Negro History* 55 (April 1970): 182–99.

New England Anti-Slavery Society

See Garrison, William Lloyd

New Granada, Abolition in

New Granada was a Spanish colony that roughly constituted the present-day South American nation of Colombia. By the late seventeenth century, it had a significant black slave population in the port region of Cartagena and in several profitable gold mines in the interior of the colony. As in most Spanish colonies, the scope of slavery was restricted as a result of political upheaval during the wars of independence from Spain in the 1810s and 1820s, but outright abolition was not achieved until 1851.

Early Slavery

Compared to the English, French, and Portuguese colonies in the New World, slavery was of minor significance in the majority of Spain's colonies. Spain had officially eliminated the slavery of indigenous peoples in 1548, and, although slavery continued in different forms on a small scale, Amerindian slaves were never the main laboring force in any region. Amerindian tribute labor became the preferred form of labor organization in most of the Spanish colonies. Though the Spanish Crown, the Catholic Church, and the colonial elites were prepared to halfheartedly accept the intrinsic humanity of Amerindians—and thus protect them from outright slavery—long-standing prejudices about the inherent inhumanity of blacks eventually resulted in the considerable use of African slaves in some colonies.

Black slaves were more expensive than the tribute labor of Amerindians, so they were often restricted to skilled occupations, construction labor, and domestic service in the cities or worked as laborers and overseers in the silver and gold mines. By the mid-eighteenth century, slaves constituted a significant portion of the urban populations of Mexico City, Quito, Caracas, Arica, and Lima. In New Granada, the northern port city of Cartagena had a significant black slave population. Yet it was in the gold-mining districts of the interior of New Granada that large numbers of black slaves dominated the labor force. By the eighteenth century, gold mining formed the principal economic activity in three provinces: Antioquia, Popayán, and Chocó.

By the 1590s, slave traders were bringing as many as 1,000 slaves a year into the colony to pan the rivers of the interior for gold. By the 1780s, there were 45,000 black slaves in the colony as a whole and at least 17,000 in the gold-producing regions, altogether composing 5 percent of the colony's population. The slave population's relatively low growth rate can be explained by high mortality, gender imbalance (the vast majority were male), escape, and the high number of slaves who were able to purchase their own freedom. In 1778 in Chocó, for example, 35 percent of the

Simón Bolívar, called "The Liberator," led the fight that brought independence to New Granada (now Colombia) and neighboring states. His actions hastened the demise of slavery throughout South America. *(©Caracas, Venezuela/Ken Welsh/The Bridgeman Art Library)*

province's 8,916 blacks were free; by 1808, the share of free blacks had soared to 75 percent of the population. A significant number of slaves also escaped in the sixteenth and seventeenth centuries, forming fugitive communities called *palenques.*

Slaves in New Granada's gold-mining operations were organized into labor gangs of both men and women under the direction of a captain, often a slave himself. Larger operations used male and female slaves to work on farms to provide food for the miners. Conditions in the gold mines were atrocious: Much of the backbreaking work was done in the rivers, where tropical diseases were easily contracted. Adult slaves were not expected to live more than seven or eight years.

Stirrings of Abolition

The question of the abolition of slavery first emerged during the drawn-out wars of independence from Spain during the 1810s and 1820s. The native-born white leaders of the independence movements expressed rhetorical commitments in favor of gradually ending slavery, although they were not prepared to support outright abolition and often stalled on the limited promises they made. In addition to an entrenched set of racial prejudices against blacks, they were not prepared to confront the considerable economic and po-

litical power of slave owners, many of whom were ardently behind the independence struggles.

The 1812 Constitution of the independent nation of New Granada mentioned the importance of slaves' well-being and formally supported the decline of slavery, but it never called for outright abolition. It banned the slave trade and announced the possible establishment of a manumission fund, but it specifically stated that slaves would not be emancipated without the consent or indemnification of their owners. For complex ideological and political reasons, the large free population of color who had won some political and economic rights during the independence struggles had never made the abolition of slavery a priority.

The personal history of Simón Bolívar neatly illustrates this lax process of gradual abolition. Bolívar was the chief military leader and politician who led the protracted wars of independence to liberate present-day Venezuela, Colombia, Ecuador, and Peru from Spanish colonialism. After a series of defeats in the first battles of the war from 1811 to 1815, Bolívar fled to Haiti, where blacks had led the first successful war against slavery and imperialism. In Haiti, he sought advice and military support, which was given by the government of President Alexandre Sabès Pétion in return for the promise that Bolívar would free the slaves in the colonies he liberated. A slave owner himself, Bolívar was forced to confront what historian Robin Blackburn has called the "deep-seated prejudices and taboos of his class." Bolívar agreed to Pétion's request, and the assistance of the Haitians helped kick-start a renewed series of successful military campaigns to liberate the American colonies from Spain.

Manumission

From 1816 on, Bolívar adopted a policy of military manumission whereby black slaves would be conscripted into the revolutionary armies in return for their freedom. This policy was widely adopted in all of the Spanish American colonies. He urged a more general policy of abolition among his supporters and freed the 100 slaves he personally owned.

Though the rhetoric of abolition on the part of Bolívar and other leaders was often just that, these acts did have consequences for the system of slavery. Even if only a minority survived the wars, some escaped, and few slave soldiers were ever re-enslaved. Indeed, slave and ex-slave soldiers would be crucial in defeating the forces that were loyal to Spain, and the republican victories spurred numerous revolts from 1820 to 1822 among thousands of slaves who believed liberation was at hand.

Nevertheless, the elites resisted Bolívar's policy of military manumission and gradual abolition of slavery throughout the wars of independence, and slave revolts were brutally suppressed by local authorities. In 1813–1814, for example, an independent government was established in the gold-mining region of Antioquia, and its leader declared that all children born of slave mothers would be henceforth free, yet the law was slow to be practically implemented. When independence armies conquered the mining area of the Cauca, Bolívar urged military manumission, but local leaders failed to challenge the powerful slave owners in the region. Bolívar himself played on racial prejudice when he argued that if slaves were not permitted to die for their country, then the African influence on the continent would be even greater.

A formal manumission law decreeing that the children of slaves would be automatically free was passed in 1821 in the independent territory that would later constitute Venezuela, Colombia, and Ecuador. Government-controlled Manumission Boards were also established that had the power to buy the freedom of slaves from their owners. However, emancipated children were still required to work for their mother's owner until the age of eighteen, and slave owners and the governing elites in the newly independent countries devised legal and illegal means to circumvent the laws. Indeed, a small-scale trade in slaves among Colombia, Ecuador, and Peru lasted until the late 1840s.

The final abolition of slavery in Colombia did not occur until 1851, following persistent slave revolts, mounting international pressure to end the slave trade, a steep decline in the number of slaves (to a nominal 16,000), and the development of a sizable mixed-race free labor force. By that time, the limited actions taken during the independence wars, constant slave resistance, and the gradual economic weakening of the institution had already undermined the foundations of the institution.

Sean Purdy

See also: Bolívar, Simón; New Granada, Emancipation in.

Further Reading

Blackburn, Robin. *The Overthrow of Colonial Slavery, 1776–1848.* New York: Verso, 1988.

Bushnell, David. "The Independence of Spanish South America." In *The Cambridge History of Latin America*, vol. 3, ed. Leslie Bethell. Cambridge, UK: Cambridge University Press, 1984.

Klein, Herbert S. *African Slavery in Latin America and the Caribbean.* New York: Oxford University Press, 1986.

Mellafe, Rolando. *Negro Slavery in Latin America.* Berkeley: University of California Press, 1975.

Rout, Leslie B., Jr. *The African Experience in Spanish America, 1502 to the Present Day.* Cambridge, UK: Cambridge University Press, 1976.

New Granada, Emancipation in

Slavery was officially abolished in the Spanish colony of New Granada (the present-day nation of Colombia) in 1851, but emancipation—the granting of rights and freedoms to former slaves and their freedom from forced labor—was a complex process that began with the struggles of fugitive slaves in the late sixteenth century. By the early 1800s, a majority of blacks in the Spanish colony were legally free, yet a strict racial hierarchy had developed that constrained their aspirations. The gradual abolition of slavery during the first half of the nineteenth century was similarly restricted by formal and informal limitations on the social, political, and economic mobility of former slaves.

A significant black slave population worked in domestic service, construction, and farming operations in and around the port city of Cartagena, the main entry point for forced African labor in South America. In the gold-mining districts of the provinces of Antioquia, Popayán, and Chocó, however, black slaves dominated the labor force. By the 1780s, there were 45,000 black slaves in the colony—composing 5 percent of the colony's population—although by this time, the majority of people of African origin were free.

Rise of Palenques

The first slaves to emancipate themselves were fugitives fleeing the appallingly unsafe gold-mining ventures. As early as 1576, slaves revolted against their masters in Antioquia, fleeing to remote swamps where they created fortified settlements known as *palenques*. In 1603, military conflict between Spanish troops and the *palenqueros* (residents of the palenques) of La Matuna in the province of Cartagena, led by the legendary black leader Domingo Benkos Biohó, forced the colonial governor to sign an official peace settlement.

In the 1690s, renewed military campaigns against runaway slaves in Cartagena revealed the existence of a dozen significant palenques, including four with more than 200 inhabitants each. Serious clashes led to a stalemate, and, in 1691, the Spanish king officially granted unconditional freedom to the palenqueros of the region. Slaves continued to escape intermittently throughout the colonial period, but the palenques flourished only until the beginning of the eighteenth century, largely because of the decline of slavery and the diminishing frontier.

Many of the palenques were coherently organized, evading the control of colonial powers or forcing them to formally recognize the rights of ex-slaves and their communities. Many were organized with kings and religious leaders following African traditions, whereas subsistence farming and hunting were ordered along familial lines. These self-emancipated communities frequently raided mining camps, ranches and farms, shipping routes, and towns for food and supplies.

Nevertheless, incursions by colonial troops constantly put the palenques on the defensive, often resulting in their re-enslavement or forcing them to flee to even more far-flung hideaways. As slavery steadily declined and the free black population increased in the 1700s, many former palenqueros were absorbed into the local economy as laborers, artisans, tenant farmers, and itinerant miners. Today, a number of black communities along the Pacific and Caribbean coasts of Colombia retain distinctive languages, cultures, and modes of social organization based on the African traditions preserved in the palenques.

Manumitted Slaves

By the time the wars of independence from Spain began in the 1810s, the vast majority of slaves had already been freed by manumission (legal freedom granted by owners or the Spanish Crown) or had bought themselves out of slavery. In the mining regions, for instance, many blacks were able to save enough money through private gold mining to purchase their freedom. Gradually, they formed a majority, together with runaways and mulattoes, and continued to work in the mining industry as independent gold washers or free laborers. Similar processes of self-purchase were common in urban centers such as Cartagena, involving both men and women in a variety of occupations.

Spanish law formally recognized all slaves' right to manumission, and it occurred at a much faster rate than in the Anglo-Saxon slave societies. Slave masters both voluntarily and involuntarily manumitted their slaves. There were cases in which slaves were manumitted on humanitarian grounds because of advanced age, sickness, or personal friendship, and, sometimes, the children of slave women were freed for similar reasons. During periods of economic depression, it was sometimes in the best economic interest of masters to free their slaves, given that they were legally required to provide for them.

Freed blacks still faced an uphill battle for full inclusion in society. Colonial society was strictly organized along race, class, and gender lines that severely limited opportunities. Black slaves were at the bottom of these hierarchies, but free blacks and those of mixed race also suffered occupational discrimination and exclusion from high positions in the government, the Catholic Church, and the military.

During the wars of independence, some free blacks and mulattoes made important political advances through their prominent roles as citizen soldiers in the battles against Spain. Yet they also maintained long-standing class and color divisions, by seeing themselves as an intermediate social level below the white elites but manifestly above the lower classes of black slaves and indigenous peoples. Despite their considerable power at key moments during the battles for independence, they never demanded the abolition of slavery. As part of the Constitution of 1812 drafted in Cartagena, white lawmakers, under pressure from free blacks, decreed the humane treatment of slaves and expressed a desire for the gradual abolition of slavery, but there was no mention of complete abolition. The complex class and racial divisions that permeated colonial society would continue in the following decades, delaying the final abolition of slavery and sustaining the continued inequality of blacks long after abolition.

New Granada, like most of the newly independent South American nations, adopted a policy of military manumission whereby black slaves would be conscripted into the revolutionary armies in return for their freedom. The motivations for this practice were mostly racist in origin, but it did free large numbers of slaves. Black soldiers played a critical role in defeating the forces that were loyal to Spain, and those blacks who survived were rarely re-enslaved.

Some independence leaders encouraged freedom for the slaves in New Granada and successfully pressured for a series of laws that decreed manumission under government auspices and the gradual abolition of slavery from the 1820s onward. Powerful local leaders tied to the "slavocracy," however, were able to delay and undermine, both legally and illegally, all such legislation until the 1840s. By that time, only 17,000 slaves remained in New Granada, and economic and political pressures at the local, national, and international level encouraged politicians to end slavery once and for all.

Because of the severe political and economic uncertainty facing the new nation of Colombia and its deeply ingrained racism, no practical measures were enacted to help the freed slaves. Those who were liberated from mines and farms became subsistence farmers or continued to work for their former masters as laborers under stringent labor contracts. Most urban blacks continued to live with the social and economic restrictions that had developed out of the racist ideologies of colonialism. Top economic and social positions were denied to all but a few blacks and mulattoes. Full suffrage was denied to the vast majority of poor Colombians until the 1930s, effectively disenfranchising the bulk of the black population, which altogether constituted 30 percent of the population at the time.

Emancipation in New Granada was a long and drawn-out process, involving complex patterns of resistance and accommodation among blacks, as well as the shifting ideas, politics, and economic structures of the colonial system. The formal legal freedoms won by blacks and slaves were significant, but thoroughgoing social and economic emancipation has not yet been fully achieved in the early twenty-first century.

Sean Purdy

See also: Bolívar, Simón; New Granada, Abolition in.

Further Reading

Helg, Aline. "The Limits of Equality: Free People of Colour and Slaves During the First Independence of Cartagena, Colombia, 1810–1815." *Slavery and Abolition* 20 (August 1999): 1–30.

Klein, Herbert S. *African Slavery in Latin America and the Caribbean.* New York: Oxford University Press, 1986.

Lockhart, James, and Stuart B. Schwartz. *Early Latin America: A History of Colonial Spanish America and Brazil.* Cambridge, UK: Cambridge University Press, 1983.

Mellafe, Rolando. *Negro Slavery in Latin America.* Berkeley: University of California Press, 1975.

Rout, Leslie B., Jr. *The African Experience in Spanish America, 1502 to the Present Day.* Cambridge, UK: Cambridge University Press, 1976.

West, Robert C. *Colonial Placer Mining in Colombia.* Baton Rouge: Louisiana State University Press, 1952.

New York City Draft Riot (1863)

Among the bloodiest urban upheavals of the nineteenth century, the New York City draft riot of July 1863 erupted in the midst of the U.S. Civil War. The violence was spurred by resentment for the emancipation of slaves and the implementation of the federal Conscription Act. These changes in government policy combined with already-brewing racial and economic tensions to spark outrage among New York's immigrant and working-class residents.

During five days of unrest, the rioters targeted government officials, draft offices, the wealthy, and African Americans. Each group was viewed as a beneficiary of government favoritism or a threat to the advancement of the immigrant and laborer populations.

The Dilemma

Faced with declining enlistments in the Union army, the U.S. Congress passed the Conscription Act on March 3, 1863. The first mandatory conscription bill in the nation's history, the act required all men between twenty and thirty-five years of age and unmarried men between thirty-five and forty-five years of age to register for the draft. Blacks were exempt from conscription, as they were not yet considered American citizens.

New York governor Horatio Seymour echoed the reaction of many of his constituents, calling the legislation unjust and unconstitutional. The stipulation that draftees could avoid military service for a $300 commutation fee further excited animosity toward the government and the wealthy few who were capable of avoiding military service. Immigrants, particularly the Irish, reacted forcefully to the law's enactment in July 1863. A number of areas with large foreign populations saw demonstrations against the legislation, though New York City became the epicenter of the unrest.

There was considerable sympathy for the Confederacy among urban Northerners during the war, providing encouragement to those who disapproved of emancipation and the draft. At first, many had supported President Abraham Lincoln and the Union cause, but opinion shifted as the war brought with it economic downturn caused by the cessation of trade with the Southern states. Stagnant wages and increasing costs for goods and services caused many to favor an end to the war, even if it meant the independence

Draft offices, government buildings, and homes of the wealthy came under attack during the New York draft riot of July 1863. The major bone of contention was conscription legislation that allowed draftees to avoid service by paying a "commutation fee" of $300. *(Library of Congress)*

of the Confederacy. Popularly known as Peace Democrats or Copperheads, many in the Democratic Party supported an end to the hostilities.

The Democratic press in New York aligned itself with the Copperheads, often placing the immigrant working class in opposition to the city's African Americans. Distaste for abolitionism was particularly strong among the Irish, who feared increased competition for jobs once slavery was abolished. Issued just over six months before the riots, the Emancipation Proclamation was still on the minds of immigrants who feared a black exodus to the North. Though many had supported the war as necessary to upholding the U.S. Constitution, far fewer supported a war aimed at the abolition of slavery.

Religious differences combined with political strife, as abolitionist views were often identified with evangelical Protestantism. Some abolitionists rallied against Roman Catholicism, the religion of most Irish immigrants and a sizable number of New York's German residents.

The Spark

The names of the first individuals drafted for military service were drawn in New York City on Saturday, July 11, 1863. Though there was little reaction from the crowd that had gathered that day, the weekend allowed the anger of those opposed to the draft to ferment. The violence began the following Monday, July 13, when a mob of mostly unskilled Irish laborers attacked the Ninth District draft office, setting it ablaze. With the police in retreat, the mob searched for other targets, looting the nearby armory. The rioters targeted well-dressed gentlemen (so-called $300 men), draft officials, and government employees, as well as abolitionists and those who appeared sympathetic to blacks.

Though the riot began as a violent reaction to the draft and to symbols of government power, by Monday evening, race largely determined the mob's targets. The burning of New York's Colored Orphan Asylum was perhaps the most stunning act of the riot. More than 200 children living in the home were successfully evacuated before the rioters ransacked the building and set it on fire on the afternoon of July 13. Fortunately, the mob did not attack any of the children fleeing the asylum.

Some called the riot a "black pogrom," but the rioters' targeting of blacks was far from systematic—although any African American in the mob's path was at risk. Blacks on the streets and those riding streetcars were assaulted, and the homes and boardinghouses of African Americans were targeted. The rioters were particularly vicious toward young African American men, whom they believed represented the threat of black economic gain at the expense of immigrant laborers. In retribution for the hiring of black longshoremen to replace striking Irish workers, the mob attacked some 200 African Americans who were working on the docks. By the evening of July 13, a substantial number of blacks had either gone into hiding or exited the city.

The Aftermath

Both force and persuasion were required to quell the violence. At the request of Governor Seymour, John Hughes, the Roman Catholic archbishop of New York, addressed the city's residents on July 17. He pleaded with them to end the violence and to voice their displeasure with the government through other means. The local police had proved too few to break up the mob, and consequently, the state militia and ten Union army regiments were called in to subdue the rioters. By the evening of Friday, July 17, an uneasy peace had been attained in New York City.

During the course of the riots, about 150 people were killed, two-thirds of whom were rioters, though the official count of those killed by the mob was only eighteen, including eleven blacks. The number of wounded or injured was estimated to total an additional 300.

The riot's impact on economic and civic life in New York cannot be exaggerated. Commerce was interrupted for weeks, and damage estimates were calculated at $5 million. Though hundreds of rioters were arrested, most were never convicted of any crime.

The impact on the black community was also substantial. African Americans left New York City in large numbers in the aftermath of the riot, reducing labor competition and thus fulfilling at least one of the rioters' objectives. For months after the riots, blacks were reluctant to be seen in public within the city.

The New York City draft riot was an unprecedented event, attesting to the fear of economic competition from black laborers, the strength of Democratic and immigrant sympathy with the Confederacy, and the power of political discontent. The event magnified the racial tension of the era and the threat of violence in the heavily polarized environment of the urban North.

David J. Endres

See also: Emancipation Proclamation (1863).

Further Reading

Bernstein, Iver. *The New York City Draft Riots: Their Significance for American Society and Politics in the Age of the Civil War.* New York: Oxford University Press, 1990.

Cook, Adrian. *The Armies of the Streets: The New York City Draft Riots of 1863.* Lexington: University Press of Kentucky, 1974.

Harris, Leslie M. *In the Shadow of Slavery: African Americans in New York City, 1626–1863.* Chicago: University of Chicago Press, 2003.

McCague, James. *The Second Rebellion: The Story of the New York City Draft Riots of 1863.* New York: Dial, 1968.

Newton, John (1725–1807)

A sailor and sea captain who worked in the slave trade, John Newton underwent a religious conversion and became an ordained minister, vocal abolitionist, and writer of Christian hymns. He is perhaps best known for writing the lyrics to the hymn "Amazing Grace," set to an old African slave tune.

Newton was born in London on July 24, 1725, to a stern sea captain and his devout Christian wife, who taught the boy to read at a young age. His mother died when Newton was seven, his father soon remarried, and the boy was sent off to boarding school in Essex. His father took him on his first voyage when he was only eleven, followed by many more voyages in the next six years. Newton took up the life of a sailor.

During his years aboard, Newton had little to anchor his life and conduct, and he led an irresolute existence in which he seldom acted responsibly. As a midshipman on one voyage, he deserted his post and was arrested. Although he had not had any religious upbringing, he saw religion as a means of escaping damnation. He enjoyed his waywardness, however, and, for many years, his personal morality swung between excess and sobriety. He eventually found work aboard English vessels that were involved in the transatlantic slave trade.

Newton noted May 10, 1748, as the date of his religious conversion, which occurred after he experienced a fierce storm at sea on one of his many slaving voyages. Fearing for his life, as well as that of the others on board, he penned the words that would be immortalized in the Christian hymn "Amazing Grace." Although the lyrics were based on Bible verses, scholars have noted its personal application to Newton's life and spiritual quest in phrases such as "I once was lost, but now am found."

Having endured a near-shipwreck and death, Newton began the spiritual journey that would eventually lead him to the ministry. Even while engaging such new thoughts, however, he continued working in the slave trade for six years as a crew member and eventually as captain of the *Duke of Argyll*. Newton believed that God's providence kept him safe through treacherous times and that the same providence cared for the slaves. But because of his constant use of chains and shackles, along with other measures to subdue the slaves, Newton began to see himself as a jailor. Although he had been thinking of ending his involvement in the slave trade for several years, it was his physical condition, after suffering a seizure, that brought about his resignation in 1754.

Newton taught himself Latin, Greek, Hebrew, and Syriac as he contemplated religious studies to pursue a life in the ministry. He sought ordination in the Church of England from the archbishop of York but initially was denied because of his lack of formal education. Newton made numerous attempts to obtain ordination and even considered joining the Dissenters. He was finally ordained under the bishop of Lincoln in 1764 and appointed to the parish of Olney, the home of the poet William Cowper. Newton held the position for nearly sixteen years.

In the years before his ordination and during his time at Olney, Newton published several volumes of sermons, letters, and ecclesiastical history. He also published *Olney Hymns* (1779), some co-authored with Cowper. In 1778, he published *Thoughts Upon the African Slave Trade,* in which he attacked the political and moral evils of slavery.

The following year, Newton moved on from Olney to Saint Mary Woolnoth parish in a favorable section of London. Although this pulpit brought him to national prominence, Newton took care not to rest on the opulence around him and warned his parishioners to do the same. His reputation became such that the University of New Jersey awarded him a doctor of divinity degree in absentia in 1790. He used his influence to help found the Church Missionary Society of the Church of England in 1799.

During his years as a minister, Newton became a frequent correspondent of such noted ministers as John Wesley and George Whitefield. Newton also became close with William Wilberforce, the well-known Member of Parliament and Christian philanthropist who effectively led the antislavery movement in Great Britain. Newton often preached against slavery in his sermons, coinciding with Wilberforce's efforts in Parliament to abolish it.

In his later years, Newton expressed embarrassment at having been an accomplice in the slave trade and at not having spoken out more forcefully and publicly for its abolition. He preached his last sermon in October 1806 and died on December 21, 1807.

David B. Malone

See also: Church Missionary Society; Wesley, John; Wilberforce, William.

Further Reading

Bull, Josiah. *John Newton of Olney and St. Mary Woolnoth.* London: Religious Tract Society, 1869.

Hindmarsh, D. Bruce. *John Newton and the English Evangelical Tradition.* Oxford, UK: Clarendon, 1996.

Martin, Bernard. *John Newton: A Biography.* London: Heinemann, 1950.

Newton, John. *Out of the Depths: An Autobiography.* New Canaan, CT: Keats, 1981.

Phipps, William E. *Amazing Grace in John Newton: Slave-Ship Captain, Hymnwriter, and Abolitionist.* Macon, GA: Mercer University Press, 2001.

North Star, The

Founded in December 1847 by Frederick Douglass in Rochester, New York, *The North Star* was one of the most influential antislavery newspapers in the United States between 1848 and 1851. Douglass, together with his partners Martin Robison Delany and William Cooper Nell, created the African American–owned and operated paper because they believed it would perform critical work for the antislavery cause while serving as a weekly rejoinder to arguments claiming the inferiority of people of African descent.

As much as *The North Star* played an important role in the struggle against slavery and racial prejudice in the United States, it was also a critical vehicle for Douglass personally. Although his editorship of *The North Star* eventually alienated Douglass from his white mentor, William Lloyd Garrison, and his colleagues in the American Anti-Slavery Society, it was crucial in forging his identity as a leading—and independent—voice in the antislavery struggle.

Douglass first formulated his plan to start an antislavery journal while promoting his *Narrative of the Life of Frederick Douglass* (1845) on a speaking tour of Great Britain between 1845 and 1847. The tour

was a resounding success: Douglass drew significant crowds in England, Ireland, and Scotland, gaining an international reputation by the time he returned to the United States. In addition, Douglass earned the support of influential British abolitionists, who helped raise money both to purchase his freedom from his former master and to support the publication of his own antislavery newspaper.

Douglass's British supporters thought they were helping him build "the most powerful lever for the attainment of emancipation," but his Boston colleagues in the American Anti-Slavery Society insisted that a new black-run antislavery journal was entirely unnecessary. A number of other African American antislavery papers already existed, the Garrisonians argued,

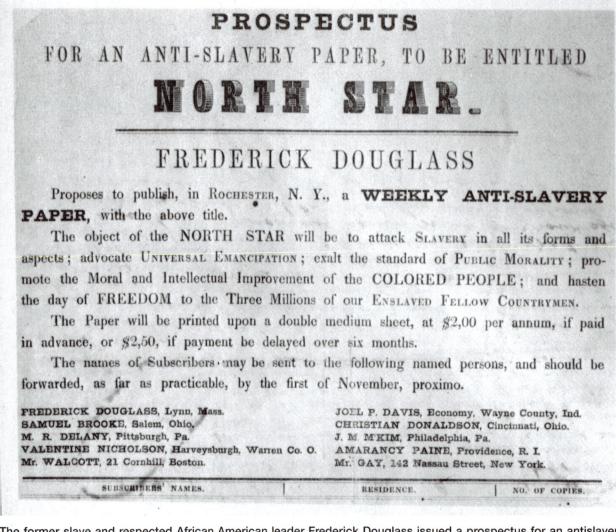

The former slave and respected African American leader Frederick Douglass issued a prospectus for an antislavery newspaper, to be called *The North Star*, in 1847. Published from that December to 1851, the influential paper was entirely black-owned and black-operated. *(Photographs and Print Division, Schomburg Center for Research in Black Culture, The New York Public Library, Astor, Lenox, and Tilden Foundations)*

and, furthermore, Douglass lacked the necessary experience to succeed in publishing his own paper. Most of all, though, Douglass's Boston colleagues maintained that the journal would distract Douglass from his important role as an antislavery lecturer—a June 1847 issue of *The Liberator,* for example, insisted that "his extraordinary powers can be the most successfully employed for the promotion of the anti-slavery cause."

Initially, Douglass seemed to take the advice of his fellow abolitionists, suspending his plans and touring Ohio and western New York with Garrison in summer and fall 1847. But by the end of the tour, Douglass had made up his mind to publish the paper that would be called *The North Star.* By the end of the year, Douglass had relocated to Rochester, New York, and set up shop with funds from his British supporters.

A bustling city on the Erie Canal, Rochester was located in the "Burned-Over District" of western New York, so called because it was home to waves of revivalism during the early nineteenth century and became fertile ground for a range of reform movements, from communitarianism to abolitionism. Douglass enlisted Delany, a black abolitionist from Pittsburgh who had published his own antislavery weekly, to join him as co-editor and recruited Nell, a black Garrisonian from Boston, to serve as *The North Star*'s publisher (though he actually functioned more as its printer).

The first issue of *The North Star* was published on December 3, 1847. Although it was dedicated primarily to the destruction of slavery, the new antislavery newspaper, Douglass insisted, would address a range of reform topics from temperance to capital punishment. *The North Star*'s primary goal, however, was the effacement of American racial prejudice. "The general contempt with which my people are regarded," Douglass wrote, "the low estimate entertained of the negro's mental and moral qualities among the white people of this land—and the absences of any very striking confutation of the disturbing and depressing theories . . . led me to establish this paper."

If Douglass and his partners were able to establish a successful black antislavery paper, they surmised that they could strike a blow against the prevailing racist assumptions about black Americans. Douglass therefore recruited solely African American correspondents for *The North Star,* including James McCune Smith, Samuel Ringgold Ward, and William Wells Brown.

The North Star was well received in most antislavery circles, and it quickly circulated across the United States and as far overseas as Great Britain and Aus-

tralia. In just a few years, the paper built a subscription list that included many well-known antislavery figures in America, including Lucretia Mott, Harriet Beecher Stowe, and Lewis and Arthur Tappan. Still, the newspaper was costly to produce, and Douglass had to dip into his own savings to keep it afloat. Ironically, though it was a black-run newspaper, *The North Star*'s subscribers were overwhelmingly white, and Douglass relied heavily on gifts from white supporters of the paper, especially the wealthy New York abolitionist Gerrit Smith. Fortunately, with the help of British supporter Julia Griffiths, Douglass was able to put *The North Star* on relatively sure economic footing by the early 1850s.

Although Douglass succeeded in keeping *The North Star* solvent, he was unable to convince his former colleagues and mentors in the American Anti-Slavery Society to support the paper, financially or otherwise. Their objections rested not merely on his choice to ignore their advice, leave his position as a lecturer for the society, and strike out on his own but also on a growing philosophical rift between the two parties. Increasingly, Douglass had doubts about Garrison's uncompromising rejection of political abolitionism.

By 1851, Douglass had publicly rejected the Garrisonian interpretation of the U.S. Constitution as a proslavery document, formally endorsed political abolitionism in *The North Star,* and announced that he planned to merge the paper with the *Liberty Party Paper,* a Liberty Party journal bankrolled by Smith. These decisions transformed what had been a small squabble into a vituperative war of words between Douglass and the Garrisonians that lasted for several years.

The North Star ceased publication in summer 1851, when Douglass officially renamed his antislavery weekly *Frederick Douglass' Paper.* Although Douglass had played the lead in the creation and production of *The North Star* from the very beginning, this titular change reflected Douglass's increasing celebrity and ever-growing role in the newspaper. Both Delany and Nell departed in the early 1850s, leaving control of the paper solely in Douglass's hands.

From 1851 to 1860, the antislavery editor published *Frederick Douglass' Paper* on a weekly basis. Thereafter, Douglass produced a monthly version of his antislavery newspaper, known as *Douglass' Monthly,* until 1863.

Ethan J. Kytle

See also: Delany, Martin Robison; Douglass, Frederick; Garrison, William Lloyd; Nell, William Cooper; Smith, Gerrit; Ward, Samuel Ringgold.

Further Reading

Fishkin, Shelly Fisher, and Carla L. Peterson. "'We Hold These Truths to Be Self-Evident': The Rhetoric of Frederick Douglass' Journalism." In *Frederick Douglass: New Literary and Historical Essays*, ed. Eric J. Sundquist. Cambridge, MA: Cambridge University Press, 1990.

Foner, Philip S. *Life and Writings of Frederick Douglass.* 5 vols. New York: International Publishers, 1950.

McFeely, William S. *Frederick Douglass.* New York: W.W. Norton, 1991.

Perry, P.B. "Before the *North Star:* Frederick Douglass' Early Journalistic Career." *Phylon* 35 (March 1974): 96–107.

Northup, Solomon (1808–1863)

Solomon Northup was the best-known free black to be kidnapped and sold into slavery during the antebellum era. His autobiographical account of the experience, *Twelve Years a Slave* (1853), was a powerful reminder that the security of one's freedom was always questionable in a society that used the badge of race as an excuse to make a commodity of one's liberty.

Northup was born a free black man in Minerva, New York, in 1808. He was employed as a day laborer doing carpentry work, and he was recognized in the community as an accomplished fiddler. In 1834, Northup and his wife, Anne Hampton, moved to Saratoga Springs, New York, where they raised a family of three children. The demands of supporting his growing family brought Northup to Washington, D.C., where he had been promised work as a musician with a traveling circus.

In March 1841, Northup was kidnapped in Washington, D.C. The circumstances of his capture indicate the level of duplicity employed in the kidnapping of free blacks, who were then sold as slaves in the South. Northup was offered a drink by a white patron in a tavern in Washington, D.C. He accepted the offer, not realizing that the drink had been drugged. When he awoke, he had been removed from the tavern, bound, and placed in a basement to await transport aboard a vessel that would set sail for New Orleans. Shortly after his arrival in New Orleans, Northup was sold at auction. Despite his pleas that he was a free man, Northup became a slave.

Northup adroitly described the New Orleans slave pen managed by Theophilus Freeman and noted the customary business practices that were associated with the flesh trade. It was common, according to Northup, for slaves to be made to "walk briskly back and forth, while customers would feel of our hands and arms and bodies, turn us about, ask us what we could do, make us open our mouths and show our teeth, precisely as a jockey examines a horse which he is about to barter for or purchase." His account also described the painful separation of families that was a regular occurrence at these auctions.

Northup was sold for $1,000 at the New Orleans auction, and he spent the next twelve years of his life working as a slave on three cotton plantations in the parishes of central Louisiana's Red River Valley. He was owned by and worked the plantations of William Ford, John M. Tibeats, and Edwin Epps.

Northup's account of his life as a slave is valuable for its level of detail, which far exceeds that of most traditional slave narratives. His recollection of events demonstrates the fluid communication that took place within the slave quarters; slaves in the region knew much of what was occurring in the region of Avoyelles and Rapides parishes. Northup even suggests that there was an institutional memory in the oral traditions of the plantation, as slaves in the area still discussed a failed slave revolt conspiracy that Lew Cheney had organized in 1837.

During Northup's enslavement, Northern abolitionists conducted a sustained letter-writing campaign on his behalf. Northup wasted no time in using Northern merchants as intermediaries to communicate his plight to sympathetic antislavery advocates in the North who might work to bring about his freedom. In addition, Samuel Bass, a Canadian émigré living on a nearby plantation, felt sympathy for Northup's plight and wrote letters on his behalf to abolitionists and public officials in New York State in 1852. Despite these efforts, Northup's continued enslavement was a constant reminder to free blacks in early nineteenth century America that there were no ironclad means by which to prove one's status as a free person.

Northup finally gained his freedom in January 1853, after Northern abolitionists were able to convince his Louisiana owner that they were willing to purchase the unfortunate slave in order to set him free and allow him to return to his home and family in the North. In March 1853, Northrop's story was published as *Twelve Years a Slave.* The narrative sold 27,000 copies, with multiple printings taking place during its first two years on the market.

Junius P. Rodriguez

See also: Manumission.

Further Reading

Nichols, Charles H., Jr., "Who Read the Slave Narratives?" *Phylon* 20 (Second Quarterly 1959) 149–62.

Northup, Solomon. *Twelve Years a Slave.* 1853. Ed. Sue Eakin and Joseph Logsdon. Baton Rouge: Louisiana State University Press, 1968.

Wilson, Carol. *Freedom at Risk: The Kidnapping of Free Blacks in America, 1780–1865.* Lexington: University Press of Kentucky, 1994.

Norton, John Treadwell (1795–1869)

John Treadwell Norton was an American industrialist who held leadership positions in the American Anti-Slavery Society. He devoted much of his time and fortune to the cause of abolition during the late 1830s and early 1840s, and he personally intervened on behalf of the *Amistad* captives. When a schism developed within the American abolitionist movement following the 1840 World Anti-Slavery Convention in London, Norton tried unsuccessfully to heal the rift.

A prominent merchant in Albany, New York, Norton was a partner in the mercantile firm of Corning and Norton from 1825 to 1829. He became financially involved in the early railroad industry and served as president of the newly established New York Central Railroad. Highly successful as an entrepreneur, he amassed a small fortune from his business ventures.

Norton faced personal tragedy in 1829 when his young wife, Mary Pitkin Norton, died of consumption at the age of twenty-six. Her death marked a turning point in his life. Three years later, he moved to Farmington, Connecticut, and built Barney House, the largest mansion in town.

His business success continued, as he became involved with local internal improvement projects (roads, bridges, and harbor improvements) that proved financially lucrative. He became a key proponent of the Farmington Canal and Dam and subsequently established the Farmington River Water-Power Company. Norton supplemented his income by raising a herd of Jersey cattle—he was only the second American to do so—and sold the butter produced by his herd to the Astor House in New York City. A man of affluence in community affairs, Norton also served in the Connecticut legislature.

Norton joined an antislavery society as early as 1837, but it was the events of 1839 that transformed his involvement in the abolitionist cause. The Spanish slave vessel *Amistad* was brought ashore near Farmington in 1839, and, for eight months, the captive Africans who were fighting to win their freedom were unexpected residents of the town that Norton called home. He used much of his financial resources to fund the legal expenses of the *Amistad* Africans. Additionally, his son, John Pitkin Norton, kept a daily diary describing the experiences of the *Amistad* Africans' day-to-day life in Farmington.

Because of his generous financial support for the abolitionist movement in general and his specific work on behalf of the *Amistad* captives, Norton was elected vice president of the American Anti-Slavery Society in 1839 and 1840.

Norton participated in the 1840 World Anti-Slavery Convention in London, which was attended by abolitionist delegates from the United States and Great Britain. Upon returning from London, he caused a stir when he published a letter in the *Friend,* a Philadelphia Quaker periodical, in which he stated that free blacks were treated better in Britain than they were in the United States. Not wanting his newspaper to be viewed as radical on the race question, the paper's publisher later issued an editorial retraction in which he denied supporting Norton's statement.

Norton sought to reunite the American abolitionist factions by issuing a circular letter, dated December 12, 1842, to abolitionist leaders William Lloyd Garrison, Joshua Leavitt, John Greenleaf Whittier, Lewis Tappan, Gerrit Smith, and Theodore Dwight Weld. Believing that the abolitionists had more commonalities that united them than minor differences that divided them, Norton proposed a conference of the principal leaders of all factions to try to repair the damages before the antislavery cause became hindered by divisiveness. The proposed meeting was never held.

Rebuffed in his attempt to make peace among factions, Norton's active involvement in the abolitionist cause waned. Until his death in 1869, he devoted more attention to his business ventures.

Junius P. Rodriguez

See also: *Amistad* Case (1841).

Further Reading

Birney, James Gillespie. *Letters of James Gillespie Birney, 1831–1857.* 2 vols. Ed. Dwight L. Dumond. New York: D. Appleton-Century, 1938; Gloucester, MA: P. Smith, 1966.

Novels, Antislavery

During the mid-nineteenth century, the antislavery novel reached the high point of its popularity in the transatlantic world as the American abolitionist movement flourished. Harriet Beecher Stowe's great antislavery novel *Uncle Tom's Cabin* (1852) was a worldwide success, and it was followed by a number of works, including the first novels of former slaves themselves, that brought the antislavery message to a growing audience.

Antislavery themes had been prominent in other literary forms, such as poetry, moral tales, religious sermons, personal narratives, and children's books, since the eighteenth century. But it was the relatively new and popular form of the novel that succeeded in inflaming the antislavery passions of the general reading public.

One of the first prose narratives in English literature focused on the theme of slavery, although it did not explicitly criticize the institution. Aphra Behn's short novel *Oroonoko* (1688) tells the story of an African slave uprising in the British colony of Suriname in South America. Its main characters include the black slave Oroonoko, a former African prince, and the narrator, a white English woman living among the colonial planter aristocracy. Though it never openly condemns slavery, the novel's sympathetic portrayal of its hero offers an implicit critique. In fact, *Oroonoko* was considered an antislavery novel by many abolitionists until the late nineteenth century.

As the novel form matured during the eighteenth century, English novelists writing in the "sentimental tradition" used their fiction to criticize aspects of slavery. Sentimentalist fiction emphasized personal feeling—as opposed to reason—as the principal guide to truth. Despite their superficial romantic plots, the sentimentalist novels also considered the raging political debates of the day.

The most celebrated of the sentimental novelists, Laurence Sterne, drew on his extensive correspondence with the contemporary African writer Ignatius Sancho to punctuate his most acclaimed novel, *Tristram Shandy* (1759), with arresting images of the suffering and exploitation caused by slavery. Sarah Scott's *The History of Sir George Ellison* (1766) and Henry Mackenzie's *Julia de Roubigné* (1777) likewise explored the human degradation caused by the slavery of black Africans. Scott's novel focuses on a kind slave master in the West Indies, Mr. Ellison, who eases the harsh punishments normally meted out to his slaves and receives their admiration in return. As the literary his-

torian Markman Ellis has argued, however, "sentimental benevolence enriches the giver as much as, or even more than, the receiver," and the sentimentalist critique of slavery was self-serving and ultimately muted. It never really addressed the underlying structures of slavery as a social and economic system.

Still, the strong moral messages contained in sentimental texts proved to be an inspiration to the burgeoning abolitionist movement in Great Britain and the United States. Romantic treatments of love and adventure were evident in the first antislavery novel by an American, the anonymously authored *Humanity in Algiers, or The Story of Azem* (1801). Though the plot revolves around the adventures of Azem, a former Senegalese slave in Algiers who grows rich as a trader, the novel's real critique is aimed at the United States and its hypocrisy in "freeing" North Africa from oppression while practicing slavery in its own country.

By the 1830s, novelists were drawing on a new source for their plots: the autobiographical narratives of former slaves. These firsthand accounts provided authentic details, such as the dialects of African Americans, the daily abuses and brutalities of slavery, and heroic stories of resistance and escape. The first antislavery novel set in the United States, Richard Hildreth's *The Slave, or Memoirs of Archy Moore* (1836), recounts the tale of a slave who heroically escapes his master, flees to Europe, and eventually redeems his slave wife in the United States. Similarly, the first American woman antislavery novelist, Emily Catharine Pierson, used sentimental themes to condemn slavery in *Jamie Parker, The Fugitive* (1851). Other novelists who were not primarily concerned with slavery, such as Herman Melville, incorporated bitter critiques of slavery into their novels; such works include Melville's *Mardi* (1849) and *Moby Dick* (1851).

It was the publication of Harriet Beecher Stowe's *Uncle Tom's Cabin* in 1852 that provided a lasting literary form and stance for antislavery novelists in the decades immediately preceding abolition throughout the transatlantic world. In her stirring tale of freedom from bondage, Stowe used more realistic and dramatic narratives of the struggle against slavery and infused them with powerful Christian arguments about its inherent inhumanity. *Uncle Tom's Cabin* was the first American book to sell more than 1 million copies, and it reached huge audiences in many countries. The enormously popular novel spawned no fewer than twenty-seven proslavery novels, including children's books, that were written specifically in response to Stowe in the period preceding the U.S. Civil War.

CHAPTER XL.

THE MARTYR.

"Deem not the just by Heaven forgot!
Though life its common gifts deny,—
Though, with a crushed and bleeding heart,
And spurned of man, he goes to die!
For God hath marked each sorrowing day,
And numbered every bitter tear;
And heaven's long years of bliss shall pay
For all his children suffer here."

BRYANT.

THE longest way must have its close,—the gloomiest night will wear on to a morning. An eternal, inexorable lapse of moments is ever hurrying the day of the evil to an eternal night, and the night of the just to an eternal day. We have walked with our humble friend thus far in the valley of slavery; first through flowery fields of

Slave hunters track the runaways Cassy and Emeline in chapter 40 of *Uncle Tom's Cabin*. Dramatic narrative helped make Harriet Beecher Stowe's novel a powerful antislavery tract and the best-selling book of the nineteenth century after the Bible. *(Library of Congress)*

Stowe's antislavery vision has been described as "romantic racialism." As Sterling Brown wrote in *The Negro in American Fiction* (1937), Stowe saw blacks as "natural Christians whose soft emotionalism and gentle passivity were destined to temper the harshness of Anglo-Saxon culture." Indeed, her melodramatic writing encouraged black stereotypes and limited itself to an abstract appeal to moralism in the fight for abolition. Later generations of African Americans would use the term "Uncle Tom" derisively to describe blacks who are passive in the face of oppression.

Although it has often been criticized for its stereotypical portrayal of blacks and its literary deficiencies, *Uncle Tom's Cabin* was a rich and influential document of social protest. Many antislavery novels published in the 1850s and 1860s explicitly or implicitly adopted Stowe's work as their model.

The first African American novelists, Harriet E. Wilson and William Wells Brown, were similarly influenced by Stowe's sentimental appeals to the im-

morality of slavery. Wilson's *Our Nig* (1859) centers on racism in the pre–Civil War North, and Brown's *Clotel, or The President's Daughter* (1853) is a melodramatic commentary on interracial love. As in *Uncle Tom's Cabin,* these works display a tension between the impulse toward realism and the Christian conception of social redemption, which was largely designed to attract the sympathy of whites. Yet they proved to be important literary testaments to the growing abolitionist sentiment in the United States and helped create a favorable climate for reform.

Antislavery novels were thus the products of the social and political struggle against slavery and the overall development of the novel as a literary form. They stand out not only as rich testimonies to contemporary literary trends, but also as significant primary documents in the history of slavery and abolition.

Sean Purdy

See also: Brown, William Wells; Novels, Proslavery; *Oroonoko* (1688); Stowe, Harriet Beecher.

Further Reading

Brown, Sterling. *The Negro in American Fiction.* Port Washington, NY: Kennikat, 1937.

Ellis, Markman. *The Politics of Sensibility: Race, Gender, and Commerce in the Sentimental Novel.* New York: Cambridge University Press, 1996.

Oldfield, John R. "Anti-Slavery Sentiment in Children's Literature, 1750–1850." *Slavery and Abolition* 10 (May 1989): 44–59.

Sundquist, Eric J., ed. *New Essays on* Uncle Tom's Cabin. Cambridge, UK, and New York: Cambridge University Press, 1986.

Tompkins, Jane. *Sensational Designs: The Cultural Work of American Fiction, 1790–1860.* New York: Oxford University Press, 1985.

Novels, Proslavery

Proslavery sentiment was evident in English literature before the nineteenth century, but the proslavery novel arose specifically in response to the growing abolitionist movement in the United States during the 1850s. Proslavery writers produced a number of novels specifically in reaction to Harriet Beecher Stowe's phenomenally successful antislavery novel *Uncle Tom's Cabin* (1852).

Such racist protest novels generally drew on paternalistic arguments about the benefits of slavery, ideologies of white superiority, and alarmist appeals regarding the consequences of abolition for American society, especially the threat of miscegenation and racial assimilation. Though they were nowhere near as popular as abolitionist fiction, proslavery novels reached a considerable audience in the North and South and played a part in the turbulent propaganda battle surrounding abolition in the years before the U.S. Civil War.

Among the first explicitly proslavery novels, George Tucker's *The Valley of the Shenandoah* (1824) and John Pendleton Kennedy's *The Swallow Barn* (1832) can be placed in the context of a developing regional tradition in American literature. Both set in rural Virginia, these novels were early examples of the so-called plantation tradition in American literature, which would flourish in the late nineteenth century. The plantation novel focused on the characters, dialects, customs, and physical landscape of the white South, extolling Southern manners, tradition, and conservatism.

Authors such as Tucker and Kennedy painted an idyllic portrait of Southern life and institutions, idealizing slavery on the grounds that blacks were inherently inferior and dependent on white masters. They mythologized the slave plantation as a "family" and generally saw blacks as simple, harmless, and happy in a state of bondage. White Virginians were portrayed as courageous defenders of women, honor, and their region, often in the face of economic adversity, whereas black slaves, as the main character of *The Swallow Barn* says, "could never become a happier people" than they are under slavery. Both novels enjoyed modest popularity and foreshadowed many of the themes that would be taken up by the proslavery novels of the 1850s.

The publication of Stowe's *Uncle Tom's Cabin* and the proliferation of abolitionist sentiment and organizations in the 1850s prompted a flurry of responses from proslavery writers in the North and South. Literary scholars have observed that at least twenty-seven proslavery novels, including children's books, were written in response to Stowe's work between 1852 and the Civil War. Differing somewhat in terms of plot and literary style, they shared a view of slavery and plantation society as honorable, moral, and beneficial and saw blacks as either contented with slavery or unfit for freedom. Laced with sentimentality and "blood and tears romances," they often contrasted "scenes of bliss in the plantation" with "scenes of squalor in the Free North." Some attention was paid to realistic portrayals of white culture and the domestic situations of women, but the depiction of African American physical characteristics, customs, and dialects were mostly crude and stereotypical.

A common polemical strategy of proslavery novelists was to forcefully counter the image of slavery as harsh and demeaning to blacks. Southern reviewers of *Uncle Tom's Cabin* were particularly critical of Stowe's supposed mischaracterization of the harshness of slavery, arguing that abusive masters were rare. To counter an image that they recognized as damaging to the institution of slavery, proslavery novelists went to great lengths to portray the slave master as kind and generous and slave life as prosperous and contented.

In Mrs. Henry R. Schoolcraft's *The Black Gauntlet* (1860), slaves live in spacious and airy homes with "sitting and sleeping rooms" and enjoy plenty of food and their own garden plots. Martha Haines Butt's *Antifanaticism: A Tale of the South* (1853) invites Northerners to visit the South to witness firsthand the kindness of the masters and the carefree lives of the contented slaves. Caroline Lee Whiting Hentz's *The Planter's Northern Bride* (1857) similarly emphasizes the guiding paternalism of slavery and its benevolence toward slaves. When the Northern bride arrives on the plantation and the slaves respond with cries of adoration, she exclaims, "Oh! My husband! I never dreamed that slavery could present an aspect so tender and affectionate." In the vision of the proslavery novelists, African American slaves did not resent their situation; indeed, they considered themselves part of the wider plantation family.

Contrasting the peaceful order of the Southern plantation with the ruthlessness of industrial capitalism in the Northern states was another prominent theme in proslavery literature. Mary Eastman's *Aunt Phillis's Cabin; or Southern Life as It Is* (1852) aims to show how Northern laws did not protect free workers, who were, in fact, treated no better than the slaves in the South. The novel describes a reminiscence of Mr. Chappman, a Southern plantation owner, in which the foreman of a Northern construction company punches an Irish worker. When asked about the laws protecting workers from such abuse, the foreman answers, "Laws! Why railroads have to be made, and have to be made the right way. I ain't afraid of the laws. I think no more of knocking an Irishman, sir, than I do of eating my dinner." In a fictional debate between an abolitionist and slaveholder, the latter responds to the abolitionist claim that Southerners have no legal right to hold slaves by analogizing that Northerners also stole the land of the Native Americans and have similarly used it to their profit. In *The Planter's Northern Bride*, the author claims that slave women were better off than the "Northern woman-workers" whom industrial society had all but abandoned.

Underlying all of the proslavery novels was a belief that whites are inherently superior to blacks. This is reflected in their frequent use of racist stereotypes to describe the physical characteristics of blacks and in their sociocultural representations of the slave character as simple, dull, and uncreative. Several novels show how fugitive slaves and free people of color were unable to fend for themselves outside the world of the Southern plantation. For example, W.L.G. Smith's *Uncle Tom's Cabin as It Is; or, Life at the South* (1852) recounts the story of a runaway slave who escapes to the North and then to Canada, finds life unbearable, and finally begs his master to return. In *The Black Gauntlet,* slave mothers are exposed as negligent and unable to care for their children without the help of whites.

Proslavery novels also defended slavery as the only means to prevent miscegenation and racial assimilation. Interestingly, the contemporary fact of racial mixing in both the North and South was almost completely absent in proslavery novels. Yet their racist characterization of blacks reflected an implicit and widespread fear of the consequences of ending slavery on ideas of racial purity among white society.

In the decades after abolition, proslavery novels continued to be published, especially those written in the plantation tradition, which harked back to the supposed glory days of the Southern plantation and slavery. Novelists such as Thomas Nelson Page (*In Ole Virginia,* 1887), Thomas Dixon (*The Clansman,* 1905), and Joel Chandler Harris (*Uncle Remus: His Songs and Sayings,* 1881) favorably contrasted the impoverished and potentially dangerous blacks of the post-Reconstruction years with the happy-go-lucky plantation slaves of the pre–Civil War years. Like their predecessors in the 1850s and 1860s, these writers employed racist stereotypes and dubious interpretations of the reality of the slave system, reflecting long-standing racial prejudices in American literature and society.

Sean Purdy

See also: Novels, Antislavery.

Further Reading

Brophy, Alfred L. " 'Over and Above . . . There Broods a Portentous Shadow, the Shadow of the Law': Harriet Beecher Stowe's Critique of Slave Law in *Uncle Tom's Cabin.*" *Journal of Law and Religion* 13 (1996/1997): 406–512.

Brown, Sterling. *The Negro in American Fiction.* Port Washington, NY: Kennikat, 1937.

Kaplan, Amy. "Nation, Region, and Empire." In *The Columbia History of the American Novel,* ed. Cathy N. Davidson. New York: Columbia University Press, 1991.

O'Connell, Daniel (1775–1847)

Through his leadership of the Irish nationalist movement in the early nineteenth century, Daniel O'Connell helped create nationwide networks that were capable of electing Irish nationalists as Members of Parliament and mobilizing support for campaigns against discriminatory legislation. His life's work was dedicated to the reform of the Irish government and Catholic emancipation, whereby Roman Catholics in the British Isles were relieved of oppressive civil regulations that had been placed on them by statutes dating back to Henry VIII. These efforts earned O'Connell the nickname "the Liberator."

O'Connell was born in County Kerry on August 6, 1775. After a successful career as a lawyer, he formed the Catholic Association in 1823. This organization was aimed at eliminating legal restrictions on the professional posts that Roman Catholics could occupy and the land they could own, as well as repealing the 1801 Act of Union that joined Ireland to Britain politically (after a short period in which there was an Irish parliament). O'Connell was elected as a Member of Parliament in 1828, but as a Roman Catholic, he was prevented from taking his seat. The momentum gained during the campaign, however, contributed to passage of the Catholic Emancipation Act in 1829.

O'Connell's interests extended beyond national issues. As well as being interested in India's colonial situation, he was a committed abolitionist from the mid-1820s on. He used the network of repeal associations to campaign for the abolition of slavery in the United States. In the 1840s, American abolitionists, including Frederick Douglass and Charles Lenox Remond, carried out speaking tours in Ireland and England.

In 1842, the Irish abolitionist movement sent a petition with nearly 60,000 signatures to the United States, calling on Irish Americans to declare their opposition to slavery. O'Connell had signed the petition after meeting Remond in Dublin. The ambivalent response that the petition received from recent immigrants revealed the complexities of their identification with Ireland and America, as well as the marginal social status they occupied in the United States at the time. O'Connell was horrified at the weak response of his compatriots, whom he accused of joining "the filthy aristocracy of skin."

O'Connell's stance on abolition was a combination of principle and expediency. As the leader of the Irish nationalist Members of Parliament, he divided his efforts between advancing the cause of Irish independence and Roman Catholic emancipation and the cause of antislavery. He made an alliance with the British Whig Party to support abolition in return for favorable treatment, yet he could not guarantee that the Irish Members of Parliament would all back the Whigs' antislavery bills. His support for abolition earned him disapprobation not only in the American South but also in New York and other eastern U.S. seaboard towns with close economic links to the South.

O'Connell's relations with American and Irish antislavery organizations (especially the Quaker-dominated Hibernian Anti-Slavery Society) were frequently difficult. Irish nationalists, anxious about the support of America against the British, feared that O'Connell's outspokenness would jeopardize solidarity—or worse, place them in a temporary alliance with the British (who were critical of slavery in the United States after 1838). On the other hand, for many religious abolitionists, slavery was viewed as a sin, and avoiding criticism or backtracking (construed as moral wavering) was equivalent to committing that sin.

In 1843, O'Connell canceled a mass rally at Clontarf to show the British authorities that the repeal movement was not traitorous. The more radical nationalists of the Young Ireland movement interpreted this as a failure of nerve. They criticized his conservative attitude toward social questions and argued that antislavery should not take such a high place on the agenda.

One of the key elements of mid-nineteenth-century Irish nationalism was the move toward armed resistance or physical force against the British. O'Connell rejected this approach, pursuing instead moral force. Moreover, his uncompromising stance on the abolition of slavery threatened to sour relations between Irish Americans and the nationalist movement in Ireland. America was seen as a lucrative source of funding and a rival power to support the cause. O'Connell's unwillingness to sideline the issue may be contrasted with the direction taken by proslavery Young Irelander John Mitchel, for example.

One of the most vocal abolitionists of the transatlantic world, O'Connell did not live to witness the changes he championed. He died in Genoa, Italy, on his way to Rome on May 15, 1847.

Steve Garner

See also: Hibernian Anti-Slavery Society.

Further Reading

Macintyre, Angus D. *The Liberator: Daniel O'Connell and the Irish Party, 1830–1847.* New York: Macmillan, 1965.

Olmsted, Frederick Law (1822–1903)

Best known as the founder of modern landscape architecture and the designer of New York City's Central Park, Olmsted also made significant contributions to the abolitionist movement. His published descriptions of life in the South during the years leading up to the U.S. Civil War helped educate many Northerners about slavery, convincingly showing the institution's deleterious effects on both the physical and social landscape of the region.

Born in Hartford, Connecticut, on April 26, 1822, Olmsted was the son of a wealthy merchant who paid for private tutoring, world travels, apprenticeships, and a farm on Staten Island for the youth. Having inherited a fervid love of natural beauty, horticulture, and landscaping from his father, Olmsted made a career designing some of the most renowned parks, campuses, and estates in the United States.

In the 1850s, Olmsted made two sightseeing trips to the slave states, beginning in Washington, D.C., and ultimately traveling southwest all the way through Texas. He described what he saw to *The New York Times* in a series of letters, which the paper published weekly. In 1856, Olmsted's first collection of Southern writings was published in book form as *A Journey in the Seaboard Slave States; With Remarks on Their Economy,* followed by two more collections, *A Journey Through Texas* (1859) and *A Journey Through the Back Country* (1860).

His musings on slavery and its effects on the Southern people greatly influenced the common perception in the Northern states, especially among abolitionists and Free Soilers, that the South was backward because of its "peculiar institution." His writings, along with those of abolitionists such as Harriet Beecher Stowe and Hinton Rowan Helper, contributed to the rise of the Republican Party, as Northern voters began to see the slavery controversy as more immediate and serious than the nativistic issues espoused by the American (Know-Nothing) Party.

Olmsted also raised funds to support Free Soilers who sought to keep slavery out of Kansas and other Western territories that had not already succumbed to proslavery forces. The Southwest, by virtue of its frontier condition, was a more primitive society than a Northeast sojourner such as Olmsted was accustomed to. Yet Olmsted could only equate the sad state of economic and cultural affairs on the Southwestern frontier to the presence of slavery.

The physical ugliness Olmsted perceived in the Southwest prompted him, upon his return to the North, to try to beautify the cities of the region. In so doing, he believed he could prove the superiority of the North to the South, and, in effect, the free labor system to the slave labor system.

During the Civil War, President Abraham Lincoln appointed Olmsted to head the U.S. Sanitary Commission, which supervised the health and hygiene of Union army camps and hospitals, a position he held until summer 1863. In that capacity, he again traveled to the South, where he observed the helpless condition of 8,000 slaves who had been left behind at Port Royal, South Carolina, when their masters fled before the advance of Union troops. He pleaded with the Lincoln Administration to formulate a comprehensive plan for the slaves' welfare, but no such plan was enacted. Wrangling in the U.S. Congress and among Lincoln's cabinet led to only temporary solutions for such refugees, until the Freedmen's Bureau was created in 1865.

After Lincoln issued the controversial Emancipation Proclamation on January 1, 1863, Olmsted helped organize the Union League Clubs of New York City and Philadelphia in support of the Republican administration. Formed throughout the North, the clubs distributed Civil War literature, raised money for soldier relief, and recruited black and white soldiers for the Union army.

At the same time, Olmsted began working with his partner E.L. Godkin on the creation of a new antislavery publication called the *Nation*. The two finally launched the publication in 1865, with Godkin as editor and Olmsted as assistant editor. Against Olmsted's wishes, Godkin gradually changed the focus of the periodical away from black issues toward Gilded Age political, economic, and social issues.

In the post–Civil War and Reconstruction years, Olmsted returned to his first love, landscaping. During the 1880s, he designed the campus of Stanford University in California; the first public park at Niagara Falls, New York; and the immaculate grounds of the Biltmore Estate in Asheville, North Carolina. He retired in 1895, not realizing that he was to have an even greater impact on posterity than on his own generation.

Although he is remembered mainly for his contributions in the field of landscape architecture, Olmsted's role in precipitating the Civil War and freeing the slaves was perhaps his greatest accomplishment. He died on August 28, 1903.

Thomas Adams Upchurch

See also: Education of Former Slaves; Port Royal Experiment.

Further Reading

Beveridge, Charles E., and Charles Capen McLaughlin, eds. *The Papers of Frederick Law Olmsted.* Vol. 2, *Slavery and the South, 1852–1857.* Baltimore: Johns Hopkins University Press, 1981.

Olmsted, Frederick Law. *A Journey in the Seaboard Slave States; With Remarks on Their Economy.* 1856. Chapel Hill: University of North Carolina Press, 2001.

Schlesinger, Arthur M., ed. *The Cotton Kingdom: A Traveler's Observations on Cotton and Slavery in the American Slave States.* New York: Da Capo, 1996.

White, Dana F., and Victor A. Kramer. *Olmsted South: Old South Critic/New South Planner.* Westport, CT: Greenwood, 1979.

Oroonoko (1688)

The 1688 novel *Oroonoko, or the History of the Royal Slave* was written by Aphra Behn, who is often referred to as the first professional female English writer. By presenting a sympathetic literary portrait of slavery's victims, *Oroonoko* may have indirectly hastened the end of the slave trade and the eventual abolition of slavery in the nineteenth century. The story's popularity is partly attributable to Thomas Southerne's successful 1696 stage adaptation, which was performed throughout the eighteenth century.

Until the twentieth century, Behn's story was considered a condemnation of slavery and a forerunner of Harriet Beecher Stowe's famous antislavery novel *Uncle Tom's Cabin* (1852). Abolitionists considered *Oroonoko* a literary manifesto and praised Behn for her views against slavery. They stressed that Behn had portrayed the slaves as simple yet morally superior to the Christian colonizers, who are presented as hypocritical and untrustworthy. Behn may have shown compassion for her hero's fate, however, the novel cannot avoid sharing the racist and colonial sentiments that were deeply embedded in seventeenth-century English culture.

The plot of the novel, which combines elements of memoir, romance, and exotic travel narrative (perhaps based on Behn's experience in the colony of Suriname in the West Indies), focuses on the noble Oroonoko, the grandson of an African king who falls in love with the beautiful Imoinda, a member of the king's harem. Unfortunately, the king is also in love with Imoinda, and he is so enraged when she tells him that she loves Oroonoko that he sells her into slavery. Oroonoko is captured by an English slaver, and he, too, becomes enslaved.

In the colony of Suriname, Oroonoko and Imoinda are reunited. Oroonoko leads the slaves to revolt against their masters, but they are forced to surrender, and their leader is heavily flogged. The humiliation prompts Oroonoko to seek revenge. Because he knows that his plan will lead to his death, he decides, with her consent, to kill Imoinda so that she will not be left at the mercy of her white owner. When her corpse is found, Oroonoko is still at her side. He is captured and executed.

The modern literary critic Laura Brown points out that *Oroonoko* has been "recognized as a seminal work in the tradition of antislavery writings from the time of its publication down to our own period." Other twentieth-century critics, on the other hand, have been less sympathetic, focusing on the discrepancies and contradictions that obscure a clear rejection of slavery. Indeed, the work never directly criticizes slavery as an institution, though the hero's victimization can be interpreted as an indirect critique.

Whatever its contemporary criticisms, scholars agree that *Oroonoko* played an influential role in the development of the English novel, particularly for its introduction of the idea of the "noble savage," an archetype that would later be developed by the French philosopher and writer Jean-Jacques Rousseau.

Luca Prono

See also: Behn, Aphra; Novels, Antislavery.

Further Reading

Behn, Aphra. *Oroonoko*. Ed. Joanna Lipking. New York: W.W. Norton, 1997.

Brown, Laura. "The Romance of Empire: *Oroonoko* and the Trade in Slaves." In *The New Eighteenth Century*, ed. Felicity Nussbaum and Laura Brown. London: Methuen, 1987.

Ferguson, Margaret. "Juggling the Categories of Race, Class and Gender: Aphra Behn's *Oroonoko*." *Women's Studies* 19 (1991): 159–81.

Hunter, Heidi, ed. *Rereading Aphra Behn: History, Theory, and Criticism*. Charlottesville: University of Virginia Press, 1993.

Ottoman Emancipation

The emancipation of slaves in the Ottoman Empire was a slow, incremental process of restricting the slave-owning class. Emancipation was complicated and delayed by the status of slavery in Islamic law; it had played a fundamental role throughout the Ottoman Empire since its founding in the late fourteenth century.

By the nineteenth century, the *devsirme,* the collection from which the elite Janissary corps of slave soldiers and administrators were selected, had ceased, but the belief that conquered populations were liable to enslavement and the customs surrounding household slavery persisted. Ottoman subjects believed that their form of slavery was particularly humane, because it barred the separation of mothers and children, allowed slaves to pass on property to their children, and forbade forced marriages. Slavery was often based on contracts that allowed manumission after a set term of years or payments, and Ottoman bureaucrats insisted that slavery provided an essential "socialization" of peoples into the Ottoman upper class. The fact that many Ottoman administrators of the nineteenth century were former slaves, or the husbands and children of manumitted slaves, muddied the waters even further.

In 1839, the sultanate took the first steps toward limiting slavery by issuing a royal decree on November 3, restricting the sultan's ability to confiscate estates and execute at will. In 1846, Sultan Abdulmecid ordered the end of the Istanbul slave market, largely because of its rampant corruption and the difficulty of policing it for violations such as selling women into prostitution and dealing in children. In 1847, the slave trade with Egypt was restricted, a move that had less to do with slavery than with reigning in the Mameluk vassal leaders of Egypt, who depended on the slave trade for manpower. Meanwhile, Ottoman generals had ceased enslaving prisoners of war in 1829, and the sultan discouraged tributes of slaves from his vassals in the Crimea and the Persian Gulf.

Under pressure from Great Britain during the Crimean War (1853–1856), the Ottoman state worked to discourage the Georgian-Circassian slave trade in central Asia. This was difficult to accomplish, as the Circassians sold themselves into slavery, often grooming their daughters for harem marriages through this process. The trade in African slaves to the Ottoman Empire was cut off in 1857, when the sultan succumbed to British pressure (though the British were later forced by local tradition to allow Egyptians to continue owning slaves after taking over administration from the caliph in 1882). The actual practice of slavery continued in households and through clandestine buying and selling that was nearly impossible to police.

The Ottoman Empire's 1876 constitution, although short-lived, specified that all subjects were equal under the law and re-issued the 1857 ban on the African trade, but it preserved the Islamic laws on slavery. In 1880, the Ottoman Empire participated in the Brussels Slave Trade Conference, avoiding censure by surrendering to Britain the right of search and seizure on Ottoman vessels. In 1889, the sultan promulgated a law allowing slaves to demand their freedom if they had been sold after 1857 and provided a way to punish slave traders. Freed slave self-help societies, largely geared to African women, were established in Istanbul to assist slaves in going to the police authorities to demand their freedom and to help them set up independent lives.

In 1909, the Young Turks, a group of Western-influenced nationalistic modernizers, returned to the 1876 constitution, officially dismantling the harem of Sultan Abdülhamid II and manumitting hundreds of women, eunuchs, and palace workers. Slavery was gradually phased out, and, by 1920, there were few slaves in Ottoman Turkey. Turkey's 1924 civil constitution and the reforms of Mustafa Kemal Ataturk, the founder of the Turkish Republic and its first president, formally abandoned Islamic law and ended slavery.

Margaret Sankey

Further Reading

Erdem, Y. Hakan. *Slavery in the Ottoman Empire and Its Demise, 1800–1909*. Basingstoke, UK: Palgrave Macmillan, 1996.

Lewis, Bernard. *Race and Slavery in the Middle East*. Oxford, UK: Oxford University Press, 1990.

Toledano, Ehud. *The Ottoman Slave Trade and Its Suppression, 1840–1890.* Princeton, NJ: Princeton University Press, 1982.

Owen, Robert Dale (1801–1877)

A Scottish-born legislator and social reformer, Robert Dale Owen was an advocate of American emancipation in the late 1850s. The son of Robert Owen, founder of the utopian community of New Harmony, Indiana, he was raised with "a belief which existing abuses cannot shake nor worldly scepticism destroy, an abiding faith in human virtue and in social progress." Although his abolitionist views were moderate as a young adult, they became more radical by the beginning of the U.S. Civil War.

Owen was born in Glasgow, Scotland, on November 9, 1801. In 1825, his father, a prominent in-

An inveterate social reformer, newspaper editor, and antislavery politician, Robert Dale Owen is said to have influenced the thinking of President Abraham Lincoln with the arguments in his pamphlet *The Policy of Emancipation. (Hulton Archive/Getty Images)*

dustrial reformer, educational theorist, and socialist, purchased the failed religious commune of Harmony, Indiana. He soon redeveloped the settlement as the utopian community of New Harmony based on his principles of social reform, which included cooperative living and rational education.

In New Harmony, the younger Owen taught school and edited the *New Harmony Gazette.* By July 1826, the elder Owen, an agnostic, had alarmed observers by publishing a "Declaration of Mental Independence," which denounced religion, private property, and marriage. By the following year, the group of intellectuals who formed the core of the community had splintered into separate settlements.

After New Harmony's disintegration, Owen met the abolitionist and women's rights advocate Frances Wright, who, several years prior, had founded Nashoba, a community devoted to the gradual emancipation of slaves, near Memphis, Tennessee. Together, they transformed the *New Harmony Gazette* into a freethinking newspaper, and, by 1830, they were editing the *Free Enquirer,* a New York paper denouncing organized religion and calling for sweeping social change.

Meanwhile, Owen's book *Moral Physiology* (1830) had branded him as a radical supporter of birth control. Despite his radical beliefs on religion and women's rights, Owen's antislavery stance was moderate. He criticized William Lloyd Garrison's belief in immediate abolition of slavery as unrealistic and impractical.

After serving in the Indiana state legislature from 1836 to 1839, Owen successfully ran for a seat in the U.S. House of Representatives as a Democrat in 1843. He became a proponent of Manifest Destiny, supporting sole U.S. possession of the Oregon Territory and the annexation of Texas, for which he was accused of being proslavery. Owen, however, maintained that American liberty would spread through the U.S. acquisition of Texas. Horace Greeley's *New York Tribune* insinuated that Owen had voted against the 1846 Wilmot Proviso—which proposed prohibiting slavery in any lands acquired from Mexico—in order to receive a patronage diplomatic appointment, an allegation that Owen denied.

In 1847, Owen's failure to win a third term in the House prompted him to write several face-saving letters to a Princeton, Indiana, newspaper, the *Democratic Clarion*, denouncing slavery. In addition, he used his position as an Indiana delegate at the 1848 Democratic convention in Indianapolis to deliver an attack on slavery. He dismissed the increasingly popular Free Soil Party stance—which opposed the extension of slavery into the Western territories—as unnecessary, stating the apparent illegality of slavery's spread to new territories. Instead, Owen supported Democratic candidate Lewis Cass, whose concept of popular sovereignty allowed residents to determine whether their territory would have slavery. At the 1851 Indiana constitutional convention, Owen initially supported the right of blacks to vote, but the delegates settled on a clause excluding blacks from settling in the state.

After serving out an appointment as diplomat to the Kingdom of Naples from 1853 to 1859, Owens returned to the United States, which was on the brink of civil war, with a committed abolitionist stance. Three weeks before Abraham Lincoln's inauguration as president in 1861, Owen delivered a speech in the Indiana legislature advocating peace and compromise at all costs. Once Confederate forces attacked Fort Sumter in April 1861, however, he changed his stance: Owen argued that the war should be carried out relentlessly in order to encourage the secessionists to negotiate for reunion. Soon after the war's outbreak, Owen became Indiana's agent for purchasing armaments.

In 1861 and 1862, his position took him east, where he made new abolitionist contacts, including Treasury Secretary Salmon P. Chase. In July 1862, he wrote a letter to Secretary of War Edwin M. Stanton, arguing that the sectional conflict could only end once and for all with the compensated emancipation of all slaves. He also wrote to President Lincoln on September 17 of that year, urging him to end slavery: "It is within your power . . . as the instrument of the Almighty, to restore to freedom a race of men." These letters were published as a part of the pamphlet *The Policy of Emancipation* (1863). Owen's increasingly radical abolitionist stance and his support of Lincoln's 1863 Emancipation Proclamation upset his former Indiana constituency.

Stanton named Owen chair of the American Freedmen's Inquiry Commission, along with James McKaye and Samuel Gridley Howe. The commission inspected the condition of former slaves who had escaped to Union forces. Owen's report on the freedmen in Washington and the Southeast, *Preliminary Report Touching the Condition and Management of Emancipated Refugees,* recommended that the Union army employ refugee slaves in these areas as soldiers and laborers.

A second report, *The Wrong of Slavery, the Right of Emancipation, and the Future of the African Race in the Americas,* published in May 1864, traced the brutal history of slaves in the Americas, optimistically characterized their postwar prospects, and emphasized the importance of equal rights for freed slaves. Although controversial, the report gained supporters, such as abolitionists Wendell Phillips and Lewis Tappan, and eventually contributed to the establishment of the Freedmen's Bureau in 1865.

During the congressional debate over Reconstruction in early 1866, Owen drafted what would become the Fourteenth Amendment, which granted citizenship to recently freed slaves, and submitted it to the Radical Republican Thaddeus Stevens; however, the clause ensuring freedmen's suffrage by 1876 was written out of Owen's proposal in committee. Owen died on June 24, 1877, in Lake George, New York, at the age of seventy-five.

Brian M. Ingrassia

See also: Wright, Frances ("Fanny").

Further Reading

Leopold, Richard William. *Robert Dale Owen: A Biography.* Cambridge, MA: Harvard University Press, 1940.
Owen, Robert Dale. *Threading My Way: Twenty-Seven Years of Autobiography.* 1874. New York: Augustus M. Kelley, 1967.

Pacheco, Luís (1800–1895)

Luís Pacheco was a black slave who worked as an interpreter for the U.S. Army in the 1830s during its military engagements with the Seminoles, a Native American nation in Florida. He later joined the Seminoles, and, after the federal government forcibly removed the majority of that nation to Indian Territory in present-day Oklahoma, he participated in a revolt of black slaves against their Cherokee Indian masters. Pacheco's life illustrates the complex interrelationships among European settlers, black slaves, and indigenous peoples in mid-nineteenth century America.

Pacheco was born in 1800 to African parents on the New Switzerland Plantation in the northern part of the Spanish territory of Florida. He learned to read and speak English, French, and Spanish. Through his brother, who had been raised in a Seminole community, he also learned to speak the Seminole language, which he used to facilitate trade relations between his owner and local natives. Pacheco escaped his master but was later captured; his owner contracted his services as an interpreter to the army in the late 1830s.

The Seminoles were a new Amerindian nation of migrants and refugees formed during the early eighteenth century in Florida by members of the Lower Creek Nation who originally came from Georgia and South Carolina. In the following decades, runaway black slaves from other Southern states also fled to Florida, where they established close personal, cultural, and political ties with the Native Americans. Some blacks intermarried and became full-fledged members of the native communities, some were enslaved, and still others formed autonomous communities connected to the Seminoles by political alliances.

By the early nineteenth century, white American settlement had begun to encroach on the Seminole lands in Florida. The strong black presence among the Seminoles worried whites, and they pressured the U.S. government to intervene. In 1818,

General Andrew Jackson led a force of army troops and allied native warriors into Florida, inflicting military defeat on several Seminole settlements and massacring many civilians. Known as the First Seminole War, the conflict forced the natives to sign a peace treaty and establish a reservation system. The preferred solution for whites, however, was forcible removal, a federal government policy that had begun in the 1820s with Native American nations east of the Mississippi River. Through outright lies and legal sleight-of-hand, government negotiators convinced some Seminoles to agree to removal in 1836, but the majority formed an armed resistance movement.

In 1835, Pacheco was working as an interpreter for U.S. Army Major Francis Dade, who was involved in stamping out Seminole armed resistance to the removal policy. The great Seminole leader Osceola wiped out Dade's column in a major battle, but Pacheco survived. He later would employ his valuable language skills in the service of the Seminoles.

The U.S. Army used its overwhelming military might to crush all armed resistance by 1842, but at a loss of $20 million and 1,500 dead soldiers—the most costly military engagement to that date in U.S. history. A few hundred Seminoles remained hidden in the Everglades, but the vast majority was transported to Oklahoma, where they lived within the larger Creek and Cherokee nations.

Pacheco's history after removal is little known. The Black Seminoles were still under the threat of being enslaved, both by whites and by Indian tribes that had adopted chattel slavery in Oklahoma. There is evidence that Pacheco was living during the late 1840s in a free Afro-Indian community in Oklahoma that provided a safe haven for black slaves who had revolted from their Cherokee masters.

Pacheco's life is an example of the intricate links that developed between some blacks and Native Americans in the early history of the United States. Facing the brutal subjugation of slavery and ethnic cleansing, a significant number of these two oppressed groups united to preserve their unique cultural traditions and customs, eventually establishing Afro-Indian communities that still survive in Texas and Oklahoma.

Sean Purdy

See also: Brazil, Abolition in.

Further Reading

Colburn, David R., and Jane L. Landers. *The African American Heritage of Florida.* Gainesville: University Press of Florida, 1995.

Green, Michael. "The Expansion of European Colonization to the Mississippi Valley, 1780–1880." In *The Cambridge History of the Native Peoples of the Americas,* ed. Bruce G. Trigger and Wilcomb E. Washburn. Cambridge, UK: Cambridge University Press, 1996.

Paine, Thomas (1737–1809)

The Anglo-American writer, philosopher, and abolitionist Thomas Paine is best known for his 1776 pamphlet advocating American independence, *Common Sense.*

Paine was born in Thetford, England, on January 29, 1737. His mother, Frances, belonged to the Church of England, and his father, Joseph, was a Quaker. Paine's Quaker heritage is clearly reflected in his later writings and humanitarian ideals.

After completing a basic education and working at various trades, Paine gained employment as a collector of excise taxes, a position from which the British government dismissed him on two separate occasions. His experience as a tax collector inspired his first inflammatory writing on behalf of improved working conditions and higher salaries for excise men. His controversial tracts on the subjects of liberty, equality, and education made Paine a household name in both Britain and America by the end of the eighteenth century.

Paine immigrated to America in 1774, encouraged by Benjamin Franklin, whom he had met in London. Upon arriving in the colonies, Paine became an avid supporter of the American cause, writing on behalf of independence and donating his time and finances to assist the Continental army. His pamphlet *Common Sense* played a decisive role in persuading members of the Continental Congress, as well as common folk throughout the colonies, to choose independence from Great Britain over reconciliation. Throughout the American Revolution, Paine linked the colonial struggle for independence with the plight of slaves,

The revolutionary firebrand Thomas Paine argued against slavery from before the nation's founding. He compared the plight of slaves to the colonial struggle for independence. *(Time & Life Pictures/Getty Images)*

writing a number of articles that illuminated the similarities between the two issues.

A letter of introduction from Franklin helped Paine to obtain employment as co-editor of the *Pennsylvania Magazine.* His radical views increased the magazine's distribution but instigated a conflict with its proprietor, Robert Aitkin. The *Pennsylvania Journal* published Paine's first antislavery article, "African Slavery in America," in 1775. Aitkin would not allow the article to appear in *Pennsylvania Magazine,* because he felt Paine's assessment of slavery was too extreme for his magazine's audience. Signed "Justice and Humanity," the editorial denounced slavery and proclaimed the intelligence and abilities of blacks, a highly volatile subject in the late eighteenth century. Paine argued that the slave trade opposed Christianity and that references made by proslavery advocates to the history of slavery among the Jews were unbiblical. His diatribe against the evils of human bondage labeled Britain as the chief perpetrator of slavery. Paine blamed Europeans for introducing Africans to alcohol and found Americans culpable for allowing the slave trade to continue.

One month later, shortly after the publication of "African Slavery in America," Paine joined other abolitionists in forming the first antislavery society in America. Founded in Philadelphia, the Pennsylvania Society for Promoting the Abolition of Slavery boasted a membership of colonial elites such as Franklin and Benjamin Rush. Paine continued to promote the emancipation of slavery within the colonies, publishing *A Serious Thought* in October 1775, in which he described slavery as "the most horrid of all traffics, that of human flesh." Certain that America would break way from Great Britain, Paine, writing under the pseudonym "Humanus," proposed that Americans show their gratefulness to God by emancipating slaves.

As Paine's writings gained attention in both revolutionary and antislavery circles, he became the focus of a heated debate in the Pennsylvania elections of 1779. His radical abolitionist views made him a source of dissension during the campaign, even though he was not himself a candidate for office. When the Pennsylvania Assembly met for the first time after the elections on November 2, 1779, it elected Paine to the position of clerk. Shortly thereafter, it passed a bill requiring the gradual emancipation of slaves in the state. Paine contributed to the legislation by authoring the preamble to the Act for the Gradual Abolition of Slavery, passed by the Pennsylvania Assembly on March 1, 1780. Although he had hoped for immediate emancipation, Paine took great pride in the bill, considering it the first step toward universal emancipation.

American success in the Revolutionary War did not end Paine's resolve to free the subjugated peoples of his own land. During the early nineteenth century, he turned his attention to the brewing conflict among the French citizens of Louisiana, who demanded statehood and the freedom to use African slaves for labor. Paine responded to the French complaints in an article that Virginia congressman John Randolph ordered printed and distributed to the inhabitants of the state. In the tract, Paine rebuked the residents of Louisiana for claiming the right to statehood and the protection of the United States while refusing the same rights to slaves. When Robert Livingston and James Monroe completed the Louisiana Purchase in 1803, Thomas Jefferson solicited Paine's advice on the matter of slavery within the newly acquired territory.

Although Paine did not write extensively on slavery after the American Revolution, he continued to promote equality and emancipation for oppressed persons throughout the remainder of his life. He spent his last years in New York City, where he read daily and wrote on behalf of various causes. He requested a burial plot in a local Quaker cemetery, but the church refused his application, because he was a deist. Paine died in New York City on June 8, 1809, and was buried at his farm in nearby New Rochelle.

Melinda M. Hicks

See also: American Revolution (1775–1781); Quakers (Society of Friends).

Further Reading

Edwards, Samuel. *Rebel! A Biography of Tom Paine.* New York: Praeger, 1974.

Foot, Michael, and Isaac Kramnick, eds. *The Thomas Paine Reader.* New York: Penguin, 1987.

Keane, John. *Tom Paine: A Political Life.* New York: Grove, 2003.

Paine, Thomas. *The Complete Writings of Thomas Paine.* Ed. Philip S. Foner. New York: Citadel, 1945.

Palladium of Liberty, The

Ohio's oldest known black newspaper, *The Palladium of Liberty* was published weekly by the African American abolitionist David Jenkins from December 27, 1843, until November 13, 1844. "It may be argued by some," the first issue stated, "that a press cannot affect anything; but we look to the press for future good . . . and hope through it to affect much [to] ameliorate our condition." It was a mission to which the paper adhered to throughout its brief period of publication.

Jenkins was born in Lynchburg, Virginia, in 1821. His father was either a white slaveholder or a free black man who provided a tutor for his son's education, though the education was informal and imperfect. Jenkins moved to Columbus, Ohio, in 1837 and worked as a successful self-employed house painter, glazier, and paper hanger, as well as a farmer and barber.

He was active in the Underground Railroad during a time when Ohio enforced a strict policy of social segregation and discrimination. Under a series of Black Laws enacted in 1803, African Americans were forbidden to use public institutions, were not allowed to vote, and their testimony was limited in the courts. Jenkins sought to change this by arguing for the assimilation of free blacks into society and by advocating the abolition of slavery.

The paper was inspired by the August 1843 Ohio State Convention of Colored People, which Jenkins had convened. He founded *The Palladium* with a group of free blacks from the Columbus area. Generally running only four pages in length and poorly written and edited, it nonetheless was a powerful voice throughout Ohio and the Northeast.

The Palladium discussed moral as well as political issues and commented on such social concerns as the education of African American children, temperance, and civil and voting rights for free blacks. It featured articles on fugitive slaves, the annexation of Texas, laws against free blacks, educational opportunity, the slave trade, colonization, and presidential candidates. It promoted respect for black womanhood and urged free black men to educate their children, as in this appeal published April 17, 1844:

> We call upon our colored brethren through out our entire country, to educate their children and give them mechanical trades. The great evil among us is this, when our children get large enough to put to trades, at this time the parent thinks that his boy, or boys can do him much good; in this way his sons are raised up to manhood without education.

The newspaper reported on the meetings and celebrations of concerned African Americans, particularly in Columbus. It also published an assortment of poetry, petitions, and letters to the editor while providing editorial commentary on issues that affected African American life. *The Palladium* enjoyed wide circulation throughout Ohio and parts of Pennsylvania, New York, Massachusetts, Indiana, and Michigan.

Charles A. D'Aniello

See also: Underground Railroad; U.S. Colored Troops.

Further Reading

Bell, Howard H., ed. *Minutes of the Proceedings of the National Negro Conventions, 1830–1864.* New York: Arno, 1969.

Foner, Philip S., and George E. Walker, eds. *Proceedings of the Black State Conventions, 1840–1865.* Vol. 1, *New York, Pennsylvania, Indiana, Michigan, Ohio.* Philadelphia: Temple University Press, 1969.

Ripley, C. Peter, et al., eds. *The Black Abolitionist Papers.* 5 vols. Chapel Hill: University of North Carolina Press, 1985–1992.

Palmares

The Negro Republic of Palmares was established in northeastern Brazil in 1603 and rapidly became the largest community of runaway slaves in the Americas. In the seventeenth century, the most common display of slave resistance in Brazil was the establishment of fugitive slave settlements, commonly known as *quilombos* in Portuguese and *cimarrones* in Spanish. During the 1630s, civil wars between the Portuguese and Dutch settlers in northern Brazil contributed to the high number of runaway slaves and consequently to the growth of quilombo communities. Slaves from the captaincies of Pernambuco and Bahia escaped their plantations and villages to organize their own communities. Palmares was established in the captaincy of Alagoas. The name "Palmares" derives from its location in an isolated forested area where palm trees were abundant.

Fugitive slaves developed self-ruling communities in the mountains of Brazil. They selected remote locations with strategic geographic advantages that allowed them to defend their settlements from invasion. Palmares flourished into a semi-autonomous kingdom, larger than any other quilombo in Brazil; historians estimate that its population reached 20,000 fugitive slaves. The community included people of African ancestry, mostly from the territory that is modern-day Angola and the Congo. Because most of the runaway slaves were men, they frequently raided nearby plantations for women.

Given its large population, Palmares was not a single village but a collection of settlements ruled by a group of local chiefs and a commonly selected king. Residents attempted to develop egalitarian communities following their African customs, although they also incorporated aspects of European, Indian, and Catholic social practice. Their economic structure relied on slash-and-burn agriculture for subsistence, but they also ventured into nearby farms, markets, and villages to trade their surplus produce for other basic necessities, as well as for rifles and ammunition for their defense.

Palmares survived from 1603 to 1694, during which time it endured periodic attacks from both the Portuguese and Dutch colonial powers. The Dutch viewed Palmares as a threat, and, from 1644 to 1645, under the command of Rodolfo Baro, they made several failed attempts to destroy and take control of the settlements. Palmares suffered significant losses during the Dutch military raids, but the communities were quickly rebuilt.

The Portuguese attacked the region again in 1676 and managed to destroy most of it. Nevertheless, the former slaves persevered and rebuilt Palmares once again. During the decade of the 1670s, Palmares was under attack almost every year, prompting its leaders to consider a peace agreement with the new governor of Pernambuco in 1678.

The persistence of the quilombos and the danger of slave revolts posed a serious threat to the Portuguese Crown in Brazil during the seventeenth century. These rebel communities undermined the institution of slavery and colonial rule in the northern part of the country. Initially, the Portuguese military attempted to offer peace treaties. The leaders of the runaway slave communities quickly rejected these treaties, as their main stipulation was that all slaves return to their masters. As a result, most of the small quilombos were overpowered and destroyed by the Portuguese military in a massive show of force.

King Ganga Zumba of Palmares signed a peace treaty with the Portuguese in 1678 that would have allowed the settlement to remain intact but to return any other slaves who arrived in the future. It quickly became obvious, however, that the Portuguese had no intention of following the stipulations of the agreement. The treaty was not well accepted in Palmares, and the king's nephew, Zumbi, ordered his uncle's execution and took the throne himself. He immediately nullified the peace treaty and refused to make any further deals with the Portuguese colonial leaders.

Finally, in 1685, the *bandeirante* Domingos Jorge Velho of São Paolo received authorization to destroy Palmares completely. In February 1694, the largest quilombo in Brazil was defeated after a two-year-long battle in which thousands of runaway slaves died, and many others committed suicide rather than capitulate. In the aftermath of the battle, more slaves were captured and eventually sold again in another captaincy of Brazil.

Zumbi, the king of Palmares at the time, managed to escape the brutal attack, but he was later caught on November 25, 1695. He was decapitated and his head displayed in the public square to send a clear message: Do not challenge the slavery system in Brazil.

The quilombos in Brazil eventually came to an end when Princess Regent Isabel of Brazil signed the *Lei Áurea* (Golden Law) on May 13, 1888, abolishing slavery in the country. Even though slavery had declined in importance by the time the law was signed, Brazil had the infamous reputation of being the last nation in the Western Hemisphere to abolish slavery.

Javier A. Galván

See also: Fugitive Slaves; *Lei Áurea* (Golden Law, 1888); Maroons.

Further Reading

Conrad, Robert E. *Children of God's Fire: A Documentary History of Black Slavery in Brazil.* Princeton, NJ: Princeton University Press, 1983.

Meltzer, Milton. *Slavery: A World History.* New York: Da Capo, 1993.

Schwartz, Stuart B. *Slaves, Peasants, and Rebels.* Urbana: University of Illinois Press, 1992.

Palmerston Act (1839)

The Palmerston Act was a measure enacted by the British Parliament to suppress the international slave trade by granting British naval vessels the unilateral right to stop and search Portuguese ships suspected of involvement in the transport of slaves. The legislation was prompted by the Portuguese government's refusal to cooperate with the British in efforts to end the trade.

After abolishing the slave trade within the British Empire in 1807, the British government led an attempt to end the international slave trade. It deployed naval units to suppress the trade, but in order to stop the ships of other countries, the British had to arrange treaties with those nations. If negotiated, the treaties allowed ships of the Royal Navy to stop and seize any ships that were carrying, loading, or unloading slaves. In addition, through a treaty provision known as the "equipment clause," British ships could also stop and impound ships that were outfitted as slaving vessels. Hence, if a ship was en route to buy slaves, it could be stopped and seized.

By 1838, the only major powers that had not signed broad antislavery treaties with Great Britain were Portugal and the United States. In 1815 and again in 1817, the Portuguese signed antislavery treaties with the British that allowed the Royal Navy to search and seize Portuguese ships involved in the slave trade north of the equator; the treaties did not cover ships sailing south of the equator.

Portugal's two main slave-exporting colonies in Africa, Mozambique and Angola, and its main slave-importing colony, Brazil, all lay below the equator. After Brazil became independent in 1822, Portugal remained the main supplier of slaves to the new nation. Because the overwhelming majority of its slave trade occurred below the equator, Portugal's treaties with Great Britain were essentially meaningless. Enforcement of other existing antislavery treaties was complicated for the British because ships from other nations would use Portuguese or American flags in an effort to trick the Royal Navy's antislavery patrols.

eighteen months) widened British abolitionist aims beyond the West Indies. The same year, following the death of Britain's leading abolitionist, William Wilberforce, Price wrote an introduction to one of his works and a memoir of him. Price made a successful series of public lectures on religious history, published in 1836 as *A History of Protestant Nonconformity in England from the Reformation under Henry VIII.*

New controversy erupted in 1835, when Baptist minister F.A. Cox, a noted abolitionist, on a deputation from the Baptist Union with instructions to admonish slavery in America, bowed to proslavery pressure and abstained from speaking on the issue. Price knew Cox well but became one of his fiercest critics.

As a result of throat disease, by 1836, Price could no longer preach and resigned the pulpit, but he continued campaigning with his pen. In July 1836 he launched a new monthly, *Slavery in America,* a "magazine of information" that chronicled the development of transatlantic abolitionist thought. Its aim was to link British and American abolitionism through the publication of narratives, statistics, and reports, especially resolutions by British churches supporting religious pressure on their American brethren.

In 1836, Price published a letter by escaped slave Moses Roper and organized meetings for him during his visit to Britain. Thus, Price naturally stood in as a replacement editor for Roper's autobiography, writing the preface to his *Narrative of the Adventures and Escape of Moses Roper,* published in London in 1837.

Originally, the emphasis of Price's monthly magazine was on American slavery, but as it published more accounts of slavery worldwide, it showed that Britain was still deeply implicated, leading Price to question its relevance. After thirteen months, he ended the publication.

In 1837, Price became the editor and proprietor of the *Eclectic Review,* a widely read Nonconformist literary periodical. He edited the *Review* for the next nineteen years, using it to question the British political establishment and review abolitionist works. In 1839, Price became a founder and energetic committee member of the British and Foreign Anti-Slavery Society, which espoused universal abolitionism. In 1844, he also helped found the Liberation Society, which advocated stronger Nonconformist political pressure on the Anglican establishment.

Beginning in 1848, Price suffered from heart disease. His poor health further reduced his public activities, until his death in 1868.

Gwilym Games

See also: Jamaica, Abolition in; Jamaica Rebellion (1831–1832).

Further Reading

Harwood, Thomas F. "British Evangelical Abolitionism and American Churches in the 1830s." *Journal of Southern History* 28 (August 1962): 287–306.

Priestley, Joseph (1733–1804)

One of the great men of science in the eighteenth century, known chiefly for the discovery of oxygen, Joseph Priestley was an intellectual of substantial range who taught classics and literature, wrote extensively on radical theology, and was an ordained minister. He is regarded as a founder of both English Unitarianism and the modern science of chemistry. A lifelong abolitionist, he also wrote an influential pamphlet advocating the end of the slave trade.

The eldest son of a cloth dresser, Priestley was born in Yorkshire, England, on March 13, 1733. His mother died when he was six years old, at which time his father sent him to live with a wealthy aunt. He attended a Calvinist academy, where he studied classical languages, but left school early because of poor health. He chose to pursue a career in the clergy and was ordained as a Calvinist minister at the age of twenty-two.

Priestley's relations with his congregation were impaired by his increasingly heterodox religious views, which eventually led him to embrace Unitarianism. In 1761, he left the ministry to teach at the Warrington Academy, an intellectually rigorous institution referred to as the Athens of the north of England. It was at Warrington that he first became interested in science and befriended Benjamin Franklin. He published his first scientific treatise, *The History and Present State of Electricity,* in 1767, and subsequent work at a brewery in Leeds inspired his interest in gases.

From 1767 to 1791, Priestley returned to and left the ministry several times and served as the librarian for the earl of Shelburne. It was a period of active writing and publishing during which he produced his most significant political work, *An Essay on the First*

A scientist and theologian best known as the discoverer of oxygen and founder of English Unitarianism, Joseph Priestley also wrote a powerful and widely read sermon against the slave trade in 1788. (*©National Portrait Gallery, London, UK/The Bridgeman Art Library*)

Principles of Government (1768), a defense of political liberty that influenced the political philosopher and founder of utilitarianism, Jeremy Bentham.

Having written *History of the Corruptions of Christianity* (1782) and being a vocal supporter of both the American and French revolutions, Priestley saw his home and laboratory in Birmingham burned in 1791 by a mob that feared his radicalism. Three years later, he and his family fled to the United States. There, he was feted as a man of science by Thomas Jefferson and George Washington, among others. He eventually settled in Northumberland, Pennsylvania, where he spent much of the rest of his life.

Priestley was committed to the antislavery cause throughout his adult life. He was a member of the Lunar Society, an informal group of men of letters who met in Manchester on the Monday nearest the full moon. Although it was not a political organization, members of the Lunar Society were advocates of some of the most politically advanced sentiments of the day, including the antislavery cause; a number of members, such as Thomas Day and Erasmus Darwin, were prominent abolitionists. Though his personal correspondence is filled with references to the evils of slavery, Priestley published only one work on the subject, a sermon that he delivered when a petition was circulating in Birmingham calling for abolition.

Priestley's *Sermon on the Subject of the Slave Trade* (1788) was a broad attack on the institution of slavery. Although many of his contemporaries in the abolitionist movement had trouble believing that Africans were their moral equals, Priestley emphasized the common humanity of Africans and Europeans. He implicitly condemned the position of fellow Lunar Society member and inventor James Watt, who, though a critic of slavery, sold his steam engine to slave owners in the West Indies. For Priestley, the moral argument against slavery superseded any prospect of economic gain or advantage. He regarded slavery as more than a crime committed by the slave trader or plantation owner but also an indictment of all those who benefited from it—those "who in order to have our sugars and other West-India commodities, a little cheaper, connive at, and encourage, these iniquitous proceedings."

Priestley died on February 6, 1804, in Northumberland, Pennsylvania.

Kenneth Pearl

See also: Day, Thomas.

Further Reading

Clark, John Ruskin. *Joseph Priestley: A Comet in the System.* Northumberland, PA: Friends of Joseph Priestley House, 1994.

Gibbs, F.W. *Joseph Priestley: Revolutions of the Eighteenth Century.* Garden City, NY: Doubleday, 1967.

Graham, Jenny. *Revolutionary in Exile: The Emigration of Joseph Priestley to America, 1794–1804.* Philadelphia: American Philosophical Society, 1995.

Prigg v. Pennsylvania (1842)

A landmark in the ongoing controversy over fugitive slaves in America, the court case *Prigg v. Pennsylvania* (1842), which arose from an interstate dispute over runaway slave Margaret Morgan, served as the first legal test of the Fugitive Slave Law of 1793. The case's progression from the lower courts to the highest court in the land was rapid. An act of the Pennsylvania Assembly attached special importance to the *Prigg* case, which pushed the appeals process—and the case—directly to the U.S. Supreme Court.

In 1837, four men, including slave catcher Edward Prigg, entered York County, Pennsylvania, from Maryland seeking to reclaim Morgan, a fugitive slave. Morgan had arrived in the state five years earlier from Harford County, Maryland, with her free black husband. In accordance with Pennsylvania's personal liberty laws, Prigg and his associates obtained a warrant for her capture from a local justice of the peace. Under an 1826 Pennsylvania fugitive slave law, such a warrant was necessary, because the state extended the right of habeas corpus to persons of color.

After finally apprehending Morgan, Prigg returned to the local justice to have the case heard and to establish Morgan's status as a slave. The justice stunned Prigg when he refused any further consideration of the case. (Mistakenly, the local justice of the peace had made the warrant returnable to himself, a technical violation of Pennsylvania's 1826 law.)

Either unable or unwilling to wait for another warrant, Prigg and his company left Pennsylvania and returned to Maryland with the captured runaway. In doing so, they forcibly and unlawfully took the woman from the Commonwealth of Pennsylvania with the intention of selling her or otherwise disposing of her into slavery. A Pennsylvania court indicted Prigg and his associates on charges of kidnapping, but despite repeated requests, the governor of Maryland refused to extradite the four men.

Only after further negotiation did the two states reach an agreement. Maryland extradited Prigg on the condition that any verdict in the case could be automatically appealed to the U.S. Supreme Court. In 1840, twelve jurors in a Pennsylvania trial found Prigg guilty of kidnapping, a conviction that was upheld by the Pennsylvania Supreme Court in 1841.

By 1842, the case had reached the U.S. Supreme Court, where the state of Maryland argued that Pennsylvania's fugitive slave law interfered with a slave owner's right to property and therefore was unconstitutional. The U.S. Constitution clearly supported the right to slave property in Article IV, Section 2, which declared that a slaveholder need only claim his or her slaves for them to be delivered. But the clause was ambiguous as to who held the right of enforcement.

In 1793, the U.S. Congress had enacted legislation under the federal Fugitive Slave Law to amend the Constitution. Under this legislation, Maryland argued that Pennsylvania's law was unconstitutional. Pennsylvania countered that the Fugitive Slave Law had failed to account for free persons of color who held the right of habeas corpus within its borders.

Thus, the legal challenge boiled down to a question of states' rights versus federal powers.

According to the Court's decision, written by Justice Joseph Story, the Fugitive Slave Law of 1793 was constitutional, and all state fugitive slave laws therefore violated rather than supported the Constitution. He further concluded that only federal authorities were legally compelled to enforce the Fugitive Slave Law and that the states were not required to participate in the process of returning fugitive slaves. Although all of the justices concurred with Story that Pennsylvania's statute violated the Constitution, they disagreed as to why the statute was inviolate and wrote seven individual decisions.

Controversial from beginning to end, the case only exacerbated tensions between the free and slave states and prompted the passage of personal liberty laws in the North, whereby states could avoid enforcing the unpopular federal law within their jurisdictions. Angry Southerners responded by pressing for congressional action, leading to the more restrictive Fugitive Slave Law of 1850, which forbade states from interfering in the capture of fugitive slaves.

Timothy Konhaus

See also: Fugitive Slave Act of 1793; Personal Liberty Laws.

Further Reading

Burke, Joseph C. "What Did the *Prigg* Decision Really Decide?" *Pennsylvania Magazine of History and Biography* 93 (January 1969): 73–85.

Finkelman, Paul. "Story Telling on the Supreme Court: *Prigg v. Pennsylvania* and Justice Joseph Story's Judicial Nationalism." *Supreme Court Review* (1994): 247–94.

Morris, Thomas D. *Free Men All: The Personal Liberty Laws of the North, 1780–1861.* Baltimore: Johns Hopkins University Press, 1974.

Nogee, Joseph L. "The *Prigg* Case and Fugitive Slavery, 1842–1850." *Journal of Negro History* 39 (July 1954): 185–93.

Pritchard, "Gullah" Jack (?–1822)

Jack Pritchard, known as "Gullah Jack," was a slave and religious leader associated with the 1822 slave insurrection organized by the free black tradesman and lay pastor Denmark Vesey in Charleston, South Carolina. Gullah Jack reputedly used his skills as a conjurer to convince the slaves who participated in the conspiracy that they would be invincible to harm from whites. The slave revolt of 1822 was one of the largest ever planned, involving an estimated 9,000 slaves. In the aftermath, Gullah Jack was one of the thirty-five men sentenced to death for their participation.

Historians believe that Gullah Jack arrived in Charleston in 1806 after having been taken as a prisoner of war in East Africa and sold into slavery. Soon after his arrival, Gullah Jack began to labor for his master, Paul Pritchard, in his carpentry shop at the Charleston wharves. During the period from 1803 to 1808, nearly 39,000 African slaves were imported into the American South. Many of them passed through Charleston's wharves or nearby entry points.

After the suppression of religious activity at the African Methodist Episcopal (AME) Church in 1818, Gullah Jack joined with Vesey to form a conspiratorial circle among a section of skilled slave artisans. Their plan for violent insurrection took shape as blacks, who dominated the AME Church and outnumbered whites in Charleston, believed they had some chance of success because of their large population.

The group's morale was further bolstered by Gullah Jack's use of protective amulets and charms, which ostensibly made the slaves immune from death. Conjurers such as Gullah Jack, who appealed to slaves through their native religions, were both highly esteemed and feared in the slave community. The insurgents' ability to use conjuring techniques also led some slaves to believe that the conspirators in Charleston could rely on military assistance from the free black republic of Haiti. All that remained was for the insurgents to make the first move or conjure this assistance into existence.

The conspiracy was discovered days before the insurrection was to begin. Gullah Jack was arrested and tried. According to testimony given at his trial, he had been involved in directing several aspects of the conspiracy, including finding housing for insurgents coming from outlying plantations, organizing a band of insurgents under his leadership, and developing a plan to poison the water supply of the whites. The most widely cited example of Jack's use of conjure came from testimony about his distribution of crab claws to members of his band of insurgents. He had instructed them that by inserting the claws into their mouths, they would become invincible to the bullets of their white opponents. Sentenced to death on July 9, 1822, Gullah Jack was executed on July 12.

Gullah Jack's ability to combine African religious thought and notions of freedom inspired by the Haitian Revolution is an important example of how Charleston's slave community hoped to win its freedom through force. In the end, however, the words of the judge at Gullah Jack's conspiracy trial rang true: "You represented yourself as invulnerable . . . and that all who fought under your banner would be invincible. . . . Your boasted charms have not preserved yourself and of course could not preserve others."

William A. Wharton

See also: Haitian Revolution (1791–1804); Vesey, Denmark.

Further Reading

Kennedy, Lionel H., and Thomas Parker, eds. "An Official Report of the Trials of Sundry Negroes, Charged with an Attempt to Raise an Insurrection in the State of South Carolina." In *The Trial Record of Denmark Vesey,* introduction by John Oliver Killens. Boston: Beacon, 1970.

Raboteau, Albert J. *Slave Religion: The "Invisible Institution" in the Antebellum South.* Oxford, UK: Oxford University Press, 1978.

Silverman, Susan S., and Lois A. Walker, eds. *A Documented History of Gullah Jack Pritchard and the Denmark Vesey Slave Insurrection of 1822.* Lewiston, NY: Edwin Mellen, 2000.

Smith, Theophus H. *Conjuring Culture: Biblical Formations of Black America.* Oxford, UK: Oxford University Press, 1994.

Prosser, Gabriel (ca. 1775–1800)

Gabriel Prosser was the leader of an unsuccessful Virginia slave rebellion in late summer 1800. The plan for the rebellion centered on taking Richmond by force and kidnapping the governor of the state so that, as Prosser stated, "We might conquer the white people and possess ourselves of their property." This revolutionary vision of a new society—with Gabriel at its head—was foiled by inclement weather and by two slaves revealing the plot to authorities. The discovery of the plot and its subsequent suppression led to the deaths of dozens of rebels and precipitated a heightened state of alert among whites in Virginia and other slave states in the U.S. South.

Gabriel was born on the plantation of slave owner Thomas Prosser in Henrico County, Virginia, on the eve of the American Revolution. The Prosser plantation was located just six miles north of Richmond, Virginia, a thriving city of roughly 5,000 by 1800. Richmond served a dual role during the early nineteenth century as the seat of local and state government and the trade center for plantations throughout Henrico County and neighboring regions.

By the time he turned twenty-four, Gabriel had become a literate blacksmith and, because of the trusting relationship he had with his owner, was allowed much mobility. Gabriel frequently visited Richmond to hire out his services to whites. This freedom brought him into contact with ideas and individuals that helped in the formulation of his conspiracy to end slavery in Virginia.

Described as a man of considerable stature, physical strength, and intelligence, Gabriel was respected by both slaves and whites. His literacy, apparently the result of efforts by Prosser's wife, allowed Gabriel to receive inspiration from the Bible, as well as the political rhetoric of classical liberalism. The freedom of movement he enjoyed as a trusted craftsman put Gabriel into contact with radical French immigrants, disgruntled slaves, and free blacks throughout Richmond. The infectious revolutionary zeal generated by the American, French, and Haitian revolutions in the last decades of the eighteenth century provided additional ideological motivation to the young slave.

Despite his relatively high status and rank, by early 1799, Gabriel apparently had begun making plans to organize a slave insurrection. After a violent clash occurred with a white overseer on a neighboring plantation, Gabriel—who had escaped the encounter unscathed—may have viewed this incident as the proverbial last straw.

When Absalom Johnson, an overseer working on Colonel Nathaniel Wilkinson's nearby plantation, assaulted a slave named Jupiter for reportedly stealing a hog, Gabriel and his brother Solomon confronted Johnson. Solomon threatened to set fire to the overseer's property, and Gabriel physically assaulted him, biting off a portion of Johnson's left ear. Less than a year later, the two brothers would conspire in the Richmond uprising; as court officials later revealed, the conspirators involved in the 1800 plot specifically targeted Johnson as one of the first whites they would kill.

Their plan to take Richmond was remarkable in its sophistication. Bolstered by the skills that both Gabriel and Solomon had as blacksmiths, the conspirators planned to make, buy, or steal hundreds of weapons. According to trial testimony, dozens of swords were crafted from scythe blades and ploughshares, and Jupiter agreed to provide his master's keys to one of Richmond's arsenals.

The outbreak of violence was to begin on August 30, 1800, at midnight. Although Gabriel claimed that some 2,000 men had joined the plot, in all likelihood, fewer combatants were recruited. After the Prosser plantation and neighboring estates were sacked, the combatants would descend on Richmond in multiple waves. Once lower Richmond was set ablaze, the slaughter of whites would commence. In one version of the plan, all whites except for the French, Quakers, Methodists, poor, and non-slaveholding women were to be killed. In addition, all white men who were spared would have one arm amputated. The rebels also planned to attack the city arsenal, the penitentiary, and the governor's house and to capture the current governor, James Monroe. Once Richmond was taken, Gabriel would become the "king" of Virginia, and a provisional government would be established. Afterward, he would work to negotiate or force an end to slavery throughout the state.

On the day of the intended rebellion, two events undermined the plans laid out by Gabriel and his followers. First, two slaves owned by Mosby Sheppard—Tom and Pharaoh—betrayed the plot to their master. The same day, Sheppard managed to inform Governor Monroe of the impending danger. Immediately, Monroe ordered nearby militia units to strategic locations throughout Richmond. Even with these swift and decisive actions, Richmond may not have been spared if not for a second event that destroyed all hopes of a successful revolt. Just after sunset, the area around Richmond witnessed a torrential rainfall that washed away bridges and flooded some of the major roads between Prosser's plantation and Richmond.

Despite the inclement weather, several hundred slaves armed with clubs, scythe-swords, knives, and guns reportedly assembled at designated rendezvous locations. Once the attack was delayed, however, scores of men were arrested and Gabriel was forced into hiding. While attempting to escape the area on a schooner named *Mary*, Gabriel was captured in Norfolk in September 1800.

Despite interrogation by Governor Monroe, Gabriel provided no additional information, and he was sentenced and executed on October 7. Almost two dozen fellow conspirators received the same fate, and dozens of others were transported out of state, pardoned, or found not guilty. The state of Virginia reimbursed the owners of the condemned slaves almost $9,000 for their losses.

Gabriel Prosser and the slave conspiracy to take Richmond served as a warning and a wake-up call for the slaveholding South, which would see a similar attempt near New Orleans in 1811, an attempt by Denmark Vesey in South Carolina in 1822, and a significant slave revolt led by Nat Turner in Virginia in

1831. With each rebellion, the states responded with force and increased regulations further limiting the freedoms of their enslaved populations as well as the free black community.

Walter Rucker

See also: Mott, James, and Lucretia Coffin Mott; Turner, Nat.

Further Reading

Aptheker, Herbert. *American Negro Slave Revolts.* New York: International Publishers, 1993.

Carroll, Joseph Cephas. *Slave Insurrections in the United States, 1800–1865.* 1938. New York: Negro Universities Press, 1968.

Egerton, Douglas R. *Gabriel's Rebellion: The Virginia Slave Conspiracies of 1800 and 1802.* Chapel Hill: University of North Carolina Press, 1993.

Mullin, Michael. *Africa in America: Slave Acculturation and Resistance in the American South and the Caribbean, 1736–1831.* Chicago: University of Chicago Press, 1992.

Schwarz, Philip. "Gabriel's Challenge: Slaves and Crime in Late Eighteenth-Century Virginia." *Virginia Magazine of History and Biography* 90 (July 1982): 283–87.

Sidbury, James. *Ploughshares into Swords: Race, Rebellion, and Identity in Gabriel's Virginia, 1730–1810.* New York: Cambridge University Press, 1997.

Tate, W. Carrington. "Gabriel's Insurrection." *Henrico County Historical Society Magazine* 3 (Fall 1979): 13–15.

Pugh, Sarah (1800–1884)

An abolitionist and a suffragist, Sarah Pugh was most closely associated with the Philadelphia Female Anti-Slavery Society, the vanguard of female grassroots organizing in the mid-nineteenth-century antislavery movement and the model for many other female abolitionist groups of the era. Her work with early women's rights activist Lucretia Mott helped build awareness of the nascent women's movement. Although she was not as famous as other women abolitionists, Pugh played a prominent role in the Philadelphia Female Anti-Slavery Society, and her enduring commitment to African American freedom secured her a place of importance in the history of the American antislavery movement.

She was born in Virginia in 1800 to Jessie and Catherine Pugh. Her father died while she was a child, prompting Sarah and her mother to move in with her maternal grandfather, in Philadelphia, Pennsylvania. Her grandfather was an early abolitionist, and his antislavery stance had a great influence on his young granddaughter. At the age of twelve, Sarah entered the Westtown Boarding School, and in 1821, she began teaching at the Society of Friends Twelfth Street Meeting House. She remained there until 1828, when she started her own school with a friend, Rachel Pierce.

As a Quaker, a sect that afforded women some measure of equality, Sarah Pugh was brought up to think and act according to her own wishes. Though she had always been sympathetic to the abolitionist cause, she was moved to become publicly involved in the movement after attending a lecture by George Thompson in 1835.

Thompson's speech prompted Pugh to join the Philadelphia Female Anti-Slavery Society. The first abolitionist organization to include both white and black women, the society was founded in 1833 by Lucretia Mott and Mary Ann McClintock. Pugh would remain a member for thirty-six years, functioning as its presiding officer for many years, until it was dissolved following the U.S. Civil War. Pugh also joined the American Anti-Slavery Society, attended the Anti-Slavery Convention of American Women in 1837, and she later served as a board member of the Philadelphia Female Anti-Slavery Society.

The environment for abolitionists, especially women, was dangerous in the decades immediately preceding the Civil War. While attending a meeting at the newly constructed Philadelphia Hall in 1838, the women were threatened and the building was burned down. Fearing for the safety of the black women in attendance, Pugh and the other women linked arms with the black women, one white woman with one black woman, and walked out of the building and through the mob without sustaining physical injury. The next day, the meeting was continued at Pugh's school, with only a few protesters in attendance.

In 1840, Pugh, along with fellow Philadelphians Mott, Mary Grew, Elizabeth Neall, and Abby Kimber, were sent as American delegates to the World Anti-Slavery Convention in London. Their attendance provoked a volatile debate about the place of women in the abolitionist movement. When they issued invitations to attend the conference, John Bull and the conservative antislavery circles in England had never envisioned that women might attend the conference. After heated debate and contentious deliberation, a vote upheld the view that women had no place in the convention and would not be allowed to attend as recognized delegates. They were allowed to remain in the building but were seated in the gallery and denied permission to participate in the proceedings.

Pugh remained in Europe for a year, touring and lecturing on abolition and the role of women in the abolitionist movement. Upon her return to Philadelphia, she was more determined than ever to keep fighting for the end of slavery, but her experience at the convention and the continuing prohibition against women speaking in public and serving as officers in social organizations convinced her, as well as the other women delegates, that women's rights also needed to be addressed.

After the Civil War, Sarah supported the Moral Education Society, worked with freed slaves, and sought to improve the status of women. Until her death in 1884, she attended many women's rights conferences, including the Twentieth Anniversary of the Inauguration of the Woman Suffrage Movement in New York City in October 1870.

Robin Hanson

See also: Vesey, Denmark; Women's Rights and the Abolitionist Movement.

Further Reading

James, Edward T., and Janet W. James, eds. *Notable American Women 1607–1950: A Biographical Dictionary.* Boston: Harvard University Press, 1974.

Yellin, Jean Fagan, and John C. Van Horne, eds. *The Abolitionist Sisterhood: Women's Political Culture in Antebellum America.* Ithaca, NY: Cornell University Press, 1994.

Purchasing Freedom

In virtually all locations where slavery was practiced in the Americas, it was customary to allow slaves to purchase their freedom. Depending on the location, the practice varied from a tenuous cultural tradition to a clearly defined statutory process.

In the United States, laws in the slaveholding states became stringent during the antebellum era, as states tried to limit the number of slaves who were allowed to purchase their freedom. Certain legislative provisions, such as those requiring self-emancipated slaves to move out of the state or resettle in Africa, created cost-prohibitive barriers for those seeking emancipation.

There were several means by which slaves could accumulate the wealth needed to effect self-emancipation. On most plantations and farms, it was customary to allow each slave household a small plot of ground, widely referred to as the "provision ground," on which supplemental foodstuffs could be grown. Allowing slaves to grow crops to feed themselves was a means of reducing overhead costs for plantation owners, and the practice also fostered a

healthier workforce. On occasion, individuals who produced excess vegetables in their provision grounds were permitted to sell their produce in the community. Depending on the whims of their owners, slaves were allowed to keep all or part of the income generated through these sales. Industrious slaves might be able to save enough money to purchase their own freedom (or that of a spouse or child) through accumulated savings over a number of years.

Other slaves were recognized as artisans who possessed specialized skills that were in demand not only on the plantation but also in the larger community. A slave with skills in carpentry, for example, might find his labors hired out by his owner to individuals in the nearby community. Most slave owners had a financial understanding with skilled slaves whereby wages earned through their efforts in the community would be divided between the owner and the slave.

Denmark Vesey, a slave in South Carolina during the early nineteenth century, found a more resourceful means by which he could purchase his freedom. Vesey won $1,500 in a lottery and was able to use his winnings to purchase his freedom and to establish himself as a free black merchant in the area of Charleston. Two decades after obtaining his freedom, Vesey was implicated in an 1822 plot to foment slave insurrection in South Carolina.

Slaves who entered into arrangements with their owners to purchase their freedom faced a number of risks. Because slave literacy was prohibited throughout the plantation South, agreements tended to be verbal rather than written, often amounting to nothing more than a promise and a handshake. In some cases, slaves took part in a pay-as-you-go installment plan, hoping that they would eventually reach the amount needed to purchase their freedom. In some cases, unscrupulous owners simply pocketed the payments and refused to emancipate the slaves when the appointed time came. In addition, the value of the verbal contract was limited by the life of the owner who had made the initial promise. Because slaves were regularly sold as disposable property to settle an estate when a plantation owner died, slaves who had verbal agreements to purchase their freedom often found themselves sold to another owner rather emancipated.

Not all slave owners operated in bad faith when making arrangements for self-purchase with their slaves. It was common practice for owners to set a predetermined price that would have to be paid for the slave to achieve self-emancipation. The price might be the cost of replacing the slave with another at current market prices. Other owners sometimes determined, especially for elderly slaves, the slave's amortized value over the years of service. In this fashion, slaves would only be expected to pay the value of the work they had yet to perform in the service of the owner.

On some occasions, the purchase of freedom was effected after the fact, once a slave had escaped to the North. Fugitive slaves who chose to remain in the Northern states lived a precarious existence, as they could be legally recaptured and returned to servitude in the South.

It was not uncommon for fugitive slaves to negotiate with their former owners through an intermediary to determine a price that would remove the stigma of being a fugitive. Even Frederick Douglass took part in this practice of self-emancipation, as British abolitionists helped him raise the funds necessary to purchase his freedom in 1847. It was also common for such fugitives to purchase the freedom of a spouse, child, or other family member.

As Southern states became increasingly concerned about the presence of a growing free black population in their midst, state legislatures responded by limiting manumission opportunities and making self-emancipation more difficult to effect. These measures, coupled with the passage of the Fugitive Slave Law of 1850, greatly reduced the opportunities for Southern slaves to achieve their freedom through legal means.

Junius P. Rodriguez

See also: Douglass, Frederick; Fugitive Slave Act of 1793; Manumission; Vesey, Denmark.

Further Reading

Schafer, Judith Kelleher. *Becoming Free, Remaining Free: Manumission and Enslavement in New Orleans, 1846–1862.* Baton Rouge: Louisiana State University Press, 2003.

Whitman, T. Stephen. *The Price of Freedom: Slavery and Manumission in Baltimore and Early National Maryland.* Lexington: University Press of Kentucky, 1997.

Purvis, Robert (1810–1898)

A freeborn African American from South Carolina, Robert Purvis was a leading progressive voice for emancipation and civil rights from the early 1830s through the American Civil War. He was one of only three blacks to help organize the American Anti-Slavery Society, and he also headed the Philadelphia Vigilant Committee, which assisted fugitive slaves on the Underground Railroad.

Born to a white father and mulatto mother in South Carolina, Robert Purvis became an active abolitionist both publicly and behind the scenes. He helped found the American Anti-Slavery Society in 1833 and aided hundreds of runaways on the Underground Railroad. *(General Research & Reference Division, Schomburg Center for Research in Black Culture, The New York Public Library, Astor, Lenox, and Tilden Foundations)*

Purvis was born on August 4, 1810, in Charleston, South Carolina, to Harriet Judah, a free mulatto, and William Purvis, a wealthy white cotton broker who had emigrated from Britain. At the age of nine, Robert, his parents, and two brothers moved from the slave South to Philadelphia, where the boy attended private school and read his father's books on abolitionism.

Purvis's father died in 1826, bequeathing his middle son $120,000, years of private schooling, business savvy, and a passion for abolitionism. Purvis continued his education at Amherst College in Massachusetts and later returned to Philadelphia. By his early twenties, he had become a vocal leader in the abolitionist movement, believing in the concept of immediate, uncompensated emancipation as professed by William Lloyd Garrison.

Purvis married into a prominent African American abolitionist family, wedding Harriet Forten (the daughter of James Forten) in 1831. He joined with Garrison in the founding of the American Anti-Slavery Society in 1833, and he was a signer of its Declaration of Sentiments. He soon traveled to Britain, where he spoke and wrote in an effort to gain support for abolitionism and raise money for the cause.

Purvis also focused on state and local projects promoting abolitionism and civil rights. He became the first black member of the Pennsylvania Society for Promoting the Abolition of Slavery and served as president of the Pennsylvania Anti-Slavery Society for five terms (1845–1850). He fought for African Americans' right to vote in Pennsylvania in his *Appeal of Forty Thousand Citizens Threatened with Disenfranchisement* (1838). He also fought to promote black schools and libraries, despite his personal desire for racial integration.

Among his greatest passions was the assistance of runaway slaves. In addition to running the Vigilant Committee of Philadelphia, Purvis and his wife prepared a secret room in their home where runaways could rest safely before continuing their migration northward. Their home would remain an important station on the Underground Railroad from the early 1830s until the end of the Civil War.

Purvis welcomed the Civil War as a means to end slavery, and he strongly advocated black enlistment in the Union forces. He publicly criticized President Abraham Lincoln's delayed emancipation and the Union army's propensity to have white officers command regiments of black troops. Purvis also disagreed with Lincoln's stance on black colonization outside the United States.

After the Civil War, Purvis's activism faded, and he took pleasure in his home, garden, and family in Philadelphia. He did, however, make headlines for publicly criticizing the ratification of the Fifteenth Amendment in 1870, objecting to the fact that it disallowed women from voting. In 1883, he presided over the fiftieth anniversary of the American Anti-Slavery Society. Purvis died at his home in Philadelphia on April 15, 1898.

Nathan R. Meyer

See also: Garrison, William Lloyd; Underground Railroad.

Further Reading

Borome, Joseph A. "Robert Purvis and His Early Challenge to American Racism." *Negro History Bulletin* 30 (May 1967): 8–10.

Quarles, Benjamin. *Black Abolitionists*. New York: Oxford University Press, 1969.

Smedley, R.C. *History of the Underground Railroad in Chester and the Neighboring Counties of Pennsylvania*. New York: Arno, 1969.

Sumler-Harris, Janice. "The Forten-Purvis Women of Philadelphia and the American Anti-Slavery Crusade." *Journal of Negro History* 66 (1981/1982): 281–88.

Putnam, Caroline F. (1826–1917)

Caroline F. Putnam was an abolitionist and an educator who devoted her life to helping those who had been limited by the oppression of slavery. Following the U.S. Civil War, she operated schools in Virginia that educated African American children and adults in an effort to assist the former slaves.

Putnam was born in 1826 in Massachusetts to a Unitarian physician, who died while Caroline was a small child, and his wife Eliza (Carpenter) Putnam. Eliza's second marriage to Levi Peet in 1840 moved the family to southwestern New York. Little is known of Caroline's early life until she enrolled at Oberlin College in 1848. While attending Oberlin, she met Sarah (Sallie) Holley, who would remain her constant companion for more than forty years.

In 1851, when Holley completed her degree, Putnam decided to forgo her last year at the school so that the two could leave Oberlin together. Although both women were staunch abolitionists and believed in the immediate emancipation of all slaves, Putnam was not comfortable in the public view and thus served as a road manager while Holley toured the country speaking about abolition.

It was shortly after the Civil War that Putnam found her true calling. In November 1868, Putnam, a former member of the American Anti-Slavery Society, moved to Lottsburg, a town in rural Virginia. Upon her arrival, she started a freedmen's school, naming it the Holley School.

Although the school was named for Holley, Putnam was the heart and soul of the endeavor. Her ability to adapt her curriculum and pedagogy to the cultural expectations and environmental constraints of the people in the community led her to a teaching career that spanned thirty-six years and included four generations of students. Children were taught during the day and adults were welcomed in the evenings; during the harvesting and planting seasons, attendance expectations were relaxed to accommodate the need for added labor in the fields.

Holley joined Putnam in Lottsburg, but she spent a great deal of time traveling throughout New England to raise money for the school. A limited amount of money was available from the Freedmen's Bureau, and the cost and expense of running the school far exceeded the bureau's contribution. To provide more local funds, Putnam became the town's postmistress in 1869.

The local white community was not pleased to see Northerners educating the recently freed slaves, so Putnam used her position as postmistress to engage and educate the surrounding white community about her school. By locating the post office in a room at the school, local residents were required to stop by the school to pick up their mail. While at the school, the suspicious, but curious, whites had the opportunity to observe the children in the classrooms. Consequently, many gained a grudging appreciation for Putnam and her work.

Putnam worked diligently to educate the black population, but she was also a proponent of anticolonialism, temperance, and animal rights. She shared her experiences in Virginia in letters to friends and acquaintances, as well as in articles in magazines such as the *National Anti-Slavery Standard*. Although she was more timid in her approach than Holley, she was an outspoken opponent of Booker T. Washington's call for black accommodation, which proposed that blacks temper their quest for social and political equality and instead concentrate on economic opportunities and progress.

Putnam never married, and her thirty-six years of teaching at the Holley School constituted one of the longest tenures in a freedmen's school. Even after retiring from teaching, she remained in Lottsburg to oversee the operation of the school. She died in 1917 and was buried in the cemetery directly across from the school and community she had grown to love.

Robin Hanson

See also: Education of Former Slaves; Freedmen's Bureau; Holley, Sallie.

Further Reading

Butchart, Ronald E. "Caroline F. Putnam." In *Women Educators in the United States, 1820–1993: A Bio-Bibliographical Sourcebook,* ed. Maxine Seller. Westport, CT: Greenwood, 1994.

Quakers (Society of Friends)

Officially named the Society of Friends, the religious community that came to be known as the Quakers played a significant role in the history of abolitionism in the transatlantic world. Some of the most eloquent and persuasive antislavery advocates were inspired by the tenets of the Quaker faith, as they demonstrated, both in word and in deed, the unholy nature of the slave trade and slaveholding.

The Society of Friends first formed in England during the 1650s. It was an outgrowth of the Anabaptist Reformation, whose adherents were dissatisfied with the theological beliefs of many of the mainline Protestant denominations. In particular, Quaker founder George Fox believed that true spirituality came from an "inner light" that emerged through personal communion with God.

Viewed as part of a religious fringe in England, many of the Quakers were persecuted, and a significant number emigrated to the English colonies in North America. Fox encouraged his American brethren to embrace "the duty of converting the slaves" and later demonstrated his personal commitment to this ideal by ministering to slaves in the West Indies.

The Quaker William Penn established a colony in Pennsylvania that was to be a "holy experiment" in which people of all faiths were welcome to settle. Yet, in spite of these egalitarian beliefs, the Quaker community remained influential within the colony. English Quaker William Edmondson addressed a general letter to the slaveholders of England's North American colonies in 1676. In the letter, Edmondson argued that Christianity was incompatible with slaveholding, and he urged his colonial brethren to separate themselves from the vile institution of slavery.

The Quakers soon developed a reputation for their antislavery views. The Virginia House of Burgesses passed a statute in 1685 that prohibited slaves within the colony from participating in any of the Quaker meetings that were held for educational purposes.

On February 18, 1688, the famous "Germantown Protest" was published when a group of Pennsylvania Mennonite Quakers openly declared at their monthly meeting that slavery was contrary to Christian principles and signed an antislavery resolution to that effect. The document was prepared by Francis Daniel Pastorius and his Quaker brethren. This antislavery tract was the first public condemnation of the institution and practice of slavery in the Western Hemisphere and one of the first examples of nonviolent protest in American history.

Generally well educated and articulate, the Quakers used every means at their disposal to proselytize their views on slavery. Quaker George Keith published *An Exhortation and Caution to Friends Concerning Buying or Keeping of Negroes* (1693). It was Keith's desire that Quakers who owned slaves should free them as soon as possible.

During their annual meeting in 1696, American Quakers admonished their membership for participating in the importation of slaves and threatened those who continued to import slaves with expulsion from the Society of Friends. Two years later, Pennsylvania Quaker William Southeby petitioned his coreligionists in Barbados to stop shipping blacks to Pennsylvania to work as slaves. As a result of his sustained efforts in the fight against slavery, Southeby was eventually expelled from the Society of Friends, thus reflecting how divisive the slavery question remained among the Quakers.

During the eighteenth century, the Quakers began to make efforts to provide religious instruction to slaves throughout the colonies. In Pennsylvania, William Penn organized a monthly meeting for blacks. In 1711, at the insistence of the Quakers and Mennonites, the Pennsylvania colonial assembly outlawed slavery, but the action was immediately overruled by the British Crown.

Quaker Ralph Sandiford published an antislavery tract titled *A Brief Examination of the Practice of the Times, By the Foregoing and the Present Dispensation* (1729). The work was published in Philadelphia by

Benjamin Franklin, who supported efforts to abolish the institution of slavery.

In the New Jersey colony, John Woolman, an itinerant Quaker clergyman, delivered a series of sermons in 1743 calling for an end to slavery and urging greater consideration of racial equality. Woolman eventually published his ideas in *Some Considerations on the Keeping of Negroes* (1754), and he would carry his antislavery message to Quaker meetings in several colonies.

Having previously taken a denominational stand against the practice of slavery, in 1755, American Quakers excluded from their denomination all members who continued to import slaves. Shortly thereafter, antislavery supporter Anthony Benezet and other Pennsylvania Quakers began meeting yearly to discuss and plan strategies for the abolitionist crusade. This group became the core of the Society for the Relief of Free Negroes Unlawfully Held in Bondage, which was later organized in Philadelphia in April 1775.

The Quakers continued to provide a cadre of leadership for many of the abolitionist groups that emerged in the early nineteenth century. Antislavery advocates such as Benjamin Lundy, Elijah P. Lovejoy, Thomas Garrett, Lucretia Mott, and Levi Coffin were all drawn to the cause by the tenets of their faith.

During the 1840s, the Quakers in the United States became divided, as the split between advocates of immediate emancipation and proponents of gradual emancipation that had divided the abolitionist movement was mirrored within the Society of Friends. Some Quakers who found the doctrine of immediatism unchristian voted their more radical colleagues out of the religious community as a result of this internal debate within the Society of Friends.

Junius P. Rodriguez

See also: Benezet, Anthony; Coffin, Levi; Fox, George; Garrett, Thomas; Germantown Protest (1688); Lovejoy, Elijah P.; Lundy, Benjamin; Mott, James, and Lucretia Coffin Mott; Woolman, John.

Further Reading

Aptheker, Herbert. "The Quakers and Negro Slavery." *Journal of Negro History* 25 (July 1940): 331–62.

Barbour, Hugh, and J. William Frost. *The Quakers.* Westport, CT: Greenwood, 1988.

Braithwaite, William. *The Second Period of Quakerism.* 2nd ed. Cambridge, UK: Cambridge University Press, 1961.

Drake, Thomas. *Quakers and Slavery in America.* New Haven, CT: Yale University Press, 1950.

Frost, J. William. "The Origins of the Quaker Crusade Against Slavery: A Review of Recent Literature." *Quaker History* 67 (1978): 42–58.

Hewitt, Nancy A. "Feminist Friends: Agrarian Quakers and the Emergence of Women's Rights in America." *Feminist Studies* 12 (Spring 1986): 27–49.

Knee, Stuart E. "The Quaker Petition of 1791: A Challenge to Democracy in Early America." *Slavery and Abolition* 6 (September 1985): 151–59.

Soderlund, Jean R. *Quakers and Slavery: A Divided Spirit.* Princeton, NJ: Princeton University Press, 1985.

Queiros Law (1850)

With the passage of the Queiros Law in 1850, Brazil officially ended its involvement in the transatlantic slave trade. In spite of this measure, slavery continued in Brazil for another generation until it was finally abolished in 1888.

Efforts to end Brazil's slave trade began in 1826. The Brazilian legislature passed a law known as the Convention of 1826, which declared that any importation of slaves after 1829 would be considered piracy. The law guaranteed freedom for any captured African slaves. This law had its origins in an 1817 treaty between Britain and Portugal that allowed the Royal Navy to search and seize Portuguese ships involved in the slave trade north of the equator. Enforcement of the Brazilian law and the bilateral treaty, however, proved difficult. Portugal remained the main supplier of slaves to Brazil, and Brazil had the largest number of slaves anywhere in the Western Hemisphere—almost 40 percent of all African slaves traded.

The Brazilian legislature passed another anti–slave trade law in 1831. Under pressure from Britain to enforce the previous law and treaty, the 1831 measure was more comprehensive. It called for specific sanctions against traders delivering slaves to the Brazilian coast. Still, the Brazilian government lacked a navy to prevent the trade, and the powerful planter community opposed any measures restricting their receipt of slaves. Moreover, the government virtually ignored past illegal shipments of African slaves.

An 1837 anti–slave trading law did little to stop the traffic. Although this law also called for sanctions, local juries seldom convicted anyone of trafficking in slaves. According to some estimates, more than 300,000 slaves entered Brazil from Africa between 1842 and 1851.

Brazilian minister of justice Eusebio de Queiros inherited his reformist tradition from a generation of predecessors who had also fought to end the slave trade. As Brazil's justice minister from 1848 until

1852, Queiros used his position to put pressure on the powerful coffee planters, who relied on the slave trade. Other Brazilians, however, were concerned about a large-scale slave revolt if more slaves continued to arrive.

In an 1849 memo to the Brazilian cabinet, Queiros called for new legislative initiatives to restrict slave traders and vigorous prosecution (without pardon) for Brazilians involved in the trade. He recognized that the powerful coffee interests exerted considerable pressure to maintain the trade, but he promised sanctions against any growers who resisted. Queiros noted that the existing laws lacked strong enforcement and began a concerted effort to end the slave trade by rallying popular support for the cause.

In a May 1850 speech to the Chamber of Deputies, Queiros remarked that most of the Brazilian public favored abolition. He asked the body to move forward on a bill submitted in September 1848 that would have outlawed the transatlantic slave trade but had been stalled for nearly two years. Despite his prodding, the legislative body did not vote on the bill. Two months later, Queiros invited the Chamber of Deputies to meet in secret to consider the antislavery trade bill. With some modifications, the 1848 bill represented an improvement over previous measures: It declared slave traders pirates and gave the government the right to seize ships used in the slave trade. Meeting behind closed doors, Queiros hoped, would permit discussion without interference from the powerful planter class. Responding to his urgent plea for support, proponents of the bill defeated a last-ditch effort by planters to maintain the trade.

On July 17, the Chamber of Deputies sent the bill to the Senate. After a series of debates—once again conducted in secret—the Senate approved the anti–slave trade measure. Queiros presented the law to Emperor Dom Pedro II, who had already declared his support for ending the traffic in African slaves. On September 4, 1850, the legislation that had become known as the Queiros bill became law.

Critics of the law complained that Queiros had yielded to pressure from the British, a charge that he denied. He argued that British influence had not been responsible for the passage of the strong 1850 anti–slave trade law. The piracy provision in the measure, borrowed from previous legislation, now gave the government the power to seize Brazilian as well as foreign vessels that violated the law. Unlike the earlier laws, the Queiros bill empowered the small Brazilian navy to take control of ships loaded with slaves in territorial waters. In addition, Brazilian judges promised to enforce the measure. Moreover, the British navy had threatened to enforce the older law with or without the aid of the Brazilian government.

Although rumors of continuing slave trafficking persisted after Queiros retired from the cabinet, there was little evidence of smuggling into Brazilian ports or harbors. According to one source, about a dozen ships landed slaves illegally between 1850 and 1856. After the latter date, there is no record that any slave vessels arrived.

The suppression of the transatlantic slave trade to Brazil owes much of its success to the efforts of the liberal Queiros. More important, his bill laid the foundation for the eventual abolition of Brazilian slavery.

Jackie R. Booker

See also: Benezet, Anthony.

Further Reading

Bethell, Leslie. *The Abolition of the Brazilian Slave Trade: Britain, Brazil and the Slave Trade Question, 1807–1869.* Cambridge, UK: Cambridge University Press, 1970.

Nabuco, Joaquim. *Abolitionism: The Brazilian Anti-Slavery Struggle.* Trans. and ed. Robert Conrad. Urbana: University of Illinois Press, 1977.

Skidmore, Thomas E. *Brazil: Five Centuries of Change.* New York: Oxford University Press, 1999.

Quock Walker Case

See Commonwealth v. Jennison (1783)

Racism

A perennial dispute in the debate over slavery in the Americas is the role that racism played in the origins, development, and maintenance of the institution. Although slavery in the transatlantic world became associated exclusively with Africans and persons of African descent, this practice was inconsistent with that of other slave-based societies in world history. In addition, this viewpoint does not take into account some anomalous cases in which Native Americans and white Europeans were enslaved in the Americas.

The debate that emerges challenges whether racism is a necessary precondition for the enslavement of a particular group of individuals. Or is racism a cultural invention that was developed and became enshrined as a form of pseudo-scientific rationalism to justify the enslavement of certain groups of people?

In the ancient slave societies of Mesopotamia, Greece, and Rome, factors such as race or ethnicity had no bearing on who was enslaved and who was free. In these early societies, the condition of enslavement fell on those who were either war captives or residents of polities that had been defeated in battle. According to this practice, it was misfortune on the battlefield that made one person the property of another.

In societies in which race was not the basis for enslavement, opportunities existed for a smooth transition between slavery and freedom. The manumitted slave bore no badge of dishonor upon being freed, and he or she was welcomed into the free community without question or required sanction. It was only later, when race became associated with slavery, that emancipated slaves remained marginalized—sometimes viewed as "slaves without masters"—and were not readily welcomed into the free community with the full rights and privileges of that status.

The formulation of the concept of distinct races led to the development of typologies. These classifications first focused on observable bodily characteristics but later used subjective determinations (which could not be sustained) to describe character flaws associated with certain classes of people. Formalized in the writings of several eighteenth- and nineteenth-century scholarly works, the idea of race became so widely accepted that many in contemporary society still scoff at the notion that race is a culturally created status that has little connection to reality.

Some scholars of the history of racism believe the idea of race was born sometime around the eleventh century, when European warriors embarked on a series of wars known as the Crusades. As a result of their encounters with peoples of different ethnic origins, the Europeans came to realize that they were "outnumbered," as the populations of Asia and of Africa seemed more vast and expansive than those of Western Europe. The Europeans formulated a doctrine whereby they declared themselves superior to other peoples whom they had encountered. They subsequently turned to innovation and technology to fashion a self-fulfilling prophecy that, in spite of their poor numbers, the peoples of Western Europe held an advantage over other, supposedly lesser peoples.

During the Enlightenment, the philosopher David Hume published *Of National Characters* (1754), in which he affirmed the superiority of the Teutonic peoples over the peoples of Africa. The cultivation of such beliefs was readily apparent in European society. In 1770, the *Oxford English Dictionary* included the word "race" for the first time. The racial attitudes that Hume and other European intellectuals expressed became commonly accepted. These views influenced the development of the slaveholder's identity while fashioning the slave's persona by reinforcing the prevailing stereotypes.

During the early nineteenth century, slavery apologists such as Josiah Nott of Mobile, Alabama, and Dr. Samuel Cartwright of New Orleans, Louisiana, published supposedly scholarly studies that affirmed the inferiority of the African and posited that slavery was a benevolent institution that served to uplift lesser peoples. Such racist arguments became central to the

Slavery in the ancient world was generally a function of military or political captivity rather than race or ethnicity. But in commercial slave societies from ancient Rome (depicted here) to the antebellum American South, slaves were used for manual labor. *(©Index, Barcelona, Spain/Index/The Bridgeman Art Library)*

Southern proslavery argument, which was honed to counter the growing antislavery sentiment coming from Northern abolitionists.

But racism was not a habit of mind that was exclusive to the slaveholder or to the Southerner. Many individuals who opposed the idea of slavery on moral principle still could not bring themselves to view Africans or African Americans as their social equals. Even within the ranks of the abolitionist movement, there existed a soft bigotry that caused unease among many antislavery supporters who found it difficult to reconcile their hearts and minds when it came to the institution of slavery.

Junius P. Rodriguez

See also: Enlightenment; Ku Klux Klan; Lynching; Novels, Proslavery; Reconstruction.

Further Reading

Dumond, Dwight Lowell. "Race, Prejudice, and Abolition: New Views on the Antislavery Movement." *Michigan Alumni Quarterly Review* 41 (April 1935): 377–85.

Inikori, Joseph E., ed. *Forced Migration: The Impact of the Export Slave Trade on African Societies.* London: Hutchinson, 1982.

Inikori, Joseph E., and Stanley L. Engerman, eds. *The Atlantic Slave Trade: Effects on Economies, Societies, and Peoples in Africa, the Americas, and Europe.* Durham, NC: Duke University Press, 1992.

Miers, Suzanne, and Igor Kopytoff, eds. *Slavery in Africa: Historical and Anthropological Perspective.* Madison: University of Wisconsin Press, 1977.

Roediger, David R. *Towards the Abolition of Whiteness: Essays on Race, Politics, and Working Class History.* New York: Verso, 1994.

Van den Berghe, Pierre L. *Race and Racism: A Comparative Perspective.* New York: Wiley, 1967.

Ralston, Gerard (ca. 1800–ca. 1880)

Gerard Ralston was a British abolitionist who supported colonization plans to return freed slaves to established African homelands, such as Sierra Leone and Liberia, in the early nineteenth century. When the British government established diplomatic relations with the Republic of Liberia in 1847, Ralston was appointed consul general.

As a financial patron of the colonization movement, Ralston was rewarded with an honorary appointment to the board of directors of the American Colonization Society at the urging of Elliott Cresson, the society's agent. In addition to his financial support of the endeavor, Ralston also provided ideas to Cresson that might make the venture more successful. One of those ideas was a plan to name towns in Liberia after British donors who pledged £2,000 or more to the American Colonization Society. Another was the introduction of sugar cultivation in Liberia so that British markets, which were fond of selling "free produce," would have a ready supply of sugar.

One of Ralston's more noteworthy efforts in his association with the American Colonization Society was the testimony he gave to win the freedom of Fulani prince Abduhl Rahhahman, who had been enslaved for forty years in Natchez, Mississippi. The case of the "Moorish prince" attracted newspaper attention in the United States and Great Britain.

Ralston later co-authored an abolitionist propaganda pamphlet based on an apocryphal correspondence between two Americans (in fact, both writers were Englishmen). The work was titled *The African Race in America, North and South. Being a Correspondence on That Subject Between Two Pennsylvanians {G. MacHenry and G. Ralston}. With an Appendix Containing Extracts in Reference to the Right of Secession, From the Writings of the Late W. Rawle . . . ; and the Views of Senator Bayard, of Delaware, on the Antagonism of the Caucasian and African Races* (1861). Ralston also published *On the Republic of Liberia, Its Products and Resources* (1862) after presenting a paper on the topic before the British Society for the Encouragement of Arts, Manufactures, and Commerce.

In April 1862, Ralston was a member of a delegation representing the British and Foreign Anti-Slavery Society that met with American minister Charles Francis Adams in London. Tensions between the United States and Great Britain were high at the time because of unresolved diplomatic issues associated with the Trent Affair, an incident in which Confederate diplomats were seized from a British ship that was intercepted on the high seas. The meeting with Adams was largely a publicity opportunity to demonstrate the solidarity that still existed between abolitionist forces on both sides of the Atlantic.

As an officer of the British Foreign Office in West Africa, Ralston worked with associates to assist freed slaves in making the transition from slave labor to wage labor. In addition, the presence of Ralston and other diplomatic agents in West Africa served to diminish the possibility that new domestic slave trading enterprises might take root.

Junius P. Rodriguez

See also: American Colonization Society; Liberia.

Further Reading

Anstey, Roger. *The Atlantic Slave Trade and British Abolition, 1760–1810*. London: Macmillan, 1975.

Ramsay, James (1733–1789)

The Anglican churchman James Ramsay was one of the most influential British abolitionists writing in the 1780s, the first decade to see a popular campaign against the slave trade. His *Essay on the Treatment and Conversion of African Slaves in the British Sugar Colonies* (1784) helped stir initial debate in British society over the moral justification of the slave trade and the institution of slavery.

Ramsay was born on July 25, 1733, in Fraserburgh, Scotland, and educated at King's College, Aberdeen, between 1750 and 1755. He then moved to London, where he trained as a surgeon. In 1757, he became a ship's surgeon aboard the Royal Navy warship *Arundel*.

On November 21, 1759, Ramsay's life was transformed by two simultaneous incidents. Boarding a slave ship afflicted by an epidemic, he was horrified by the conditions in which the slaves were transported; the experience marked him for life. Upon returning to the *Arundel*, he fell and was badly injured; the accident left him permanently disabled. No longer able to serve at sea, Ramsay entered the Anglican Church and took orders as a clergyman.

In 1762, Ramsay settled into a living on the Caribbean island of Saint Christopher (now Saint Kitts), where, in addition to attending to the spiritual needs of his parish, he also practiced medicine. The financial success of his parish was derived from the slave-based sugar plantations attached to the church. Ramsay broke with established practice by ameliorating the conditions of the slaves and attempting to convert them to Christianity. Even more controversially, he denounced the harsh measures employed by his white parishioners and urged them to follow his lead.

Ramsay came under attack for these liberal ideas. Letters were written to local newspapers, an angry notice was pinned to the church door, his church was boycotted, and he was threatened with violence. Although Ramsay held out for fifteen years, he finally grew weary of the conflict.

In 1777, he accepted a naval chaplaincy before returning briefly to Saint Christopher in the (mistaken) hope that the conflict there might have come to an end. He left the island for the last time in August 1781, taking with him his personal servant, a black slave named Nestor, and returning to England, where, under the patronage of Sir Charles Middleton, he became vicar of Teston in Kent.

Ramsay took advantage of his political contacts in Middleton to inform many influential people about the conditions in which slaves labored in the British colonies. At the same time, he wrote *An Essay on the Treatment and Conversion of African Slaves*, which was widely read. Although he stopped short of calling for the outright abolition of slavery and the slave trade, both ideas were strongly implied throughout the book, which brought together the legal, scriptural, philosophical, practical, economic, and humanitarian arguments against slavery. However, the chief strength

The treatment of African slaves in the Sugar Islands of the British West Indies led Anglican clergyman and former naval surgeon James Ramsay to write a firsthand account and moral condemnation that sparked widespread public concern in the 1740s. (*©Private Collection/The Bridgeman Art Library*)

of the book was its authority. Not only was Ramsay a respected Anglican churchman, but he also had personal experience with the institution he condemned. Moreover, he had made vocal enemies in Saint Christopher and elsewhere who published a series of books attacking both Ramsay's arguments and his personal integrity.

Among these apologists for slavery, the most fluent was James Tobin, who addressed three books to Ramsay between 1785 and 1788, beginning with the much-reviled *Cursory Remarks Upon the Revd. Mr. Ramsay's Essay on the Treatment and Conversion of African Slaves in the Sugar Colonies, By a Friend to the West India Colonies and Their Inhabitants* (1785). Ramsay replied, and altogether, he published eight books on the topic of slavery during the decade. In his later publications, he explicitly supported the abolition of the slave trade. Some of these publications, including *A Letter to James Tobin, Esq. Late Member of His Majesty's Council in the Island of Nevis, From James Ramsay* (1787), directly refuted the arguments made against him. Others, such as *An Address on the Proposed Bill for the Abolition of the Slave Trade* (1788), were published to support the popular campaign against the slave trade that had been growing throughout the 1780s.

Ramsay's contribution to the upsurge in antislavery sentiment cannot be overestimated. His books sold well and were widely reviewed in the periodical press, bringing abolitionist discussion to the widest possible audience in the mid-1780s. Of more lasting consequence, both the tone and the arguments of his *Essay* were widely imitated by later abolitionist writers, such as William Lloyd Garrison. Ramsay's influence can be detected in books written on both sides of the Atlantic well into the nineteenth century.

Ramsay's most lasting contribution was to initiate a public debate on slavery and the slave trade—a debate that ultimately led the British Parliament to abolish the slave trade and later slavery itself. Ramsay remained active and influential until the end, working with such leading lights of the British antislavery movement as Thomas Clarkson and William Wilberforce.

His health was failing, however, and, in spring 1789, he retired to Teston, where he continued to write. Ramsay died on July 20, 1789, and was buried in Teston churchyard, not far from the grave of his servant Nestor.

Brycchan Carey

See also: Clarkson, Thomas; Wilberforce, William.

Further Reading

Carey, Brycchan. *British Abolitionism and the Rhetoric of Sensibility: Writing, Sentiment, and Slavery, 1760–1807.* Basingstoke, UK: Palgrave Macmillan, 2005.

Ramsay, James. "An Essay on the Treatment and Conversion of African Slaves in the British Sugar Colonies." In *Slavery, Abolition and Emancipation: Writings in the British Romantic Period,* ed. Deborah Lee and Peter Kitson. London: Pickering & Chatto, 1999.

Shyllon, Folarin O. *James Ramsay: The Unknown Abolitionist.* Edinburgh, UK: Canongate, 1977.

Watt, James. "James Ramsay, 1733–1789: Naval Surgeon, Naval Chaplain and Morning Star of the Anti-Slavery Movement." *Mariner's Mirror* 81 (May 1995): 156–70.

Ray, Charles B. (1807–1886)

Charles B. Ray was one of the most influential African American abolitionists of the early nineteenth century. As a journalist, an officer in several antislavery organizations, and a conductor on the Underground Railroad, Ray worked to hasten the abolition of slavery in the United States.

Born on December 25, 1807, in Falmouth, Massachusetts, Ray was the son of a mailman. At the age of twenty-three, he experienced a religious awakening and decided to pursue the ministry within the Methodist Church. He was educated at the Wesleyan Academy in Massachusetts and later entered Wesleyan University in Connecticut, which offered training to Methodist teachers and preachers. Ray soon left Wesleyan, however, not wishing to endure his classmates' severe racism. In 1832, he relocated to New York City, where he opened a boot and shoe store. Ray was ordained as a Congregationalist minister in 1845, and he organized the Bethesda Congregational Church, serving as its pastor for nearly twenty years.

Ray's first known political activity began in 1837, when he became a member of the Young Men's Anti-Slavery Society. In December 1837, the young activist took a stand on the pending split within the American Anti-Slavery Society and the abolitionist movement at large. Though most black New Yorkers supported the Tappan brothers—the less radical wing of the American Anti-Slavery Society that advocated moral suasion and political action to combat slavery—Ray did not abandon William Lloyd Garrison. Garrison and his followers were more radical than others; they denounced the U.S. Constitution as supportive of slavery and called for a new government that disallowed slavery. In addition, Garrison and his adherents took the radical view that women should be full members of the national and state abolitionist societies. Ray tried to remain neutral and maintain ties with both factions, because he felt it was in the black community's best interest to associate with anyone who acted on behalf of the abolitionist cause.

In 1839, Ray assumed the editorship of a black weekly newspaper called *The Colored American,* a position he held until the paper folded in 1842. In August 1840, he was selected as chairman of a statewide gathering to gain suffrage for black men. The movement faced internal conflict, however, largely in response to the New York State legislature's refusal to take action on the petitions submitted. Frustrated black leaders formed the American Reform Board of Disfranchised Commissioners, which was more militant in its language. Ray openly attacked the organization, calling its efforts a failure. Despite these conflicts, Ray advocated black suffrage rights throughout the 1840s and supported both the Liberty Party and the Radical Abolition Party.

In 1843, Ray represented New York at the National Convention of Colored Citizens in Buffalo. Although he was a staunch abolitionist, Ray attacked Henry Highland Garnet's "Address to the Slaves," in which Garnet argued that slaves should use violence if necessary to end their submission to slave owners. Ray argued that Garnet's position was too radical and that moral suasion would ultimately prevail over the threat of confrontation. Garnet and Ray faced off again in 1849 at a public meeting held in New York City to discuss colonization. Garnet was becoming increasingly concerned about the future of the black race in the United States, whereas Ray asserted that black people had a long and proud history in the country.

Throughout the 1840s, Ray was a conductor on the Underground Railroad and remained committed to the cause of the fugitive. In 1847, he joined the New York Vigilant Committee, a statewide organization dedicated to assisting and protecting fugitives. That year, he cofounded, with fellow abolitionist and educator Charles L. Reason, the Society for the Promotion of Education Among Colored Children to educate black students in public schools. In 1850, Ray also joined the Committee of Thirteen, which was concerned with fugitives, colonization, and suffrage.

By the 1850s, Ray was making fewer public appearances, but he remained committed to education in the black community. In 1850, he helped form the American League of Colored Laborers, which advocated for education and training in mechanical skills as a way of improving conditions for African Americans. Three years later, he represented New York City at the 1853 Colored National Convention and focused his efforts on education. For many years, he served as a city missionary for the American Missionary Association, ministering in the free black community. Ray died on August 15, 1886.

Leslie M. Alexander

See also: American Missionary Association; *Colored American, The;* Hopper, Isaac Tatem; Underground Railroad.

Raynal, Guillaume-Thomas-François (1713–1796)

The French philosopher and historian Abbé Guillaume-Thomas-François Raynal's *Histoire philosophique et politique des établissements et du commerce des Européens dans les deux Indes* (Philosophical and Political History of the Settlements and Trade of the Europeans in the East and West Indies) was one of several works that influenced the eighteenth-century debate about slavery and the slave trade in France. Spanning three major editions (1770, 1774, 1781), this collaborative project helped frame the terms of the growing abolitionist movement in the second half of the eighteenth century. Essentially a celebration of European expansion in Asia and the Americas, Raynal's *History* was similar to Denis Diderot's more popular *Encyclopédie* (Encyclopedia) in that it was a laboratory of ideas advanced during the Enlightenment. Although it bears Raynal's name and editorial influence, many of the positions it advocates were supplied by philosophers such as Jean de Pechméja and Diderot.

Born on April 12, 1713, in Saint-Geniez, France, Raynal published his multivolume history of European colonization anonymously in French in 1770. The earl of Orford, Horace Walpole, commented, "It tells one everything in the world," from the history of the tea and coffee trades to the history of Greek and Roman slavery. Raynal's attacks on the clergy and his staunch denunciation of European colonization shocked French society, setting off a firestorm of controversy.

The French Crown immediately prohibited the work's sale on the grounds that it contained "propositions that are impudent, dangerous, rash, and contrary to good morals and the principles of religion" and ordered Raynal into exile. Parliament ordered the book publicly burned in 1781. Despite Raynal's notoriety—or perhaps because of it—the book became a best-seller, with twenty approved and fifty pirated editions appearing in print by the time of his death on March 6, 1796.

The irony of the eighteenth-century French debate over slavery was that the humanitarian and reformist ideals of the Enlightenment increasingly clashed with the growing economic focus of a colonial system that was based on forced labor. The mercantilist French economy profited from its plantation-based colonies, especially Saint-Domingue in the Caribbean, which was the leading producer of sugarcane in the world. With Saint-Domingue, Guadeloupe, and Martinique, France controlled more than half a million black slaves; from French port cities, more than 4,000 slaving ships visited Africa between 1650 and 1850 to procure workers for the colonies. Beginning with the satirical critique of slavery offered by Baron de La Brède et de Montesquieu in his *Spirit of the Laws* in 1748, an abolitionist movement emerged in France to denounce both slavery and the slave trade that made it possible. After Montesquieu's *Spirit of the Laws,* Raynal's *History* was consulted among writers as the most relevant discussion of antislavery.

The merit of Raynal's *History* lay in its extensive description of the system of enslavement from Africa to the Antilles. It defeated all of the major proslavery arguments: Religions had no right to support slavery for the purpose of conversion; blacks were not born slaves or for slavery; it was despotic governments that claimed the right to sell their own; prisoners of war were created by European-sponsored conflicts to produce captives; and blacks were not happier in the Americas, as their many forms of protest had demonstrated. Raynal's basic principle of liberty was that "if man belongs to himself, he has the right to dispose of himself." At its core, the system of transatlantic slavery did not allow this choice, and Raynal called on the world's monarchs to oppose slavery.

But this was not an egalitarian perspective. Like most of his contemporaries, Raynal saw his project as part of a "civilizing mission" to regenerate an Africa that was yet in its historical infancy. This effort would parallel the reforms that he had recommended in the American colonies. In the third edition of the *History,* he even recommended mixed marriages between French subjects and natives in other lands as a way of civilizing the latter.

Raynal's position of gradual emancipation was influenced by economic philosophers known as *physiocrats,* who argued that slavery was both contrary to natural law and unprofitable and advocated free labor over servile labor. Raynal extolled the advantages of cultivation by Africans in Africa; he did not favor the immediate liberation of present slaves but, oddly, recommended the continued importation of those who were enslaved in Africa so that they could become free in America. Blacks who were already enslaved in the colonies would not be emancipated, as they were unprepared for freedom. Younger slaves would have to work until the age of twenty and then for an additional five years with salary for the same master; then they could become independent cultivators or agricultural laborers. Female slaves could be emancipated once they had produced enough children to augment the colonial population.

Raynal (or Pechméja) warned that if the condition of the blacks in the colonies were not ameliorated, the result would be a slave uprising that would lead to reprisals and destruction. Only a courageous leader was missing, a "Black Spartacus" who would restore human rights and perhaps, in vengeance, replace the black code with a white code.

Raynal's increasingly radical solution to slavery did not survive long past his third edition. In 1785, it was no longer the voices of Pechméja and Diderot speaking through the pages of the *History;* Raynal had submitted to the influence of Victor-Pierre Malouet, an associate and colonial official. In his *Essay on the Administration of Saint-Domingue,* Raynal's program better reflected his own attitude toward blacks, whom he had come to believe were happier as slave laborers than as victims of their own barbaric and hostile society in Africa. Caribbean agricultural products could be cultivated only by blacks, Raynal argued, and until they could produce a Montesquieu among themselves, blacks were closer to humanity as slaves than in their own lands: "Servitude, and what is necessary to maintain it, has marked an immense distance from the white man to the black man."

As a collective enterprise spanning three major editions, struggling through an era in which humanitarian ideals were balanced with economic realities, the *History* was frequently inconsistent. But even with its contradictions, Raynal's *History* embodied the discussion of slavery and its abolition in the eighteenth century. To its contemporaries, it was a synthesis of Enlightenment antislavery ideas within a global framework and animated by strong advocacy. On balance, Abbé Raynal was regarded as a kind of oracle in the march toward abolition.

William H. Alexander

See also: Enlightenment.

Further Reading

Hunt, Lynn, ed. and trans. *The French Revolution and Human Rights: A Brief Documentary History.* New York: Bedford/St. Martin's, 1996.

Muthu, Sankar. *Enlightenment Against Empire.* Princeton, NJ: Princeton University Press, 2003.

Realf, Richard (1834–1878)

An agent of Free Soil expansion into Kansas, a confidant of the radical abolitionist John Brown, a distinguished Union officer, and a poet, journalist, and lecturer, Richard Realf was one of the most charismatic figures of the antislavery movement in the United States.

Realf was born to a peasant family in East Sussex, England, on June 14, 1834. His early verses attracted the attention of the literary set of Brighton, including Lady Byron and the celebrated poet Samuel Rogers, both of whom assisted in the publication of a slim volume of his poetry, *Guesses at the Beautiful,* in 1852.

After an ill-fated love affair in Britain, Realf traveled to America in 1854 and worked at the Five Points House of Industry in the notorious slum district of New York. He became a staunch supporter of the abolitionist movement, traveling to Kansas in 1856 with the escort party of an emigrant group of Free Soil settlers, most of whom were farmers who opposed slavery in the region.

In Kansas, Realf worked as a reporter for several Northern newspapers and was intent on furthering the cause of abolition. He wrote a series of poems for local newspapers, later published under the title *Richard Realf's Free State Poems* (1900). He became an intimate and supporter of John Brown and was named secretary of state in Brown's provisional government, which was outlined at the Chatham Convention in 1858.

Returning to Britain on a fund-raising mission, Realf had a change of heart regarding Brown's plans, and he returned to America via New Orleans in order to witness the institution of slavery firsthand. He thereby escaped involvement in Brown's disastrous Harpers Ferry raid of October 1859, though he was later arrested in Texas under suspicion of compliance in the incident and investigated by a Senate commission before being discharged.

For Realf, the U.S. Civil War was clearly about slavery, and he fought with distinction in the Union army, serving with the Eighty-eighth Illinois Volunteer Infantry. He later served as a white officer with the Fiftieth Regiment of the U.S. Colored Troops, and his name appears on the African American Civil War Memorial in Washington, D.C. After the war, Realf worked for the Freedmen's Bureau, which was established by the War Department in 1865 to oversee relief efforts and educational activities related to refugees and freedmen.

In 1869, Realf resumed his career as a lecturer, journalist, and poet, writing for the leading journals and magazines of the day. In Graniteville, South Carolina, he set up a school for blacks. He spent his leisure time teaching children by day and their parents in the evening in a thatched-roof shed, because no one would rent him a room. Intimidation from the local white population, threats by the Ku Klux Klan, and a lack of support from his spouse caused him to abandon his educational efforts.

Realf's subsequent career and private life were fraught with difficulties. Destitute, in failing health, and facing a charge of bigamy from his wife, he committed suicide in San Francisco on October 28, 1878.

Realf had appointed his friend Richard J. Hinton as his literary executor. Few manuscripts of Realf's poetry existed, and Hinton set about the task of collecting copies. A volume of Realf's poetry, together with an emotionally charged memoir by Hinton, was finally published in 1898 as *Poems by Richard Realf, Poet, Soldier, Workman.*

Carole Realff

See also: Brown, John; U.S. Colored Troops.

Further Reading

Stimson, John Ward. "An Overlooked American Shelley." *The Arena,* July 1903, 15–26.

Reason, Charles L. (1818–1893)

Charles L. Reason was one of the most influential African American abolitionists of the early nineteenth century. As an educator, an officer in several antislavery organizations, and a critic of the African colonization movement, he worked to hasten the end of slavery in the United States.

Born on July 21, 1818, to Haitian immigrant parents, Reason attended New York City's African Free School as a young boy and developed a talent for mathematics. When he was only fourteen years old, he became an instructor at the school and used his salary to hire additional tutors. As a young man, Reason wished to pursue a future in the ministry, but he was denied entrance into the General Theological Seminary of the Protestant Episcopal Church because of his race. Disillusioned, he left the church and enrolled at McGrawville College in upstate New York. Beyond his brother, Patrick (who became a famous artist and engraver), little is known of Reason's private life except that he was married and widowed three times and that his third wife was named Clorice Esteve.

Reason began his political career in December 1833 when he joined the New York Anti-Slavery Society, a branch of the American Anti-Slavery Society, and embraced a radical policy of immediate abolition and black civil rights. In August 1837, Reason became committed to the cause of suffrage and, along with other concerned activists, such as Henry Highland Garnet and Charles Downing, attended a public meeting of young black activists. The goal of the Young Men's Convention was to challenge the restrictive suffrage clause of the New York State constitution, which set a $250 property requirement in order for blacks to vote. Three years later, Reason, along with Charles B. Ray, issued a call for a state convention of black men to discuss strategies for gaining voting rights. The outcome was a series of state conventions, the first of which was held in Albany in August 1840.

The following August, another state suffrage convention was held, at which Reason and Garnet were asked to draft a public address. The two men quickly found themselves at odds. Reason was disturbed by a passage that he felt too strongly suggested violent resistance. In response, Garnet became extremely annoyed, and a raucous debate ensued. In fact, the discussion lasted all night and was not resolved until the following morning, when the convention elected to adopt the controversial passage. Yet Reason drafted another address at the convention that was directed to the black community, urging its members to action. The message especially targeted black men, who, Reason claimed, needed to stand up for their manhood and defend their families against injustice. Particularly strong words were directed at black ministers, who, in his view, had not sufficiently used their influence and position to advance the cause of the race.

Reason's commitment to black rights in the United States also fueled his opposition to colonization. In 1851, he attacked the Liberian Agricultural and Emigration Society, and in 1860, he strongly criticized Garnet for his support of African colonization.

For Reason, the key to uplifting his race was black education. He advocated the creation of manual labor schools and, in 1850, helped form the American League of Colored Laborers, which focused on industrial education. In 1847, Reason and Ray established the Society for the Promotion of Education Among Colored Children to promote black control of education and self-help in the black community, and in 1848, Reason served as a school superintendent.

In 1849, Reason became the first black college professor in the United States when he was hired to teach at New York Central College in McGrawville, New York. Three years later, Reason resigned to become principal of Philadelphia's Institute for Colored Youth. The following year, he represented Pennsylvania at the Colored National Convention.

In 1855, Reason returned to New York City, where he served as a teacher and school administrator. He launched a successful crusade against the city's policy of segregated schools in 1873. A year after retiring, he died in New York City on August 16, 1893.

Leslie M. Alexander

See also: Garnet, Henry Highland; Ray, Charles B.; Reason, Patrick H.

Further Reading

Mayo, Anthony R. "Charles Lewis Reason." *Negro History Bulletin* 5 (June 1942): 212–15.
Simmons, William J. *Men of Mark: Eminent, Progressive, and Rising.* 1887. Chicago: Johnson, 1970.

Reason, Patrick H. (ca. 1816–1857)

Patrick Henry Reason was an African American abolitionist and artist whose engravings of kneeling slaves became powerful symbols in the transatlantic abolitionist movement. Reason also advocated strongly for the right of free black men to vote.

Reason was born in New York City about 1816 to parents who had fled from Haiti. As a child, he attended the African Free School, where the teachers quickly recognized his talent for art. He was soon apprenticed to a white engraver who taught him the craft. At the age of thirteen, Reason received special attention for designing the frontispiece for Charles C. Andrews's *The History of the African Free School* (1830). Little is known of his personal life, and it is not certain whether he ever married or had children. What is clear is that Reason made art his life's work, creating engravings, lithographs, and pencil and wash drawings of abolitionists and escaped slaves.

His most famous pieces were two copper engravings. "Am I Not a Woman and a Sister?" (depicting a chained woman kneeling in prayer) was frequently used as a letterhead by abolitionists from the mid-1830s on. Its companion piece, "Am I Not a Man and a Brother?" (depicting a male slave in tattered clothing kneeling in prayer) appeared on the membership certificates of the Philadelphia Vigilant Committee, a group of African American activists who aided escaped slaves.

Reason's art was often used as frontispieces for the autobiographies of escaped slaves, such as *The Narrative of James Williams* (1838) and *The Narrative of the Life and Adventures of Henry Bibb* (1849). He also received portrait commissions from such noted abolitionists as the British reformer Granville Sharp, New York governor DeWitt Clinton, and James McCune Smith.

As a young man, Reason became involved in the abolitionist movement when he joined the New York Anti-Slavery Society, a branch of the American Anti-Slavery Society that embraced a radical policy of immediate abolition and black civil rights. When the Tappan brothers, two wealthy New York activists, withdrew from the national organization to protest the nomination of a woman to its executive council, Reason and a number of other black New Yorkers were among the dissenting faction. Reason worked with the Tappans in 1840 to create a new organization, the American and Foreign Anti-Slavery Society, in order to foster abolitionism in the nation's churches.

Beyond abolition, Reason was also deeply concerned about suffrage rights for free black men. On July 27, 1840, the black community gathered at Philomathean Hall in New York City to discuss the upcoming state convention and to select delegates. Under his leadership, the group attempted to pass resolutions supporting the convention and the need for political elevation for free blacks through the expansion of suffrage. The meeting quickly devolved into argument and dissension. John Peterson offered a resolution stating that because of overwhelming prejudice, it was unreasonable to believe that black people could advance their cause through any separate action. Although Reason declared the motion out of order, Peterson and James McCune Smith refused to be silenced. During the rest of the night, Peterson and Smith attempted to pass a series of resolutions opposing the state convention, but they were unable to gain adequate support. The debates persisted until late that night, when they were forced to adjourn without any conclusive decisions.

Despite the dispute in the days before the state meeting, the convention of 1840 was successful.

Convened in August in Albany, black delegates came from throughout the state to discuss the condition of their people and to make plans for obtaining their suffrage. The New York City delegation dominated the convention, with Charles B. Ray serving as chairman and Patrick Reason, his brother Charles L. Reason, William Johnson, and Theodore Wright holding influential positions. Patrick Reason was also one of the conveners of the second state convention in 1841.

Throughout most of the 1840s, Reason committed himself to his art, re-emerging briefly in 1857 to support another suffrage convention. The event was a dismal failure, as the New York State legislature refused to consider the petitions submitted. Shortly thereafter, in late 1857, Reason died in New York City.

Leslie M. Alexander

See also: Reason, Charles L.

Further Reading

Bolden, Tonya. *Strong Men Keep Coming: The Book of African American Men.* New York: Wiley, 1999.

Goodman, Paul. *Of One Blood: Abolitionism and the Origins of Racial Equality.* Berkeley: University of California Press, 1998.

Stauffer, John. *The Black Hearts of Men: Radical Abolitionists and the Transformation of Race.* Cambridge, MA: Harvard University Press, 2001.

Rebouças, André (1838–1898)

André Rebouças was a Brazilian intellectual who opposed slavery because he believed that it was inconsistent with the development of a modern industrial nation. As a mulatto, he faced the sting of racism, but Rebouças expressed his opposition to slavery in economic terms.

Rebouças was born in Cachoeira in the state of Bahia, Brazil, in 1838. He was the son of Antônio Pereira Rebouças and Carolina Pinto Rebouças, daughter of a wealthy merchant. His father was a deputy who was known for defending the political participation of mulattoes, and, in 1847, he became the first mulatto to have permission to work as a lawyer in Brazil.

In 1846, Rebouças moved with his family to Rio de Janeiro, the capital of the empire. In Rio, he attended the university and graduated as a military engineer. In 1860, he traveled with his brother Antônio to Europe, where they stayed until the end of 1862. Soon after their return, Rebouças joined the army, and, as a lieutenant in the engineering corps, he fought in the Paraguay War from 1865 to 1866.

After the war, Rebouças returned to Rio and became a professor at the Polytechnic School, teaching zoology, botany, architecture, and accounting. He joined the Engineering Club and the National Industrial Society, where he advocated the adaptation of certain crops, such as wheat, to the Brazilian climate. He also called for the improvement of the quality and volume of Brazilian exports. With his brother, Rebouças displayed his engineering skill by leading the expansion of Rio's water supply and the construction of two major sea docks between 1866 and 1871.

About this time, Rebouças became involved with the abolitionist movement in Rio de Janeiro. In 1880, together with other important antislavery activists in Brazil, such as Joaquim Nabuco and José do Patrocínio, Rebouças founded the Brazilian Anti-Slavery Society (*Sociedade Brasileira Contra a Escravidão*), which helped secure the emancipation of elderly slaves after 1885.

He supported the modernization of Brazil along European standards of freedom, economic development, and industry. According to Rebouças, modernity and freedom were essential to development, and as a consequence, there was no justification for slavery. He criticized slavery in economic terms. For him, the abolition of slavery was essential to the diversification of the economy and the standardization of labor. Without these two prerequisites, modernization was impossible. Full abolition could be accomplished only if education and land ownership were liberalized and made available to the masses.

Although a monarchist, Rebouças criticized the political and economic policies of the Brazilian monarchy, especially Brazil's agro-export economy, and warned of the danger of dependency on outside powers. Similarly, he condemned the immigration policy under which millions of Africans had been introduced, arguing that Brazil did not need extra laborers so much as improvements in education, industry, and communications. He published several articles in newspapers in which he tried to convince slave owners that wage labor was more productive. In 1883, after a one-year stay in Europe, he wrote the manifesto of the Abolitionist Confederation (*Confederação Abolicionista*) with Patrocínio. In the manifesto, Rebouças and Patrocínio called for the adoption of the U.S. model of industrial expansion in Brazil.

Though he was a rich and politically powerful man, Rebouças was also a victim of racism. As his political power increased, he suffered attacks from members of the elite, who were unsatisfied with the achievements that a mulatto man had accomplished in Brazil. Rebouças's diary describes the problems that he faced in New York as a black man; for example, on one occasion, he was only accepted in a hotel after the direct intervention of the Brazilian consulate.

In 1889, after the proclamation of the Brazilian Republic, which was dominated by Brazil's landholding elite, Rebouças departed in self-exile to Lisbon, Portugal, where he worked as a foreign correspondent for the *Times* of London. In 1892, he went to Luanda in modern-day Angola, where he spent fifteen months. From there, he migrated to Funchal in the Madeira Islands, where he died in 1898.

Mariana P. Candido

See also: Brazil, Abolition in; Nabuco, Joaquim; Patrocínio, José do.

Further Reading

Haberly, David T. *Three Sad Races: Racial Identity and National Consciousness in Brazilian Literature.* Cambridge, UK: Cambridge University Press, 1983.
Spitzer, Leo. *Lives in Between: The Experience of Marginality in a Century of Emancipation.* New York: Hill and Wang, 1999.

Reconstruction

The term *Reconstruction* refers to the period in American history immediately following the U.S. Civil War—from 1867 to 1877—during which efforts were made to assist former slaves as they made the transition from slavery to freedom. In spite of federal legislative initiatives and three new constitutional amendments extending civil liberties to African Americans, much of the Reconstruction effort remained incomplete when federal troops left the South in 1877.

As divisive and destructive as the Civil War was, the process of Reconstruction perpetuated the sectional strife between North and South. The perceived imposition of punitive restrictions upon the liberties of white Southerners, coupled with the legislated expansion of rights to the recently emancipated blacks, stirred much discontent in the South. Though many questions confronted the nation during this pivotal period, the single most important issue concerned the social and economic status of former slaves. Reconstruction presented an opportunity to define freedom in America in new, more inclusive ways. Instead, the final result helped establish a system whereby former slaves and their descendants were systematically denied equality. Thus, Reconstruction was both an unprecedented opportunity and a great tragedy.

Because blacks greatly outnumbered whites in the state, South Carolina's first Reconstruction assembly in 1870 had an African American majority. There and elsewhere in the South, black empowerment was met with white violence. *(Hulton Archive/Getty Images)*

Lincoln and the Ten Percent Plan

In many ways, Reconstruction began before the war was over and, indeed, even before the Union's victory was assured. By summer 1862, President Abraham Lincoln had begun to consider freeing the slaves in the South. Although he personally deplored slavery, Lincoln envisioned emancipation primarily as a measure that would undermine the Confederacy's ability to wage war. He announced the Emancipation Proclamation on September 22, 1862, shortly after the Union victory at Antietam, declaring his intent to free all slaves in areas in rebellion against the United States on January 1, 1863.

Although the Emancipation Proclamation was important to the Union war effort in many ways—including its allowing for the enlistment of black soldiers—it also set the agenda for Reconstruction. It meant that if the Union won the war, slavery would be abolished, and people in both the North and South would be forced to deal with the fallout.

As early as 1862, the Union army began to take control of large tracts of Confederate territory, and Lincoln pondered ways to re-establish Southern state governments in order to speed the process of emancipation. Hoping to achieve a peaceful and expedient reconciliation, he devised a policy for wartime Reconstruction called the "Ten Percent Plan." Under its terms, former Confederate states could be re-admitted to the Union if 10 percent of voters registered in 1860 signed an oath of loyalty to the federal government. Once this was achieved, voters could elect a constitutional convention that, among other things, was required to follow federal law, including the Emancipation Proclamation. By 1864, state governments formed under the Ten Percent Plan existed in Arkansas, Louisiana, and Tennessee, despite opposition from some in the U.S. Congress who believed the president's policy was too lenient. Clearly, the eradication of slavery and the way emancipation was handled would play prominent roles in shaping the political realities of the post–Civil War South.

The collapse of the Confederacy and Lincoln's assassination in spring 1865 altered the course of Reconstruction and, with it, the course of African American freedom. The new president, Andrew Johnson of Tennessee, wanted to punish elite white Southerners for their role in the war, but he did not embrace the cause of civil rights for former slaves. Neither did he support federal efforts to redistribute abandoned plantation lands to newly freed slaves.

As early as 1864, Union army officers in places such as the South Carolina Sea Islands had declared plantations owned by citizens who supported the Confederacy to be forfeited. Such land was subdivided and given to former slaves in the hope that they would forge new lives on these plots. As the new president pardoned many former Confederates in order to move the nation forward and beyond the divisiveness of the war, he also restored their property rights, thus ending hopes that the federal authorities would provide for the freedmen's economic future. Initial efforts had led the former slaves to expect such assistance, giving rise to the myth that the government had promised to provide each head of household "forty acres and a mule" with which to build a life after slavery.

Congressional Response

As some black Southerners were forced to return land to their former masters, new governments assumed power in the states of the former Confederacy. The leaders of these new governments, chosen by a white electorate, had played prominent roles in the Confederate government, indicating to many Northerners that white Southerners were unwilling to abandon the past and look to the future. Although Congress refused to recognize new Southern members such as former Confederate vice president Alexander H. Stephens, the new state legislatures dominated by the traditional elite began to assert their political power.

The most telling examples of their recalcitrance were bodies of laws called Black Codes. These statutes dictated the social and legal parameters that black Southerners were expected to follow. Such codes varied from state to state, but most did not allow blacks to bring suit in court or own most types of property. They also placed severe limits on other civil liberties. Most states prevented blacks from carrying firearms or possessing alcohol, outlawed interracial marriage, and further limited black testimony in court.

The harshest restrictions, however, were economic. Some of these codes required black Southerners to sign annual labor contracts with white landowners; if they refused, they could be jailed. Children of impoverished parents were often forced to become apprentices to white tradesmen. Petty criminals could be forced to labor for white landowners who paid their fines. In short, the Black Codes were designed to control the social status of former slaves while simultaneously creating a labor system—oppressive and grounded in white supremacy—to replace slavery.

Northern white political leaders, especially Republicans such as Thaddeus Stevens, Benjamin Wade, and Charles Sumner, saw such actions as undermining the progress achieved by the war. Labeled Radical Republicans, they began to push for congressional control of Reconstruction and a political agenda that included civil rights and social protections for former slaves. In December 1865, the states ratified the Thirteenth Amendment, formally ending slavery in the United States. In 1866, the Radical Republicans passed—over President Johnson's veto—the Civil Rights Act, which was designed to negate the Black Codes by providing equality for all under the law.

In 1866, the Radicals also pushed successfully for the creation of the Bureau of Refugees, Freedmen and Abandoned Lands within the Department of War. The first federal social welfare agency, the Freedmen's Bureau attempted to help black Southerners negotiate labor contracts, acquire an education, and sometimes just find food and shelter. In addition, private groups such as the American Missionary Association took up the cause of black education in the South, often cooperating with Freedmen's Bureau officials to build schools.

For the Radical Republicans, such efforts were not enough. In 1867, Congress seized control of Reconstruction in a series of laws known as the Reconstruction Acts. These laws divided the South into five military districts, set more stringent criteria for readmission to the Union, and placed the legislative rather than the executive branch in control of the process. Although President Johnson's impeachment trial the next year solidified congressional control of Reconstruction, the Reconstruction Acts had the more immediate effect of providing for black male suffrage under new Southern state constitutions (later expanded to include all the states by the Fifteenth Amendment, ratified in 1870). Congress passed the Fourteenth Amendment, which was ratified by the states in 1868, making blacks citizens and providing for equal protection under the law.

Generally, the Republicans rose to dominance in the new state governments organized under the Reconstruction Acts. Both Northern whites and Southern whites—derided as "carpetbaggers" and "scalawags," respectively—held most of the political power at this stage of Reconstruction. But the Republican Party also aggressively cultivated newly enfranchised black voters. Local organizations called Union Leagues mobilized this segment among the electorate at the grassroots level.

Black voters not only helped the Republicans gain control of every state government in the former Confederacy, but they even brought black Southerners to public office. Hiram Revels of Mississippi won a seat in the U.S. Senate, Francis L. Cardozo was elected secretary of state of South Carolina, and countless other black leaders filled offices at the federal, state, and local levels.

Some white Southerners responded to black social, political, and economic empowerment with violence. Through organizations such as the Ku Klux Klan, whites across the South sought to re-assert white supremacy and intimidate black voters by committing lynchings and other acts of violence against black Southerners and their white allies. By 1870, the violence had become so widespread that Congress began formal inquiries and eventually passed laws designed to bring the Klansmen to justice.

Unfortunately for black Southerners, such efforts were unsuccessful. Often, Klan leaders and white politicians worked together to punish Republicans of both races. In North Carolina in 1871, for example, Klan leaders and Conservative Party politicians cooperated to impeach Republican governor William Woods Holden because of his support for black rights and opposition to the Klan.

Legacy

By the mid-1870s, all Confederate states except Louisiana, South Carolina, and Florida had been readmitted to the Union. Troops were withdrawn, Freedmen's Bureau agents went home, and race relations evolved in an environment that was devoid of direct federal supervision.

Once freed of voting restrictions, white Southerners rose to dominate state governments, displacing Republicans of both races. The Republican Party in the South began a precipitous decline; in the years following Reconstruction, the South became the nation's most solidly Democratic region. This left black voters without a viable political voice and helped pave the way for the disenfranchisement and segregation that were in place at the end of the nineteenth century.

In 1876, controversies over disputed electoral votes in Louisiana, South Carolina, and Florida set the stage for the end of Reconstruction. In exchange for allowing these electoral votes to go to Republican Rutherford B. Hayes, Southern Democrats demanded that federal troops be removed from the three states and that other concessions be made. The Northern

Republicans agreed, choosing political expediency over loyalty to black Southerners.

Thus ended Reconstruction. For a brief period, at least, former slaves enjoyed equality under the law, the right to vote, and personal freedom as they had never known before. Although black Southerners had gained their freedom, they still lacked equality, economic opportunity, and legal protection.

Richard D. Starnes

See also: Amendments, Reconstruction; "Forty Acres and a Mule"; Freedmen's Bureau; Ku Klux Klan; Stevens, Thaddeus; Sumner, Charles; Wade, Benjamin Franklin.

Further Reading

Carter, Dan T. *When the War Was Over: The Failure of Self-Reconstruction in the South, 1865–1867.* Baton Rouge: Louisiana State University Press, 1985.

Foner, Eric. *Reconstruction: America's Unfinished Revolution.* New York: Harper & Row, 1988.

Lemann, Nicholas. *Redemption: The Last Battle of the Civil War.* New York: Farrar, Straus and Giroux, 2006.

Trelease, Allen W. *White Terror: The Ku Klux Klan Conspiracy and Southern Reconstruction.* Baton Rouge: Louisiana State University Press, 1971, 1995.

Religion and Abolitionism

Throughout the history of slavery, religious communities worldwide were conspicuously silent in their criticism of the institution and their apparent disinterest in advocating the cause of emancipation. Although this action may seem at odds with our modern sensibility, which views slavery through the twin lenses of morality and ethics, the churches' position must be considered within the context of times in which church and state were not separate but were often in league with one another to achieve a common purpose. From the time of Saint Augustine onward, those who sought to advance the celestial "city of God" found themselves beholden to sustain the temporal "city of man" in all its manifestations. Therefore, any challenge to the established social order that slavery represented was not in the best interest of the religious class.

The three great religions of the Western world—Judaism, Christianity, and Islam—readily accepted that slavery was sanctioned as an acceptable practice, with only minor restrictions found in the scriptures. The Hebrew Torah makes reference to the term for which slaves should be held (generally seven years) and includes a special provision that all slaves should be freed in the year of the Jubilee, which occurred every fifty years. The Christian Bible does not criticize slavery; in fact, it contains particular references suggesting that slaves should accept their appointed lot with Christian humility (later understood as an acceptance of planter paternalism). Such advice is found, for example, in Ephesians 6:5, which urges slaves "to obey your earthly masters with fear and trembling, in singleness of heart, as you obey Christ." Muslims were not permitted to enslave fellow believers, but the Koran does permit the enslavement of infidels (all non-Muslims, according to the Islamic view).

The peoples of Western Europe became Christianized during and immediately after the fall of the Roman Empire. As new rulers were crowned in the incipient European states, they sought to demonstrate their legitimacy through a close alliance with Christian belief and custom. In their so doing, church and state buttressed one another during this critical era. This arrangement was largely one of convenience, but it would prove to have far-reaching consequences many centuries down the line.

As the theological foundations of Western Christianity were organized in the writings of Saint Augustine and Thomas Aquinas, neither of the early church fathers found cause to criticize the labor practices of slavery or serfdom. In fact, Aquinas's doctrine of "just war," which he developed to justify the actions of Christian knights fighting in the Crusades against Muslim forces who had conquered the Holy Land, would later be employed to sanctify the actions of European slave traders who plied the coast of West Africa seeking human cargo. This practice became enshrined in church policy when Pope Nicholas V issued the bull *Dum Diversas* in June 1452, which authorized King Alfonso V of Portugal to enslave West African "pagans" and other "unbelievers."

Roman Catholicism was not alone in its apparent endorsement of slavery. During the Protestant Reformation of the sixteenth century, neither Martin Luther nor John Calvin found reason to criticize the system of transatlantic slave trading that was taking shape contemporaneously with their religious movements. It would be left to other more radical reformers to broach the issue and to question the morality of the slave trade and slaveholding. Reformers such as the Quakers (Society of Friends) and the Methodists would find themselves challenged by the mainline Protestant denominations, which criticized such reformers for being too concerned with worldly affairs to be true people of faith.

Quakers on both sides of the Atlantic were some of the earliest abolitionists. They recognized that slavery was a violation of a secular ethic—the essential question of good versus evil—while many coreligionists of more traditional Protestant denominations struggled with the understanding that slavery was a biblically sanctioned practice. Although most of the mainline denominations would later divide over the issue of slavery, the faith communities of the Anabaptist tradition remained largely unified during the religious schisms that would characterize subsequent abolitionist debates.

By the mid-eighteenth century, new religious denominations such as the Methodists, the spiritual followers of John Wesley, had splintered from the Anglican (Church of England) communion, and members of these denominations took a more active stance against the perceived sin of the slave trade. In true missionary endeavors, men such as Wesley and Thomas Coke would attempt to convert slave owners to the abolitionist perspective through persistent argument and moral suasion.

Slave owners were careful to prevent religion from interfering with the economic viability of slavery and the immense profits that it generated. The Virginia House of Burgesses enacted a law in 1682 that reduced all non-Christian bond servants to permanent status as slaves regardless of any future religious conversion experiences. The new law allowed slaves who were Christians at the time of their arrival in Virginia to be enslaved for life. By 1793, the General Committee of Virginia Baptists had reached the conclusion that because emancipation was a political question, it should be addressed by legislative action, not through pronouncements agreed on by church convocations.

In many respects, there seemed to be a disconnect between the thoughts and practices of many slaveholders regarding the proper place of religion. Most slave owners believed that it was desirable for their slaves to acquire religion—they believed that religion would make slaves more docile and accepting of their condition—yet these same owners wanted to maintain rigid control over who could preach to their slaves and the religious messages that were delivered. In the same breath, owners praised religion for helping slaves to accept their plight, while also fearing that the Christian message of deliverance might incite slaves to resist the authority of their masters.

Softening its previous antislavery tone, the Methodist Church stated its intention in 1836 to refrain from interfering in civil and political relationships between masters and slaves. The slavery question began to cause a schism in many religious communities in the United States as early as 1844, when the Methodist Episcopal Church divided over the question of whether bishops within the church should be allowed to hold slaves. This debate grew out of a decision by Georgia bishop James O. Andrews to continue holding his slaves after church authorities had told him to manumit them or else give up his bishopric.

As a result of this division, white Southerners formed the Methodist Episcopal Church, South. A similar disruption would take place in most mainline Protestant denominations during the 1850s.

Junius P. Rodriguez

See also: Allen, Richard (African American bishop); Anabaptists; Beecher, Henry Ward; Finney, Charles Grandison; Great Awakening; Quakers (Society of Friends); Second Great Awakening; Society for the Propagation of the Gospel in Foreign Parts; Wesley, John.

Further Reading

Banner, Lois W. "Religion and Reform in the Early Republic: The Role of Youth." *American Quarterly* 22 (December 1971): 677–95.

———. "Religious Benevolence as Social Control: A Critique of an Interpretation." *Journal of American History* 60 (June 1973): 23–41.

Carroll, Bret E. Review of *The Religious World of Antislavery Women: Spirituality in the Lives of Five Abolitionist Lecturers,* by Anna M. Speicher. *Journal of American History* 88 (December 2001): 1068–69.

Griffin, Clifford S. "Religious Benevolence as Social Control, 1815–1860." *Mississippi Valley Historical Review* 44 (December 1957): 423–44.

Hammond, John L. "Revival Religion and Antislavery Politics." *American Sociological Review* 39 (April 1974): 175–86.

McKivigan, John R., ed. *Abolitionism and American Religion.* New York: Garland, 1999.

Van Deburg, William L. "William Lloyd Garrison and the 'Pro-Slavery Priesthood': The Changing Beliefs of an Evangelical Reformer." *Journal of the American Academy of Religion* 43 (June 1975): 224–37.

Rock, John Sweat (1825–1866)

John Sweat Rock was one of the youngest black abolitionists to lend his voice to the movement against slavery in the United States. Broadly talented, he became a teacher, dentist, medical doctor, and lawyer—all in a short life. Although he earned his income from these sources, he also lectured widely on antislavery and abolition and lobbied for African American civil rights. Rock unsuccessfully petitioned the Committee on Federal Relations of the Massachusetts House of Representatives to remove the word *white* from the state's militia code. After the U.S. Congress approved the creation of black units to fight in the U.S. Civil War, Rock worked to recruit black men for the Fifty-fourth and Fifty-fifth Regiments of the Massachusetts Volunteer Infantry and subsequently lobbied for equal pay for African American troops. On February 1, 1865, the day after Congress passed the Thirteenth Amendment abolishing slavery, Rock became the first African American attorney to be admitted to the bar to practice law before the U.S. Supreme Court.

Rock was born on October 13, 1825, into a free black family in Salem, New Jersey, that had sufficient means to permit him to study in the local schools until the age of nineteen. He loved to read and, while still a student himself, started teaching others in his community. For four years, Rock taught in a one-room schoolhouse in Salem.

Rock's health was poor throughout his life, and his natural interest in medicine stemmed from his desire to remedy his own condition. He studied with two local physicians in the hope that he could prepare himself to attend medical school, but he discovered that he was barred from admittance because of his race. Undaunted, Rock decided instead to pursue a career in dentistry, which he mastered by 1849. That same year, Rock first became involved with the abolitionist movement, when he addressed the Pennsylvania Anti-Slavery Society. In 1851, Rock became the director of Philadelphia's Apprentices' High School, a night school for the city's black population.

Rock practiced dentistry in Philadelphia from 1849 until 1853, when he decided to relocate to Boston. Most likely through the influence of white doctors in his community, Rock was permitted to enroll in the American Medical College in Philadelphia, from which he graduated with a medical degree in 1852.

Rock was only twenty-eight years old when he arrived in Boston, but he soon found himself swept up in the vigorous antislavery movement that was headquartered there. He became involved in local abolitionist societies and was a member of the Boston Vigilance Committee, which took care of fugitive slaves in transit to freedom. In October 1855, Rock served as a delegate to the Colored National Convention in Philadelphia.

Of his many antislavery speeches, the most famous and most controversial was delivered at Boston's Faneuil Hall on Crispus Attucks Day, March 5, 1858.

Rock delivered a speech in which he praised his race and all of the physical qualities associated with it while disparaging the lesser qualities of whites. Rock proudly asserted, "I would have you understand, that I not only love my race, but am pleased with my color." Although the surviving transcript is incomplete, some have asserted that this speech represented the first use of the "Black Is Beautiful" slogan popularized in the 1960s. Rock continued to lecture widely, speaking at events such as the 1862 meeting of the Massachusetts Anti-Slavery Society and the 1864 National Convention of Colored Men.

Rock traveled to France for surgery in May 1858, returning to the United States the following year. His failing health required him to suspend his medical and dental practice; Rock began to study law. Under the tutelage of Robert Morris, Boston's best-known African American lawyer, Rock passed the bar in 1861 and was permitted to practice in Massachusetts.

Rock continued to press the antislavery agenda during the Civil War years. He was initially dissatisfied with President Abraham Lincoln because of the president's seemingly slow pace in addressing the slavery question. Once Lincoln announced the Emancipation Proclamation in September 1862, Rock became a supporter. In 1863, he worked to recruit black troops for the two regiments, the Fifty-fourth and Fifty-fifth Massachusetts Volunteer Infantry, that had been authorized by Governor John Albion Andrews. Though Rock praised the use of black troops, he criticized attempts by the federal government to pay them less than white troops.

With the assistance of Massachusetts senator Charles Sumner, who petitioned Supreme Court Justice Salmon P. Chase on Rock's behalf, Rock was admitted to the bar of the Supreme Court in February 1865. Both activists and the press commented on the significance of the decision, which was perceived by many as a repudiation of the infamous *Dred Scott* decision (1857), in which the Supreme Court had denied the right of citizenship to African Americans. If a black man was granted the right to appear before the Supreme Court, they argued, how could the *Dred Scott* decision hold up?

Rock never argued a case before the Supreme Court. He died of tuberculosis on December 3, 1866, at the age of forty-one.

Junius P. Rodriguez

See also: Chase, Salmon P.; Massachusetts Fifty-Fourth Regiment.

Further Reading

Quarles, Benjamin. *Black Abolitionists.* New York: Oxford University Press, 1969.

Roper, Moses (1815–?)

An escaped slave from the United States, Moses Roper became a prominent abolitionist speaker in Great Britain. His *Narrative of the Adventures and Escape of Moses Roper, From American Slavery* (1837) describes the brutality of slavery and one man's determination to obtain freedom.

Like many fugitive slave biographies, much of the information that historians know comes from Roper's own narrative. Roper was born in Caswell County, North Carolina. His mother was a house slave of mixed African and Native American descent, and his father was a white master, Henry Roper. After his father's death, Moses, then six years old, was separated from his mother and sold in 1821. Thus began his life under a series of nearly fifteen owners and informal masters across the South; the most notable was a brutal South Carolina planter, John Gooch, for whom Roper worked as a cotton hand from 1829 to 1832.

Harsh treatment prompted Roper to make several unsuccessful attempts at escape, transgressions for which he was flogged and kept in irons for extended periods. Despite these oppressive measures, he finally succeeded in escaping in 1831. Playing on his ability to pass as white, he traveled as far as North Carolina, where he visited his mother and extended family. Roper was recaptured and subjected to Gooch's harsh punishments, which included burning him and the removal of some of his fingernails and toenails.

After Roper had made more than nine escape bids, Gooch sold him in 1832 to a Mr. Beveridge of Apalachicola, Florida. Beveridge worked Roper as a steward on a steamboat before going bankrupt.

In a final escape from yet another new master, Roper headed North to Savannah, Georgia, getting work in mid-1834 as a steward on a ship to New York and working his way to New England. For more than a year, Roper traveled in search of employment in upstate New York, Vermont, and New Hampshire. During this time, he started attending church, learned to read, and made contact with American abolitionists in Boston, where he signed the American Anti-Slavery Society's constitution. Afraid of being recaptured, he set sail for England in November 1835.

Accompanied by a letter from an unnamed American abolitionist who described him as "excellent . . . [possessing] uncommon intelligence, sincere piety, and a strong desire to preach the gospel," Roper arrived in London. There, he was aided by prominent British abolitionists and forward-thinking ministers, most notably John Morrison and Francis Cox, who furthered his education in London in 1836.

Roper recounted his adventures in a number of abolitionist meetings and wrote an account of his life, *A Narrative of the Adventures and Escape of Moses Roper, From American Slavery.* The book was edited by the Reverend Thomas Price, who also contributed the preface to the first edition, which was published in 1837. In 1838, a second London edition was published, as well as the first American edition. Widely distributed and read, the narrative went through ten editions, was translated into Welsh, and sold more than 30,000 copies on both sides of the Atlantic.

Roper's story combines depictions of a wide range of horrific and remarkable events with an appealing portrayal of his own resourcefulness, awakening piety, and stoic suffering in defiance of slaveholder hypocrisy and cruelty. As the 1830s witnessed the rise of antislavery societies and tract associations, Roper's narrative was introduced to sympathetic Philadelphia readers, ushering in an era of slave narratives, including those of Lunsford Lane, Moses Grandy, and Frederick Douglass.

Roper had delivered more than 2,000 lectures in support of his book by 1844, at which time he immigrated to Canada. He returned to Britain briefly in 1846 and again in 1854 to lecture. The date of Roper's death is unknown.

Gwilym Games

See also: Fugitive Slaves.

Further Reading

Andrews, William L., ed. *North Carolina Slave Narratives: The Lives of Moses Roper, Lunsford Lane, Moses Grandy, and Thomas H. Jones.* Chapel Hill: University of North Carolina Press, 2003.
Ripley, C. Peter, et al., eds. *The Black Abolitionist Papers.* 5 vols. Chapel Hill: University of North Carolina Press, 1985–1992.

Rousseau, Jean Jacques (1712–1778)

Jean Jacques Rousseau was a Swiss-born philosopher, author, and political theorist whom historians rank as one of the greatest figures of the eighteenth-century

The French Enlightenment philosopher Jean Jacques Rousseau argued against slavery on the grounds that all persons are equal in nature. "Man is born free," he observed in *The Social Contract* (1762), "and everywhere he is in chains." *(Hulton Archive/Getty Images)*

French Enlightenment. His thought ranged widely. He was a major Enlightenment thinker, but he also had an influence on the Romantic movement, educational philosophy, and political theory. He is connected to antislavery thought mainly through his works *Discours sur l'origine et les fondements de l'inégalité parmi les hommes* (Discourse on the Origin of Inequality, 1755) and *Du contrat social* (The Social Contract, 1762).

Rousseau was born in Geneva, Switzerland, on June 28, 1712. He lived a transient and haphazard life until settling in Paris in 1741. There, he became acquainted with the encyclopedist Denis Diderot and joined the circle that included Baron de La Brède et de Montesquieu.

In his early writing—beginning with his prize-winning essay *Discours sur les Arts et les Sciences* (Discourse on the Arts and Sciences, 1750) and continuing in *Discourse on the Origin of Equality*—Rousseau voiced the harmful effects of modern civilization. He contended that man is essentially good, a "noble savage" when in the "state of nature," which he defined as the state that animals are in, or the condition man was in before the creation of civilization and society. He believed that good people are made unhappy and become "corrupted" by their experiences in society. As he explains in the *Origin of Equality,* the state of nature ended with the first person who enclosed property and claimed ownership. Ownership, sanctioned by law, leads to competition, failure of compassion, war, and "pillaging the poor." Those who become rich exercise arbitrary power, "subduing and enslaving their neighbors."

Contrary to his earlier work, Rousseau's *Social Contract* maintains that the state of nature is a brutish condition without law or morality and that good men exist only as a result of society. In this work, Rousseau views the social order more positively as "a sacred right that serves as a foundation for all others." The social order is not part of nature but a result of human convention or agreement—that is, a social contract.

According to Rousseau, human freedom and natural equality are grounded in nature, but they are compromised by the social contract, which guarantees only political liberty. He argues against "the pretended right of slavery" on two grounds: the natural equality of all at birth and reasonable logic. The first axiom is the premise for the logical arguments against slavery that Rousseau develops in the fourth chapter of book 1.

Rousseau opens *The Social Contract* with the famous words, "Man is born free, and everywhere he is in chains." According to this dictum, life in bondage stands for human life under the social contract. Though the universal metaphor need not obscure its particular relevance, Rousseau was, in fact, more concerned with the limitations that states impose on individual freedom than he was with the horrors of actual chattel slavery. Rousseau questioned the assumption that the will of the majority is always correct, and he argued that the purpose of the government should be to secure and preserve freedom, equality, and justice for all people living within its society.

The spread of the Enlightenment ideas of Rousseau, Montesquieu, and others, along with rising democratic sentiment in the United States, led to a growing attack on the slave trade. Rousseau's thought provided much of the material for the antislavery arguments. His exposure of the contradiction between principles of natural equality and the realities of convention undermined proslavery arguments grounded in notions of the "naturalness" of slavery and in scripture.

Yet locating direct, acknowledged influences on antislavery writers and abolitionist organizations who cited Rousseau is more difficult. One such writer was Thomas Day, author of the first antislavery poem in English, "The Dying Negro," whose second edition included an antislavery essay dedicated to Rousseau. Rousseau's thought also influenced the French philosophers Diderot and Abbé Raynal, who, in turn, influenced the German philosophers Immanuel Kant and Johann Gottfried von Herder.

By 1762, Rousseau had published his didactic novel *Émile,* which was condemned by the Parliament of Paris and burned. Rousseau was forced to take sanctuary in Britain with philosopher David Hume in 1765. In 1770, he finally returned to Paris. No longer pursued by the authorities, he lived as a music copyist and wrote his autobiography, *Les Confessions* (published posthumously in 1781). He died on July 2, 1778, in Ermenonville, near Paris.

Riva Berleant and Gina Misiroglu

See also: Enlightenment.

Further Reading

Muthu, Sankar. *Enlightenment Against Empire.* Princeton, NJ: Princeton University Press, 2003.

Rousseau, Jean-Jacques. *Discourse on the Origin of Inequality.* 1754. Trans. Henry J. Tozzer, ed. Lester G. Crocker. New York: Simon & Schuster, 1967.

———. *The Social Contract.* 1762. Trans. and ed. Lester G. Crocker. New York: Simon & Schuster, 1967.

Rush, Benjamin (1745–1813)

The physician and patriot Benjamin Rush was a humanitarian engaged in many areas of social reform. An antislavery activist, opponent of capital punishment, and temperance advocate, Rush published his views in the Pennsylvania press and voiced his opinions openly and often. A professor of chemistry and medicine at the College of Philadelphia (today the University of Pennsylvania Medical School), Rush was the best-known physician of his day. As such, he was an active member of Pennsylvania society, joining the Pennsylvania Abolition Society, opening the Philadelphia Dispensary (the first free dispensary in the United States), and campaigning against public and capital punishment and for general penal reform. He also advocated women's education and a national educational system capped by a national university. As a delegate from Pennsylvania to the Second Continental Congress in 1776, Rush signed the Declaration of Independence.

Benjamin Rush was born on December 12, 1745, in Philadelphia to farmers John and Susanna Rush. He was baptized Anglican, but after his father's death in 1751, the family became members of the Presbyterian Church. Susanna's brother, Samuel Finley, was a Great Awakening Presbyterian minister and master of the West Nottingham Academy in Colora, Maryland, which Rush attended from age eight to thirteen. In 1759, he entered the College of New Jersey (now Princeton University); the thirteen-year-old junior became an admirer of the college's president, Samuel Davies, who opposed slavery on the grounds that Africans could be educated.

Rush graduated in 1760 and was apprenticed to Philadelphia doctor John Redman from 1761 to 1766. During this period, Rush attended lectures at the College of Philadelphia and decided to study at the University of Edinburgh. He received his medical degree in 1768, and, during a trip to London, he met Benjamin Franklin, who urged him to travel to Paris.

In 1769, Rush returned to Philadelphia, where he practiced medicine, served as a professor of chemistry at the College of Philadelphia, and became a member of the American Philosophical Society. In 1772, he decided to remain in Philadelphia, rather than practice in Charleston, partly because he did not want to live in a slave society. Engaged in early prerevolutionary movements, Rush wrote for the press on the colonist's rights, associating with the Patriot leaders Thomas Paine, John Adams, and Thomas Jefferson.

Rush also participated in antislavery causes. At the request of Quaker abolitionist Anthony Benezet, Rush supported a 1773 Pennsylvania Assembly bill that doubled the tariff on imported slaves. Rush anonymously published *An Address to the Inhabitants of the British Settlements on the Slavery of the Negroes in America,* a pamphlet in which he equated revolutionary and antislavery ideals.

He argued that Africans were not mentally inferior to Europeans but that the harsh conditions of slavery caused slaves' mental capacities to deteriorate. Rush's understanding of the conditions of slavery was likely informed by John Coakley Lettsom, a young British doctor from the West Indies whom he had met in London. Rush dismissed as absurd the idea that dark skin was the result of blacks' descent from Cain and instead used environmentalist theory, first advocated by John Locke, to argue that Africans' skin color helped them tolerate their home continent's hot climate. He believed in educating young slaves in republican ideals so that gradual manumission might be successful. In response to a proslavery rebuttal by Philadelphian Richard Nesbit, Rush published a second pamphlet, titled *A Vindication.*

Rush participated in many significant political events. In 1775, he argued that Great Britain aimed to "enslave" Americans, and, in June 1776, he was elected to attend the provincial conference to send delegates to the Continental Congress. He was appointed to represent Philadelphia that year and was one of fifty-six men who signed the Declaration of Independence. Rush envisaged the new republic's potential for social reform. In 1782, he began advocating temperance, rejected Calvinist predestination in favor of universal salvation, and resumed his antislavery stance.

In 1782, Rush joined the Pennsylvania Society for Promoting the Abolition of Slavery (also known as the Pennsylvania Abolition Society), and he was elected one of its secretaries. The society proposed that the new U.S. Constitution include a ban on the slave trade. Rush later served as a member of the Pennsylvania ratifying convention. In 1789, he and James Wilson began a campaign that secured for Pennsylvania a more liberal and effective state constitution, the last achievement of Rush's political career. Demonstrating his commitment to gradual emancipation, in 1788, Rush declared his personal slave William—whom he had likely purchased in 1770—free as of 1794.

In 1789, Rush became a professor of medicine at the College of Philadelphia (after 1791, the University of Pennsylvania). He subsequently played a significant role in treating the victims of Philadelphia's yellow fever epidemic in 1793.

One of America's first psychiatrists, Rush published *Medical Inquiries and Observations Upon the Diseases of the Mind* in 1812. As a psychiatrist, he argued that slave owners' irrationality resulted in "negromania," a form of insanity. He also contended that slavery led to physical maladies such as dietary disorders, lockjaw, and melancholy. Rush died in Philadelphia on April 19, 1813.

Brian M. Ingrassia

See also: Benezet, Anthony; Declaration of Independence (1776); Paine, Thomas.

Further Reading

Hawke, David Freeman. *Benjamin Rush: Revolutionary Gadfly.* Indianapolis, IN: Bobbs-Merrill, 1971.

Rush, Benjamin. *An Address to the Inhabitants of the British Settlements on the Slavery of the Negroes in America.* Philadelphia: John Dunlap, 1773; New York: Arno, 1969.

Russwurm, John B. (1799–1851)

An African American journalist and educator, John Brown Russwurm helped establish the first black newspaper in the United States, *Freedom's Journal,* in the late 1820s. In line with the opinion of most abolitionists, the paper initially opposed the American Colonization Society, which sponsored Liberia as a home for blacks. Russwurm later became a staunch supporter of colonization, however, stating, "We consider it mere waste of words to talk of ever enjoying citizenship in this country." He relocated to Liberia, becoming the superintendent of public schools there and governor of the Maryland colony in Cape Palmas.

Russwurm was born in Jamaica on October 1, 1799, to an enslaved mother and a white merchant father who moved the young John to Quebec when he was eight years old. Shortly thereafter, the family moved to Maine, where his father married. Russwurm lived and was educated in Maine at the Hebron Academy. In 1824, he enrolled in Bowdoin College; when he graduated in 1826, Russwurm was among the first black college graduates in the United States. Significantly, he was selected to deliver the commencement address, titled "The Condition and Prospects of Haiti." Immediately after graduation, Russwurm moved to Boston, where he taught at the Primus Hall School for black children.

As an educated, articulate, and outspoken member of the black community, Russwurm was chosen to co-edit *Freedom's Journal* with Samuel Cornish. Although the paper had been founded in New York City in 1827, its influence reached far beyond the city and state, gaining the support of some of the most recognized black activists in the country. *Freedom's Journal* was founded, in part, as a response to the racist depictions of blacks that regularly appeared in mainstream newspapers. Thus, when the first issue of *Freedom's Journal* appeared on March 16, the editors wanted it to be the voice of the black leadership. They felt compelled to present an accurate view of their people to combat the racist attacks on their character.

Freedom's Journal provided international, national, and regional news; published editorials denouncing slavery, lynching, and other social injustices to blacks; and featured biographies of prominent African Americans, including Paul Cuffe (a black Bostonian who owned a trading ship staffed by free black people), Haitian revolutionary leader Touissant L'Ouverture, and poet Phillis Wheatley. It was soon circulating in eleven U.S. states, Canada, Western Europe, and Haiti.

The newspaper promoted the movement to uplift African Americans by improving black education. In 1828, Russwurm became the secretary for the African Dorcas Society, an organization designed to provide necessities to young children who hoped to attend school. In 1829, Russwurm wrote, "more general efforts should be made for the education of our rising youth, for it is upon them that all our hopes for the future respectability of our people are fixed." Respectability was a matter of serious concern for Russwurm, who routinely denounced the tradition of black parades.

Most famously, Russwurm gave a biting indictment of blacks in Brooklyn for holding an emancipation parade in 1828. Although they had participated in the New York celebration, Brooklyn's blacks resolved to have a parade in the streets of their own neighborhood. Russwurm argued that the Brooklyn parade reflected poor taste and brought out the "lower orders of society," and he was particularly frustrated by the behavior of women. He seemed especially concerned with the parade's frivolity and perceived lack of morality. He urged his brethren to consider their actions more seriously, "has any man yet been held in estimation on account of his *fine dress?* is it mark of *prudence* to put all our earnings upon our backs? and finally, from this imprudence, to be *unprovided* with the *food,* and *clothing,* and *fuel* during the chilling blasts of winter?"

Although Russwurm was deeply committed to respectability and proper conduct, his most powerful commitment was to the cause of emigration. In fact, it was his belief in colonization that caused division among the staff members of *Freedom's Journal*. Cornish had begun to use *Freedom's Journal* to actively speak out against colonization, and, as an alternative, he advocated black settlement in rural areas; however, Russwurm supported emigration. Their conflicting

ideologies soon collided. By September 1827, Cornish had resigned from the paper, and Russwurm continued to edit *Freedom's Journal* on his own. After Cornish's departure, Russwurm received many complaints about the quality and content of the paper.

In the last issues of the paper, Russwurm publicly endorsed colonization. Despite the severe racism of the colonizationists, Russwurm's argument contained a logical and accurate critique of life in the United States, in which he argued that the mark of race would always prevent black people from achieving full equality. He advocated immigration to Liberia rather than remaining in the United States, where "the mere name of colour, blocks up every avenue . . . and from which it is impossible to rise, unless he can change the Ethiopian hue of his complexion."

The black community responded angrily, believing that Russwurm had become a pawn of the white racists. The final issue of *Freedom's Journal* appeared on March 28, 1829. Russwurm's departing words were bitter, alleging that he had been mistreated and misunderstood by his community.

Just a few months after *Freedom's Journal* disintegrated, Russwurm fulfilled his dream of emigration and accepted a position as superintendent of schools in Liberia. He was well received in Africa; there, he edited a newspaper, the *Liberia Herald.* In 1833, he married Sarah McGill, the daughter of the lieutenant governor of Monrovia. Together, they had three sons and a daughter. By 1836, he had become governor of the Maryland colony in Cape Palmas, Liberia. Russwurm remained in that position until his death on June 17, 1851.

Leslie M. Alexander

See also: Cornish, Samuel E.; Liberia.

Further Reading

Borzendowski, Janice, and Nathan Irvin Huggins. *John Russwurm.* New York: Chelsea House, 1989.
Sagarin, Mary. *John Brown Russwurm; The Story of Freedom's Journal, Freedom's Journey.* New York: Lothrop, Lee & Shepard, 1970.

San Martín, José Francisco de (1778–1850)

José Francisco de San Martín was a legendary South American military leader known for securing the independence of several South American countries from Spain. A disciplined professional soldier, San Martín is often discussed in the same historical context as Simón Bolívar, the Venezuelan revolutionary who also fought for independence from Spain.

San Martín was born on February 25, 1778, in Tupambac, a remote post in what is today northeastern Argentina. His father was a Spanish military officer who was assigned to administer the area in 1770 after King Charles III of Spain expelled the Jesuits from the Americas. His father moved the family back to Spain in 1785, where San Martín pursued a career in the armed forces. He served in military ventures throughout Spain and gained a reputation for being a meticulous battle planner.

When he learned of the revolt against Spain in his native Argentina, San Martín resigned from the Spanish army and sailed for Buenos Aires in 1812 to join the patriot forces. Because of his vast military experience, he was appointed to lead the army controlling Upper Peru, a territory that roughly comprises modern-day Bolivia.

San Martín organized his own battalions, and about 50 percent of his men were former slaves. They were recruited from Buenos Aires and western Argentina according to laws approved in 1813 authorizing the *rescate* (redemption or exchange) of slaves to increase enrollment in the army. The government mandated that slave owners contribute 30 percent of their slaves to the nation, in exchange for which they received token compensation. The slaves often wanted to be recruited, because they received their freedom after five years of service. Although this practice appears to have been a benevolent gesture, it did not translate into tangible freedom for many slaves; most died during the independence struggles and civil wars.

In 1814, San Martín received approval for his request to become governor of the province of Cuyo, located at the foot of the Andes Mountains. He valued Argentina's capital city of Mendoza for its strategic position across the Andes from Chile. He began to build a larger army, collect taxes, and gather provisions. In his efforts to liberate South America from Spanish control, San Martín proposed marching over the Andes from Argentina into Chile, where rebel leader Bernardo O'Higgins was struggling against the Spanish army; however, his ultimate goal was to reach Lima and to defeat the remaining Spanish forces in South America. San Martín believed that Argentina could not be safely independent unless Spanish forces were driven out of Chile, Peru, and Bolivia.

On January 5, 1817, San Martín began to cross the Andes with an army of almost 4,000 men, including the famous Seventh and Eighth Infantry battalions, which were composed of almost 2,000 former slaves. He succeeded in taking control of Santiago, Chile, and dislodging the Spaniards, but he refused the people's offer that he proclaim himself leader of the country. Instead, he left O'Higgins in charge and prepared his forces for a final push into Lima, Spain's power center and the seat of the oldest viceroyalty in South America. With his victory in Santiago, San Martín set in motion the final stages of the war of independence.

In 1820, San Martín and his recruits sailed from Valparaiso to attack Peru from the sea. Upon landing, they won several isolated battles on the outskirts of Lima. The Spanish troops were almost entirely defeated. Meanwhile, San Martín continued to recruit local Indians and blocked entry into the port city of Callao, preventing the Spaniards from receiving any reinforcements.

Within a year, San Martín had occupied the capital, and on July 28, 1821, he proclaimed Peru's independence from Spain. By popular request, he accepted the position of supreme protector of Peru on August 3. In an effort to completely drive the Spaniards out of the country, San Martín requested the support of Bolívar's armies, which had just liberated Venezuela, Colombia, and Ecuador.

Although San Martín reformed Peru's social institutions and created new ones—he approved the freedom of religion, abolished the *mita* (Indian forced labor system), and approved the 1871 *Libertad de Vientres* (Free Womb Law) to provide freedom to the children of slave parents—his approach to governance had mixed results. On September 20, 1822, following a disagreement with Bolívar over the best way to run the newly liberated nation, San Martín resigned in front of the National Assembly, leaving Bolívar the undisputed leader of Peru.

San Martín went to Chile and then to Buenos Aires, where he was neither appreciated nor socially accepted. Having become disillusioned, San Martín and his daughter sailed to Europe in 1823. He died in France on August 17, 1850.

Javier A. Galván

See also: Bolívar, Simón.

Further Reading

Adams, Jerome R. *Latin American Heroes: Liberators and Patriots from 1500 to the Present.* New York: Ballantine, 1991.

Andrews, George Reid. *The Afro-Argentines of Buenos Aires, 1800–1900.* Madison: University of Wisconsin Press, 1980.

Sancho, Ignatius (1729–1780)

A British domestic worker and man of letters, Ignatius Sancho is perhaps best known for the large volume of letters he exchanged with men and women of eighteenth-century British society. A collection of his correspondence appeared in 1782, two years after his death, and became an immediate best-seller. An amateur musician and composer, Sancho was the first black musician to publish music in Britain. He is also notable for being the first Afro-Briton to vote in a British election.

Sancho was born a slave in 1729 during his African parents' Middle Passage on a slave ship traveling from West Africa to South America. His mother died soon after his birth, and his father chose to commit suicide rather than live as a slave. At the age of two, Sancho was taken from Colombia to Britain, which was home to approximately 14,000 blacks during the eighteenth century. Most were servants, slaves, or former slaves brought to Britain by the owners of New World plantations. Associated with the riches of empire, black slaves and servants were particularly desired in wealthy households, where they served as exotic indicators of the status of the owners and employers.

Sancho was given as a gift to three maiden sisters who lived in Greenwich. The Catholic bishop of Cartagena, in what is today Colombia, had baptized him Ignatius; an imaginary resemblance to Don Quixote's squire led the sisters to give him the surname Sancho.

The sisters subjected Sancho to rigorous discipline and deemed it imprudent to give him an education. However, their neighbor John, the second duke of Montagu and former governor of Jamaica, was an enlightened aristocrat who performed benevolent acts to prove that Africans were as capable of education as Europeans. He encouraged Sancho's learning, and the adolescent displayed an unusual intelligence and a love of books, paintings, and music. After John's death in 1749, Sancho successfully beseeched the nobleman's widow to take him into her household as a butler, an important and lucrative position.

John's widow, Mary Churchill, the duchess of Montagu, died in 1751, leaving Sancho a small

Ignatius Sancho.

Born a slave, Ignatius Sancho was an Afro-British musician, actor, and best-selling author of the mid-eighteenth century. Abolitionists pointed to him as an example of the refinement and sophistication of which Africans were capable. *(The Bridgeman Art Library/Getty Images)*

inheritance and an annuity to augment his savings. Gambling, women, and theater soon exhausted the young man's resources, forcing Sancho to resume domestic service with the Montagu family. For the next twenty years, he was employed as a butler for John's son-in-law, the new duke, George Brudenell, and his wife, the duchess Mary. In 1758, Sancho married Anne Osborne, a woman of West Indian origin, with whom he had seven children.

Sancho became an extraordinary and respected member of London's emerging black middle class. He wrote poetry, essays, and dramas; composed music; appeared on the stage; and entertained many famous figures of literary and artistic London. For eighteenth-century British opponents of slavery, the sophisticated and devoutly Christian Sancho demonstrated the sort of humanity and moral refinement in Africans that many of their fellow Britons disputed.

In 1768, Thomas Gainsborough, perhaps the greatest British painter of the century, painted portraits of Sancho and his employers. Sancho's friends included David Garrick, the century's foremost British actor; Joseph Nollekens, the most fashionable English portrait sculptor of his day; and Laurence Sterne, the novelist who wrote *Tristram Shandy* (1760).

In his letters to Sterne, Sancho conveyed his appreciation for Sterne's criticism of slavery in his novels and urged him to continue to defend the African slaves who were bound in servitude in the British colonies. Sancho's letters to other correspondents emphasized his strong moral condemnation of slavery and described the African community in England.

About 1773, Sancho's health began to fail. He retired from domestic service to live as an independent grocer in London's fashionable Mayfair district on Charles Street in Westminster. There, he spent his last years penning letters to the esteemed members of his social circle, relating his unique view of British life. The letters reflect Sancho's engagement with the social and political issues of the age, including his challenges with slavery and racial discrimination. After Sancho died at his shop in 1780, his obituary appeared in the prestigious *Gentleman's Magazine*.

Two years after Sancho's death, one of his correspondents collected his letters and published them in two volumes as *Letters of the Late Ignatius Sancho, an African* (1782). One reviewer noted Sancho's contributions, saying, "Let it no longer be said by half informed philosophers, and superficial investigators of human nature, that Negers, as they are vulgarly called, are inferior to any white nation in mental abilities." A fifth edition of the exceedingly popular work was published in 1803 by Sancho's son, William, who was then pursuing a career as a bookseller in his father's old shop.

David M. Carletta

Further Reading

Carretta, Vincent, ed. *The Letters of the Late Ignatius Sancho, An African.* New York: Penguin, 1998.

King, Reyahn, ed. *Ignatius Sancho: An African Man of Letters.* London: National Portrait Gallery, 1997.

Wright, Josephine R.B., ed. *Ignatius Sancho (1729–1780), An Early African Composer in England: The Collected Editions of His Music in Facsimile.* New York: Garland, 1981.

Schoelcher, Victor (1804–1893)

A French colonial administrator, author, and abolitionist, Victor Schoelcher helped colonial inhabitants in Guadeloupe and Martinique make the transition from slavery to freedom when emancipation was effected on those islands in 1848. By incorporating his personal views about abolition, which were fashioned from his firsthand observations of slaveholding societies in the Americas, Schoelcher deftly implemented a successful policy of emancipation that came to be known as "Schoelcherism" in the French West Indies. Rather than recognizing abolition simply as the end point of enslavement, Schoelcher believed that inculcating republican principles among the newly emancipated and making productive citizens of them was the key work of abolitionism.

Schoelcher was born in Paris, France, on July 21, 1804, to a wealthy Alsatian porcelain manufacturer. He could have enjoyed a privileged life free of the concerns of antislavery agitation, but he was drawn to the call of social reform.

In 1829–1830, Schoelcher traveled to the United States, Mexico, and Cuba. Although his travels were ostensibly associated with the family business, Schoelcher could not help but notice that the institution of slavery dominated much of the social, economic, and political life of the regions that he visited. His observations led him to publish a series of antislavery tracts during the 1830s and 1840s and to participate actively in French antislavery societies.

An astute observer of French political affairs, Schoelcher became increasingly critical of the supposedly liberal government of King Louis-Philippe, as it lost sight of the republican principles that had led to its formation in the revolutionary days of 1830. Accordingly, Schoelcher supported the efforts of the French revolutionaries who overthrew the decrepit monarchy in 1848 and instituted the Second Republic.

Schoelcher was named undersecretary of state for the colonies in the provisional government that took control in France, a position that permitted him to author and implement the French abolition decree that went into effect on April 27, 1848. He labored strenuously to ensure that the civil rights guaranteed to slaves in the decree would be more than empty promises. In addition, his policies enhanced the development of the sugar industry in the colonies by encouraging the emigration of French farmers to the islands.

Schoelcher became disenchanted with French political affairs after the December 1851 coup d'état of Louis-Napoleon Bonaparte, and he opted to live as a political exile in Belgium and London until 1870. During his period of exile, Schoelcher continued to support reform causes and became increasingly drawn to the idea of socialism, a notion that perhaps was influenced by his long friendship with the author Victor Hugo.

During the final years of his life, Schoelcher worked on a biography of Toussaint L'Ouverture, the Haitian military leader who had helped to effect Haiti's independence in 1804, which he finally published in 1889. He also encouraged French colonial administrators in Africa to do everything within their power to end slavery and the slave trade in areas where it had re-emerged.

Schoelcher died on December 24, 1893, in Houilles, France. He was recognized as one of the leading French authorities on slavery and abolitionism when, in May 1949, his remains were moved to the Panthéon in Paris, where many of the greatest French heroes are interred.

Junius P. Rodriguez

See also: French West Indies, Abolition and Emancipation in the; Toussaint L'Ouverture, François-Dominique.

Further Reading

Dorigny, Marcel. *The Abolitions of Slavery: From Léger Félicité Sonthonax to Victor Schoelcher, 1793, 1794, 1848.* New York: Berghahn, 2003.

Welborn, Max. "Victor Schoelcher's Views on Race and Slavery." Ph.D. diss., Ohio State University, 1965.

Second Great Awakening

An era of renewed evangelical religious revivalism in the United States, the Second Great Awakening stirred the religious consciousness of many and attracted new adherents to the antislavery cause. Beginning in the first decade of the nineteenth century and lasting for nearly thirty years, the Second Great Awakening shook the very foundation of American life.

Like its predecessor, the Great Awakening of the eighteenth century, this series of revivals called on Americans to ponder religious matters in a new light. Stirred by the fiery preaching of men such as Charles Grandison Finney and Peter Cartwright at revivals and camp meetings throughout the nation, people embraced the movement's evangelism, emotionalism, and emphasis on personal salvation. Church attendance increased, and the role of religion in American life became more prominent. Like other social institutions, slavery was not immune to the changes wrought by this extended period of religious revival.

The revival movement shaped slavery through its renewed focus on individual salvation. Slave masters in the United States had long been interested in encouraging Christianity among their slaves. The Second Great Awakening gave new life to this idea, and owners began to view the religious welfare of their slaves as their responsibility. Churches opened their doors to slaves—though they required them to sit in segregated sections—and slave owners brought ministers to preach on their plantations.

For the owners, these activities were more than an attempt to fulfill their responsibilities as evangelical Christians. They also used religion as a way to control their slaves, emphasizing the themes of obedience, loyalty, and rewards in the world to come. For their part, slaves embraced the emotionalism of the Second Great Awakening, as well as its focus on individual salvation. Slave preachers told their congregants of God's love and the promise of heaven, and they often equated freedom with salvation, though outside the master's hearing.

The Second Great Awakening also shaped the way Americans viewed social reform. Causes such as temperance and care for the indigent and insane sprang from this movement in the late nineteenth century, as social reform became a vital part of the civic culture. Likewise, some religious people came to identify slavery as a moral blight on the country, thus linking the religious revival movement with the cause of abolition.

Increasingly, religious leaders in the North condemned the institution as unchristian. By the 1830s, ministers such as Henry Ward Beecher were condemning slavery and emerging as leaders of the budding abolitionist movement.

Centered in the Northeast, abolitionism found its greatest appeal among Congregationalists, though Baptists, Methodists, Wesleyans, Presbyterians, and members of other denominations also joined its ranks. The Second Great Awakening provided a theological basis for abolitionism, as its emphasis on personal responsibility, morality, and salvation made many Americans question the dichotomy between slavery and their religious faith. Writers such as Theodore Dwight Weld published popular tracts arguing that the Bible condemned slavery, a position that ministers in countless pulpits trumpeted to their congregations. Organizations such as the American Missionary Association, American Tract Society, and American Colonization Society blended the abolitionist message with evangelical zeal. Abolitionists succeeded in linking their sacred responsibility as evangelists with their secular moral agenda, bringing the cause of eradicating slavery into the public spotlight. Abolitionism emerged as the largest and most influential reform movement spawned by the Second Great Awakening.

As time passed, the nation grew more and more divided over the issue of slavery. Interestingly, this division caused schisms within the very religious groups that benefited most from the evangelism of the Second Great Awakening. As a result of countless revivals and camp meetings, by the 1840s, the Baptists and Methodists had grown to be the largest, most vibrant Protestant denominations. They also were bitterly divided over slavery.

Since the late eighteenth century, Methodists had forbidden clergymen from owning slaves. As the Second Great Awakening spread in the South, church leaders often ignored this rule in an effort to appoint qualified ministers to their growing numbers of pulpits. In 1844, the General Conference of the Methodist Episcopal Church became aware that the bishop of Georgia owned two slaves, and abolitionists within the church demanded that he rid himself of his slaves or resign. He refused, and the clash led to the division of the church into bodies in the North and in the South (the latter body encompassed the slaveholding states). This sectional separation among Methodists persisted until 1939.

The issue of slavery came to a head among the Baptist ranks in 1845. Conflict over slavery within the denomination had been brewing since the early 1830s, as some Northern church leaders opposed the appointment of slave owners as missionaries and questioned the morality of slavery in general. These differences led to sectional divisions within the Home Mission Society, the largest of the denomination's evangelical efforts. As tensions grew among the factions, Southern church leaders decided to form their own organization, splitting off to form the Southern Baptist Convention on May 8, 1845. These two religious rifts, rooted in differences over slavery, not only affected church institutions and individual believers but also prophesied larger sectional divisions as the nation moved closer to civil war.

The Second Great Awakening was a tumultuous phase of American religious history, recasting questions of salvation and morality in new ways. Prompted partly by the new nation's attempt to reconcile personal freedom with religious belief, the movement both influenced and was influenced by the institution of slavery. This internal conflict demonstrates both the centrality of slavery in antebellum America and the role of religion in shaping American society.

Richard D. Starnes

See also: American Colonization Society; American Missionary Association; American Tract Society; Beecher, Henry Ward; Finney, Charles Grandison; Religion and Abolitionism; Weld, Theodore Dwight.

Further Reading

Heyrman, Christine L. *Southern Cross: The Beginnings of the Bible Belt.* New York: Alfred A. Knopf, 1997.

McKivigan, John R., ed. *Abolitionism and American Religion.* New York: Garland, 1999.

———. *The War Against Proslavery Religion: Abolitionism and the Northern Churches, 1830–1865.* Ithaca, NY: Cornell University Press, 1984.

Seward, William H. (1801–1872)

A Northern abolitionist, William Henry Seward became an early leader in the Republican Party and served as U.S. secretary of state from 1861 to 1869. He vied with Abraham Lincoln for the Republican Party's presidential nomination in 1860, but his greatest fame came as a member of Lincoln's cabinet, in which he deftly managed the nation's foreign policy during the U.S. Civil War and prevented European recognition of the Confederacy.

Seward was born on May 16, 1801, in Orange County, New York, to a wealthy and prominent family.

He became a successful lawyer and an ardent member of the Whig Party, emerging as a leading abolitionist. He was elected to the state legislature in 1830 and soon became the leader of the Whigs in that body. He ran unsuccessfully for governor in 1834 but won election to that office in 1838. Seward served two terms as governor, retiring after the Democrats captured both houses of the legislature.

Remaining active in party politics, Seward was generally regarded as the foremost abolitionist in the state of New York. On the strength of his antislavery stance, he was elected to the U.S. Senate in 1848. During his time in the Senate, Seward acquired a national reputation for his opposition to the expansion of slavery into the Western territories.

Following the demise of the Whig Party in 1854, he joined the new Republican Party, which supported abolition, and was instrumental in convincing former Whigs to follow him. He soon emerged as one of the leading figures in the Republican Party and led the opposition to President James Buchanan's policies toward Kansas. He also denounced the U.S. Supreme Court's decision in the 1857 *Dred Scott v. Sandford* case and tried to advance legislation to effectively reverse the ruling.

In 1859, Seward decided to run for the presidency, and he campaigned vigorously even before announcing his candidacy in February 1860. However, opposition from Horace Greeley and members of the Whig Party who had joined the American (Know-Nothing) Party before entering the Republican ranks cost him the nomination. Lincoln won the party nod at the national convention in Chicago. Seward campaigned extensively on Lincoln's behalf and lent crucial support in attracting voters from the former Whig Party.

In the months after Lincoln's victory, Seward tried unsuccessfully to craft compromise legislation in the Senate to prevent the outbreak of hostilities between the North and South. The new president promptly invited Seward to become secretary of state; he undertook the duties of this position on March 5, 1861. Seward had considerable influence in the cabinet, and Lincoln consulted with him frequently on issues related to both foreign and domestic policy. For example, it was Seward, not the attorney general, who developed the administration's policy that suspended habeas corpus in September 1862. Seward campaigned diligently for Lincoln's re-election in 1864, and the president reappointed him to his cabinet post.

On the night of Lincoln's assassination, Seward was also attacked in his home by a would-be assassin and suffered severe stab wounds. Upon his recovery, he continued as President Andrew Johnson's secretary of state, engineering the purchase of Alaska from Russia in 1867.

Seward retired in 1869 and spent several years touring Europe and Asia. He died on October 10, 1872, at his home in Auburn, New York.

Tom Lansford

See also: Civil War, American (1861–1865); Johnson, Andrew; Lincoln, Abraham.

Further Reading

Bancroft, Frederic. *The Life of William H. Seward.* Gloucester, MA: P. Smith, 1967.

Burgan, Michael. *William Henry Seward: Senator and Statesman.* Philadelphia: Chelsea House, 2002.

Taylor, John M. *William Henry Seward: The Definitive Biography of Abraham Lincoln's Controversial Secretary of State.* New York: HarperCollins, 1991.

An abolitionist from New York whom Abraham Lincoln defeated for the Republican presidential nomination in 1860, William H. Seward exerted his greatest influence as Lincoln's secretary of state by maintaining good relations with Europe. *(Library of Congress)*

Shadd Cary, Mary Ann (1823–1893)

The first African American woman in North America to edit a weekly newspaper, the *Provincial Freeman,* Mary Ann Shadd Cary was one of the most influential black women to advocate for the abolition of slavery in the United States.

Mary Ann Shadd was born on October 9, 1823, in Wilmington, in the slave state of Delaware. Both her parents had been born free. Her father, Abraham Shadd, was a shoemaker and abolitionist whose home served as a station on the Underground Railroad. His antislavery activities included selling subscriptions to the abolitionist newspaper *The Liberator* and serving as president of the National Convention for the Improvement of Free People of Color in the United States. The elder Shadd believed strongly in activism and education for blacks, two areas that young Mary would soon gravitate toward.

Less than a decade after Mary's birth, the Shadds migrated to West Chester, Pennsylvania, where she was educated by Quakers until she completed high school at the age of sixteen. In 1838, she opted to return to Wilmington, where she established a school for black children. Her desire to educate blacks led to teaching stints in New York City and Trenton, New Jersey.

In letters to the editors of newspapers, Shadd sought to express her views on subjects of interest to free blacks. In 1849, she published the pamphlet *Hints to the Coloured People of the North,* an appeal for blacks to become independent, take initiative in charting their destiny, and discontinue their reliance on philanthropic individuals and organizations.

Following the passage of the Fugitive Slave Law of 1850, which gave slave owners the right to organize a posse anywhere in the United States to aid in recapturing runaway slaves, many blacks fled to Canada. Settling in Windsor, Ontario, in 1851, Shadd advocated for black emigration, joining her many contemporaries, including Henry Bibb and Martin Delany, who supported the emigration movement and called blacks to relocate. Her pamphlet *A Plea for Emigration, or Notes on Canada West* (1852) circulated in the United States and aided the emigration campaign; by the end of the 1850s, more than 15,000 blacks had fled the United States to Canada.

Shadd refused to teach in segregated schools, which were common in Upper Canada (present-day Ontario). Likewise, she did not support the existence of all-black settlements such as the Dawn Settlement, founded by Josiah Henson, instead advocating for blacks' integration and assimilation into white Canadian society.

In Windsor, she opened a school for disadvantaged fugitives, which was financially supported by the American Missionary Association. By 1852, Shadd had forged a close relationship with the Reverend Samuel Ringgold Ward, an orator and black minister who served a white congregation and edited the *Provincial Freeman,* a black newspaper in Chatham. Shadd willingly assumed the majority of the paper's workload as publisher, editor, and subscription agent. As editor, she advocated for emigration and urged free blacks and fugitives to settle permanently in Canada. During this time, Shadd toured Canada, publicly condemning slavery in the United States and advocating emigration.

In 1854, the newspaper's headquarters and Shadd moved to Toronto, the city with the largest black population. The public was unwilling to accept a woman as the editor of a newspaper, and she relinquished the position to a male editor at Chatham in 1855. She returned to the United States to join the antislavery lecture circuit; during this time, she became the first black woman to be admitted as a member of the 1855 Convention of African Americans in Philadelphia. These lecture tours were educational for Shadd, who applied the knowledge she gained of African American social conditions to editorials she continued to write for the *Provincial Freeman.*

At Saint Catharines, Canada, in 1856, she married Thomas Cary, a barber from Toronto. In August 1857, she gave birth to a daughter, an event that marked the temporary stoppage of her contributions to the *Provincial Freeman,* but she resumed her abolitionist writings in June 1858.

In early 1864, Mary Ann Shadd Cary assisted in recruiting Canadian blacks to fight in the U.S. Civil War. For much of the rest of her life, she actively worked for women's suffrage as a member of the National Woman Suffrage Association, taught in public schools in Washington, D.C., and wrote for papers such as the *New National Era* and *The Advocate.*

In 1883, she earned a law degree from Howard University. A decade later, on June 5, 1893, she died in Washington, D.C.

Jerome Teelucksingh

See also: Canada; Ward, Samuel Ringgold; Women's Rights and the Abolitionist Movement.

Further Reading

Alexander, Ken, and Avis Glaze. *Towards Freedom: The African-Canadian Experience.* Toronto, Ontario, Canada: Umbrella, 1996.

MacDonald, Cheryl. "Mary Ann Shadd in Canada: Last Stop on the Underground Railroad." *The Beaver* 70 (February/March 1990): 32–38.

Shadrach Fugitive Slave Case (1851)

The second Fugitive Slave Act, enacted in 1850 in the United States, not only angered the antislavery contingency but also agitated the growing animosity between the North and the South. The law required that any escaped slaves be returned to their owners. It did not take long for abolitionists to challenge this law in an effort to liberate African Americans from the bondage of slavery. The first case that brought freedom to one former slave, Shadrach Minkins, occurred in Boston, Massachusetts, in 1851.

Minkins was a house servant in Norfolk, Virginia. His owner, John Debree, was a purser in the U.S. Navy. Minkins escaped in May 1850 and fled to Boston, where he earned money by waiting tables. While doing so, he sometimes used a false name, Frederick Wilkins, to avoid being discovered and sent back to Norfolk.

Debree, however, did not give up trying to find his escaped servant and hired a Norfolk constable, John Caphart, to bring him back. On February 12, 1851, Caphart found Minkins in Boston and sought a warrant for his arrest. Boston's federal fugitive slave commissioner, George Ticknor Curtis, issued the warrant. Within a week, Minkins was apprehended and arrested by a U.S. marshal.

Because the Fugitive Slave Act called for timeliness, a hearing was held immediately. A local interest group, the Boston Vigilance Committee, assisted Minkins in securing legal representation for his defense. Among the six lawyers who were serving on Minkins's behalf, one, Robert Morris, was black. The legal team petitioned the court for a continuance so that they could adequately prepare Minkins's defense; they were granted three days.

On February 15, 1851, once the courtroom was cleared of everyone except Minkins and Morris, a large group of blacks from the area barged in and grabbed Minkins. He was removed from the building and taken to the African American neighborhood of Beacon Hill. Quickly, he disappeared. A few days later, Minkins arrived safely in Montreal, Canada.

President Millard Fillmore demanded that all parties found to be accomplices in Minkins's disappearance be tried in federal court under the Fugitive Slave Act. After an investigation, a handful of Boston abolitionists were arrested, including Morris and Lewis Hayden. They were all tried in U.S. district court during May and June 1851.

Initially, five defendants were released because of insufficient evidence. The remaining three defendants were retried the following year, and eventually they were found not guilty. The case was an embarrassment to the federal government and served to widen the chasm of distrust between the North and the South.

Philine Georgette Vega

See also: Fugitive Slave Act of 1850; Fugitive Slaves.

Further Reading

Collison, Gary. *Shadrach Minkins: From Fugitive Slave to Citizen.* Cambridge, MA: Harvard University Press, 1997.

Sharp, Granville (1735–1813)

A prolific writer on the slavery question, particularly its legal aspects, Granville Sharp was one of the leading advocates of abolitionism in Great Britain during the late eighteenth century. His extensive writings and political activism helped convince Parliament to abolish the slave trade in 1807.

Sharp was born on November 10, 1735, in Durham, England, the youngest son of the archbishop of Northumberland and the grandson of the archbishop of York. Destined for a trade, Sharp received only a grammar school education. He remained intellectually curious throughout his life, however, and taught himself Greek and Hebrew in order to better understand the Bible.

In 1758, Sharp took a government position with the ordnance department, but he resigned in 1776 in opposition to the war with the American colonies. For the remainder of his life, he lived off the largesse of his more prosperous brothers.

The direction of Sharp's life was altered in 1765, when he met Jonathan Strong, a slave who had been abused and then abandoned on the streets of London by his owner, David Lisle, a Barbados planter. Strong, who had been beaten on his head so badly that he nearly lost his sight, had gone to see Sharp's brother William, a physician with a reputation for helping the indigent.

Granville Sharp brought Strong home. After restoring Strong's health, Sharp found him a job and thought his involvement in the black man's life was over. Strong, however, had the misfortune of running into Lisle, who, upon seeing his former slave was physically revitalized, had him seized and then sold to James Kerr, a Jamaican planter. Somehow, Strong was able to contact Sharp, who appealed to the lord mayor of London and obtained Strong's release.

This incident prompted Sharp to aid other slaves living in England. At the time, England was home to approximately 15,000 slaves, many of them brought by West Indian plantation owners who used their slaves as personal servants. In order to assist them, Sharp needed to overturn the 1729 joint opinion by Attorney General Sir Philip Yorke and Solicitor General Charles James Talbot that stated slavery was legal in England.

For two years, Sharp studied the law in his spare time. In an early edition of Blackstone's *Commentaries on the Laws of England,* he found an opinion from an old case, *Smith v. Brown and Cooper,* that stated, "As soon as a negro comes into England he becomes free." Although a later edition of the *Commentaries* excluded the passage, Sharp used it as the basis for his pamphlet on the legal justification for emancipation, *A Representation of the Injustice and Dangerous Tendency of Tolerating Slavery* (1769).

With his growing expertise in the law, Sharp was consulted on a number of cases in which escaped former slaves who had been living in England were kidnapped and placed on ships bound for the West Indies. In several of these instances, such as the cases of Mary Hylas (1766) and Thomas Lewis (1770), the individuals were rescued and the courts set them free. Nevertheless, Sharp was disappointed with the outcome in these cases, as the judges were careful not to issue a definitive ruling on the legality of slavery in England.

In 1772, Sharp hoped for a better result when he became involved in the case of James Somersett, a slave owned by Charles Stewart, a customs officer from Boston. Somersett had escaped from Stewart but had been recaptured and placed aboard a ship bound for Jamaica. Sharp intervened and was able to get Somersett brought before the Court of King's Bench. The case was argued before William Murray, Lord Mansfield, who ruled in *Knowles v. Somersett* that slaves in England could not be forcibly returned to their owners.

Knowles v. Somersett was less than a complete victory, as it still allowed for the practice of slavery in England, and the authorities did little to intervene when escaped slaves were forcibly returned to their owners. Failure to enforce the law led former slave and writer Olaudah Equiano to ask for Sharp's help in rescuing John Annis, a kidnapped former slave, but they were unable to win Annis's freedom.

Equiano also brought to Sharp's attention the mass murder on the slave ship *Zong* in 1781, during which the ship's captain ordered more than 100 slaves thrown overboard to collect insurance on lost cargo rather than be liable for the value of slaves who died on his ship due to a lack of water. A trial was held to decide who was to pay for the loss of the Africans thrown overboard. Sharp failed in his attempt to have the captain and crew prosecuted for murder.

Sharp also became involved in a plan for the repatriation of former slaves in Sierra Leone, after hearing the report of Henry Smeathman, a naturalist who returned from West Africa in 1786. For Sharp, this was the perfect opportunity to show that blacks could live useful and productive lives under civilized conditions, and he wrote a pamphlet in support of the plan. The colony met with mixed success, and by 1791, the Saint George's Bay Company had been formed in London to take responsibility for the colony. In Sharp's honor, the capital city of Granville Town was established and repopulated with 1,100 former slaves who had fought for Britain during the American Revolution. In 1808, Sierra Leone became a British Crown colony.

After reaching out to the staunchly abolitionist Quaker community, Sharp was convinced of the need to form an organization to aid in the fight against slavery. In 1787, he became the first chairman of the Society for Effecting the Abolition of the African Slave Trade. As a matter of expediency, the society decided to attack only the slave trade and not slavery, a position that Sharp vigorously opposed.

Always a deeply religious man, in his later years, Sharp became increasingly involved with the evangelical branch of the Church of England. He died on July 6, 1813.

Kenneth Pearl

See also: Abolition of the Slave Trade Act (1807); Sierra Leone; Society for the Abolition of the Slave Trade; *Somersett* Case (1772); Wilberforce, William.

Further Reading

Lascelles, Edward Charles Ponsonby. *Granville Sharp and the Freedom of Slaves in England.* New York: Negro Universities Press, 1969.

Sharpe, Samuel (1801–1832)

Samuel Sharpe was a lay Baptist preacher and a national hero of Jamaica. He is best known as the planner and leader of the 1831–1832 labor strike that became a violent revolt, which erupted on December 27, 1831.

A Creole born in Jamaica, Sharpe was named after his enslaver, the owner of Cooper's Hill on the outskirts of Montego Bay, Saint James, Jamaica. Historians believe that his parents arrived from Africa some time between 1787 and 1801. Sharpe was among a group that historians characterize as the "slave elite," as they were artisans, domestic servants, and supervisors. A convert to Christianity, Sharpe became a deacon in the First Baptist Church in Montego Bay, now the Burchell Memorial Baptist Church. He is said to have possessed great oratorical skills and the ability to inspire his listeners.

The revolt that Sharpe led was one of the largest slave uprisings in the history of the British-colonized Caribbean. Known variously as the Christmas Uprising, the Baptist War, and the Great Jamaican Slave Revolt, the 1831–1832 uprising was unparalleled in Jamaican history. Its effective design and planning brought ruin and misery to many of the island's planters.

The ten-day rebellion, which mobilized as many as 60,000 slaves, began as a nonviolent strike when Sharpe, aided by other black leaders from the church, informed a core group of his followers that they should sit down and refuse to work unless given wages. When the elite planter class forced them to work as slaves, fighting erupted. The Jamaican plantocracy and its forces suppressed the rebellion with relative ease. The conflict resulted in the death of a dozen whites and hundreds of rebels, the majority of whom were killed by the judgment of military tribunals held after the rebellion ceased.

In April 1832, Sharpe was tried, found guilty, and sentenced to death for his role in the revolt. The testimonies of nine other slaves were used as evidence against him. Joseph Martin, for example, testified that "[t]he first place I saw Sharpe was at Retrieve—did not see any other person swear the people [on the Bible] but Sharpe—he had the Book read it and gave it to them—he gave them the Book and said they must take their oath not to work after Xmas unless they know what they are to work for."

Sharpe was hanged in the Montego Bay town square by order of the colonial government in Jamaica on May 23, 1832, at the age of thirty-one. His owner was compensated with £16, 10 shillings of Jamaican currency, the value that the jury placed on the loss of Sharpe's life.

Several people witnessed Sharpe's execution or spoke with him in prison, and they left written accounts. According to these accounts, Sharpe, dressed in a new white suit, walked in a dignified manner to the gallows. After a short speech, he knelt and prayed. Before he was hanged, he uttered the words, "I now bid you farewell! That is all I have to say."

Verene A. Shepherd

See also: Jamaica Rebellion (1831–1832).

Further Reading

Craton, Michael. *Testing the Chains: Resistance to Slavery in the British West Indies.* Ithaca, NY: Cornell University Press, 1982.

Reid, C.S. *Samuel Sharpe: From Slave to National Hero.* Kingston, Jamaica: Bustamante Institute for Public and International Affairs, 1988.

Shepherd, Verene, and Ahmed Reid. "Rebel Voices: Testimonies from the 1831–32 Emancipation War in Jamaica." *Jamaica Journal* 27 (May 2004): 54–63.

Sierra Leone

Sierra Leone was originally colonized by British slave traders, but after the American Revolution, it became the center of efforts to suppress the African slave trade and to resettle former slaves and black Loyalists. The perceived success of Sierra Leone led the United States to attempt to replicate it in the colony of Liberia.

Early Colonization Efforts

The British made the first formal effort to colonize the territory that became Sierra Leone in 1628, although the Portuguese had explored the coastal areas as early as the 1460s. British traders established a post on Sherbro Island, where they traded manufactured goods and metal products in exchange for slaves. Slaves quickly became the principal export, as the traders negotiated concessions from the local chiefs and created one of West Africa's largest slave markets.

Slave merchants formed the Royal African Company in 1672 to expand the slave trade in the area and to coordinate other commercial ventures. The company was extremely profitable at the outset, but a series of military clashes quickly made the region far

After becoming a Crown colony in 1808, Sierra Leone was the focus of British efforts to end the international slave trade and, later, to suppress slavery itself. In 1849, the Royal Navy sent in troops to destroy slave factories on the Gallinas River. *(Hulton Archive/Getty Images)*

less lucrative and led the British to abandon their efforts to move into the interior regions.

In addition to an ongoing armed struggle against the native peoples, many of the trading posts were destroyed by French raids. In 1728, the Royal African Company ceased trying to develop large posts. Instead, a succession of small, privately owned slave factories emerged along the coast. Throughout the remainder of the century, the volume of exported slaves continued to grow, as did the number of slave factories.

Meanwhile, the British government increasingly sought to develop a long-range plan to resettle former slaves and free blacks. Such efforts were spurred by public pressure on the government and the British Crown to take steps to prevent the emergence of a large class of free blacks in Britain. In 1772, Lord Mansfield ruled in the *Somerset* case that masters could not reclaim former slaves within Britain.

In addition, several large groups of free blacks found themselves in legal limbo, as the government debated where to settle them. These groups included the maroons in Jamaica, who had achieved a form of

de facto autonomy after a series of revolts beginning in 1739, and later large numbers of former slaves and free blacks who had fought on the side of the British military during the American Revolution in exchange for promises of freedom. Large numbers of both maroons and black American Loyalists had been transported to Nova Scotia, but the government saw this as a temporary solution and sought to resettle the groups in Africa.

In 1787, Henry Smeathman proposed resettling all former slaves and free blacks in the territory of Sierra Leone. Under Smeathman's plan, a refuge, dubbed the "Province of Freedom," would be created for free blacks who agreed to act as settlers on behalf of the British. Parliament approved Smeathman's proposal, and approximately 400 free blacks left London to establish a settlement there.

The original settlement fared poorly, as disease ravaged the population, but subsequent settlements proved more successful. In a second attempt led by the abolitionist Thomas Clarkson, Freetown was founded, and eventually it became the capital of the colony. The settlers established farms and soon made the colony self-sufficient in terms of food and other staples.

The venture's early promise prompted the formation of the Sierra Leone Company in 1791 as a semi-public entity to oversee the economic development of the region and to coordinate resettlement efforts. The company was also responsible for the protection of the colony, and it established a militia that ultimately defeated the indigenous tribes that had prevented earlier efforts at colonization of the interior. Within five years, more than 1,000 freed slaves had settled in the area. In addition, large numbers of free blacks from Nova Scotia were transported to the region. By 1802, 800 black American Loyalists and 900 maroons had been relocated to Sierra Leone.

A British Colony

In 1807, the British government abolished the slave trade and dispatched a small naval force, the African Squadron, to interdict suspected slave vessels. As it was unclear what should be done with the slaves freed from captured slave ships, the British government decided to resettle the former slaves in Sierra Leone. Consequently, in 1808, Parliament formally took control of the colony from the Sierra Leone Company and made Sierra Leone a Crown colony.

Sierra Leone subsequently became the main base for the Africa Squadron and the center for British efforts to suppress the international slave trade. A naval station was established at Freetown, and a court system was created to adjudicate cases involving suspected slavers and captured slave ships.

Freed slaves continued to be released in the colony. By 1815, some 6,000 former slaves had been resettled in Sierra Leone; by the 1820s, the Royal Navy was releasing an average of 3,000–4,000 slaves per year in the colony. An estimated 50,000 former slaves had been resettled in the colony by the 1860s.

Although the British government continued to transport newly freed slaves to Sierra Leone, the colonial infrastructure was unable to accommodate the influx of people, who spoke different languages and had diverse cultures and religions. There was an ongoing shortage of developed land that was suitable for agriculture, and the colonial government had difficulty providing employment for the new citizens.

Reports of such problems prompted Parliament to try other relocation programs. For example, at one point, some 10,000 freed slaves were transported to colonies in the West Indies. The proximity of Sierra Leone to the African Squadron's base made the colony the most practical site for newly freed slaves, however; therefore, the colony remained the main destination for slaves freed by the British navy.

The British moved steadily into the interior, and, by 1896, the entire present-day area of Sierra Leone was under British control. The country remained a British colony until it won its independence in 1961. Contemporary politics continue to be dominated by the struggle between the Creole class, made up of descendants from the transported former slaves, and the native African peoples.

Blueprint for Liberia

The early success of the Sierra Leone colony prompted a group of Americans to attempt to replicate the colony. In 1810, Paul Cuffe, a wealthy African American, visited the colony and decided that the area would be an ideal site for free blacks in the United States to settle and thus avoid the racial discrimination experienced in many U.S. states. In 1812, Cuffe organized a group of American settlers who had agreed to travel to Sierra Leone and create an enclave.

It was not until 1820, three years after Cuffe's death, that the expedition was launched. The Americans initially settled in a disease-ridden area, resulting in high mortality rates among the colonists. They decided to relocate the settlement to what would become Liberia, which emerged as an American counterpart to Sierra Leone.

Tom Lansford

See also: Clarkson, Thomas; Liberia.

Further Reading

Eltis, David. *Economic Growth and the Ending of the Transatlantic Slave Trade.* New York: Oxford University Press, 1987.

Fyfe, Christopher. *A History of Sierra Leone.* New York: Oxford University, 1962.

Howell, Raymond. *The Royal Navy and the Slave Trade.* New York: St. Martin's, 1987.

Lloyd, Christopher. *The Navy and the Slave Trade: The Suppression of the African Slave Trade in the Nineteenth Century.* London: Longman, Green, 1949; London: Frank Cass, 1968.

Miers, Suzanne. *Britain and the Ending of the Slave Trade.* London: Longman, 1975; New York: Africana, 1975.

Peterson, John. *Province of Freedom: A History of Sierra Leone.* London: Faber, 1969.

Schama, Simon. *Rough Crossings: Britain, the Slaves, and the American Revolution.* New York: Ecco, 2006.

Wilson, Ellen Gibson. *The Loyal Blacks.* New York: Capricorn, 1976.

Simcoe, John Graves (1752–1806)

John Graves Simcoe was a British military officer who served as lieutenant governor of the British colony of Upper Canada (present-day Ontario) from 1792 to 1794. His term in Canada was distinguished by the introduction and consolidation of British civil government and the practical abolition of slavery well before its demise in the British Empire.

Born on February 25, 1752, in Cotterstock, England, Simcoe was raised in a wealthy English family and studied at the prestigious Eton boys' school and later at Oxford University. He entered the army as a low-level officer in 1771 and first saw action in Boston during the American Revolution. He was hailed as one of the most successful officers on the British side and eventually earned the command of the British Loyalist unit, the Queen's Rangers, which fought in New York and Virginia during the war. After being wounded and taken prisoner, he eventually returned to Britain in 1781 as a lieutenant colonel but returned to Canada a decade later as lieutenant governor.

Simcoe was personally opposed to slavery, advocated the recruitment of blacks by the British military, and ardently supported the leading British abolitionist of the late eighteenth century, William Wilberforce. There is no direct evidence of the exact nature of his antislavery ideas, but it appears that Simcoe drew on essentially religious arguments, believing that slavery was contrary to Christian teachings.

Unlike the British colonies elsewhere in the Western Hemisphere, slavery was uncommon in Canada. The few slaves who existed in early Canada were largely domestic servants and played no significant role in the colonial economy. Their numbers were boosted, however, by the arrival of slaves owned by Loyalist refugees from the American Revolution in the 1770s and 1780s.

Simcoe introduced a bill to the Legislative Assembly of Upper Canada in 1793 proposing the complete abolition of slavery. William Renwick Riddell, one of Simcoe's early biographers, claimed that he was encouraged to take action after hearing of individual cases of slaves being bought and sold in the colony. Simcoe's legislation, however, met stiff opposition from influential Loyalists and wealthy, landowning politicians—many of whom were slave owners—forcing the abolitionist to work out a compromise. He responded by supporting legislation that called for gradual abolition. Existing slaves would remain enslaved until death, no new slaves would be allowed in Upper Canada, and children born to female slaves would be legally freed at the age of twenty-five.

By 1810, no slaves remained in the colony, and in the midst of the War of 1812 between the British colonies in Canada and the United States, the attorney general of Upper Canada declared all blacks in the colony legally free. Simcoe's legislation was superseded in 1833 by the Abolition of Slavery Act (commonly known as the British Emancipation Act), which eliminated slavery in all British territories.

Upper Canada was the first British colony to abolish slavery in practice, although slave labor was never crucial to the colonial economy. After 1800, Upper Canada became a beacon for fugitive slaves from the United States, who eventually established forty separate communities totaling 30,000 people. Historians of the early African Canadian community have established, however, that free blacks in the colony continued to face entrenched discrimination from Simcoe and other white elites. In the 1790s, for example, Simcoe ignored a petition from free blacks requesting equal land rights in the colony.

One of Simcoe's last postings, as governor of Santo Domingo (today Haiti) in 1797, was to suppress the great slave uprising led by Toussaint L'Ouverture. Simcoe died on October 26, 1806, in Exeter, England.

Sean Purdy

See also: Canada; Toussaint L'Ouverture, François-Dominique.

Further Reading

Fryer, Mary Beacock, and Christopher Dracott. *John Graves Simcoe, 1752–1806: A Biography.* Toronto, Ontario, Canada: Dundurn, 1998.

Hill, Daniel G. "Black History in Early Toronto." *Polyphony* (Summer 1984): 28–30.

Johnson, J.K. *Becoming Prominent: Regional Leadership in Upper Canada, 1791–1841.* Kingston, Ontario, Canada: McGill-Queen's University Press, 1989.

Riddell, William Renwick. *The Life of John Graves Simcoe: First Lieutenant-Governor of the Province of Upper Canada, 1792–96.* Toronto, Ontario, Canada: McClelland and Stewart, 1926.

Smalls, Robert (1839–1915)

A U.S. Civil War hero and pioneering African American congressman, Robert Smalls is best remembered as the slave who stole the Confederate ship *Planter* in May 1862 and piloted it into Union hands in Charleston Harbor. Despite this and other acts of courage and loyalty on behalf of the United States, he remained largely a forgotten figure and unsung hero for nearly a century.

Born to an unknown white father and a slave mother in Beaufort, South Carolina, on April 5, 1839, Smalls grew up in Charleston, where he was hired out by his master. He worked his way into the thriving shipping industry of Charleston, agreed to a deal with his master that made him largely autonomous, and married a slave girl whose freedom he sought to purchase with $700.

By 1862, Smalls had earned promotion to pilot aboard the steamboat *Planter.* The 150-foot ship had been built in 1860 to haul cotton down the Pee Dee River to Charleston Harbor, but it was put into service for the Confederacy in late 1861. From November 1861 to May 1862, Smalls was compelled to serve the Confederacy as "wheelman" of the *Planter*, as only whites could be called "pilot."

After Union forces occupied Beaufort and the neighboring Sea Islands, Smalls plotted with fellow black crewmen to steal the ship and turn it over to the Union navy. Sneaking his family aboard at night, he succeeded in his daring venture, for which he was immediately hailed as a hero by the Northern press. He and his ship were photographed, and his fame spread rapidly by word of mouth and in print. Abolitionists used his feat as evidence of the average slave's ability to fend for himself outside the instruction of a white master.

The Union navy eagerly employed Smalls to captain the *Planter* as a troop transporter, supply carrier, and mail runner. Although his official status in the navy cannot be verified, it is believed that he was initially given the rank of lieutenant and become captain by promotion. (Later in life, he enigmatically would be referred to by some as "General.") Smalls participated in a total of seventeen battles and performed admirably by all accounts, but he still suffered racial discrimination and segregation throughout his two-year active stint in the navy.

Soon after escaping slavery in 1862, Smalls traveled to New York City, where he worked on behalf of

An 1862 issue of *Harper's Weekly* recounts the exploits of South Carolina slave and steamboat helmsman Robert Smalls, who commandeered the Confederate frigate *Planter* and delivered it to the Union navy in Charleston Harbor. *(Library of Congress)*

the refugees in the Port Royal area of South Carolina (who had been abandoned by their masters when Union troops arrived), seeking charitable donations for their welfare. There, he met the African American abolitionist Henry Highland Garnet and made his first acquaintance with other abolitionists. In 1864, he traveled to Philadelphia and became involved in the abolitionist movement as a public speaker and fund-raiser. At the war's end, he returned to his native South Carolina and received a small honorarium for his service in giving the United States possession of the *Planter*.

In 1865, Smalls put his energies into the new Freedmen's Bureau. He opened a cooperative store, a church, a school, and a "poor farm" for the benefit of the freedmen. He also became a successful real estate proprietor, even acquiring the property of his former master. Local whites envied his business acumen, detested his entrepreneurial success, and loathed the ostentatious display of his newfound wealth.

In 1868, Smalls enjoyed his first great political success when he was elected to the South Carolina state legislature, where he served three terms. In 1874, he was elected to the U.S. Congress, where he served until 1878. In 1877, he was convicted of taking a bribe while serving in the state legislature and sentenced to three years in prison. He appealed without success to the South Carolina Supreme Court and again to the U.S. Supreme Court. Ultimately, the Democratic governor of South Carolina agreed to pardon him in exchange for a promise from the administration of Rutherford B. Hayes to drop all charges against Democratic miscreants in his state.

Smalls lost his bid for re-election to Congress in 1878 and again in 1880, although in the latter election he successfully appealed the outcome based on alleged Democratic fraud. In 1882, as a result of Democratic gerrymandering, he lost again but managed to win back his seat one final time in 1884. By 1886, white southern Democrats were beginning the wholesale disfranchisement of blacks, and, by 1895, the state of South Carolina had effectively legalized disfranchisement through a new constitution. These actions ended Smalls's career in local politics.

Smalls spent much of the remainder of his life as the U.S. Customs collector at the port of Beaufort, first appointed by President Benjamin Harrison in 1889 and thereafter re-appointed by Presidents William McKinley, Theodore Roosevelt, and William H. Taft between 1898 and 1913. He died in Beaufort in 1915, disillusioned by the regression he had witnessed in race relations from Reconstruction through the early Jim Crow period.

Thomas Adams Upchurch

See also: Civil War, American (1861–1865); Freedmen's Bureau; Port Royal Experiment; Reconstruction.

Further Reading

Escott, Paul D., David R. Goldfield, Sally G. McMillen, and Elizabeth Hayes Turner, eds. *Major Problems in the History of the American South.* Vol. II, *The New South.* 2nd ed. Boston: Houghton Mifflin, 1999.

Uya, Okon Edet. *From Slavery to Public Service: Robert Smalls, 1839–1915.* New York: Oxford University Press, 1971.

Smith, Gerrit (1797–1874)

Gerrit Smith was a businessman and congressman who became a leading figure in the abolitionist movement in the United States. As he sensed the movement's failure to effect reform through traditional means, Smith's antislavery views became increasingly more radical. By 1859, he had become one of the "Secret Six" abolitionists who backed John Brown's insurrection at Harpers Ferry, Virginia.

Born on March 6, 1797, in Utica, New York, Smith was the son of Peter Smith, a fur trader and land speculator, and Elizabeth Livingston Smith, daughter of James Livingston, the cousin of American diplomat Robert R. Livingston. In 1806, the Smith family moved to the village (Peterboro) and town (Smithfield) bearing Peter Smith's name. There, Gerrit Smith worked beside enslaved blacks, who, he later wrote, were the "companions and playmates of [my] childhood."

In 1818, Smith graduated as valedictorian from the academy at Hamilton, hoping to become a writer or a lawyer. Instead, he was forced into the world of commerce in 1819, when his father retired and transferred his sizable estate to him; as a result, Smith became one of the state's largest landholders.

Like many others in western New York's "Burned-Over District" (so named for the frequency and intensity of religious revivals held there) in the 1820s, Smith and his second wife, Ann Fitzhugh Smith, became concerned with their spiritual health. Supporters of the Sunday School movement and the American Bible Society in the early 1820s, they experienced conversion in 1826, joined Peterboro's Presbyterian Church, and became sympathetic to the plight of the enslaved and intemperate.

In 1827, Smith proposed a manual labor school in Peterboro for blacks who planned on serving as missionaries in Africa for the American Colonization Society; the school opened in 1834 and lasted a year. Concerned over the American Colonization Society's refusal to acknowledge slavery's sinfulness and call for its immediate abolition, Smith established closer ties with abolitionists.

After witnessing a proslavery mob break up the New York Anti-Slavery Society's inaugural meeting in Utica on October 21, 1835, he invited the delegates to reconvene in Peterboro. There, Smith condemned the mob for attacking free speech and declared his affinity for abolitionist principles. He joined the American Anti-Slavery Society and severed ties with the American Colonization Society in November 1835.

After the panic of 1837, which left Smith reeling from financial losses, he intensified his commitment to abolitionism but began to question the American Anti-Slavery Society's strategy. Realizing that candidates' connections with national parties tethered them to weak positions on slavery, Smith, abolitionist Myron Holley, philanthropist Arthur Tappan, Ohio anti-slavery agitator and attorney Salmon P. Chase, and others organized a third party committed to radical abolitionism in late 1839. Smith suggested its name—the Liberty Party—in a February 1840 letter to the *Friend of Man* and was chosen as its gubernatorial nominee in 1840 and 1842.

At the same time as he was organizing the new party, Smith focused his attention on activism at home in Madison County. Liberty Party votes increased three-fold in the county in 1843, but, in 1844, the party's votes declined in ten of its fourteen towns. Believing that the lack of support from local clergymen inhibited the success of the party and the abolitionist movement, Smith started his own free church, the Church of Peterboro, in 1843. In 1844, Smith published an opinion favoring the antislavery interpretation of the U.S. Constitution, and, in 1850, he debated abolitionist Charles C. Burleigh on the subject in Syracuse, New York.

Though he supported the Liberty Party's one-issue platform as late as 1846, Smith and others called for a new, multicomponent platform the following year. Smith had become interested in land reform, anti-Masonic, and pacifist causes, and the new platform reflected his varied interests. Supporters of the new Liberty League nominated Smith for president in 1848, but he declined the nomination.

One of the most prominent and radical figures in the antebellum abolitionist movement, Gerrit Smith of New York resigned his seat in Congress after the Kansas-Nebraska Act of 1854 and supported John Brown's plans for a slave insurrection in 1859. *(Library of Congress)*

In 1849, Smith announced his intent to distribute 120,000 acres in the Adirondacks to 3,000 blacks as part of a land reform initiative, and about 200 blacks settled on his North Country lands. John Brown assisted the farmers, but the land's quality was poor, and the settlement, called Timbuctoo, was short-lived.

A longtime supporter of the Underground Railroad, Smith also agitated against the Fugitive Slave Law of 1850. Soon after its passage, Smith and others rescued the runaway slave William "Jerry" Henry from federal custody in Syracuse after he was arrested on October 1, 1851.

With support from Frederick Douglass, who had befriended Smith after arriving in Rochester in 1847, he was elected to the U.S. Congress as an independent in 1852. Voters gave Smith, likely elected for his support of free trade (his district included the port of Oswego), a national stage for reform activism. In Congress, he lobbied for Cuba's annexation and lobbied against a federal postal system, war, the sale of liquor in Washington, D.C., and the Kansas-Nebraska Act of 1854.

Though he was disgusted by the intemperance of some congressmen, Smith became well known for his hospitality to all politicians, regardless of their party affiliation or opinion on slavery. As a radical abolitionist standard-bearer in Congress, his every move was scrutinized, and Smith's graciousness toward proslavery men upset some abolitionists. Expressing a need to tend to personal financial matters, he resigned his congressional seat in 1854, soon after the passage of the Kansas-Nebraska Act.

In the years that preceded the U.S. Civil War, Smith wrote on religion and agitated for abolition, temperance, land reform, and women's dress reform. In 1858, he accepted the nomination for governor on the People's State Ticket.

A financial supporter of Brown and the Kansas Aid movement, Smith hosted Brown and abolitionist Franklin Sanborn in 1858 to discuss Brown's plan for mounting a slave insurrection. Although it is likely that Smith, Sanborn, and the other "Secret Six" members knew of Brown's plan to attack the arsenal at Harpers Ferry, Smith proclaimed his ignorance when he was later identified as Brown's financial backer. Frantic that he would be arrested, he suffered a nervous breakdown (some critics claimed that he faked his illness) and spent almost two months in Utica's New York State Lunatic Asylum.

After his recovery, Smith was less visible in the fight against slavery. When he did speak, Smith expressed regret in 1861 that slavery was "going out in blood." Nevertheless, he supported the Lincoln Administration and viewed the war as necessary for the Union's preservation. At the war's end, he favored compensating former slaves and enfranchising blacks to prevent their re-enslavement. Believing that Jefferson Davis was entitled to a fair trial and hoping to ease the rift between North and South, Smith signed Davis's bail bond in 1867.

Declaring in 1869 that "slavery is dead, but drunkenness stays," Smith focused his efforts on temperance during the late 1860s and early 1870s. He electioneered for the Anti-Dramshop Party, but fearing that the Democrats would reverse Republican achievements, he supported Ulysses Grant in the 1872 presidential election. In 1873 and 1874, he continued to lobby for the annexation of Cuba and supported woman suffrage.

Smith died on December 28, 1874, in New York City. He was survived by his wife, a son, and a daughter.

Hadley Kruczek-Aaron

See also: American Colonization Society; Brown, John; Fugitive Slave Act of 1850; Harpers Ferry Raid (1859); Liberty Party.

Further Reading

Dyson, Zita. "Gerrit Smith's Effort in Behalf of Negroes in New York." *Journal of Negro History* 3 (October 1918): 354–59.

Friedman, Lawrence J. "The Gerrit Smith Circle: Abolitionism in the Burned-Over District." *Civil War History* 26 (March 1980): 18–38.

Harlow, Ralph V. *Gerrit Smith: Philanthropist and Reformer.* New York: Henry Holt, 1939.

McKivigan, John R., and Madeleine L. McKivigan. "'He Stands Like Jupiter': The Autobiography of Gerrit Smith." *New York History* 65 (April 1984): 189–200.

Stauffer, John. *The Black Hearts of Men: Radical Abolitionists and the Transformation of Race.* Cambridge, MA: Harvard University Press, 2001.

Strong, Donald. *Perfectionist Politics: Abolitionism and the Religious Tensions of American Democracy.* Syracuse, NY: Syracuse University Press, 2000.

Smith, Goldwin (1823–1910)

A noted journalist and historian in England, the United States, and Canada, Goldwin Smith was a passionate advocate for the end of slavery and played a considerable role in popularizing abolitionist arguments during the 1860s. Strongly influenced by Victorian liberalism during the U.S. Civil War period, he became famous by the end of the nineteenth century as a conservative historian and virulent anti-Semite.

Smith was born into a wealthy family in Reading, England, on August 13, 1823. His father was a prominent physician and director of two railway companies. Studying at the exclusive Eton boys' school and later at Oxford University, Smith excelled in his studies and became a fellow at Oxford at the age of twenty-three. In addition to writing and lecturing about history and advocating education reform in the United Kingdom during the 1850s and 1860s, he took a keen interest in the burning political issues of the broader English-speaking world.

Smith largely adhered to the rational liberalism of mid-nineteenth-century philosophers such as John Stuart Mill. He supported the capitalist market economy and believed that it worked best within a democratic political system with formal rights and freedoms. According to this view, social and economic systems such as slavery were politically irrational and economically backward, not to mention profoundly immoral. Like many abolitionists of the day, he maintained a paternalistic stance toward blacks, seeing them as pathetic victims of an immoral system. Smith retained stereotypical racist ideas about the culture and ideas of black people, and he was mainly concerned that slavery was neither paternalistic nor rational.

Though motivated by Christianity, he regularly appealed to rational arguments rather than emotional sentiments and, according to historian Paul Phillips, "saw his mission to elevate and direct the public attention to what he deemed the great issues facing humanity, past and present." From the 1840s to the 1860s, his reputation among abolitionists in England and the United States grew considerably, as he penned numerous antislavery newspaper and periodical articles. In 1862, Mill observed, "I am much mistaken if Goldwin Smith will not grow into a power in this country."

In the early 1860s, Smith addressed a crowd of 6,000 people at the Manchester Union and Emancipation Society, arguing that the Civil War in the United States was a monumental struggle between aristocracy and democracy: "The cause of emancipation is not that of the Negro race alone. It is the cause of civilization, of Christian morality, of the rights of labour and the rights of man."

As a result of the popularity and influence of his forceful antislavery journalism and activism, Smith was invited to conduct a three-month lecture tour in the United States in 1864. He became a media star, as abolitionists flocked to his fervent antislavery speeches. In Washington, D.C., he stayed with Secretary of State William Henry Seward, interviewed Union General Ulysses S. Grant, and had a personal audience with President Abraham Lincoln.

Returning to England, Smith dedicated himself to improving the treatment of freed slaves in the British colonies. Along with Charles Darwin, Thomas Huxley, and other notable British intellectual and political figures, he was a founding member of the Jamaica Company, formed to raise money for the prosecution of Jamaica's governor, Edward John Eyre, who had brutally suppressed an 1865 rebellion by ex-slaves on the island. Smith advocated a colonial system based on paternalistic rule by the enlightened administrators of the British Empire.

Smith left England to teach at Cornell University in New York City from 1868 to 1871, and he eventually settled in Toronto, Canada. There, he played a key role in the establishment of the Department of History at the University of Toronto and founded and edited several magazines. He wrote prolifically on history, politics, and social questions, publishing numerous books and hundreds of articles.

By the 1890s, the resolute liberalism of Smith's antislavery days had been replaced by blatantly discriminatory attitudes toward women, Catholics, non-Europeans, and, especially, Jews. He died in Toronto on June 7, 1910.

Sean Purdy

See also: Mill, John Stuart; Morant Bay Rebellion (1865).

Further Reading

Phillips, Paul. *The Controversialist: An Intellectual Life of Goldwin Smith.* Westport, CT: Praeger, 2002.

Tulchinsky, Gerald. "Goldwin Smith: Victorian Liberal Anti-Semite." In *Antisemitism in Canada: History and Interpretation,* ed. Alan Davies. Waterloo, Ontario, Canada: Wilfrid Laurier University Press, 1992.

Wallace, Elizabeth. *Goldwin Smith: Victorian Liberal.* Toronto, Ontario, Canada: University of Toronto Press, 1957.

Sociedad Abolicionista Española, La

La Sociedad Abolicionista Española was a Spanish abolitionist society founded by the Puerto Rican Julio L. de Vizcarrondo y Coronado in Madrid, Spain, in 1864. During the second half of the nineteenth century, the *Sociedad* fought to end slavery throughout the Spanish Empire.

Born in San Juan, Puerto Rico, in 1830, Vizcarrondo became a journalist, abolitionist, and tireless champion of the underprivileged in both Puerto Rico and Spain. After being banished from Puerto Rico by the governor for antislavery agitation, Vizcarrondo moved to the United States at the age of twenty. He spent four years in the United States, where he married an American woman. Returning with his wife to Puerto Rico, he freed his slaves and began to condemn the extralegal cruelties of slaveholders before the courts.

Thwarted in his abolitionist efforts in Puerto Rico, where the colonial government anxiously guarded against a free press, Vizcarrondo decided to take his message directly to the Spanish government in Madrid, which legislated for the colonial possessions of Cuba and Puerto Rico. When the Vizcarrondos moved to Spain in 1863, they encountered a generation of Spanish liberals who, following the revolution of 1854, had struggled together with their liberal counterparts throughout Europe to enhance political democratization and economic liberalization. Vizcarrondo arrived in Madrid eager to take part in the burgeoning liberal movement and associational culture that would provide the organizational and ideological precedents for *La Sociedad Abolicionista Española.*

The liberal political and economic thought of Spain's middle-class social thinkers and activists established a foundation for abolitionist mobilization. Vizcarrondo ably unified the growing antislavery sentiment in Madrid, organizing the first meeting of the *Sociedad* on December 7, 1864. The society was formally constituted on April 2, 1865, in the Academy of Jurisprudence and Legislation. The society's original members included many influential Spanish and Antillean liberals.

Under Vizcarrondo's leadership, the society successfully fostered abolitionist activism in Spain. Events in North America made their efforts easier. By the end of 1863, most Spanish-speaking observers had come to believe that the slaveholding Confederacy was lost. Thus, in 1864, a year before the Union victory in the U.S. Civil War brought about the abolition of slavery in North America, two organizations in Spain, the Free Society of Political Economy and the Academy of Jurisprudence and Legislation, were emboldened to discuss the abolition of slavery in public for the first time.

La Sociedad Abolicionista Española took as its symbol a beseeching black man on bended knee with chained hands. Under Vizcarrondo's leadership, the society launched its first newspaper, *El Abolicionista Español* (The Spanish Abolitionist), and began holding organizational meetings in theaters throughout Spain. Branches were soon founded in other Spanish cities, and Vizcarrondo's wife, Harriet Brewster, organized a female chapter whose membership included many prominent society ladies. The liberal newspapers helped the cause by printing columns penned by abolitionists. Within a year of its founding, the society claimed some 700 members. Using the mottoes "free labor" and "moral redemption of the slaves," the society argued for immediate rather than gradual abolition of slavery and strove to be a secular organization with neither religious nor political party affiliations.

The most radical abolitionist in nineteenth-century Spain was Rafael María de Labra y Cadrana, the son of a Creole mother and a Spanish father. A charter member of *La Sociedad Abolicionista Española,* Labra became the society's president in 1869. Two years later, he was elected to represent Puerto Rico as a member of the Spanish Cortes (Parliament), where he confronted the proslavery colonial establishment. During his long career in the Cortes, Labra fought not only for abolition but also for many other reforms aimed at liberalizing the Spanish colonial administration. A professor at the University of Madrid, a prolific author, and member of many literary and scientific institutions, Labra considered slavery the most reprehensible aspect of Spanish colonial policy.

Both Labra and Vizcarrondo lived to see the abolitionist cause triumph. Slavery was abolished in Puerto Rico in 1873, and, in 1886, slavery and the suppressive *patronato* (slave tutelage system) were abolished in Cuba by royal decree.

David M. Carletta

See also: Cuba, Abolition in; Cuba, Emancipation in; Spanish Abolition Acts (1880, 1886).

Further Reading

Corwin, Arthur F. *Spain and the Abolition of Slavery in Cuba, 1817–1886.* Austin: University of Texas Press, 1967.
Schmidt-Nowara, Christopher. *Empire and Antislavery: Spain, Cuba, and Puerto Rico, 1833–1874.* Pittsburgh: University of Pittsburgh Press, 1999.

Société des Amis des Noirs, La

La Société des Amis des Noirs (Society of Friends of the Blacks) was the first abolitionist society in France. Founded by the journalist and future revolutionary Jacques-Pierre Brissot de Warville and his associate, the banker Étienne Clavière, the group first convened on February 19, 1788, in Brissot and Clavière's Paris apartments. Although the society functioned under its own bylaws and according to social and political conditions that were peculiar to France, its members never considered the organization independent of the international antislavery movement in the North Atlantic with which it coordinated its activities.

The initiative to form *La Société des Amis des Noirs* in fact came from Britain. The London-based Society for the Abolition of the Slave Trade, founded in May 1787, sought from the beginning to expand its influence beyond national borders. As a matter of strategic policy, the British chose to attack the slave trade alone, believing that the practice of slavery itself would eventually die away once the trade was abolished. To pursue this policy internationally, the British maintained contact with the principal American abolitionist societies and, from 1788 on, closely monitored the activities of *La Société des Amis des Noirs.* As a result of intense British involvement, the antislavery movement in the North Atlantic remained primarily focused on abolition, rather than emancipation, in the eighteenth century.

Despite charges from the French proslavery lobby that *La Société des Amis des Noirs* was part of a British plot to destabilize French control over its colonies in the West Indies, Brissot and Clavière never attempted to hide their British connections. The British abolitionists contacted Brissot during his visit to London in fall 1787 and convinced him to open a Parisian branch of the London society. Brissot and Clavière later confirmed they were members of the London society and considered themselves its "ambassadors" in France. They took their direction primarily from Thomas Clarkson, who remained in constant correspondence and traveled to Paris to oversee the French abolitionist activity. The London society also authorized the use of its seal (depicting a kneeling slave and the words "Am I not a man and a brother?" which the French replaced with *Ne suis-je pas ton frère?*) and provided translated documents and pamphlets detailing the atrocities and long-term economic infeasibility of the slave trade. Historians have argued that the London society so closely monitored the activities of the *Société* that the first French abolitionist movement rarely corresponded to the actual French situation.

Brissot and Clavière's abolitionism was part of a larger effort to transform the Atlantic world politically and economically. In January 1787, Brissot, Clavière, and a few companions founded the Gallo-American Society to promote economic relations between France and the United States and to introduce the French to the principles of American liberty. Although the society engaged in the sort of unrestrained enthusiasm for America that was common in Paris after the American Revolution, it nevertheless promoted a coherent foreign policy, outlined in Brissot and Clavière's April 1787 publication, *De la France et des États-Unis* (Of France and the United States).

Following this manifesto, the Gallo-American Society promoted financial investment as a way of drawing the two nations together without excluding Britain. In the second half of 1788, Brissot traveled to "Free America" (the thirteen states) to establish contacts and invest in American property.

The Gallo-American Society made up the core membership of *La Société des Amis des Noirs.* By early 1789, the *Société* had enrolled some 141 members, largely from the social and intellectual elite of Paris, including the comte de Mirabeau, the marquis de Lafayette, the marquis de Condorcet, François de la Rochefoucauld, and Abbé Grégoire. Imbibing the Enlightenment rhetoric of Baron de La Brède et de Montesquieu, Jean-Jacques Rousseau, and Voltaire, these men regarded African slavery not only as a violation of natural law, but also as a particularly heinous symptom of the tyranny and injustice that pervaded French society.

Questioning both its effectiveness and methods, some historians have accused *La Société des Amis des Noirs* of being an elitist philanthropic society that failed to organize effective popular political opposition to slavery and succeeded only in arousing the alarm of the proslavery lobby. A fair evaluation of the *Société* must take into account the conditions in France, however. The society modeled itself as a political action committee along British lines, but the kind of overt political action that was possible in Great Britain would have been out of the question in France at the time. The London society could and did propose a bill in Parliament to abolish the slave trade, but the *Société* had no such influence with King Louis XVI and could do little before 1789 except disseminate information on the economic and ethical realities of the trade. Mirabeau, Lafayette, and Clavière attempted to use their personal connections to influence the French Ministry of the Navy, which had jurisdiction over the French slave trade, but failed to affect policy. Nevertheless, the *Société* did provide its members—many of whom would later serve in the revolutionary assemblies—with an apprenticeship in political activism and coordination that would prove invaluable after 1789.

La Société des Amis des Noirs continued to function as a political society until spring 1793. It argued for the exclusion of colonial planters from the Estates-General in 1789, formally demanded that the National Assembly abolish the slave trade in 1790, and campaigned successfully for laws granting citizens' rights to free "persons of color" in 1791 and 1792.

The *Société*'s close association with Brissot, however, led to its suppression when the Jacobins purged

Brissot's faction (the Girondins) from the National Convention in early summer 1793. Brissot and Clavière were guillotined; others were driven underground. The *Société* thus had no direct role in the National Convention's decision on February 4, 1794, to emancipate all of France's colonial slaves.

At the instigation of Abbé Grégoire, a small remnant of the society regrouped in 1796 under the name *La Société des Amis des Noirs et des Colonies* (hoping vainly to avoid charges of being unpatriotic) but exercised little influence. Napoleon Bonaparte suppressed all abolitionist activities after his coup d'état in 1799 and re-instituted slavery in 1802. A few of the original members of the *Société*, particularly Abbé Grégoire and Lafayette, continued to serve the abolitionist movement into the 1820s.

Gregory Matthew Adkins

See also: Clarkson, Thomas; Enlightenment; Grégoire, Abbé Henri.

Further Reading

Jennings, Lawrence C. *French Anti-Slavery: The Movement for the Abolition of Slavery in France, 1802–1848.* Cambridge, UK: Cambridge University Press, 2000.

Quinney, Valerie. "Decisions on Slavery, the Slave Trade and Civil Rights for Negroes in the Early French Revolution." *Canadian Journal of History* 17 (1982): 447–67.

Resnick, Daniel P. "The Société des Amis des Noirs and the Abolition of Slavery." *French Historical Studies* 7 (Autumn 1972): 558–69.

Society for the Abolition of the Slave Trade

The Society for the Abolition of the Slave Trade, sometimes called the Society for Effecting the Abolition of the Slave Trade, was founded in Great Britain in May 1787. The society became the first fully developed pressure group and succeeded in bringing about the abolition of the transatlantic slave trade.

By the eighteenth century, the transatlantic slave trade was reaping enormous benefits for the British Empire. Most people in British society accepted the romanticized stories of the adventurous lives of traders on the high seas, so there was little opposition to the trade in human lives. By the late eighteenth century, however, the Society of Friends (Quakers) and other religious groups had begun to question the morality of the trade. In 1783, the Quakers were the first group to petition Parliament on the subject of outlawing the trade. Their efforts were unsuccessful, but they did bring great attention to the abolitionist cause.

A far more successful attempt to abolish the transatlantic slave trade began in 1787. Thomas Clarkson, an Anglican priest and the son of a clergyman, developed a strong antislavery stance that led him into a lifelong friendship with fellow Anglican Granville Sharp. In 1787, the two joined with nine Quakers to form the Society for the Abolition of the Slave Trade. Members of this new society included such influential figures as John Wesley and Josiah Wedgwood.

With an extensive organization and a fully developed network of local chapters, the society became a dramatic force for change; its London chapter, called the London Committee, became its center. The society created a nationwide constituency through the distribution of abolitionist literature, pamphlets, prints, and artifacts. The London Committee effectively developed a network of local contacts, known as *agents* or *county committees*, who were responsible for spreading the abolitionist message.

As the London Committee's traveling agent, Clarkson became the central figure in spreading this message. He traveled the nation, providing a vital link between London and the provinces, organizing committees, distributing literature, and offering advice and encouragement to hundreds of grassroots organizations.

Clarkson widened the campaign by writing *Summary View of the Slave Trade, and the Probable Consequences of Its Abolition*, published in 1787. The work included interviews with more than 20,000 sailors and ship captains. He collected thousands of pieces of equipment used on slaves, such as iron handcuffs, leg shackles, branding irons, and other implements of torture. The text remains one of the most important pieces of literature on the horrors of the slave trade.

Support for the cause of abolition stretched across all classes and regions in the British Isles, from high-powered men such as Member of Parliament William Wilberforce to industrial workers in places as far-flung as Bristol and Scotland. The society's ability to raise funds and diversity of support allowed it to mount the largest petition campaign attacking the slave trade the nation had ever seen. In 1788, in the first of these campaigns, more than 100 petitions, collected in less than three months, were presented to the House of Commons in London. In 1792, the society's London Committee presented an astounding 519 petitions to the House of Commons, the largest

William Wilberforce, chosen to lead the Society for the Abolition of the Slave Trade at its founding in 1787, used this model of the slave ship *Brookes* and other evidence to demonstrate to Parliament the immorality of the Middle Passage. (*©Wilberforce House, Hull City Museums and Art Galleries, UK/The Bridgeman Art Library*)

number ever submitted to the House on a single subject or in a single session.

Wilberforce, who led the campaign in the House of Commons, hoped the mass petitioning would exert enough pressure on Parliament to abolish the trade. In a vote of 230 to 80, the House of Commons passed a resolution to gradually abolish the trade in human beings. Although the resolution was eventually overturned, Sharp, Clarkson, and their allies continued their campaign.

In the end, world events shaped the course of abolition. The acquisition of new territories in the West Indies encouraged many of the old planter elites, who were growing increasingly concerned about foreign competition, to become abolitionists. Capitalizing on this change of heart and the entry into Parliament of a new group of liberal Irish members, the abolitionists recharged their campaign in 1804.

In 1805, a bill providing for the abolition of the slave trade in conquered territories passed both the House of Commons and the House of Lords. The following year, the bill was superseded by a stronger measure that outlawed the British transatlantic slave trade altogether. This new measure, known as the Abolition of the Slave Trade Act, became law in 1807.

With its success, the Society for the Abolition of the Slave Trade changed its name to the African Institution in 1807. The primary aim of this new group was to ensure that the legislation was enforced and that other countries followed Britain's example.

In 1823, Clarkson, Wilberforce, and Zachary Macaulay set out to form yet another organization, the Anti-Slavery Society, to foment support for the abolition of slavery throughout the British Empire. The efforts of Clarkson, Sharp, and Wilberforce to end the Atlantic slave trade marked them as some of the most noted abolitionists in history. The Society for the Abolition of the Slave Trade remained one of the most successful pressure groups and provided a model of how grassroots organizations could effect widespread social change.

Melissa Anyiwo

See also: African Institution; Clarkson, Thomas; Dolben's Act (1788); Quakers (Society of Friends); Sharp, Granville; Wedgwood Cameos; Wilberforce, William.

Further Reading

Davidson, Basil. *The African Slave Trade: Pre-Colonial History, 1450–1850.* Boston: Little, Brown, 1961.

Society for the Civilization of Africa

Abolitionists on both sides of the Atlantic believed that the key to ending slavery lay in the complete eradication of the transatlantic slave trade and the economic elimination of a market for captives in the coastal states of West Africa. Sir Thomas Fowell Buxton, one of the great leaders of the British antislavery movement, proposed the creation of the Society for the Extinction of the Slave Trade and the Civilization of Africa—more commonly known as the Society for the Civilization of Africa—in the early 1840s to help achieve these lofty objectives. Buxton presented his ideas at the World Anti-Slavery Convention in London in 1840, but he was met with opposition from convention delegates and British parliamentarians, and the society was short-lived.

Buxton was a Quaker businessman and philanthropist who had been active in the antislavery cause for many years. In 1824, he succeeded the aging William Wilberforce as leader of the abolitionist movement in Great Britain. Buxton served as a Member of Parliament representing Weymouth from 1818 to 1837. During this time, he supported a variety of reform movements, including prison reform and abolitionism, and expressed a desire to improve social conditions for Africans.

Buxton believed that only Great Britain was powerful enough to direct the necessary actions to end the slave trade in Africa and begin to improve the conditions of life that Africans faced. Rather than viewing this power in military terms, he believed that the twin forces of economic preeminence and commanding moral authority would bring about a transformation of conditions in West Africa. This approach satisfied Buxton's pacifism, which was inspired by his religious heritage, but many questioned whether such changes could be brought about without military support.

Buxton's plans for the Society for the Civilization of Africa were based on quasi-imperialistic notions rooted in nineteenth-century paternalism and racism, presuming that Africa's future could be improved only if it were relegated to the oversight of outside powers. The key to Africa's uplift, in Buxton's view, was the creation of a sustainable economic base that could wean Africans away from the necessity of trading in war captives, a practice that perpetuated the slave trade.

It would be necessary, in Buxton's view, for British authorities to meet with local rulers along a 1,000-mile stretch of West Africa's coastal states to negotiate agreements that would place the British in control of the coastline. These agreements established terms related specifically to trade and economic development; political power remained in the hands of the local rulers. Subsequently, coastal trading depots would be established to facilitate the transfer of locally produced agricultural goods for British-made manufactured products. It was believed that the health of such a trading network would preclude the necessity for a slave trade. In addition, Buxton wanted to provide missionaries and teachers to Africa to aid the region in moral and social development; however, the creation of economically viable communities was more central to Buxton's proposed system than the religious impulse to save individual souls.

Buxton's ideas stemmed from a career of research and observation, during which he had honed a comprehensive plan to stimulate the economic and social development of the African peoples. Many of his plans for the Society for the Civilization of Africa first appeared in works such as *The African Slave Trade and its Remedy* (1939).

Buxton presented his plans publicly at the 1840 World Anti-Slavery Convention in London. The plan received enthusiastic support among many, but others questioned the cost of such an endeavor and its potential efficacy. In addition, some abolitionists criticized the plan as a cleverly disguised attempt to repackage the old idea of colonization, which, by 1840, had acquired an odious reputation in many circles of the antislavery movement.

In fact, representatives of the American Colonization Society (ACS) perceived a commonality between their efforts and the ideas proposed by Buxton. Ralph Randolph Gurley, an agent of the ACS, traveled to London to meet with Buxton about joining forces, but American abolitionists who were in London for the 1840 convention discredited the idea of colonization and dissuaded Buxton from any effort to join with the ACS.

Despite vocal opposition from certain parliamentarians, the British government adopted Buxton's suggestions and outfitted an 1841 expedition to the Niger River delta to begin its work. Although a missionary headquarters was established, an extremely high casualty rate among project participants forced the abandonment of the effort within a few years.

In several respects, Buxton's ideas were well ahead of their time. During the late twentieth century, many of the economic policies included in structural adjustment programs created by the World Bank and the International Monetary Fund employed the same economic measures that Buxton had envisioned. In addition, the work of Peace Corps volunteers provided much of the secular missionary effort that Buxton had argued was necessary for social and economic development in West Africa.

Junius P. Rodriguez

See also: Buxton, Thomas Fowell; World Anti-Slavery Convention (1840).

Society for the Propagation of the Gospel in Foreign Parts

Established by royal charter in 1701, the Society for the Propagation of the Gospel in Foreign Parts was founded in London by the Reverend Dr. Thomas Bray. The society represented the missionary arm of the Church of England. Its primary role was to minister to white settlers in all English colonies, but, over the course of time, the ministry expanded to include the religious conversion of Native American peoples and persons of African descent in the English colonies. The society was never an institution that supported abolition or emancipation, and its ideology, which reflected the Church of England's conservative position, did not consider Christianity and slavery as being incompatible.

The society's mission was predicated on the assumption that the wild nature of the exotic areas that had been colonized influenced the colonists who moved to those regions, making them somehow tainted by the wilderness that they inhabited. Henry Compton, the bishop of London, was concerned about the lack of religious activity in the colonies, and he appointed Bray commissary for Maryland in 1696. Bray's observations there convinced him that the spiritual welfare of the English settlers in the colonies was at risk.

Bray was instrumental in helping to organize the society and writing its charter. Committed to ensuring "that sufficient mainteynance [sic] be provided for an orthodox clergy to live amongst the colonists and that such other provision be made as may be necessary for the propagation of the gospel in those parts," the society provided missionaries, teachers, Bibles, Books of Common Prayer, and other religious literature to the settlers in the English colonies.

Society missionaries ministered to the Native Americans and slaves whom they encountered in the English colonies. In the case of the Native Ameri-

cans, the requirements of living along the harsh frontier were too demanding for many missionaries, and that ministry faltered. Many slave owners purposefully prevented the missionaries from having any direct contact with their slaves. Some planters allowed the society's missionaries to speak to slaves only if the meeting was held in the owner's presence.

Even in cases in which society missionaries could have acted in the slaves' best interests, they often failed to do so. In 1710, for example, the wealthy planter Colonel Christopher Codrington died on Barbados and willed two plantations to the society. It was Codrington's wish that the land be used to build a college to educate the island's slaves. He hoped such a college would prove that slavery and Christianity could coexist. The missionaries ignored his wish.

In the English North American colonies, the society's missionaries were not always welcome in the colonial settlements. New England Puritans had done their best to disestablish themselves from the Church of England and viewed the society's efforts to proselytize in Puritan-dominated regions as suspect. The missionaries did not fare much better in the Middle and Southern colonies, where religious conformity was not highly valued in the early eighteenth century. These difficulties, along with the hardship of frontier life, the problems of transportation and communication, and the uncertainties of the weather, made the work of the Church of England missionaries arduous.

In 1729, the Society for the Propagation of the Gospel in Foreign Parts reorganized itself and changed its name to Dr. Bray's Associates. The name change reflected a more secular, service-oriented emphasis, but the work of the organization still focused on the spiritual uplift of colonial inhabitants who were at risk.

Occasionally, the organization did meet with success. In Charleston, South Carolina, Mr. Garden's School was established in 1743 to teach black youth in the city. The school was supported by both free black and white residents of Charleston. In the same year, another school, one specifically designed to train black missionaries, was established in Charleston by the missionaries associated with Dr. Bray's Associates. By 1755, the school had seventy students enrolled.

By 1752, British missionaries from Dr. Bray's Associates had arrived in the Gold Coast region of West Africa. They conducted their missionary activities from Cape Coast Castle, one of the locations where the business of the slave trade was conducted.

Tragically, the missionaries never took an active role in any of their colonial settings to work against the institution of slavery and support the work of abolition and emancipation. The Church of England had issued a policy statement in 1727 indicating that it would not associate itself with the pro-emancipation forces that were then beginning to organize themselves in Great Britain. As a result, the missionaries who were associated with the Church of England did not question slavery in terms of morality and ethics. Many of the prevailing racist assumptions—especially the notion that slavery was a necessary step in the civilizing of Africans—characterized the work of the Church of England missionaries.

After the American Revolution, the work of the Church of England missionaries in North America was curtailed substantially, with the exception of their ongoing work in Canada. At the time, many of the missionaries began to concentrate their activities on the plantation colonies of the British West Indies. Because the missionaries often relied on the financial patronage of wealthy planters, they made no effort to upset the social conditions of life in the British West Indies by questioning the moral legitimacy of slavery.

Junius P. Rodriguez

See also: Religion and Abolitionism.

Further Reading

Bellot, Leland J. "Evangelicals and the Defense of Slavery in Britain's Old Colonial Empire." *Journal of Southern History* 37 (February 1971): 19–40.
Wood, Forest G. *The Arrogance of Faith: Christianity and Race in America from the Colonial Era to the Twentieth Century.* Boston: Northeastern University Press, 1990.

Society of Friends of the Blacks

See Société des Amis des Noirs, La

Somersett Case (1772)

One of the most important legal proceedings in England during the eighteenth century—a time when the African slave trade was thriving—the case of *Knowles v. Somersett* is widely understood as having ended slavery in England.

Practically speaking, the case considered the question of a simple wrongful detainment: Could a man who had committed no criminal act be forcibly detained with a view toward being removed from the country? As it happened, the detained man and the ship's captain who secreted him aboard a vessel anchored in the Thames River each represented key social, political, and economic forces of the time.

Arrayed on opposing sides, on one hand were James Somersett (the enslaved), his legal counsel in support of liberty, and the antislavery personage Granville Sharp; on the other hand were Charles Stewart (the slave master), John Knowles (the ship's captain), and the West Indian planters in support of slavery. At the center sat William Murray, Lord Mansfield, in the position of chief justice of the Court of King's Bench.

The case was tried during a time when conceptions of and debates about liberty—particularly individual natural rights—were of deep concern. Therefore, the arguments set forth by Somersett's legal counsel and by Stewart provide a window into an important element of the eighteenth-century ideological framework regarding liberty and slavery and the ways in which the law reinforced or contributed to the dismantling of that framework.

Background

In the late 1740s, Somersett was purchased in Virginia by Stewart, a British subject. Stewart and Somersett resided in Virginia for several years before moving to Massachusetts. In 1769, Stewart returned to England with Somersett in tow. For two years, Somersett lived with Stewart in London without incident.

In autumn 1771, Somersett ran away. Although he managed to evade capture for nearly two months, he was ultimately caught and, at the behest of his master, secured below the decks of the *Ann and Mary*, a ship captained by John Knowles and bound for Jamaica, then one of Britain's Caribbean plantation colonies. Somersett could easily have been spirited away, with few in London the wiser for his disappearance. But his abduction did not go unnoticed, and a writ of habeas corpus (granted based on affidavits asserting that Somersett had been bound in irons) directed Knowles to present the captive before Mansfield and to state the reason for detaining him. The wheels of the case were thus set in motion, and it proceeded for six months until a conclusion was reached in June 1772.

Lord Mansfield, who heard the case, was no stranger to the issue of slavery in England, having presided over similar cases in the 1760s and 1770s. The legal status of Africans had bedeviled the English courts at least since 1677—the earliest recorded judicial determination involving Africans on the question of slavery. As a form of involuntary servitude, the English understood the medieval concept of *villeinage* (legal status or condition of servitude associated with feudal serfdom); slavery, however, was another matter. Although the financial benefits reaped by Britain as a result of the African slave trade could not be denied (making it clear that they had no fundamental scruples against trading in human beings), it was the question of slavery on English soil that demanded scrutiny in this particular case. Thus, English law did not assume that Africans were, by definition, slaves.

For centuries, English law had taken no notice of Africans, because there were few in their midst. By the late eighteenth century, however, Britain had become the preeminent European power in the African slave trade. The growing presence of Africans in England, the status of Africans in relation to the law, and the possible limits of the transatlantic slave trade all compelled the English and the English courts to address the problem of slavery—at least within the borders of England's green and pleasant land.

Arguments

Among Somersett's legal counsel team, the arguments of Francis Hargrave dominated. Hargrave's opening observations responded directly to the statement provided by Knowles, wherein the captain had accounted for his detention of Somersett. In the statement, Knowles had argued for Somersett's continued slave status: If the buying and selling of slaves was sanctioned, why should Stewart not continue in his right to Somersett?

Hargrave countered Knowles's argument by addressing Stewart's claimed right to the person of Somersett and by questioning Stewart's authority to enforce such a right through Somersett's imprisonment and removal from England. In challenging Stewart's right to detain Somersett, Hargrave effectively brought before the court the lawfulness of slavery in England; Stewart's claim in the return to the writ was founded principally on the legitimacy of slavery as a state of being.

In a demonstration of tactical brilliance, Hargrave redirected the standard argument against slavery (moral grounds) to make an argument against the presence of slavery specifically *in England*. As the difference between servanthood and slavery had been frequently elided in England in the past, and as

villeinage as a species of perpetual bondage was argued to have been dissolved, Hargrave focused on the inadvisability of admitting a new species of bondage into England—namely, colonial slavery. Listing the general characteristics of slavery and its destructive effects allowed Hargrave to assert that slavery corrupted the state and its citizens.

To present-day sensibilities, such specificity of argument might appear to be more cowardly than cunning, given the heinous nature of the slave trade and Britain's eager participation. Hargrave recognized, however, that there was little chance of slavery being abolished in Britain's New World colonies; thus, his strategy was to countenance the institution grudgingly. The goal, after all, was to keep England free of slavery. It was precisely the specificity of the argument that had the greatest potential to hold sway: It could condemn the condoning of slavery within certain boundaries, while reluctantly giving some quarter to England's West Indian planters, who profited mightily from the trade.

Ruling

The decision rendered by Lord Mansfield—in a case that he was disinclined to try at all—proved to be narrow in its application and expansive in its ability to be misconstrued. During the course of the trial, he refused to countenance the notion of a contract—by nature, a relationship entered into voluntarily—between an enslaved person and his master; it was a refusal that effectively weakened the arguments of Stewart's legal counsel. However, the core of the case was not a question of contract between Somersett and Stewart. Instead, the issue was Stewart's claim to the *person* of Somersett and the right to remove him at will from the English metropole to the plantation colonies.

Dismissing the often-invoked Yorke-Talbot opinion of 1729, which guaranteed the West Indian planters a continued right to their enslaved property while in England, Mansfield ruled that although slavery existed and that the power of a master over a slave varied in time and space, slavery as an institution had not been explicitly introduced (by positive law) in England. Thus, the case could not be approved by English law, and James Somersett, who had been detained solely on the basis of his presumed enslaved status, was set free.

T.K. Hunter

See also: Hargrave, Francis; Sharp, Granville.

Further Reading

Gerzina, Gretchen. *Black London: Life Before Emancipation.* New Brunswick, NJ: Rutgers University Press, 1995.

Scobie, Edward. *Black Britannia: A History of Blacks in Britain.* Chicago: Johnson, 1972.

Shyllon, Folarin O. *Black Slaves in Britain.* London: Oxford University Press, 1974.

Sons of Africa

As the first antislavery organization to be established in the Atlantic world by former slaves who had been born in Africa, the Sons of Africa was a bold venture to advance the cause of abolitionism.

The notion that the "sons of Africa" had a moral obligation to redeem their native continent from the abuses it faced was a significant part of the cultural ethos of the Pan-African movement that developed in the late nineteenth and early twentieth centuries. That movement, motivated by a spirited sense of "negritude" (awareness and pride in the African cultural heritage), focused on the liberation of Africa from the clutches of the European colonial powers that had occupied the continent for the better part of a century. The first manifestation of this attitude appeared in the late eighteenth century in Britain, as African expatriates, themselves the victims and survivors of the transatlantic slave trade, organized to assist the crusade to end the evil institution of slavery. The Sons of Africa was the first abolitionist group to be organized and led by black abolitionists.

Founded in London in 1787, the Sons of Africa was established by twelve blacks living in Great Britain who hoped to make an important contribution to the vital issues of their time. More than just another antislavery organization, the Sons of Africa is regarded by modern historians as the first civil rights organization in the transatlantic world. The black abolitionists who formed the society viewed their antislavery work as more than a mere reform-oriented pastime; it was a vital and urgent calling inspired by their own life experiences.

The former-slaves-turned-abolitionists Quobna Ottobah Cugoano and Olaudah Equiano were the chief organizers of the Sons of Africa. In the aftermath of the famous *Somersett* case of 1772, in which slavery was effectively outlawed in England, free blacks became a significant, if small, presence in London and other urban centers. Recognizing that the moment was right to organize in support of incipient efforts by British abolitionists working to have Parliament outlaw the transatlantic slave trade, free blacks such as Cugoano and Equiano realized that they could contribute to the discussion on the merits of abolition.

Both Cugoano and Equiano had already exerted an important influence on the antislavery discourse in Great Britain. Cugoano had published his *Thoughts and Sentiments on the Evil and Wicked Traffic of the Slavery and Commerce of the Human Species* (1787), and Equiano had followed with publication of *The Interesting Narrative of the Life of Olaudah Equiano* (1789). Both works were widely read and distributed by white abolitionists in Britain.

The rhetoric of these first-person narratives animated the message that the Sons of Africa hoped to deliver to British society, which was not yet committed to the cause of abolitionism. The former slaves could give powerful testimony to the inhumanity inherent in the institution, making it more than an academic issue that affected others beyond Britain's shores. In addition, they could emphasize the moral dictum that silence on such a great moral tragedy was tantamount to complicity in the crime. Such heady moralism was powerful, but it was also dangerous, because it challenged the religious sensibilities of the times.

Members of the Sons of Africa traveled in England, Scotland, and Ireland, lecturing on the horrors of the slave trade they had experienced firsthand. In addition, members of the society mounted a sustained campaign to collect signatures for antislavery petitions that were presented to the Prince of Wales and Queen Charlotte, the wife of English king George III. Through these activities, as well as letters published in newspapers such as the *Public Advertiser,* the Sons of Africa gave proof that Africans could be articulate and impassioned spokesmen for the abolitionist cause.

Granville Sharp, one of the leading white abolitionists in Great Britain, believed that the work of Cugoano, Equiano, and their compatriots was an important contribution to the efforts that he and other abolitionists had already begun. He applauded their efforts and their methods.

One of the ironies of the abolitionist movement, however, is that the efforts of groups such as the Sons of Africa were never fully appreciated or effectively utilized, a result of the fundamentally racist tendencies of many of the white reformers who called themselves abolitionists. Many who sincerely opposed the slave trade and slavery did so because they equated these activities with sin on an intellectual level, but, on a purely social level, they could not accept blacks as their equals. Although such parsing of morality and personal ethics seems disingenuous by modern-day standards, it was a fact of life in the abolitionist movement and often prevented the movement from mounting a singular, sustained voice against the perpetuation of the transatlantic slave trade and slavery.

Junius P. Rodriguez

See also: Cugoano, Quobna Ottobah; Equiano, Olaudah; Sharp, Granville; *Somersett* Case (1772).

Further Reading

Gerzina, Gretchen. *Black London: Life Before Emancipation.* New Brunswick, NJ: Rutgers University Press, 1995.

Scobie, Edward. *Black Britannia: A History of Blacks in Britain.* Chicago: Johnson, 1972.

Shyllon, Folarin O. *Black Slaves in Britain.* London: Oxford University Press, 1974.

Sonthonax, Léger Félicité (1763–1813)

Léger Félicité Sonthonax was a key figure in the decolonization of Haiti and the abolition of slavery in the French Empire. He was directly responsible for the abolition of slavery in the French colony of Saint-Domingue in 1793 and worked diligently to effect equal rights for free blacks in the colony.

Born in 1763 in Oyonnax, France, close to the Swiss border, Sonthonax earned a degree in law from the University of Dijon in 1784. His father, a wealthy trader, bought him a position as a parliamentary lawyer. In Paris, he encountered the duc d'Orléans and his entourage, one of whom was Jacques-Pierre Brissot de Warville, founder of the abolitionist *Société des Amis des Noirs* (Society of Friends of the Blacks).

In spring 1789, Sonthonax began writing for a radical (i.e., antiroyalist and pro-Jacobin) paper, *Les Révolutions de Paris.* He addressed the subject of slavery for the first time in an article published in September 1790, arguing for its abolition, and he was soon acknowledged as the colonial affairs expert of the Jacobin Club. He was also the protégé of Brissot, who drafted French foreign policy from October 1791.

In August 1791, Saint-Domingue witnessed a revolt involving 50,000 of the island's 450,000 slaves; an initial mission involving three commissioners failed to stem the crisis. In March 1792, the new National Assembly in Paris overturned the 1791 Constitution, thus recognizing equal rights for all free blacks; it passed a law to this effect the following month. Sonthonax and two other civilian commissioners were sent to the Caribbean to implement the law by setting up a national guard and preparing for local elections. From the moment they arrived, they encountered plots hatched by the colonists. The commissioners ended up seeking the support of fugitive slaves, promising them freedom in return.

On August 29, 1793, Sonthonax unilaterally declared the abolition of slavery in Saint-Domingue. Having done this, the commissioners now had to return order to the island, resist British and Spanish attempts to invade, and get the National Assembly to accept Sonthonax's decision. Sonthonax endorsed the election of three black, three white, and three mixed-race deputies to be sent to Paris to defend his stance. On February 4, 1794, after hearing the arguments presented by these deputies, the National Assembly voted to abolish slavery.

Events in Paris soon took precedence over the governance of Saint-Domingue. Although the British had taken Port-au-Prince in June 1794 and the Spanish had invaded the north of the island (now Santo Domingo), aided by rebel leader Toussaint L'Ouverture, Sonthonax and others were recalled to Paris to face corruption charges stemming from the collapse of the Brissot faction's administration. They arrived in France two days after the execution of French revolutionist Maximilien de Robespierre in July 1794.

After a long trial carried out by representatives of the Saint-Domingue colonists, the charges against Sonthonax were dropped in October 1795. In the meantime, Toussaint had again joined the French in expelling British and Spanish troops, and the revolutionary culture in Saint-Domingue had stabilized. The new government (the Directory) sent Sonthonax back to head a five-man mission to the island, where he arrived triumphantly in May 1796.

For the next year, Sonthonax attempted to resist the powers of the many generals who had emerged during the slave war and leaned on Touissant for guidance. However, the country was disintegrating into militarized fiefdoms, and Sonthonax's Jacobin objective of unitary nationhood could not be achieved.

In August 1796, Sonthonax was elected deputy for Saint-Domingue, but a year later Toussaint forced his return to France. The latter was seeking independence, a goal that was anathema to the Jacobin Sonthonax. He continued his antislavery activities in France under the surveillance of the government. Napoleon Bonaparte's coup d'état in November 1799 effectively ended his political career. Sonthonax was arrested and spent the next few years in exile within France.

He returned to Paris from 1806 to 1813, before again being ordered to leave. He died in his hometown of Oyonnax in 1813.

Steve Garner

See also: Haitian Revolution (1791–1804); *Société des Amis des Noirs, La;* Toussaint L'Ouverture, François-Dominique.

Further Reading

Dorigny, Marcel. *The Abolitions of Slavery: From Léger Félicité Sonthonax to Victor Schoelcher, 1793, 1794, 1848.* New York: Berghahn, 2003.

Stein, Robert Louis. *Léger Félicité Sonthonax: The Lost Sentinel of the Republic.* Rutherford, NJ: Fairleigh Dickinson University Press, 1985.

Spanish Abolition Acts (1880, 1886)

The emancipation of slaves in Cuba was effected through a process of gradual abolition that was set in motion by the Spanish Abolition Act of 1880 and completed by the Spanish Abolition Act of 1886. The 1880 act created a system of *patronato* (compulsory apprenticeship) that was to be in effect on Cuba's plantations and farms for eight years. The measure was similar to the system of apprenticeship that had been implemented in the British West Indies when that region was emancipated in 1834. In the face of increasing hostility to the abuses of the patronato system, and with the support of the king, the Cortes (Spanish Parliament) subsequently passed the 1886 act, which reduced the period of servitude to six years and effectively abolished slavery and unfree servitude throughout the Spanish colonies.

Because of the enormous profits reaped from sugar cultivation and a feeling of obligation to maintain the system of slavery that had made such riches possible, Spain was the last of the European powers to abolish slavery through positive law in the late nineteenth century. The Spanish movement toward emancipation was motivated neither by diplomatic suasion nor by enlightened benevolence but rather by military necessity.

The Spanish Crown had used the force of arms to maintain its colonial authority in Cuba, the richest of the sugar islands, despite the growth of an incipient movement in the colony for political autonomy and independence. The growing insurgency became more difficult for the Spanish to counter as the nineteenth century progressed. For a time, the Spanish feared that they might lose the colony to the United States, which seemed eager to extend its notion of "manifest destiny" beyond its continental boundaries.

Although the Spanish government had shown itself capable of crushing independence movements in Cuba, the Ten Years' War (1868–1878) proved to be a sustained guerilla war that threatened to drive the Spanish authorities out of Cuba. Facing the possible loss of the colony, the Spanish government enlisted allies in the royalist cause by promising the island's slaves that if they supported the Spanish and helped defeat the Cuban insurgents, they would receive their freedom at the successful conclusion of the war. Large numbers of Cuban slaves flocked to the Spanish cause, and Spain delivered on its promise when the war ended.

The cause of emancipation was aided by *La Sociedad Abolicionista Española* (Spanish Abolitionist Society), which was formed in 1864 and advocated for the abolition of slavery throughout the Spanish Empire. During the 1860s and 1870s, an increasing number of liberal reformers were elected to the Cortes, and they, too, began to agitate for the cause of emancipation. In 1870, the Cortes enacted the Moret Law, which established a procedure for the gradual abolition of slavery in Puerto Rico, but the measure had no impact on slavery in Cuba. Therefore, the Spanish Abolition Act of 1880 was enacted.

Although the measure had the most direct impact on Cuba, it also affected other Spanish colonial possessions, including the Philippine Islands, Guam, and portions of the Western Sahara. With the adoption of the Spanish Abolition Act of 1886, the Spanish government joined other European powers in their effort to eradicate forms of slavery that lingered in parts of Africa and Asia.

Junius P. Rodriguez

See also: Cuba, Abolition in; Cuba, Emancipation in; *Sociedad Abolicionista Española, La.*

Further Reading

Corwin, Arthur F. *Spain and the Abolition of Slavery in Cuba, 1817–1886.* Austin: University of Texas Press, 1967.

Schmidt-Nowara, Christopher. *Empire and Antislavery: Spain, Cuba, and Puerto Rico, 1833–1874.* Pittsburgh: University of Pittsburgh Press, 1999.

Spooner, Lysander (1808–1887)

Lysander Spooner was a Massachusetts lawyer who was noted for his vigorous opposition to the state's encroachment on individual liberty. He wrote widely on the unconstitutionality of slavery, and his treatise of that name became campaign literature of the Liberty Party, the first antislavery political party organized by abolitionists in 1840.

Spooner was born on January 19, 1808, outside Athol, Massachusetts. He began studying the law in 1833 in Worcester. Spooner set up office in Worcester and immediately challenged a law mandating that nongraduates serve in a lawyer's office for five years as opposed to the three required for college graduates.

Spooner's legal training was fairly common in the annals of abolitionary history. Much of the abolitionist writing in the United States centered on the nation's legal system and its use to defend the practice of slavery. Among the many splits that developed within the antislavery camp, legal differences related to the U.S. Constitution were central. William Lloyd Garrison, editor of *The Liberator*, called the Constitution "a covenant with death and an agreement with hell" for its sanction of slavery. Garrison's view of the Constitution led him to oppose any political activity by abolitionists. Spooner's treatise *The Unconstitutionality of Slavery* (1845, reprinted with a second part added in 1847) took a different approach.

Spooner insisted that law in its most basic sense refers to natural law. According to natural law, all human beings are born with the inalienable right of freedom. Freedom, in one of its most essential aspects, means that no human being can own another human being. Spooner argued that the Constitution supported this notion in its application of the rights of citizenship to all persons, thereby invalidating slavery.

Spooner responded to the passage of the Fugitive Slave Act in 1850 by publishing *A Defense for Fugitive Slaves* the same year. In this tract, Spooner argued that rescuing individuals from an assault or restraint on their liberty—without the authority of natural law—was morally and legally "a meritorious act." Given the unjustness of the act, any slave who faced prosecution should be exonerated by the jury. Faced with the Kansas-Nebraska Act (1854), which introduced the idea of popular sovereignty into previously "free" territory, and the *Dred Scott* decision (1857), which held that slavery could be maintained anywhere in the nation, Spooner penned his assault on the Fugitive Slave Law in an 1858 broadsheet that was a bold blueprint for insurrection in the South.

Although Spooner and radical abolitionist John Brown had met before the Harpers Ferry raid, Spooner had little prior knowledge about the takeover of the U.S. Army arsenal. Furthermore, historians generally agree that the 1858 broadsheet was withheld from circulation at Brown's request, lest it forewarn Southerners of Brown's plans for guerrilla action. Spooner expressed confidence that the raid would be a success and later extolled Brown as a model of just action.

Spooner subsequently participated in a conspiracy to free Brown. His plan was to kidnap the governor of Virginia and hold him for ransom in exchange for Brown. The kidnapping never came to fruition, however, as Spooner's associates were unable to muster the courage or money to go through with it. After Brown was hanged on December 2, 1859, Spooner began to view politicians and the legal process with increasing disdain.

Spooner's most controversial publication—and one that ran counter to the ideas of most abolitionists in the United States—was *No Treason* (1867–1870). In it, Spooner argued that the Constitution, "having no inherent authority or obligation," was a contract of government that had been violated during the U.S. Civil War and therefore was void. The essay also contained a legal defense against the crime of treason intended for former Confederate soldiers, arguing that "no treason" had been committed by Southerners during the war.

Nearly the entire abolitionist movement, including men such as Garrison, who was opposed to political action, had supported the North during the Civil War. What differentiated Spooner was his distinction between the evil of slavery and the right of secession. Spooner chided those who felt that the war was fought over slavery. Rather, he maintained, the conflict began "for a purely pecuniary consideration . . . control of the markets in the South."

Though Spooner's legalistic attacks on the "peculiar institution" of slavery clearly differentiated him from the Garrisonian moralists, his uncompromising insurrectionary stance and support for the South during the Civil War placed him at the margins of the constitutionalist camp as well. He died on May 14, 1887.

Evan M. Daniel

See also: Brown, John; *Dred Scott* Case (1857); Liberty Party.

Further Reading

Barnett, Randy E. "Was Slavery Constitutional Before the Thirteenth Amendment? Lysander Spooner's Theory of Interpretation." *Pacific Law Review* 28 (Summer 1997): 977–1014.

Martin, James Joseph. *Men Against the State: The Expositors of Individualist Anarchism in America, 1827–1908.* De Kalb, IL: Adrian Allen, 1953.

Perry, Lewis. *Radical Abolitionism: Anarchy and the Government of God in Antislavery Thought.* Ithaca, NY: Cornell University Press, 1973; Knoxville: University of Tennessee Press, 1995.

Shively, Charles, ed. *The Collected Works of Lysander Spooner.* Weston, MA: M & S, 1971.

Smith, George H., ed. *The Lysander Spooner Reader.* San Francisco: Fox and Wilkes, 1992.

Sprading, Charles T. *Liberty and the Great Libertarians: An Anthology on Liberty, A Hand-Book of Freedom.* New York: Arno, 1972.

Wiecek, William M. *The Sources of Antislavery Constitutionalism in America, 1760–1848.* Ithaca, NY: Cornell University Press, 1977.

Stanton, Elizabeth Cady (1815–1902)

Women's rights pioneer Elizabeth Cady Stanton was also an active member of the antislavery movement, using her education and talents to promote racial equality and black suffrage. Although Stanton's legacy as a women's rights advocate has often overshadowed her contributions to abolition, her efforts on behalf of racial equality inspired other women to join the fight against slavery during the most controversial decade of the nineteenth century.

Stanton was born in Johnstown, New York, on November 12, 1815. The daughter of prominent Johnstown judge Daniel Cady, she completed her formal education at the Troy Female Seminary under the direction of the noted educator Emma Willard. Disturbed by her inability to pursue a college education because of her gender, Elizabeth studied independently and became a prolific writer and orator.

As a young woman, she became acquainted with the abolitionist movement through her first cousin, Gerrit Smith. Smith, a staunch social reformer and a supporter of the radical abolitionist John Brown, opened Stanton's eyes to the injustices of slavery. Smith also introduced Elizabeth to her husband, abolitionist Henry B. Stanton, at his home in Peterboro, New York. After their marriage in 1840, the couple honeymooned in London, where they attended the World Anti-Slavery Convention.

While in London, Stanton met women's rights leader Lucretia Mott; both women were denied the opportunity to participate fully in the Anti-Slavery Convention because of their gender. The controversy aroused by the convention inspired Stanton and Mott to plan the 1848 Seneca Falls Convention, a landmark conference devoted to promoting the equality of women.

Stanton's involvement in the abolitionist and women's rights movements was restricted during the early years of her marriage by the birth of her five sons and two daughters. Despite her inability to attend reform meetings, Stanton actively campaigned for the rights of women, and she often wrote speeches that fellow reformer Susan B. Anthony presented on her behalf. For the Seneca Falls Convention, Stanton penned the "Declaration of Sentiments," a document that closely resembled the Declaration of Independence. Stanton's declaration proclaimed the right of women to vote and listed women's grievances against male tyranny.

Although the Seneca Falls Convention focused solely on women's issues, the women's movement maintained a close connection with abolitionism during the nineteenth century. As the United States drew nearer to war in the second half of the century, many advocates of women's rights laid aside their gender platforms to campaign for emancipation.

In 1850, the second Fugitive Slave Law inspired heated controversy between abolitionists and proslavery advocates in the United States. Although Stanton was well acquainted with abolitionism through her husband's work, she did not participate fully in the movement until the 1850s, when she formally joined the American Anti-Slavery Society.

During the 1860 presidential election, many male abolitionists committed themselves to the Republican Party, hoping to influence Abraham Lincoln to pursue the emancipation of slaves in the American South. In the absence of male leaders, the American Anti-Slavery Society asked Stanton and Anthony to travel throughout central New York in 1861 to promote abolition. Their brief tour brought about little change, as crowds verbally assaulted them and interrupted their speeches. Stanton did not allow her audience's response to deter her, but instead she continued to speak and write on behalf of minority rights.

Although Stanton had vigorously defended the rights of women prior to the 1860s, the U.S. Civil War forced her to lay aside the promotion of women's rights in order to support the Union. In May 1863, Stanton and Anthony formed the Women's National Loyal League to promote the abolition of slavery. Joined by other suffragists, such as Angelina Grimké, the league petitioned the U.S. Congress for the total emancipation of slaves. Although the league enjoyed some success, it was later enveloped by the American Equal Rights Association.

At a speech delivered at the annual meeting of the American Anti-Slavery Society during the early 1860s, Stanton compared the treatment of slaves and women and noted that both groups existed in a subjugated condition. Although Stanton initially espoused the idea of black suffrage, the women's rights movement divided over the issue during Reconstruction when Congress added the Fourteenth and Fifteenth Amendments to the Constitution, granting suffrage and citizenship to former male slaves. Stanton and other female reformers believed that black male suffrage had taken precedence over women's struggle for the vote. Although William Lloyd Garrison and the American Anti-Slavery Society had allowed women to maintain an equal role within the abolitionist movement, they refused to sacrifice black male suffrage in order for women to receive the vote.

In response, Stanton and Anthony split from the organization and founded the National Woman Suffrage Association in 1869. Stanton served as president of the organization until it merged with Lucy Stone's American Woman Suffrage Association in 1890. The new association, the National American Woman Suffrage Association, also elected Stanton president, a position she maintained until 1892.

During her career as a social reformer, Stanton argued on behalf of women's education, abolition, temperance, and divorce rights for women. Labeled a radical for her criticism of the Old Testament and her publication of *The Woman's Bible*, she actively strove for equal rights until her death on October 26, 1902.

Melinda M. Hicks

See also: American Anti-Slavery Society; Anthony, Susan B.; Smith, Gerrit; Women's Rights and the Abolitionist Movement.

Further Reading

Banner, Lois W. *Elizabeth Cady Stanton: A Radical for Woman's Rights.* Boston: Little, Brown, 1980.
Griffith, Elisabeth. *In Her Own Right: The Life of Elizabeth Cady Stanton.* New York: Oxford University Press, 1984.
Sigerman, Harriet. *Elizabeth Cady Stanton: The Right Is Ours.* New York: Oxford University Press, 2001.
Stanton, Elizabeth Cady. *Eighty Years and More; Reminiscences, 1815–1897.* 1898. New York: Schocken, 1971.

Stevens, Thaddeus (1792–1868)

Among all of the abolitionists in the United States, Thaddeus Stevens may have been the most sincere advocate of equal rights for all people, regardless of race. During the Reconstruction era, he endeavored to pass federal legislation that would ensure equal rights for all citizens.

Stevens was born on April 4, 1792, in Danville, Vermont. He was the second of four sons born to Joshua and Sarah (Morrill) Stevens. Stevens was born with a clubfoot, and his father abandoned the young family when the boy was twelve, leaving the task of rearing the sons to Stevens's mother. Sarah Stevens was an intensely religious woman, but Thaddeus remained irreligious throughout his life.

Although Sarah Stevens lacked financial resources, she saw to it that Thaddeus received a first-rate education. After attending a grammar academy in Vermont, he enrolled at Dartmouth College, where he graduated in 1814. From Dartmouth, Stevens moved to York, Pennsylvania, where he began reading the law with attorney David Cassat.

After passing the bar examination in nearby Maryland, Stevens moved to Gettysburg, Pennsylvania, where he quickly established himself as a competent and successful attorney. Stevens used the money earned through his legal work to finance a variety of other business pursuits, including investments in the iron forging industry. After spending more than twenty years in Gettysburg, he would eventually relocate to the larger town of Lancaster, where he would reside for the rest of his life.

In the early 1830s, Stevens ran for the Pennsylvania state legislature. Although his political beliefs were akin to those of the Whig Party, Stevens entered politics on a wave of anti-Masonic sentiment. The Masons were widely disliked for their secrecy, elaborate rituals, and alleged elitism. Though Stevens showed an interest in antislavery principles during his tenure in the state legislature, it was his desire to cripple the Masons that motivated his political activities during the 1830s. When the wave of anti-Masonry subsided in the mid-1830s, so did Stevens's popularity, and he was defeated for re-election in 1836. Winning back his seat in 1838, he served two more terms in the legislature before retiring from politics. He then moved to Lancaster and began to focus on his law practice.

As a seven-term Congressman from Pennsylvania, Thaddeus Stevens led Radical Republicans during the Civil War and Reconstruction. He viewed the end of slavery as the legitimate purpose of the war and called for full civil rights for African Americans. *(Hulton Archive/Getty Images)*

It was during the 1840s that Stevens's devotion to the cause of abolition became more pronounced. One of the principal concerns of his legal career was defending fugitive slaves and preventing them from being forcibly returned to the South. In 1850, when the U.S. Congress passed the Fugitive Slave Law, Stevens handled a prominent case that involved the prosecution of two Quakers who were accused of failing to aid a slaveholder in recovering his slaves in Christiana, Maryland. The skilled attorney won an acquittal for his two clients.

Unlike many antislavery advocates, Stevens did not join the Free Soil Party. Although he would employ many of the same arguments used by such prominent Free Soilers as Joshua Giddings, Charles Sumner, and Salmon P. Chase, Stevens instead joined the Whig Party. Elected to Congress in 1848, he

devoted considerable energy to contesting the spread of slavery. During the crisis over the organization of the New Mexico Territory in 1850, Stevens spoke out repeatedly on the right of Congress to prohibit slavery in territories of the United States. A determined opponent of the Fugitive Slave Law, he excoriated proponents of the bill for requiring citizens to aid federal marshals in the pursuit of fugitive slaves.

Stevens also ridiculed slavery apologists who contended that the institution was a blessing for African Americans and that slaves were better off than free laborers in the North. "Let the slaves, who choose, go free; and the free, who choose, become slaves," Stevens told the U.S. House of Representatives. "If these gentlemen believe there is a word of truth in what they preach, the slaveholder need be under no apprehension that he will ever lack bondsmen."

When the Whig Party collapsed after the passage of the Kansas-Nebraska Act (1854), Stevens temporarily dabbled with the American (Know-Nothing) Party before joining the Republican Party. Elected to the House as a Republican in 1858, he would serve continuously until his death in 1868.

When Abraham Lincoln's election prompted the secession crisis, Stevens was one of the foremost Northern radicals to oppose compromise. After shots were fired at Fort Sumter, Stevens argued that the ending of slavery was a legitimate goal of the war. He abstained when the Crittenden-Johnson resolution was put to vote in the House after the first Battle of Manassas; the resolution explicitly stated that the war's purpose was not the abolition of slavery.

Throughout the U.S. Civil War, Stevens supported every major piece of legislation aimed at weakening slavery, including the First and Second Confiscation Acts in 1861 and 1862, the abolition of the Fugitive Slave Law in 1862, the abolition of slavery in the territories in 1862, and the Thirteenth Amendment in 1865. Often at odds with the president, Stevens was critical of Lincoln when he overruled generals, such as John C. Frémont and David Hunter, who challenged the "peculiar institution" by attempting to emancipate slaves. At the same time, Stevens was highly critical of the army's conservative West Point leadership. "I cannot approve of setting generals who sympathize with slavery at the head of our armies," he told the House.

Though Stevens supported Lincoln's Emancipation Proclamation and begrudgingly supported the sixteenth president for re-election in 1864, the two men differed markedly in their opinions on Reconstruction.

Stevens endorsed a "state suicide" theory that would allow the federal government to impose rigorous conditions for re-admittance to the Union. Such conditions would include the abolition of slavery, as well as full civil and political rights for African Americans, including suffrage. The untimely death of Abraham Lincoln put Stevens on a collision course with the new president, Andrew Johnson. The latter believed that states could be restored to the Union with minimal conditions—excluding black suffrage.

Stevens became one of the prominent leaders of Radical Reconstruction throughout the 1860s. He was one of the principal proponents of the impeachment of President Johnson when the latter resisted the wishes of the Republican Congress.

Shortly after Johnson's impeachment trial concluded, Stevens grew ill. Confined to his sickbed in his Washington apartment, he passed away on August 11, 1868. By his request, he was buried in Schreiner's Cemetery in Washington, D.C., because it did not practice segregation in burial.

Bruce Tap

See also: Confiscation Acts (1861, 1862); Fugitive Slave Act of 1850; Reconstruction.

Further Reading

Brodie, Fawn N. *Thaddeus Stevens, Scourge of the South.* New York: W.W. Norton, 1966.
Korngold, Ralph. *Thaddeus Stevens: A Being Darkly Wise and Rudely Great.* New York: Harcourt, Brace, 1955,
Palmer, Beverly Wilson, and Holly Byers Ochoa, eds. *The Selected Papers of Thaddeus Stevens.* 2 vols. Pittsburgh: University of Pittsburgh Press, 1997.
Trefousse, Hans L. *The Radical Republicans: Lincoln's Vanguard for Racial Justice.* New York: Alfred A. Knopf, 1969.
———. *Thaddeus Stevens: Nineteenth-Century Egalitarian.* Chapel Hill: University of North Carolina Press, 1997.

Steward, Austin (1793–1869)

The African American abolitionist Austin Steward devoted much of his career to assisting fugitive slaves who settled in the northern United States and Canada. In his writings and speeches, he called for the abolition of slavery and the expansion of civil rights for free blacks in the United States.

Austin Steward was born enslaved in Virginia in 1793 but moved to New York State with his owner in 1800. By 1816, he had successfully petitioned for his freedom and moved to Rochester, New York, where he would become a successful grocer and prominent figure in the Northern black abolitionist community.

Steward first came to the attention of the Northern black population on July 5, 1827, when he delivered the city of Rochester's Emancipation Day Address. On that day, Rochester blacks joined other African Americans in communities across New York in a celebration marking the July 4, 1827, emancipation of the state's remaining slaves. The themes on which Steward dwelled in his address crystallized the beliefs and strategies that were popular with the period's Northern African American leadership.

In addition to joining abolitionist organizations, Northern African Americans promoted the creation of schools, newspapers, and moral reform societies and fought to attain civil and political equality, which had been denied to the free black community. They did so in the hope that their success would not only improve the status of free blacks but also create living examples of free African American achievement and progress that would undermine the rhetoric of the increasingly popular proslavery theorists. In his Emancipation Day speech, Steward advised his newly freed brothers and sisters to improve themselves intellectually, morally, and economically and comport themselves as industrious and honest freedmen and women. At the same time, he urged them to remember the plight of those who were still enslaved and to work and pray on their behalf.

Steward would act on this broad interpretation of abolitionist activism throughout his career. His concern for the position of Northern blacks led him to attend the national convention of the Free Persons of Colour in Philadelphia in 1830 and to serve as the organization's vice president. Convened to discuss the plight of African American refugees who had taken refuge in Ontario, Canada, after being driven from Cincinnati, the meeting inspired Steward to work on their behalf. After the convention, Steward closed his Rochester business and moved to the Canadian settlement, at that time called the Wilberforce Colony. He served as the president of the colony's board of managers from 1830 to 1835, but eventually he returned to the United States after disputes with agents whom he suspected of mismanaging the colony's funds.

Despite his inability to create a model settlement at Wilberforce, Steward remained a respected figure in the Northern black community. After returning to New York, Steward settled in Canandaigua and remained active in abolitionist activities. He regularly invited antislavery speakers to visit and give public lectures, and he mentored young black abolitionists such as William Wells Brown.

In summer 1840, Steward served as president of the Convention of the Colored Inhabitants of the State of New York, and he continued to campaign for black enfranchisement throughout the next few decades. He published a narrative of his life, *Twenty-Two Years a Slave and Forty Years a Free Man* (1857), which went through three editions in three years.

Although scholars have long assumed that Steward died in 1860, recent scholarship has revealed that he lived on through much of the decade and continued to work on behalf of the abolitionist movement. Beginning in 1861, the first year of the U.S. Civil War, he traveled throughout the Northeast with his daughter Barbara giving antislavery lectures. As the war ended, Steward hoped to join his African American colleagues who moved to the South during Reconstruction. His age and health prevented him from doing so, however, and he died of typhoid fever on February 15, 1869, at the age of 76.

Erica L. Ball

See also: Brown, William Wells; Canada.

Further Reading

Bethel, Elizabeth Rauh. *The Roots of African-American Identity: Memory and History in Free Antebellum Communities.* New York: St. Martin's, 1997.

Horton, James Oliver, and Lois E. Horton. *In Hope of Liberty: Culture, Community, and Protest Among Northern Free Blacks, 1700–1860.* New York: Oxford University Press, 1997.

Quarles, Benjamin. *Black Abolitionists.* New York: Oxford University Press, 1969.

Rael, Patrick. *Black Identity and Black Protest in the Antebellum North.* Chapel Hill: University of North Carolina Press, 2002.

Steward, Austin. *Twenty-Two Years a Slave and Forty Years a Free-man.* 1857. Syracuse, NY: Syracuse University Press, 2002.

Still, William (1821–1902)

An African American abolitionist and community activist, William Still was an agent of the Underground Railroad who assisted hundreds of runaway slaves in their flight to freedom from his home in Philadelphia. To profile some of the fugitives he encountered, Still published *The Underground Railroad* in 1872.

Still was born on October 7, 1821, near Medford in Burlington County, New Jersey, the youngest of eighteen children of Levin and Sydney Still. Levin had purchased his freedom from slavery around 1800, but his wife, then known as Charity, and his children remained enslaved. After Charity and two of her children escaped, the couple changed their last name from Steel to Still and settled in New Jersey.

William worked on his father's farm throughout childhood, teaching himself to read and write as time would allow. In 1844, he moved to Philadelphia, then home to a large free black and fugitive slave community. Working as a day laborer and then as a house servant, Still eventually found employment as a clerk with the Pennsylvania Society for the Abolition of Slavery in Philadelphia in 1847.

For many years, Philadelphia had been the destination or way station for thousands of runaway slaves seeking freedom. In 1850, with the passage of the Fugitive Slave Law, safety and permanent freedom became far less certain, and regional antislavery efforts expanded dramatically to help fugitives make their way farther north to Canada, where freedom was more secure. Still's position with the Pennsylvania Abolition Society led him to become personally involved in aiding and hiding runaway slaves in his own home. In 1852, Still became secretary of the Philadelphia Vigilant Committee, a group of black and white antislavery activists associated with the society who committed their resources—and in some cases their livelihoods and even their lives—to helping runaway slaves with food, shelter, and transportation to safe havens farther north.

Compelled by his own family's tragic story of liberation and loss, Still was determined to keep records of the names and details of each fugitive who passed through the society's office so that relatives could trace their family members in the future. The keeping of such records was highly dangerous, and, on at least one occasion, Still's records had to be secreted in a local cemetery for protection.

It was Still's own fateful reunion with his brother Peter—after more than forty years of separation—that led him to devote his efforts to this meticulous record keeping. Once free from his life of slavery in the Deep South, Peter set out to find the family he had been separated from as a child. He arrived in Philadelphia in 1851 and was directed to Still's office, where he was assured he would find help. When Still heard Peter's story, he realized this man was the long-lost brother his family had been missing. Through William's help and the efforts of Philadelphia's abolitionist circles, money was raised to purchase Peter's wife and children and bring them north.

Throughout the 1850s, Still and a well-coordinated network of black and white supporters helped thousands of runaway slaves find their way to freedom. Still's vast network spanned great distances, from local safe houses in Philadelphia and neighboring cities and towns to New Jersey, New York, Connecticut, Massachusetts, New Hampshire, and Canada. These runaways came mostly from Maryland, Delaware, Virginia, and North Carolina, though a few from Georgia and South Carolina also found their way to Still's office.

Perhaps his most famous associate was Harriet Tubman, who conducted many of her rescue missions through his office. Still's relationship with Thomas Garrett, the famous Quaker of Wilmington, Delaware, who is credited with aiding more than 2,700 slaves to freedom over a forty-year period, also proved to be one of his most important colleagues. Correspondence between the two men reveals a constant flow of fugitives from Garrett to Still throughout the 1850s.

An astute businessman, Still began acquiring property during the 1850s. When he stepped down from his position with the Philadelphia Vigilant Committee in 1861, he opened a stove business. During the U.S. Civil War, he actively recruited African American men for Union regiments at Camp William Penn outside Philadelphia. He expanded his coal business after the war and remained an active political and community activist, fighting for African Americans' right to vote and promoting business ownership in the black community.

After years of working on behalf of blacks, Still published *The Underground Railroad*, a compendium of stories, names, places, and events recorded during his days as secretary of the Philadelphia Vigilant Committee. In addition to the narratives of the fugitive slaves, Still included newspaper articles, runaway advertisements, correspondence, and character sketches of abolitionists and Underground Railroad agents with whom he had worked closely.

Still continued to fight discrimination and injustice throughout the remainder of his life. He also helped found several educational, social, and health care institutions for African Americans in the Philadelphia area. In 1896, Still returned to the Pennsylvania Abolition Society as its vice president. He died on July 14, 1902, from complications of kidney disease.

Kate Clifford Larson

See also: Fugitive Slaves; Garrett, Thomas; Tubman, Harriet; Underground Railroad.

A free black from Philadelphia, William Still helped countless runaway slaves as a conductor on the Underground Railroad. His 1872 book on the subject remains one of the most authoritative and compelling accounts of that system and the people it saved. *(Hulton Archive/Getty Images)*

Further Reading

Blockson, Charles L. *The Underground Railroad: First-Person Narratives of Escapes to Freedom in the North.* New York: Prentice Hall, 1987.

Kashatus, William C. *Just Over the Line: Chester County and the Underground Railroad.* West Chester, PA: Chester County Historical Society, 2002.

McGowan, James A. *Station Master on the Underground Railroad: The Life and Letters of Thomas Garrett.* Moylan, PA: Whimsie, 1977; rev. ed., Jefferson, NC: McFarland, 2005.

Pickard, Kate E.R. *The Kidnapped and the Ransomed: The Narrative of Peter and Vera Still After Forty Years of Slavery.* 1856. Lincoln: University of Nebraska Press, 1995.

Quarles, Benjamin. *Black Abolitionists.* New York: Oxford University Press, 1969.

Ripley, C. Peter, et al., eds. *The Black Abolitionist Papers.* 5 vols. Chapel Hill: University of North Carolina Press, 1985–1992.

for the Pittsburgh *Spirit of Liberty*, a newspaper that was associated with the abolitionist Liberty Party.

Her marriage was contentious, and she and her husband frequently quarreled over finances. After providing care for Jane's dying mother, James Swisshelm attempted to sue the Cannon estate for compensation for his wife's services. He also sought to collect his wife's share from the sale of her mother's property. In response, Jane Swisshelm successfully lobbied the Pennsylvania legislature in 1847 to recognize a married woman's right to property.

Using money from her mother's estate, she established the *Pittsburgh Saturday Visiter*, a six-column abolitionist paper, in late 1847. Under the motto, "Speak unto the children of Israel that they go forward," the *Visiter* provided Swisshelm with a means of expressing her fervent support of abolitionism, temperance, and women's suffrage. Writing "most passionately, but with rare ability, for the freedom of the negro slave and of the white wife," Swisshelm attacked slavery on a number of fronts, arguing that the institution harmed the economic health of the nation and that it bred a class of subservient people. The newspaper gained 6,000 subscribers nationwide and brought Swisshelm national attention as a leading voice against slavery. In 1848, the *Visiter* endorsed Martin Van Buren for the presidency, praising the Free Soil Party's opposition to the expansion of slavery.

In 1850, Horace Greeley hired Swisshelm to write for the *New York Tribune* as a news correspondent in Washington, D.C. There, she wrote articles attacking the private life of Daniel Webster, which may have contributed to his failure to receive the Whig nomination for president in 1852.

Swisshelm sold the *Visiter* in 1857 and abandoned her husband the same year. With only her infant daughter accompanying her, she traveled to Saint Cloud, Minnesota, to live with her sister Elizabeth and her husband. The following year, she established the *St. Cloud Visiter* with the financial backing of Sylvanus B. Lowry, a slave owner and former Tennessean who served as the Democratic boss in Minnesota.

When Lowry insisted that the *Visiter* endorse James Buchanan for the presidency, Swisshelm did so, but with such sarcasm and irony that it soon became clear that she was actually publishing an abolitionist newspaper. In response, Lowry withdrew his support of the paper, and his attorney, James C. Shepley, held a public lecture in which he presented a veiled attack on Swisshelm's femininity. In the following issue of the *Visiter*, Swisshelm replied with an attack on Shepley's wife. Lowry's supporters destroyed Swisshelm's press and threatened her life.

As a result of public outrage over the destruction of the press, a public meeting was held, at which Swisshelm was given the opportunity to give her account of her conflict with Lowry. Under repeated death threats, she completed a will before traveling to the meeting and sought the companionship of Miles Brown, a noted marksman whom she instructed to shoot her in the head if she were taken alive by an angry mob. To her surprise, Swisshelm found a warm audience at the event, and she received funds to purchase a new press.

Shepley then filed a $10,000 suit against the *Visiter*, demanding that Swisshelm publish a retraction of her attack on his wife. She agreed to this stipulation, but within a week, she had republished the offending article in a new publication, the *St. Cloud Democrat*. The controversy generated national interest and served to portray proponents of slavery as violent opponents to freedom of the press. Swisshelm later traveled across Minnesota, recounting her experiences and promoting the Republican Party.

During the U.S. Civil War, Swisshelm moved back to Washington. There, she became one of the first female clerks to work in the quartermaster general's office of the War Department, and she nursed Union soldiers in the field hospitals surrounding the city. In 1866, she established the radical newspaper *The Reconstructionist*. In this publication, her attacks on President Andrew Johnson were so fierce that he dismissed her from government service.

Swisshelm continued to write and speak in favor of women's suffrage, but her intense individualism and continued devotion to biblical teaching on the role of women put her at odds with other prominent suffragists. She spent her last days in Wilkinsburg, Pennsylvania, where she completed her autobiography. She died on July 22, 1884.

J. Brent Etzel

See also: Greeley, Horace; Reconstruction; Women's Rights and the Abolitionist Movement.

Further Reading

Endres, Kathleen. "Jane Grey Swisshelm: 19th Century Journalist and Feminist." *Journalism History* 2 (Winter 1975–1976): 126–32.

Hoffert, Sylvia D. *Jane Grey Swisshelm: An Unconventional Life, 1815–1884*. Chapel Hill: University of North Carolina Press, 2004.

———. "Jane Grey Swisshelm, Elizabeth Keckley, and the Significance of Race Consciousness in American Women's History." *Journal of Women's History* 13 (Autumn 2001): 8–33.

Pierson, Michael D. "Between Antislavery and Abolition: The Politics and Rhetoric of Jane Grey Swisshelm." *Pennsylvania History* 60 (July 1993): 305–19.

Swisshelm, Jane Grey Cannon. *Crusader and Feminist: Letters of Jane Grey Swisshelm, 1858–1865.* Ed. Arthur J. Larsen. St. Paul: Minnesota Historical Society, 1934.

———. *Half a Century.* 2nd ed. New York: Source Book, 1970.

Walker, Peter F. *Moral Choices: Memory, Desire, and Imagination in Nineteenth-Century American Abolition.* Baton Rouge: Louisiana State University Press, 1978.

Tacky's Rebellion (1760–1761)

Claude Stuart Park in Port Maria, Jamaica, features a monument to Tacky, an enslaved Coromantee chief from southern Ghana on the West African coast who led the most serious and bloody slave rebellion in the history of that island nation. Whereas most slave rebellions were short-lived and local, Tacky's Rebellion lasted for six months and spread across all of Jamaica.

Jamaica had a long history of black resistance to slavery. The maroons resisted so effectively that the British had been forced to sign treaties in 1739 guaranteeing the Windward and Leeward maroons land and autonomy. Throughout the eighteenth century, slave uprisings occurred nearly every five years, inspired, in part, by the maroons' example of freedom and sustained by the heavy influx of newly enslaved Africans from the most warlike societies of the continent's West Coast. Of the 3,000 to 4,000 slaves who arrived in Jamaica each year, most were Coromantee.

The rebellion began in 1760 when a band of approximately 150 Coromantee slaves attacked the fort of Port Maria, triggering other revolts across Jamaica. The rebels' ultimate goal was to expel all whites from Jamaica and create an independent state. By the end of the uprising in 1761, more than 400 enslaved blacks had been killed, 600 slaves had been transported to British Honduras (now Belize), and some sixty whites and sixty free blacks had died. Abolitionists in Great Britain used Tacky's Rebellion to underscore the cruelty and high cost of Caribbean slavery.

Tacky began his revolt on April 7, Easter Sunday, taking advantage of the relaxed vigilance of the holiday. His position as overseer on the Frontier Estate gave him an opportunity to recruit followers. The original plan called for simultaneous uprisings in six parishes.

Cultural ties proved as important as logistics in determining the success of the movement, as the Coromantee were Akan-speaking and Ga-speaking slaves from the Gold Coast of West Africa who rebelled with unparalleled frequency in eighteenth-century Jamaica. African shaman-type leaders called *Obeahmen* helped lead the rebellion; they sprinkled white powder on the rebels and declared them immune to injury, thus bolstering their confidence. In addition, women played a prominent role as both insurgents and leaders, particularly an enslaved woman named Cubah, a plotter of the rebellion.

Tacky and his followers first seized control of the Frontier and Trinity estates. They killed many of the whites but spared the overseer of the Trinity plantation, Abraham Fletcher. Next, they seized the armory at Fort Haldane, where weapons for the defense of Port Maria were stored, killed the guard on duty, and appropriated four barrels of gunpowder and forty muskets with shot. By dawn on Monday, the rebels had overrun the plantations at Heywood Hall and Esher, and hundreds of men and women had joined Tacky.

After their initial triumph, however, the rebels' situation deteriorated quickly. A slave who had been liberated from Esher alerted the authorities to the pending danger. The lieutenant governor, Sir Henry Moore, mustered two companies of regular soldiers and two troops of mounted militia to put down the rebellion. They were joined by a number of the Scott's Hall and Leeward maroons, fugitive slaves who were living independently in the interior of Jamaica; under the terms of a peace treaty with the British government signed in 1739, the maroons were obligated to serve as slave catchers.

Early in the revolt, an Obeahman was caught and killed, and his body was displayed in public, demoralizing some rebels who had counted on the invulnerability of Obeah. Many rebels surrendered, but Tacky and twenty-five of his followers continued to fight.

Tacky was killed by a renowned maroon marksman named Davy, and his head was displayed on a pole in Spanish Town until a sympathizer spirited it away for proper burial. Two of the key coconspirators, Kingston and Fortune, were hanged in the square until they starved. Some twenty-five survivors of the original band retreated to a cave near Tacky Falls, where they committed suicide rather than return to slavery. Although the leaders of the revolt were dead, the rebellion spread to other parishes, where new bands of rebels inflicted damage and injury for months to come. The British finally suppressed the revolt in October 1761.

To the extent that the enslaved people of Jamaica wrought emancipation by making slavery untenable, Tacky's Rebellion contributed significantly. The Baptist War of 1831 finally pushed the British to abolish slavery on August 1, 1834.

Teresa M. Van Hoy

See also: Jamaica, Emancipation in; Jamaica Rebellion (1831–1832); Maroons.

Further Reading

Craton, Michael. *Testing the Chains: Resistance to Slavery in the British West Indies.* Ithaca, NY: Cornell University Press, 1982.

Curtin, Philip D. *The Atlantic Slave Trade: A Census.* Madison: University of Wisconsin Press, 1969.

Schuler, Monica. "Ethnic Slave Rebellions in the Caribbean and the Guianas." *Journal of Social History* 3 (Summer 1970): 374–85.

Tailors' Revolt (1798)

The Tailors' Revolt (*Conjuração dos Alfaiates*) of 1798 was a failed attempt to establish the state of Bahia as an independent nation, separate from Brazil.

In the eighteenth century, Brazil experienced multiple revolts in the cities of Minas Gerais, Pernambuco, and Salvador. During this period, Afro-Brazilian culture was centered in the state of Bahia, in the northeastern section of Brazil. Because a large number of slaves congregated there, the potential for rioting and rebellion was high. In addition, the Brazilian aristocracy was fearful of the legacy of the Haitian Revolution (1791–1804), in which slaves and mulattoes spearheaded a successful bloody revolt against the ruling class.

The so-called Conspiracy of the Tailors was so named for the large number of tailors who were arrested for participating in the revolt. Most of the people who took part in the insurgency movement were skilled workers such as soldiers, artisans, carpenters, and tailors. In comparison with previous revolts in Brazil, such as the Minas Gerais Conspiracy (*Inconfidência Mineira*) of 1756, most of the rebels were not slaves but free mulattoes who lived in extreme poverty. They resented the Portuguese for their domination of the country, as well as the apparent wealth that had been accumulated by a handful of free Brazilians.

The Tailors' Revolt was inspired by the events and ideology of the French Revolution, especially the ideals of equality and independence. As a result, its demands were different from those of previous rebellions. The leaders presented specific requests: full independence, the creation of a republic, racial equality, and the complete abolition of slavery. The general goal was to build an egalitarian and democratic society in which the color of a person's skin would not restrict his or her potential for social and economic advancement.

As the mulatto soldier Lucas Dantas do Amorim Tôrres explained to the judges who tried him for his role in the rebellion, "We want a republic in order to breathe freely because we live subjugated and because we're colored and we can't advance, and if there was a republic there would be equality for everyone." This ideology represented a tangible threat to the Brazilian political system and its existing social hierarchy.

The Brazilian government had crushed other revolts in the sugar state of Bahia. But what allowed the government to take control of the Tailors' Revolt was the existence of a traitor within the leadership ranks of the rebels and disagreement among the participants about how best to achieve their goals. The government responded quickly and squashed the insurgency through the use of force.

In less than two weeks, the governor of Bahia captured more than forty people who were directly tied to the conspiracy. Most of the detainees were free mulatto artisans, a few were soldiers, and more than a dozen were slaves. The three main leaders were arrested and hanged in a public display that was intended to intimidate the masses. The governor reported to Portugal that the riot was completely under control and that the organized revolt had been limited to the lower classes of society.

The revolt failed to achieve its objectives, and the slaves saw no tangible improvement in their social condition or way of life. Instead, the result was a conservative backlash in Brazil; the government responded with curfews and other civil restrictions intended to limit the possibility of further disruption to the slavery system. The elites feared complete abolition, because it represented a challenge to their social order, which provided them with privileges and economic prosperity.

The slaves nevertheless continued to actively participate in protests, riots, and rebellions, accelerating the process of abolition in Brazil. The end of slavery finally came on May 13, 1888, when Princess Regent Isabel signed the *Lei Áurea* (Golden Law).

Brazil was the last nation in the Western Hemisphere to grant the complete emancipation of slaves.

Javier A. Galván

See also: Brazil, Abolition in; Brazil, Emancipation in; Haitian Revolution (1791–1804).

Further Reading

Schwartz, Stuart B. *Sugar Plantations in the Formation of Brazilian Society: Bahia, 1550–1835.* Cambridge, UK: Cambridge University Press, 1985.

Tallmadge, James, Jr. (1778–1853)

New York congressman James Tallmadge, Jr., instigated a national debate over the expansion of slavery in 1819 when he sought to prohibit Missouri from entering the Union as a slave state. After nearly two years of debate, the U.S. Congress eventually adopted the Missouri Compromise of 1820 to resolve the issue.

Tallmadge was born on January 28, 1778, in Stanfordville, New York. After graduating from Brown University in 1798, he became secretary to Governor DeWitt Clinton of New York. He left this position to practice law in Poughkeepsie and New York City.

During the War of 1812, Tallmadge commanded a company of New York militia, enjoying considerable success and rising to the rank of general. He then parlayed his military success into political advancement, winning election to the 15th Congress as a National Republican. Tallmadge entered the House of Representatives on June 6, 1817, as the representative for the district that included his hometown of Poughkeepsie.

The greatest contributions that Tallmadge made during his one term in Congress were his efforts to restrict the westward expansion of slavery. The first battle came when the Illinois Territory sent its proposed constitution to Congress for consideration in 1818. Illinois had been carved from the Northwest Territory and thus had to adhere to the strictures of the Northwest Ordinance of 1787, in particular the sixth article, which forbade slavery. Tallmadge became concerned when he read some of the provisions of the state's proposed constitution, which permitted the hiring of slaves from nonresident slaveholders for one-year terms until 1825. Slaves hired before the approval of the constitution were not mentioned in the document. Tallmadge urged Congress to reject the constitution and to use its powers to keep slavery out of Illinois. Despite his plea, the House voted overwhelmingly in favor of the proposed Illinois constitution.

In February 1819, Tallmadge offered an amendment to the Missouri statehood bill that called for a ban on the further introduction of slavery or involuntary servitude and granted freedom to the children of slaves already living in Missouri once they reached the age of twenty-five. He used the same arguments he had made during the battle over the Illinois constitution, as well as some new ones. Tallmadge criticized Southern slaveholders for their treatment of slaves, such as forbidding them to learn to read. He believed that the enmity between slaves and their masters created a weakness that enemies of the United States could use if the republic were invaded, as it had been during the War of 1812.

In addition, Tallmadge objected to the westward expansion of the three-fifths clause of the U.S. Constitution, which counted five slaves as the equivalent of three white men for the purposes of taxation and representation. Should Missouri enter the Union as a slave state, the South would gain political power the founding fathers had never dreamed of, nor sought.

Tallmadge's Missouri amendment sparked two days of spirited debate in the House of Representatives, which voted in favor of it. The Senate rejected it, however, and the bill died when the two houses failed to reach an agreement before the end of the congressional session. Even though it failed to pass, the amendment set off a political firestorm that raged for two years.

Tallmadge left the House in 1819, served as a delegate to the New York State Constitutional Convention in 1821, and finished his political career serving as lieutenant governor of New York. He died on September 29, 1853.

James C. Foley

See also: Missouri Compromise (1820); U.S. Constitution (1789).

Further Reading

Moore, Glover. *The Missouri Controversy, 1819–1821.* Lexington: University Press of Kentucky, 1953.

Tappan, Arthur (1786–1865)

One of America's foremost abolitionists and a successful businessman, Arthur Tappan used his wealth to champion many social causes, including the antislavery movement. He served as an officer of many reform

Promoting the doctrine of immediate abolition, New York businessman Arthur Tappan cofounded the American Anti-Slavery Society with William Lloyd Garrison in 1833 and served as its first president. *(Library of Congress)*

organizations, working on behalf of temperance, eliminating prostitution, fostering education, and founding churches and schools. Working with his brothers Lewis and Benjamin, he dedicated his life to the betterment of humankind.

Tappan was born on May 22, 1786, in Northampton, Massachusetts, into a strict Calvinist household. He began his business career in Boston at the age of fifteen as an apprentice clerk in a wholesale exporting store; by age twenty-one, he had established a dry goods business. In 1826, he started the silk-importing firm Arthur Tappan and Company in New York City, with Lewis as his business partner. He imported silk that he sold to rural shopkeepers for cash at a low fixed price, an unusual business practice for the time, and wealth followed.

As soon as he became successful, Tappan seriously began to consider his "obligations as a steward for the Lord." He gave both his time and money to humanitarian and religious causes, including the

American Sunday School Union, the American Tract Society, and the American Education Society. In 1827, he founded the short-lived daily paper the *New York Journal of Commerce* as a means of delivering both the news and a moral message to New York's business community.

Moved by a concern for the well-being of African Americans, Tappan became a member of the American Colonization Society, but he soon left to pursue a more radical approach to abolition. Dedicated to the elimination of slavery at all costs, Tappan embraced William Lloyd Garrison's radical doctrine of immediate abolition and financially supported Garrison's abolitionist paper, *The Liberator.*

In 1833, Tappan helped organize the New York Anti-Slavery Society and the American Anti-Slavery Society, which called for an immediate end to slavery and advocated equal rights for African Americans. He served as the latter organization's president from its founding until 1840, when he resigned from the society, because it had become too radical and its focus had drifted to other causes, such as women's rights. After withdrawing his support from the American Anti-Slavery Society, Tappan helped form the American and Foreign Anti-Slavery Society, a conservative organization that was dedicated to moral suasion and political action as a means of ending slavery.

Through his association with these two key abolitionist groups, Tappan gave financial aid to several black abolitionist weeklies, such as the *Genius of Universal Emancipation* and *The Emancipator.* In 1847, he founded the *National Era* under the auspices of the American and Foreign Anti-Slavery Society.

Convinced that slavery could be terminated through political action, he supported the establishment of the Liberty Party in 1840 and its presidential candidate, James G. Birney. In 1846, concerned that the leading missionary organizations were not advocating abolition, Tappan helped found the American Missionary Association, which promoted political activity and encouraged a strong Christian antislavery sentiment in its mission work. After the passage of the second Fugitive Slave Law in 1850, which demanded that fugitive slaves be returned to their owners and imposed heavy fines on citizens who aided fugitives, Tappan helped fund the Underground Railroad, an informal network of abolitionists and safe houses that assisted escaped slaves from the South flee to freedom in the North.

Tappan was also dedicated to furthering education. Early in his career, he paid the tuition for many divinity students at Yale College. He also contributed financially to the founding of Kenyon College in Gambier, Ohio; the Auburn Theological Seminary in Cincinnati, Ohio; and the Lane Theological Seminary in Cincinnati. In 1835, after several Lane students withdrew from the seminary because of the school's restrictions on the discussion of slavery, Tappan established Oberlin College and helped arrange for African American students, including the so-called Lane Rebels, to be admitted.

Although Tappan retired from his business endeavors in the mid-1850s, he continued his philanthropic efforts. He retired to New Haven, Connecticut, where he died on July 23, 1865.

Charles A. D'Aniello and Gina Misiroglu

See also: American and Foreign Anti-Slavery Society; American Anti-Slavery Society; American Colonization Society; American Missionary Association; Garrison, William Lloyd; Immediatism; Liberty Party; Tappan, Benjamin; Tappan, Lewis; Underground Railroad.

Further Reading

Friedman, Lawrence J. *Gregarious Saints: Self and Community in American Abolitionism, 1830–1870.* New York: Cambridge University Press, 1982.

Havas, John M. "Commerce and Calvinism: The *Journal of Commerce, 1827–65.*" *Journalism Quarterly* 38 (Winter 1961): 84–86.

Southall, Eugene Portlette. "Arthur Tappan and the Anti-Slavery Movement." *Journal of Negro History* 15 (April 1930): 162–97.

Tappan, Lewis. *The Life of Arthur Tappan.* 1870. Westport, CT: Negro Universities Press, 1970.

Wyatt-Brown, Bertram. *Lewis Tappan and the Evangelical War Against Slavery.* Cleveland, OH: Press of Case Western Reserve University, 1969.

Tappan, Benjamin (1773–1857)

A senator from Ohio, Benjamin Tappan joined his abolitionist brothers Arthur and Lewis Tappan as a leader in the fight against slavery. A supporter of a wide range of educational activities, Benjamin was the first president of the Historical and Philosophical Society of Ohio. His 1844 Smithsonian Institution bill became a basis for the Smithsonian's development, and he oversaw the publication of the reports of explorer Charles Wilkes's expedition, which surveyed the Pacific Ocean between 1838 and 1842.

Tappan was born in Northampton, Massachusetts, on May 25, 1773, the oldest son of Benjamin and Sarah Tappan, both devout Calvinists. He prepared to enter Harvard College but instead chose to pursue a wide-ranging self-education that included studying law under the tutelage of Gideon Granger. Tappan was admitted to the Connecticut bar in 1799. He first pursued a career in law in a small firm in Steubenville, Ohio, and then entered politics.

Having embraced the ideals of the Enlightenment and Jeffersonian democracy, Tappan began his political career as a Jacksonian Democrat, later becoming a Free Soiler and then a Republican. He was floor leader in the Ohio state senate from 1803 to 1805, was appointed president judge of Ohio's Fifth Circuit Court of Common Pleas in 1816, and was appointed Ohio's canal commissioner from 1822 to 1836. An ardent supporter of Andrew Jackson—who appointed him to a federal judgeship in 1833—Tappan was a pivotal figure in Ohio's Democratic Party. He was elected to the U.S. Senate in 1838, serving just one term.

While sitting as the chief magistrate of Ohio in 1818, Tappan proclaimed from the bench, "I will never sanction any doctrine which directly or indirectly contravenes that principle on which our Government rests, that all men are created free and equal," a statement he held to throughout his political career.

As a senator, Tappan affirmed that it was not moral suasion that would end slavery but the skillful use of political power that came from the people. Benjamin told his brother Lewis, "I am as much in favor of giving freedom to slaves as you are, but I will not sacrifice the union of the states and the only hope of maintaining free government among whites to accomplish that object." Benjamin refused to present antislavery petitions on the Senate floor, maintaining that Ohioans, as constituents of a free state, should not interfere with local institutions in other parts of the country.

In 1844, Secretary of State John C. Calhoun's letter to the British minister in Washington, which extolled the benefits of slavery with regard to the proposed treaty for the annexation of Texas, infuriated Tappan. Working with Lewis, Benjamin worked to see the document published in the *New York Evening Post* in April of that year. Despite the effort, westward expansion enthusiast James K. Polk was given the Democratic nomination; he ran on a ticket supporting annexation, and the breakup of the Democratic Party began. Although Tappan supported the annexation of Texas in 1845, he did not endorse slavery.

When Tappan's Senate term ended in 1845, he returned to Steubenville to practice law. He helped organize Ohio's Free Soil Party, a breakaway faction of the Democratic Party that opposed the expansion of slavery into the territories.

Though they were increasingly in agreement on slavery, the Tappan brothers continued to disagree on politics and religion. Seven months before his death on April 20, 1857, Benjamin wrote to Lewis, urging him to support the Republican Party's stand against the spread of slavery and arguing that it was the first step toward slavery's extinction.

Charles A. D'Aniello and Gina Misiroglu

See also: Free Soil Party; Tappan, Arthur; Tappan, Lewis.

Further Reading

Feller, Daniel. "Benjamin Tappan: The Making of a Democrat." In *The Pursuit of Public Power: Political Culture in Ohio 1787–1861,* ed. Jeffrey P. Brown and Andrew R.L. Cayton. Kent, OH: Kent State University Press, 1994.

———. "A Brother in Arms: Benjamin Tappan and the Antislavery Democracy." *Journal of American History* 88 (June 2001): 48–74.

Ratcliffe, Donald J. "The Autobiography of Benjamin Tappan." *Ohio Historical Quarterly* 85 (Spring 1976): 109–57.

Tappan, Lewis (1788–1873)

Lewis Tappan was a wealthy New York businessman, entrepreneur, and antislavery supporter who worked with his brothers Arthur and Benjamin Tappan to further abolitionist and humanitarian causes.

Tappan was born in Northampton, Massachusetts, on May 23, 1788, into a devout Calvinist household. He was educated locally before embarking on what would become a successful business career, one that was closely intertwined with that of his older brother Arthur. The two entered into a partnership in 1826 in the silk business, with Lewis acting as credit manager. After the panic of 1837, the younger Tappan established the Mercantile Agency, the first commercial credit-rating agency in the United States; it would eventually become Dun & Bradstreet, the world's largest global commercial business information database.

Tappan's business acumen allowed him to support humanitarian causes, such as the American Colonization Society, and the Tappan brothers were among the founders of the New York Anti-Slavery Society and American Anti-Slavery Society, established in Philadelphia in 1833. Lewis served on the American Anti-Slavery Society's executive committee, where his significant business and organizational skills were vital to the society's operations, and he led

the group's fund-raising efforts. The publication of the group's newspaper, *The Emancipator*, was made possible in large part because of the Tappans' financial support.

Before long, the Tappan brothers fell victim to anti-abolitionist violence. Both ignored the death threats and negative press, but, in July 1834, Lewis's house was vandalized by a mob and Arthur's business was nearly ransacked. The attacks served to bring national attention to the abolitionist cause.

In 1835, the brothers gave financial support for the founding of Oberlin College in Ohio, whose purpose was to spread radical ideas through education. Lewis fueled the flames even further that year, when he initiated a nationwide mailing of abolitionist materials, mainly to leading clergymen. Huge crowds—led primarily by Democratic politicians—gathered in Northern cities, denouncing the Tappans and what was perceived as their threat to national unity over the issue of slavery. In the South, the mailings predictably led to the burning of antislavery literature by angry mobs. Undaunted, Tappan continued as an active

Lewis Tappan

Lewis Tappan, the younger brother of abolitionists Arthur and Benjamin Tappan, established the nation's first commercial credit-rating agency (later Dun & Bradstreet). His antislavery activities included support for the *Amistad* mutineers. *(Hulton Archive/Getty Images)*

speaker and pamphleteer for the antislavery cause, as well as a constant contributor to *The Emancipator* and other publications of the abolitionist movement.

If the Tappans wanted to bring more national attention to the antislavery movement, they could not have planned a better strategy. Northern sympathies naturally sided with the abolitionists, and from 1836 to 1838, Lewis helped organize antislavery petitions drives, calling on an army of volunteers to gather support and bringing the antislavery cause before the federal government. The congressional Gag Rule—established to prohibit discussion of antislavery measures on the House floor—doomed the effort, however, and coincided with a decline in the Tappans' influence.

By 1840, the Tappans were no longer a formidable force in the American Anti-Slavery Society. When the society began to advocate women's rights and elected feminist Abby Kelley to the executive committee, the Tappans left and formed a rival organization, the American and Foreign Anti-Slavery Society, for which Lewis served as the first treasurer.

During this time, Tappan's energies were devoted to the Amistad Committee, formed to gain the freedom of African captives aboard the slave ship *Amistad* who had mutinied before being recaptured and taken prisoner in a Connecticut jail. Tappan and his colleagues on the committee convinced former president John Quincy Adams to argue on behalf of the *Amistad* mutineers before the U.S. Supreme Court. In 1841, the Court ruled to free the captives and return them to Africa.

Tappan continued his antislavery campaign throughout the 1840s. He helped to found the American Missionary Association in 1846, which was responsible for the establishment of institutions that educated freedmen, including Berea College in Berea, Kentucky; Fisk University in Nashville, Tennessee; and Howard University in Washington, D.C.

Tappan published the pamphlet *Address to the Non-Slaveholders of the South, on the Social and Political Evils of Slavery* (1843), challenging Southerners who were not slaveholders to help end slavery. He pushed for the establishment of Texas as a slaveless republic under British protection—yet another unpopular cause, especially in the South. Yet through all of his earnest efforts to bring about the total demise of slavery, Tappan and the other abolitionists never grasped the regional intensity of those who did not own slaves but were nevertheless ardent supporters of slavery and slave owners.

In 1870, Tappan published his brother's biography, *The Life of Arthur Tappan*, suffering a stroke as the book went to press. He never fully recovered, and he died in Brooklyn, New York, on June 21, 1873.

Boyd Childress and Gina Misiroglu

See also: American and Foreign Anti-Slavery Society; American Anti-Slavery Society; American Colonization Society; American Missionary Association; *Amistad* Case (1841); Foster, Abigail Kelley; Gag Resolution; Tappan, Arthur; Tappan, Benjamin.

Further Reading

DeBoer, Clara Merritt. *Be Jubilant My Feet: African American Abolitionists in the American Missionary Association, 1839–1861.* New York: Garland, 1994.
Mayer, Henry. *All on Fire: William Lloyd Garrison and the Abolition of Slavery.* New York: St. Martin's, 1998.
Wyatt-Brown, Bertram. *Lewis Tappan and the Evangelical War Against Slavery.* Cleveland, OH: Press of Case Western Reserve University, 1969.

Taylor, John W. (1784–1854)

New York congressman John W. Taylor was one of the first political figures to argue that the U.S. Constitution provided the Congress with the power to keep slavery out of both the territories and future states. Although his arguments did not sway opinion during the debate over the Missouri Compromise of 1820, his views would be reconsidered during the 1840s and 1850s.

John W. Taylor was born on March 26, 1784, in Charlton, New York. He graduated from Union College, then studied law and opened a practice in Ballston Spa, New York, in 1807. He served in the state assembly in 1812–1813 and quickly gained election to the U.S. House of Representatives as a Republican. His constituents elected him to ten consecutive terms between 1813 and 1833. Twice during his career, he served as Speaker of the House.

It was the issue of slavery and its westward expansion that gained Taylor renown, as he joined James Tallmadge, Jr., and Rufus King in voicing opposition to the expansion of slavery into the proposed state of Missouri in 1819–1821. Taylor also led an unsuccessful effort in 1819 to bar slavery from the newly created Arkansas Territory.

In his defense of the Tallmadge Amendment, which sought to ban further slave importation into Missouri and begin the process of gradual emancipation in the proposed state, Taylor argued that Congress possessed the power to regulate slavery in the territories under Article IV, Section 3, of the Constitution. Congress also had the power to admit new states to the Union with certain stipulations; Illinois, Indiana, and Ohio, for example, had entered the Union as free states because they had been carved out of the territory covered by the Northwest Ordinance of 1787. Taylor maintained that Congress needed to exercise these powers in order to preserve the honor and national character of the United States as a land devoted to liberty.

During the first Missouri debates, Taylor challenged the "diffusion" argument put forth by Kentucky senator Henry Clay, who claimed that westward expansion would ameliorate the conditions of slavery and lead to gradual emancipation. On the contrary, Taylor asserted that the westward expansion of slavery would only bolster the illegal slave trade by creating a vast new market for slaves. Taylor advanced an argument based on the principles of free soil and free labor, contending that slavery debased free white labor and discouraged white migration to the Western territories, because white laborers would refuse to work in areas where they had to compete with slave labor. A majority of House members sided with Taylor, but the Senate rejected the Tallmadge Amendment. With both sides standing firm, the Missouri bill died in 1819 and awaited renewed action in the 16th Congress.

In winter 1820, Taylor led the campaign against slavery in the proposed state of Missouri, asserting many of the arguments he had made during the previous session of Congress. Taylor drove home the point that the nation's moral power derived from its yeoman farmers, laborers, and mechanics. Even more explicitly than before, he linked antislavery and republicanism through founding documents such as the Declaration of Independence and the Northwest Ordinance of 1787. Despite his best efforts, the House ultimately sided with the Senate and passed a measure—known as the Missouri Compromise of 1820—that admitted Maine as a free state, permitted Missouri to form a state government and write a constitution without restrictions on slavery, and banned slavery north of the 36°30' parallel.

At the start of the next session of Congress, Taylor was elected Speaker of the House. His personal success ultimately hurt the antislavery cause, as he played a neutral role as Speaker during the final Missouri debates. Taylor's tenure as Speaker was short-lived: He lost his bid for re-election in fall 1821,

thanks largely to opposition from other factions in New York.

Taylor returned to state politics and the law after 1833. He later moved to Cleveland, Ohio, where he died on September 18, 1854.

James C. Foley

See also: Missouri Compromise (1820); U.S. Constitution (1789).

Further Reading

Moore, Glover. *The Missouri Controversy, 1819–1821.* Lexington: University Press of Kentucky, 1953.

Thirteenth Amendment

See Amendments, Reconstruction

36°30' North Latitude

The boundary established at the 36°30' north latitude line, which separated Missouri (except for the so-called boot heel region) from the Arkansas Territory, became one of the most significant dividing lines within the United States during the antebellum era. Under the terms of the Missouri Compromise of 1820, this line of demarcation limited the expansion of slavery in the Louisiana Territory to points south; lands above the line became free territory in which slavery was prohibited.

Within the Louisiana Territory, the Missouri Compromise only permitted slavery above the 36°30' line in Missouri, which was admitted to the Union as the twenty-second state in 1821. The later passage of the Kansas-Nebraska Act of 1854 repealed the antislavery provision for the territories of Kansas and Nebraska, and the decision issued by the U.S. Supreme Court in the case *Dred Scott v. Sandford* (1857) would effectively nullify the provision of the Missouri Compromise that created the line of demarcation between slave and free territory.

The designation of the 36°30' boundary allowed slavery to expand only into the territory that eventually formed the states of Arkansas and Oklahoma. This restriction, coupled with the South's desire for additional territory where cotton and slavery might expand, encouraged Southern interest in Texas and other lands of the Southwest that belonged to Mexico. When the United States and Mexico went to war in 1846, Congressman David Wilmot (D-PA) introduced an unsuccessful resolution—known as the

Wilmot Proviso—that sought to prohibit the expansion of slavery into any territory acquired from Mexico. In 1848, when the United States defeated Mexico and acquired the vast Mexican cession territory in the Treaty of Guadalupe Hidalgo, some Northern political leaders hoped that the 36°30' boundary might be extended westward to the Pacific Ocean.

By 1848, Northern Democrats such as Lewis Cass of Michigan and Stephen A. Douglas of Illinois believed the slavery controversy could be best settled by imposing an inflexible line of demarcation and deferring to an ingenious new concept they termed "popular sovereignty." According to this approach, the people of a territory seeking statehood would have the opportunity to vote for or against slavery in a popular referendum.

The Kansas-Nebraska Act of 1854, which included a specific provision for popular sovereignty, ran counter to the decision reached in the Missouri Compromise by allowing the possibility that slavery might become established in lands north of 36°30' if territorial residents expressed that will in a popular referendum. The Kansas-Nebraska Act re-ignited the largely sectional debate over slavery's expansion into the territories, and in so doing, it furthered the resolve of the Free Soil movement in the United States, inspired the creation of the Republican Party, and led the nation to the brink of civil war.

Protests for and against the 36°30' line became moot in 1857, when the Supreme Court ruled in the *Dred Scott* case that slavery could exist anywhere in the United States.

Junius P. Rodriguez

See also: *Dred Scott* Case (1857); Missouri Compromise (1820).

Further Reading

Fehrenbacher, Don E. *Sectional Crisis and Southern Constitutionalism.* Baton Rouge: Louisiana State University Press, 1980.
Ray, Perley Orman. *Repeal of the Missouri Compromise, Its Origin and Authorship.* Cleveland, OH: Arthur H. Clark, 1909.

Tocqueville, Alexis de (1805–1859)

A French jurist, statesman, and social theorist, Alexis de Tocqueville was a leading abolitionist during the July Monarchy (1830–1848) of King Louis-Philippe. He is widely known for his classic study of the culture and politics of the United States, *Democracy in America* (1835–1840), the first analysis of American government written by a foreigner. As a chronicler of U.S. democracy, Tocqueville "sought the image of democracy itself, with its inclinations, its character, its prejudices, and its passions, in order to learn what we have to fear or hope from its progress."

Born on July 29, 1805, in Paris to an aristocratic family and trained in the law, Tocqueville became a magistrate at the court of Versailles in 1827. Following the revolution of 1830, he reluctantly took an oath of loyalty to the new constitutional monarch, Louis-Philippe, and later became a deputy judge. Despite his oath, Tocqueville's professional position remained uncertain. As a result, he obtained a leave of absence to study the U.S. penal system.

Accompanied by his colleague and friend Gustave Auguste de Beaumont, Tocqueville visited the United States over a period of nine months, from May 1831 to February 1832. In addition to a joint volume on the American penitentiary system, Beaumont and Tocqueville published individual works based on their voyage. Beaumont's novel, *Marie, or Slavery in the United States* (1835), laid bare the physical and emotional toll of the institution on enslaved blacks in America. Tocqueville's well-received two-volume study, *Democracy in America,* contained a substantial chapter on slavery and race relations in the United States. The views that Tocqueville developed with regard to slavery in the United States became the basis for his political activism in favor of abolition.

In *Democracy in America,* Tocqueville criticized slavery from an economic and sociological standpoint. Unlike ancient slaves, who had been allowed or even encouraged to develop their intellect, modern slaves labored under a system of intellectual and physical tyranny. Tocqueville believed that slavery had a damaging effect on the United States as a whole and on the Southern states in particular. In the South, he maintained, the reliance on unfree labor retarded social, economic, and intellectual development, because both blacks and whites could not benefit from the fruits of their own labor; in the Northern states, by contrast, self-interest and self-improvement were the vital forces driving progress.

Equally troubling, in Tocqueville's view, were the deleterious effects of the racial prejudice born of slavery, which he believed led whites to practice forms of racial despotism that were at odds with the American principles of liberty and justice. Although Tocqueville's economic and sociological arguments against slavery took center stage, he also opposed slavery from a philosophical and religious standpoint. Chattel slavery not only conflicted with Christian principles of social equality, he argued, it also contradicted the political philosophies of the American and French revolutions.

Upon his return to France, Tocqueville became active in the moderate abolitionist movement. In 1835, he joined the *Société pour L'abolition de L'esclavage* (Society for the Abolition of Slavery), founded a year earlier by the duc de Broglie. Tocqueville was elected to the French Chamber of Deputies in March 1839, and he soon joined other abolitionists on a parliamentary commission charged with developing a report on the gradual emancipation proposals of Hippolyte Passy and Victor Destutt de Tracy. Tocqueville wrote the commission's final report, which was presented in July 1839.

In this report, the commission called for the general emancipation of all slaves in the French colonies. The arguments for emancipation were couched in pragmatic terms—drawing chiefly on the recent abolition of slavery in the British West Indies—and the arguments against progressive emancipation were refuted. The plan would resolve the problems associated with emancipation by having the state take the leading role in the process and by having slaves finance planter indemnification through taxes on their wages.

Despite Tocqueville's efforts to have the report discussed in the Chamber of Deputies, it never reached the chamber floor. Instead, another parliamentary commission was established in May 1840 to study anew the question of abolition. Tocqueville also joined this body, which was known as the Broglie Commission. Though he advocated a general emancipation, the majority of the commissioners favored a gradual approach. The Broglie Commission report, issued in March 1843, presented the commissioners' recommendations on both emancipation options to the government, but in the end, no action was taken.

In response to the French government's continued inaction on abolition, Tocqueville penned a series of anonymous articles in an opposition newspaper, *Le Siècle (The Century),* in 1843. In them, he argued for the adoption of three recommendations put forth by the Broglie Commission: that a definite date for slave emancipation be established, giving the colonies ten years to prepare; that the government establish a set price for colonial sugar following emancipation; and that slave owners be compensated. He also suggested that former slaves be prohibited from buying land

in order to prevent a collapse of the large plantation operations. In these articles, Tocqueville linked the abolition of slavery with the economic future of France's overseas colonies and the nation's international prestige, which had been overshadowed by Great Britain's abolition of slavery in 1833.

In 1845, Tocqueville made a final effort in the Chamber of Deputies on the question of emancipation. During a debate over laws aimed at improving conditions for slaves, he reminded his fellow deputies of the philosophical principles of the French revolutions of 1789 and 1830. He argued that he would vote in favor of the proposed changes to the slave laws (*Code Noir*) in the belief that this would allow the French legislature to decide the question of emancipation at a future date.

Following the overthrow of the constitutional monarchy in 1848, the French provisional government issued a decree on April 27, 1848, freeing all slaves in the French colonies within two months. Tocqueville served on the parliamentary commission charged with studying the question of indemnity for former slaveholders before retiring from politics in 1852.

Tocqueville's public advocacy for abolition diminished with his health, but as the abolitionist movement in the United States gathered steam, he joined with other European abolitionists in writing letters of support that were printed in American antislavery publications. He died on April 16, 1859, in Cannes, France.

Melinda Marie Jetté

See also: French West Indies, Abolition and Emancipation in the.

Further Reading

Bonetto, Gerald. "Tocqueville and American Slavery." *Canadian Review of American Studies* 15 (Summer 1984): 123–39.

Gershman, Sally. "Alexis de Tocqueville and Slavery." *French Historical Studies* 9 (Spring 1976): 467–84.

Jennings, Lawrence. *French Anti-Slavery: The Movement for the Abolition of Slavery in France, 1802–1848.* New York: Cambridge University Press, 2000.

Stanley, John L. "Majority Tyranny in Tocqueville's America: The Failure of Negro Suffrage in 1846." *Political Science Quarterly* 84 (1969): 412–35.

Strong, Robert A. "Alexis de Tocqueville and the Abolition of Slavery." *Slavery and Abolition* 8 (September 1987): 204–15.

Tocqueville, Alexis de. *Democracy in America.* 2 vols. New York: Alfred A. Knopf, 1945.

Torrey, Charles Turner (1813–1846)

In a life span of only thirty-three years, the Reverend Charles Turner Torrey had a major influence on the abolitionist movement in the United States. His death in a Maryland penitentiary on May 9, 1846, after years of working with the state's Underground Railroad network, made him a martyr to the antislavery cause.

Born in Scituate, Massachusetts, on November 21, 1813, Torrey was raised in a Congregationalist household and eventually felt a calling to the ministry. He studied theology at Yale College and graduated in 1830, and then served briefly as a pastor at Congregationalist churches in Princeton, New Jersey, and Salem, Massachusetts. It was in the cause of abolition, however, that he found his true mission in the ministry.

Like many antislavery advocates of the early 1830s, and Torrey was drawn to the cause of abolition by the enthusiastic efforts of William Lloyd Garrison, founder of the American Anti-Slavery Society and a proponent of the immediate emancipation of all slaves. Torrey eventually broke ranks with Garrison during the schisms that fractured the American abolitionist movement. In particular, Torrey believed that Garrison's efforts to include women's rights as part of antislavery agitation would only serve to weaken the force of the abolitionist message and limit its effectiveness.

Torrey viewed the antislavery effort as his life's great purpose, and he devoted tireless energy to active advocacy. He became involved in the work of the Underground Railroad in Maryland, establishing standard routes that could be used to aid fugitive slaves in their efforts to escape. Previously, the Underground Railroad had operated more or less as a spontaneous effort to assist fugitives, but Torrey sought to regularize its activities in Maryland to facilitate the escape of more fugitives.

Torrey's efforts in Maryland were largely successful: He was credited with aiding in the escape of 400 slaves from plantations in Virginia and Maryland. His success, however, made him a marked man, as he operated his network primarily within Maryland, a Southern slave state. In addition to his clandestine efforts to aid fugitives in their escape, Torrey also took a public stand on African American civil rights. During winter 1841, when he was operating from Washington, D.C., Torrey only worshiped in the area's black churches, because he did not approve of the segregation that characterized the other churches in the nation's capital.

Hoping to learn more about his adversaries, Torrey attended a meeting of slaveholders held in Baltimore in 1844. He was recognized at the gathering and subsequently arrested for aiding the escape of slaves. A slave owner from Winchester, Virginia, brought charges against Torrey, and he was placed in the penitentiary in Baltimore to await trial.

During Torrey's trial, which lasted through November and December 1844, he was convicted and sentenced to six years in prison with hard labor. Antislavery groups from around the country raised money to support his defense, and some groups petitioned the governor of Maryland to intervene on Torrey's behalf and pardon him.

From his prison cell, Torrey wrote, "Shall a man be put into the Penitentiary for doing good? That is the real question at issue, and it is one which will shake down the whole edifice of slavery, even if there were no other issue." Although he might have been freed if he had renounced his earlier efforts to help slaves escape, he refused to do so. Torrey viewed himself as a prisoner of conscience and his incarceration as an act of civil disobedience. His health deteriorated rapidly in the unsanitary conditions of the penitentiary, prompting increased calls from antislavery advocates urging that the clergyman be freed.

On May 9, 1846, Torrey died of tuberculosis in prison. His remains were taken to Boston, where his funeral became a public spectacle. He was buried at Mount Auburn Cemetery in Cambridge, Massachusetts; his grave became a holy place for many abolitionists.

In subsequent years, American abolitionists used the expression "Torrey's blood crieth out" to remind the nation that a martyr had given his life for the cause. Like newspaper publisher Elijah P. Lovejoy before him and radical abolitionist John Brown after him, Charles Turner Torrey assumed a larger place in death than he had in life.

Junius P. Rodriguez

See also: Garrison, William Lloyd; Underground Railroad.

Toussaint L'Ouverture, François-Dominique (ca. 1743–1803)

Born into slavery and raised on a plantation, François-Dominique Toussaint L'Ouverture led the only successful slave rebellion in history in the French colony of Saint-Domingue on the island of Hispaniola between 1791 and 1804. The country that he helped to establish—Haiti—stands out as the longest-lived republic in the region, the second in the Americas (after the United States), and the first founded by former slaves who defeated their colonial masters.

Toussaint, as he is commonly known, was born between 1743 and 1746 on the Bréda plantation of Saint-Domingue's Northern Plain. His father is said to have been the son of an African chieftain. In his early years, Toussaint's master, Bayon de Libertas, gave him the rare opportunity to learn to read and write.

As a young man, he studied the books in his master's library, including the works of Julius Caesar, but for the most part he worked in the fields with the other slaves. He also served as his master's coachman and sometimes as the plantation's veterinarian. In the course of his education, Toussaint acquired knowledge of medicinal herbs and plants, and he earned a reputation as a healer.

Revolutionary Leader

Inspired by the egalitarian doctrines of the French Revolution of 1789, the Saint-Domingue insurrections broke out in 1791 as plantation slaves began to revolt against French colonial control and demand their rights as free citizens. Having been granted his freedom after thirty years as a slave, Toussaint was in his forties when he joined the officer ranks of the resistance against the proslavery planters and white royalists.

Because he was literate, Toussaint qualified for a leadership position, especially as he had also studied military strategy: He rose quickly in the ranks due to his skill in leadership and maneuvering the forces under his command. For championing the struggle for emancipation as he did, Toussaint would earn the designations "Negro Spartacus" and "Black Napoleon." It was his destiny, historian Eric Williams writes, "to raise the sacred standard of liberty and restore the rights of the black race." Thanks in great part to his leadership, the colony would eventually gain its independence as the Republic of Haiti.

In 1792, Toussaint joined the pro-Spanish forces led by Jean-François, who at this early stage of the rebellion fought as a royalist against the French Republicans. Toussaint was promoted to the position of colonel, and as a commander, he repulsed a French offense on November 17, 1792. Once the French Republican forces took over Cap-Français in April 1793, they had to face the assault of the Spanish forces led by Toussaint, who was third in command over an army of

4,000 blacks, trained with the assistance of French deserters. Toussaint's army reconquered the northern regions as far as Gonaïves and would eventually take control of the entire north-central zones of the French portion of the colony. It was during this time that Toussaint assumed the surname "L'Ouverture"—a reference either to the "opening" he had made in the forces of the enemy, the path to liberty, or the gap between his two front teeth.

Toussaint showed great skill in military strategy and leadership while fighting for the Spanish but, disillusioned with Spanish and British reinstatements of slavery in 1794, decided to switch to the French Republican side. It was General Étienne-Maynard Laveaux who, organizing resistance against attacks by British and Spanish, contacted Toussaint and persuaded him to return to the French side and lead the fight as a general in the French army, this time against British and Spanish incursions. Most of Toussaint's lieutenants went to the French side as well. The French National Assembly abolished slavery on February 4, 1794, and welcomed black and mulatto deputies to represent Saint-Domingue in their meetings.

After the British invaded Port-au-Prince in 1794 with white royalist aid, Toussaint surrounded the port city, forcing the British to withdraw. The mulattoes André Rigaud and Villate, meanwhile, gained control of the South and Cap Haitien as Toussaint held the center. Toussaint succeeded in rescuing the French governor, held by Villate, and was rewarded with an appointment as the colony's lieutenant governor.

In May 1796, a commission headed by Léger-Félicité Sonthonax was sent to restore French control over the colony. Villate was expelled, and Rigaud continued to command in the South. Toussaint, as general in chief of the Saint-Domingue army, headed an alliance of planters, émigrés, and royalists that marched on Sonthonax and forced his return to France. Sonthonax was replaced by Gabriel-Marie Hédouville. Hédouville wanted to gain control of Toussaint and Rigaud and to stand up against the British, who controlled Port-au-Prince and the West.

Rise to Prominence and Capture

By 1798, Toussaint commanded Saint-Domingue while continuing to swear allegiance to France but staying committed to defending the freedom of the former slaves. After the insurrection against Hédouville, sparked by a rumor that he planned to reinstate slavery, the French commissioner withdrew, allowing Toussaint to defeat Rigaud with the help of arms and transport provided by U.S. president John Adams. Clashes took place between the black forces of Toussaint and those of Rigaud and the mulattoes in the South. Rigaud attacked on June 16, 1799, initiating the so-called War of Knives, a race war with devastating effects.

Prevailing in the end, Toussaint mustered the troops to invade and easily conquer Santo Domingo in January 1801. He declared himself governor for life of Saint-Domingue and Santo Domingo and declared the island *une et indivisible* (one and indivisible). With the whole island temporarily and loosely united under Toussaint's command, Saint-Domingue continued to be considered part of France. As ruler of the two nations, Toussaint granted freedom to the slaves of the Spanish side and dismissed the French officials, though he never went so far as to declare the island's independence from French control.

At Toussaint's orders, a constitutional assembly composed of seven whites and three mulattoes was convened. The outcome of the assembly was Toussaint's appointment as governor for life and the abolition of slavery throughout the island in 1801. Toussaint established a military administrative system, with a Central Assembly invested with the power to legislate and laws ratified by the governor. Backed by the constitution, Toussaint appropriated land that had been abandoned by the French and mulattoes; in order to rebuild the war-shattered economy, he reinforced the system tying former slaves to plantations but gave them allowances for medical care, meager wages, and lodging. Under Toussaint's administration, the color distinction was banished in the civil service for good, and large landholdings (*latifundia*) were given to officers and senior officials of the government.

The 1801 constitution not only made Toussaint governor for life, but it also gave him the right to name his successor. In the eyes of the French government, the constitutional arrangement constituted a dangerous condition of autonomy.

Flush from recent victories in Italy, Napoleon Bonaparte looked hungrily to Saint-Domingue as a potential beachhead from which to launch a campaign to take control of the Louisiana Territory. Yet one great impediment stood in his way: Although Saint-Domingue was officially French, Toussaint dominated. Napoleon had officially recognized Toussaint as captain general in March 1801, but he did not know the blacks would get as far as they did: He ac-

cepted neither abolition nor autonomy for the colony, nor did the naming of a black as leader of the colony sit well with the first consul's plans for building an empire in America.

When Toussaint sent him the constitution, Napoleon rejected it, accusing the black governor general of seeking personal gain. Toussaint wrote back:

> You ask me if I desire consideration, honours, riches. Certainly: but not from you. I put my consideration in the respect of my fellow-citizens, my honours in their love, my fortune in their disinterested fidelity. . . . The power which I hold has been as legitimately acquired as your own, and nothing but the expressed wish of the people of San Domingo will force me to give it up.

To remedy the situation, Napoleon sent his brother-in-law, Charles-Victor-Emmanuel Leclerc, to command a fleet whose mission was to retake the island for the French. Leclerc led an expedition of 22,000 experienced troops, the largest force ever sent abroad by France, and counted on the support of Rigaud and the mulattoes against Toussaint and the other "black Jacobin" leaders in 1802.

Leaders Toussaint, Jean-Jacques Dessalines, and Henri Christophe kept up a guerrilla war against Leclerc's invasion from the interior of the island. Christophe eventually surrendered, but Toussaint came to an understanding with Leclerc, who had captured the main ports, and Dessalines joined them later.

Through deceit, however, Toussaint was arrested by French authorities in June 1802 and transported to France. Aboard the ship, he declared in resounding words, "In overthrowing me, you have cut down in San Domingo only the trunk of the tree of liberty. It will spring up again by the roots for they are numerous and deep."

In the cold of his castle prison in Joux, set in the French Alps near the Swiss border, deprived of food and sick with pneumonia, Toussaint died alone. His lifeless body was found by the fireplace on April 7, 1803.

Some two centuries after his death, the ideal of freedom and equality for which Toussaint L'Ouverture created the opening remains intact. Yet, it is still a distant goal for which the impoverished Haitian masses continue to struggle.

Eugenio Matibag

See also: Haitian Revolution (1791–1804); Sonthonax, Léger Félicité.

Further Reading

Bellegarde-Smith, Patrick. *Haiti: The Breached Citadel.* Boulder, CO: Westview, 1990.

Heinl, Robert Debs, Jr., and Nancy Gordon Heinl. *Written in Blood: The Story of the Haitian People, 1492–1995.* 2nd ed. Lanham, MD: University Press of America, 1996.

Knight, Franklin W. *The Caribbean: The Genesis of a Fragmented Nationalism.* New York: Oxford University Press, 1990.

Trelawney Town Maroons

See Maroon Wars, Jamaica (1729–1739, 1795–1796)

Truth, Sojourner (ca. 1797–1883)

One of the most inspirational leaders of the abolitionist movement, the former slave Sojourner Truth became a powerful voice in the nineteenth-century abolitionist and women's rights movements in the United States. Although she was not directly involved in either movement at the political level, her fiery speaking skills were invaluable because of the attention she was able to draw to their causes.

Early Life

The woman we know as Sojourner Truth was born about 1797 in Hurley, Ulster County, New York. Given the name Isabella Baumfree at birth, she was one of thirteen children born to slaves James and Elizabeth, who served a wealthy Dutch patroon, Charles Hardenbergh. At the age of eleven, Baumfree was sold from her family, and she subsequently passed through the hands of several owners. Speaking only Dutch and forced to learn English quickly, she relied on her deep Christian faith, instilled in her by her mother, to support her through the difficult experience. This unwavering devotion would be the hallmark of her life's work as a preacher, abolitionist, and feminist.

In 1810, Baumfree was sold to John Dumont of New Paltz, New York. A harsh master, Dumont forced her to marry another slave named Thomas. During her time in the Dumont household, Baumfree bore at least five children by Thomas. In 1827, a year before New York mandated the legal emancipation of slaves in the state, Dumont reneged on a promise to grant Baumfree her freedom the following year. She fled the Dumont household and sought refuge with the nearby Quaker family of Isaac and Maria Van Wagener, whose surname she adopted. In 1829, she moved to New York City with her two youngest children.

Her time in New York City was a transforming period in her life. Working as a domestic servant in an unfamiliar and unwelcoming environment, she maintained her strong religious beliefs. She considered herself a mystic, had visions, and heard voices that she assumed to be those of God. Sometime between 1829 and 1831, she was introduced to Elijah Pierson, a wealthy religious fanatic who had dedicated himself to the conversion of prostitutes in the city's notorious slums. She joined Pierson's crusade and attracted public attention through her street preaching. Nearly six feet tall, slender, and speaking with a Dutch accent, she stood out from the crowd in her public proselytizing.

In 1832, Van Wagener and the Pierson family were introduced to Robert Matthews, a mystic who referred to himself as Matthias. In 1833, they all moved to Ossining, New York, to join Zion Hill, a commune that Matthews had established. However, the commune folded only two years later, after Pierson's mysterious murder and charges of scandalous behavior among its residents. Van Wagener returned to New York City, where she continued to support her children through domestic work.

Orator

In 1843, inspired by her continued mystic visions and voices, she changed her name to Sojourner Truth and committed her life to preaching the message of God's love to anyone who would listen. Although she was illiterate, she was extremely knowledgeable in biblical scripture and preached a simple message of God's love and man's duty to love one another.

In June 1843, Truth toured Long Island and Connecticut on foot, spreading her religious message. She camped at night, worked part-time when she needed money, and gained comfort and support from strangers.

In the winter of that year, Truth traveled to Northampton, Massachusetts, where she joined the Northampton Association of Education and Industry, a utopian communal farm founded by George Benson, brother-in-law of the abolitionist William Lloyd Garrison. At the Northampton commune, Truth was introduced to the abolitionist movement and prominent leaders such as Garrison and Frederick Douglass.

After the farm ceased operation in 1846, Truth remained with Benson and traveled throughout Massachusetts delivering abolitionist speeches. In her orations, she offered recollections of her enslaved youth,

Adopting a name that reflected her spiritual mission, former New York slave Sojourner Truth traveled throughout the country delivering passionate speeches on behalf of abolition, women's rights, and other social causes. *(National Portrait Gallery, Smithsonian Institution/Art Resource, New York)*

preached and sang gospel songs, and called for the emancipation of all slaves. Because of her firsthand experience with slavery and her public speaking skills, abolitionist leaders began to publicize her speeches and travels in their literature.

Starting in 1850, Truth traveled through the Midwest spreading the abolitionist message. In states such as Ohio, Missouri, and Kansas, she appeared with fellow activists, including Douglass and Parker Pillsbury. Her statuesque appearance and charisma attracted large crowds of listeners. Despite her popularity, however, those who opposed her abolitionist stance often attacked her. Heckled and sometimes physically attacked, she was publicly questioned on whether she was actually a female. Directly confronting the issue, Truth boldly bared her breast to the audience at a convention in Indiana. The public jeers served only to heighten her resolve to do everything in her power to bring an end to slavery.

In spite of her antagonistic audiences, Truth continued to publicly advocate abolition. Introduced to the women's rights movement at a convention in Worcester, Massachusetts, in 1850, she quickly added the issue to her public-speaking repertoire. One of her most notable contributions to the women's rights movement was her famous "Ar'n't I a Woman?" speech, delivered at a women's rights convention in Akron, Ohio, in 1851. Challenging the widely held notion that men are superior to women, she relived her harsh experience under slavery to dramatize women's strength and the injustice of treating them as second-class citizens.

Advocate of Free Slaves

By 1857, Truth had moved to Battle Creek, Michigan, which would serve as her home base for the remainder of her life. During the U.S. Civil War, she traveled throughout Michigan, soliciting donations of clothing and supplies for black troops. In 1864, she traveled to Washington, D.C., where President Abraham Lincoln received her as a guest at the White House.

After the war ended in 1865, she turned her attention to advocating for the rights of the newly freed slaves, actively supporting the creation of a Negro state. Supporters of that concept called for public land in the West to be set aside for settlement by former slaves. In addition to speaking on the matter, she created, circulated, and ultimately submitted a petition for a Negro state to President Ulysses S. Grant in 1870.

Though a Negro state never materialized, Truth nonetheless continued to serve as an advocate for the rights of African Americans during Reconstruction. She visited black settlements, offered advice, and preached a message of cleanliness and godliness to recently emancipated African Americans. Continuing to travel the United States, she advocated equal rights for African Americans and women. To support herself and her campaign, she sold photographs of herself and copies of her dictated memoirs, *The Narrative of Sojourner Truth*, which had been compiled by fellow abolitionist Olive Gilbert in 1850.

In 1875, her traveling companion, grandson Sammy Banks, fell ill, and she was forced to retire from the lecture circuit and return to Battle Creek. Truth died on November 26, 1883, in Battle Creek and was buried in Oak Hill Cemetery.

Jennifer Searcy

See also: Women's Rights and the Abolitionist Movement.

Further Reading

Mabee, Carlton, with Susan Mabee Newhouse. *Sojourner Truth: Slave, Prophet, Legend.* New York: New York University Press, 1995.

Painter, Nell Irvin. *Sojourner Truth: A Life, a Symbol.* New York: W.W. Norton, 1996.

————. "Sojourner Truth in Life and Memory: Writing the Biography of an American Exotic." *Gender and History* 2 (Spring 1990): 3–16.

Truth, Sojourner. *Narrative of Sojourner Truth: A Bondswoman of Olden Time.* Ed. Olive Gilbert. New York: Oxford University Press, 1991.

Tubman, Harriet (ca. 1820–1913)

Harriet Tubman was known by many names: Fellow slaves called her "Minty," fugitive slaves called her "Moses," abolitionists called her "Heroine," slave owners called her "Criminal," radical abolitionist John Brown called her "General," black soldiers called her "Nurse," and the rebel army called her "Spy." As a fugitive slave who helped more than 300 slaves reach freedom through the Underground Railroad, she became a legendary figure in the history of the antislavery movement in the United States.

She recruited volunteers to assist Brown in his raid on the Harpers Ferry arsenal in 1859, worked with the Union army as a reconnaissance agent and guide, and helped her people adjust to freedom during Reconstruction, as she worked to establish schools and a home for the aged and infirm. Well known in New England abolitionist circles, she spoke at antislavery meetings of her experiences, which were later published in *Scenes in the Life of Harriet Tubman* (1869).

Early Life

Harriet Tubman was born as Araminta Ross ("Minty") in Bucktown, Dorchester County, on Maryland's eastern shore, sometime around 1820. Her father, Benjamin Ross, and her mother, Harriet Greene Ross ("Old Rit"), worked hard to strengthen family ties among their twelve children at a time when families were frequently separated by slave owners. Growing up on the plantation, Minty, who assumed the name Harriet early in life, listened to the tales of an elderly slave who talked about the Declaration of Independence and its guarantee of equality, life, liberty, and happiness. Young Harriet also heard stories about Quakers who helped slaves escape.

When she was six years old, Harriet was hired out to a neighboring plantation, where Miss Susan, the plantation mistress, beat her daily. After six months, the young girl was returned to her parents, battered, sick, and unable to work. As tragic as the experience was, Harriet learned protection skills that would serve her well in later years. She cunningly encouraged the idea that she was mentally deficient to avoid the exploitation of slave breeding by her master, who was sure that any children Harriet had would be half-witted.

Interfering in the attempted murder of a fellow slave when she was in her teens, Harriet was hit in the head with weights from a scale, causing her to have "sleeping seizures" for the rest of her life. At the time of the injury, the only medical help she received came from her mother. Years later, she underwent surgery at Massachusetts General Hospital in Boston to relieve some of the pressure on her brain.

Although she never learned to read or write, Harriet possessed enormous physical strength and a

Referred to as the "Moses of Her People," Harriet Tubman escaped slavery in Maryland and became a legendary figure of the Underground Railroad. She made nineteen journeys back into slave territory to lead hundreds of fugitives to freedom. *(Hulton Archive/Getty Images)*

good deal of native ingenuity. She convinced her owner to hire her out as a field hand. After paying her master $1 a day, the rest of the money belonged to her. She worked so hard that she was able to buy two steers for $40 and hoped to earn enough money to buy her freedom. In 1844, Harriet married John Tubman, a free black man, who joined her in the plantation's slave quarters.

After seeing two of her sisters sold farther into the South, Tubman began to have visions. In the first vision, she saw a group of horsemen riding into the slave quarters in the dead of night; the slaves cried out in agony as children were torn from their parents' arms. In another vision, she saw her own escape, clearly seeing the faces of her liberators. Tubman later said that the faces in her vision were actually those of the members of the Underground Railroad who helped her on her road to freedom. During this period, her dreams of freedom were filled with "green fields and lovely flowers, and beautiful white ladies, who stretched out their arms to me over the line." These visions, coupled with a rumor that she and her brothers were to be sold, gave her the courage to flee her master.

In 1849, Tubman ran away with no clear idea of where she was going or how she would survive. Scared and suspicious, she visited the home of a local Quaker woman who directed her out of Maryland. Tubman followed the North Star, traveling by night and often walking in water to cover her tracks. Along the way, she learned that a lantern attached to a hitching post indicated a safe house where she would be welcomed.

She was first directed toward Camden, Delaware, to the home of Eliza and Ezekiel Hamm. From Camden, Tubman was sent to Wilmington, Delaware, where she was assisted by the noted Quaker abolitionist Thomas Garrett. From there, she traveled to Philadelphia, where she had her first real taste of freedom.

Conductor of the Underground Railroad

In Philadelphia, Tubman worked as laundress, scrubwoman, cook, and seamstress to earn enough money to support herself and to finance her trips to the South for the Underground Railroad. She realized that she would not be truly free as long as members of her family were still slaves: "I was free," she said, "but there was no one to welcome me to the land of freedom."

Her first trip as a conductor on the Underground Railroad was made to free one of her sisters and the sis-

ter's two children. On the next trip, Tubman freed her brother and two others. In 1851, Tubman returned to guide her husband John to safety but found him living with another woman and uninterested in freedom. Undaunted, Tubman led eleven slaves out of bondage, including another brother and his family.

She made nineteen trips into Maryland, Delaware, and Virginia, never being captured and never losing a passenger, making her the most effective conductor of the Underground Railroad in history. All told, slave owners lost tens of millions of dollars in property on her account, leading Southern legislatures to call for her capture, dead or alive, and placing a $40,000 bounty on her head (approximately $200,000 in contemporary terms). Despite the price placed on her head, Tubman continued to come to the aid of fleeing slaves, who swore that she had the eyesight of an eagle, the hearing of a deer, and the ability to quell vicious dogs at a glance.

In 1850, defenders of slavery persuaded the U.S. Congress to pass the Fugitive Slave Law, which required that all escaped slaves be returned to their masters without question or trial. The Underground Railroad reacted by increasing its efforts to help slaves escape to Canada. The new law sent Tubman back on the road to avoid capture.

From Philadelphia, she was sent to Rochester, New York, by black abolitionist William Still. In Rochester, she met abolitionist and women's rights advocate Susan B. Anthony, who sent her on her way toward Lake Erie. After crossing Lake Erie, Tubman entered Saint Catharines, Canada, where she made her home from 1851 to 1857. Making two trips a year to the South, she eventually succeeded in freeing her entire family, including her aging parents.

Later Life

From 1862 to 1864, Tubman worked for the Department of the South, located on a group of islands off the coast of South Carolina where Reconstruction had already begun. In addition to acting as a secret agent and scout, she served as a liaison between the Union army and local slaves.

After returning to Auburn, New York, to live with her parents in a house she had bought from Senator William Seward (later U.S. secretary of state), Tubman struggled financially. Her friends, led by schoolteacher Sarah Hughes Bradford, lobbied Congress for a veteran's pension for her because of the work she had done for the Union army.

Much of what historians know about Tubman's early life comes from a series of interviews that Bradford conducted with her at this time. The interviews were published in 1869, and the $1,200 profit was given to Tubman to pay off her mortgage on the Auburn house.

That same year, Tubman married Nelson Davis, a man twenty years her junior. When he died on October 14, 1888, Congress granted the elderly Mrs. Nelson Davis a pension of $20 a month—though it never officially acknowledged her contributions to the nation. In her final years, Tubman sold vegetables door to door, never refusing an invitation to come inside and tell her stories.

Tubman died on March 10, 1913, in Auburn, New York. In 2003, New York governor George Pataki established March 10 as Harriet Tubman Day in the state of New York to honor this heroine's life and legacy.

Elizabeth Purdy

See also: Fugitive Slave Act of 1850; Fugitive Slaves; Still, William; Underground Railroad.

Further Reading

Bradford, Sarah H. *Scenes in the Life of Harriet Tubman.* 1869. Salem, NH: Ayer, 1999.

Friedman, Dorothy Sterling. *Freedom Train: The Story of Harriet Tubman.* Garden City, NY: Doubleday, 1954.

Nies, Judith. *Seven Women: Portraits from the Radical Tradition.* New York: Penguin, 1977.

Petry, Ann. *Harriet Tubman: Conductor on the Underground Railroad.* New York: Thomas Y. Crowell, 1955.

Thompson, Priscilla. "Harriet Tubman, Thomas Garrett, and the Underground Railroad." *Delaware History* 22 (September 1986): 1–21.

Turner, Nat (1800–1831)

A slave and lay preacher from Southampton County, Virginia, who was recognized for his mystical religious powers, Nat Turner organized and led one of the largest and bloodiest slave revolts in the history of the United States in August 1831. Although the state authorities were able to restore order, the rebellion was so influential that in 1831–1832, the Virginia legislature debated whether to maintain the institution of slavery in the state.

Turner was born on October 2, 1800, on the plantation of Benjamin Turner in Southampton, Virginia. Turner's mother, a "saltwater" or African-born slave, hated the institution of slavery so much that she tried to abort her son in order to spare his life from bondage.

Turner survived, grew up, worshiped in a local church, and learned to read and write. Like Denmark Vesey and Gabriel Prosser, who had made earlier unsuccessful attempts to free their fellow slaves, Turner found his inspiration in the teachings of the Bible.

Turner's rebellion, called "Old Nat's War" or "Nat's Fray" by the natives of Southampton County, began on his owner's plantation near Flat Swamp, in the western part of the county, during the predawn hours of Monday, August 22, 1831. The initial army of rebels totaled seven conspirators, including Turner. With a hatchet and a broadax, the men killed Turner's owner, Joseph Travis, and his family.

Vowing that no white people of any age or gender would be spared, the slaves—who quickly numbered between sixty and eighty men—made their way from plantation to plantation. As they moved toward nearby Jerusalem, they killed approximately fifty-five whites along the way.

Within two days, the U.S. Army and the U.S. Marines had squelched the rebellion. The white militiamen, arriving in Jerusalem, began indiscriminately killing blacks. When they were done, the death count totaled several hundred victims. Turner escaped the barrage, while the South succumbed to an atmosphere of fear and outrage.

Turner, who also called himself the "Prophet"—he said he had heard from the Spirit, as the prophets in the Bible had—dictated his story to Thomas Gray, who visited Turner after his capture and later published his account of the events, *The Confessions of Nat Turner* (1832). Gray recounted that Turner felt destined by God to deliver his people from bondage. He shrouded himself in mysticism, isolating himself from other slaves, and did not attend social functions so as to set himself apart from other captives in the territory. In his testimony, Turner claimed that he had been waiting for a "sign in the heavens" to identify the point at which the rebellion was to begin; he believed that he had received the sign in the form of a solar eclipse.

After the rebellion, Turner eluded an extensive manhunt until his capture in mid-October. Judge Jeremiah Cobb sentenced him in early November, and Turner was hanged on November 11, 1831. Turner had prophesied that his death would cause a darkening of the sky and rain, and, in fact, there was an unusual shift in the weather at the time.

In the aftermath of the rebellion, Southern legislatures passed laws against black preachers, banned the education of slaves, and made the manu-

HORRID MASSACRE IN VIRGINIA.

The Scenes which the above Plate is designed to represent, are—Fig 1. a Mother intreating for the lives of her children.—2. Mr. Travis, cruelly murdered by his own Slaves.—3. Mr. Barrow, who bravely defended himself until his wife escaped.—4. A comp. of mounted Dragoons in pursuit of the Blacks.

The bloody slave uprising led by Nat Turner in Virginia in August 1831 raised fears among whites throughout the South. The incident provoked both repressive new measures against blacks and public debate on the future of slavery. *(Hulton Archive/Getty Images)*

mission of slaves almost impossible. One Virginia legislator described the climate of the South during that time: "We have, as far as possible, closed every avenue by which light might enter their minds. If you could extinguish the capacity to see the light, our work would be completed . . . and we should be safe!" This mind-set provoked a public debate on emancipation in Virginia, as the House of Delegates debated the future of slavery in the state for two weeks.

Imelda Hunt

See also: Prosser, Gabriel; Vesey, Denmark; Virginia Slavery Debate (1831–1832).

Further Reading

Clarke, John H. *William Styron's Nat Turner: Ten Black Writers Respond.* Boston: Beacon, 1968.

Foner, Eric. *Nat Turner.* Englewood Cliffs, NJ: Prentice Hall, 1971.

French, Scot. *The Rebellious Slave: Nat Turner in American Memory.* Boston: Houghton Mifflin, 2003.

Greenberg, Kenneth S. *The Confessions of Nat Turner and Related Documents.* Boston: St. Martin's, 1996.

Oates, Stephen B. *The Fires of Jubilee: Nat Turner's Fierce Rebellion.* New York: Harper & Row, 1990.

Stampp, Kenneth M. *The Peculiar Institution: Slavery in the Ante-Bellum South.* New York: Random House, 1956.

Tragle, Henry Irving. *The Southampton Slave Revolt of 1831: A Compilation of Source Material.* Amherst, MA: University of Massachusetts Press, 1971.

Uncle Tom's Cabin (1852)

No book published in the United States during the nineteenth century had as great an impact on American politics and society as the antislavery novel *Uncle Tom's Cabin; or, Life Among the Lowly* (1852), written by the New England abolitionist Harriet Beecher Stowe in the decade preceding the U.S. Civil War. When President Abraham Lincoln welcomed Stowe at the White House in 1862, he reportedly commented, "So this is the little lady who started this great war." The causes of the war were many and complex, as no one knew better than Lincoln, but there is no doubt that *Uncle Tom's Cabin* played a vital part in drawing attention to the inhumanity of slavery.

Stowe's chief contribution to the cause of abolition was to present slavery as a real human experience rather than an ideological issue. She dramatized the stories of slaves in emotional terms, hoping that Northerners would rise up against the institution of slavery, which she believed violated Judeo-Christian beliefs, basic human dignity, and the tenets of the U.S. Constitution.

Stowe's Christian faith was an integral part of her worldview and heavily influenced her characterizations in *Uncle Tom's Cabin*. In 1851, while attending morning services in Brunswick, Maine, she reportedly had a vision that provided the basis for *Uncle Tom's Cabin*. She told her family that in her vision, she had seen a slave being viciously beaten. As he died, this Christlike figure asked God to forgive his murderers. Immediately upon reaching home, Stowe began to write. She regarded her work as that of a painter, presenting vivid pictures of the evils of slavery to an indifferent or unaware population.

Uncle Tom's Cabin was first printed in serial form in the abolitionist newspaper the *National Era,* with the initial installment appearing on June 5, 1851, and the concluding segment on April 1, 1852. Stowe received $300 for the serial rights. On September 4, 1851, it was announced that John P. Jewett would publish *Uncle Tom's Cabin* in book form. Jewett felt that the Stowe family should share in the venture and asked them to pay half the publishing costs, which would have proved financially successful for the Stowes. The family had no money to contribute, however, so Harriet settled for a 10 percent royalty on all sales.

Uncle Tom's Cabin was released on March 20, 1852. Readers had the choice of a paper cover for $1, a cloth cover for $1.50, or an edition with lavender cloth and full gilt for $2; later, a deluxe edition sold for $5. Jewett published a total of 5,000 copies on the first run, of which 3,000 were sold in just the first few days. Within three weeks, 20,000 copies of the book had been sold, and three printing presses ran twenty-four hours a day, six days a week to meet the demand.

By the following January, *Uncle Tom's Cabin* had sold more than 200,000 copies in the United States alone, in addition to thousands of copies in Great Britain. Lending libraries throughout the North kept multiple copies on hand. Enormously popular in its time, *Uncle Tom's Cabin* would later be translated into twenty-five languages and would be widely read for more than a century.

The novel was well received throughout the North, bringing its author enthusiastic praise from fellow writers such as Henry Wadsworth Longfellow, John Greenleaf Whittier, James Russell Lowell, and Ralph Waldo Emerson. The African American leader Frederick Douglass wrote that *Uncle Tom's Cabin* was marked by the "finger of God." Acclaim also came from politicians such as Senator Charles Sumner of Massachusetts and Senator William Seward of New York, who called Stowe's novel "the greatest book of all time."

Southern critics, on the other hand, called the book "scandalous," and Stowe was roundly criticized for using fiction to present her abolitionist views. Generally, Southerners denied that slave owners were as cruel as those portrayed in the novel and tried to prohibit the distribution of the book. In Alabama, a bookseller was run out of town for selling *Uncle Tom's Cabin,* and the University of Virginia sponsored public burnings of the novel. In Maryland, a free black was sentenced to ten years in prison for possessing a copy.

This copy of *Uncle Tom's Cabin*, once owned by Susan B. Anthony, carries the signatures of several noted abolitionists, including Anthony and Lydia (Lucretia) Mott. Harriet Beecher Stowe's novel inspired the leaders of the movement as well as public sentiment. *(Library of Congress, Rare Books and Special Collections Division)*

The preface to *Uncle Tom's Cabin* establishes the author's purpose from the outset: "The scenes of the story lie among a race hitherto ignored by the associations of polite and refined society." Stowe admitted that the work was polemic, informing her readers that her object was "to awaken sympathy and feeling for the African race" and "to show their wrongs and sorrows, under a system so unnecessarily cruel and unjust as to defeat and do away the good effects of all that can be attempted for them."

Despite the impact that *Uncle Tom's Cabin* had on American politics and society, the novel has been widely criticized for its literary style—or, as some critics claim, its lack thereof. Stowe was so emotionally involved in her subject that she never intended to write a literary masterpiece. She drew on her love of debate and tendency to moralize as she presented the institution of slavery as inherently evil and depicted the horrible reality that slaves were treated as property rather than human beings. Because she felt so strongly about her characters, she imbued them with such animation that they became real to her readers, who laughed and cried by turns as they read about Uncle Tom, Eliza, Topsy, and Little Eva.

The novel, which opens on the Shelby Plantation in Kentucky, contains two parallel story lines. The first centers on the slave Tom, who experiences life in the Deep South under the hand of the treacherous Simon Legree. The second story line involves Eliza and her young son, Harry, who flee a life of bondage by crossing the Ohio River, eventually reaching safety in Canada.

Although the name "Uncle Tom" came to be viewed as a derogatory term, representing an African American who kowtows to whites, Stowe's Uncle Tom is good because of his strong faith. Stowe presents Tom as an intelligent black man who refuses to rebel against slavery because of his innate goodness.

Stowe portrays the character of Eliza, on the other hand, as a black woman struggling against her subservient role who runs away rather than see her child torn from her arms. Along the way, Eliza and her family are helped by members of the Underground Railroad, an organization that assisted thousands of slaves in their flight to freedom. Ironically, the novel was criticized during the nineteenth century for its promotion of women's rights, yet in the twentieth century, Stowe was vilified for her portrayal of women as bound to home and family.

Legree is the epitome of evil, not only in his violent treatment of Tom but also in his behavior toward his black female slaves, but not all of Stowe's slave owners are evil. Mr. Shelby, Tom's original owner, sells him out of economic necessity rather than greed. Tom's next owner, Augustine Saint Clare, has every intention of freeing Tom but dies before he can do so. Master Shelby, who recognizes Tom's worth as a human being, represents the awakened slave owner who acknowledges the evils of slavery.

The character of Eva Saint Clare, based on a daughter whom Stowe lost, symbolizes the Southerner who is too young to have accepted the traditional Southern attitudes about slavery. Miss Ophelia, Saint Clare's sister, represents the enlightened Northerner who abhors slavery. Topsy, a young slave girl, is depicted as a caricature, at times lending comic relief to the tragedy of slave life.

Stowe's characters have stood the test of time to become part of America's literary tradition. Although Stowe published additional novels, essays, and studies of social life, her later works never reached the level of popularity and prominence that *Uncle Tom's Cabin* attained.

Elizabeth Purdy

See also: Novels, Antislavery; Stowe, Harriet Beecher; Underground Railroad.

Further Reading

Adams, John R. *Harriet Beecher Stowe*. Boston: Twayne, 1989.

Gossett, Thomas F. Uncle Tom's Cabin *and American Culture*. Dallas, TX: Southern Methodist University Press, 1965.

Kirkham, E. Bruce. *The Building of* Uncle Tom's Cabin. Knoxville: University of Tennessee Press, 1977.

Stowe, Harriet Beecher. *Uncle Tom's Cabin*. 1852. Boston: Houghton Mifflin, 1951.

Sundquist, Eric J., ed. *New Essays on Uncle Tom's Cabin*. Cambridge, UK, and New York: Cambridge University Press, 1986.

Underground Railroad

The vast, informal network of people who helped slaves escape from the American South to the American North and as far as Canada was known as the Underground Railroad. Those involved in this dangerous endeavor played a substantial role helping thousands of slaves reach freedom during the early to mid-1800s.

All slaveholding societies have had to deal with fugitives who ran away to liberate themselves from enslavement, but the situation for slaves in the United States differed from others in the transatlantic world during the period following the American Revolution. Because all of the original states from Pennsylvania northward instituted some form of gradual emancipation after the war, whereas states to the south of Pennsylvania retained slavery, the United States was fashioned from the beginning as a nation that was half slave and half free. Accordingly, the possibility that fugitive slaves from the Southern states might seek refuge in the Northern states was an issue that the founders reckoned with during the early years of the American republic.

The principle of "comity" (respect for the laws of other states) was ill defined during the period when the United States was governed by the Articles of Confederation (1781–1789). But specific language included in the U.S. Constitution made clear that Southern slaveholders had the right to claim their property should their slaves escape to free states and that Northern states were bound to respect the legality of slavery in states where it continued to exist.

These measures were further defined when Congress passed the Fugitive Slave Act of 1793, which provided a mechanism by which Southern slave owners could legally reclaim fugitives who had escaped to free territory. Although the law protected the right of Southern slaveholders to retrieve fugitives, there certainly was no universal acclaim for this practice in the Northern states. Many found the practice of "redention" (the returning of fugitives) to be morally reprehensible and vowed to take part in acts of civil disobedience that ignored the legal provisions and provided aid and comfort to escaping slaves.

Long before the term "Underground Railroad" came into common usage, the practice of aiding fugitives was a well-established fact that many Quakers and other persons of faith implemented out of benevolent necessity. Indeed, in 1786, George Washington noted that one of his runaway slaves had been helped by a "society of Quakers, formed for such purposes." In a detailed proposal that would foreshadow the Underground Railroad of the nineteenth century, Quaker Isaac T. Hopper of Philadelphia promoted a plan in 1787 whereby Northerners could aid slaves trying to escape from Southern states.

It appears that the name Underground Railroad was used for the first time to describe the system in 1831, shortly after the first appearance of the locomotive in the United States. The metaphor was apt, as the mysterious network swept fugitives away from

Information along the Underground Railroad was communicated by means of special signs and signals. The hitching post was a common means of conveying messages. A lighted lantern or a bright cloth hanging from it meant that all was clear. *(Louie Psihoyos/Science Faction/Getty Images)*

the snare of hired slave catchers and delivered them to safe destinations in free states and territories.

The metaphor was extended over time as those involved in aiding the fugitives began to describe themselves as "agents" and "conductors," while the safe houses where fugitives were kept became known as "stations." Geography dictated the most advantageous routes to freedom, and, as a result, the Underground Railroad was especially active in Pennsylvania, Ohio, Indiana, and Illinois, although all of the Northern states and territories took part in the work of aiding fugitives.

Levi Coffin of Newport, Indiana (and later Cincinnati, Ohio), was the self-described "president" of the Underground Railroad, although no formal leadership structure existed, as there was no real organization to the practice. Thomas Garrett became one of the best-known conductors in the vicinity of northern Delaware and Philadelphia.

As local abolitionist societies began to form in many of the Northern states, it became common for members of these groups to aid fugitive slaves who happened to come their way in escaping to freedom. Very few societies kept accurate records (or any records) of how many fugitives were aided, so it is difficult to estimate the total number of fugitive slaves who found assistance via the Underground Railroad. Despite the lack of comprehensive data, scholars estimate that as many as 100,000 slaves obtained some type of support in their escape through agents of the Underground Railroad.

The black abolitionist William Still, an active conductor on the Underground Railroad, began keeping statistical records of escaped fugitives in August 1850. The passenger records that Still kept are some of the best source materials available for determining the effectiveness of the Underground Railroad.

Although the work of the Underground Railroad was conducted by private individuals, it was indirectly aided by the actions of some state and local governments, which enacted measures that were designed to obstruct Southern slave catchers' efforts to retrieve fugitive slaves. In response to the Fugitive Slave Act of 1793, many Northern states had enacted so-called personal liberty laws that made the detention of fugitives problematic. Even after the U.S. Supreme Court declared personal liberty laws illegal in its *Prigg v. Pennsylvania* (1842) decision, most Northern state governments continued to ignore their obligations under the Fugitive Slave Act.

Much of the intrigue associated with the Underground Railroad stems from the remarkable figures who were associated with the effort. Perhaps none of these individuals is more impressive than Harriet Tubman, who escaped from slavery in Maryland during summer 1849. After escaping, she became active in the Underground Railroad, which helped fugitive slaves make their way to freedom in the Northern states and eventually Canada. Tubman is reported to have made nineteen trips back to the states of the Upper South, helping more than 300 slaves escape to freedom. For this heroic action, she became known as the "Moses" of her people.

In the decades following the U.S. Civil War and emancipation, much of the history of the Underground Railroad became shrouded in myth. Many individuals claimed to have been abolitionists who participated in the Underground Railroad, though the rigor of historical analysis does not always bear out these claims.

In addition, early histories of the Underground Railroad told the story from the perspective of white abolitionists, who often were portrayed as larger-than-life heroes, while the participation and involvement of free blacks and the fugitives themselves were excluded from the historical record. Over time, scholarship has pointed to the involvement of both free blacks and fugitive slaves themselves, who played a central role in their personal emancipation and then helped others on the path to freedom.

Junius P. Rodriguez

See also: Coffin, Levi; Fugitive Slave Act of 1793; Fugitive Slave Act of 1850; Fugitive Slaves; Garrett, Thomas; *Prigg v. Pennsylvania* (1842); Still, William; Tubman, Harriet.

Further Reading

Blockson, Charles L. *The Underground Railroad: First-Person Narratives of Escapes to Freedom in the North*. New York: Prentice Hall, 1987.

Bordewich, Fergus M. *Bound for Canaan: The Underground Railroad and the War for the Soul of America*. New York: Amistad, 2005.

Buckmaster, Henrietta. *Let My People Go: The Story of the Underground Railroad and the Growth of the Abolition Movement*. New York: Harper & Brothers, 1941; Columbia: University of South Carolina Press, 1992.

Cooley, Verna. "Illinois and the Underground Railroad to Canada." *Transactions of the Illinois State Historical Society* 23 (1917): 76–98.

Gara, Larry. *The Liberty Line: The Legend of the Underground Railroad*. Lexington: University Press of Kentucky, 1996.

Lumpkin, Katherine DuPre. "The General Plan Was Freedom: A Negro Secret Order on the Underground Railroad." *Phylon* 28 (Spring 1967): 63–77.

Siebert, Wilbur H. *The Underground Railroad From Slavery to Freedom*. New York: Macmillan, 1898; New York: Arno, 1968.

Still, William. *The Underground Railroad*. 1872. Chicago: Johnson, 1970; Medford, NJ: Plexus, 2005.

U.S. Colored Troops

In July 1862, the U.S. Congress passed the Militia Act, which provided for the recruitment of black soldiers. Because of reservations on the part of the Union army, ranging from lack of military success to doubts about the continued loyalty of the border states, President Abraham Lincoln refused to implement the policy. It was not until the Emancipation Proclamation, which was announced in September 1862 and took effect on January 1, 1863, that Lincoln embraced the idea.

By incorporating the U.S. Colored Troops (USCT)—the banner name given to most black units who fought in the U.S. Civil War—into the Union army, the Lincoln administration increased its manpower. It also bolstered African American demands for equality by providing an arena in which blacks could exercise their courage and patriotism on the battlefield.

Shortly after Lincoln issued the Emancipation Proclamation, the Union army launched a recruitment drive that raised a total of 165 black regiments—145 of infantry, seven of cavalry, twelve of heavy artillery, and one of engineers. Altogether, 7,122 officers and 178,895 enlisted men served in the USCT. The Union War Department established the Bureau of Colored Troops in May 1863 to oversee black recruitment and to screen applicants for commission in black regiments. The majority of USCT officers were white, although the number of African Americans eventually numbered around 110.

African American recruits encountered discrimination on many levels, starting with their monthly pay of $10—$3 less than the pay their white counterparts received. In addition, African American soldiers had $3 deducted from their monthly pay to cover the cost of clothing. Not until June 1864 did Congress pass a measure that guaranteed equal pay, though the increase applied only to men who had been free at the beginning of the war. This restriction remained in force until March 1865.

Reaction to the recruitment of the USCT was mixed throughout the North and in the Union army.

Though Lincoln viewed it as a way to sap the Confederacy's will to continue the war, Frederick Douglass interpreted the recruitment of black soldiers as a necessary step toward full citizenship for African Americans. General Ulysses S. Grant argued that the enlistment would be one in a series of steps in which blacks' actions would disabuse whites of their racial notions and stereotypes. Understood in a military context, Grant believed, the recruitment was part of a broader mobilization of all available resources to achieve victory. Although General William T. Sherman was privately dissatisfied with the policy, he remained silent in public.

It is impossible to generalize in reference to the reaction among white Union soldiers. Some protested so loudly that they were expelled from the service. Others remained skeptical as to whether blacks could exercise the skills necessary for successful battlefield performance.

Questions surrounding the effectiveness of black soldiers initially kept them away from combat. Many Union generals thought the USCT should be used exclusively as labor and garrison battalions. Many of the units were issued inferior weapons, and their overall care was second rate, as black regiments lost 29,000 men to disease, nine times as many as perished from wounds. Part of the problem can be traced to the federal commanders' decision to station the USCT units in the unhealthiest posts; they justified this move on the grounds that blacks possessed a special resilience to diseases prevalent on the coast and along rivers and swamps. In addition, African American soldiers were supplied with inferior medical facilities and care.

In May 1863, the new units saw combat. That month, two black Union regiments from Louisiana assaulted Port Hudson. On June 7, Confederates attacked a training camp for black recruits at Milliken's Bend, Louisiana. Perhaps the most famous engagement involving black soldiers took place at Battery Wagner, South Carolina, in July 1863. Throughout the spring and early summer, the Union high command had tried to gain a foothold near Charleston Harbor. Attempts to secure the beachhead had failed, leading to a joint expedition in July during which the army would attempt to secure several outlying forts while the navy followed with a forced entrance into the harbor.

The capture of Battery Wagner, located south of the harbor, was essential to the success of the operation. When it did not fall to naval bombardment, Union commanders planned a ground attack at night. Leading the attack was the Fifty-fourth Regiment of the Massachusetts Volunteer Infantry, which was composed of free blacks and former slaves under the command of Colonel Robert Gould Shaw. Shaw firmly believed that the only way to silence critics of emancipation and those skeptical of black soldiers' fighting abilities was to show that they could indeed fight for their freedom. The regiment commenced its attack on the night of July 18. In the assault that followed, the Fifty-fourth Regiment failed to take the fort and suffered heavy casualties; among them was Shaw, who was killed in the attack.

The events at Port Hudson, Milliken's Bend, and Battery Wagner provided evidence that not only could African Americans fight for their freedom, but they could fight on the same level as whites and were willing to die for their cause. Although the performance of blacks on the battlefields altered the perception of their white comrades, black soldiers' performance in combat had a minimal effect on broader racial prejudice of the time.

In reaction to the recruitment of African American soldiers, Confederate officials warned that captured black soldiers would be re-enslaved or executed and that USCT officers could expect to be treated as war criminals for inciting slave insurrection. Lincoln's threat that Union troops would respond in kind against Confederate prisoners of war forced the Richmond authorities to back off of this policy in 1863. Authorities in Richmond could not, however, stop Confederate soldiers from killing black soldiers on the spot rather than taking them as prisoners of war.

On April 12, 1864, at Fort Pillow, Tennessee, along the Mississippi River, a Confederate force under the command of Nathan Bedford Forrest attacked and captured the fort, which was manned in part by black soldiers. Though the events that followed are still open to speculation, it seems apparent that Confederate cavalrymen gunned down blacks who were attempting to surrender. The evidence suggests that Forrest did not give the order himself but that he probably was not disturbed by it, as he had already made public his belief that the battle would show that USCT could not stand up to Southerners.

Fort Pillow was but one instance in which USCT soldiers experienced mistreatment at the hands of Confederates. In July 1864, black soldiers in the division led by Brigadier General Edward Ferrero were massacred at the Battle of the Crater during the Petersburg siege. In October of the same year, Confederates put black prisoners of war to work on fortifications at Petersburg, within range of Union artillery.

By the end of the war, African Americans made up 12 percent of the Union army. They participated in more than forty major battles and close to 500 other actions. Roughly 37,000 black soldiers died in service.

The USCT proved invaluable to the Union cause. At a time when half of all recruits refused to re-enlist, new sources of manpower were critical to the Northern war effort. The U.S. Colored Troops both filled the demand and contributed significantly to the defeat of the Confederacy.

Kevin M. Levin

See also: Civil War, American (1861–1865); Lincoln, Abraham; Massachusetts Fifty-Fourth Regiment.

Further Reading

Glatthaar, Joseph T. *Forged in Battle: The Civil War Alliance of Black Soldiers and White Officers.* New York: Free Press, 1990; Baton Rouge: Louisiana State University Press, 2000.

McPherson, James M. *The Negro's Civil War: How American Negroes Felt and Acted During the War for the Union.* Urbana: University of Illinois Press, 1965.

Smith, John David, ed. *Black Soldiers in Blue: African American Troops in the Civil War Era.* Chapel Hill: University of North Carolina Press, 2003.

Trudeau, Noah A. *Like Men of War: Black Troops in the Civil War, 1862–1865.* Boston: Little, Brown, 1998.

Wilson, Keith P. *Campfires of Freedom: The Camp Life of Black Soldiers During the Civil War.* Kent, OH: Kent State University Press, 2002.

U.S. Constitution (1789)

The issue of slavery influenced the creation and history of the government of the United States. The first frame of American government, the Articles of Confederation (ratified and in force 1781), contained a scant reference to slavery, proportionate to the limited amount of political power the document granted to the national government. The weaknesses of the Articles had become apparent by summer 1787, when the Constitutional Convention convened in Philadelphia to create a new frame of government.

The amount of national power under the proposed Constitution was considerably greater than that granted under the Articles, which emphasized state sovereignty, and Southern delegates were concerned that a national government with enlarged powers might threaten the institution of slavery. At one point, James Madison even proposed a bicameral legislature in which one house would be based on free population and the other based on both free and slave population, but this suggestion did not receive serious consideration. America's internal divisions—political, social, and moral—were demonstrated as the delegates sought compromises to overcome great differences. What emerged from the debate was a document that contained three compromise provisions that dealt directly with slavery and five provisions that dealt with it indirectly. Each offered some form of protection to the institution.

Much of the political debate about slavery at the Constitutional Convention focused on the question of representation in the U.S. Congress. Once the decision was made to establish a bicameral legislature with equal representation in one house and proportional representation based on state population in the other, Southern delegates began to argue that the slave states should be allowed to count their slaves as part of their population. They contended that if only the white population was counted, they would always be outvoted in the House of Representatives by the more populous Northern states, which had much larger white populations. The Northern states argued that if slaves were considered property, then they could not be counted when determining the number of representatives states could send to the House. Resolution came through compromise.

Direct Provisions Regarding Slavery

The first direct provision regarding slavery to be included in the Constitution was commonly known as the "three-fifths compromise." According to Article I, Section 2 of the Constitution, "Representatives and direct Taxes shall be apportioned among the several States which may be included within this Union, according to their respective Numbers, which shall be determined by adding to the whole Number of free Persons, including those bound to Service for a Term of Years, and excluding Indians not taxed, three fifths of all other Persons." For the purposes of determining the number of representatives that each state could send to the House, each slave would count as three-fifths of a person.

The choice of three-fifths as the proportion was not arbitrary. The fraction was known as the "federal ratio" and had been considered in 1783 during a debate on a proposed amendment to the Articles of Confederation. The Northern states had argued that slaves should be counted for the purposes of apportioning expenses among the states, whereas the Southern states held that they should not because slaves were property. In the end, it was decided that three-fifths of the slaves would be counted.

The importance of representation resonated over the next half century, as new states were added to the Union. When the balance of slave states and free states in Congress was threatened by the addition of a new state, intense political debate resulted. The Missouri Compromise (1820) and the Compromise of 1850 were outcomes of this tension. The three-fifths compromise was rendered obsolete by the ratification of the Thirteenth Amendment in 1865.

The second direct provision eased Southern concerns that the new Congress might try to suffocate the institution of slavery by prohibiting the slave trade. Again, compromise resolved the issue. Article I, Section 9 protected the slave trade for twenty years after the ratification of the Constitution: "The Migration or Importation of such Persons as any of the States now existing shall think proper to admit, shall not be prohibited by the Congress prior to the Year one thousand eight hundred and eight, but a Tax or duty may be imposed on such Importation, not exceeding ten dollars for each Person." Although Congress banned the slave trade in 1808, the illegal trade in slaves continued until the eve of the U.S. Civil War.

Runaway slaves were addressed by the third direct provision regarding slavery in the Constitution. Article IV, Section 2 stated, "No Person held to Service or Labour in one State, under the Laws thereof, escaping into another, shall, in Consequence of any Law or Regulation therein, be discharged from such Service or Labour, but shall be delivered up on Claim of the Party to whom such Service or Labour may be due."

During the antebellum period, the maturation of the abolitionist movement and the success of runaway slave networks such as the Underground Railroad stimulated a Southern response in Congress. A stronger Fugitive Slave Act was passed by Congress as part of the Compromise of 1850.

Indirect Provisions

The first indirect provision authorized the government to suppress domestic insurrections by raising a militia. Among the powers granted to Congress by Article I, Section 8 was the authority "[t]o provide for calling forth the Militia to execute the Laws of the Union, suppress Insurrections and repel Invasions." This provision empowered the government to use force to crush slave uprisings, a perpetual fear in the South.

The second indirect provision, articulated in Article I, Section 9, protected the fruits of slave labor by prohibiting the government from levying export duties: "No Tax or Duty shall be laid on Articles exported from any State." This language ensured that the economic benefits of slavery would be protected from federal legislative action.

The third indirect provision can be found in the structure of the electoral college. Under this system, each state is apportioned a number of electors equal to the number of senators and representatives that state has in Congress. The three-fifths compromise inflated the Southern vote in the electoral college, offering some protection of slavery by executive action.

Article V contains the fourth indirect provision. Amending the Constitution requires the approval of three-fourths of the states, granting Southern states effective veto power over any potential amendment that would aim to ban slavery. Only two parts of the Constitution were specifically protected from alteration or elimination by future amendment: each state's right to equal representation in the Senate and the clauses dealing with the slave trade in Section 9 of Article I.

The fifth indirect provision regarding slavery, contained in Article IV, Section 2, excludes noncitizens from the legal rights granted by the Constitution and by state governments: "The Citizens of each State shall be entitled to all Privileges and Immunities of Citizens in the several States."

One of the privileges of citizenship is the right to sue in court, an issue that featured prominently in the U.S. Supreme Court case of *Dred Scott v. Sandford* (1857). Scott, a slave who had lived in the free state of Illinois and the free territory of Wisconsin, had appealed to the Supreme Court in the hope of being granted his freedom. The Court ruled that because Scott was black, he was not, in fact, a citizen of the United States, and therefore he had no right to sue in court.

The *Dred Scott* decision was a victory for proslavery forces in the years leading up to the Civil War. It would not be until the ratification of the Constitution's Thirteenth, Fourteenth, and Fifteenth amendments—which outlawed slavery, granted citizenship to blacks, and guaranteed voting rights to blacks, respectively—that issues of freedom and equality for African Americans would be addressed.

Scott Wignall

See also: Amendments, Reconstruction; *Dred Scott* Case (1857); Fugitive Slave Act of 1793; Fugitive Slave Act of 1850; Missouri Compromise (1820); Personal Liberty Laws.

Further Reading

Alvis, John. "The Slavery Provisions of the U.S. Constitution: Means for Emancipation." *Political Science Reviewer* 17 (Spring 1987): 241–65.

Commanger, Henry Steele. "Constitutional History and Higher Law." *Pennsylvania Magazine of History and Biography* 62 (January 1938): 20–40.

Cover, Robert. *Justice Accused: Antislavery and the Judicial Process.* New Haven, CT: Yale University Press, 1975.

Morriss, Thomas D. *Free Men All: The Personal Liberty Laws of the North, 1780–1861.* Baltimore: Johns Hopkins University Press, 1974.

Tushnet, Mark V. *The American Law of Slavery, 1810–1860: Considerations of Humanity and Interest.* Princeton, NJ: Princeton University Press, 1981.

Wiecek, William M. *The Sources of Antislavery Constitutionalism in America, 1760–1848.* Ithaca, NY: Cornell University Press, 1977.

Valdés, Gabriel de la Concepción (1809–1844)

Celebrated for his Romantic writings, the Cuban poet Gabriel de la Concepción Valdés—known as Plácido—is also remembered for his legendary death at the hands of a colonial administration bent on suppressing an antislavery revolt on the island in 1843.

Valdés was born in Havana, Cuba, on March 18, 1809, the illegitimate son of a white Spanish dancer, Concepción Vázquez, and a mulatto hairdresser, Diego Ferrer Matoso. As an infant, he was left by his mother at the Casa de Beneficencia y Maternidad, where he was given the name of the orphanage's founder, Valdés. Relatives on his father's side took care of him. Although he had little formal schooling, he wrote his first poem, "A una bella" (To a Beauty) at the age of twelve.

Having started his literary career at an early age, Valdés renamed himself Plácido (meaning "placid" or "serene"), after the novel of the same name by Madame de Genlis. He would grow up to become one of the elite manumitted Creole blacks and a poet. Distinguished by his high hairline, light skin, and pencil-thin mustache, he cut a striking figure in Cuban colonial society. Apart from writing poetry, he made a living fashioning hair combs and typesetting between 1826 and 1832. He would go on to publish almost all of his writings in the periodicals of Matanzas and Villa Clara.

In 1834, Plácido won first prize in the Fête de Aroyo Apolo, a celebration held in honor of the liberal Spanish poet Francisco Martínez de la Rosa; his winning entry was the octosyllabic "La siempreviva" (Everlasting Flower). In 1837, he worked for the newspaper *La Aurora de Matanzas*, drawing his salary for writing a poem a week. He published his first book, *Poesías de Plácido*, in 1838, and his second, *Poesías escojidas de Plácido*, in 1842. He was later credited with the ballad "Jicoténcal" and the sonnet "La flor de la caña" (The Flower of the Cane).

An admirer of the Romantics Quintana and Martínez de la Rosa, Plácido read deeply in the literature of abolitionism and liberal ideology. A free mulatto, Plácido formulated his own solution to the racial question: It lay in the integration of the races, a celebration of hybridity that regarded the European Hispanic as the foundation of a multiethnic nation that included the African component in its *unión sagrada* (sacred union).

To express his abolitionist views, Plácido resorted to writing fables. In his poem "El Juramento" (The Oath), said to have been improvised in the company of friends, he speaks of drinking from a fountain in the shade of a tree in a "wide valley." There, at the "altar" and "[b]efore the sacred code of life," he swears to fight tyranny, at the sacrifice of his own life if necessary, "in order to break the yoke."

Plácido published the chivalric tale *El hijo de maldición* in 1843. The same year, he was accused of involvement in the Conspiración de la Escalera (Ladder Conspiracy), a major slave revolt and abolitionist uprising. The investigation revealed that a conspiracy instigated by British abolitionist and consul David Turnbull had drawn the poet into its plot: In 1841, Plácido had hid Turnbull's agent from Santo Domingo, Luis Gigaut (known as Jigó), the founder of the Matanzas cell of the revolt, in his house at Matanzas and later introduced him to other *gente de color* (people of color) sympathetic to the twin causes of abolition and independence.

Subsequent to Plácido's arrest, in 1844, the government responded to the rumors of conspiracy by unleashing a campaign of terror against the upper class of mulattoes and manumitted slaves. Innocents and subversives alike were persecuted under the preemptive operation, which consisted of arrests, executions, and exiles. The *pardos* and *morenos libres* (free blacks and mulattoes), even those who had joined the militia and held the rank of officer, were the targets of suits, accused of attending secret meetings and denounced for selling paraphernalia for the purpose of witchcraft.

By summer 1843, Plácido was jailed in La Ferrolana de Trinidad, where he would remain until October of that year. As part of the so-called Ladder Conspiracy, he and others were falsely accused of collaboration with Miguel Flores and other Havana blacks who led the revolt against the island's whites, for he indeed belonged to (but did not frequent) the abolitionist circle of Cuban patriot Domingo del Monte. At his trial, Plácido admitted only to sheltering Jigó and attending clandestine meetings, denying any deeper involvement in the conspiracy and rejecting the accusation that he harbored any racist hatred against the whites. Nevertheless, he was implicated in the secret plot along with those whom Jigó had recruited.

The irony of the sentence lay in the fact that Plácido had always advocated racial integration and harmony. His poem "Plegaria a Dios" (Supplication to God) referred to the accusation as a *sello ignominioso* (ignominious seal) and a *mancha* (stain) that he refused to accept.

He reflected on his own merciless destiny in the poem "La fatalidad" (Fatality): "Devoid of any clemency of pity / thou hast with spines encircled me, blind Deity, / As a font whose marge displays for its array / the thorny, pungent cacti and wild maguey." Here, the poet regards himself as a source or spring surrounded by adversity.

Plácido was executed by firing squad, along with other mulattoes of Matanzas, on June 28, 1844.

Eugenio Matibag

See also: Cuba, Abolition in.

Further Reading

Anderson Imbert, Enrique. *Spanish-American Literature: A History.* Trans. John V. Falconieri. Detroit, MI: Wayne State University Press, 1963.

Paquette, Robert. *Sugar Is Made With Blood: The Conspiracy of La Escalera and the Conflict Between Empires Over Slavery in Cuba.* Middletown, CT: Wesleyan University Press, 1988.

Van Buren, Martin (1782–1862)

The eighth president of the United States (1837–1841), Martin Van Buren faced increasing challenges, as slavery became a contentious political issue in national affairs. The institution of the congressional Gag Rule, which prohibited the discussion of antislavery petitions, and the capture of the slave ship *Amistad* heightened tensions during his administration.

Van Buren was born on December 5, 1782. His father, Abraham, was a tavern keeper and slave-owning farmer in a small Dutch village called Kinderhook, lo-

cated on the Hudson River in New York. Van Buren's love of politics grew out of his listening to political conversations between tavern patrons, such as Aaron Burr and Alexander Hamilton, who often stopped in for a drink as they traveled between New York City and Albany. Likewise, his proslavery sentiments were forged by the experience of growing up in a slaveholding household.

Van Buren worked as a lawyer for a brief time before devoting himself completely to politics. During the presidency of Andrew Jackson, Van Buren served as vice president from 1833 to 1837, and with Jackson's strong endorsement, he ran for president in 1836.

The twin issues of territorial expansion and the possible spread of slavery played an important role

Slavery became an increasingly contentious national issue during the presidency of Martin Van Buren (1837–1841). A Democrat from New York, he opposed the expansion of slavery but vowed to resist federal intervention in the South. *(Getty Images News/Getty Images)*

in the 1836 campaign. That same year, Texans won the Battle of San Jacinto, the last major battle of the Texas Revolution, and they immediately applied for admission into the Union. But Jackson did not want to upset Northern voters (and Van Buren's chances of being elected) by adding more Southern territory to the Union during an election year. Furthermore, he was concerned that the annexation of Texas could lead to war with Mexico, which did not recognize the independence of its former territory. Jackson and Van Buren thought it wise to preserve the balance between free and slave states under the Missouri Compromise (1820), and both opposed the annexation of Texas.

During the presidential campaign, Van Buren believed that Jackson's popularity and support would be enough to guarantee a win at the polls, and he avoided the slavery issue by not adopting the Democratic Party platform. The maneuver worked, but the slavery issue did not go away.

At his inauguration, Van Buren attempted to address the growing problem in a way that would placate both Northern abolitionists and Southern slaveholders. He stated that he would block any attempt to abolish slavery in the District of Columbia and in the South; in his opinion, the Southern states had the right to decide the matter for themselves. Likewise, he indicated, the Northern states could refuse to allow slavery within their borders. Van Buren sought to preserve the status quo, fearing that a change in the balance might endanger the Union.

During his presidency, Van Buren was confronted with the *Amistad* case as the Justice Department determined how to proceed in the matter. Prior to *Dred Scott v. Sandford* (1857), *Amistad* was the most important legal case involving slavery to date. In this case, the slave ship *Amistad* was seized in 1839 by an American vessel off the coast of Long Island. It was discovered that fifty-three Africans, who had been purchased illegally as slaves, had killed two men and taken control of the ship that was bound for Cuba. Hoping to brush the matter aside quickly, Van Buren favored extraditing the Africans to Cuba. Abolitionists, however, pushed for a trial in the United States. Former president John Quincy Adams defended the African captives before the U.S. Supreme Court in 1841 and won their freedom.

Van Buren's refusal to annex Texas, a slave state, coupled with the economic panic of 1837, cost him re-election in 1840. In 1844, President

John Tyler and President-Elect James K. Polk both favored annexation.

Van Buren responded by becoming the leader of the Free Soil Party, which opposed slavery in the new Western territories. In 1848, he ran unsuccessfully for president as the Free Soil candidate. He died on July 24, 1862.

Rolando Avila

See also: *Amistad* Case (1841); Free Soil Party; Gag Resolution.

Further Reading

Wilson, Major L. *The Presidency of Martin Van Buren.* Lawrence: University of Kansas, 1984.

Varela y Morales, Félix (1788–1853)

The Cuban priest, social activist, and humanitarian Félix Varela y Morales was an antislavery polemicist for whom the causes of abolition and independence were inseparable. His provocative writings influenced the Cuban patriot José Martí, who called Varela "the one who first taught us to think."

Varela was born in Havana, Cuba, on November 20, 1788. The son of a Spanish officer stationed in Saint Augustine, Florida, Varela lived there for his first fourteen years but returned to Cuba when his father was transferred to the island. Varela then entered the San Carlos y San Ambrosio Seminary, excelling in its curriculum of Latin and philosophy under the direction of Padre José Agustín Caballero, a Creole opponent of slavery.

Joining what would later be called the "Creole revolution" on the island, Varela learned the doctrine of political autonomy and emancipation not only from Caballero but also from his mentor, Juan José Díaz de Espada, the Basque social reformer and bishop of Havana. The liberal Díaz, a follower of the French physiocrats and the *iluminismo* of statesman and author Gaspar Melchor de Jovellanos, was responsible for developing the Seminary of San Carlos. Varela went on to earn a bachelor's degree in theology at the University of Havana, and, in 1811, he was ordained as a Roman Catholic priest. Soon thereafter, he came to occupy the chair of professor of philosophy at San Carlos.

As a professor in the seminary, the center of intellectual reform and modernization in Havana, Varela taught philosophy, ethics, and physics. He disseminated his liberal ideas in the classroom—where his students included José Antonio Saco, who would later replace him in the chair, as well as Domingo del Monte and José de la Luz y Caballero—and in his extensive philosophical writings and plays.

In 1817, Varela joined the *Real Sociedad Económica* (Royal Economic Society) and was awarded the title *socio de mérito* (member of honor). He published abolitionist speeches and articles in the *Diario de Gobierno*, *El Observador Habanero*, and *Memorias de la Real Sociedad Económica de La Habana*. Synthesizing and applying ideas from the authors of the French Enlightenment, the North American abolitionists, and the Spanish liberals of the period, Varela characterized the perspective of free Cubans of color in this fashion:

The image of their enslaved cohorts [*semejantes*] torments them, because it recalls the opprobrium with which one looks upon their origin, and it is very natural that these men endeavor by all means to remove that obstacle to their happiness by liberating their equals.

Encouraged by Díaz, Varela campaigned for election as a representative in the Spanish Cortes (Parliament). He was elected deputy on May 13, 1821, but then hesitated to carry out his office: He refused to advance the proslavery agenda of the aristocracy that supported him in the consulate and the Havana City Council. Varela declared that he would not serve the interests of the wealthy commercial and landowning class but instead would serve those of *la patria* (the country or fatherland), declaring his ardent opposition to slavery. Besides the error that whites committed in regarding blacks as inferior brutes, he warned of the danger, should slavery continue in Cuba, of provoking the kind of upheaval that had overwhelmed the French colony of Saint-Domingue. Varela eventually accepted his seat in the legislature but continued his work as a radical abolitionist.

In the Cortes, Varela proposed abolition along with independence for the nations of Latin America. In 1822, he published the political essay "*Observaciones sobre la constitución política de la monarquía española*" (Observations on the Political Constitution of the Spanish Monarchy). In his speeches, he identified the anticolonial struggle with the cause of emancipation: "Constitution, liberty, equality are synonyms," he wrote in *Memorias sobre la Esclavitud* (1822), drawing on the Enlightenment doctrine of natural rights.

Varela's antislavery views thus followed rationalist and democratic lines: Cubans, for the most part (predominantly mulatto or black at this time), wanted freedom for slaves, he argued; the interests of the slave owners and the "the security of the public order" were protected in the call to end slavery on the island. On this latter point he erred—at least one gentleman called for the deputy's tongue to be pulled out—and roused the ire of King Fernando VII, who ordered his arrest and imprisonment.

For his advocacy of emancipation, Varela was accused and tried for sedition in 1822. Later that same year, he rejected an offer of amnesty from the Spanish government, refusing to abjure his pro-independence stance as a condition of the pardon. Sentenced to death, he escaped to Gibraltar and then to New York. He lived the rest of his life in the United States.

Life in North America did not stop Varela's activism. In Philadelphia, this forefather of Cuban abolitionism published the newspaper *El Habanero*—which returnees introduced as contraband in Cuba—and from which the writer castigated the sugar aristocracy of Cuba and its mercantile mentality. Varela also collaborated with José Antonio Saco to edit *El Mensajero Semanal*, a weekly newspaper that sent word of abolitionism back to Cuba and other Hispanic countries. He used the paper to defend Catholicism against Protestant attacks in the periodical the *Protestant Abridger and Annotator*.

In addition, Varela collaborated on the journals *El Revisor Político y Literario*, *Revista Bimestre Cubana*, and *La Moda*; he founded orphanages, schools, and churches; and he participated in a host of church-related programs. In 1837, he was named vicar of New York, and, in 1841, he earned his doctorate in theology. He also worked with Charles C. Pise to edit the monthly *Catholic Expositor and Literary Magazine*.

In the 1840s, Varela published a number of articles on religious subjects, including the series *Cartas a Elpidio* (Letters to Elpidio), which attacked superstition and fanaticism. He also produced articles on pedagogy, made translations of parliamentary procedures texts, and published the first edition of Manuel de Zequeira's book of poetry.

In declining health, Varela left New York City for Saint Augustine, where he had been raised. He died there on February 25, 1853.

In the 1990s, a movement to canonize him arose within the church, and a postage stamp was issued in his honor in the United States. Today, the Félix

Varela Cultural Award, given for the highest achievements in the arts, commemorates the clergyman's contribution to Cuba's humanistic heritage. In 2002, a Cuban dissident group named in his honor, Proyecto Varela, submitted a petition with 11,000 signatures to Fidel Castro's government demanding democratic reforms in Cuba. Varela's biographer, Antonio Hernández Travieso, has called him "the one who forged the Cuban conscience."

Eugenio Matibag

See also: Cuba, Abolition in.

Further Reading

Levinson, Sandra. "Talking About Cuban Culture: A Reporter's Notebook." In *The Cuba Reader: The Making of A Revolutionary Society,* eds. Philip Brenner, William M. Leogrande, Donna Rich, and Daniel Siegel. New York: Grove, 1989.
Martínez-Fernández, Luis, D.H. Figueredo, Louis A. Perez, Jr., and Luis González, eds. *Encyclopedia of Cuba.* Vol. 1, *People, History, Culture.* Westport, CT: Greenwood, 2003.

Vaux, Roberts (1786–1836)

Quaker activist Roberts Vaux was one of the most active members of the Pennsylvania Abolition Society. He authored the biographies of several leading abolitionists, including Benjamin Lay, Ralph Sandiford, and Anthony Benezet.

Vaux was born on January 21, 1786, the son of a wealthy Philadelphia merchant who died when the boy was four years old. Vaux's education included both private tutors and attendance at the Friends Select Academy. He was apprenticed to a Philadelphia countinghouse in 1802 and opened his own dry goods business in 1807. Following the deaths of his sister and mother, Vaux determined to devote his life solely to humanitarian concerns. His inheritance provided him with the means to close his business in 1814 and immerse himself in the cause of improving society.

During his career in public service, Vaux participated in thirty-six local and state organizations and held memberships in eleven groups located outside Pennsylvania. Though Vaux is best remembered for his role in creating the public school system and his work in the field of penal reform, he was also active in the antislavery movement and became a member of the Pennsylvania Abolition Society in 1807.

Although Pennsylvania had passed its Gradual Abolition Act in 1780, the Pennsylvania Abolition Society offered assistance to free blacks, petitioned legislatures, lobbied individual politicians, and circulated pamphlets in an effort to persuade others to oppose slavery. Vaux served as corresponding secretary of the society for two years and worked on committees concerned with fraudulent enslavement and education for freed blacks. In 1809 and 1812, he represented the society at the conventions of various antislavery societies, and, in 1813, he helped found a school for black children in Philadelphia.

In addition to his work with the Pennsylvania Abolition Society, Vaux wrote biographies of the early Quaker abolitionists. His *Memoirs of the Lives of Benjamin Lay and Ralph Sandiford* was published in 1815, followed two years later by *Memoirs of the Life of Anthony Benezet.* It is evident that Vaux modeled himself after these men and hoped their pioneering work in the abolitionist movement would inspire others. In his biography of Benezet, Vaux outlined his own plan for ending slavery, calling for the passage of gradual emancipation laws that would give slaves adequate time to prepare for a life of freedom. Because the free states were so unwelcoming to former slaves, Vaux believed it would be necessary to settle them in some territory under U.S. authority or send them to Africa.

Vaux also became actively involved in efforts to prevent the expansion of slavery. In 1819, as the U.S. Congress debated Missouri's admission into the Union, he organized a public meeting in Philadelphia to support a free Missouri, and he successfully lobbied the Pennsylvania legislature to pass a resolution in favor of the same.

In 1823, when proslavery forces in Illinois began a movement to call a new constitutional convention for the purpose of allowing slavery, Vaux provided valuable aid to Edward Coles, the antislavery governor of that state. In addition to writing a pamphlet that pointed out the disastrous economic consequences of slavery, he commissioned two others and subsidized their publication. Illinois voters rejected the proposed convention in an 1824 referendum.

Despite the victory in Illinois, Vaux became increasingly disheartened by the antislavery movement's lack of progress. After representing the Pennsylvania Abolition Society at a national convention of antislavery societies in 1824, he largely withdrew from the movement.

Although Vaux feared widespread slave rebellions and believed that racial prejudice would prevent former slaves from achieving true equality in the United States, he did not join the American Colonization Society. He also remained unwilling to abandon his gradual, moderate approach and adopt the more revolutionary methods espoused by immediatist groups such as the American Anti-Slavery Society. He died on January 7, 1836.

Matt Norman

See also: Benezet, Anthony; Coles, Edward; Lay, Benjamin; Quakers (Society of Friends).

Further Reading

Drake, Thomas. *Quakers and Slavery in America.* New Haven, CT: Yale University Press. 1950.
Soderlund, Jean R. *Quakers and Slavery: A Divided Spirit.* Princeton, NJ: Princeton University Press, 1985.

Veney, Bethany (ca. 1815–?)

Bethany "Aunt Betty" Veney was a black woman who spent forty-three years as a slave in Virginia before gaining her freedom in 1858. Four decades later, she dictated her life story to a writer, known only as M.W.G., who produced a brief biography, *The Narrative of Bethany Veney, A Slave Woman* (1889). Published more than twenty years after slavery was abolished in the United States, Veney's narrative was intended to remind African Americans of the horrors of slavery. Her story motivated others to continue the struggle for social, political, and economic equality for freedmen and their descendants.

Veney was born around 1815 on James Fletcher's plantation in Luray, Virginia, near the Blue Ridge Mountains. Veney was owned by at least three masters, all of whom lived in or near the town of Luray. Though she described her life as "uneventful," it was filled with enough tragedy to move even the hard-hearted to tears. Under slavery, wives and husbands were regularly separated, and mothers were torn from their children when plantation property was settled through wills or public auctions to pay the debts of insolvent masters.

The narrative presents a candid view of social classes in the antebellum South. Veney described free blacks as "the one class despised by everybody." She explained that slave owners despised free blacks because "they could not subject them to their will quite in the same way as if they were slaves," whereas slaves hated them for "possessing a nominal freedom . . . [slaves] were denied."

Veney also described the complex economic relationships that sometimes formed in the days of slavery. Her third owner trusted her enough to allow her to hire herself out in the community as a washerwoman, housekeeper, and cook. As long as she provided $30 per month to her owner, she was permitted to keep the remainder of the money for herself.

Veney and her son Joe became free on December 27, 1858, when an antislavery sympathizer named G.J. Adams purchased the pair from their Virginia owner for $775, with the plan of relocating them to Rhode Island, where they would be emancipated. Veney established her first free homestead in Providence, Rhode Island. Though she cherished her freedom, she felt some remorse that she was so distant from her family and familiar surroundings. Despite these misgivings, she noted: "Never could I forget to be grateful for my escape from a system under which I had suffered so much."

In the years following the U.S. Civil War, Veney returned to Virginia on four occasions to visit former slaves and slave owners, as well as to locate long-lost family members. As a result of her visits, she was able to convince sixteen members of her extended family to return with her to the North.

Narratives such as Veney's are as important for what they include as what they omit. She mentions that she was able to escape from Virginia before the reaction to John Brown's failed raid at Harpers Ferry in 1859. Her narrative makes no mention of Nat Turner and the local response to his insurrection, but the Blue Ridge Mountains were a world away from Southampton County, where Turner's rebellion took place.

Several individuals provided testimonials to the sincerity and authenticity of the text. The Reverend Bishop Willard Francis Mallalieu of the Methodist Episcopal Church in New Orleans wrote the introduction, attesting to the historical importance of Veney's story. In the preface, M.W.G. comments that the truest value of the work is that it may inspire "the generation now coming upon the stage of action," those who were already one generation removed from slavery but living in a society defined by Jim Crow segregation. V.A. and Elizabeth Cooper, Veney's former pastor and his wife, suggest one course of action, noting "the simplest act of justice [would be] to pension all the remaining slaves."

Junius P. Rodriguez

See also: Manumission.

Further Reading

Blassingame, John W., ed. *Slave Testimony: Two Centuries of Letters, Speeches, Interviews, and Autobiographies.* Baton Rouge: Louisiana State University Press, 1977.

Davis, Charles T., and Henry Louis Gates, Jr., eds. *The Slave's Narrative.* New York: Oxford University Press, 1985.

Vermont Constitution (1777)

The constitution of Vermont was the first state constitution to prohibit slavery. In the years between the American Revolution and the U.S. Civil War, the state of Vermont was home to a strong antislavery movement, and it became one of the main transit lines on the Underground Railroad.

The state of Vermont was formed out of a disputed section of land between Lake Champlain and the Connecticut River that was known as the New Hampshire Grants. The region was claimed by New York, but the majority of the settlers who lived there had come from New England. By 1775, they had formed a small army to resist "Yorker" authority in their territory.

Finally, in July 1777, a group of settlers met at Windsor to declare an independent republic and write a constitution. Vermont maintained its status as an independent republic until 1791, when it was admitted to the Union as the fourteenth state. The state's constitution, adopted on July 9, 1793, retained the wording of the 1777 constitution with regard to slavery.

Chapter 1, Article 1 of the Vermont Constitution, which is titled "A Declaration of the Rights of the Inhabitants of the State of Vermont," reads as follows,

> That all men are born equally free and independent, and have certain natural, inherent and unalienable rights, amongst which are enjoying and defending life and liberty; acquiring, possessing and protecting property, and pursuing and obtaining happiness and safety. Therefore, no male person, born in this country, or brought from over sea, ought to be holden by law, to serve any person, as a servant, slave or apprentice, after he arrives to the age of twenty-one Years, nor female, in like manner, after she arrives to the age of eighteen years, unless they are bound by their own consent, after they arrive to such an age, or bound by law, for the payments of debts, damages, fines, costs, or the like.

The constitution granted immediate manumission to any slave residing in the new state. It also prohibited anyone held as a slave in another state to continue to be held in bondage after moving to Vermont.

The constitution's Declaration of Rights was extraordinary by the standards of its time. Vermont's founders were guided by the same Enlightenment principles that influenced lawmakers across colonial America, but they stated these principles much more forthrightly than many others. Many Enlightenment thinkers believed in the abstract notion of the natural rights of man, but few were willing to codify those rights in a document that granted equality to all men, regardless of social rank, and fewer still were willing to extend those rights to people of color.

On the other hand, Vermont's founders did not lose sight of the practical realities of government. Age limits ensured that children under a specified age could be "bound out" as laborers (and thus kept off the state's dole), and the constitution did not prohibit the state from requiring debtors to enter involuntary servitude in order to repay creditors. These provisions allowed some blacks to be held in bondage for such specific reasons.

Although the Vermont constitution was certainly an important step forward in the abolitionist movement, there is little evidence that the document actually freed any slaves. The only evidence to the contrary is a 1790 census that lists sixteen slaves living in Bennington County. That particular county borders on both Massachusetts (which did not abolish slavery until 1783) and New York State (which did not abolish slavery until 1799); in theory, some settlers could have kept their slaves when they moved into Vermont. Other evidence contradicts the census, however, and, in 1870, a Vermonter who happened to be chief clerk of the Census Bureau changed the record to list the slaves as "free blacks."

Heather K. Michon

See also: Enlightenment; Manumission; Underground Railroad.

Further Reading

Jones, Matt B. *Vermont in the Making, 1750–1777.* Hamden, CT: Archon, 1968.

Melish, Joanne Pope. *Disowning Slavery: Gradual Emancipation and "Race" in New England, 1780–1860.* Ithaca, NY: Cornell University Press, 1998.

Sherman, Michael, ed. *A More Perfect Union: Vermont Becomes a State, 1777–1816.* Montpelier: Vermont Historical Society, 1991.

Vesey, Denmark (ca. 1767–1822)

As a former slave who had purchased his freedom, Denmark Vesey was able to travel freely in and around Charleston, South Carolina. He used his freedom of movement and association with free blacks and slaves to organize a vast conspiracy that was designed to foment a slave insurrection in Charleston in 1822.

Though he spent the majority of his life in Charleston, Vesey's ideas, activities, and experiences are best understood in a broader transatlantic context. He was born either in the Caribbean or in Africa sometime between 1767 and 1770, and he spent much of his childhood aboard commercial vessels traveling between Africa, the Caribbean, and the mainland United States. Historians believe that during this time, he was called Telemaque—Denmark may have been a corruption of this name that was recorded upon his arrival in Charleston. Ship captain Joseph Vesey purchased Denmark in the Caribbean in 1781 and settled in Charleston in the early 1780s.

During his time as an enslaved worker in Charleston, Denmark was employed in various tasks as a domestic servant to the Vesey family. After winning a lottery ticket, he purchased his freedom from Joseph Vesey for $600 in 1800; he invested the rest of his winnings in a carpentry shop.

Denmark Vesey's newfound freedom led him to become involved in the recently organized African Methodist Episcopal (AME) Church as a teacher of scripture. A conversation between Vesey and fellow conspirator Jack Pritchard (known as "Gullah Jack") following the suppression of church activity in 1818 by city officials is thought to have been a catalyst for the formation of a conspiratorial circle among a group of skilled slave and free black artisans. In late 1821, the Charleston authorities closed the local Hampstead AME Church, and Vesey began to plan his rebellion in earnest.

During conspiratorial meetings held throughout 1822, Vesey relied on his literacy and familiarity with Christian theology to mix a radical vision of the freedoms afforded by the Haitian Revolution and motivational tales of classical antiquity (such as the fable of Hercules) with the black Christianity of the AME Church. His vision of freedom called for a general uprising of rural and urban slaves, motivated by the supposedly imminent arrival of military assistance from the free black republic of Haiti. Vesey issued a call to action to his followers that "we must not stand with our hands in our pockets" as this imagined liberation army advanced on Charleston.

A plan was formulated to seize weapons from the city battery and to combine armed urban slaves with a "Black Army" that would march on Charleston from the countryside. The insurgents would then leave Charleston by ship and head toward freedom in the Caribbean, perhaps in Haiti. In the subsequent conspiracy trials, witnesses testified that Vesey, along with fellow conspirator Monday Gell, had penned a letter to Haitian president Jean-Pierre Boyer informing him of the plan.

Vesey's preparations were stymied in May 1822, when two slaves informed their masters of the conspiracy. More than 100 individuals were arrested, 35 were hanged, and 37 others were exiled. Vesey was arrested on June 22 and received a two-day trial.

Ironically, most of what is known about Vesey comes from the testimony of the witnesses who helped to convict him. "He would speak of the creation of the world in which he would say all men had equal rights, black as well as whites," testified Benjamin Ford, a white teenager. Frank, a slave witness, testified that, despite the fact that Vesey was free and could have migrated to Africa as part of the newly formed colonization movement, "He wanted to stay and see what he could do for his fellow creatures." According to a more hostile witness, "He studies all he can to put it into the heads of the Blacks to have a rising against the Whites." Vesey and several other conspirators were executed on July 3, 1822.

It was precisely the values highlighted by the witnesses who testified against him—self-sacrifice, religiosity, and education—that ensured Vesey's persistence as a symbol of slave resistance in the antebellum South. His name returned to the public discourse in 1863, when Frederick Douglass invoked Vesey as an example of bold self-sacrifice during an inspirational speech to the all-black Fifty-fourth Regiment of the Massachusetts Volunteer Infantry as it headed off to fight in the U.S. Civil War. Although he was often associated with fellow slave rebels Gabriel Prosser and Nat Turner, Vesey's political theology of liberation, which was so influenced by the Haitian Revolution, points to a connection between American slaves and notions of freedom that were operative in the larger transatlantic world.

William A. Wharton

See also: Haitian Revolution (1791–1804); Pritchard, "Gullah" Jack; Prosser, Gabriel; Turner, Nat.

group held meetings across London and sponsored public debates on the meaning of social equality and the avenues by which it might be realized among the English working classes.

Because Spencean philosophy advocated revolution, the organization was deemed a credible threat to the interests of the British government and the ruling classes. Therefore, in 1816, the government enlisted spies to infiltrate the organization and report on its activities. According to informants, the Spenceans planned to overthrow the government.

As a result, Wedderburn, who had established a Unitarian chapel as a forum for spreading his radical ideology, became a figure of major interest. He used the chapel meetings to offer a critique of capitalism that called for the end of slavery and for a working-class revolution. After a government spy reported on a sermon in which he supported a slave's right to kill a master, Wedderburn was arrested on charges of sedition and blasphemy and sent to Newgate Prison. He was released in short order, however, after his followers raised money for bail.

Just as Wedderburn's social commentary was informed by the transatlantic context, his revolutionary thought also had transnational implications. In 1817, he published a weekly series of volumes titled *The Axe Laid to the Root; or, a Fatal Blow to Oppressors, Being an Address to the Planters and Negroes of the Island of Jamaica,* in which he called for a slave revolution against the abuses and exploitation committed by Jamaican sugar planters. To suppress the potentially explosive consequences of his rhetoric, the Jamaican Assembly offered a reward to any slave who came forth with copies of Wedderburn's tracts. In many instances, colonial officials rewarded such slaves with freedom. Just as the British government viewed Wedderburn's scathing denunciation of capitalist exploitation as a threat to social stability, Jamaican colonial officials similarly recognized that his ideas directly challenged the inequities of the slave regime in Caribbean society.

In 1824, Wedderburn published *The Horrors of Slavery,* which included vivid accounts of the rape of his mother, the brutal flogging of his aging grandmother, and other violent incidents. Not only did the narrative provide fuel for the antislavery movement, it also highlighted his experiences as a target of the British government's efforts to subdue working-class radicalism.

In 1831, as he continued to promote free speech, antislavery, and working-class revolution, Wedderburn was arrested and jailed. Although the date of his death is unknown, he is known to have spent his final years in Giltspur Street Prison in London.

Kennetta Hammond Perry

Further Reading

Linebaugh, Paul. "A Little Jubilee? The Literacy of Robert Wedderburn in 1817." In *Protest and Survival: The Historical Experience, Essays for E.P. Thompson,* ed. John Rule and Robert Malcolmson. London: Merlin, 1993.

McCalman, Ian, ed. *The Horrors of Slavery and Other Writings by Robert Wedderburn.* Edinburgh, UK: Edinburgh University Press, 1991.

Wedgwood Cameos

No other symbol so succinctly captured the moral urgency of the transatlantic abolitionist movement as the Wedgwood cameo. Portraying the image of a suppliant, kneeling slave burdened by shackles, the cameo symbolically rendered the question, "Am I not a man and a brother?"

Named for Josiah Wedgwood, the noted British abolitionist and famous potter and manufacturer of porcelain ware, the antislavery cameo was first created in 1787. It was likely designed by William Hackwood or Henry Webber, both master modelers at the Wedgwood factory in Staffordshire, England. Though Wedgwood's factory produced the cameos, it originated neither the image nor the famous question.

The Quaker-led Society for the Abolition of the Slave Trade first produced the image on medallions minted in 1787, when abolitionist supporters in Great Britain pressed for parliamentary action to abolish the transatlantic slave trade. The Wedgwood modelers borrowed the image and motto used on these medallions and designed a cameo made of Jasperware, a material consisting of fine-grained, unglazed stoneware, said to resemble jasper stone in its appearance and its hardness. The cameos were widely distributed in Britain, and several were sent to Benjamin Franklin for display in the United States.

The Wedgwood cameos represented a late-eighteenth-century marketing campaign in support of the antislavery crusade. They were worn by female abolitionist supporters as an item of fashion adornment, either as broaches or as ornamental hairpins. Over the course of time, the cameos were added to other common household items, such as jewelry boxes or even snuffboxes. The sale of the cameos, as

The image of a kneeling slave in chains, as rendered in cameos by the British potter Josiah Wedgwood, became an icon of the transatlantic abolitionist movement. The cameos were sold to raise money for antislavery efforts. *(©Wilberforce House, Hull City Museums and Art Galleries, UK/The Bridgeman Art Library)*

well as other cameo-adorned items, provided profits to finance the ongoing antislavery efforts of British abolitionists.

The cameos were bought and sold at antislavery bazaars held to support the abolitionist movement. In many families, as daughters became involved in the antislavery cause, mothers would pass their cameos along to their daughters as treasured family heirlooms. During his lifetime, Wedgwood preferred to give the cameos away rather than sell them, because he never wanted anyone to be able to say that he had profited from slavery.

The popularity of the cameos was not limited to the British Isles. Women in the United States who supported the antislavery cause also purchased and wore the Wedgwood cameos to publicly assert their solidarity with the abolitionist cause. For many American women in the early nineteenth century—an era when public speaking by women was frowned on—wearing the cameo was a bold assertion and a daring social and political statement against the entrenched powers of their day.

As the women's movement in the United States began to grow out of the antislavery movement, another cameo was created in the same vein. This one pictured a female slave in chains with the question, "Am I not a woman and a sister?" The iconic power of the symbol was evident, and other groups began to adopt it for their causes. British laborers, for example, created a medallion of their own after the infamous Peterloo Massacre (1819), in which workingmen were killed as they advocated for political reform.

Junius P. Rodriguez

See also: Society for the Abolition of the Slave Trade.

Further Reading

Wedgwood, Julia. *The Personal Life of Josiah Wedgwood the Potter.* Ed. C.M. Herford. London: Macmillan, 1915.

Weekly Anglo-African Magazine, The

The Weekly Anglo-African Magazine was a unique publication of the mid-nineteenth century, initially published in New York City by Thomas Hamilton. The policy of the *Anglo-African* was that only the works of black authors would be published in its pages. In maintaining this race-exclusive policy, the magazine became one of the first venues to demonstrate the power of racial self-sufficiency.

In the first issue of the paper, Hamilton ran a policy statement that argued cogently for racial exclusiveness. Blacks, he argued, "in order to assert and maintain their rank as men among men, must speak for themselves; no outside tongue, however gifted with eloquence, can tell their story; no outside eye, however penetrating, can see their wants."

In addition to Hamilton, prominent black abolitionists and men of letters such as Charles B. Ray, George B. Vashon, and James McCune Smith lent their support to the publication and were regular contributors. Some of the leading black women authors of the era, including Frances E.W. Harper and Sarah Mapps Douglass, also wrote literary pieces for the publication.

As its name implied, it was clear from the beginning that *The Weekly Anglo-African Magazine* would not be a typical weekly newspaper. Although the publication focused on the news of the day and provided editorial commentary as needed, it also championed the literary arts and celebrated the accomplishments of black authors. In this role, the publication hoped to showcase the contributions and elevate the position of black writers in the United States.

In terms of its political views, the *Anglo-African* criticized both Democrats and Republicans for failing to address the issue of slavery and ignoring the plight of free blacks in America. In a March 1860 editorial, Hamilton delivered a scathing attack on Republicans, noting "their opposition to slavery means opposition to the black man—nothing else. Where it is clearly in their power to do anything for the oppressed colored man, why then they are too nice, too conservative, to do it."

Hamilton began publication of the *Anglo-African* in July 1859 and continued to edit the newspaper through its March 1861 issue. There was a brief hiatus in publication during the secession spring and summer, but it was back in print in August 1861 under the editorial direction of Robert Hamilton, a brother of Thomas. Robert Hamilton continued to publish the newspaper until December 1865.

The newspaper emphasized the importance of black cultural life and focused attention on some of the key social and political questions of the day. Once the U.S. Civil War began, the *Anglo-African* took a more activist stance in defending the rights of blacks. After the Emancipation Proclamation was issued on January 1, 1863, and the U.S. Colored Troops were organized, the offices of the *Anglo-African* in New York City began to serve as a recruitment office to bring black troops into the military. African Americans in the ranks kept abreast of news during the war by reading the *Anglo-African,* which often printed letters from soldiers that provided a unique perspective on the operations and conduct of the war.

In 1865, *The Weekly Anglo-African Magazine* became associated with the National Equal Rights League, a civil rights organization that supported Radical Reconstruction policies. When the *Anglo-African* finally ceased publication in December 1865, advocates of civil rights for blacks lost an influential voice in the crusade for social justice.

Junius P. Rodriguez

See also: Douglass, Sarah Mapps; Harper, Frances Ellen Watkins; Ray, Charles B.; U.S. Colored Troops.

Further Reading

Aptheker, Herbert, ed. *A Documentary History of the Negro People in the United States.* Vol. 1, *From the Colonial Times Through the Civil War.* New York: Citadel, 1951.

Weld, Theodore Dwight (1803–1895)

The American reformer and editor Theodore Dwight Weld was an influential leader of the antislavery movement. Historians have noted his far-reaching influence as an organizer of the American and Foreign Anti-Slavery Society and many antislavery conventions, including the 1836 American Anti-Slavery Convention, where he spoke to dozens of agents in training. He also mentored leaders in the movement, including the abolitionist orators Sarah M. and Angelina E. Grimké, and published widely on behalf of the antislavery cause.

Weld was born on November 23, 1803, in Hampton, Connecticut, where his father, the Reverend Ludovicus Weld, was a Congregationalist minister. Weld attended the Andover Academy for one year but soon left school to lecture on mnemonics, an occupation that allowed him to develop the oratorical skills that would later help him preach against slavery.

In 1825, the Weld family moved to Western New York—the "Burned-Over District," so named for the frequent religious revivals that took place there. It was at this time that Weld met his longtime friend and abolitionist interlocutor, Charles Stuart. The following year, he first experienced the Reverend Charles Grandison Finney's religious revivals in Rochester. Although he initially resisted Finney's evangelism, Weld eventually became a close ally, speaking on millennialism and temperance throughout New York in the late 1820s. This alliance lasted until the mid-1830s, when Weld shifted his energy and focus to the cause of antislavery.

Weld became an advocate of manual labor in 1830. Adherents of this movement contended that theological education combined with physical labor would help bring about the Christian millennium. Weld began studying at the Oneida Institute in Whitesboro, New York, the most influential manual labor seminary of the Second Great Awakening. In 1831, abolitionist and reformer Lewis Tappan appointed Weld general agent for the Society for the Promotion of Manual Labor in Literary Institutions; one of his duties was to locate a site for the National Manual Labor Seminary. Weld chose Lane Theological Seminary in Cincinnati, Ohio, enlisting the prominent New England Finneyite minister Lyman Beecher as its president.

A number of Oneida students transferred to Lane, which was soon thrust into turmoil. Weld, inspired by his manual labor ideology to promote egalitarianism, began crusading against slavery, along

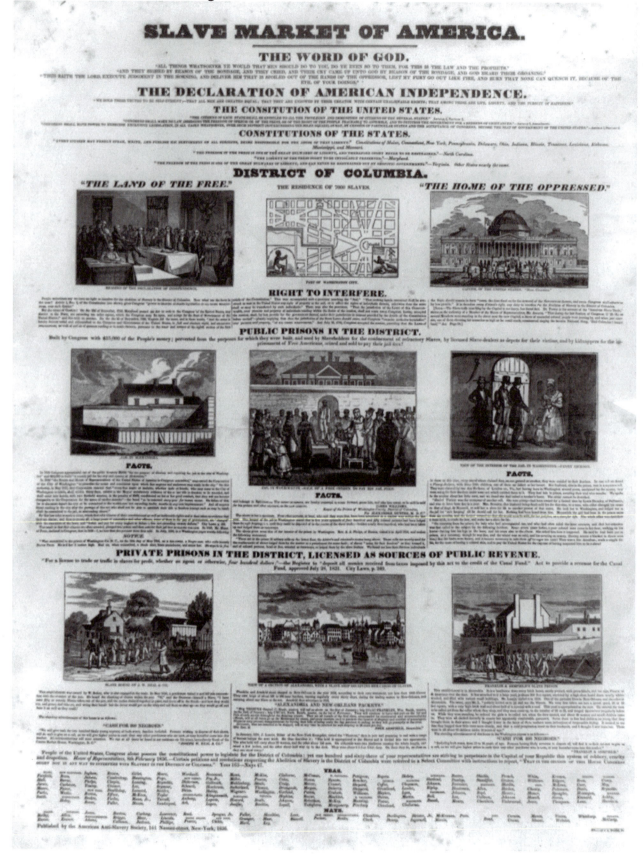

Among the most effective organizers in the American abolitionist movement, Theodore Dwight Weld helped wage a national petition campaign against slavery. This broadside of 1836 calls on Congress to end slavery in the District of Columbia. *(Library of Congress)*

with Garrisonian abolitionists then working in Ohio, such as Beriah Green, Elizur Wright, and Charles B. Storrs. Weld argued that colonization plans were unfavorable: Colonization was too big a task, and it was a solution that neither recognized the slaves' humanity nor atoned for the dual sins of slavery and racism.

In 1834, Weld founded Lane's antislavery society, which advocated voluntary manumission, and began circulating abolitionist literature in the section of Cincinnati known as Little Africa. He organized the 1834 "Lane debates," a well-planned argument against slavery that served to crystallize the growing disagreement between the seminary's Garrisonian students and colonizationist trustees. When the trustees limited student involvement in abolitionist activities, Weld and other students left the school for Finney's new college in nearby Oberlin, Ohio.

In 1835 and 1836, Weld canvassed Ohio and New York for antislavery converts. He was mobbed in Troy, New York, a setback that merely strengthened his resolve and increased his stature among abolitionists. In November 1836, he chaired the American Anti-Slavery Convention in New York, a three-week-long intensive training convention led by Weld to prepare fieldworkers to tour the Northern states and promote abolitionism. Attendees included William Lloyd Garrison, James G. Birney, and the Grimké sisters, the only women in attendance and the first female agents of the society.

The convention was a turning point for Weld. After speaking to fifty agents in training, the well-known antislavery orator lost his voice and rarely spoke in public for the rest of his life. In 1837, though, Weld published *The Bible Against Slavery,* which attacked contemporary biblical proslavery arguments. Weld contended that the Bible never depicted Hebrew slavery as being as pervasive and cruel as racial slavery in the American South.

In 1838, Weld married Charlestonian abolitionist and women's rights advocate Angelina Grimké. The following year, Weld and the Grimké sisters authored *American Slavery as It Is: Testimony of a Thousand Witnesses,* one of the era's most influential antislavery tracts. Written under the auspices of the American Anti-Slavery Society, the book compiled accounts of slavery from personal narratives and Southern newspapers. Although it was distinctly abolitionist in flavor, the book asserted its own objectivity. The preface declared, "That [slave owners] should utter falsehoods, for the sake of proclaiming their own infamy, is not probable."

During subsequent years, Weld and the Grimkés lived a largely private life, although they remained committed to a broad slate of reform principles. In 1841, Weld traveled to Washington, D.C., to fight the Gag Rule, which prohibited the discussion of antislavery petitions on the congressional floor, and he succeeded in influencing Representative John Quincy Adams. But by 1844, Weld had effectively retired as a public reformer. The lecture "Truth's Hindrances" (1844) marked the beginning of his introversion and estrangement from other abolitionists. His isolation fostered an intensely personal faith shaped by Swedenborgianism, transcendentalism, and spiritualism.

In October 1848, Weld and the Grimké sisters began their careers as educators with the opening of the Weld Institute. In addition to teaching his own children at the co-educational academy, Weld also educated the children of abolitionists James G. Birney, Henry B. Stanton, and Gerrit Smith. In 1852, Weld and the Grimkés moved to the Fourierist Raritan Bay Union in New Jersey. There they took over the Eagleswood School, and Weld preached egalitarianism in Sunday morning lessons. Some community members tended to endorse racial exclusivity and phrenology, despite the town's explicit commitment to equality.

A year into the U.S. Civil War, the school closed and Weld briefly raised the abolitionist banner once again. On November 9, at the suggestion of Garrison, Weld spoke at the Boston Music Hall on "The Conspirators: Their False Issues and Lying Pretences." The success of this speech prompted him to traverse New England, Pennsylvania, Ohio, and New York in 1863, stumping for abolitionism and the Republican Party. That year, Weld and the Grimkés moved permanently to Boston, where they taught at the Young Ladies' Boarding School in nearby Lexington until it burned down in 1867.

Weld continued his advocacy for freedmen's and women's rights, as well as temperance, until his death on February 3, 1895, at the age of ninety-one.

Brian M. Ingrassia

See also: American and Foreign Anti-Slavery Society; Finney, Charles Grandison; Gag Resolution; Garrison, William Lloyd; Grimké, Angelina Emily; Grimké, Sarah Moore; Tappan, Lewis; Wright, Elizur.

Further Reading

Abzug, Robert H. *Passionate Liberator: Theodore Dwight Weld and the Dilemma of Reform.* New York: Oxford University Press, 1980.

Thomas, Benjamin P. *Theodore Weld: Crusader for Freedom.* New Brunswick, NJ: Rutgers University Press, 1950.

Weld, Theodore Dwight. *The Bible Against Slavery; or, an Inquiry Into the Genius of the Mosaic System, and the Teachings of the Old Testament on the Subject of Human Rights.* 1837. Pittsburgh: United Presbyterian Board of Publication, 1864; Detroit, MI: Negro History, 1970.

Wellington, Arthur Wellesley, First Duke of (1769–1852)

The duke of Wellington was a renowned British field marshal who defeated Napoleon Bonaparte at the Battle of Waterloo in 1815 and served as British prime minister from 1828 to 1830.

Born on May 1, 1769, in Dublin, Arthur Wellesley was raised in Ireland and London as a member of an impoverished family of the Irish gentry. He embarked on a military career under the guidance of his brother, Richard Wellesley, the earl of Mornington, who, in March 1787, purchased a commission for him in the Seventy-third Foot, a Scottish regiment about to leave for India.

Wellington proved to be a natural leader. His successful command in India from 1796 to 1805 was followed by victory in the Peninsular War of 1808–1814. The defeat of Napoleon led to Wellington's appointment as British ambassador to Bourbon France in 1814, with instructions to press for the abolition of the French slave trade. Wellington consulted with William Wilberforce and Thomas Clarkson to convince them of his sincerity and then commenced a methodical reading of the abolitionist literature, which he continued later in life. Although the abolition of the slave traffic conformed to Wellington's firm sense of justice, he took a measured stance, believing that the populism aroused by the issue actually hindered attempts to end the trade by antagonizing opponents.

In France, Wellington faced the overwhelming influence of colonial merchants and plantation owners, who demonized the abolitionist cause as British triumphalism and trickery. There was a real abolitionist movement in France, so Wellington encouraged the formation of one with Wilberforce's help. At the same time, he applied diplomatic pressure on King Louis XVIII, hinting at a possible incentive in the form of a subsidy or West Indian island. The eventual result was that Louis promised to abolish the trade in five years, a pace that was still too slow for British abolitionists.

Even this offer was soon rendered irrelevant, however, for in March 1815, Napoleon returned and instantly abolished the slave trade (reversing his previous policy) in a failed attempt to drive a wedge between the Bourbons and Britain. After Napoleon was defeated at Waterloo in 1815, the restored Bourbons confirmed the law, in part because of Wellington's prestige and position as commander of the occupying forces.

Together with Lord Castlereagh, Wellington played an important part in pressing British demands for international suppression of the slave trade as part of the Concert of Europe at the Congresses of Vienna (1814–1815) and Aix-la-Chapelle (1818). Castlereagh's suicide left Wellington in charge of British efforts at the Congress of Verona in 1822. Although the abolitionists had confidence in him, Russia's failure to support Britain as promised, which infuriated Wellington, meant the results were limited as before to a joint declaration against slavery rather than firm action.

As a Tory prime minister, Wellington's main achievement was Catholic emancipation in Ireland. His downfall—and that of his government—was a reactionary opposition to the reform of Parliament. Given the focus of Wellington's government, little was done to address the popular demand for the emancipation of West Indian slaves. In the 1830 election, reform and abolitionism became closely associated, and the creation of the Reformed Parliament of 1833, which Wellington accepted only after a bitter struggle, crushed the proslavery lobby.

Wellington's dislike of extremism led him to oppose the abolition bill in 1833; he believed that it threatened private property and was badly organized, especially following the recent revolt in Jamaica. He felt the passage of the bill would cause disorder and economic collapse in the West Indies, where ex-slaves, just like the British lower classes, needed supervision to prevent idleness, and the antagonized planter class would be expected to enforce the law.

Wellington was echoing some of the radical abolitionist criticisms of the bill, though from a more conservative stance, but his stubbornness again left him isolated from the popular mood of the reform period. In August 1833, Parliament passed the Abolition of Slavery Act, which provided for the freedom of all slaves in the British colonies.

Ever loyal to his Tory convictions, Wellington continued to oppose the liberal policies of the Whigs in the 1830s and 1840s. Upon his death in 1852, he was given a state funeral, an honor bestowed upon only the greatest of English statesmen.

Gwilym Games

See also: Abolition of Slavery Act (1833); Clarkson, Thomas; Congress of Vienna (1814–1815); Wilberforce, William.

Further Reading

Fladeland, Betty. "Abolitionist Pressures on the Concert of Europe, 1814–1822." *Journal of Modern History* 38 (December 1966): 355–73.

Longford, Elizabeth. *Wellington.* London: Weidenfield, 1992.

Putney, Martha. "The Slave Trade in French Diplomacy from 1814 to 1815." *Journal of Negro History* 60 (July 1975): 411–27.

Wells-Barnett, Ida B. (1862–1931)

A distinguished journalist and civil rights activist, Ida B. Wells-Barnett was one of the most outspoken, radical, and militant African American voices during the Jim Crow era. Although she would make her most enduring contribution as a crusader against the crime of lynching, she spent her life fighting the injustice of racial discrimination in its many forms.

Born on July 16, 1862, in Holly Springs, Mississippi, Wells was the daughter of a Native American father and a slave mother. Her parents were deeply religious, politically aware, and strongly committed to educating their children, and they instilled these values in Wells at an early age. She began her education at the Methodist Church–sponsored freedmen's school in Holly Springs (then called Shaw University but today named Rust College). She later took classes at Fisk University in Nashville, Tennessee.

In 1879, at the age of sixteen, Wells became a teacher in Holly Springs, and, five years later, she moved about forty miles up the road to Memphis to teach. There she encountered her first life-changing experience with racial injustice. She was forcibly removed from a train on the Chesapeake, Ohio, and Southwestern line for sitting in the white section and refusing to move to the Jim Crow car designated for black passengers. She immediately showed the pluck and resolve that would characterize her life by fighting back against the system, suing the railroad company and winning, before the Tennessee Supreme Court reversed the ruling.

While continuing to teach, Wells founded and began editing a black weekly newspaper, the *Memphis Free Speech,* in 1889, and she was elected president of

Born to slave parents in Mississippi, Ida Wells-Barnett went on to edit a newspaper in Memphis and used it to launch her decades-long crusade against lynching. She was also a founder of the NAACP. *(Hulton Archive/Getty Images)*

the Afro-American Press Association the same year. In 1891, a campaign that she waged in print against the segregated and discriminatory Memphis public school system got her fired from her teaching job. That year, however, she stumbled on the issue that would become the hallmark of her long career: lynching.

In 1891, the lynching of a black man in Kentucky and the subsequent lynching of three black friends in Memphis provoked Wells's righteous indignation like no other cause had done. She began compiling statistics on lynching nationwide, an effort that culminated in the pamphlet *Southern Horrors: Lynch Law in All Its Phases,* which was published in 1892 by T. Thomas Fortune's *New York Age* press.

For her exposé of lynching and her proposed remedy for it—that blacks arm themselves and fight back—the white establishment of Memphis destroyed Wells's office and press, banished her from town, and threatened her life should she ever return. She then moved to Chicago, where she met the prominent abolitionist and civil rights leader Frederick Douglass; together, they co-authored a scathing indictment of the 1893 World's Columbian Exposition, which had banned black participation. In 1895, she married the editor of the *Chicago Conservator,* attorney Ferdinand L. Barnett, with whom she had four children.

Even as a wife and mother, Wells-Barnett continued her crusade to stamp out the injustice of lynching, publishing *A Red Record: Tabulated Statistics and Alleged Causes of Lynching in the United States* (1895), *Lynch Law in Georgia* (1899), and *Mob Rule in New Orleans* (1900). Besides writing about lynching, Wells-Barnett also traveled the United States and England, speaking out publicly against the crime. In 1894 alone, she spoke at more than 100 public meetings in Great Britain. The British people and press accepted her work at a time when white Americans and the mainstream American press would not. Despite her activism, the cancer of lynching continued to metastasize back home in the Southern states.

In 1909, Wells-Barnett attended the fourth annual Niagara Conference in New York City, along with W.E.B. Du Bois and other black and white leaders, and helped launch the National Association for the Advancement of Colored People (NAACP). That organization adopted her antilynching crusade as its own—thanks mainly to the efforts of Walter White—and continued it long after Wells-Barnett died until finally achieving the reforms in the justice system that she had spent her life seeking. In the meantime, Wells-Barnett and the NAACP leadership came to disagree about the tactics that should be used in the antilynching movement, and she turned her attention to other organizations and pursuits.

In 1910, Wells-Barnett was influenced by her good friend Jane Addams, founder of Chicago's Hull-House for indigent women, to found the Negro Fellowship League of Chicago, a kind Hull-House for black men. The league provided counseling, job services, and inexpensive housing to disenfranchised blacks in Chicago's inner city.

After Marcus Garvey founded his Universal Negro Improvement Association in 1914 to colonize American blacks in Africa, Wells-Barnett became one of the few black leaders to see no contradiction in supporting the mission of both the NAACP and the dubious and doomed Universal Negro Improvement Association. Yet she never supported the other great black leader of the day, Booker T. Washington, whom she considered a sellout to her people because of his cautious, conservative approach to social reform.

During the height of the women's suffrage movement in the 1910s, Wells-Barnett became an active suffragette, finally joining a reform movement that would bear more immediate fruit than any other she would be involved with. In 1913, she formed the first black women's suffrage organization in Chicago, called the Alpha Suffrage Club, and tried to work within the framework of the Republican Party.

In 1930, only eleven years after the passage of the Nineteenth Amendment, which granted nationwide women's suffrage, Wells-Barnett ran unsuccessfully for a seat in the Illinois state senate as an independent. She died on March 25, 1931, in Chicago, at the age of sixty-nine. Her autobiography was published posthumously in 1970.

Thomas Adams Upchurch

See also: Lynching; Women's Rights and the Abolitionist Movement.

Further Reading

Edwards, Linda McMurray. *To Keep the Waters Troubled: The Life of Ida B. Wells.* New York: Oxford University Press, 1998.

Escott, Paul D., David R. Goldfield, Sally G. McMillen, and Elizabeth Hayes Turner, eds. *Major Problems in the History of the American South.* Volume II, *The New South.* 2nd. ed. Boston: Houghton Mifflin, 1999.

Holt, Thomas C., and Elsa Barkley Brown, eds. *Major Problems in African-American History.* Vol. 2, *From Freedom to "Freedom Now," 1865–1990s.* Boston: Houghton Mifflin, 2000.

Schechter, Patricia Ann. *Ida B. Wells-Barnett and American Reform, 1880–1930.* Chapel Hill: University of North Carolina Press, 2001.

Wells, Ida B. *Crusade for Justice: The Autobiography of Ida B. Wells.* Ed. Alfreda M. Duster. Chicago: University of Chicago Press, 1991.

Wesley, John (1703–1791)

John Wesley, the founder of Methodism, a tireless evangelist, and a prolific writer, was an early opponent of slavery.

Wesley was born on June 17, 1703, the fifteenth child of Samuel and Susanna Wesley, in the village of Epworth in Lincolnshire, England, where his father was the rector. When Wesley was rescued from the burning rectory in 1709, Susanna reasoned that God had a special purpose for her son and focused her attention on his education. In 1720, Wesley left the Charterhouse School and arrived at Christ Church College at Oxford University. By 1726, he had become a fellow of Lincoln College and a Greek lecturer.

Wesley was ordained as a deacon in 1725 and as a priest of the Church of England in 1728. He became the leader of a small group called the "Holy Club," first organized by his brother Charles and mockingly referred to by other Oxford students as "Methodists" for its members' methodical life of Bible study and prayer. (Wesley would later embrace the name for his religious movement.) The group also strove to aid the poor and bring the word of God to the imprisoned.

Upon his father's death in 1735, Wesley traveled to Georgia, at the time a colony closed to slavery and founded as a refuge for the poor, to do missionary work. His brother Charles served as secretary to Governor James Oglethorpe. Because of disagreements with the colonists and his lack of success at converting the Native Americans, however, Wesley's time in the colonies was a disappointment. Nevertheless, he was proud of his achievements among the black slaves, though he was shocked by the slave conditions and the lack of Christian education provided by the slave owners. As a precursor to his future travels in England, Wesley traversed slave regions, moving from plantation to plantation and recording his evangelical successes with slaves who were eager to learn of Christianity.

During a storm-tossed sea voyage to the Georgia colony, Wesley had been impressed by the devotion and courage of a group of Moravians, members of a religious sect formed around the teachings of Czech reformer Jan Hus. When Wesley returned to England in 1738, he began to attend the meetings of the Moravian Church on a regular basis. During one such a meeting on Aldersgate Street in London, Wesley felt an unusual assurance of salvation and determined to bring that feeling to as many people as possible. Thus, the great Methodist evangelical movement began under his leadership, but not without resistance.

Disturbed and frightened by Wesley's zeal and the emotional reaction of congregations to his preaching, parish priests closed their church doors to him, forcing Wesley to hold his meetings in the open. At first, he met with harassment and threats from mobs, but he gained new adherents and ultimately preached to as many as 30,000 people at a time. During his tours across Britain, Wesley traveled up to 250,000 miles and delivered 40,000 sermons on his practical theology. While denying any desire to break from the Church of England, he founded Methodist chapels, schools, and hospitals for the poor, and he wrote books and pamphlets on subjects ranging from theology to geology.

In 1774, Wesley published his *Thoughts Upon Slavery,* a tract cataloging slavery's horrors and injustices and ending with an impassioned appeal directly to slave traders and owners. Although the work reflected the influence of Anthony Benezet's *Some Historical Account of Guinea,* published in Philadelphia in 1771, *Thoughts Upon Slavery* sparkled with the Wesleyan flourish, along with his direct logic and the understanding of one who had witnessed slavery in America firsthand.

In *Thoughts Upon Slavery,* Wesley rejected the argument that slavery was a natural and permanent institution, arguing that it had fallen into decline until the discovery of America and the coasts of Africa, and that the modern version of slavery included horrors that were unequaled in ancient history. Far from a backward, desolate continent, Wesley asserted that Africa had once been a fertile place and that Africans were industrious, civilized, religious, and just. It was the slave traders who brought waste, war, and injustice in order to gain prisoners and misled Africans regarding their intent. Wesley reviewed the inhumane treatment on slave ships and plantations, refuting any argument that slavery was compatible with natural law or justice. He further rejected the notion that slavery was economically necessary but argued that even if there were some economic benefit, it was better to live in poverty than to profit from such misery and evil. He concluded with a warning that those who traded or owned slaves would face God's judgment.

Wesley continued to oppose slavery in his voluminous writings and letters, arguing that the slave trade was Great Britain's greatest sin. In 1787, Wesley wrote to the English abolitionist Granville Sharp to praise his efforts to establish a colony for freed slaves in Sierra Leone, and he stated that he had detested slavery from the moment he first knew of it.

Wesley wrote his last letter on February 24, 1791, to the English reformer William Wilberforce. In it, he condemned colonial laws that prevented the sworn testimony of a black man from standing against that of a white man, and he once again attacked slavery, especially in America. Wesley encouraged Wilberforce to continue the antislavery struggle as an instrument of God.

Wesley died an Anglican priest, yet having initiated the inevitable breach between the Methodists and the established church by ordaining his own American clergy in 1784. These early Methodist leaders continued Wesley's campaign against slavery in the United States.

Russell Fowler

See also: Benezet, Anthony; Religion and Abolitionism; Sharp, Granville; Wilberforce, William.

Further Reading

Baker, Eric W. *A Herald of the Evangelical Revival.* London: Epworth, 1948.
Baker, Frank. *John Wesley and the Church of England.* Nashville, TN: Abingdon, 1970.
Pudney, John. *John Wesley and His World.* New York: Scribner's, 1978.

West Africa, Abolition in

Just as outside interests shaped West African slavery, so, too, must abolition in West Africa be interpreted in the context of the transatlantic world. European interference in West Africa resulted in twin ironies: For most of the nineteenth century, Europeans pushed for abolition in Africa while simultaneously reinforcing slavery in their own colonies. Then, in the 1890s, the European powers used the persistence of slavery to justify their conquest of Africa, only to tolerate or protect slavery in their colonial territories elsewhere.

Historical Background

Slavery in West Africa became more pervasive as local elites mobilized to gain advantage from the transatlantic slave trade. The Dahomey Kingdom conquered the rival Whydah on the Bight of Benin in the early eighteenth century in order to control the slave trade, while the Asante pressed for greater control over the Gold Coast. By the mid-nineteenth century, the slave trade had become virtually a royal monopoly, sometimes exploited directly and other times commissioned to brokers. The African kings secured favorable terms by playing rival European and African slave traders against each other.

Although the transatlantic slave trade consolidated the power of the local elites, the imported textiles that were distributed as patronage reinforced the elite control perhaps more than the importation of arms and alcohol. Nor were the textiles necessarily of European manufacture. At one time, fabrics from India accounted for some 55 percent of imports, whereas alcohol, muskets, and powder amounted to less than one-third, as measured by their value in European currency.

The consolidation of power achieved by the rulers of the major African states of this period—the Segu, Asante, Dahomey, and Oyo—owed as much to domestic slavery as to the transatlantic slave trade. African elites retained slaves to increase their own retinues and armies, as well as those of their clients. The domestic slave trade proved countercyclical to the Atlantic slave trade. As the latter decreased, African elites retained greater numbers of captives to produce the commercial goods that were endorsed by the British as "legitimate trade."

The domestic market favored female captives. Female slaves cost 10 percent to 50 percent more than male slaves through the 1880s, thanks to high demand for their sexual and reproductive services, their agricultural labor, the provisioning of the burgeoning caravan trade, and their military service. The British envoy to the kingdom of Dahomey reported at mid-century that King Guezo had 18,000 royal wives and that Dahomey women distinguished themselves as soldiers and warriors. The West African preference for female captives recasts the nature of the transatlantic slave trade as driven more by supply from Africa than by demand from the Americas.

European Influence

Britain's suppression of the maritime slave trade during the nineteenth century succeeded in expanding domestic slavery rather than abolishing it. Slaves produced palm and peanut products for legitimate export trade. Both Africans and Europeans defended domestic slavery as necessary to this commodities trade. Africans sought to sustain their power and wealth in the new economy and condemned the hypocrisy of Europeans' moral condemnation of their slave trade. In 1849, Vice Consul John Duncan reported to the British foreign secretary, "The King admits the injustice of slave-trading, but remarked that we were a long time finding it out to be wrong."

Nearly fifty years later, French merchants complained to the director of native affairs in Senegal that actions against the slave trade would undermine the growth of peanut exports by depriving the economy of slave labor. That labor was required not just for producing palm and peanut products; the export of cash crops and the importation of European goods also increased the demand for slave porters. Pack animals could not absorb the greater freight volume because of the scarcity of fodder and prevalence of disease-carrying tsetse flies. The labor of free porters became more expensive as the exchange of goods of low value relative to weight and bulk increased.

The increased volume of trade simultaneously gave rise to greater currency requirements in the economy. Given the scarcity of coin, slaves served as currency, as they had lower transportation costs than other units such as livestock, iron, or puncheons of oil. Suppression of the transatlantic slave trade also increased the desert trade, as the export of humans was reoriented across the Sahara from Senegambian "ports."

Prior to the "Scramble for Africa" in the late nineteenth century, Europeans' efforts at abolition in West Africa proved partial, gradual, and weakly enforced. The British tolerated slavery in the areas under their indirect rule, including slaveholding by British officials. The commandant of Fort James owned hundreds of slaves at the time of his death in the late 1830s.

In 1848, France finally succeeded in permanently abolishing slavery in all its possessions, including its small outposts in West Africa. In Walo and Dimar, however, France permitted slavery to trump even imperialism. When confronted with outcomes that were deemed undesirable—fugitive slaves seeking refuge and masters fleeing to protect their slaveholdings—local French authorities unannexed the territories and turned them into protectorates subject to local laws that permitted slavery.

The Portuguese began to abolish slavery in their territories in 1858, but they required slaves to remain in unpaid service until 1878. Afterward, the former slaves' rights as freed people were weakly enforced.

King Leopold of Belgium and other colonizers justified conquest as a means to end the slave trade and slavery in Africa, yet they avoided decisive action. The General Act of the Brussels Conference Relative to the African Slave Trade, signed on July 2, 1890, did not commit the Europeans to effect immediate abolition, despite conferring broad powers on them to regulate labor practices in the areas they controlled. Ironically, the immediate consequence of European colonial expansion in Africa was a brief explosion of enslavement.

In Nigeria, the Europeans emancipated the slaves but often with harsh restrictions or major gaps. After conquering northern Nigeria, the British military leader and colonial administrator Frederick Lugard prohibited slavery but invoked the specter of lawlessness and diminished food production to weaken freedmen's rights. He required slaves to purchase their freedom and limited their mobility and access to land. Well into the twentieth century, Islamic courts in northern Nigeria continued to recognize aspects of masters' power over slaves. Overall, the European governments did not actively emancipate slaves; instead, they abolished the legal status of slavery.

Although the Europeans generally proved to be reluctant abolitionists, their gradualist measures enacted before and after the conference of 1890 did succeed in eroding slavery in West Africa. Perhaps most effective was legislation stipulating that no colonial or indigenous court could legally recognize slavery. Masters could not enforce claims over slaves who managed to press their cases in court. Other piecemeal measures such as "free womb" laws, bans on local slave trade, and release from bondage upon a master's death further contributed to abolition. Certain developments during colonial rule also served to undermine slavery indirectly. Slave porters became superfluous as Europeans built roads, bridges, and railways.

Unlike the French colonies, where the alienation of any person's liberty was outlawed, a small number of Africans kidnapped in the British colonies continued to be sold into slavery well into the twentieth century. Although the Europeans used abolition to legitimate annexation and conquest, they avoided disrupting slavery lest abolition threaten colonial rule.

Slavery Abolished

Slaves themselves undermined slavery in West Africa. By the twentieth century, the nature of slave resistance had changed. Whereas slaves in the late eighteenth and early nineteenth centuries had rebelled—the Blood Men of Calabar, Yalunka slaves against their Fula masters, Koranko slaves against their Susu masters—West African slaves by the late nineteenth century resisted by running away. When market forces encouraged harsher forms of slavery during the first two decades of the twentieth century, as much as half the total slave population fled their masters.

Others redeemed their relatives. Relations, including fictive kinships, were renegotiated between masters and former slaves remaining nearby. Some former slaves departed for neighboring communities, where chiefs let them settle on vacant land. Others fled to missions or new urban areas. When the holding of property in humans was prohibited in French West Africa in 1905, an estimated 1 million slaves left their masters within a few years. Above all, slavery was abolished de facto in West Africa as local elites and colonial officials lost the ability to coerce enslaved peoples.

Vestiges of slavery persisted, however, well into the 1930s. As in the United States after the Civil War, the power holders in West Africa limited access to economic resources in order to force former slaves to provide noncompensated labor. The crisis in the world market of the 1930s caused a resurgence in the pawning of humans. Pawn labor served as interest payments until the debtor redeemed them.

In some cases, the stigma of slavery remained long after the institution had disappeared. Even after slavery no longer played an economic role in West Africa, its status continued to be invoked to reinforce hierarchies of power and subordination.

Teresa M. Van Hoy

Further Reading

Coates, Tim, ed. *King Guezo of Dahomey, 1850–52: The Abolition of the Slave Trade on the West Coast of Africa.* London: Her Majesty's Stationery Office, 2001.
Lovejoy, Paul E., and A.S. Kanya-Forstner, eds. *Slavery and Its Abolition in French West Africa: The Official Reports of G. Poulet, E. Roume, and G. Deherme.* Madison: University of Wisconsin–Madison, African Studies Program, 1994.

Wheatley, Phillis (ca. 1753–1784)

Known as the first black poet in America, the slave Phillis Wheatley wrote a number of poems that reflect the religious and classical influences of her New England upbringing. In her writing, she expressed a strong antislavery sentiment, stating in a 1774 letter published in the *Connecticut Gazette,* "In every human breast God has implanted a principle . . . it is impatient of oppression, and pants for deliverance." Although she produced only one book of poetry, *Poems on Various Subjects, Religious and Moral* (1773), her work brought her fame, freedom, and the recognition of being the first African American of her time to publish a book of poetry in English.

Wheatley was born in Senegal, West Africa, in about 1753. On July 11, 1761, she was brought from Africa to Boston aboard the schooner *Phillis.* Later that month, Susanna Wheatley, the wife of John Wheatley, a prominent merchant from King Street, Boston, purchased the young woman and took her to their home. With the help of Mary, the Wheatleys' daughter, she learned to speak English, Latin, and Greek. Sixteen months after her arrival in America, she was able to read passages from the Bible, the Western classics, and

British literature, and she began to write letters and poems to her friends.

Wheatley wrote her first poem at about the age of thirteen. Dated 1765, the poem, titled "On Messrs Hussey and Coffin," was published in Newport, Rhode Island, in December 1767. That same year, Wheatley wrote an elegy on the popular evangelical preacher George Whitefield, published under the title "A Poem by Phillis Wheatley, a Negro Girl, on the Death of Reverend Whitefield" in 1770. She became an overnight sensation in Boston.

Over the course of the next four years, she completed a full volume of poetry titled *Poems on Various Subjects, Religious and Moral.* When her master showed her manuscript to Boston printers, they expressed doubts about Wheatley's authorship. According to historian Henry Louis Gates, Jr., sometime in October 1772, eighteen men, including Thomas Hutchinson, the governor of Massachusetts, met with Wheatley in Boston's Town Hall to "verify the authorship of her poems and to answer a much larger question: was a Negro capable of producing literature." The book was published in England in 1773 with the assistance of Countess Selina Hastings of Huntingdon, a friend of Whitefield's.

Wheatley's poetry deals with a variety of themes, including slavery, Africa, and the right of African Americans to achieve freedom. In "To The Right Honourable William [Legge], Earl of Dartmouth, His Majesty's Principal Secretary of State for North America," she describes slavery as a system that is inimical to the ideals of justice and freedom that America represents.

No more, *America,* in mournful strain
Of wrongs, and grievance unredress'd complain,
No longer shall thou dread the iron chain,
Which wanton *Tyranny* with lawless hand
Had made, and with it meant t' enslave the land.

In Wheatley's view, ending slavery would allow America to become a free nation in which justice and law prevail. In making America's freedom contingent on the emancipation of the slaves, she developed a rhetoric that appealed to clergymen and abolitionists on both sides of the Atlantic.

In her writing, Wheatley also discussed her relationship to Africa. In poems such as "Mæcenas," "Afric," "Hymn," "Ethiop," and "To The University," she identified herself as originating from either "Ethiop" (Africa) or the "sable race" (Africans). This identification with Africa helped Wheatley oppose

Brought from Africa and sold into slavery as a child, Phillis Wheatley became the first black poet to be published in America. Her verse, which appeared in the 1770s, revolves around classical and Christian themes; slavery and Africa are also frequent topics. *(Library of Congress)*

the view that blacks were an inferior race. At the same time, her representation of Africa is ambiguous. In "On Being Brought From Africa to America" (1773), for example, she calls Africa a "*Pagan* land" with people who "May be refin'd, and join th' angelic train." A zealous Christianity thus tainted her views about Africa and, to some contemporary readers, her relevance to African American identification with the mother continent.

Wheatley was emancipated in 1773, and she married a free black man in 1778. Despite her talent and success, however, she could not support her family and died in poverty in Boston on December 5, 1784. Her memoirs were published in 1834, and the *Letters of Phillis Wheatley, the Negro-Slave Poet of Boston* appeared thirty years later.

Babacar M'Baye

See also: American Revolution (1775–1781).

Further Reading

Gates, Henry Louis, Jr. *The Trials of Phillis Wheatley: America's First Black Poet and Her Encounters With the Founding Fathers.* New York: Basic Civitas, 2003.

Levernier, James A. "Phillis Wheatley and the New England Clergy." *Early American Literature* 26 (March 1991): 21–38.

Mason, Julian D. *The Poems of Phillis Wheatley.* Chapel Hill: University of North Carolina Press, 1989.

Salisbury, Cynthia. *Phillis Wheatley: Legendary African-American Poet.* Berkeley Heights, CA: Enslow, 2001.

Wheatley, Phillis. *The Collected Works of Phillis Wheatley.* Ed. John C. Fields. New York: Oxford University Press, 1988.

Whitfield, James Monroe (1822–1871)

James Monroe Whitfield was a free black poet and author whose writings frequently appeared in leading abolitionist newspapers of the early nineteenth century. Politically and socially active in seeking equal rights for African Americans, he was drawn to the idea of emigration (the creation of independent free black communities outside the United States) advocated by black nationalist Martin R. Delany in the 1850s.

Whitfield grew up in a free black household in New Hampshire, where he obtained his education. Little is known of his early life, but by the late 1840s, he was living in Buffalo, New York, where he worked as a barber. He wrote verse as a hobby, but it was the income from his barbershop that allowed him to pay the bills and provide for his family.

Whitfield's poetry was published in William Lloyd Garrison's *Liberator* and Frederick Douglass's *North Star* and *Frederick Douglass' Paper* during the 1840s and 1850s. Douglass was so impressed with Whitfield's talent that he suggested the young writer abandon his barbershop and write professionally. Despite such high praise, Whitfield continued to write on a part-time basis.

His greatest achievement as a poet was the publication of *America and Other Poems* (1853), which received much critical acclaim. In its introduction, Whitfield describes himself as "the humble colored man, who hath wrought it out amid the daily and incessant toil necessary for the maintenance of a family, who are dependent upon the labor of his hands for support." The book was dedicated to Martin Delany, whose political rhetoric matched the pained despair found in many of Whitfield's poems. He praises Delany out of "respect for his character, admiration of his talents, and love of his principles."

The year before Whitfield's book appeared, Delany had published *The Condition, Elevation, Emigration, and Destiny of the Colored People of the United States* (1852), a work that had a profound influence on Whitfield's thinking. Delany believed that institutional racism in America was so deep that free blacks could never attain the rights enjoyed by white citizens. It was Delany's position that remaining in a country where second-class citizenship was the best a person could hope for was not a viable option for free blacks. He argued that emigration to another country where they might begin their own free communities was the most promising solution.

When Frederick Douglass publicly opposed Delany's ideas on emigration, Whitfield wrote letters to Douglass defending the position; the extended correspondence was published in *Frederick Douglass' Paper*. Whitfield attended the July 1854 convention that Delany held in Cleveland, Ohio, to promote the idea of emigration and traveled with Delany in 1859–1861 to visit sites in Central America that might be suitable locations for black nationalist emigration communities.

The admiration between Delany and Whitfield was mutual. When the former published his serialized novel, *Blake,* in the *Weekly Anglo-African Magazine* (1859 and 1861–1862), Whitfield was honored to discover that the black revolutionaries in Delany's book chanted Whitfield's poetry as they organized slave rebellions.

Whitfield moved away from the idea of emigration during the U.S. Civil War, regarding the conflict as a war of emancipation. He moved to the West in the 1860s and spent his final years in Oregon and California, where he supported himself by operating a barbershop. His last published poem, which appeared in the *San Francisco Elevator* in April 1870, was an untitled ode to American liberty. Whitfield died in San Francisco in 1871.

Junius P. Rodriguez

See also: Delany, Martin Robison; Douglass, Frederick.

Further Reading

Sherman, Joan R. "James Monroe Whitfield, Poet and Emigrationist: A Voice of Protest and Despair." *Journal of Negro History* 57 (April 1972): 169–76.

Whittier, John Greenleaf (1807–1892)

John Greenleaf Whittier, one of the nineteenth century's most famous poets, was an abolitionist, journalist, and humanitarian. Although he edited several antislavery journals, Whittier's primary contribution to the abolitionist movement was his poetry. In dozens of poems, including "The Yankee Girl," "The Slavery-Ships," "The Hunters of Men," "Massachusetts to Virginia," and "Ichabod," he spoke out against the injustices of slavery.

Born on December 17, 1807, in Haverhill, Massachusetts, Whittier grew up on a farm and received his early religious training through the Society of Friends (Quakers), of which both of his parents were practicing members. His early education consisted of reading the books and journals housed at the Friends Meeting House.

He later claimed that the first book of poems he had read was a volume by Robert Burns, which influenced his learning of the Scottish dialect and inspired him to write rhymes and imaginative stories of his own. In addition to Burns, Whittier admired other authors, including Edmund Spenser, William Shakespeare, John Milton, William Wordsworth, and Lady Caroline Lamb. In particular, the work of the English poet Milton inspired him to write on the themes of freedom and righteous living.

Whittier was also inspired by his acquaintance with the abolitionist leader William Lloyd Garrison, who published Whittier's first poem, "The Exile's Departure," in the *Newburyport Free Press* in June 1826. The two men sustained a friendship that would later spark Whittier's involvement in politics. Whittier attended the Haverhill Academy in 1827 after Garrison and Abijah W. Thayer, editor of the *Haverhill Gazette* (later the *Essex Gazette*), persuaded Whittier's father to allow him to further his education. During his time at Haverhill, Whittier wrote poems that appeared in the *Free Press* and the *Essex Gazette,* as well as in the *Boston Statesman,* edited by Nathaniel Greene. As an advocate for the antislavery cause, Whittier edited the *American Manufacturer* in Boston, the *Essex Gazette,* and the *New England Weekly Review* in Hartford, Connecticut.

In his writing and in his work as an editor, Whittier fought against the evils of slavery and promoted the cause of emancipation. The work that catapulted him to prominence in the abolitionist movement was an anticolonization pamphlet titled *Justice and Expediency* (1833), which began a thirty-year run of writing connected to slavery and abolition. On the basis of *Justice and Expediency,* Whittier was selected as a delegate to the Philadelphia Anti-Slavery Convention in 1833, at which the American Anti-Slavery Society was founded. The first collection of his antislavery poetry, *Poems,* was published in Philadelphia in 1838. From 1838 to 1840, he edited the *Pennsylvania Freeman,* to which he contributed bold antislavery editorials. Sponsored by the American Anti-Slavery Society in Boston, he transcribed, crafted, and wrote the preface to *The Narrative of James Williams* (1838).

In 1840, Whittier broke ties with Garrison and joined the American and Foreign Anti-Slavery Society, cofounded the Liberty Party (which was committed to electing abolitionists to political office), and ran for the U.S. Congress on the party's ticket two years later. In 1846, *Voices of Freedom,* his last and perhaps most celebrated collection of antislavery poems, was published. The following year, Whittier became corresponding editor of the Washington, D.C.–based *National Era,* to which he contributed most of his poems and articles during the next decade.

As a result of his prolific output and dedication to the antislavery cause, a number of African American abolitionists cited his antislavery poems in their publications, and several of his poems came to be sung as hymns. In her journals, Charlotte Forten Grimké, who taught former slaves in the Port Royal Experiment on Hilton Head Island, South Carolina, especially praised a poem that Whittier had written as a Christmas song. The educational curriculum of the Port Royal Experiment encouraged newly freed slaves to learn about those helping to advance their race, and Whittier was among those singled out for study.

Frederick Douglass included lines from two of Whittier's poems in his celebrated autobiography, *Narrative of the Life of Frederick Douglass* (1845). He used an excerpt from the antislavery poem "Farewell of a Virginia Slave Mother to Her Daughters, Sold Into Southern Bondage" (1838) to describe the pain and suffering felt by slaves upon the loss of their children, grandchildren, and great-grandchildren: "Gone, gone, sold and gone / To the rice swamp dank and lone." Douglass also used an excerpt from the poem "Clerical Oppressors" (1836), which lambastes the ministers of the gospel who preach God's word yet sanction slavery.

Whittier remained a voice for abolitionism throughout the course of the U.S. Civil War, producing polemics and patriotic verse in support of the cause. He died in Hampton Falls, New Hampshire, on September 7, 1892.

Lena Ampadu

See also: American and Foreign Anti-Slavery Society; American Anti-Slavery Society; Liberty Party.

Further Reading

Whittier, John Greenleaf. *Essays and Pamphlets on Antislavery.* Westport, CT: Negro Universities Press, 1970.

Whitting, William (1788–1862)

William Whitting was a Massachusetts businessman and a staunch supporter of the antislavery cause who advocated William Lloyd Garrison's call for immediate emancipation. Whitting served as a leader of several abolitionist groups and used his personal financial resources to support radical means of hastening the end of slavery.

Whitting was born in Sterling, Massachusetts, but lived most of his life in Concord, where he began operating a harness and carriage-making shop at the age of about twenty. His home and shop were destroyed by fire in 1823, but the business was thriving again by the early 1830s and the economic expansion of the Jacksonian era. It was during this time that Whitting became attracted to the antislavery movement as he began to read abolitionist literature.

As a man of affluence in his community, Whitting became involved in a variety of civic causes in Concord. He joined the local Masonic lodge in 1819 and took an active role in the benevolent work of that organization. He helped found the Concord Academy in 1822 and later became active in the Concord Lyceum and the Concord Social Circle. He held the rank of lieutenant colonel of artillery in the Massachusetts militia and was known locally as Colonel Whitting.

At the age of about forty, Whitting joined the Unitarian Church and became religiously active in the community, teaching Sunday school, supporting the temperance movement, and advocating equal education for boys and girls. Politically, Whitting moved from being a Federalist in his early years toward the Whig Party's probusiness stance. As he became more involved in the antislavery movement, he found himself drawn to the Free Soil and Republican parties.

Whitting was so pro-Garrisonian in his antislavery views that he kept a picture of Garrison as if it were a religious icon on the wall of his home. From 1835 on, he was a diligent reader of Garrison's *Liberator,* and he corresponded regularly with Garrison and other leaders of the American abolitionist movement. A member of several antislavery groups, he served as president of the Middlesex County Anti-Slavery Society for many years, and, for a time, he was vice president of the Massachusetts Anti-Slavery Society.

Ever the gracious host to his fellow abolitionists, Whitting opened his home to such frequent guests as Garrison, Wendell Phillips, and John Brown. Whitting provided financial support to John Brown and other antislavery advocates during the agitation in "Bleeding Kansas" of the mid-1850s. Certain that immediate action was the only viable means to end the scourge of slavery, Whitting was willing to support all means, including violence, to destroy the institution. More than a passive financial supporter of abolition, he was willing to take risks in support of his beliefs. He was known to assist fugitive slaves who passed through Concord on their way to freedom, even though such action was prohibited by the Fugitive Slave Law of 1850.

Whitting's abiding admiration for Garrison and his generous financial support for the antislavery cause were rewarded publicly at the time of his death. Garrison published an obituary in *The Liberator* of October 10, 1862, that described Whitting as a "thorough-going and out-spoken abolitionist." By pure coincidence, the same issue carried the announcement of President Abraham Lincoln's decision to issue the Emancipation Proclamation, ending slavery in the United States.

Junius P. Rodriguez

See also: Brown, John; Garrison, William Lloyd; Immediatism.

Further Reading

Stewart, James Brewer. *William Lloyd Garrison and the Challenge of Emancipation.* Arlington Heights, IL: Harlan Davidson, 1992.

Wilberforce, William (1759–1833)

A Christian reformer and longtime Member of Parliament, William Wilberforce led the campaign to end the slave trade and to abolish slavery throughout the British Empire. His lifetime of agitation helped convince Parliament to pass the Abolition of Slavery Act in 1833 (commonly known as the British Emancipation Act), which freed all slaves in the British colonies on August 1 of the following year.

Wilberforce was born on August 24, 1759, in Hull, England. Although he felt a call to the Methodist ministry at an early age, his mother wanted to ensure that he received a well-rounded education. After attending Saint John's College at Cambridge University, he embarked on a career in politics as a Member of Parliament, serving in the House of Commons from 1780 to 1825.

Wilberforce became an evangelical Christian in 1785, and he believed that part of his calling was to work for the abolition of slavery. In 1787, he made what was perhaps his greatest single contribution to the cause, when, at the invitation of Prime Minister William Pitt, he led a parliamentary campaign for the abolition of the slave trade. In May of that year, the Committee for the Abolition of the African Slave Trade was born. Armed with evidence of slaving atrocities supplied by fellow committee members, including Thomas Clarkson and others, Wilberforce petitioned Parliament on behalf of the cause. Wilberforce fell ill just as he was to present his resolution to the House, forcing Pitt to do so on his behalf.

The foreign slave trade bill was first introduced in 1788. The following year, Wilberforce made an impassioned speech against the slave trade, in which he suggested that all men were guilty of man's inhumanity to man. He argued that abolishing the slave trade would allow slaveholders to treat their charges more kindly. The resolution was defeated each time it was brought up over a period of eighteen years, in spite of mounting evidence documenting the cruelties of slavery.

Wilberforce became associated with a group of antislavery advocates known as the "Clapham Sect" (so called for the location where they held their meetings), which included abolitionists Clarkson, Granville Sharp, Zachary Macaulay, and Hannah More. Under Clarkson's leadership, the group appealed to the masses by launching a campaign against the slave trade, distributing antilavery pamphlets and cameos (produced by potter Josiah Wedgwood), and promoting the boycotting of sugar from the West Indies, among other means.

Ultimately, Wilberforce sought to convince the House of Commons that the West Indian planters

As a longtime member of Parliament (1780–1825), William Wilberforce was the preeminent figure in the campaign to end the British slave trade. He committed himself to the cause after what he described as a religious awakening. *(Hulton Archive/Getty Images)*

could survive economically without slave labor. By the late 1790s, however, England had become preoccupied with conflict in France. Although Pitt personally supported Wilberforce's petitions, the West Indies slave trade interests were a key component of Pitt's Whig coalition, and the House of Commons tabled the discussion of abolition until after the war against France. During this time, Wilberforce was personally threatened by supporters of the proslavery West Indian lobby.

In April 1797, Wilberforce published *A Practical View of the Prevailing Religious System of Professed Christians in the Higher and Middle Classes in this Country Contrasted with Real Christianity,* in which he suggested that the conflict Britain was experiencing was the result of its failure to practice true Christianity. It was an argument he also used in reference to Britain's participation in the slave trade.

A social activist, Wilberforce was a member of several missionary and Bible societies, and he supported missionary work in India and British child labor laws. He also was one of many directors of the African Institution and the Sierra Leone Company.

The African Institution, which replaced the Committee for the Abolition of the African Slave Trade in 1807, aimed to ensure that the new laws against the slave trade were properly enforced and to encourage legitimate trade with Africa. Through its well-connected members, including the duke of Gloucester as its president, the committee lobbied Parliament to send out naval patrols to monitor boats leaving Africa. The Sierra Leone Company, on the other hand, intended to "civilize" Africa through the efforts of missionaries. Blacks from Nova Scotia were sent there to colonize the area and founded Freetown, which became stable only after a minor insurrection, malaria outbreaks, and an attack by American-led French troops.

Wilberforce had more political success in the early 1800s. He proposed a slave trade limitation bill in 1804 that was meant to protect Africa from slave traders. Although this bill did not pass, the Abolition of the Slave Trade Act became law in 1807, as a more liberal government coalition led by Charles James Fox united liberals and evangelicals behind the law. Under the Slave Trade Act, British captains found to be transporting slaves were subject to a fine of £100 for every slave on board.

Although the slave trade was illegal in the British colonies, it continued actively and without regulation through Spanish, French, and Portuguese traders, who were now responsible for most of the traffic. Around 1816, Wilberforce devised a notion for registering enslaved Africans throughout the British colonies as a way of ensuring the 1807 law was being enforced, but the measure never passed. It became apparent to Wilberforce and his colleagues that more stringent measures were needed.

In 1823, Wilberforce, along with Clarkson and Macaulay, organized the Society for the Mitigation and Gradual Abolition of Slavery throughout the British Dominions. More commonly called the Anti-Slavery Society, this organization sought to improve conditions in the West Indies and laid out a plan for the gradual emancipation of British slaves.

Thomas Fowell Buxton, who had succeeded Wilberforce as leader of the antislavery campaign in Parliament, presented a bill recommending that all enslaved blacks be freed and then apprenticed to their masters for a specified period of time. In addition, the planters would be compensated £20 million for the eventual loss of labor.

Wilberforce died in London on July 29, 1833. One month later, Parliament passed the Abolition of Slavery Act, granting freedom to all slaves in the British Empire.

Denise Lovett

See also: Abolition of Slavery Act (1833); Abolition of the Slave Trade Act (1807); African Institution; Buxton, Thomas Fowell; Clarkson, Thomas; Macaulay, Zachary; Sharp, Granville; Sierra Leone.

Further Reading

Coupland, Reginald. *Wilberforce: A Narrative.* New York: Negro Universities Press, 1968.
Furneaux, Robin. *William Wilberforce.* London: Hamish Hamilton, 1974.
Warner, Oliver. *William Wilberforce and His Times.* London: B.T. Batsford, 1962.

Williams, Peter, Jr. (1786–1840)

In the 1820s and 1830s, a large portion of America's abolitionist leadership was composed of black ministers, including men such as Peter Williams, Jr., who was the pastor at Saint Philip's Episcopal Church in Harlem from 1826 to 1840. A proponent of emigration, Williams supported groups such as the American Colonization Society, which sought to create settlements of free blacks in Africa. He spoke out against injustices to African Americans in both speeches and from the pulpit.

Williams was born as a free man in 1786 in New York City. His father, Peter Williams, Sr., was a respected activist in New York's black community, known for establishing the independent African Methodist Church in New York City in 1796. As a child, Williams attended the African Free School, and his social activism began while he was still a young man. At the age of twenty-two, Williams delivered "An Oration on the Abolition of the Slave Trade," a powerful political statement describing the horrors of the slave trade and the duties of free blacks. The address was given in the New York African Church on January 1, 1808, the same day that U.S. legislation barring the African slave trade went into effect. Just six months later, he helped reorganize the most enduring autonomous black organization in New York City, the African Society for Mutual Relief.

In 1809, Williams rebelled against the Methodist tradition of his father and became a lay reader for a black Episcopalian church in New York City. In October 1820, he became the first black man to be ordained by the Episcopal Church, and, in July 1826, he became the first black Episcopal priest.

In addition to his religious contributions, Williams remained an activist. He became deeply involved in the American effort during the War of 1812, and he called on his black brothers and sisters to help fortify the city of New York against the British.

By 1816, however, Williams had become an advocate of emigration. Concerned about the black community's future in the United States, he became the leader of the New York City branch of the African Institution and began a regular correspondence with black emigrationist Paul Cuffe. The latter relied on Williams to dispense information and rally support for the cause of emigration. In 1824, Williams became president of the New York Haytien Emigration Society and visited Haiti as a possible émigré community. In 1827, he helped establish *Freedom's Journal,* a black-owned abolitionist newspaper.

In 1830, Williams delivered another speech in which he declared his disappointment with the shortcomings of legal emancipation, and he urged his community to fight for its rights but also to consider their options in case they were forcibly removed from the United States. Around this time, Williams shifted his focus from Haiti as a prospective emigration settlement and encouraged his people to consider Canada as a potential home.

By 1833, Williams had become active in the American Anti-Slavery Society; the following year, he faced his most serious challenge in the form of an anti-abolition riot. The mob, which numbered 7,000 to 8,000 at its peak, descended on black neighborhoods in New York City. Perhaps the most vehement rage was directed against Williams and Saint Philip's Church, as rioters believed that Williams had performed an interracial marriage ceremony there.

The 1834 riot marked the end of Williams's public career as an abolitionist and agitator for black civil rights. His mentor, Bishop Benjamin T. Onderdonk, demanded that he resign from the American Anti-Slavery Society and refrain from future public appearances relating to abolition or statements on political matters. Williams was compelled to obey his bishop. He continued in his role as minister of Saint Philip's Church until his death in 1840.

Leslie M. Alexander

See also: African Institution; Cuffe, Paul.

Further Reading

Mabee, Carleton. *Black Freedom; The Nonviolent Abolitionists From 1830 Through the Civil War.* New York: Macmillan, 1970.

Wilmot Proviso (1846)

The Wilmot Proviso was a legislative attempt to prohibit slavery in the territories acquired by the United States as a result of the Mexican-American War (1846–1848). On August 8, 1846, Congressman David Wilmot, a Pennsylvania Democrat, introduced an amendment to an army appropriations bill to ban slavery and involuntary servitude in all territories acquired during the war.

The debate over the Wilmot Proviso deeply divided Americans no less than it did the major political parties. The bitterness it engendered helped set the stage for the U.S. Civil War, which would begin less than two decades later. Although the House of Representatives twice passed the proposed amendment, Southerners were able to block the measure in the Senate.

Many members of the Whig Party opposed the war between the United States and Mexico, because they believed that President James K. Polk had instigated the conflict in order to expand slavery into new territories. The admission of Texas as a slave state in 1845 seemed to confirm this fear for most Whigs, who initially opposed the acquisition of any new territory as a result of the war.

The Democrats, members of the other major political party of this period, were split over whether slavery should be allowed in new areas of the country. Northern Democrats supported retaining the areas conquered during the war, including California and New Mexico, but opposed the expansion of slavery into those areas. Southern Democrats supported both territorial expansion and the spread of slavery. With congressional elections forthcoming in 1846, Northern Democrats were afraid that abolitionists in the North would support the Whigs, risking a significant electoral loss for their own party.

When it became clear that the United States would win the war, Polk asked the U.S. Congress for the funding and political authorization to negotiate a settlement with Mexico. In 1846, an army appropriations bill was submitted to the House of Representatives that allocated $2 million for Polk to end the war. Wilmot saw an opportunity to attach his proviso to this appropriations bill. The language of the amendment was taken from the provisions of the Northwest Ordinance of 1787, which prohibited slavery in areas such as Ohio and Michigan.

Polk bitterly opposed the proviso and sought to separate the issue of slavery from the effort to negotiate an end to the war. He warned Congress that any delays would cause the war to continue unnecessarily. Most Southerners joined Polk in his opposition of the proviso, as they supported slavery and states' rights. Both Southern Democrats and Southern Whigs argued that individual states, not the federal government, should decide the question of slavery for themselves. This position became known as "popular sovereignty."

The abolitionists in the Whig and Democratic parties outnumbered the proslavery and states' rights proponents in the House, and the amendment was passed. In the Senate, however, Southerners were able to block its passage, and the Senate adjourned without approving the proviso.

Undeterred, Wilmot reintroduced the measure the following year as an amendment to a $3 million appropriations bill that was under consideration in the House. Again, the measure passed in the House but was defeated in the Senate; the latter drafted its own appropriations bill.

The Treaty of Guadalupe Hidalgo was ratified by the Senate in March 1848, and the question of slavery in the new territories was left open. Amid preparations for the presidential and congressional elections in 1848, the leadership of both parties decided not to endorse the Wilmot Proviso for fear of antagonizing voters.

The Democrats embraced popular sovereignty as a campaign plank. Among the Whigs, the party's failure to support the proviso led to increased dissatisfaction among abolitionists and helped speed the demise of the party. Disaffected Whigs left the party and formed the Free Soil Party, for which the Wilmot Proviso became a core policy platform.

The Compromise of 1850, which admitted California as a free state but also imposed the Fugitive Slave Law, did not end the controversy, as it failed to address whether slavery would be allowed in the territories that would eventually become Arizona, New Mexico, Nevada, and Utah. Instead, the doctrine of popular sovereignty would be applied to future territories that sought to enter the Union.

Wilmot became a leader of the Free Soil Party, but he was defeated in the congressional race of 1850, a result of his efforts to stop the expansion of slavery. In 1851, he was appointed as a judge in Pennsylvania, and, in 1854, he helped found the Republican Party. As one of the early Republican leaders, he ensured that the party adopted a strong position against the expansion of slavery into newly acquired territories. From 1850 on, Northern state legislatures instructed their state's congressional delegations to propose or support the terms of the Wilmot Proviso on any new territory brought into the Union. Southern states increasingly promised secession if such a measure was adopted.

The continuing efforts of abolitionists to pass the Wilmot Proviso led the preeminent politicians of the day to seek alternative plans to deal with the slavery question in new territories after the Compromise of 1850. However, the antagonism and sectional rivalry wrought by the proviso made each future compromise more and more precarious.

Tom Lansford

See also: Free Soil Party.

Further Reading

Fehrenbacher, Don E. *The South and Three Sectional Crises.* Baton Rouge: Louisiana State University Press, 1980.

Foner, Eric. "The Wilmot Proviso Revisited." *Journal of American History* 61 (September 1969): 269–79.

Goings, Charles Buxton. *David Wilmot, Free-Soiler: A Biography of the Great Advocate of the Wilmot Proviso.* Gloucester, MA: P. Smith, 1966.

Morrison, Chaplain W. *Democratic Politics and Sectionalism: The Wilmot Proviso Controversy.* Chapel Hill: University of North Carolina Press, 1967.

Rayback, Joseph. *Free Soil: The Election of 1848.* Lexington: University Press of Kentucky, 1971.

Wilson, Harriet E. (ca. 1820s–1863)

Critically neglected for more than a century, Harriet E. Wilson is finally acknowledged as the first African American woman to publish a novel—*Our Nig; or, Sketches From the Life of a Free Black, in a Two-Story White House, North, Showing That Slavery's Shadows Fall Even There* (1859), which was originally published anonymously. The novel offers a rare insight into the treatment of African American women in the antebellum North and their precarious existences, which were constantly endangered by the Fugitive Slave Law of 1850.

Born in New Hampshire sometime in the 1820s, Harriet, whose maiden name was Adams, spent her childhood working as an indentured servant for the Haywards, a farming family with strong abolitionist connections living near Milford. This experience is the foundation of the plot of *Our Nig,* which is set in the free state of Massachusetts.

The main character, Frado (diminutive for Alfrado, also referred to as "Our Nig"), is deserted by her white mother after the death of her black father and becomes an indentured servant for the Bellomonts, who treat her cruelly. At the age of eighteen, in another turn that closely parallels the author's own experience, Frado leaves the Bellomonts and marries a young African American who deserts her after she gives birth to his child. Her ensuing impoverishment forces her separation from the child, who is taken under the care of a charity, and the book describes Frado's attempt to earn enough money to recover her child.

The end of the story finds Frado focused "on her steadfast purpose of elevating herself," constantly threatened by slave-hunting kidnappers, and "maltreated by professed abolitionists, who didn't want slaves at the South nor niggers in their own houses, North." This concluding sentence is a powerful indictment of both the Fugitive Slave Law, which gave slave hunters a pretext for capturing *any* African American found in the North, and Northern racism and hypocrisy.

The suffering that Frado endures during her years with the Bellomonts exposes African American oppression in the antebellum North, where domestic service was the main form of employment for free blacks, particularly for women. Wilson's statement in the preface that she has "purposely omitted what would most provoke shame in our good antislavery friends at home" may signify that she avoided reference to the abolitionist sympathies of the Bellomonts, who were modeled on the abolitionist Haywards.

The narrative of *Our Nig* is shaped by the dominant mode of African American writing of the time, the slave narrative. The text reaches its climax as Frado realizes that she has the ability to change her own life, an epiphany that has innumerable counterparts in traditional slave narratives. Still, Wilson's novel deviates from that genre—most notably, by depicting a main character who is female and has never experienced, to quote Frederick Douglass's phrase, "the bloody arms of slavery" but nevertheless becomes conscious of "the stirring of free and independent thoughts."

Our Nig focuses on the growing awareness of a servant girl who becomes a woman, casting light on the unique plight of African American women in a racist context. Since Wilson's novel was rediscovered in 1983, it has stood at the center of African American women's writing.

Luca Prono

See also: Fugitive Slave Act of 1850; Novels, Antislavery.

Further Reading

Davis, Cynthia J. "Speaking the Body's Pain: Harriet Wilson's *Our Nig*." *African American Review* 27 (Fall 1993): 391–404.

Stern, Julia. "Excavating Genre in *Our Nig*." *American Literature* 67 (September 1995): 439–64.

White, Barbara A. "*Our Nig* and the She-Devil: New Information About Harriet Wilson and the 'Bellomont Family.'" *American Literature* 65 (March 1993): 19–52.

Wilson, Harriet E. *Our Nig; or, Sketches From the Life of a Free Black.* 1859. Ed. Henry Louis Gates, Jr. New York: Vintage Books, 1983.

Wilson, Hiram (1803–1864)

Trained as a Congregationalist minister, Hiram Wilson was a passionate antislavery advocate and educational innovator who devoted his life to ministering to fugitive slaves in western Ontario. Wilson's mission in the city of Saint Catharines, Canada, came to be known as the northern terminus of the Underground Railroad.

Wilson was born in 1803 in Acworth, New Hampshire, but he moved west as a young man. He graduated from the Oneida Institute in Whitesboro,

New York, and began his preparation for the ministry in 1833 at Lane Theological Seminary in Cincinnati, Ohio. Shortly after arriving in Cincinnati, he joined the group of young antislavery activists who became known disparagingly as the "Lane Rebels." When the activities of these reformers ran afoul of the more conservative leadership at the seminary, Wilson and other like-minded students left the institution and completed their ministerial studies at Oberlin College, Ohio's pro-abolition institution of higher education.

Wilson completed his studies at Oberlin College in 1836 and decided to continue his ministry through efforts in support of the abolitionist cause. He joined the American Anti-Slavery Society and became one of the "seventy agents" whom Theodore Dwight Weld sent out on the lecture circuit. Wilson traveled extensively throughout Ohio, lecturing and recruiting new members for the abolitionist organization. He was an effective agent, but his religious training called him to minister, and he believed that he could do more to aid the antislavery cause in another capacity.

Wilson's work for the antislavery cause eventually brought him to Toronto, Canada, where he assisted fugitive slaves from the United States as they adjusted to their new home. He spent the next six years traveling in Upper Canada (present-day Ontario), during which time he founded ten schools.

Recognizing the importance of education and training to newly freed blacks as they made the transition from slavery to wage labor, he founded the British-American Institute of Science, a manual labor school in the Dawn Fugitive Slave Settlement near present-day London, Ontario. Wilson and fellow abolitionists Josiah Henson and James Canning Fuller had conceived the institute in 1838, but it took several years of fund raising before the school opened its doors in 1842. Wilson served as principal until 1849.

The Canadian branch of the American Missionary Association supported Wilson's efforts at the Dawn Fugitive Slave Settlement, and enrollment at the British-American Institute of Science had increased from fourteen to sixty students by 1852. Although Wilson had conceived the school primarily as a fugitive slave facility, it later expanded its mission to accept interested white and American Indian students. The school offered essential services that were rare on what was then Canada's western frontier. Besides providing training in manual labor, the school made an invaluable contribution to the spiritual and physical well-being of many fugitive slaves who found refuge in Canada. Unfortunately, internal division among the school's leaders led to its decline after 1855.

Wilson left the Dawn Settlement in 1850 after the death of his wife Hannah. He contemplated returning to the United States but realized that his services were desperately needed in Canada. With the passage of the new Fugitive Slave Law in 1850, he understood that even more fugitive slaves from the United States would be making their way to freedom in Canada. Wilson moved to Saint Catharines and founded an evening school, where he taught, preached, and operated a relief station for fugitive slaves. He worked with local authorities to permit supplies for the refugees to enter Canada, exempt from custom duties. He died in 1864.

Junius P. Rodriguez

See also: American Missionary Association; Canada; Fugitive Slaves; Underground Railroad; Weld, Theodore Dwight.

Further Reading

Siebert, Wilbur H. *The Underground Railroad From Slavery to Freedom.* New York: Macmillan, 1898; New York: Arno, 1968.
Woodson, Carter G. *The Education of the Negro Prior to 1861.* Salem, NH: Ayer, 1986.

Women's Rights and the Abolitionist Movement

Although scholarship points to the 1848 Seneca Falls Convention as the birthplace of the women's rights movement, in fact, women's political and social activism began in the early decades of the nineteenth century. During a period when they lacked the right to vote and could not be employed in many professions, women became America's social and moral guardians in their roles as wives and mothers. Many women—mostly white and middle class—extended their responsibilities beyond the private sphere of the family by joining or initiating reform organizations to promote temperance, curb prostitution, and abolish slavery. In support of their causes, they organized fairs, raised money, wrote pamphlets and books, and lifted their voices. As abolitionist women entered into the male domain of antislavery work in the 1820s and 1830s, they carved out new social roles for women and laid the groundwork for future feminists.

The nineteenth century in the United States was an era during which the accepted, appropriate roles assigned to men and women were well established. Men were public entities, owing to their role as breadwinners and protectors of their families. Men operated in the public realm: They went to work at jobs located outside the home; they conducted business in the marketplace; and they traveled, both to and from their jobs and more extensively. Men were responsible for creating and maintaining the political and cultural infrastructure that allowed economic and intellectual commerce to occur; they were worldly beings, and their sphere of operation and influence was the public sphere.

Women, on the other hand, were considered to operate within the domestic sphere. Child bearing and child rearing, cleaning, cooking, sewing, and laundering the family's clothing—whether undertaken directly or through the direction of household servants—were among women's responsibilities, as were the happiness and, even more importantly, the moral welfare of those in their households. Ironically, this restrictive domestic sphere was in many ways responsible for women's engagement in the abolitionist movement.

As early as the mid-1820s, women's voices were heard in defense of the rights of American slaves. Elizabeth Heyrick, an Englishwoman, and the Scottish American Frances Wright wrote publications calling for the abolition of slavery in 1824 and 1825, respectively; Elizabeth Margaret Chandler regularly contributed antislavery articles to the press starting the following year. By 1828, Wright was speaking publicly on antislavery topics to groups of women, and Maria Stewart, a free black woman, followed her lead in 1831. However, the efforts of these early female abolitionists were not particularly effective—not surprising in light of the era's cultural climate. Detractors were quick to find reasons to discount these women's activities: Heyrick was a foreigner and a detested Quaker, as was Chandler; Stewart, as an African American, was discounted out of hand by many observers; and Wright, a woman of decidedly unconventional personal appearance, beliefs, and conduct, was frequently ridiculed by the critical public.

The origins of women's public voice came through the work of local groups of ordinary ladies in New England. As early as 1829, a group of Philadelphia women organized to monitor and eventually boycott the use of cotton grown by slave labor. Soon, similar groups began to meet informally in the homes of women throughout New England, and word of such gatherings was spread through the exchange of letters among friends and family members, an accepted activity for women. The skills that women gained by maintaining such correspondence, by organizing these groups, and by conducting their informal meetings gave the participants a taste of the kind of work that previously had bee undertaken only by men. These same skills also readied the women for the explosion of formal activist work that was to come in the ensuing years.

The 1830s saw a dramatic increase in the number of women's social reform groups, the earliest of which were involved with the abolition of slavery. In 1832, Maria Weston Chapman and her sisters started the Boston Female Anti-Slavery Society to complement William Lloyd Garrison's newly formed all-male New England Anti-Slavery Society; Lucretia Coffin Mott organized the Philadelphia Female Anti-Slavery Society the following year. Soon, nearly every city and town across New England boasted its own female antislavery society; in 1838, the Massachusetts Anti-Slavery Society alone recorded more than forty female auxiliaries. In fact, such groups had their greatest success in the northeastern United States. They were understandably off-limits in the South, and women living in the Western regions of the nation were so consumed with the realities of frontier life that there was little time for the luxury of socializing, no matter the cause or event.

These societies allowed women to experience the best of both spheres of activity: By discussing the question of slavery and how best to end it, they were engaging in decidedly "male" work, and many groups took their interests one step further to express their concerns through petitions addressed to the U.S. Congress. On the other hand, their "female" concern for moral issues was tailor-made for the growing abolitionist view of slavery as a sin against God and one's fellow human beings. Additionally, the domestic arts that were so familiar to all respectable women of the day—sewing, painting, embroidery and other fancy-work, baking, cooking, candy making—were put to good use in support of the cause as the women's societies held their popular antislavery fairs, the equivalent of modern-day church bazaars, which raised funds to be used in spreading the abolitionist message.

Of course, not all Americans welcomed the rise of the female abolitionist societies. Many men—and a substantial number of women as well—felt threatened by these women's growing activism. Indeed, Garrison's commitment to ensuring that women played a significant role in the American Anti-Slavery Society would later spur a major split in the organization. In some cases, female antislavery societies were attacked from the pulpit, on the grounds that they were addressing an issue that was of no concern to Northerners, that they caused women to usurp men's work, or that they drew women away from their important God-given work of caring for their families.

The popularity of the female antislavery societies led to another phenomenon that immeasurably advanced the cause of women's rights: the rise of the female antislavery lecturer. Although several women had spoken on antislavery topics prior to the emergence of these groups, none had the impact of the Grimké sisters on the presence of women in the public sphere.

Sarah M. Grimké and her younger sister Angelina E. Grimké were the daughters of a slaveholding judge from South Carolina. Both women had become Quakers as adults, and both had moved to the North in the late 1820s because of their opposition to the conditions they had witnessed in the South. Sarah, long convinced that the conventional separation of men's and women's spheres was contrary to the teachings of scripture, assisted her sister in writing and editing a number of essays and speeches against the evils of slavery. Angelina, the more compelling speaker of the two, took to the stage for some eighteen months during the late 1830s, touring New England with Sarah and her future husband, the abolitionist Theodore Dwight Weld. Angelina was, by all contemporary accounts, a powerful and confident orator, although her diaries and letters reveal her insecurities and misgivings; as a white woman speaking before "mixed" (black and white) and "promiscuous" (male and female) audiences, she was subject to a barrage of personal attacks, including several that endangered her physical safety.

As the 1830s drew to a close, abolitionist men and women aggressively debated the "socially correct" role of women in the antislavery movement. Because abolitionists were wrestling with the issue of racial equality, they created a climate that was ripe for discussion of equality between the sexes. In the following decade, women such as Lucretia C. Mott, Elizabeth Cady Stanton, and Lucy Stone would birth the women's rights movement as they lectured, wrote newspaper articles, and organized women's rights conventions.

Indeed, two antislavery events in 1840—Abigail Kelley's appointment to the executive committee of the male-dominated American Anti-Slavery Society and the rejection of women delegates at the World Anti-Slavery Convention in London—prompted women to agitate for rights specific to their gender. The feminists of the mid-nineteenth century borrowed from their predecessors' antislavery rhetoric and determination as they stepped into a new era that fought for the civil rights of women.

Barbara Schwarz Wachal

See also: American Anti-Slavery Society; Anthony, Susan B.; Chandler, Elizabeth Margaret; Chapman, Maria Weston; Foster, Abigail Kelley; Grimké, Angelina Emily; Grimké, Sarah Moore; Heyrick, Elizabeth; Mott, James, and Lucretia Coffin Mott; Stanton, Elizabeth Cady; Stone, Lucy; Wright, Frances ("Fanny").

Further Reading

Hersh, Blanche Glassman. *The Slavery of Sex: Feminist-Abolitionists in America.* Urbana: University of Illinois Press, 1978.

Lerner, Gerda. *The Grimké Sisters From South Carolina: Pioneers for Women's Rights and Abolition.* Chapel Hill: University of North Carolina Press, 2004.

Yellin, Jean Fagan, and John C. Van Horne, eds. *The Abolitionist Sisterhood: Women's Political Culture in Antebellum America.* Ithaca, NY: Cornell University Press, 1994.

Woolman, John (1720–1772)

Most of what historians know of John Woolman, one of the earliest antislavery partisans in North America, comes from his journal, which he began writing in 1756. Quaker journals were meant to be religious and spiritual documents, and Woolman's is counted as a classic in the spiritual autobiography genre. The entries show that his revulsion toward slavery rested on the Quaker convictions of divine love, human equality, and moral law based on scripture. These beliefs infused his daily life and behavior, much of which were dedicated to the cause of antislavery. As a Quaker, Woolman worked to bring fellow members of the Society of Friends to the principles of pacifism and equality.

Woolman was born on October 19, 1720, into a Quaker farm family in Burlington County, New Jersey, the fourth of thirteen children. At the age of about eighteen, he left farming and went to work as a shop clerk. He later became a prosperous shopkeeper but turned to tailoring as a means to greater independence. By his own account, his first antislavery emotions were aroused at the age of twenty-two, when his employer asked him to write a bill of sale for a slave. He did as he was told, but he was, as he reported in his journal, "afflicted in mind" by the moral dilemma.

Woolman began his lifelong antislavery campaign in 1746 while on a missionary journey on horseback through Maryland, Virginia, and North Carolina. Many of the Quaker households that received him lived luxuriously on slave labor. In his understated tone, he wrote, "my exercise was often great, and I frequently had conversations with them in private concerning it."

One result of Woolman's journey was the pamphlet *Some Considerations on the Keeping of Negroes,* published in 1753 by the Philadelphia Yearly Meeting and distributed to Quakers in America and Britain. It was the first antislavery literature to be disseminated broadly and became a prototype for English and American abolitionist pamphlets. The pamphlet argued from Genesis 3:20 that "all nations are of one blood." Thus, "to consider mankind otherwise than brethren, to think favours are peculiar to one nation and exclude others, plainly supposes a darkness in the understanding" of God's universal love.

A succeeding essay, *Part Second of Considerations on the Keeping of Negroes,* appeared in 1762. This time, Benjamin Franklin published the pamphlet, which Woolman paid for himself. Addressed to all Christians, the essay rallied the abolitionist movements in America, Great Britain, and beyond.

Woolman helped to gradually end slavery among members of the American Society of Friends. In 1755, he convinced the Philadelphia Yearly Meeting to censure members who were still implicated in slavery in any way. That meeting influenced others to follow suit. Even the Yearly Meeting in Virginia, acting under Woolman's influence, barred its members from commercial slave trading, though not from slave ownership. In 1758, the Philadelphia Yearly Meeting barred slaveholding members from responsible Quaker offices. In 1760, Woolman visited Newport, Rhode Island, a center of the slave trade, and talked to individual Quakers, persuading them to stop buying and selling slaves. In 1770, New England Quakers removed themselves from the trade. Finally, in 1784, twelve years after Woolman died, American Quakers became the first organized group to free their slaves.

Woolman carried his antislavery efforts to Great Britain, arriving at the London Yearly Meeting in 1772. During the voyage, he wrote the essay *On the Slave Trade.* From London, he traveled by stagecoach to meetings all over England. So distressed was he by the brutality inflicted by the coach service on both the horses and the postboys that he asked correspondents at home to send only the most necessary mail. Woolman's last journal entry is dated September 29, 1772, in the city of York, where he lay "so weak in body that I know not how my sickness may end." He died of smallpox on October 7, 1772.

Woolman's journal was published in 1776. Steeped in Quaker thought, the text extended his thoughts to the abolitionist movement as a whole. Woolman's followers, including Quaker abolitionist and publisher Benjamin Lundy, continued their anti-slavery missionary work in the early 1800s and, in turn, inspired other leading American abolitionists, such as William Lloyd Garrison.

Riva Berleant

See also: Lundy, Benjamin; Quakers (Society of Friends); Religion and Abolitionism.

Further Reading

Sox, David. *John Woolman: Quintessential Quaker, 1720–1772.* Richmond, IN: Friends United Press, 1999.
Woolman, John. *The Journal and Major Essays of John Woolman.* Ed. Phillips P. Moulton. New York: Oxford University Press, 1971.

World Anti-Slavery Convention (1840)

Hundreds of abolitionists from Great Britain, the United States, and elsewhere gathered in London in June 1840 to seek common ground so that transatlantic abolitionists might hasten the end of slavery in the Americas and all other areas where it still thrived.

The convention coincided with the end of the apprenticeship system in the British colonies and the successful emancipation of all British colonial possessions as a result of the passage of the Abolition of Slavery Act (commonly known as the British Emancipation Act) in 1833. Buoyed by the optimism of this singular achievement, antislavery advocates on both sides of the Atlantic believed that slavery might be abolished in the United States, Brazil, Cuba, Suriname, and elsewhere if similar legislative remedies were pursued.

The idea of holding such a convention was promoted by Joseph Sturge and John Scoble, representatives of a new generation of leaders within the ranks of British abolitionists who held positions in the recently formed British and Foreign Anti-Slavery Society. To these reformers, the purpose of the gathering was "to open an active correspondence" with abolitionists worldwide and "to encourage them by every means in our power." Accordingly, delegates from the United States, Canada, and France were invited to take part in the convention. The convention's goal was to usher in a new era of international cooperation in the struggle against slavery, and it succeeded to a degree in opening dialogue toward that end.

Nearly 500 delegates attended the World Anti-Slavery Convention, held from June 12 to June 23 in London's Freemason's Hall. The eighty-year-old Thomas Clarkson presided over the gathering, though his role was more ceremonial and symbolic than real; the true business of the convention was conducted by vice chairmen and standing committees.

William Lloyd Garrison, the editor and publisher of *The Liberator,* a popular antislavery newspaper, led the delegation of American abolitionists who journeyed to London for the convention. Because the convention was held amid the litigation associated with the *Amistad* affair in the United States, some prominent American abolitionists, such as Lewis Tappan, were unable to attend. Since the American Anti-Slavery Society had already begun to experience internal dissension, some anti-Garrisonian abolitionists worried that Garrison might stack the delegation with only like-minded supporters. These opponents realized that while Garrison was viewed as a fanatic by some in the United States, he was widely respected in Britain; the convention, they feared, might only enhance his reputation.

Several black abolitionists were invited to be a part of the American delegation to the London meeting, but they faced discrimination in myriad ways during the course of their travels. Some were initially denied passports; others, such as Charles Lenox Remond, were forced to travel in steerage during the transatlantic crossing.

The delegation of abolitionists from the United States included a number of women who were active in local antislavery societies throughout the New England region. This group included Lucretia C. Mott, Lydia Maria Child, and Abigail Kelley Foster. Upon their arrival, the American women were dismayed to learn that they would not be allowed to participate actively in the meeting; the formal deliberations were limited to men only. The women were permitted to sit behind a screen in the gallery where they might hear the debates, but they were not permitted to add their voices. Believing that the American women were being treated unfairly, Garrison opted to sit with them in the gallery as a nondelegate.

One reason for this gender segregation was the schism that had appeared within the Quaker (Society of Friends) community in the United States. Orthodox Quakers had parted ways with the more liberal Quakers (known as Hicksites), who favored direct action in several social reform movements of the day. The Hicksite Quakers supported greater opportunities for women, and many of the female delegates who traveled to London belonged to that faction. In Britain, however, Hicksite Quakers were viewed as heretics, and it was widely believed that permitting the women delegates to be seated within the convention would do irreparable harm to the British antislavery movement.

In advance of the convention, abolitionists in the United States had collected a wealth of statistical data on slavery. Much of it was included in the publication *Slavery and the Internal Slave Trade in the United States* (1841), which was subsequently published in London by the British and Foreign Anti-Slavery Society.

Junius P. Rodriguez

See also: Abolition of Slavery Act (1833); Child, Lydia Maria Francis; Clarkson, Thomas; Foster, Abigail Kelley; Garrison, William Lloyd; Mott, James, and Lucretia Coffin Mott; Quakers (Society of Friends).

Further Reading

Kennon, Donald R. "'An Apple of Discord': The Woman Question at the World's Anti-Slavery Convention of 1840." *Slavery and Abolition* 5 (Winter 1984): 244–76.

Maynard, Douglas H. "The World's Anti-Slavery Convention of 1840." *Mississippi Valley Historical Review* 47 (December 1969): 452–71.

Usrey, Mirian L. "Charles Lenox Remond: Garrison's Ebony Echo at the World's Anti-Slavery Convention 1840." *Essex Institute Historical Collections* 106 (April 1970): 112–25.

World Anti-Slavery Convention (1843)

A second World Anti-Slavery Convention was held in London in June 1843, three years after the first such event took place. Hundreds of abolitionists from the United States, Britain, and the Caribbean region gathered to find common ground in their efforts to end slavery in areas where it still existed in the Americas.

When members of the British and Foreign Anti-Slavery Society decided to host a second convention, they purposely avoided revisiting the controversial

"woman question" that had plagued the 1840 gathering. Specifically, only those delegates who were directly invited by the society were welcomed to attend the convention and participate in its deliberations. As a result of this decision, American women abolitionists and the male abolitionists who supported their participation did not receive invitations.

This course of action did not meet with unanimous approval from abolitionist groups in the United Kingdom. In particular, delegates from the Hibernian Anti-Slavery Society boycotted the event entirely; delegates from Glasgow, having initially refused to attend, reluctantly agreed to participate only after last-minute coaxing by society officials.

Noticeably excluded from the invitation list were William Lloyd Garrison and other leaders of the American Anti-Slavery Society. Instead, members of the British and Foreign Anti-Slavery Society invited anti-Garrisonian abolitionists, many of whom came from the ranks of the American and Foreign Anti-Slavery Society, to head the American delegation. Lewis Tappan, Joshua Leavitt, Amos Phelps, Jonathan Blanchard, and James W.C. Pennington were some of the key antislavery delegates who traveled to London from the United States.

The British and Foreign Anti-Slavery Society also sought to have a more structured program than the 1840 convention and determined beforehand that specific issues would be discussed at the gathering. Several leading American abolitionists were tasked with collecting data and preparing preliminary reports on various slavery-related topics, including agriculture, commerce, literature, law, moral and social habits, religion, and missionary endeavors.

Joseph Sturge and John Scoble were again the chief organizers of the event among the British abolitionists, as they had been in 1840. In many respects, the 1843 convention proved to be a turning point within the leadership of the British antislavery movement. Noticeably absent due to fading health were such giants of the movement as Thomas Clarkson and Thomas Fowell Buxton. The important role of such leaders was legendary, but their battles—ending the transatlantic slave trade and abolishing slavery in the British Empire—were now regarded as the battles of an earlier generation. Sturge, Scoble, and their contemporaries hoped that the future of the movement might bring greater transatlantic support and end slavery in all parts of the world where it remained active.

The goals and the rhetoric of the British and American abolitionists belied the true nature of the movement in the early 1840s. There was a real and growing schism among the ranks of the American abolitionists, and the British and Foreign Anti-Slavery Society's decision to exclude Garrison and his supporters further broadened the gap of factionalism. In addition, the society saw little value in seeking a political solution to the slavery question. Still rooted in the evangelical fervor of an earlier generation, the British abolitionists continued to believe that moral suasion was a sufficient method to bring an end to slavery. More and more people in the United States abolitionist movement were turning toward a political approach at the very time that British abolitionists were discouraging such measures.

One of the key points of contention that animated the debates between the American and British abolitionists was that of fair trade and its relationship to slavery. Many American abolitionists argued that the British government, through its continued support of the Corn Laws, perpetuated the existence of slavery in the states of the American South. By refusing to import wheat, corn, or other forms of grain from the American South, the British government was indirectly forcing the continued reliance on cotton—and effectively urging the continuation of slavery, the labor force upon which this crop was based. Samuel Webb, an abolitionist from Philadelphia, argued, "*You* buy the slaveholder's cotton—you hire him to chain, to whip and to work his slaves to death! *You* stimulate him by your money—by your patronage—by your commerce!"

Although free trade was one of the key points of debate at the World Anti-Slavery Convention, it was not the most controversial issue to arise there. The question of Texas—specifically, whether it should be annexed to the United States or allowed to remain independent and sovereign—was an important concern throughout the gathering. British abolitionists considered a proposal whereby foreign interests, primarily antislavery-leaning British corporate and financial houses, might provide sufficient loan guarantees to the Republic of Texas so that it might remain independent and sovereign. This plan would be contingent on two points: that Texas would abolish slavery and that it would relinquish any plans to annex itself to the United States.

Consideration of this scheme, coming just one year before a contentious American presidential election in 1844, did substantial harm to the incipient Liberty Party movement and made it seem as though the British were meddling in a purely American political matter. Abolitionists from the United States had to fend off charges that they were scheming with the British in a matter that was a domestic concern.

There was no immediate result in the wake of the World Anti-Slavery Convention of 1843. The British government did abolish the Corn Laws within a few years, but many viewed that victory as being associated with the ongoing negotiations between the United States and Britain over the joint occupancy of the Oregon Country, and not the result of the abolitionists' debates. Likewise, Texas was annexed to the United States in 1845, laying to rest any hope among the British abolitionists that slavery might be abolished there through the financial schemes that had been discussed in 1843.

The divisive political issue of slavery within the United States—and the heated discourse that it inspired—made it far less likely that foreign abolitionist organizations could have any real impact on the slavery question in America. After calling World Anti-Slavery Conventions in 1840 and again in 1843, the British and Foreign Anti-Slavery Society attempted no such gatherings again.

Junius P. Rodriguez

See also: Blanchard, Jonathan; Hibernian Anti-Slavery Society; Pennington, James W.C.; Tappan, Lewis.

Further Reading

Fladeland, Betty. *Men and Brothers: Anglo-American Antislavery Cooperation.* Urbana: University of Illinois Press, 1972.

Wright, Elizur (1804–1885)

The American reformer and activist Elizur Wright spent his life as an advocate for many causes. Though he is remembered as a pioneer in the insurance industry, his political views led him to assist in the founding of a national antislavery society and to author numerous publications protesting slavery.

Wright was born in South Canaan, Connecticut, on February 12, 1804. His father, Elizur Wright, Sr., had studied mathematics, graduated from Yale College in 1781, and passed his antislavery views on to his children. After moving the family to a farm near Tallmadge, Ohio, the elder Wright taught at a local academy that his son attended. The Wright home was a stopover on the Underground Railroad and often harbored fugitive slaves, instilling in young Elizur strong abolitionist sentiments.

After following his father's footsteps to Yale and graduating in 1826, Wright taught at the Groton Academy in Groton, Massachusetts. He later became a professor of mathematics and natural philosophy at the Western Reserve Academy, a hotbed of social and political activism then located in Hudson, Ohio. In 1831, Wright accepted an offer from abolitionist Arthur Tappan to edit *The Emancipator*, a position he held for the next eight years.

Wright also became the corresponding secretary of a group that was preparing to form a national anti-slavery organization. For two years, he wrote to abolitionists in other states seeking support for this group, and, in December 1833, Wright attended the Philadelphia convention at which the American Anti-Slavery Society was born. Its membership included abolitionists Theodore Dwight Weld, James G. Birney, and William Lloyd Garrison. Wright was chosen as the society's secretary and placed in charge of publications, including editing the society's main publication, the *Anti-Slavery Reporter.*

An early advocate of the American Colonization Society (ACS), Wright gradually changed his views and began to question the ACS's motives in the pages of *The Emancipator.* In 1832, he published *The Sin of Slavery, and Its Remedy; Containing Some Reflections on the Moral Influences of African Colonization.* He founded a paper called *Human Rights* in 1834–1835 and edited the *Quarterly Anti-Slavery Magazine* from 1835 to 1837.

Wright proposed the appointment of American Anti-Slavery Society agents to distribute literature, promote equal rights for blacks, and speak to the public on the cause of antislavery; early agents included Garrison, Amos Phelps, and Samuel J. May. An advocate of immediatism, Wright called for "a moral embargo" on the South in his 1835 publication *On Abstinence From Products of Slave Labor.* With a distribution goal of 20,000–50,000 free pamphlets per week, Wright helped disseminate antislavery writings wherever possible, from churches to steamboats, and to thousands through every mailing list he could secure.

Many of these pamphlets found their way into slave states, prompting new laws in the South banning antislavery rhetoric. In response to these efforts, Wright spoke openly that he welcomed such challenges to defend free speech. Many abolitionist writers became the targets of retaliatory mobs, however; by the time Elijah P. Lovejoy was murdered in Illinois in 1837, Wright had installed bars on his windows and extra locks on his doors.

By 1839, several factions were emerging within the ranks of the American Anti-Slavery Society. Other causes were being advocated, including women's rights and anticlericalism, and much of the division was fueled by Garrison's rhetoric. Wright pleaded with fellow abolitionists to abandon other causes until their goal of ending slavery was met. He even attempted to publish some anti-Garrison articles, but Garrison's current popularity made him an extremely powerful figure. When a group of Massachusetts abolitionists left the American Anti-Slavery Society to form their own group, Wright followed.

Wright moved to Boston and became editor of the *Massachusetts Abolitionist* in 1839. Now married with a family, he turned to other nonpolitical work to earn money, translating the fables of French writer Jean de la Fontaine in 1842.

In 1846, he created and edited a daily antislavery, antitariff newspaper in Boston, the *Weekly Chronotype,* continuing to follow his antislavery sentiments. In February 1851, he was among a group of abolitionists who were arrested in Boston for aiding in the rescue of runaway slave Shadrach Minkins, the first fugitive slave to be arrested in New England under the Fugitive Slave Law of 1850. A hung jury resulted in the abolitionists' acquittal.

Moving on to other interests, Wright edited the *Railroad Times* from 1853 to 1858 and patented several inventions, including a spike-making machine. Using his mathematical skills, he turned his focus to the insurance industry. In the 1850s, he published a series of insurance valuation tables, secured an act of the Massachusetts legislature to create an insurance commission, and, in 1858, became the state's insurance commissioner, a post he held until 1866. His contributions in actuarial science include numerous publications, and he is considered by many to be the father of life insurance.

Wright published two additional books on slavery, *An Eye-Opener for the Wide Awakes* in 1860 and *The Programme of Peace, by A Democrat of the Old School* in 1862. He returned to the political scene in 1876 when he attended a conference of the National Liberal League, a group that supported state secularization. He served as the group's second president and was re-elected to two more terms.

He continued writing for the remainder of his life, publishing *Myron Holley, and What He Did for*

Liberty and True Religion in 1882. Wright died in Medford, Massachusetts, on November 21, 1885.

Jane S. Groeper

See also: American Anti-Slavery Society; American Colonization Society; Tappan, Arthur; Tappan, Lewis.

Further Reading

Buckmaster, Henrietta. *Let My People Go: The Story of the Underground Railroad and the Growth of the Abolition Movement.* New York: Harper & Brothers, 1941; Columbia: University of South Carolina Press, 1992.

Buley, R. Carlyle. *The American Life Convention, 1906–1952: A Study in the History of Life Insurance.* New York: Appleton-Century-Crofts, 1953.

Dumond, Dwight Lowell. *Antislavery: The Crusade for Freedom in America.* Ann Arbor: University of Michigan Press, 1961.

Goodheart, Lawrence B. *Abolitionist, Actuary, Atheist: Elizur Wright and the Reform Impulse.* Kent, OH: Kent State University Press, 1990.

Kraditor, Aileen S. *Means and Ends in American Abolitionism: Garrison and His Critics on Strategy and Tactics, 1834–1850.* New York: Pantheon, 1969.

Nye, Russel B. *William Lloyd Garrison and the Humanitarian Reformers.* Boston: Little, Brown, 1955.

Sorin, Gerald. *Abolitionism: A New Perspective.* New York: Praeger, 1972.

Wright, Frances ("Fanny"; 1795–1852)

Frances "Fanny" Wright was an abolitionist known for her failed attempt to gradually free slaves at her Southern community of Nashoba on the Wolf River in Tennessee. She lectured widely on the principles of the Nashoba Settlement and various controversial social reforms, including the abolition of marriage and organized religion.

Wright was born in Dundee, Scotland, on September 6, 1795, the eldest of two daughters of James and Camilla (Campbell) Wright. Both of her parents died before Fanny was four years old, leaving the children to be raised by relatives in England and Scotland. To cope with her loneliness and isolation, Fanny immersed herself in learning. She became an admirer of America and its promise of freedom, and, in August 1818, she and her sister Camilla left for a tour of the young republic.

The Wright sisters were well received in New York and Philadelphia social circles, and they toured the Northeast to the Canadian border. When they re-turned home in May 1820, Fanny wrote a book about their experiences, *Views of Society and Manners in America.* Published in 1821, it was one of the most popular travelogues of the nineteenth century, an uncritical paean to the raw new country and its people.

In her book, Wright also criticized slavery, calling it "odious beyond all that the imagination can conceive." During her second visit to the United States in 1825, she wrote *A Plan for the Gradual Abolition of Slavery in the United States Without Danger of Loss to the Citizens of the South,* urging the U.S. Congress to set aside public land that slaves could work, thereby earning money to buy their eventual freedom. The tract, which she sent to political leaders across the United States, received a uniformly polite, but noncommittal, response. In Washington, D.C., Wright was inspired by Scottish social reformer Robert Dale Owen, whom she heard speak on his plans for his utopian community New Harmony, Indiana.

In 1826, Wright put her plans into action. She formed the Emancipating Labor Society, and, with the encouragement of the Marquis de Lafayette and advice of General Andrew Jackson, Wright purchased a 640-acre tract of land thirteen miles southeast of the small community of Memphis along the Wolf River. She named her plantation Nashoba, the Chickasaw word for "wolf," and announced her intention to open it as a community for slaves who would work for their freedom. Slave owners from across the South were invited to donate their slaves to the experiment, which included training the slaves in a trade, teaching them to read and write, and educating their children.

The community grew, but it did not prosper. Slave owners used Nashoba as a dumping ground for their less productive slaves. Poor soil, swamps infested with mosquitoes, and inadequate finances contributed to the eventual failure of Nashoba. Wright left Camilla and a Scottish overseer in charge when she traveled to England to recover from malaria in May 1827. While she was gone, word spread that the community practiced "free love" (sex outside marriage), and any sense of order to the plantation was lost.

Wright returned to the United States in November 1827 with a friend, Frances Trollope. Believing Wright's claims about a utopia on the Wolf River, Trollope and her children planned on living at Nashoba for a few months. When they arrived in January 1828, however, Trollope found the settlement to be a bleak clearing in the wilderness with no decent housing, no productive land, and no safe drinking

Scottish-born Fanny Wright settled in the United States in 1825 and established the Nashoba Settlement, a plantation settlement in Tennessee where slaves could be educated and work for their freedom. A variety of factors contributed to its demise. *(National Portrait Gallery, Smithsonian Institution/Art Resource, New York)*

water. She and her children quickly decamped for Cincinnati, Ohio. When it became apparent that Nashoba could not thrive, Wright, along with Camilla and several of the community's leaders, moved to Owen's New Harmony, leaving some thirty slaves behind to fend for themselves.

Wright launched a lecture tour that made her one of the most notorious figures of the era. In reaction to the religious revivals then sweeping the nation, which she believed were contrary to the democratic principles of the republic, she began to espouse controversial reforms, including free love, the abolition of marriage and organized religion, interracial sex, and birth control. For all this, she earned the sobriquet "Great Red Harlot of Infidelity."

Wright settled in New York City in 1828. There, she became involved in education reform and the organization of workingmen's unions. She began editing, with Robert Dale Owen, the *New Harmony Gazette.* All the while, however, she felt a need to complete her work at Nashoba. At great personal ex-

pense, she fulfilled her promise to the slaves who had come to the community, purchasing them from their owners and transporting them to freedom in Haiti during the early 1830s.

On the trip to Haiti, Wright met William Phiquepal D'Arusmont, a fellow reformer; she married D'Arusmont in France in July 1831. Their first daughter died in infancy, but a second child, Sylvia, was born in Paris in 1832.

The last two decades of Wright's life proved sad. Her health was poor, and she suffered frequent depressions. Wright settled in Cincinnati in the late 1840s, and she occasionally reappeared on the national scene. Time and controversy had marginalized her influence, however, and she was rarely sought out as a speaker or writer. Wright died on December 13, 1852, at the age of fifty-seven.

Heather K. Michon

See also: Lafayette, Marquis de; Owen, Robert Dale.

Further Reading

Lane, Margaret. *Frances Wright and the "Great Experiment."* Totowa, NJ: Rowman & Littlefield, 1972.
Morris, Celia. *Fanny Wright: Rebel in America.* Cambridge, MA: Harvard University Press, 1984.

Wright, Henry Clarke (1797–1870)

Henry Clarke Wright was a radical abolitionist who was active in a variety of reform movements, including the abolition of slavery, women's rights, temperance, the peace movement, and anti-Sabbatarianism (which denounced the movement that espoused that one day of the week should be observed for religious observance, as dictated by Old Testament Sabbath law).

Wright was an influential abolitionist, contributing much to the thinking of William Lloyd Garrison. In fact, some of the strategies and opinions expressed in *The Liberator* that came to be considered Garrisonian were ones that Wright had helped develop. In particular, the emphasis on nonresistance as the guiding principle for achieving the immediate goal of full emancipation was a concept that Wright developed. He wrote extensively on sociological matters related to matrimony, childbirth, and child rearing while also earning the reputation of a nineteenth-century pioneer in eugenics.

Wright was born in 1797 in Sharon, Connecticut, though the family moved to New York when he was a child. He grew up in the "Burned-Over

District," so named for the frequent religious revivals that took place there during the Second Great Awakening. After facing an emotional crisis, Wright abandoned his trade as a farmer and an apprenticed hatmaker, and accepted the calling of ministry. He graduated from the Andover Theological Seminary in Massachusetts and was licensed to preach in 1823. He accepted a position as a Congregationalist pastor in West Newbury, Massachusetts, where he frequently lectured on behalf of the American Sunday School Union, a nondenominational organization that established Sunday schools.

Wright joined the American Anti-Slavery Society in 1835 and became one of the "seventy agents" whom Theodore Dwight Weld sent out on the lecture circuit, but he was fired two years later because of his outspoken views on the need for immediate abolition. After being similarly rejected by the American Peace Society, for which he had also been lecturing, Wright helped organize the New England Non-Resistance Society, a splinter group of the American Peace Society founded by Garrison and Adin Ballou in 1838.

James G. Birney, an American abolitionist who disagreed with Wright, criticized his "multiplied writing and his violent spirit" when Wright supported what conservatives considered the fanatical efforts of Angelina and Sarah Grimké to draw women into the public sphere. Despite this criticism, Wright continued to support the cause of women's rights and would later attend the 1848 Seneca Falls Convention, which marked the start of the organized women's rights movement in the United States.

Wright traveled to Great Britain in the early 1850s to confer with like-minded abolitionists there, but his radicalism made him unpopular among many of the more conservative abolitionists. Wright criticized the Church of Scotland for accepting financial support from American slave owners and demanded that such gifts be returned. His support for temperance did not sit well with many British antislavery advocates, whom Wright described on one occasion as drunkards.

Although he was an avowed pacifist, Wright became increasingly militant and argued that abolitionists should provide weapons to the slaves so that they might foment insurrection. After the failure of John Brown's 1859 raid on the U.S. arsenal at Harpers Ferry, Virginia, Wright became even more vocal in his support of the armed overthrow of slavery. He published a pamphlet in which he argued, "Whereas, Resistance to tyrants is obedience to God; therefore,

Resolved, That it is the right and duty of the slaves to resist their masters, and the right and duty of the people of the North to incite them to resistance, and to aid them in it."

In the final years of his life, Wright began to support pacifist efforts by helping to create the Universal Peace Union in 1867. He died three years later in Pawtucket, Rhode Island.

Junius P. Rodriguez

See also: Garrison, William Lloyd; Immediatism; Second Great Awakening; Weld, Theodore Dwight.

Further Reading

Curti, Merle E. "Non-Resistance in New England." *New England Quarterly* 2 (January 1929): 34–57.
Perry, Lewis. *Childhood, Marriage, and Reform: Henry Clarke Wright, 1797–1870.* Chicago: University of Chicago Press, 1980.
Sokolow, Jayme A. "Henry Clarke Wright: Antebellum Crusader." *Essex Institute Historical Collections* 3 (April 1975): 122–37.

Wright, Theodore Sedgwick (1797–1847)

The Reverend Theodore Sedgwick Wright was a black abolitionist who called on antislavery crusaders to consider the true significance of race in American society. He made history in 1828 by becoming the first African American to graduate from the Princeton Theological Seminary. As a minister ordained by the Albany Presbytery, he represented the vanguard of black evangelicals whose work in proclaiming the gospel called them to challenge the great national sin of slavery. Other black ministers, including Samuel E. Cornish, Henry Highland Garnet, and Samuel Ringgold Ward, would join Wright in preaching the brotherhood of man while reminding their congregations that God was indeed just and that a day of reckoning would surely come.

Born into a free black family in Schenectady, New York, in 1797, Wright came of age during the religious enthusiasm of the Second Great Awakening. During the period of his ministry, it was clear that Wright brought a sense of evangelical urgency to his sustained efforts to achieve social justice. He spent most of his professional career as pastor of New York City's Shiloh Presbyterian Church, during which time he gained distinction as a theological scholar.

Despite his academic training and position of respect within the free black community, Wright was not immune to the racial animosity of New York's white residents. On one occasion, he was thrown out of a meeting of a literary society at the Alumni of Nassau Hall because of his race.

Wright was not afraid to take up the thorny issue of racial superiority, which, he supposed, held sway even among some white abolitionists. Addressing a meeting of the New York Anti-Slavery Society in 1837, he declared, "to call the dark man a brother . . . to treat the man of color in all circumstances as a man and a brother—that is the test." Directly challenging the audience, he stated that if all people "burn out this prejudice, live it down," the outcome would be the destruction of slavery.

Wright was one of the first black abolitionists to criticize the motives of the American Colonization Society, which encouraged free blacks to return to Africa and settle in Liberia, the colony that the society had established there. Wright and Cornish established America's first black-owned and black-operated newspaper, *Freedom's Journal* (1827–1829), in order to provide an editorial voice in opposition to the idea of colonization. Wright and Cornish later published an anticolonization pamphlet titled *The Colonization Scheme Considered, in Its Rejection by the Colored People, in Its Tendency to Uphold Caste, in Its Unfitness for Christianizing and Civilizing the Aborigines of Africa, and for Putting a Stop to the African Slave Trade* (1840).

In addition to helping establish the American Anti-Slavery Society in 1833, Wright supported other social causes as well. He was a strong supporter of the temperance movement and an advocate of providing missionary assistance to the peoples of Africa. In 1841, he served as the founding treasurer of the Union Missionary Society, which raised funds to return the *Amistad* slaves to Africa and recruited African American missionaries to accompany them. Wright was one of four African Americans who served on the board of the American Missionary Association when that group was chartered in 1846 to help educate and train slaves.

In addition to his involvement with these formal organizations, Wright helped organize the National Negro Convention movement during the 1840s as free blacks began to discuss what they might do independently of the abolitionist societies to hasten the end of slavery.

Junius P. Rodriguez

See also: American Anti-Slavery Society; American Colonization Society; *Amistad* Case (1841); Cornish, Samuel E.; Garnet, Henry Highland; Liberia; Ward, Samuel Ringgold.

Further Reading

Gross, Bella. "Life and Times of Theodore S. Wright, 1797–1847." *Negro History Bulletin* 3 (June 1940): 133–38.